Social Psychology

Fourteenth Edition

Nyla R. Branscombe
University of Kansas

Robert A. Baron
Oklahoma State University

P Pearson

330 Hudson Street, NY NY 10013

VP, Product Development: *Dickson Musslewhite*
Director, Content Strategy and Development:
Sharon Geary
Editor in Chief: *Ashley Dodge*
Managing Editor: *Sutapa Mukherjee*
Sponsoring Editor: *Tanimaa Mehra*
Content Manager: *Carly Czech*
Editorial Project Manager: *Melissa Sacco*
Lumina Datamatics, Inc.
Development Editor: *Micah Newman*
Asset Development Team: *LearningMate Solutions, Ltd.*
VP, Director of Marketing: *Maggie Moylan*
Director, Project Management Services: *Etain O'Dea*
Project Team Lead: *Vamanan Namboodiri*

Project Manager: *Sudipto Roy*
Director of Field Marketing: *Jonathan Cottrell*
Senior Marketing Coordinator: *Susan Osterlitz*
Operations Manager: *Mary Fischer*
Operations Specialist: *Carol Melville*
Associate Director of Design: *Blair Brown*
Interior Design: *Kathryn Foot*
Cover Design: *Lumina Datamatics, Inc*
Cover Art: *AntoinetteW/Shutterstock*
Full-Service Project Management and
Composition: *Saraswathi Muralidhar,*
Lumina Datamatics, Inc.
Printer/Binder: *RRD Willard*
Cover Printer: *Phoenix Color*

Acknowledgements of third party content appear on pages 481–484, which constitutes an extension of this copyright page.

Library of Congress Cataloging-in-Publication Data

Names: Branscombe, Nyla R., author. | Baron, Robert A., author.
Title: Social psychology / Robert A. Baron, Oklahoma State University,
Nyla R. Branscombe, University of Kansas.
Description: Fourteenth edition. | Boston : Pearson, [2016] | Includes
bibliographical references and index.
Identifiers: LCCN 2016010431| ISBN 9780134410968 (alk. paper) | ISBN 0134410963 (alk. paper)
Subjects: LCSH: Social psychology.
Classification: LCC HM1033 .B35 2016 | DDC 302--dc23
LC record available at https://lccn.loc.gov/2016010431

1   16

Student Edition:
ISBN 13: 978-0-13-441096-8
ISBN 10:   0-13-441096-3

Book Ala Carte:
ISBN 13: 978-0-13-456198-1
ISBN 10:   0-13-456198-8

Dedication

To Phil Schlaman, my best friend and essential social support;
You make it all worthwhile.

—Nyla R. Branscombe

To the people I care about most and who care most about me—
Rebecca, Ted, Melissa, Samantha, Randy, Paul and Leah;
And to the colleagues who helped make my life's journey such a happy one—
Donn Byrne, Roger Black, Jim Naylor, John Capaldi, and Mike Morris

—Robert A. Baron

Brief Contents

Contents

Preface

Social Psychology in a Changing World

"Education is the most powerful weapon which you can use to change the world."

–Quote by Nelson Mandela

"As we go forward, I hope we're going to continue to use technology to make really big differences in how people live and work."

–Quote by Sergey Brin, co-founder of Google

"Psychology cannot tell people how they ought to live their lives. It can, however, provide them with the means for effecting personal and social change."

–Quote by Albert Bandura

The aims identified in these quotations are truly impressive ones, and we most assuredly share their faith in the transformative power of education. We agree that equipping people with new ways of understanding themselves and interacting with the world has far-reaching consequences. And—more importantly—we believe that social psychology does provide powerful means of comprehending why people think, feel, and act as they do, and these ideas, in turn, illuminate how the social world shapes who we are and the processes by which we can achieve change, in ourselves and the social world. As you know, the goal of changing the world through technology, at least in terms of its implications for how we interact with other people and access our accumulated knowledge, has in fact been met—to "google" something has become a verb in everyday language, and Facebook and other social media have changed much about how we interact with each other. Just try to imagine life without the many forms of social media we use practically every hour of every day. Probably you cannot because digital technology has become woven into the very fabric of our lives so that we take them for granted and use them as though they are extensions of ourselves. While the founders of Google and Facebook sought to change how people interact with the world, social psychologists seek to illuminate the many "hidden processes" that shape how people influence each other. By providing you with a comprehensive overview of social psychological theory and research, we believe the information in this book offers you a valuable means of learning about yourself and the social world in which we live.

The social world, which is the primary focus of this book, has changed tremendously in recent years, perhaps more quickly and dramatically than at any time in the past. That includes how we interact with each other, and a key point we will emphasize throughout the book is this: These changes have important implications for how we think about ourselves and other people. *Social psychology* is the branch of psychology that studies all aspects of our behavior with and toward others, our feelings and thoughts about them, and the relationships we develop with them. The central message for social psychology as a field, and for any book that seeks to represent it, is simple: Keep up with these technological changes in terms of their implications for social life, and this is precisely what we do with this 14th edition.

We are happy to report that social psychology provides many important insights crucial to understanding the social changes we have described thus far and can provide you with the means of understanding how to create further—and beneficial—social change. The field continues to be the vibrant and adaptable one it has always been and, we predict, always will be. The scope of social psychological research (and knowledge acquired) has expanded rapidly in the past few years—in fact, much has been learned since the publication of the previous edition of this book—and this new edition fully reflects the many changes now occurring all over the world.

Our central goal for this new edition was to illustrate just how well our field has—and does—adjust to and reflect the changing social world. Technology is not simply changing the way we carry out certain tasks: It is also changing the way we live and—most important—how we interact with each other. Although many basic principles of social life remain, in essence, unchanged—for instance, the nature of love, hate, and emotions in-between—the ways in which these principles are *expressed* and *experienced* have changed drastically.

So, how, precisely, did we set out to reflect these major trends while fully and accurately describing the core of our field—the knowledge and insights that social psychologists have gathered through decades of systematic research? As the 2015 *White House Social and Behavioral Sciences Team Report* indicates, social psychological research consists of an impressive body of knowledge about how people actually think, feel, and behave toward other people, and the accumulated knowledge identifies how changing social conditions can influence those responses, often with an eye to improving life for us all. Indeed, social psychological research has taught us much about the "human animal" that can and is being fruitfully applied in numerous domains. That is precisely what we aimed to do with this edition—illustrate how understanding social psychological processes can help to improve many aspects of life. The following is a summary of the major steps we took to accomplish these important goals.

Changes in Content
An Entirely Revamped Chapter Based on "the Science of Happiness"
Dealing with Adversity and Achieving a Happy Life (Chapter 12)

This capstone chapter is ambitious and entirely consistent with the theme of the 14th edition: *Education for achieving change*. We believe that social psychology can help *you* deal with the stresses of life and serve to guide you on the way toward achieving greater happiness. That's a tall order, but our field can indeed now provide the central ingredients for thinking about ourselves in ways that can help us be resilient when we enter new social environments and provide insight with specific strategies that, when put into practice, will improve people's well-being. Here's what you can learn from this greatly revised chapter (Chapter 12):

> *Can people be too happy? What roles do culture and age play in defining the meaning of happiness? What do we know about how the happiness of people in different nations can be improved? And, what can we do to make ourselves happier individuals and satisfied with what we have and the choices we have made? In short, this chapter describes social psychological knowledge that can help you in your quest to build the happy and fulfilling life we all seek.*

In other words, in this chapter we provide an overview of some of the important ways in which social psychology—with its scientific approach to personal and social change—can help us attain our key goals. Perhaps most important of all—we examine strategies people can use to handle the setbacks they may experience and reveal the ingredients for increasing happiness. Some of the questions we will consider are: What roles do culture and age play in defining the meaning of happiness? What do we know about how the happiness of people in different nations can

be improved? And, how do we turn adversity into strength and achievement? This chapter describes what social psychologists, with their comprehensive approach to understanding social life, have discovered, and this knowledge can help *you* in your quest to build the happy and fulfilling life we all seek. We think that some of the findings we will present are indeed surprising—for instance, the fact that increasing wealth does not necessarily make people happier, but investing in social relationships does indeed make people happier. We believe that this is a unique and important aspect of this text and one that is fully consistent with the practical credo that social psychology, as a field, has always embraced.

Changes in Content Within Each of the Chapters

Continuing a long tradition in which each edition of this textbook has included literally dozens of new topics, this 14th edition is indeed "new." In every chapter, we present new lines of research, new findings, and new theoretical perspectives. Here is a partial list of the new topics included:

Chapter 1

- An increased emphasis on the importance of social relationships for psychological well-being.
- An entirely new section on the importance of meta-analysis in assessing an existing body of knowledge on a topic.
- A new emphasis on how cultural factors shape our conceptions of the self and how that in turn affects individuals' comfort and ability to navigate different social settings.

Chapter 2

- A new section on heuristic use under conditions of economic threat.
- A new section on the "portion size effect" and how eating can reflect inadequate adjustment from a high anchor.
- New research on belief in free will and its implications for counterfactual thinking.

Chapter 3

- A new section on why we find it difficult to recognize deception in others.
- A new discussion of attributions and terrorism—how perpetrators explain their actions.
- New research on how first impressions are revised over time.

Chapter 4

- An entirely new section addresses how trying to conceal our identity can inhibit social interaction and harm well-being.

- New research addresses why introspection fails, and particularly why people apparently don't know that spending their money on others can make them happier than spending it on themselves.

- An entirely new section on how migration affects self-esteem—both international and domestic moves by students.

Chapter 5

- New research concerning the role of reactance in students' responses to instructor behaviors in the classroom.

- New research addressing how attitudes can be conditioned nonconsciously.

- New research examining when people's behavior reflects their abstract values and when it is based on their economic self-interests.

Chapter 6

- New coverage of how racial group membership affects responses to issues concerning police treatment of citizens.

- New research concerning how groups maintain a favorable view of themselves, despite treating other groups in a prejudicial fashion.

- New research illustrating how stereotypes create gender-based disparities in the workplace.

Chapter 7

- A new section on social skills—our ability to get along with others—and their importance in many aspects of social life.

- A new discussion of how even trivial similarities to others (e.g., sharing the same first names) can increase liking for them.

- New information concerning the attributes that we look for in romantic partners change over the course of our relationships with them.

Chapter 8

- A new discussion of the potential benefits of refusing to "go along", or not yielding to social pressure.

- An expanded discussion of the effectiveness of various techniques (including several new ones) for gaining compliance from others—for getting other people to say "yes" to our requests.

- An entirely new section focused on unintentional social influence: How others influence us even when they are not trying to do so.

Chapter 9

- A new discussion of "crowd-funding"—a form of online helping in which individuals donate money to entrepreneurs without ever meeting them and without expecting anything in return.

- A new discussion of the role of social class in pro-social behavior.

- New findings concerning how feelings of anonymity (produced by darkness) can reduce willingness to help others.

Chapter 10

- New research concerning the role of genes in combination with exposure to stress affects aggression in children.

- A new section on the effects of narcissism on aggression has been included.

- A new section on situational factors that encourage aggressive behavior including gun availability.

Chapter 11

- New research concerning how groups create greater cohesion among their members when their distinctiveness is threatened.

- New research on how being part of a group helps people achieve a greater sense of control in their lives has been added.

- New research on distributive justice rules and how they vary across cultures was added.

Chapter 12

- This completely revamped capstone chapter offers a "social cure" perspective for managing the stresses in our lives and illustrates the critical role of social relationships for health, well-being, and achieving a meaningful life in a changing world.

- The importance of "believing we can change" for helping us weather adversity is described.

- Why practicing self-forgiveness following mistakes can help people change.

New Special Features with Research Insights on Cutting-Edge Topics

To fully reflect current trends in social psychological research and the field's responsiveness to social change, we now include two new special sections in each chapter—ones that were *not* present in the previous edition. These new sections, which are labeled "**What Research Tells Us**

About...," integrate important new research that will capture students' attention and excite their interest in new emerging topics in social psychology. Some examples are:

- A new research insights section on "People's Preference for the Status Quo."
- A new research insights section on "Why Not Controlling Ourselves Can Make Us Feel Good."
- A new research insights section on "The Role of Nonverbal Cues in Job Interviews."
- A new research insights section on "Why Some People Conclude They Are Superior to Others."
- A new research insights section on "The Importance of Belonging and Group Ties."
- A new research insights section on "Perceived Discrimination and Self-Esteem."
- A new research insights section on "Social Modeling and Eating."
- A new research insights section on "Culture and Attitude Processes."
- A new research insights section on "Biases in Our Beliefs About Inequality."
- A new research insights section on "The Role of Existential Threat in Prejudice."
- A new research insights section on "Dramatic Differences in Appearance Between Partners: Is Love Really Blind?"
- A new research insights section on "Two Factors That Can Destroy Love: Jealousy and Infidelity."
- A new research insights section on "How Much We Really Conform."
- A new research insights section on "Using Scarcity to Gain Compliance."
- A new research insights section on "Paying it Forward: Helping Others Because We Have Been Helped."
- A new research insights section on "How People React to Being Helped."
- A new research insights section on "The Role of Emotions in Aggression."
- A new research insights section on "Aggression in the Workplace."
- A new research insights section on "Dissent and Criticism of Our Groups—"Because We Care."
- A new research insights section on "The Importance of Being Treated With Respect."
- A new research insights section on "Reducing Posttraumatic Stress Among Veterans."
- A new research insights section on "The Relationship Between Emotions and Life Satisfaction Within Different Cultures."

Student Aids

Any textbook is valuable only to the extent that it is both useful and interesting to the students using it. To make this edition even better for students, we have included several student aids—features designed to enhance the book's appeal and usefulness. Included among these features are the following:

Chapter Objectives: The aims of each major chapter section are presented. With these, students should know what they will learn before they begin each chapter.

Chapter Openings Linked to Important Trends and Events in Society: All chapters begin with examples reflecting current trends in society or real-life events that illustrate important principles of social life. Here are some examples:

1. How people must make judgments—from what college to attend to what health insurance option to select—with incomplete information (Chapter 2)

2. How many famous people have deceived the public and why their deception was so difficult to detect (Chapter 3)

3. Facebook as a medium for presenting ourselves to others (Chapter 4)

4. How our beliefs about climate change are formed (Chapter 5)

5. How protest movements such as "Black Lives Matter" emerge and why there is a racial divide concerning police treatment of citizens (Chapter 6)

6. The powerful, practical advantages of being highly likable (Chapter 7)

7. How swindlers such as Bernie Madoff, who cheated investors out of billions, use social influence for selfish purposes (Chapter 8)

8. How more than 1.5 billion people have been helped to lead better lives by being provided with more efficient—and safer—cooking stoves (Chapter 9)

9. The goals of recent mass shooting perpetrators in the United States are compared with those committing aggression as part of a group to achieve political ends (Chapter 10)

10. The critical role of sharing an identity with an audience for effective communication in groups (Chapter 11)

11. How U.S. Supreme Court Justice Sonia Sotomayor overcame adversity to achieve a happy life (Chapter 12)

Key Points: Every major section of each chapter ends with a brief review of the key points covered.

End-of-Chapter Summaries: Each chapter ends with a summary that recaps the key issues covered.

Special Labels on All Graphs and Charts: To make these easy to understand, we continue to use the "special labels" that are a unique feature of this book.

Supplementary Materials

All excellent texts are supported by a complete package of supplementary material, for both the students and the instructor. This text offers a full array of such aids including:

- **Instructor Manual:** includes chapter outlines, lecture launchers, key terms, in-class, and out-of-class activities.

- **PowerPoint Presentation:** provides a core template of the content covered throughout the text. Can easily be expanded for customization with your course.

- **Test Bank:** includes questions in multiple choice, fill-in-the blanks, short answer and essay response—formats.

- **MyTest** - Create custom quizzes and exams using the Test Bank questions. You can print these exams for in-class use. Visit: http://www.pearsonhighered.com/mytest

Some Concluding Words

Looking back over the changes we have made for this 14th edition, we absolutely believe we have done everything possible to make this edition the best one yet! We sought to create a textbook that fully captures the extent to which modern social psychology reflects, and embraces, the major changes now occurring in the world and illustrate how those affect the social side of life. But only you—our colleagues and the students who use this textbook—can tell us to what extent we have succeeded. So please do send us your comments, reactions, and suggestions. As in the past, we will listen to them very carefully and do our best to use them constructively in planning the next edition.

Our warm regards and thanks!

Nyla R. Branscombe
Nyla@ku.edu

Robert A. Baron
Robert.baron@okstate.edu

Acknowledgements

Word of Thanks

No challenging endeavor, such as writing a textbook, is completed without the assistance of many people. Now that the hard work of preparing this new 14th edition is behind us, we want to take this opportunity to thank the many talented and dedicated people whose help throughout the process has been truly invaluable.

First, our sincere thanks to the colleagues who reviewed the 13th edition and offered their suggestions for ways in which it could be improved. Their input was invaluable to us in planning this new edition: Chris Goode, University of Kansas.

Second, we wish to offer our personal thanks to our editors at Pearson. It was a pleasure to work with Carly Czech and Sutapa Mukherjee. Their helpful suggestions and good judgment were matched only by their enthusiasm and support for the book.

Third, a special thanks to Lois-Ann Freier and Micah Newman whose keen eye and attention to detail during the revision process helped us make this text accurate and more interesting reading for students. Our thanks too go to Lumina Datamatics, Inc., for very careful and constructive copyediting. Their comments were insightful and thought-provoking, which were useful for improving and clarifying our words. We look forward to working with them for many years to come.

Fourth, a very special thanks is owed to Melissa Sacco at Lumina Datamatics who handled an incredible array of details and tasks with tremendous skill—and lots of patience with the authors! In addition, we thank all of those who contributed to various aspects of the production process: to Rimpy Sharma for photo research, to Lumina Datamatics for design work, and the cover design and to Saraswathi Muralidhar for her excellent help with the page proofs and other important aspects of the production process.

We also wish to offer our thanks to the many colleagues who provided reprints of their work, and to the many students who kindly shared their thoughts about the prior edition of this textbook with us. Although these individuals are too numerous to list here, a special note is due to Lara Aknin, Craig Anderson, Manuela Barreto, Monica Biernat, Chris Crandall, Scott Eidelman, Mark Ferguson, Omri Gillath, Alex Haslam, Cath Haslam, John Helliwell, Miles Hewstone, Jolanda Jetten, Anca Miron, Ludwin Molina, Masi Noor, Tom Postmes, Valerie Purdie-Vaughns, Kate Reynolds, Michelle Ryan, Michael Schmitt, Wolfgang Stroebe and Ruth Warner whose research input we gratefully acknowledge.

To all of these outstanding people, and many others too, our warmest regards and a huge thank you!

Nyla R. Branscombe & Robert A. Baron

About the Authors

Nyla R. Branscombe is Professor of Psychology at University of Kansas. She received her B.A. from York University in Toronto, M.A. from the University of Western Ontario, and Ph.D. in 1986 from Purdue University. She has served as Associate Editor for *Personality and Social Psychology Bulletin*, *British Journal of Social Psychology*, and *Group Processes and Intergroup Relations*. In 2015, she received the University of Kansas *Byron A Alexander Graduate Mentor Award*.

She has published more than 140 articles and chapters, has been twice the co-recipient of the Otto Kleinberg prize for research on Intercultural and International Relations, and twice the co-recipient of the Society of Personality and Social Psychology Publication Award. She co-edited the 2004 volume *Collective Guilt: International Perspectives*, published by Cambridge University Press; the 2007 volume *Commemorating Brown: The Social Psychology of Racism and Discrimination*, published by the American Psychological Association; the 2010 volume *Rediscovering Social Identity*, published by Psychology Press; the 2013 volume *Handbook of Gender and Psychology*, published by Sage; and the 2015 volume *Psychology of Change: Life Contexts, Experiences, and Identities*.

Her current research addresses a variety of issues concerning intergroup relations from a social identity perspective. How people think about groups that have a history of victimization, when and why privileged groups may feel collective guilt for their past harm doing, and the consequences of experiencing discrimination for psychological well-being have been key topics investigated. She gratefully acknowledges ongoing research support from the *Canadian Institute for Advanced Research: Social Interactions, Identity, and Well-Being Program*.

Robert A. Baron is Regents Professor and the Spears Professor of Entrepreneurship at Oklahoma State University. He received his Ph.D. in social psychology from the University of Iowa (1968). He has held faculty appointments at Rensselaer Polytechnic Institute; Purdue University; the Universities of Minnesota, Texas, South Carolina, and Washington; Princeton University; and Oxford University. From 1979 to 1981, he was the Program Director for Social and Developmental Psychology at NSF. In 2001, he was appointed as a Visiting Senior Research Fellow by the French Ministry of Research (Universite de Toulouse).

He is a Fellow of APA and a Charter Fellow of APS. He has published more than 140 articles and 45 chapters and has authored/co-authored 49 books in psychology and management. He serves on the boards of several major journals and has received numerous awards for his research (e.g., "Thought Leader" award, Entrepreneurship Division, Academy of Management, 2009 the Grief award, for the most highly cited paper in the field of Entrepreneurship). He holds three U.S. patents and was founder and CEO of IEP, Inc. (1993–2000).

His current research interests focus on applying the findings and principles of social psychology to the field of entrepreneurship, where he has studied such topics as the role of perception in opportunity recognition, how entrepreneurs' social skills influence their success, and the role of positive affect in entrepreneurship.

Chapter 1
Social Psychology
The Science of the Social Side of Life

Chapter Overview

Learning Objectives

1.1 Evaluate the diverse topics that social psychology seeks to understand

1.2 Examine the major avenues that social psychology is currently exploring

1.3 Understand the methods social psychologists use to gain insight into the questions posed

1.4 Explain how theories play a key role in social psychological research

1.5 Identify how the dilemma of deception is addressed in social psychology

1.6 Outline the steps taken to make reading this book a pleasant and informative experience

Consider, for a moment, what aspect of your life impacts your health and happiness most? Did your relationships with other people come to mind? What would your life be like without your family, friends, roommates, romantic partners, professors, coworkers, sports teammates—all the people you care about and with whom you interact? The truth is human beings are a truly social species. Each of us is connected to and influenced by other people, even if we're not always consciously aware of all the ways we are affected by them. Indeed, a fundamental message of social psychology is that both the good and the bad in our lives involve other people. As evidenced in the following quotations, people from all cultures and walks of life agree that our connections to others bring happiness and meaning to our lives. At the same time, we also know that other people—when they disagree with us, exclude us, or harm us—can be the source of our worst pain.

- The Dalai Lama: "Our prime purpose in this life is to help others."
- John Lennon, former musician with the Beatles: "Count your age by friends, not years."
- Martin Luther King, Jr.: "Life's most persistent and urgent question is: What are you doing for others?"
- Bob Marley, famous reggae musician: "Truth is, everybody is going to hurt you: You just gotta find the ones worth suffering for."
- David Byrne, musician formerly of the Talking Heads: "Sometimes it's a form of love just to talk to somebody that you have nothing in common with and still be fascinated by their presence."
- Robert Alan Silverstein, author and social change activist: "In our hectic, fast-paced, consumer-driven society, it's common to feel overwhelmed, isolated and alone. . . . The sense of belonging we feel when we make the time to take an active role in our communities can give us a deeper sense of meaning and purpose."

Connecting with others—both as individuals and as part of social groups—is a major predictor not only of happiness and well-being but also of physical health. Robert Putnam summed up the importance of social connections based on extensive research reported in his book, *Bowling Alone*: "If you belong to no groups but decide to join one, you cut your risk of dying over the next year in half." If you had any lingering doubts about the importance of the social side of life, perhaps you don't anymore!

We also know that solitary confinement is so bad for mental health that it is often considered "cruel and unusual punishment." Try, for a moment, to imagine life in total isolation from others, as shown in the movie *Cast Away*, the story of a person who finds himself stranded on an uninhabited island after his plane crashes in the Pacific Ocean. After a while, he craves human company so much that he paints a face on a

Figure 1.1 Would Life in Isolation Be Worth Living?

Can you imagine what it would be like to live entirely alone, having no contact with other people? In the film *Cast Away*, a person who is stranded on an uninhabited island is so desperate for company that he "invents a person" by painting a volleyball to look like a human face. He wants to get back to his human connections so badly that he risks his life on the open seas to do so.

volleyball, gives it a name (Wilson), and talks with it regularly because it is his only friend (Figure 1.1). In the end, the character, played by Tom Hanks, decides that his life alone is not worth living, and so he risks all in an attempt to return to civilization and connect with living people again.

While we know that many people find the thought of a physically isolated existence to be disturbing, let's consider "disconnection from others" on a smaller, digital scale. Try to remember the last time you forgot your cell phone or lost access to Facebook, Twitter, or other social media outlets. How did it feel to be out of contact? Did it freak you out? Perhaps that's why it won't be surprising to learn that even these digital forms of connection to others help to satisfy our emotional needs. For example, research shows that among college students the number of Facebook friends predicts life satisfaction (Manago, Taylor, & Greenfield, 2012). It's safe to say, then, that social contact is a central aspect of our lives. In a very basic sense, it helps define who we are and the quality of our existence.

So, get ready for a fascinating journey, because the social side of life is the focus of this entire book. Social psychology is the branch of psychology that studies all aspects of our social existence—everything from love and helping people on the one hand, to prejudice, exclusion, and violence on the other. Social psychologists also investigate how groups influence us, how the social context we find ourselves in affects the way we make decisions, and how we explain ourselves and the actions of other people. As you will see, how we think about ourselves at any given point in time—our identity—is shaped by our relationships with other people, which in turn guides our social behavior. We will be addressing some questions you've probably thought about already. After all, the nature of the social world is of interest to all of us. But we believe that some of the answers concerning human social behavior that has emerged from social psychological research will nevertheless surprise and intrigue you.

Social psychology covers a lot of territory—much of what's central to human experience. What differentiates social psychology from other social sciences is its focus on explaining influences on the individual's thought and behavior. What differentiates social psychology from the informal observations of people that we all make is its scientific nature. What we mean by the science of social psychology is so crucial that we will explain it in this chapter, in terms of the different techniques that are used by social psychologists to go about answering fascinating questions about the social side of life.

We begin with a formal definition of social psychology: what it is and what it seeks to accomplish. Next, we'll describe several current trends in social psychology. These will be reflected throughout this book, so knowing about them at the start will help you understand why they are important. We'll also examine the pros and cons of different methods used by social psychologists to answer questions about the social side of life. A working knowledge of these basic methods will help you understand how social psychologists add to our understanding of social thoughts and behavior, and will also be useful to you outside the context of this course to evaluate research findings you read about in major media outlets.

In fact, social psychological research has uncovered so much useful information about human behavior that in September 2015, President Obama issued an executive order requiring federal government agencies to incorporate behavioral science insights—much of it based on social psychological research concerning factors that affect how people actually go about making decisions—into their programs (Sunstein, 2015). As you will see, social psychologists have accumulated an impressive body of knowledge about how people think, feel, and behave, along with the circumstances that influence those responses. Indeed, social psychological research has taught us much about the "human animal" that is being fruitfully applied in numerous domains. These include understanding how people make use of digital technology and social media and how people can best cope with adversity, to making it easier for low-income teens to attend college and adults to participate in retirement savings plans. Consistent with the White House's Social and Behavioral Sciences Team Report, we believe that social psychological research informs us about how reforms can be made with the aim of improving people's lives. Given the empirical and scientific approach used by social psychologists to uncover "what works and what doesn't work," we think you will see why this branch of psychology is well-placed to provide answers to many questions.

1.1: Social Psychology: What It Is and Is Not

Objective **Evaluate the diverse topics that social psychology seeks to understand**

Providing a definition of almost any field is a complex task. In the case of social psychology, this difficulty is increased by the field's broad scope. As you will see in every chapter of this book, social psychologists truly have a wide range of interests. Yet, despite this variation, most focus mainly on the following task: understanding how and why individuals behave, think, and feel as they do in social situations—ones involving the actual or symbolic presence of other people. How people define themselves and others in a given situation can alter how we behave. Accordingly, we define social psychology as the scientific field that seeks to understand *the nature and causes of individual behavior, feelings, and thoughts in social situations*. Another way to put this is to say that social psychology investigates the ways in which our thoughts, feelings, and actions are *influenced by the social environments in which we find ourselves—by other people or our thoughts about them*. We'll now clarify this definition by taking a closer look at several of its key aspects.

1.1.1: Social Psychology Is Scientific in Nature

Many people seem to believe that this term *science* applies only to fields such as chemistry, physics, and biology—ones that use the kind of equipment shown in Figure 1.2 to investigate some aspect of the physical world. If you share that view, you may find our suggestion that social psychology is a scientific discipline perplexing. How can a field that seeks to study the nature of love, the causes of aggression, the influence of groups on conceptions of ourselves, and many other topics be scientific in the same sense as physics or chemistry? The answer is surprisingly simple.

The term *science* does not refer to a special group of highly advanced fields. Rather, it refers to two things: (1) a set of values and (2) methods that can be used to study a wide range of topics. In deciding whether a given field is or is not scientific, therefore, the critical question is: *Does it adopt these values and methods*? To the extent the field does, it is scientific in nature. To the extent it does not, it falls outside the realm of science. We'll examine the procedures used by social psychologists in their research in detail in a later section, so here we will focus on the core values that all fields must adopt to be considered scientific in nature. Four of these are most important:

> *Accuracy:* A commitment to gathering and evaluating information about the world (including social behavior) in as careful, precise, and error-free a manner as possible. This means that casual "people watching" that each of us might do at a crowded event will not meet this definition. Each of us may focus on different things so there is little precision, and the observations will lack *replicability*—the same "findings" when performed by someone else may not be obtained.

> *Objectivity:* A commitment to obtaining and evaluating such information in a manner that is as free from bias as possible. This means that with casual "people watching" we may evaluate what we see differently than others would, so our observations lack objectivity.

> *Skepticism:* A commitment to accepting findings as accurate only to the extent they have been verified over and over again. Here again you should notice the importance of *replication*—where different investigators can re-produce the procedure used by others and arrive at the same conceptual conclusions.

Figure 1.2 What Is Science?

Many people believe that only fields that use equipment like that shown here (left photo) to study the physical world can be viewed as scientific. Others think that "people watching" as shown in the middle photo is a form of science. However, the term *science* actually refers to adherence to a set of basic values (e.g., accuracy, objectivity) and use of a set of methods to *systematically* examine almost any aspect of the world around us—including the social side of life. In contrast, other approaches that are *not* scientific in nature (right photo) do not accept these values or use these methods.

Open-Mindedness: A commitment to changing one's views—even those that are strongly held—if existing evidence suggests that these views are inaccurate. Social psychologists have produced plenty of surprises by conducting research, which has required us to reconsider the role of groups for our well-being, how many processes operate non-consciously, how the framing of issues can affect our attitudes and preferences, and why what actually makes people happy is often different than our expectations of what will do so. All of these have suggested revisions in assumptions about human nature.

Social psychology, as a field, is committed to these values and applies them in its efforts to understand the nature of social behavior. In contrast, fields that are *not* scientific make assertions about the world, and about people, that are not put to the careful test and analysis required by the values that guide social psychology. In such fields—ones like astrology and aromatherapy—intuition, faith, and unobservable forces are considered to be sufficient (see Figure 1.2) for reaching conclusions—the opposite of what is true in social psychology.

"But why adopt the scientific approach? Isn't social psychology just common sense?" Having taught for many years, we can almost hear you asking this question. After all, we all spend much of our lives interacting with other people and thinking about them, so in a sense, we are all amateur social psychologists. So, why don't we each just rely on our own experience and intuition as a basis for drawing conclusions about the social side of life?

Our answer is straightforward: because such sources provide an inconsistent and unreliable guide to understanding social behavior. This is so because our own experiences are unique and may not provide a solid foundation for answering general questions such as: "Why do people sometimes 'go along with the group' even when they might disagree with what it is doing?" and "How can we know what other people are thinking or feeling at any given time?" In addition, as we have learned from social psychological research, people are often unaware of what influences them. Individuals may be able to generate "theories" about how they are or are not influenced by other people, but such common sense beliefs are often biased by wishful thinking. For example, as suggested by Figure 1.3, we might want to view ourselves as "independent" and fail to see how we are actually influenced by other people, or alternatively we might want to believe a certain kind of change is possible so we claim to have been influenced by others who share our views, perhaps more than we actually are.

Figure 1.3 Being Influenced by the Actions of Other People

We can be influenced by the behavior of other people—either by seeing and being with them via social media or by physically being immersed ourselves in such events. Such exposure to others, especially when we identify with them, often exerts powerful effects on our own behavior and thought.

It is also the case that there are widely endorsed ideas about various aspects of social life that are inconsistent with each other. Only objective research evidence can provide clear answers about which of such contradictory ideas are true. For instance, consider the following statement: "Absence makes the heart grow fonder." When people are separated from those they love, they miss them and may experience increased longing for them. Many people would agree with this idea, in part because they can retrieve an instance like that from their own memory. But now consider the following statement: "Out of sight, out of mind." Is this idea true? Did you, after leaving your high school sweetheart and swearing undying love, find a new romantic interest fairly quickly upon arriving at college? Many popular songs advocate just that—for instance, Crosby, Stills, Nash, and Young's song: "If you can't be with the one you love, love the one you're with." As you can see, these two views—both suggested by common sense and popular culture—are contradictory. The same is true for many other informal observations about human behavior—they each seem plausible, but often imply opposite conclusions. How about these: "Two heads are better than one," and "Too many cooks spoil the broth." One suggests that when people work together, they perform better (e.g., make better decisions). The other suggests that when people work together, they may act in ways that actually harm the product (e.g., that they make worse decisions). Much careful systematic research has revealed that whether groups show better or worse performance than individuals depends on a variety of factors: the nature of the task, whether the work can be effectively divided up, the expertise of the group members, and how well information is shared among them (Minson & Mueller, 2012; Stasser, Stewart, & Wittenbaum, 1995; van Ginkel & van Knippenberg, 2009).

By now, our main point should be clear: Common sense often suggests a confusing and inconsistent picture of human behavior. Yet, it can offer intriguing hypotheses that can be tested in controlled research. What it doesn't tell us is *when* various principles or generalizations hold—for instance, does "absence makes the heart grow fonder," primarily among relationships that have already attained a certain level of commitment? Likewise, it doesn't tell us for *whom*, or the sort of relationships, "out of sight, out of mind" is most likely to occur. Only a scientific approach that examines social thought and behavior in different contexts and populations (such as young versus older people) can provide that kind of information, and this is one basic reason that social psychologists put their faith in the scientific method: It yields more conclusive evidence. In fact, as you'll soon see, it is designed to help us determine not just *which* of the opposite sets of predictions mentioned earlier is correct, but also *when*, for *whom*, and *why* one or the other might apply.

But this is not the only reason for not relying on common sense. As we'll note over and over again (e.g., Chapters 2, 3, 4, 6, and 8), our thinking is subject to several types of biases that can lead us badly astray. Here's one example: Think back over major projects on which you have worked in the past (writing term papers, cooking a complicated dish, painting your room). Now, try to remember two things: (1) your initial estimates about how long it would take you to complete these jobs and (2) how long it actually took. Is there a gap between these two numbers? In all likelihood because most of us fall victim to the *planning fallacy*, there is a strong tendency to believe that projects will take less time than they actually do or, alternatively, that we can accomplish more in a given period of time than is really true (Halkjelsvik & Jorgensen, 2012). Moreover, we fall victim to this bias in our thoughts over and over again, despite repeated experiences that tell us "everything takes longer than we think it will."

Why are we subject to this kind of error? Research by social psychologists indicates that part of the answer involves a tendency to think about the future when we are estimating how long a job will take. This prevents us from remembering how long similar tasks took in the past, and that, in turn, leads us to underestimate the time we need now (Buehler, Griffin, & Ross, 1994). This is just one of the many ways in which we can—and often do—make errors in thinking about other people (and ourselves). Because we are prone to such errors in our thinking about the social world, we cannot rely on introspecting about the influences on us—or rely on common sense—to solve the mysteries of social behavior. Rather, we need scientific evidence about what *most* people do, whether they realize that they do so or not, and providing such evidence is, in essence, what social psychology is all about.

1.1.2: Social Psychology Focuses on the Behavior of Individuals

Societies vary greatly in terms of their overall levels of violence; yet, social psychology focuses on explaining why individuals perform aggressive actions or refrain from doing so. Such acknowledgment of cultural differences applies to virtually all other aspects of social behavior, from conformity to helping, love as well as conflict, but social psychology aims to address the thought and emotional processes underlying those actions in individuals. This means that, as we noted earlier, because none of us are "islands" and all of us, instead, are strongly influenced by other people and the situations we find ourselves in, much research will systematically examine cultural and other contextual factors to illuminate just how those influences are exerted on the individual.

Social psychologists examine *how* groups influence individual behavior, *how* culture becomes internalized and affects individual preferences, and *how* emotions and moods affect the decisions made by the individual. Although our emphasis will be on how social factors affect the individual, as you will see throughout this book, many nonsocial factors (features of the environment; how the information we receive is framed) can exert powerful effects on us, often by influencing our emotions and social thoughts. The field's major interest lies in understanding just how social situations shape the actions of individuals.

Clearly, this does *not* mean the role that social and cultural factors play in shaping the individual is neglected. Far from it. For example, considerable research has begun to address how ethnicity and social class shape our "selves" (whether we construe it as independent from others or as interdependent with them) and, consequently, social behavior (Markus & Kitayama, 2010). This means that some institutional settings will be experienced as "friendly" or more congenial for one type of self rather than the other. For example, American universities tend to promote an independent model of self, which is more consistent with a middle-class standard of behavior than the self that is formed as a result of growing up in a working-class environment (Stephens, Fryberg, & Markus, 2012). In part because of differences in material resources, students from middle-class homes are encouraged to leave home, develop their own distinct interests, and choose their own pathway in life. In contrast, those from working-class backgrounds are more likely to live in the same place most of their lives, be more strongly embedded in familial and local social networks, and feel a need to fit in by displaying concern for the interests of others. Because of the different life experiences and selves that emerge among those whose social class origins differ, the norms prevalent in American university settings can be a good or rather poor cultural match. What this research reveals is how life experiences, which differ systematically according to social class and other group memberships, affect the individual. Because "who we are"—our identities—affects our thought and behavior, social psychological understanding of the individual is enriched by close examination of the following links.

Social Contexts/Experiences ⟹ Self-Identities ⟹ Social Behavior

1.1.3: Social Psychology Seeks to Understand the Causes of Social Behavior

Social psychologists are primarily interested in understanding the many factors and conditions that shape the social thought and behavior of individuals—their actions, feelings, beliefs, memories, and judgments. Obviously, a huge number of variables can play a role, although most fall under the five major headings described here.

THE ACTIONS AND CHARACTERISTICS OF OTHER PERSONS Consider the following events:

> *You are at a party and you notice that a very attractive person is smiling at you. In fact, this person is looking at you in a way that leaves little room for interpretation: That person is sending a clear signal saying "Hey, you look good!"*
>
> *You return from class one day and as you approach the door to your dorm room you see a friend of yours is sitting on the floor looking very down. You stop to ask if she's ok, and you see that she's been crying.*

Will these actions of others have any effect on your own emotions, thoughts, and behavior? Very likely. If you too are interested in potential romance, you may be very pleased when you see someone looking at you in a "let's get to know each other" kind of way, and you may then go over and say "Hi!" When you see that your friend has been crying, you are likely to ask "what happened?" and sit down to provide her with some comfort while you listen to her story. Instances like these, where we observe other people and respond to them, indicate that other people's emotional expressions often have a powerful impact upon us (see Figure 1.4).

Figure 1.4 When Other People Communicate Their Emotions, We Respond

We are often affected by others people's expression of emotions. Even though in one case the person is expressing positive emotion toward us and in the other the person is expressing negative feelings, in both these instances we may be motivated to approach the other person.

In addition, we are also often affected by others' appearance. Be honest: Don't you behave differently toward highly attractive persons than toward less attractive ones? Toward very old people compared to young ones? Toward people who belong to your own ethnic group compared to ones different from your own? Your answer to these questions is probably "yes," because we do often react to others' visible characteristics, such as their appearance (McCall, 1997; Twenge & Manis, 1998). In fact, research findings (e.g., Hassin & Trope, 2000) indicate that we cannot ignore others' appearance even when we consciously try to do so. So despite warnings to avoid "judging books by their covers," we are often strongly affected by other people's group memberships as indicated by appearance—even if we are unaware of such effects and might deny their existence (see Chapters 6 and 7). Interestingly, research findings indicate that relying on others' appearance as a guide to their characteristics is not always wrong; in fact, they can be relatively accurate, especially when we can observe others behaving spontaneously, rather than in posed photos (Nauman, Vazire, Rentfrow, & Gosling, 2009).

COGNITIVE PROCESSES   Suppose that you have arranged to meet a friend, and this person is late. In fact, after 30 minutes you begin to suspect that your friend will never arrive. Finally, she or he does appear and says "Sorry . . . I forgot all about meeting you until a few minutes ago." How will you react? Probably you will feel some annoyance. Imagine that instead, however, your friend says "I'm so sorry to be late. . . . There was a big accident, and the traffic was tied up for miles." Now how will you react? Perhaps you'll fell less annoyance—but not necessarily. If your friend is often late and has used this excuse before, you may be suspicious about whether this explanation is true. In contrast, if this is the first time your friend has been late, or if your friend has never used such an excuse in the past, you may accept it as true. In other words, your reactions in this situation will depend upon your memories of your friend's past behavior and your inferences about whether her or his explanation is really true. Situations like this one call attention to the fact that *cognitive processes* play a crucial role in social behavior. We try to make sense of people in our social world by attributing their actions to something about them (e.g., their traits) or something about the circumstances (e.g., unforeseeable traffic). This means we engage in lots of social cognition—thinking long and hard about other people—what they are like, why they do what they do, how they might react to our behavior, and so on (Shah, 2003). Social psychologists are well aware of the importance of such processes and social cognition is a very important area of research (Fiske, 2009).

ENVIRONMENTAL VARIABLES: IMPACT OF THE PHYSICAL WORLD   Do we become more irritable and aggressive when the weather is hot and steamy than when it is cooler and more comfortable (Bell, Greene, Fisher, & Baum, 2001; Rotton & Cohn, 2000)? Does exposure to a pleasant smell in the air make people more helpful to others (Baron, 1997)? Does simply seeing money—such as a picture of a dollar bill—interfere with our ability to enjoy small pleasures in life like the taste of chocolate (Quoidbach, Dunn, Petrides, & Mikolajczak, 2010)? Research findings indicate that aspects of the physical environment can indeed influence our feelings, thoughts, and behavior, so these variables, too, certainly fall within the realm of modern social psychology.

BIOLOGICAL FACTORS   Is social behavior influenced by biological processes? In the past, most social psychologists might have answered no, and certainly not in any direct fashion. Now, however, some suggest that our preferences, emotions, and behaviors may be linked, to some extent, to our biological inheritance (Buss, 2008; Schmitt, 2004)—although social experiences too have a powerful effect and may interact with genetic factors in generating the complex patterns of our social lives (Gillath, Shaver, Baek, & Chun, 2008).

In fact, it is becoming clear that the operation of these two factors—biology and social experience—is not unidirectional. Experiences of stress, especially early in life but also in adulthood as a function of exposure to various forms of trauma including political violence, can induce neurobiological changes that affect psychological well-being (Canetti & Lindner, 2015; Hertzman & Boyce, 2010; McInnis, McQuaid, Matheson, & Anisman, 2015). Indeed, there is now accumulating evidence that environmental factors and social experiences—through what is called *epigenetic processes*, where the operation of certain genes is turned on or off—can influence behavior, sometimes long after initial exposure (Spector, 2012).

The view that biological factors play an important role in social behavior has been emphasized among those who take an **evolutionary psychology** perspective (e.g., Buss, 2004; Buss & Shackelford, 1997). This branch of psychology suggests that our species, like all others, has been subject to the process of biological evolution throughout its history and that, as a result, we now possess a large number of *evolved psychological mechanisms* that help (or once helped) us to deal with important problems relating to survival.

Through the process of evolution, which involves the three basic components of variation, inheritance, and selection, such tendencies become part of our biological inheritance. Variation refers to the fact that organisms belonging to a given species vary in many different ways; indeed, such variation is a basic part of life on our planet. Human beings, as you already know, vary on what sometimes seems to be an almost countless number of dimensions. Inheritance refers to the fact that some of these variations can be passed from one generation to the next through complex mechanisms that we are beginning to understand only now. Selection refers to the fact that some variations give the individuals who possess them an "edge" in terms of reproduction: They are more likely to survive, find mates, and pass these variations on to succeeding generations. The result is that over time, more and more members of the species possess these variations. This change in the characteristics of a species over time—immensely long periods of time—is the concrete outcome of evolution. (See Figure 1.5 for a summary of this process.)

Social psychologists who adopt the evolutionary perspective suggest that this process applies to at least some aspects of social behavior. For instance, consider the question of mate preference. Why do we find some people attractive? According to the evolutionary perspective because the characteristics they show—symmetrical facial features; well-toned, shapely bodies; clear skin; lustrous hair—are associated with "good genes," they are likely to indicate that the people who possess them are healthy and vigorous and therefore good mates (Schmitt & Buss, 2001; Tesser & Martin, 1996). For instance, these characteristics—the ones we find attractive—potentially indicate that the persons who show them have strong immune systems that protect them from many illnesses (Li & Kenrick, 2006). Presumably, a preference for characteristics associated with good health and vigor among our ancestors increased their chances of successfully reproducing; this, in turn, could have contributed to our preference for people who possess these aspects of appearance.

Is there any reason to suppose that evolution might favor different behaviors for men and women? When asked to indicate the characteristics in potential romantic partners that they find desirable, both genders—but especially women—rate a sense of humor high on the list (e.g., Buss, 2008). From an evolutionary point of view, a sense of humor might signal high intelligence, which would make humorous people attractive (Griskevicius et al., 2009). Another possibility is that a sense of humor signals something else: interest in forming new relationships. Humor might signal that the person is available— and interested. Research by Li and colleagues (2009) found that people are more likely to use humor and laugh when they find

Figure 1.5 Evolutionary Psychology Perspective

Evolution involves three major components: variation, inheritance, and selection. Social psychologists who are guided by this perspective are particularly interested in features that might account for gendered behavior, especially those related to sexuality.

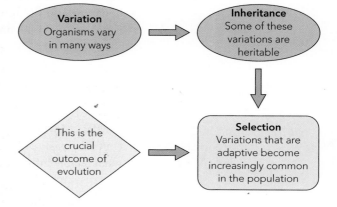

Figure 1.6 Humor: An Important "Plus" in Dating

Research findings indicate that humor is viewed as a desirable characteristic in potential romantic partners, partly because it is perceived as a sign that the person is interested in forming a new relationship. Such effects occur in many situations, including dating. So, if you want romantic partners, keep on smiling and make jokes.

another person attractive than when they do not; people who used humor during speed dating sessions were perceived as showing more romantic interest than ones who did not (see Figure 1.6).

Other topics have been studied from the evolutionary perspective (e.g., helping others; aggression; preferences for various ways of attracting persons who are already in a relationship), and we'll describe this research in other chapters. Here, we wish to emphasize the following fact: The evolutionary perspective does *not* suggest that we inherit specific patterns of social behavior; rather, it contends that we inherit tendencies or predispositions that may be apparent in our overt actions, depending on the environments in which we live. Similarly, this perspective does *not* suggest that we are "forced" or driven by our genes to act in specific ways. Rather, it merely suggests that because of our genetic inheritance, we have tendencies to behave in certain ways that, at least in the past, may have enhanced the chances that our ancestors would survive and pass their genes on to us. These tendencies, can be—and often are—overridden by cognitive factors and the effects of experience (Pettijohn & Jungeberg, 2004). For instance, what is viewed as attractive changes over time and is often very different in diverse cultures. So yes, genetic factors play some role in our behavior and thought, but they are clearly only one factor among many that influence how we think and act.

1.1.4: The Search for Basic Principles in a Changing Social World

One key goal of science is the development of basic principles that are accurate regardless of when or where they are applied or tested. Social psychologists seek to uncover the basic principles that govern social life. For instance, they'd like to determine what factors influence attraction, helping, obedience, the attitudes we form, and so on. The research they conduct is aimed to yield such knowledge—basic principles that will be true across time and in different cultures.

On the other hand, social psychologists recognize that cultures differ greatly and that the social world in which we live is constantly changing—in very important ways. For instance, cultures vary greatly with respect to when and where people are expected to "dress up" rather than dress casually. While casual is acceptable in almost all contexts in the United States, more formal "dressy" attire is often expected in other cultures. This same point applies to more important aspects of social life, too: Should teenagers be allowed to date and meet without adult supervision? Should you name your baby after a relative, or should you give your child a unique and, perhaps, unusual name? At what age should people retire, and how should they be treated after they do? Should we make choices that are the same as other people we know, or should we try to be "different" and stand out from others (see Figure 1.7)?

Cultures differ tremendously in these and countless other ways, and this complicates the task of establishing general principles of social behavior and social thought. Should we try to compliment another person to make him or her like us? This is an ingratiation tactic that, as you will see in Chapter 8, has been found to be generally effective in individualistic cultures. Yet, research has revealed that because people from some cultures value independence (being seen as unique and separate from others) while others value interdependence (being seen as similar to and connected to others), responses to such seemingly positive treatment depends on whether it implies the person is different or the same as other members of his or her group (Siy & Cheryan, 2013). So, for example, those who are Asian-born respond more negatively to treatment that implies they are different from other group members, whereas those who are U.S.-born respond more negatively to treatment that implies they are the same as other group members.

In addition, within a culture, how we interact with each other can change across time. Because of social media, and digital technology more generally, people now meet potential romantic partners in different ways than in the past when, typically, they were introduced by friends or met at dances arranged by their schools, churches, or other social organizations. Does this mean that the foundations of attraction

Figure 1.7 Cultures Differ in Many Ways—Including the Importance of Personal Uniqueness

In some cultures, it is considered important to be different from others, while in others it is seen as important to fit in with those around us.

are different today than in the past? Social psychologists believe that despite these changes, the same basic principles apply: Physical attractiveness is still a basic ingredient, even though what is deemed attractive may differ across time. Likewise, the basic principles of persuasion too remain much the same, even if messages aimed at influencing us are delivered in a different format (e.g., electronically) than in the past (e.g., print). In short, although the task of identifying basic, accurate principles of social behavior and social thought is complicated by the existence of cultural differences and rapid changes in social life, the goals of social psychological research remain the same: uncovering basic, accurate knowledge about the social side of life that applies in a wide range of contexts and situations.

In summary, social psychology focuses mainly on understanding the causes of social behavior—on identifying factors that shape our feelings, behavior, and thought in social situations. It seeks to accomplish this goal through the use of scientific methods, and it takes careful note of the fact that social behavior is influenced by a wide range of social, cognitive, environmental, cultural, and biological factors. The remainder of this text is devoted to describing some of the key findings of social psychology. We're certain that you will find it fascinating—after all, it is about *us* and the social side of *our* lives! We're equally sure that you will find the outcomes of some research surprising and that it may challenge many of your ideas about people and social relations. We predict that after reading this book, you'll never think about the social side of life in quite the same way as before.

Key Points

- Social psychology is the scientific field that seeks to understand the nature and causes of individual behavior in social situations.
- It is scientific in nature because it adopts the values and methods used in the other fields of science.
- Social psychologists adopt the scientific method because "common sense" provides an unreliable guide to predicting social behavior and because our thought is influenced by many potential sources of bias.
- Social psychology focuses on the behavior of individuals and seeks to understand the causes of their emotions,

thoughts, and social behavior. These can involve the behavior and appearance of others, environmental factors, cultural values, and even biological and genetic factors.
- Research from an **evolutionary psychology** perspective emphasizes how natural selection may have encouraged particular behavioral tendencies, especially those related to mating and sexuality.
- Social psychology seeks to establish the basic principles that govern social life, despite cultural differences and rapid changes in technology that affect how social life unfolds.

1.2: Social Psychology: Advances at the Boundaries

Objective   **Examine the major avenues that social psychology is currently exploring**

Textbooks, like fine wine, don't necessarily improve with age. So, to remain current, they must keep pace with changes in the fields they represent. Making certain that this book is current, in the best sense of this term, is one of our key goals. You can be sure that the research presented in the chapters that follow is a contemporary view of social psychological knowledge concerning the social side of life. Consistent with this goal, we will now describe several major trends in modern social psychology—themes and ideas that you will see throughout this text because they represent what is of central focus to social psychology.

1.2.1: Cognition and Behavior: Two Sides of the Same Social Coin

In the past, social psychologists could be divided into two distinct groups: those who were primarily interested in social *behavior*—how people act in social situations, and those who were primarily interested in social *thought*—how people attempt to make sense of the social world and to understand themselves and others. In modern social psychology, behavior and cognition are seen as intimately, and continuously, linked. In other words, there is virtually universal agreement in the field that we cannot hope to understand how and why people behave in certain ways in social situations without considering their thoughts, memory, intentions, emotions, attitudes, and beliefs. Similarly, virtually all social psychologists agree that there is a complex interplay between social thought and social behavior. What we think about others influences our actions toward them, and the consequences of these actions then affect our emotions and social thought. So, in trying to understand the social side of life, modern social psychology integrates both. That will be our approach throughout the book, and it will be present in virtually every chapter.

1.2.2: The Role of Emotion in the Social Side of Life

Can you imagine life without emotions? Probably not, because life without feelings would be missing a lot and not reflect humans as we know them. Social psychologists have always been interested in emotions and moods, and with good reason: They play a key role in many aspects of social life. For instance, imagine that you want a favor from a friend or acquaintance—when would you ask for it, when this person is in a good mood or a bad one? Research findings indicate that you would do much better when that person is in a good mood, because positive moods (or *affect* as social psychologists term such feelings) do increase our tendency to offer help to others (e.g., Isen & Levin, 1972). Similarly, suppose you are meeting someone for the first time—do you think your current mood might influence your reactions to this person? If you answered "yes," you are in agreement with the results of systematic research, which indicates our impressions of others (and our thoughts about them) are influenced by our current moods. More recently, social psychologists have been investigating the role of moods in a wide range of social behaviors (Forgas, Baumeister, & Tice, 2009), and overall, interest in this topic, including the impact of specific emotions, has increased. So, we include it here as another area in which rapid advances are being made at the boundaries of our current knowledge of social life.

1.2.3: Social Relationships: How Important They Are for Well-Being

If the social side of life is as important as we suggested at the start of this chapter, then relationships with others are its building blocks. When they are successful and satisfying, they add tremendously to our happiness, but when they go wrong, they can disrupt every other aspect of our lives and undermine our psychological health and well-being (Slotter, Gardner, & Finkel, 2010). Because our connections to others are so critical, social psychologists have sought to understand the nature of social relationships—how they begin and change over time, and why, gradually, some strengthen and deepen, while others weaken and end—often, causing tremendous pain to the people involved. We'll consider relationships in detail in Chapter 7, but here, to give you the flavor of this growing body of knowledge, we'll mention just a couple of lines of important and revealing research.

One such topic relates to the following question: "Is it better, in terms of building a strong relationship, to view one's partner (boyfriend, girlfriend, or spouse)

Figure 1.8 The Warm Glow of Love

When couples are in love, they often perceive each other in unrealistically favorable ways. Is that good or bad for their future relationship? The answer is complex, but research findings indicate that as long as they show some degree of reality or accuracy, it may be beneficial.

realistically, or as we often do, through "rose-colored glasses"? Folklore suggests that "love is blind," and when in love, many people do tend to see only good in their partners (see Figure 1.8). Is that tendency good or bad for their relationships? Research findings suggest that in general, it is good, but only if it is restrained by a healthy degree of reality (i.e., accuracy; Fletcher, Simpson, & Boyes, 2006). Positivity and perceived similarity between partners contributes to happiness, but accuracy does too.

Many other types of social relationships are also important for people's well-being. In fact, in the Western world, more people now spend a greater proportion of their lives living alone than ever before and people who choose to remain single are often just as happy as those who marry (DePaulo, 2008; Klinenberg, 2012). How can that be—if relationships are crucial to well-being? Research findings reveal that it is because single people often contribute more to their communities (by volunteering), they have more friends, and, crucially, they often belong to more groups. Belonging to multiple social groups that the individual values not only predicts better psychological well-being, but those who do so live longer than those who belong to few social groups (Holt-Lunstad, Smith, & Layton, 2010; Jetten et al., 2015; Putnam, 2000). Not only do the groups we belong to become an important part of "who we are," but they provide important psychological resources such as social support, which, as you'll see in Chapters 11 and 12, helps people to cope with adversity. When you came to college, did you join a sorority or fraternity, connect with others in your dorm, or perhaps even take part in your campus Psychology Club—Psi Chi? If you did, as shown in Figure 1.9, being part of such groups can help boost self-esteem.

Figure 1.9 Togetherness: Being Part of Groups Is Important for Well-Being

Connections to others that are gained by being part of different social groups is not only emotionally stimulating when the interaction is occurring but research findings indicate that when internalized as part of ourselves—our identities—they have the potential to boost self-esteem.

1.2.4: Social Neuroscience: The Intersection of Social Psychology and Brain Research

In a basic sense, everything we do, feel, imagine, or create reflects activity within our brains. Reading and understanding the words on this page is the result of activity in your brain. Are you in a good mood? Whatever you are feeling also reflects activity in your brain and biological systems. How do you know who you are? Can you remember your best friend in public school? How your first ride on a roller coaster felt? Do you have plans for the future—and do you believe you can actually achieve them? All of these memories and experiences are the result of activity in various areas of your brain.

In the past 20 years, powerful new tools for measuring activity in our brains as they function have been developed. Although they were initially developed for medical uses and have generated major advances in surgery by helping to illuminate abnormalities, as shown in Figure 1.10, magnetic resonance imaging (fMRI), PET scans, and other techniques have also allowed psychologists and other scientists to peer into the human brain as people engage in various activities, and so find out just what's happening at any given time. The result is that we now know much more about the complex relationships between neural events and psychological ones—feelings, thoughts, and overt actions.

Social psychologists, too, have begun to use these new tools to uncover the foundations of social thought and social behavior—to find out what portions of the brain and what complex systems within it are involved in key aspects of our social life—everything from prejudice and aggression, through under-performing on tasks due to "choking under pressure" (Mobbs et al., 2009), and empathy and helping (Van Berkum, Holleman, Nieuwland, Otten, & Murre, 2009). In conducting such research, social psychologists use the same basic tools as other scientists—they study events in the brain and even changes in the immune system (Taylor, Lerner, Sherman, Sage, &

Figure 1.10 Peering Inside the Head with Magnetic Resonance Imaging

As illustrated here, advances in technology have allowed social psychologists to view blood flow changes in different regions of the brain as people process different types of information. This can provide information about the interplay between types of thought and brain activity.

McDowell, 2003) in order to determine how these events are related to important social processes. The findings of this research have been truly fascinating. Here's one example of what we mean.

Attitudes and values are an important part of the social side of life; as you'll see in Chapter 5, they often shape our overt behavior and underlie powerful emotional reactions to events and people. But how are they represented in the brain, and how do they exert their powerful effects on our behavior, thought, and emotions? **Social neuroscience** research is providing intriguing answers. For example, consider a study by Van Berkum and colleagues (2009). This investigation was designed to determine what happens in the brain when people encounter statements that are consistent or inconsistent with their strongly held values and attitudes. To do this, they recruited two groups of participants known to hold opposite views on many social issues. One group (members of a strict Christian church) was known to be against euthanasia, growing equality of women in society, abortion, and the use of drugs. Members of the other group, self-described as "nonreligious," were known to hold opposite views on those issues.

Both groups were then exposed to statements relating to these attitudes on a computer screen, and while viewing them, electrical activity in their brains was carefully recorded. A key question asked by the researchers was: How quickly do people react, in terms of brain activity, to statements that disagree with their own attitudes or values?

Do they react this way as soon as they encounter a *single word* that is inconsistent with their views (e.g., "acceptable" in the statement "I think euthanasia is acceptable… " if they are against this action) or only after reading the entire statement and considering it carefully? Previous research indicated that certain patterns of activity (N400, one kind of *event-related potential*—a kind of activity in the brain) occur very quickly when individuals encounter words inconsistent with their values—only 250 milliseconds after seeing them—and indicate that intensified processing of this word is occurring. Other patterns, in contrast, occur somewhat later and reflect negative reactions to the value-inconsistent statement. It was predicted that each group would show stronger N400 reactions to words that were inconsistent with their values, so that, for instance, the Christian group would show stronger reactions to the word *acceptable* in connection with euthanasia, while the other group would express stronger reactions to the word *unacceptable* when linked to euthanasia. Results offered strong support for these predictions and suggest that we do indeed process information that disagrees with our attitudes *very* quickly—long before we can put such reactions into words. So yes, attitudes and values do indeed exert powerful and far-reaching effects on activity within our brains—and on our overt actions.

Here's another example of how social psychologists are using the tools of neuroscience to study important aspects of social thought and behavior. Have you heard of *mirror neurons*? They are neurons in our brains that are activated during the observation and execution of actions, and it has been suggested that they play a key role in *empathy*—our capacity to experience, vicariously, the emotions and feelings of other persons (Gazzola, Aziz-Zadeh, & Keysers, 2006; Iacoboni, 2009). Mirror neurons are located in a portion of the brain known as the *frontal operculum*, and in an intriguing study, Montgomery, Seeherman, and Haxby (2009) suggested that perhaps people who score high on a questionnaire measuring empathy would show more activity in this area of their brains when they viewed facial expressions of others.

To test this prediction, the researchers exposed two groups of individuals—ones who scored high or low on a measure of empathy (the capacity to take the perspective of other persons)—to video clips of others' facial expressions (e.g., smiling, frowning) or to faces that showed nonsocial movements (i.e., movements not associated with particular emotions). Activity in the brains of both groups of participants was recorded through fMRI scans. Results were clear: As predicted, persons high or moderate in empathy did indeed show greater activity in the frontal operculum (where mirror neurons are located) than persons low in empathy (see Figure 1.11).

Research in the rapidly expanding field of social neuroscience is at the forefront of advances in social psychology, and we will represent it fully in this text. We should insert one warning, however. As noted by several experts in this field (e.g., Cacioppo et al., 2003), social neuroscience cannot provide the answer to every question we have about social thought or behavior. There are many aspects of social thought that cannot easily be related to activity in specific areas of the brain—including attributions, group identities, and reciprocity (e.g., Willingham & Dunn, 2003). In principle, all of these components of social thought reflect activity in the brain, but this does not

Figure 1.11 The Neural Basis of Empathy

Individuals high or moderate on a measure of empathy (the capacity to see the world through others' eyes) showed more activity in a portion of their brains (the frontal operculum) than persons low in empathy, when watching videos of other people displaying facial expressions. In contrast, the groups did not differ in brain activity while watching videos showing nonsocial facial movements (i.e., ones unrelated to emotions).

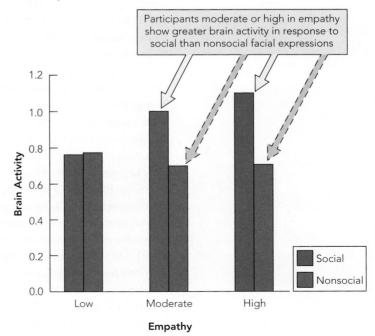

necessarily mean that it is best to try to study them in this way. In fact, the situation may be similar to that existing between chemistry and physics. All chemists agree that ultimately, every chemical reaction can be explained in terms of physics. But the principles of chemistry are still so useful that chemists continue to use them in their research and do not all rush out and become physicists. The same may well be true for social psychology: It does not have to seek to understand all of its major topics in terms of activities in the brain or nervous system; other approaches that we will describe in later chapters are more useful in terms of providing important new insights. Throughout this book, therefore, we will describe research that uses a wide range of methods, from brain scans on the one hand to direct observations of social behavior on the other.

1.2.5: The Role of Implicit (Nonconscious) Processes

Have you ever had the experience of meeting someone for the first time and taking an immediate liking—or disliking—to that person? Afterward, you may have wondered, "Why do I like (dislike) this person?" But probably, you didn't wonder for long because we are all experts at finding good reasons to explain our own actions or feelings. This speed in no way implies that we really *do* understand why we behave or think in certain ways. And, as you will see in Chapters 2 and 4, a growing theme of recent research in social psychology has been just this: In many cases we really *don't* know why we think or behave as we do in social contexts. And, partly because of errors in the way we process social information, and partly because we change greatly over time, we don't even know—with clarity—what will make us happy (Gilbert, 2006).

Indeed, our thoughts and actions are shaped by factors and processes of which we are only dimly aware, at best, and which often take place in an automatic manner, without any conscious thought or intention on our part. Consider for a minute whether you think men or women are more likely to be creative. Because this quality is deemed critical for many high-level positions, most people might be reluctant to overtly engage in gender stereotyping and state that, for example, "yes, I believe that men are more creative than women." To get at this question then, another approach is needed. Proudfoot, Kay, and Koval (2015) presented their participants with information about a male or female working in a masculine domain—architecture. After viewing the person's supposed work output—images of a building design—participants were simply asked to indicate how creative, original, and "outside-the-box" the work appeared to be. Despite the design being identical, when the name was female, it was seen as less creative than when the name was male. In another study, these investigators presented participants with information about a male or female manager who made "risky" business decisions or not. The male manager was rated as more creative when he made risky business choices than the female manager who made the same risky choices. So, this is one reason that social psychologists are reluctant to simply ask people their beliefs—such as "are women or men more creative?" We may be quite unaware of holding those beliefs, or our gender stereotypes could possibly influence the judgments we make.

Consider another example of the role of nonconscious processes, this time on first impressions. Research indicates that we form these incredibly quickly—often within mere seconds of meeting other people (Gray, 2008). Sometimes these first impressions are accurate, and sometimes they are very wrong (Carney, Colvin, & Hall, 2007). Do we know when our first impressions are likely to be accurate and when they are not? Evidence reported by Ames, Kammrath, Suppes, and Bolger (2010) indicates that we cannot intuit when these impressions are likely to be accurate and when they are not. So, nonconscious processes do influence our judgments and actions, but this occurs in ways that we often are unable to control, and they can lead us astray. Research on the role of implicit (nonconscious) processes in our social behavior and thought has examined many other topics, and we will examine them in several chapters since they represent an important focus of current research (see Chapters 2 and 6).

1.2.6: Taking Full Account of Social Diversity

There can be no doubt that the United States—like many other countries—is undergoing a major social and cultural transformation. Recent figures indicate that 64 percent of the population identifies itself as white (of European heritage), while fully 36 percent identifies itself as belonging to another group (13 percent African American, 4.5 percent American Indian, 14 percent Hispanic, 4.5 percent Asian/Pacific Islander, and 7 percent some other group). Indeed, by 2050, European Americans will lose their numerical majority status (U.S. Census Bureau, Population Division, 2012). This represents a tremendous change from the 1960s, when approximately 90 percent of the population was of European descent.

In response to these tremendous shifts, psychologists have increasingly recognized the importance of taking cultural factors into account in everything they do—teaching, research, and therapy—and social psychologists are certainly no exception to this rule. They have been increasingly sensitive to the fact that individuals' cultural, ethnic, and racial heritage often plays a key role in their conceptions of themselves (e.g., identity), and this, in turn, exerts important effects on social thought and behavior. As a result, social psychology has adopted a **multicultural perspective**—one that recognizes the potential importance of gender, age, ethnicity, sexual orientation, disability, social class, religious orientation, and many other social group dimensions. This perspective has led to important changes in the focus of social psychological research, including how behavior changes depending on which of these category memberships is used to define the self at any given moment (see Chapter 4). Social diversity and its consequences for team performance, perceptions of inequality, and discrimination are major topics that we will cover in Chapters 2, 6, and 11.

Consider for a moment how culture might modify what is considered beautiful. In a study conducted in 10 different countries around the world, people indicated what kind of body shape they find most attractive in women (Swami et al., 2010). Participants were shown drawings of different body shapes and were asked to choose the one they found most attractive. Results indicated that there were indeed cultural differences in the ratings provided by participants: Raters in Oceania, South and West Asia, and Southeast Asia preferred heavier body types than those in North America and East Asia. However, larger differences occurred within those cultures in terms of socioeconomic status: Higher SES persons (i.e., those higher in education and income) preferred slimmer body builds to those of lower SES status. This suggests that large differences exist with respect to this aspect of social perception within cultures as well as between them.

Culture can also modify the extent to which aspects of physical appearance are related to life outcomes and psychological well-being. In many studies with urban American student samples, more attractive people report being treated better by others and more positive psychological well-being as a result than those who are less attractive (Langlois et al., 2000). However, this relationship where meeting standards of attractiveness in terms of slimness in particular enables social connections and positive treatment from others is entirely absent among rural-residing Americans (Plaut, Adams, & Anderson, 2009) and residents of Ghana, Africa (Anderson, Adams, & Plaut, 2008). These cultural differences have been hypothesized as stemming from differing ways that personal relationships are constructed—as stemming from personal volition and choice or from being embedded in particular social networks. Clearly, cultures, including different social classes within cultures, can both enable and encourage people to experience the social world differently and increased recognition of this is a hallmark of modern social psychology. We will discuss research highlighting why and how culture matters for social thought and behavior at many points in this book.

Key Points

- Social psychology is the scientific branch of psychology that focuses on the social side of life.
- Social psychologists currently recognize that social thought and social behavior are two sides of the same coin, and that there is a continuous, complex interplay between them.
- There is growing interest among social psychologists in the role of emotion in social thought and social behavior.
- The importance of many types of social relationships is another major trend in the field.

- Yet another major trend involves growing interest in **social neuroscience**—efforts to relate activity in the brain to key aspects of social thought and behavior.
- Social behavior is often shaped by factors of which we are unaware. Growing attention to such implicit (nonconscious) processes is another major theme of modern social psychology.
- Social psychology currently adopts a **multicultural perspective**. This perspective recognizes the importance of cultural factors in social behavior and social thought.

1.3: How Social Psychologists Answer the Questions They Ask: Research as the Route to Increased Knowledge

Objective   **Understand the methods social psychologists use to gain insight into the questions posed**

Now that we've provided you with an overview of some of the current trends in social psychology, we can turn to the third major task mentioned at the start of this chapter: explaining how social psychologists attempt to answer questions about social behavior and social thought. Since social psychology is scientific in orientation, they usually seek to accomplish this task through systematic research. To provide you with the basic information about the specific techniques they use, we'll examine three related topics. First, we will describe basic *methods of research in social psychology*. Next we will consider the role of *theory* in such research. Finally, we'll touch on some of the complex *ethical issues* relating to social psychological research.

1.3.1: Systematic Observation: Describing the World Around Us

One basic technique for studying social behavior involves **systematic observation**—carefully observing behavior as it occurs. Such observation is not the kind of informal "people watching" we all practice from childhood onward; rather, in a scientific field such as social psychology it is observation accompanied by careful, accurate measurement of a particular behavior across people. Suppose that a social psychologist wanted to find out how frequently people touch each other in different settings. The researcher could study this topic by going to shopping malls, restaurants and bars, college campuses, and many other locations and observe, in those settings, who touches whom, how they touch, and with what frequency. Such research (which has actually been conducted; see Chapter 3) would be employing what is known as **naturalistic observation**—observation of people's behavior in natural settings (Linden, 1992).

Note that in such observation the researcher would simply record what is happening in each context; she or he would make no attempt to change the behavior of the persons being observed. In fact, such observation requires that the researcher take great pains to *avoid* influencing the people who are being observed in any way. Thus, the researchers would try to remain as inconspicuous as possible and might even try to hide behind natural barriers so as not to affect the behavior of the people they are watching.

Another technique that entails a form of systematic observation is known as the **survey method**. Here, researchers ask large numbers of persons to respond to questions about their attitudes or behavior. Surveys are used for many purposes—to measure attitudes toward specific issues such as marijuana use or abortion, to find out how voters feel about various political candidates, to determine how people feel about members of different social groups, and even to assess student reactions to professors (your college or university probably uses a form on which you rate your professor's teaching each semester). Social psychologists often use this method to assess attitudes toward a variety of social issues—for instance, gun control or affirmative action programs. Scientists and practitioners in other fields use the survey method to measure everything from life satisfaction around the globe to consumer reactions to new products.

Surveys offer several advantages. Information can be gathered about thousands or even hundreds of thousands of persons with relative ease, and the responses of different categories of people can be compared—say, do men and women differ in the prejudice they express toward Muslims, public funding for day care centers, or their reported satisfaction with life? In fact, surveys are now often conducted online, through the Internet. Because, there are now more than 1.4 billion Facebook users worldwide, it is becoming an increasingly used platform for survey research. Respondents can click on the survey from within Facebook, and doing so allows the researchers to connect their survey self-reports with many types of personal attributes (e.g., gender, number of friends, demographic details, and personal interests such as movies and books) that are available for each user (Kosinski, Matz, Gosling, Popov, & Stillwell, 2015).

Recent research on happiness is being conducted using researchers' own sites (see Figure 1.12). To take a look at how it works, just visit authentichappiness.com for one example. The surveys presented there have been prepared by well-known psychologists, and your replies—which are entirely confidential—will become part of a huge data set that is being used to find out why people are happy or unhappy, and ways it can be increased. The site has been visited by millions of people and currently has over 750,000 registered users. (We'll examine this topic in detail in Chapter 12.)

In order to be useful as a research tool, though, surveys must meet certain requirements. First, the persons who participate must be *representative* of the larger population about which conclusions are to be drawn—which raises the issue of *sampling*. If this condition is not met, serious errors can result. Suppose that the authentichappiness .com website is visited only by people who are already very happy—perhaps because unhappy people don't want to report on their feelings. Or, conversely, suppose it is visited mostly by unhappy people who want to learn how to be happier. Any results obtained would be questionable for describing Americans' average level of happiness, because they do not represent the entire range of happiness in the population as a whole.

Yet another issue that must be carefully addressed with respect to surveys is this: The way in which the items are worded can exert strong effects on the outcomes obtained. Continuing with the happiness example we have been using, suppose a survey asked people to rate, "How happy are you in your life right now?" (on a 7-point scale where 1 = very unhappy and 7 = very happy). Many people might well answer 4 or above because overall, most people do seem to be relatively happy much of the

Figure 1.12 Using the Internet to Conduct Research

Social psychologists sometimes collect survey data from sites they establish on the Internet. Many of these are set up for a specific study, but others, like the one shown here, remain open permanently and often provide data collected from hundreds of thousands of people.

time. But suppose the question asked: "Compared to the happiest you have ever been, how happy are you in your life right now?" (1 = much less happy; 7 = just as happy). In the context of this comparison to your peak level of happiness, many people might provide numbers lower than 4, because they know they have been happier sometime in the past. Comparing the results from these questions could be misleading, if the difference in wording between them were ignored.

In sum, the survey method can be a useful approach for studying some aspects of social behavior. Surveys are especially useful for capturing large samples, the questions concern topics people can easily report on, and they concern behaviors that might otherwise be difficult to learn about. However, the results obtained are accurate only to the extent that issues relating to sampling and wording are carefully addressed.

1.3.2: Correlation: The Search for Relationships

At various times, you have probably noticed that some events appear to be related to the occurrence of others: As one changes, the other changes, too. For example, perhaps you've noticed that people who drive new, expensive cars tend to be older than people who drive old, inexpensive ones or that people using social media such as Facebook tend to be relatively young (although this is now changing). When two events or attributes (age of person and age of car) are related in this way, they are said to be *correlated* or that a correlation exists between them. The term *correlation* refers to a tendency for one event to be associated with changes in the other. Social psychologists refer to such changeable aspects of the natural world as *variables*, since they can take different values.

From a scientific point of view, knowing that there is a correlation between two variables can be very useful, and it is the primary aim of many survey studies. When a correlation exists, it is possible to predict one variable from information about the other variable. The ability to make such *predictions* is one important goal of all branches of science, including social psychology. Being able to make accurate predictions can be very helpful. For instance, imagine that a correlation is observed between the amount of money people donate to charity (one variable) and how happy they are (another variable). Although there are many reasons *why* this correlation might exist, it could be very useful for organizations seeking volunteers to highlight this potential well-being benefit of helping others. In fact, we do know that in countries where there is a stronger norm of providing help to others, the well-being of the population is greater (Oarga, Stavrova, & Fetchenhauer, 2015). This might suggest that strengthening this norm (i.e., "we're the kind of people who help each other") in communities will yield improvements in the happiness of members. Similarly, suppose that a correlation is observed between certain patterns of behavior in married couples (e.g., the tendency to criticize each other harshly) and the likelihood that they will later divorce. Again, this information might be helpful in counseling the persons involved and, perhaps, improving their relationships.

The stronger the correlation between two variables, the more accurate the prediction can be made. Correlations can range from 0 to −1.00 or +1.00; the greater the departure from 0, the stronger the correlation. Positive numbers mean that as one variable increases the other increases too. For example, the more people perceive members of a prior enemy group (i.e., Muslims in Lebanon) as having changed (they are seen as different now than in the past), the more forgiveness is expressed (i.e., by Christians in Lebanon) for the harmful actions committed by the other group during the civil war (Licata, Klein, Saade, Azzi, & Branscombe, 2012). Negative numbers indicate that as one variable increases, the other decreases. For instance, the more groups with a history of conflict (i.e., Israel/Palestine; Protestants/Catholics in Northern Ireland) engage in "competitive victimhood" or claim their suffering was worse than that experienced by the other group, the less forgiving they are of the other group (Noor, Brown, Gonzalez, Manzi, & Lewis, 2008). For researchers interested in ways these sorts of intergroup conflicts might be solved and achieving peaceful reconciliation, knowing that increases in some beliefs predict greater forgiveness while increases in other beliefs predict reduced forgiveness is very useful indeed.

These basic facts underlie an important method of research sometimes used by social psychologists: the **correlational method**. In this approach, social psychologists attempt to determine whether, and to what extent, different variables are related to each other. This involves carefully measuring each variable and then performing appropriate statistical tests to determine whether and to what degree the variables are related.

Imagine that a social psychologist wants to find out whether the information posted by users on Facebook is accurate—whether it portrays the users realistically, or presents them as they would like to be (an idealized self-image). Further, imagine that on the basis of previous studies, the researcher hypothesizes that the information people post on Facebook is indeed relatively accurate. How could this idea be tested? One very basic approach, using the correlational method of research, is as follows. First, posters on Facebook could complete measures of their personality (e.g., these could include extraversion, conscientiousness, openness to experience—ones found to be important in past research). Then, raters would read the profiles on Facebook and from this information rate the posters on the same personality dimensions. As a cross-check, other people who know the posters well could also rate them on the same personality dimensions. Next, these sets of information would be compared (i.e., correlated) to see how closely they align. The higher the correlation between these ratings—the ones provided by the posters themselves and people who know them very well (i.e., self and other personality ratings)—the more accurate users of Facebook would appear to be in their self-presentations.

Because the ratings posted by people on Facebook agree with those provided by others who know them well, it suggests that there is accuracy. To test the alternative idea that posters try to present themselves in an idealized way, these individuals could be asked to describe their "ideal selves," and this information, too, could be correlated with others' ratings of their Facebook postings. These basic methods were actually used by Back et al. (2010) in a study designed to find out whether, and to what extent, Facebook postings are accurate with respect to posters' personality. Results offered clear support for the **hypothesis** that Facebook profiles are generally accurate: Posted profiles closely matched the posters' actual personalities, as measured by personality scales they themselves completed and ratings by friends and family members. There was little evidence for attempts at idealized self-presentation. On the basis of this research, we can tentatively conclude that Facebook information about posters' personality is relatively accurate; their personality scores predict their postings, and their postings predict their personality scores. But we emphasize the word *tentatively* here, for two important reasons.

First, the fact that two variables are correlated in no way guarantees that they are causally related—that changes in one *cause* changes in the other. On the contrary, the relationship between them may be due to the fact that both variables are caused by a third variable. For instance, in this case, it is possible that people who post on Facebook are simply good at self-presentation—presenting themselves to others so as to "look good." To the extent that's true, the correlation between their postings on Facebook and scores on personality tests could reflect this variable. Since they are high in self-presentation skills, their postings and their answers to personality tests *both* tend to put them in a good light. But, in fact, the two measures are unrelated to each in any direct or causal way.

There is still another complication: It is also possible that posting on Facebook leads to changes in posters' personalities, in the direction of becoming more like the information they posted. That may initially sound a little far-fetched, but we know that when people publicly make claims, they often convince themselves that it is true and, in fact, change to make it so (Higgins, 1999). Because this is a possible interpretation that correlational research cannot definitely rule out, we can only conclude that such relationships exist. Correlational research cannot establish the direction of the relationships between variables, or whether either variable causes the other.

Despite these major drawbacks, the correlational method of research is sometimes very useful to social psychologists. It can be used in natural settings where experiments might be very difficult to conduct, and it is often highly efficient: A large amount of information can be obtained in a relatively short period of time. However, the fact that it is generally not conclusive with respect to cause-and-effect relationships is a serious issue that leads social psychologists to prefer another method in many instances. It is to this approach—use of experiments—that we turn next.

1.3.3: The Experimental Method: Knowledge Through Systematic Intervention

As you have just seen, the correlational method of research is very useful from the point of view of one important goal of science: making accurate predictions. It is less useful, though, from the point of view of attaining another important goal: *explanation*. This is sometimes known as the "why" question, because scientists do not merely wish to describe the world and relationships between variables in it: They want to be able to *explain* these relationships, too.

In order to attain the goal of explanation, social psychologists employ a method of research known as **experimentation** or the **experimental method**. Experimentation involves the following strategy: One variable is changed systematically, and the effects of these changes on one or more other variables are carefully measured. If systematic changes in one variable produce changes in another variable (and if two additional conditions we'll describe later in this chapter are also met), it is possible to conclude with reasonable certainty that there is indeed a causal relationship between these variables: that changes in one do indeed *cause* changes in the other. Because the experimental method is so valuable in answering this kind of question, it is frequently the method of choice in social psychology. But bear in mind that there is no single "best" method of research. Rather, social psychologists, like all other scientists, choose the method that is most appropriate for studying a particular topic.

EXPERIMENTATION: ITS BASIC NATURE   In its most basic form, the experimental method involves two key steps: (1) The presence or strength of some variable believed to affect an aspect of social behavior is systematically changed, and (2) the effects of such changes (if any) are carefully measured. The factor systematically varied by the researcher is termed the **independent variable**, while the aspect of behavior studied is termed the **dependent variable**. In a simple experiment, then, different groups of participants are *randomly assigned* to be exposed to contrasting levels of the independent variable (such as low, moderate, and high). The researcher then carefully measures their behavior to determine whether it does in fact vary with these changes in the independent variable. If it does—and if two other conditions are also met—the researcher can tentatively conclude that the independent variable does indeed cause changes in the behavior being studied.

To illustrate the basic nature of experimentation in social psychology, we'll use the following example. Suppose that a social psychologist is interested in the following question: Does exposure to violent video games increase the likelihood that people will aggress against others in various ways (e.g., verbally, physically attacking them, spreading rumors, or posting embarrassing photos of them on the Internet; see Figure 1.13)? How can this possibility be investigated using the experimental method? Here is one possibility.

Participants in the experiment could be assigned at random to play a violent or nonviolent video game. After doing so, they would be placed in a situation where they could, if they wished, aggress against another person. For instance, they could be told that the next part of the study is concerned with taste sensitivity and they could add as much hot sauce as they wish to a glass of water that another person will drink. Participants would taste a sample in which only one drop of sauce has been placed in the glass, so they would know how hot the drink would be if they added more than one drop. Lots of sauce would make the drink so hot that it would truly hurt the person who consumed it.

If playing aggressive video games causes increases in aggression against others, then participants who played such games would use more hot sauce—and so inflict more pain on another person—than participants who examined the puzzle. If results indicate that this is the case, then the researcher could conclude that playing aggressive video games *can* increase subsequent, overt aggression. The researcher can offer this conclusion because if the study was done correctly, the only difference between the experiences of the two groups during the study is that one played violent games and the other did not. As a result, any difference in their behavior (in their aggression) can be attributed to this factor. It is important to note that in experimentation, the independent variable—in this case, exposure to one or another type of video game—is systematically changed by the researcher. In the correlational method, in contrast, variables are *not* altered in this manner; rather, naturally occurring changes in them are simply observed and recorded.

Figure 1.13 The Experimental Method: Using It to Study the Effects of Violent Video Games

Does playing violent video games, such as the one shown here, increase the tendency to aggress against others? Using the experimental method, social psychologists have gathered data to address this important issue—and in fact, found, violent video game playing does encourage aggressive responses.

EXPERIMENTATION: TWO KEY REQUIREMENTS FOR ITS SUCCESS   Earlier, we referred to two conditions that must be met before a researcher can conclude that changes in an independent variable have caused changes in a dependent variable. Let's consider these conditions now. The first involves what is termed **random assignment of participants to experimental conditions**. This means that all participants in an experiment must have an equal chance of being exposed to each level of the independent variable. The reason for this rule is simple: If participants are *not* randomly assigned to each condition, it may later be impossible to determine if differences in their behavior stem from differences they brought with them to the study, from the impact of the independent variable, or both. For instance, imagine that in the study on video games, all the persons assigned to the violent game come from a judo club—they practice martial arts regularly—while all those assigned to play the other game come from a singing club. If those who play the violent games show higher levels of aggression, what does this tell us? Not much! The difference between the two groups stem from the fact that individuals who already show tendencies toward aggression (they are taking a judo class) are more aggressive than those who prefer singing; playing violent video games during the study might be completely unrelated to this difference, which existed prior to the experiment. As result, we can't tell *why* any differences between them occurred; we have violated random assignment of persons to experimental treatments, and that makes the results virtually meaningless.

The second condition essential for successful experimentation is as follows: All factors other than the independent variable that might also affect participants' behavior must be held constant. To see why this is so, consider what will happen if, in the study on video games two assistants collect the data. One is kind and friendly, the other is rude and nasty. By bad luck, the rude assistant collects most of the data for the aggressive game condition and the polite one collects most of the data from the nonaggressive game condition. Again, suppose the results show that participants in the first group are more aggressive toward another person. What do the findings tell us? Again, virtually nothing, because we can't tell whether it was playing the aggressive video game or the rude treatment they received from the assistant that produced higher aggression. In situations like this, the independent variable is said to be **confounded** with another variable—one that is *not* under systematic investigation in the study. When such confounding occurs, the findings of an experiment may be largely uninterpretable (see Figure 1.14).

In sum, experimentation is, in several respects, the most powerful of social psychology's methods. In many ways, it is considered "the gold standard." But, it isn't perfect— for example, since it is often conducted in laboratory settings that are quite different from the locations in which social behavior actually occurs, the question of *external validity* often arises: To what extent can the findings of experiments be generalized to real-life social situations and perhaps people who are rather different (e.g., older) from those who participated in the research? And there are situations where, because of ethical or legal considerations, experiments can't be used. For instance, it would clearly be unethical to

Figure 1.14 Confounding of Variables: A Fatal Flaw in Experimentation

In a hypothetical experiment designed to investigate the effects of playing violent video games on aggression, the independent variable is confounded with another variable, the behavior of the assistants conducting the study. One assistant is polite and the other is rude. The polite assistant collects the data in the nonviolent game condition, while the rude assistant collects the data in the violent game condition. Findings indicate that people who play the violent video games are more aggressive. But, because of confounding of variables, it is impossible to tell whether this is a result of playing these games or the assistant's rude treatment. The experiment does not provide useful information on the issue it was designed to study.

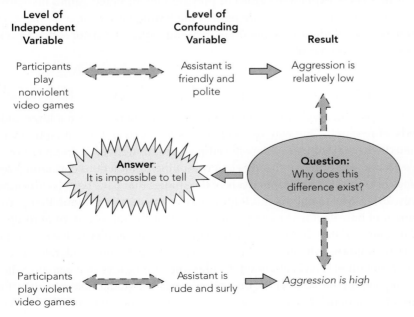

expose research participants to television programming that may cause them to harm themselves. But in situations where it *is* appropriate and is used with skill and care, however, the experimental method can yield results that help us to answer complex questions about social thoughts and behavior. Overall, though, keep the following basic point in mind: There is no single best method of conducting research in social psychology. Rather, all methods offer advantages and disadvantages, so the guiding principle is that the method that is most appropriate to answering the questions being investigated is the one that should be used. And, when a set of studies uses rather different methods that have differing strengths and weaknesses but they all point toward the same conclusion, our confidence that the answer is correct will be higher.

1.3.4: Further Thoughts on Causality: The Role of Mediating Variables

Earlier, we noted that social psychologists often use experimentation because it is helpful in answering questions about causality: Do changes in one variable produce (cause) changes in another? That is a very valuable kind of information to have because it helps us understand what situations lead to various outcomes—more or less helping, more or less aggression, more or less prejudice. Often, though, social psychologists take experimentation one step further in their efforts to answer the question "Why"—to understand *why* one variable produces changes in another. For instance, returning to video game study described earlier, it is reasonable to ask: "Why does playing such games increase aggression?" Is it because it induces thoughts about harming others? Reminds people of real or imagined wrongs they have suffered at the hands of other people? Makes them feel less empathy for the victims harmed by aggression? Convinces them that aggression is "OK" since it leads to high scores in the game?

To get at this question of underlying processes, social psychologists often conduct studies in which they measure not just a single dependent variable, but other factors that they believe to be at work—factors that are influenced by the independent variable and then, in turn, affect the dependent measures. For instance, in this study, we could measure participants' thoughts about harming others and their beliefs about when and whether aggression is acceptable to see if these factors help explain why playing violent video games increases subsequent aggression. We could also measure the degree to which empathy is felt for someone who has been hurt to determine whether that helps explain the effect of playing violent video games on subsequent aggression. If they do, then they are termed **mediating variables**, ones that intervene between an independent variable (here, playing certain kinds of video games) and changes in social behavior.

1.3.5: Meta-Analysis: Assessing a Body of Knowledge

For many topics that we will be describing in depth, there is often a large and existing body of research. One way researchers assess the extent to which two variables are related when tested in a variety of settings, the strength of an intervention, or the relative accuracy of different theories in terms of their predictions concerning research outcomes is to conduct a **meta-analysis** of the studies that have been conducted (Chan & Arvey, 2012). Meta-analysis is a highly useful statistical technique that permits an assessment of how well findings replicate—whether the same pattern of results is obtained despite variation in how particular studies were conducted. It can also point to gaps in existing research and features of research settings that moderate the strength or even direction of effects obtained. **Moderators** are factors that can alter the effect of an independent variable on the dependent variable. Moderators can also affect the strength of a relationship between two variables. Let's take an example so you can see how effective meta-analysis can be in helping make sense of existing studies (some of which may seem to be conflicting) and ensuring our science is a cumulative enterprise.

As you will see in Chapter 9, there is a long-standing interest in the question of how a person's gender might influence the extent to which he or she provides help to a person in need. There have been many studies—and theories—suggesting one gender or the other is more helpful or prosocial than the other. Eagly and Crowley (1986) undertook a meta-analysis of all the existing experiments on helping, and this provided a great deal of conceptual order to this large literature. As they noted, many social psychological studies on helping had been conducted in the context of short-term encounters with strangers that often entailed some amount of physical risk (e.g., picking up hitchhikers) or competence (e.g., repairing flat tires). By describing the nature of the body of existing literature and revealing that studies with these characteristics did indeed find greater helping on the part of men than women, their meta-analysis did a great service to the field. These researchers pointed out that caring behaviors that are prescribed by the female gender role—helping others in close relationships—tended not to be studied so the overall gender difference in helping favoring men was highly misleading. The takeaway message we offer you is that meta-analyses, whenever available, will be used to explain the findings of a large existing body of research. As we hope you can see, meta-analysis does more than just tell us what the effect is and its strength; it points to gaps and biases in the scientific literature itself.

1.4: The Role of Theory in Social Psychology

Objective   **Explain how theories play a key role in social psychological research**

There is one more aspect of social psychological research we should consider before concluding. As we noted earlier, in their research, social psychologists seek to do more than simply describe the world: They want to be able to *explain* it too. For instance, social psychologists are not interested in merely stating that racial prejudice is common in the United States: They want to be able to explain *why* some people are more prejudiced toward a particular group than are others. In social psychology, as in all branches of science, explanation involves the construction of theories—frameworks for explaining various events or processes. The procedure involved in building a theory goes something like this:

1. On the basis of existing evidence, a theory consistent with this evidence is proposed.

2. This theory, which consists of basic concepts and statements about how these concepts are related, helps to organize existing information and makes predictions about observable events. For instance, the theory might predict the conditions under which individuals acquire racial prejudice and, on that basis, how it might be reduced.

3. These predictions, known as *hypotheses*, are then tested by actual research.

4. If results are consistent with the theory, confidence in its accuracy is increased. If they are not, the theory is modified and further tests are conducted.

5. Ultimately, the theory is either accepted as accurate or rejected as inaccurate. Even if it is accepted as accurate, however, the theory remains open to further refinement as improved methods of research are developed and additional evidence relevant to the theory's predictions is obtained.

This may sound a bit abstract, so let's turn to a concrete example. Suppose that a social psychologist formulates the following theory: When people believe that they hold a view that is in the minority, they will be slower to state it and this stems not from the strength of their views, but from reluctance to state minority opinions publicly where others will hear and perhaps disapprove of them for holding those views. This theory would lead to specific predictions—for instance, the minority slowness effect will be reduced if people can state their opinions privately (Bassili, 2003). If research findings are consistent with this prediction and with others derived from the theory, confidence in the theory is increased. If findings are *not* consistent with the theory, it will be modified or perhaps rejected. This process of formulating a theory, testing it, modifying the theory, testing it again, and so on lies close to the core of the scientific method, so it is an important aspect of social psychological research (see Figure 1.15).

Two final points: First, theories are never *proven* in any final, ultimate sense. Rather, they are always open to test, and are accepted with more or less confidence depending on the weight of available evidence. Second, research is *not* undertaken to prove a theory; it is performed to gather evidence relevant to the theory. If a researcher sets out to "prove" her or his pet theory, this is a serious violation of the principles of scientific skepticism, objectivity, and open-mindedness that were described earlier in this chapter.

Figure 1.15 The Role of Theory in Social Psychological Research

Theories both organize existing knowledge and make predictions about how various events or processes will occur. *Hypotheses* are logically derived from theories and are then tested through careful research. If results agree with the predictions, confidence in the theory is increased. If results disagree with the predictions, the theory may be modified or, ultimately, rejected as false.

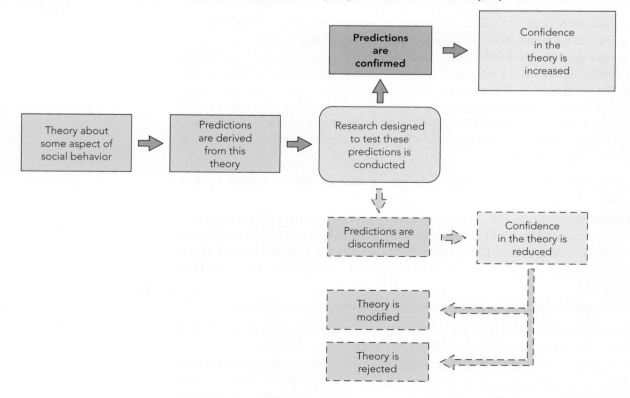

Key Points

- With **systematic observation**, behavior is carefully observed and recorded. In **naturalistic observation**, such observations are made in settings where the behavior naturally occurs, without any intervention on the part of the researcher.

- **Survey methods** often involve large numbers of persons who are asked to respond to questions about their attitudes or behavior.

- When the **correlational method** of research is employed, two or more variables are measured to determine how they might be related to one another. Variables can be positively correlated such that as one increases the other also does, or they can be negatively correlated where increases in one variable correspond with decreases in the other.

- The existence of even strong correlations between variables does not indicate that they are causally related to each other.

- **Experimentation** involves systematically altering one or more variables (**independent variables**) in order to determine whether changes in this variable affect some aspect of behavior (**dependent variables**).

- Successful use of the **experimental method** requires *random assignment of participants to conditions* and

- holding all other factors that might also influence behavior constant so as to avoid **confounding** of variables.

- Although it is a very powerful research tool, the experimental method is not perfect; questions concerning the external validity—replication of findings across populations and settings—often arise. Further, it cannot be used in some situations because of practical or ethical considerations.

- Research designed to investigate **mediating variables**—by assessing the processes that may account for the effect of the independent variable on the dependent variable—adds to understanding of how specific variables influence social behavior.

- **Meta-analysis** is a statistical technique that permits an assessment of how well findings replicate—whether the same pattern of results is obtained despite variation in how particular studies were conducted.

- **Moderators** are factors that can alter the effect of an independent variable on the dependent variable.

- Theories are frameworks for explaining various events or processes. They play a key role in social psychological research.

1.5: The Quest for Knowledge and the Rights of Individuals: Seeking an Appropriate Balance

Objective   **Identify how the dilemma of deception is addressed in social psychology**

In their use of experimentation, correlation, and **systematic observation**, social psychologists do not differ from researchers in other fields. One technique, however, does seem to be unique to research in social psychology: **deception**. This technique involves efforts by researchers to withhold or conceal information about the purposes of a study from participants. The reason for doing so is simple: Many social psychologists believe that if participants know the true purposes of a study, their behavior in it will be changed by that knowledge. Thus, the research will *not* yield valid information about social behavior, unless deception is employed.

Some kinds of research do seem to require the use of temporary deception. For example, consider the video game study described earlier. If participants know that the purpose of a study is to investigate the impact of violent games, they might lean over backward to avoid showing it. Similarly, consider a study of the effects of a person's gender on ratings of creativity or job performance. Again, if participants know that the researcher is interested in the impact of gender or likelihood of gender stereotyping, they might work hard to avoid being influenced by the person's gender. In this and many other cases, social psychologists feel compelled to employ temporary deception in their research (Suls & Rosnow, 1988). However, the use of deception raises important ethical issues that cannot be ignored.

First, there is the chance, however slim, that deception may result in some kind of harm to the persons exposed to it. They may be upset by the procedures used or by their own reactions to them. For example, in several studies concerned with helping in emergencies, participants were exposed to seemingly real emergency situations. For instance, they overheard what seemed to be a medical emergency—another person having an apparent seizure (Darley & Latané, 1968). Some participants were upset by these staged events, and others were disturbed by the fact that although they recognized the need to help, they failed to do so. Clearly, the fact that participants experienced emotional upset raises complex ethical issues about just how far researchers can go when studying even very important topics such as this one. Under current federal guidelines for the conduct of research, all such incidents would need to be immediately reported to the *Institutional Review Board*.

We should hasten to emphasize that such research represents an extreme use of deception: Generally, deception takes much milder forms such as withholding information about the true purposes of the study, what is referred to as *passive deception*. For example, in a study concerning impressions formed of persons with and without a physical disability, some participants might receive a photo of a person sitting in a wheelchair and others receive a photo of the same person without a wheelchair. With the goal of the study being to assess whether differential evaluations of the target person emerge depending on the presence of this disability cue or not; in passive deception studies, this purpose (i.e., the intention to compare these two conditions) is left unsaid.

Other forms of deception might involve providing *misleading information.* For instance, participants may receive a request for help from a stranger who is actually an assistant of the researchers, or they may be informed that most other students in their university hold certain views about a social issue when in fact they do not, or that is unknown. In other studies, experimenters may lead participants to believe that another person in the study has acted in a certain way (i.e., divided points or money in a bargaining game) when in fact a computer program is controlling what appears to be "the other person's responses." Although with this form of deception, where misleading information is presented, there is more potential for some kind of harmful effects to participants, these must be assessed against the scientific value of what might be learned from conducting the study.

Second, there is the possibility that participants will resent being "fooled" during a study and, as a result, they will acquire negative attitudes toward social psychology and psychological research in general; for instance, they may become suspicious about information presented by researchers (Kimmel, 2004). To the extent such reactions occur—and recent findings suggest they do, at least to a degree (Epley & Huff, 1998)—they have disturbing implications for the conduct of social psychology, which place so much emphasis on scientific research.

Because of such possibilities, the use of deception poses something of a dilemma to social psychologists. On the one hand, it seems essential to their research—to create an involving situation where the psychological processes of interest can be examined in a safe laboratory context. On the other, its use raises serious problems. How can this issue be resolved? Most social psychologists agree on the following points, and adhering to such guidelines is required by *Institutional Review Boards* that monitor the conduct of research conducted by university faculty and students.

First, deception should *never* be used to persuade people to take part in a study; withholding information about what will happen in an experiment or providing misleading information in order to induce people to take part in it is definitely *not* acceptable (Sigall, 1997). Second, most social psychologists agree that temporary deception may sometimes be acceptable provided two basic safeguards are employed. One of these is **informed consent**—giving participants as much information as possible about the procedures to be followed before they make their decision to participate. This is the opposite of withholding information in order to persuade people to participate. The second is careful **debriefing**—providing participants with a full description of the purposes of a study after they have participated in it, including an explanation of any deception used, and why it was necessary to employ it (see Figure 1.16).

Figure 1.16 Careful Debriefing: A Requirement in Studies Using Deception

After an experimental session is completed, participants should be provided with a thorough *debriefing*—full information about the experiment's goals and the reasons that temporary deception was considered necessary.

Fortunately, existing evidence indicates that, together, informed consent and thorough debriefing can substantially reduce the potential dangers of deception (Smith & Richardson, 1985). For example, most participants report that they view temporary deception as acceptable, provided that potential benefits outweigh potential costs and if there is no other means of obtaining the information sought (Rogers, 1980; Sharpe, Adair, & Roese, 1992). Overall, then, it appears that most research participants do not react negatively to temporary deception as long as its purpose and necessity are subsequently made clear. However, this does *not* mean that the safety or appropriateness of deception should be taken for granted (Rubin, 1985; Weathington, Cunningham, & Pittenger, 2010). On the contrary, the guiding principles for all researchers planning to use deception should be the following: (1) Use deception only when it is absolutely essential to do so—when no other means for conducting the research exists; (2) always proceed with caution; and (3) make certain that every possible precaution is taken to protect the rights, safety, and well-being of research participants. In terms of the latter, all universities in the United States who receive federal funding must have an *Institutional Review Board* to review the ethics of proposed research before it is conducted, including a cost–benefit analysis when deception is to be employed.

Key Points

- **Deception** involves efforts by social psychologists to withhold or conceal information about the purposes of a study from participants. It can entail *passive deception* where the true purpose of the research is not revealed, or presentation of *misleading information* about some aspect of the study.
- Most social psychologists believe that temporary deception is often necessary in order to obtain valid research results.

- However, they view deception as acceptable only when important safeguards are employed: **informed consent** and thorough **debriefing**.
- In the United States, an *Institutional Review Board* must review the ethics of any proposed research before it is conducted, including a cost–benefit analysis when deception is to be employed.

1.6: Getting the Most Out of This Book: A User's Guide

Objective **Outline the steps taken to make reading this book a pleasant and informative experience**

A textbook that is hard to read or understand is like a dull tool: It really can't do what it is designed to do very well. We are fully aware of this fact, so we have tried our best to make this book as easy to read as possible and have included a number of features designed to make it more enjoyable—and useful—for you. Here is a brief overview of the steps we've taken to make reading this book a pleasant and informative experience.

First, each chapter begins with a chapter-opening story that "sets the stage" and explains how the topics to be covered are related to important aspects of our everyday lives. Within each chapter, key terms are printed in **boldface** and are followed by a definition. These terms are defined in a glossary at the end of the book. To help you understand what you have read, each major section is followed by a list of *Key Points*—a brief summary of the major points covered. All figures and tables are clear and simple, and most contain special notes designed to help you understand them (see Figure 1.11 for an example). Finally, each chapter ends with a *Summary and Review*. Reviewing this section can be an important aid to your studying.

Second, this book has an underlying theme that we have already stated (see pp. 12–13), but want to emphasize again: Social psychology seeks *basic principles* concerning social thought and behavior—principles that apply very generally, across cultures and settings. But it recognizes that the *context* in which the social side of life occurs is very important. Because of the growing role of technology in our lives, the ways in which we interact with other people have changed and now often occurs via some form of digital technology rather than in face-to-face encounters. We believe that the basic principles of social psychology apply to these new contexts too, but that their accuracy in the "cyber" or "electronic" world must be established by careful research. To take account of this major change in the settings and modes of expression of social behavior, we will report research concerning use of social media and related topics throughout the book. In addition, to call special attention to research topics of growing importance, we include special sections with up-to-date research in each chapter entitled **What Research Tells Us About ...** Here are a few examples: People's Preferences for the Status Quo; Biases in Our Beliefs About Inequality; The Role of Emotion in Aggression; The Role of Nonverbal Cues in Job Interviews; and The Importance of Being Treated with Respect. We think that these sections will take account of important societal changes that are, indeed, strongly affecting the nature and form of the social side of life.

We think that, together, these features will help you get the most out of this book and your first contact with social psychology. We most assuredly hope that your first encounter with our field proves to be a rich, informative, valuable, and *enjoyable* experience.

Summary and Review

Social psychology is the scientific field that seeks to understand the nature and causes of individual thought and behavior in social situations. It is scientific in nature because it adopts the values and methods used in other fields of science. Social psychologists adopt the scientific method because "common sense" provides an unreliable guide to social behavior and because our personal thought is influenced by many potential sources of bias. Social psychology focuses on the behavior of individuals and seeks to understand the causes of social behavior, which can involve the behavior and appearance of others, our efforts to understand and interpret the actions of others, environmental factors, cultural values, and even biological factors. Social psychology seeks to establish basic principles of social life that are accurate across various cultural groups, while recognizing that "who we are"—our identities—affects our social thought and behavior. A *multicultural* approach guides social psychological research so that the principles uncovered can be applied to humans in all their diverse forms.

Social psychologists currently recognize that social thought and social behavior are two sides of the same coin and that there is a continuous, complex interplay between them. There is growing interest, among social psychologists in the role of emotion in social thought and social behavior. The role of social relationships in our well-being is another major trend in the field. Yet another major trend involves growing interest in **social neuroscience**—efforts to relate activity in the brain to key aspects of social thought and behavior. How the major changes in digital technology and social media affect how we interact with others is considered throughout this book.

Human social behavior is often shaped by factors of which we are unaware. Growing attention to such implicit (nonconscious) processes is another major theme of modern social psychology. Social psychology currently adopts a **multicultural perspective**. This perspective recognizes the importance of cultural factors in shaping who we are and social behavior.

With **naturalistic observation**, behavior is carefully observed and recorded in settings where the behavior naturally occurs. **Survey methods** often involve large numbers of persons who are asked to respond to questions about their attitudes or behavior. When the **correlational method** of research is employed, two or more variables are measured to determine how they might be related to one another. The existence of even strong correlations between variables does not indicate that they are necessarily causally related to each other.

Experimentation involves systematically altering one or more variables (**independent variables**) in order to determine whether changes in this variable affect some aspect of behavior (**dependent variables**). Successful use of the **experimental method** requires random assignment of participants to conditions and holding all other factors that might also influence behavior constant so as to avoid **confounding** of variables. Although it is a very powerful research tool, the experimental method is not perfect—questions concerning the external validity of findings so obtained often arise. Further, it cannot be used in some situations because of practical or ethical considerations.

Research designed to investigate **mediating variables** adds to understanding of how specific independent variables influence certain aspects of social behavior or social thought. **Meta-analysis** is used to synthesize a body of knowledge and point to what remains to be done. **Moderators** can change the impact or relationship between two variables. Theories are frameworks for explaining various events or processes. They play a key role in social psychological research.

Deception involves efforts by social psychologists to withhold or conceal information about the purposes of a study from participants. Most social psychologists believe that temporary deception is often necessary in order to obtain valid research results. However, they view deception as acceptable only when important safeguards are employed: **informed consent** and thorough **debriefing**.

Chapter 2
Social Cognition
How We Think About the Social World

Chapter Overview

Learning Objectives

2.1   Examine how heuristic strategies are employed to judge complex information

2.2   Describe the role of schemas in guiding our thoughts and actions

2.3   Distinguish between automatic and controlled processing modes of social thought

2.4   Evaluate the imperfections of the social cognition process

2.5   Assess the interrelation of affect and cognition

We live in an information-dense world. Yet, much of that information is ambiguous or contradictory, potentially leaving us uncertain about what to believe. How, then, do we assess the likelihood of different types of risk we might face? For example, what's our likelihood of getting into an auto accident, having our wallet (or identity) stolen, getting a cancer diagnosis, or selecting an automobile that's a "lemon"—in constant need of repairs? None of these possibilities are easy to judge. But, as you will see, a social psychological analysis of how people think about risks illuminates the processes we use to make judgments, even when we have incomplete information about the risk likelihood.

Judging our risks is just one of the challenges in life. Many of the decisions we must make require us to sift through large quantities of complex information. You probably faced a choice dilemma when deciding which college to attend. Did you try to choose rationally—create a list of all the pros and cons for each potential institution? Or, did you just choose based on a simple rule such as "which is cheaper," "which has more status," or "which one did my parents attend"? Given the high cost of college, maybe you also needed to apply for a student loan. Like the person in Figure 2.1, you no doubt learned that filling out loan applications is a complex process—one that may take even longer than applying to most colleges! After all your effort, it may still have been unclear which loan would ultimately be best for you.

After college, you will continue to face difficult choices with high-stake outcomes. These too involve wading through lots of complex information. For example, when you start a new job, you typically have to pick from a variety of seemingly incomprehensible health insurance plans and retirement savings options, all before getting a single paycheck. When you decide to purchase your first home, it will be important to understand the pros and cons of the various types of mortgage loans from which you must select one.

At first glance, it might seem wonderful that we have so many alternatives, but having lots of options can have a paralyzing effect that results in nonoptimal choices. Do we give up hope of making the "correct" decision and just blindly make a selection? Thaler and Sunstein (2009) suggest in their popular book, *Nudge,* that what we know about the social psychology of human judgment can help us make better sense of large amounts of information. It turns out, when people receive information in a way that highlights the crucial data in an accessible style, the process can be made easier and the choices people actually make for themselves can be improved.

As you will see in this chapter, people often use mental shortcuts or rules of thumb to arrive at judgments. This is especially the case when we are confronted with complex, contradictory, or difficult decisions where the "correct" answer may be hard to determine. **Social cognition**, which concerns how we think about the social world, our attempts to understand complex issues, and why we sometimes are less

Figure 2.1 Too Many Choices: When Information Is Complex and Confusing, How Do You Make a Decision?

Many of our most important life decisions require us to wade through masses of seemingly incomprehensible information. When you are faced with such complexity, do you attempt to decide "rationally," by systematically weighing all the pros and cons? Or, might you instead make a choice based on some simple strategy?

than "optimally rational," will be a major focus of this chapter (e.g., Fiske & Taylor, 2008; Higgins & Kruglanski, 1996). Research strongly suggests that our thinking about the social world often operates on "automatic"—it occurs quickly and without lots of careful reasoning. As you'll see later, automatic thought offers important advantages: It requires little or no effort and can be very efficient. Although thinking in this manner can lead to satisfactory judgments, it can also lead to important errors in our conclusions and result in suboptimal decisions.

Although we do lots of social thought on "automatic," we do sometimes stop and think much more carefully and logically about some issues (e.g., which college to attend). This more controlled way of thinking tends to occur when something is important to us or is unexpected—both of which can jolt us out of automatic, effortless thought.

In the first section of this chapter, we'll examine several rules of thumb we often use to quickly draw inferences about situations we face. We'll also consider the research conducted by social psychologists that addresses how these simple rules operate. Next, we will consider in depth the mental frameworks that we use to organize large amounts of information in an efficient manner. These frameworks can exert strong effects on social thought—effects that are not always beneficial from an accuracy point of view. We'll also examine several specific tendencies in social thought—tendencies that can lead us to false conclusions about others and the social world. Finally, we'll focus on the complex interplay between our feelings and various aspects of social cognition.

2.1: Heuristics: How We Employ Simple Rules in Social Cognition

Objective   **Examine how heuristic strategies are employed to judge complex information**

Several states have passed or are considering adopting laws that ban talking on cell phones and texting while driving. Why? As illustrated in Figure 2.2, these are very dangerous practices, particularly texting. It has been found over and over again that when drivers are distracted, they are more likely to get into accidents, and texting can certainly be highly distracting (Atchley, Hadlock, & Lane, 2012). What about global positioning systems that show maps to drivers? Do you think that they, too, can distract our attention away from fast-moving traffic and cause accidents?

At any given time, we are capable of focusing on a limited amount of information. Any input beyond our limit puts us into a state of **information overload** where the demands on our cognitive system are greater than its capacity. In addition, our processing capacity can be depleted by high levels of stress or other demands on us (e.g., Chajut & Algom, 2003). To deal with such situations, people adopt various strategies designed to "stretch" their cognitive resources—to let them do more, with less effort, than would otherwise be the case. This is one major reason that so much of our social thought occurs on "automatic"—in a quick and relatively effortless manner rather than in a careful, systematic, arduous way. We'll discuss the costs and potential benefits of this thought process later. Here, however, we'll focus on techniques we use

---

Figure 2.2 Distracted Driving: A Cause of Accidents

Because our capacity to process incoming information is limited, our ability to focus can easily be exceeded. When drivers text or talk on the telephone, their attention is drawn away from traffic. This practice has caused accidents, some fatal.

to deal quickly with large amounts of information, especially under **conditions of uncertainty** where the "correct" answer is difficult to know or would take a great deal of effort to determine. While many strategies exist for making sense of complex information, one of the most useful tactics involve **heuristics**—simple rules for making complex decisions or drawing inferences in a rapid and efficient manner.

2.1.1: Representativeness: Judging by Resemblance

Suppose that you have just met your next-door neighbor for the first time. While chatting with her, you notice that she is dressed conservatively, is neat in her personal habits, has a very large library in her home, and seems to be very gentle and a little shy. Later you realize that she never mentioned what she does for a living. Is she a business manager, a physician, a waitress, an artist, a dancer, or a librarian? One quick way of making a guess is to compare her with a **prototype**—a list of attributes commonly possessed by members of each of these occupations. How well does she resemble persons you have met in each of these fields or, perhaps, the typical member of these fields (Shah & Oppenheimer, 2009)? If you proceed in this manner, you may quickly conclude that she is likely to be a librarian; her traits seem closer to those associated with this profession than they do to the traits associated with physicians, dancers, or business executives. If you made your judgment about your neighbor's occupation in this manner, you used the **representativeness heuristic**. In other words, you made your judgment on the basis of a relatively simple rule: The more an individual seems to resemble or match a given group, the more likely she or he is to belong to that group.

Are such judgments accurate? Often they are, because belonging to certain groups does affect the behavior and style of persons in them, and because people with certain traits are attracted to particular groups in the first place. But sometimes, judgments based on representativeness are wrong, mainly for the following reason: Decisions or judgments made on the basis of this rule tend to ignore *base rates*—the frequency with which given events or categories (e.g., occupations) occur in the total population (Kahneman & Tversky, 1973; Kahneman & Frederick, 2002). In fact, there are many more business managers than librarians. Thus, even though your neighbor seemed more similar to the prototype of librarians than managers in terms of her traits, the chances are actually higher that she is a manager than a librarian.

The representativeness heuristic is also used when judging whether specific causes resemble each other and are therefore likely to produce effects that are similar in terms of magnitude. That is, when people are asked to judge the likelihood that a particular effect (e.g., either many or a few people die of a disease) was produced by a particular cause (e.g., an unusually infectious bacteria or a standard strain), they are likely to expect the strength of the cause to match its effect. However, cultural groups differ in the extent to which they rely on the representativeness heuristic and expect "like to go with like" in terms of causes and effects. In particular, people from Asia tend to consider more potential causal factors when judging effects than do Americans (Choi, Dalal, Kim-Prieto, & Park, 2003). Because Asians consider more information and arrive at more complex attributions when judging an event, they should show less evidence of thinking based on the representativeness heuristic—a judgment simplification strategy—compared to North Americans.

To test this reasoning, researchers (Spina et al., 2010) asked students in China and Canada to rate the likelihood that a high- or low-magnitude effect (few or many deaths) was caused by a virus that differed in magnitude (a strain that was treatment-resistant or a standard strain that could be controlled with medical treatment). While participants in both national groups showed evidence of expecting high-magnitude effects (many deaths) to be produced by high-magnitude causes (the treatment-resistant virus strain) and low-magnitude effects (few deaths) to be produced by low-magnitude causes (the standard strain of the virus), Canadian participants showed this effect much more strongly than the Chinese participants. Such reasoning differences could potentially result in difficulty when members of different groups seek to achieve agreement on how best to tackle problems affecting the world as a whole—such as climate change. Westerners may expect that "big causes" have to be tackled to reduce the likelihood of global warming, whereas Asians may be comfortable emphasizing more "minor causes" with substantial outcomes such as climate change.

2.1.2: Availability: "If I Can Recall Many Instances, They Must Be Frequent?"

When estimating event frequencies or their likelihood, people may simply not know the "correct" answer—even for events in their own lives. So how do they arrive at a response? Ask yourself, how often have you talked on your cell phone while driving? If you can remember quite a few instances, you'd probably conclude it happens quite often. This is an example of judging frequency based on the ease with which instances can be brought to mind.

Now consider another, non-self-related question: Are you safer driving in a huge SUV or in a smaller, lighter car? Many people would answer, "In the big SUV," thinking that if you are in an accident, you are less likely to get hurt in a big vehicle compared to a small one. While that might seem to be correct, actual data indicate that death rates (number of deaths per 1 million vehicles on the road) are *higher* for SUVs than smaller cars (e.g., Gladwell, 2004).

So why do so many people conclude falsely that they are safer in a bulky SUV? Like the cell phone–use question, the answer seems to involve what easily comes to mind when we think about this question. Most people can recall scenes in which a huge vehicle had literally crushed another smaller vehicle in an accident. Because such scenes are dramatic, we can readily bring them to mind. But this "ease-of-retrieval" effect may mislead us. We assume that because such scenes are readily available in memory, they accurately reflect the overall frequency, when, in fact, they don't. For instance, such recall does not remind us of the fact that SUVs are involved in accidents more often than smaller, lighter cars; large SUVs tip over more easily than other vehicles; and SUVs are favored by less careful drivers who are more likely to be involved in accidents.

This example, and many similar judgment errors, illustrates the operation of the **availability heuristic**, another cognitive "rule of thumb" suggesting that the easier it is to bring information to mind, the greater its impact on subsequent judgments or decisions. Use of this heuristic makes good sense much of the time. After all, the fact that we can bring some types of information to mind quite readily suggests that it may indeed be frequent or important, so it *should* influence our judgments and decisions. But relying on availability in making social judgments can also lead to errors. Specifically, it can lead us to overestimate the likelihood of events that are dramatic but rare, because they are easy to bring to mind.

Consistent with this availability principle, many people fear traveling in airplanes more than traveling in automobiles, even though the chances of dying in an auto accident are hundreds of times higher. Likewise, people tend to overestimate murder as a cause of death and underestimate more mundane but much more frequent killers such as heart disease and stroke. Because of the frequency that murder and other dramatic causes of death are seen in the mass media, instances are easier to retrieve from memory than the various natural causes of death that are rarely presented in the media.

Here's another, perhaps more troubling, example: Physicians who received information about a disease later misdiagnosed clinical cases that were superficially similar to the disease they had learned about earlier (Schmidt et al., 2014). When the media or other sources focus frequently on a particular type of illness, even doctors may show the influence of this bias because certain disease features are more readily brought to mind than others. As a result, doctors' diagnoses may reflect differences due to the ease of data retrieval—thus revealing the effect of availability heuristic use.

In what other way can the availability heuristic influence us? Research suggests that our desires can bias our decision making toward greater risk taking (Mishra, 2014). For instance, during poor economic conditions, the wisest choice might be to conserve money and make low-risk investments. But human behavior does not always conform to rational choice predictions (Akerlof & Shiller, 2009). Consider how the "need for money" might increase if you perceive your economic future to be threatened. Does the idea of taking financial risks to improve your financial condition seem more compelling? This idea is consistent with findings that people tend to overestimate the likelihood that gambling will bring financial success and gambling tends to increase during economic downturns (Canadian Gaming Association, 2011).

Experiments have tested whether economic threat can make gambling more attractive. Research by Wohl, Branscombe, and Lister (2014) first induced some students to believe that their economic future was gloomy due to the global financial crisis. In contrast, students in the control group simply read about money production at the national mint. Beliefs such as "I think of gambling like a financial investment" were assessed in both groups. Then, all participants received $10 and were given an opportunity to gamble with it at a roulette wheel. For those participants whose future financial security had been undermined, the belief that risk taking is necessary to achieve financial gains increased. That same group's willingness to gamble, and the amount of money they actually wagered, increased as well. As shown in Figure 2.3, by convincing the students their financial needs might be unfulfilled, the value of risk taking to satisfy those needs came more readily to mind. This, in turn, affected the students' willingness to gamble.

Interestingly, research suggests that there is more to the availability heuristic than merely the subjective ease with which relevant information comes to mind. The amount of information we can bring to mind seems to matter, too (e.g., Schwarz et al., 1991). The more information we can think of, the greater its impact on our judgments. Which of these two factors is more important? The answer appears to involve the kind of judgment we are making. If the judgment involves emotions or feelings, we tend to rely on the "ease" rule. However, if the judgment involves facts, or the task is inherently difficult, we tend to rely more on the "amount" rule (e.g., Rothman & Hardin, 1997; Ruder & Bless, 2003).

It is also the case that the ease of bringing instances to mind affects judgments that are self-relevant more readily than judgments about others. In fact, even judgments about objects that we are personally familiar with—such as consumer brands—are influenced by ease of retrieval more than judgments about brands that we are less familiar with (Tybout, Sternthal, Malaviya, Bakamitsos, & Park, 2005). This is because when we are aware that we have less information about other people or unfamiliar objects, making judgments about them seems more difficult, and ease of retrieval is given less weight. But when we think we are familiar with a task, know more about it, or believe the task itself is easy, then ease of retrieval is particularly likely to be the basis of our judgment. Let's see how this plays out in self-judgments.

Would you find it easier to think of two instances that indicate your own creativity, or six instances? What about listing instances of creativity that an acquaintance exhibited? In research by Caruso (2008), students found it easier to

Figure 2.3 Availability Heuristic Use: When the Value of Risk Taking Comes Readily to Mind

When people perceive an important need as unmet, the attractiveness of choosing a risky pathway to improve one's position can increase. Gambling, and the belief that it is necessary to take financial risks to achieve financial gains, may be more likely when people feel their future is insecure.

provide two examples of their own creativity compared to six examples and, as shown in Figure 2.4, this influenced ratings of their own creativity. Ease of retrieving examples of an acquaintance's creativity did not affect ratings of creativity for that other person. That's because when tasks are more difficult, which is the case when it concerns attributes of another person, subjective ease of retrieval is given less weight.

2.1.3: Anchoring and Adjustment: Where You Begin Makes a Difference

When people attempt to sell something—whether it's a house or a car, through an ad in a newspaper or online—they typically set the "asking" price higher than they really expect to get. Likewise, buyers often bid less initially than they expect to ultimately pay. This is mostly because buyers and sellers want to give themselves some room for bargaining. Often the selling price is the starting point for discussion; the buyer offers less, the seller counters, and the process continues until an agreement is reached. When a seller sets a starting price, this is an important advantage related to another heuristic that strongly influences our thinking: **anchoring and adjustment**.

Figure 2.4 Availability Heuristic Use: Perceived Creativity of the Self Depends on Ease of Retrieval

Ratings of perceived self-creativity depended on ease of retrieval. When it was easy (vs. difficult) to generate diagnostic examples for the self, then perceived self-creativity increased. The ease or difficulty of generating creative instances for another person did not affect judgments of the other's creativity.

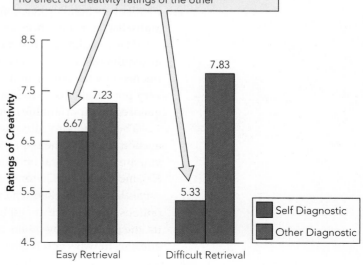

When easy to retrieve examples diagnostic of the self being creative, rated own creativity was higher than when it was difficult to retrieve creative examples for the self. Ease of retrieving examples for others had no effect on creativity ratings of the other

Figure 2.5 Anchoring and Adjustment in Legal Decisions

Experienced legal experts recommended harsher sentences when the anchors were harsh but more lenient sentences when the anchors were lenient. This was the case regardless of the relevance of the anchor source, indicating that anchoring can exert powerful effects on social thought.

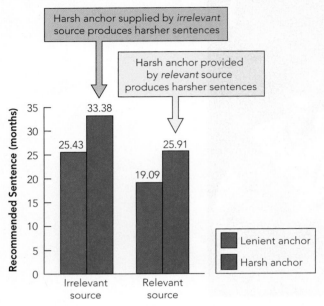

This heuristic involves the tendency to deal with uncertainty in many situations by using something we do know as a starting point (the "anchor") and then making adjustments to it. The seller's asking price provides such a starting point, to which buyers try to make adjustments in order to lower the price they pay. Lowering the price makes buyers feel they are getting a very good deal in comparison to the original asking price. This too is how "sale pricing" and highly visible "reductions" work in retail stores—the original starting point sets the anchor so shoppers feel like they are then getting a bargain in comparison.

In a sense, the existence of the anchoring and adjustment heuristic is far from surprising. In uncertain situations we have to start somewhere. What is more surprising, however, is the power of this effect—even in situations where, rationally, it should not operate. For instance, consider an unsettling study by Englich, Mussweiler, and Strach (2006) that indicates court decisions and sentences can be strongly influenced by anchoring and adjustment. Moreover, this occurs even with experienced judges!

In this research, the participants were highly experienced legal professionals. They were asked to read a very realistic court case and then learned of prison sentences recommended for the defendant. In one condition of the study, these recommendations came from a journalist—someone with no legal training. In another condition, the recommended sentences were actually generated randomly by throwing dice; the crime itself was not considered. Finally, in another condition, sentences were recommended by an experienced prosecutor.

Some of the recommendations were lenient (e.g., 1 month of probation), and others were harsh (e.g., 3 years in prison for the same crime). After receiving this information, these experienced legal participants made their own sentencing recommendations. You might expect that the recommendations of these experts would *not* be influenced by the anchors they received, especially when the sources were either irrelevant or purely random. But, as you can see in Figure 2.5, these recommendation anchors did have a significant effect on the judges. Sentences were harsher when participants were exposed to a harsh anchor but more lenient when they were exposed to a lenient anchor. Furthermore, it did *not* matter whether the source of the anchor was a journalist, an experienced prosecutor, or merely the throw of dice.

These findings, while a compelling demonstration of the power of anchoring, are also quite disturbing. If even experienced and highly trained legal experts can be influenced by anchoring and adjustment, it seems clear that this heuristic indeed has a very powerful effect—indicating how shortcuts in social thought can have real consequences in important life contexts.

There are many situations in which our behavior can be subtlety affected by an anchor. Consider the requests for donations that most of us receive. In most requests, you are given several options for an "appropriate" donation. When the first option is $50, increasing by $25 for each successive option, the organization almost certainly receives less money than when the first option is $100, with $50 increases in subsequent options. Because we are typically not conscious of the effects that anchors can have on us, the anchor set by others not only affects how much money we donate but can also affect us in ways you might not even suspect.

Consider, for example, whether the size of the meal portion you receive at a restaurant could affect how much you eat. Recent research by Marchiori, Papies, and Klein (2014) illustrates how the **portion size effect**—the tendency to eat more when a larger portion of food is received than a smaller portion—is really a good example of anchoring and *in*adequate adjustment. Participants who were given a low gram anchor as a food serving of cheese, soup, steak, and pasta estimated they would eat significantly less of those foods than the participants who were given no anchor or a large portion (high anchor). In fact, estimates of food intake were a whopping 77 percent greater in the high-anchor condition compared to the low-anchor condition. So, as shown in Figure 2.6, how much we eat may be insufficiently adjusted downward when we are presented with a large portion of food.

Why are the effects of the anchoring and adjustment heuristic so powerful? Although we do make adjustments following exposure to externally provided anchors, these adjustments are often *not* sufficient to overcome the initial impact of the anchors. Interestingly, the tendency to make insufficient judgment correction is greater when individuals are less capable of engaging in effortful thought—for instance, after consuming alcohol or when busy doing other tasks (Epley & Gilovich, 2006). Overall, then, it appears that our tendency to let initial anchors influence our judgments—in both important and mundane situations—stems, to an important degree, from a tendency to avoid the effortful work involved in making adjustments away from initial anchors.

2.1.4: Status Quo Heuristic: "What Is, Is Good"

When people are asked to make judgments and choices, they often act as though they believe the way things are currently is better than any other alternative. Similar to the availability heuristic, objects and options that are more easily retrieved from memory may be judged in a heuristic fashion as "good." In fact, these objects and options are often judged as better than ones that are new, are rarely encountered, or represent a change from the status quo. Assuming that a long-standing product on the market is superior to a new version might seem logical because over time bad products tend to be removed from the market. But, it is also true that old products sometimes stay on the market through inertia, and people may continue buying them partly out of habit. So, are marketers who put "new and improved" on packaging labels hurting their sales by doing so? In the special feature, **"What Research Tells Us About…People's Preference for the Status Quo,"** we'll see whether people really do favor the "old" or the "new."

Figure 2.6 "The Portion Size Effect": A Matter of Anchoring and Inadequate Adjustment

When people are presented with small portions of food, they estimate and eat less than when presented with large portions. The large portion serves as a high anchor that we typically fail to adjust downward, contributing to the obesity epidemic in Western countries.

What Research Tells Us About...

People's Preference for the Status Quo

In a series of studies, Eidelman, Pattershall, and Crandall (2010) addressed the question of whether people heuristically favor "old" over "new" or the opposite. Participants in one study were given a piece of chocolate to taste. Before doing so, they were either told that the chocolate was first sold in Europe in 1937 (70 years on the market) or in 2003 (3 years on the market). Participants were then asked to rate how much they enjoyed the taste of the chocolate, whether they were impressed by it, and whether they would purchase it.

Next, participants were asked about the reasons for their evaluation of the chocolate. Overwhelmingly, they rated the "older" chocolate as more delicious than the chocolate that represented a new brand. These participants seemed to be unaware that time on the market had influenced their evaluations of the chocolate. In fact, they uniformly rated brand age as the least important reason for their evaluation and taste as the most important factor. They didn't know that the chocolate was exactly the same; only the supposed length of time on the market differed!

What about when the "old" versus "new" involves people? Will the same preference for the "old" emerge? Eidelman and Crandall (2014) suggest it will, and that this may account for the well-known advantage that political incumbents have over new persons seeking elected office. To test this idea, they gave students a photograph and description of a candidate for mayor of a town in another state. For half the students, the candidate was described as "the current Mayor who was running for a second term." To the other half, the candidate was described as "running for Mayor for the first time." As with the chocolate study, participants perceived the "status quo" incumbent candidate as more attractive than the candidate who was "new" and running for office for the first time. Even though the candidate photo and information were exactly the same in both test groups, perception differed.

Additional studies have revealed that political candidates who are presented as the "new option" are consistently subjected to greater scrutiny. In other words, more questions are asked about them than the "status quo" options. Since "new" receives closer attention, potential flaws seem more obvious. Likewise, since the "status quo" is less closely scrutinized, flaws may be noticed less.

So, would marketers be better off presenting their products as "tried and true" rather than as "new and improved"? According to Eidelman and Crandall (2014), the answer is a resounding, "Yes!" For example, when they varied the length of time, a practice (acupuncture) was said to be in existence—250, 500, 1,000, or 2,000 years—the perceived effectiveness of acupuncture increased according to its apparent age. Likewise, a painting judged for its aesthetic qualities was rated more pleasing when study participants were told it was painted in 1905 compared to 2005.

So, people do seem to heuristically use the length of time a product or practice has been in existence as a cue to its goodness. Although judgments of all products are unlikely to be biased in favor of age, and occasionally novelty may win, tradition and longevity often do seem to imply heuristically that the "tried and true" is better than the new.

Key Points

- We enter a state of **information overload** when the demands on our cognitive system become greater than its capacity. To deal with this condition, we often reduce the effort we expend on **social cognition**—how we think about other persons and events.
- Given our limited capacity to process information, we often make use of simple strategies to arrive at a judgment. When information is complex and the "correct" answer is not obvious (**conditions of uncertainty**), we often make use of **heuristics**—simple rules for making decisions in a quick and relatively effortless manner.
- The **representativeness heuristic** suggests that the more similar an individual is to the typical members of a given group—the group's **prototype**—the more likely that person will be seen as belonging to the group.
- Using the representativeness heuristic can lead to erroneous decisions when *base rates* are ignored, despite their relevance.

- Not all cultural groups use representativeness to the same degree when evaluating the likelihood that a particular cause was responsible for an effect. Asians tend to expect that "like will go with like" less than Westerners do, making Asians less susceptible to this bias.
- The **availability heuristic** suggests that the easier it is to bring information to mind, the greater its impact on subsequent decisions or judgments. In some cases, availability may also involve the amount of information we bring to mind. We tend to apply the ease-of-retrieval rule to judgments about ourselves more than we do to judgments about others with whom we have less familiarity.
- The **anchoring and adjustment heuristic** leads us to use a number or value as a starting point (the "anchor") from which we then make adjustments. These adjustments may not be sufficient, perhaps because once we attain a plausible value, we stop the adjustment process. Some people

(especially sellers) may be motivated to set an anchor that will bias our judgments.

- The **portion size effect**—the tendency to eat more when a larger portion of food is received than a smaller portion—is a good example of anchoring and *in* adequate adjustment. The tendency to make insufficient judgment correction is greater when individuals are less capable of engaging in effortful thought.

- Objects and options that are more easily retrieved from memory may be judged in a heuristic fashion as "good." These objects and options are often judged as better than the ones that are new, are rarely encountered, or represent a change from the status quo.

2.2: Schemas: Mental Frameworks for Organizing Social Information

Objective   **Describe the role of schemas in guiding our thoughts and actions**

What happens when you visit your doctor? We all know it goes something like this. You enter the office and give your health insurance information. Then you sit and wait. If you are lucky, the wait is not very long and a nurse takes you into an examination room. Once there, you wait some more. Eventually, the doctor enters and talks to you and perhaps examines you. Finally, you return to the front desk and perhaps pay some part of your bill (the co-pay) on the way out.

It doesn't matter who your doctor is or where you live—this sequence of events, or something very much like it, commonly takes place. None of this surprises you. In fact, you expect this sequence to occur—including the waiting. Why? Through past experience, you have built up a mental framework containing the essential features of this kind of situation—appointments with a health professional. Similarly, you have formed other mental frameworks related to eating at restaurants, getting a haircut, shopping for groceries, going to the movies, or boarding an airplane (see Figure 2.7).

Social psychologists term these mental frameworks **schemas**: They help us to organize social information, guide our actions, and process information relevant to particular contexts. Since your personal experience in such situations is probably similar to that of others in your culture, everyone in a given society tends to share many basic schemas. Once schemas are formed, they play a role in determining what we notice

---

Figure 2.7 Schemas: Mental Frameworks Concerning Routine Events

Through experience, we acquire schemas—mental frameworks for organizing, interpreting, and processing social information. For instance, you almost certainly have a schema for events such as boarding an airplane (left photo) and going to a bar or restaurant where you have to wait to be seated (right photo). In other words, you know what to expect in these and many other situations and are prepared for these events to unfold in certain sequences.

about the social world, what information we remember, and how we use and interpret such information. Let's take a closer look at these effects, because as we'll soon see, they exert an important impact on our understanding of the social world and our relations with other people.

2.2.1: The Impact of Schemas on Social Cognition: Attention, Encoding, Retrieval

How do schemas influence social thought? Research findings suggest that schemas influence three basic processes of social cognition: attention, encoding, and retrieval (Wyer & Srull, 1994). *Attention* refers to the information we notice. *Encoding* refers to the processes we use to store noticed information in memory. Finally, *retrieval* refers to how we recover information from memory in order to use it in some manner—for example, in making judgments about other people.

With respect to attention, schemas often act as a kind of filter. Information consistent with them is more likely to be noticed and to enter our consciousness. We especially tend to rely on schemas when experiencing *cognitive load*—when we are trying to handle a lot of information at one time (Kunda, 1999). In this case, we rely on our schemas because they help us process information efficiently.

During encoding, the information that becomes the focus of our attention is much more likely to be stored in long-term memory. In general, the information that is consistent with our schemas is encoded. However, information that is sharply inconsistent with our schemas—information that does *not* agree with our expectations in a given situation—may be encoded into a separate memory location and marked with a unique "tag." Inconsistent information is sometimes so unexpected that it literally seizes our attention and almost forces us to make a mental note of it (Stangor & McMillan, 1992). Here's an example: You have a well-developed schema for the role of "professor." You expect professors to come to class, to lecture, to answer questions, to give and grade exams, and so on. Suppose that one of your professors comes to class and performs magic tricks instead of lecturing. You will certainly remember this experience because it is so inconsistent with your schema for professors—your mental framework for how professors behave in the classroom.

That leads us to the third process: retrieval from memory. What information is most readily remembered? Is it information that is consistent with our schemas, or is it information that is inconsistent with these mental frameworks? This complex question has been investigated in many different studies (e.g., Stangor & McMillan, 1992; Tice, Bratslavsky, & Baumeister, 2000).

Overall, research suggests that people tend to report remembering information that is consistent with schemas more than information that is inconsistent. However, this could potentially stem from differences in actual memory or, alternatively, from simple response tendencies. In other words, information inconsistent with schemas might be present in memory as strongly as information consistent with schemas, but people simply report the information that is consistent with their schemas. In fact, the latter appears to be the case. When measures of memory are corrected for this response tendency, or when individuals are asked to actually *recall* information rather than indicate whether they recognize it, there is a strong tendency to remember information that is *incongruent* (does not fit) with schemas. So, which do we remember better—information consistent or inconsistent with our schemas? The answer depends on the memory measure employed. In general, people *report* information consistent with their schemas, but information inconsistent with schemas may be strongly present in memory, too.

2.2.2: Priming: Which Schema Guides Our Thought?

We all develop a large array of schemas—cognitive frameworks that help us interpret and use social information. That raises an interesting question: Which of these frameworks influence our thought at any given point in time? One answer involves the strength of various schemas. The stronger and better-developed schemas are, the more likely they will influence our thinking, and especially our memory for social information (e.g., Stangor & McMillan, 1992; Tice et al., 2000).

Second, schemas can be temporarily activated by what is known as **priming**—temporary increases in the accessibility of specific schemas (Sparrow & Wegner, 2006). Suppose you have just been exposed to a "cute" product such as a "Hello Kitty" cell phone case via an advertisement. These products are known to prime mental representations of fun (Nenkov & Scott, 2014). Now, you are looking for something to eat and you notice an ice cream shop up ahead. Do you stop there and buy a sundae, perhaps even perceiving it as a "healthy choice," or do you hold out for a more nutritious salad option? Because you just had an experience that activated your schema for "fun indulgence" via exposure to cute products, you may, in fact, be more likely to perceive ice cream as healthy (and yummy). This example illustrates the effects of priming—a recent experience activates a schema, which in turn, exerts an effect on our current thinking.

Can priming be deactivated, or are we doomed to see the world in terms of the schema activated by our most recent experience? Social psychologists describe **unpriming** as a process by which thoughts or actions primed by a recent experience dissipate once they find expression. Unpriming effects are clearly demonstrated in a study by Sparrow and Wegner (2006). Participants were given a series of very easy "yes–no" questions (e.g., "Does a triangle have three sides?"). One group of participants was told to try to answer the questions randomly—*not* correctly. Another group of participants were asked to respond to the questions twice; the first time, they were told to try to answer them correctly, while the second time they were to try to answer them randomly.

It was predicted that participants in the group doing the task once would not be able to answer the questions randomly; their schema for "answering correctly" would have been activated, and this would lead them to provide the correct answers. In contrast, participants who answered the questions twice—first correctly and then randomly—would do better at responding randomly. Their first set of answers would provide expression for the schema "answer questions correctly," and so permit them to answer randomly the second time around.

The predictions proved to be accurate. Those who only answered the question once, but were told to do so randomly, were actually correct 58 percent of the time. Their activated schema prevented them from replying in a truly random manner. The participants who first answered the questions correctly and then answered randomly did much better. The second time, their answers were correct only 49 percent of the time—indicating chance performance. These findings suggest that for primed schemas that are somehow expressed, unpriming occurs, and the influence of the primed schemas disappears. Figure 2.8 summarizes the nature of unpriming. If primed schemas are *not* expressed, however, their effects may persist for long periods of time (Budson & Price, 2005; Mitchell, 2006).

2.2.3: Schema Persistence: Why Even Discredited Schemas Can Influence Thought and Behavior

Schemas are often helpful because they permit us to make sense out of a vast array of social information. However, they have an important "downside," too. By influencing what we notice, enter into memory, and later remember, schemas can produce distortions in our understanding of the social world. Unfortunately, schemas are often resistant to change. They show a strong **perseverance effect**, remaining unchanged even in the face of contradictory information (Kunda & Oleson, 1995). Perhaps even worse, schemas can sometimes be *self-fulfilling*: They influence our responses to the social world in ways that *make* our expectations come true, consistent with the schemas.

Figure 2.8 Unpriming of Schemas: Bringing the Effects of Priming to an End

When schemas are primed—activated by experiences, events, or stimuli, their effects tend to persist. In fact, they have been observed over many years even. If the schema is somehow expressed in thought or behavior, however, unpriming may occur, and the impact of the schema may decrease or even disappear.

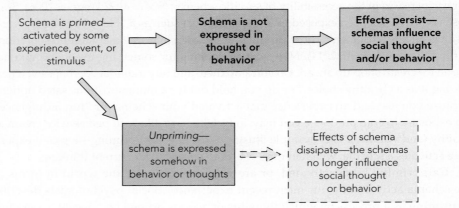

Might our cognitive frameworks—our schemas—actually shape the social world as well as reflect it? A large body of evidence suggests that this is definitely so (e.g., Smith, Jussim, & Eccles, 1999; Madon, Jussim, & Eccles, 1997). Perhaps the most dramatic evidence that schemas can be self-fulfilling was provided by Rosenthal and Jacobson (1968), in a famous study of teachers and the unintended effects of their expectations on students. These researchers went to an elementary school and administered an IQ test to all students. Then they told the teachers that some of the students had scored very high and were about to "bloom" academically. The teachers were not given such information about other students who constituted a control group. Although the researchers had chosen the names of the students for each group randomly, they predicted that this information would alter teachers' expectations about the children and their behavior toward them.

To find out if this theory was true, 8 months later the researchers tested both groups of children once again. Results were clear: Students who had been described as "bloomers" to their teachers showed significantly larger gains on the IQ test than those in the control group. In short, teachers' beliefs about the students had operated in a *self-fulfilling manner*: The students whose teachers believed they would "bloom" actually did. So schemas can be a double-edged sword. They can help us make sense of the social world and process information efficiently, but they can also lock us into acting in ways that create the world that we expect.

2.2.4: Reasoning by Metaphor: How Social Attitudes and Behavior Are Affected by Figures of Speech

A **metaphor** is a linguistic device that relates or compares a typically abstract concept to another unrelated concept, by suggesting a similarity between them. Because metaphors can activate different kinds of social knowledge, they can influence how we interpret events (Landau, Meier, & Keefer, 2010). Consider just a few metaphors:

Her presentation bombed; everyone affiliated with her tried to run for cover.

He raised the spirits of the audience; he received a warm reception.

Where is our relationship heading? Are we on the right track?

Although you may not have heard any of these specific metaphors before, you can easily understand what is being communicated. In each of these examples, abstract

Table 2.1 Metaphors Can Affect Social Attitudes and Behavior

A variety of metaphors, when primed, have been shown to affect attitudes, memory, judgments, and physical perceptions.

Metaphor Priming	Effect on Social Judgment
Nations are bodies (Landau, Sullivan, & Greenberg, 2009)	Framing U.S. as body led to harsher attitudes toward immigration in those motivated to protect their body from contamination
Good is up; Bad is down (Crawford, Margolies, Drake, & Murphy, 2006)	Positive items presented in higher location and negative items in lower location recalled best
God is up (Chasteen, Burdzy, & Pratt, 2010)	Photos of people presented in a high (vs. low) position on screen were judged as having a stronger belief in God
Social exclusion is physical cold (Zhong & Leonardelli, 2008)	Recalling a time of social exclusion (vs. acceptance) resulted in the room being perceived as 5 degrees colder
Past is backward; future is forward (Miles, Nind, & Macrae, 2010)	Backward postural sway was exhibited when thinking of the past and forward sway shown when thinking of the future

SOURCE: Based on research by Landau, Meier, and Keefer (2010).

concepts are being used to give a particular meaning to a concrete event. In the first sentence, our knowledge of warfare is being used to structure our understanding of people's response to a presentation. In the second example, both height and temperature are used to guide our understanding of an audience's response to a speaker or performer. In the last example, the concept of a journey or travel is being applied to love and relationships.

Does such metaphor use have consequences for social judgment and behavior? Research suggests this is so (Landau et al., 2010). Table 2.1 presents a selection of metaphors that, when primed, can influence a number of different types of social inferences and behavior. Let's consider an example. In order to prime the concept of body contamination for study participants, Landau, Sullivan, and Greenberg (2009) first asked them to read about the many airborne bacteria in the environment. The bacteria were described as either harmful to humans or not. Then, in a seemingly unrelated task about American domestic issues, statements related to the United States were presented either with a body metaphor ("After the Civil War, the United States experienced an unprecedented *growth spurt*") or without it ("After the Civil War, the United States experienced an unprecedented period of innovation").

In the third phase of the study, participants were asked to indicate their attitudes toward immigration. Those with a concern about "body contamination"—because they'd been told how bacteria can harm humans—expressed more negative attitudes toward immigration when the metaphor of the United States as a body had been primed, compared to when the United States had been described without this metaphor. So, how we talk—metaphorically, the pictures we paint with our words—can affect how we interpret and respond to the social world.

Can metaphors also affect our perceptions of treatment effectiveness for common problems such as depression? In several studies, Keefer, Landau, Sullivan, and Rothschild (2014) obtained evidence that supports this idea. Depressive mood is often described in terms of the metaphors "feeling down" or "a state of darkness." After one of these two metaphors was primed, the researchers wanted to find out if an antidepressant drug ("Liftix"), described as "lifting mood," would be perceived as differentially effective. As expected, the "down" metaphor priming influenced participants to judge this drug treatment as highly effective. But when the "dark" metaphor was primed, this same drug was deemed not likely to be effective. This research suggests that metaphor use in advertisements, or even as cues within product names, have the potential for driving people toward or away from various types of treatments.

Key Points

- **Schemas** are a basic component of social cognition. These mental frameworks, formed through experience, help us to organize and make sense of social information, especially when we're experiencing *cognitive load* from too much information received at one time.
- Once formed, schemas exert powerful effects on what we notice (*attention*), enter into memory (*encoding*), and later remember (*retrieval*). Individuals report remembering more information that is consistent with their schemas than information that is inconsistent with them. But in fact, inconsistent information is also strongly represented in memory.
- Schemas are often **primed**—activated by experiences, events, or stimuli. Once they are primed, the effects of schemas tend to persist until they are somehow expressed in thought or behavior. Such expression (known as **unpriming**) then reduces the likelihood that those schemas will influence further thought or behavior.
- Schemas help us to process information, but they show a strong **perseverance effect** even in the face of disconfirming information, thus distorting our understanding of the social world.
- Schemas can also exert *self-fulfilling* effects, causing us to behave in ways that create confirmation of our expectancies.
- **Metaphors**—linguistic devices that relate an abstract concept to another dissimilar concept—can shape how we perceive and respond to the social world.

2.3: Automatic and Controlled Processing in Social Thought

Objective **Distinguish between automatic and controlled processing modes of social thought**

Social thought can occur in two distinctly different ways: in a systematic, logical, and highly effortful manner known as **controlled processing**, or in a fast, relatively effortless, and intuitive manner known as **automatic processing**. This distinction has been confirmed in literally hundreds of different studies and is now recognized as an important aspect of social thought. However, these two kinds of thought are not totally independent. In fact, recent evidence suggests that automatic and controlled processing may often occur together, especially in situations that involve some uncertainty (Sherman et al., 2008). Still, the distinction between them is important and worth considering very carefully.

Perhaps the most convincing support is provided by the kind of *social neuroscience* research described briefly in Chapter 1—research that examines activity in the human brain as an individual processes social information. The findings of such research suggest that people actually possess two different neural systems for processing social information—one that operates in an automatic manner and another that operates in a systematic and controlled manner. Moreover, the operation of these two systems is reflected by activation in different regions of the brain. For instance, consider research on *evaluative reactions*—a very basic kind of social judgment relating to whether we like or dislike something (a person, idea, or object). Such evaluations can occur in two distinct ways: simple good-bad judgments that occur in a rapid and seemingly automatic manner (Phelps et al., 2001) or through more effortful thought in which we think carefully and logically, weighing all the relevant points fully and systematically (e.g., Duncan & Owen, 2000).

The first kind of reaction (automatic) seems to occur primarily in the amygdala, while the second (controlled) seems to involve portions of the prefrontal cortex, especially the medial prefrontal cortex and ventrolateral prefrontal cortex (e.g., Cunningham, Johnson, Gatenby, Gore, & Banaji, 2003). In addition, we also seem to possess two distinct brain systems for processing these types of information.

Controlled processing (reasoning, logic) occurs primarily in the prefrontal cortex areas of the brain. Emotion-related, automatic reactions occur mainly in the limbic system, structures deep inside the brain (Cohen, 2005; Fiske & Taylor, 2013).

Overall, the results of social neuroscience studies, as well as more traditional methods of social psychological research, suggest that the distinction between automatic and controlled processing is indeed real and very important. We will be illustrating this fact in many places throughout this book, but here, we will try to clarify why it is so important by examining two specific issues relating to automatic processing: the effects of automatic processing on social behavior, and the benefits provided by such processing.

2.3.1: Automatic Processing and Automatic Social Behavior

Once a concept is activated, it can exert important effects on social thought and behavior. Often, people act in ways that are consistent with their schemas, even if they do not intend to do so, and are unaware that they are acting in this manner. For example, in a well-known study by Bargh, Chen, and Burrows (1996), these researchers used priming to activate either the schema for the trait of rudeness or the schema for the trait of politeness. To do so, two groups of participants were given jumbled sentences to unscramble. The first group worked on sentences containing words related to rudeness (e.g., bold, rude, impolitely, bluntly). The second group worked on sentences with words related to politeness (e.g., cordially, patiently, polite, courteous). People in a third (control) group unscrambled sentences containing words unrelated to either trait (e.g., exercising, flawlessly, occasionally, rapidly).

After completing this task, participants in the study were asked to report back to the experimenter for additional tasks. The experimenter and another person (an accomplice) engaged in a conversation whenever a participant approached. The experimenter continued this conversation, ignoring the participant. The major dependent measure was whether or not the participant interrupted the conversation in order to receive further instructions. Persons for whom the rudeness trait had been primed were more likely to interrupt than those for whom the politeness trait had been primed. Further findings indicated that these effects occurred despite the fact that participants' ratings of the experimenter in terms of politeness did not differ across the three experimental conditions. These differences in behavior seemed to occur in a nonconscious, automatic manner. Clearly, then, automatic processing is an important aspect of social thought—one that can affect overt behavior.

Additional research suggests that the effects of automatic processing may be even more far-reaching than simply triggering particular forms of behavior. Once automatic processing is initiated (e.g., through priming), individuals may—again unconsciously—begin to prepare for future interactions with the persons or groups who are the focus of this automatic processing. As suggested by Cesario, Plaks, and Higgins (2006), activating a schema may not merely trigger behaviors consistent with that schema; it may also activate behaviors that, in a sense, "get the persons involved ready" to actually interact with others. A study conducted by Cesario et al. (2006) clearly illustrates such preparatory effects. Participants were primed with photos of men labeled as either "GAY" or "STRAIGHT." These photos were shown so quickly that participants could not actually see the images. But, as in many other studies, it was expected that the photos would prime (activate) schemas for these social categories. Then, seemingly unexpected, the computers being used by the participants locked up. Unaware that this mishap had occurred intentionally, participants were instructed to ask the experimenter for help.

When the experimenter entered, he acted in a hostile manner. The key question was: Would the heterosexual participants who had their negative stereotype (schema)

Figure 2.9 Automatic Processing Initiates Preparation for Future Interactions

Activation of schemas can trigger behaviors consistent with these cognitive frameworks. Recent research suggests that in addition, once activated, schemas may also trigger motivated efforts to prepare for interacting with the persons or groups who are the focus of these schemas. In the case of gay men, for instance, this enhances tendencies for heterosexuals to act in a hostile, aggressive manner.

Stereotypes (Schemas) Trigger Schema-Consistent Behaviors

Stereotypes (Schemas) Trigger Preparation for Interacting with Persons or Groups Who are the Focus of the Schemas

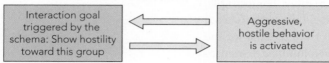

of gays primed behave more hostilely than participants who had their stereotype of heterosexuals primed? If so, this result would be directly *contrary* to the stereotype of gays, which generally suggests that gay people are passive and nonaggressive. However, *consistent* with the view that priming the gay schema motivates individuals to prepare to interact with members of that group—in this case, a group they evaluate negatively—gay priming would lead to more aggressive behavior. Indeed, the findings indicated that when interacting with the experimenter, participants showed greater hostility if they had been primed with photos labeled "GAY" rather than with photos labeled "STRAIGHT." The different predictions for both views of schema activation are summarized in Figure 2.9: (1) Schemas trigger behaviors consistent with the schemas, in which case participants shown the "GAY" label should behave nonaggressively, or (2) schemas trigger motivated preparation to interact with the group that is the subject of the schema, as evidenced by the participants shown the "GAY" label behaving aggressively.

2.3.2: Benefits of Automatic Processing: Beyond Mere Efficiency

One kind of automatic processing familiar to most people occurs when we try to remember something (someone's name, a thought we previously had)—but don't succeed. When that happens, we often turn to doing something else while the search for the information we want goes on automatically, without our conscious awareness. Often, this kind of memory search is successful, and the missing name or fact pops into mind. In such cases, we are dimly aware that *something* was happening, but can't really describe it. Research on this aspect of automatic processing confirms that we often attempt to deal with problems, and even complex decisions, while our attention is directed elsewhere (e.g., Dijksterhuis & Nordgren, 2006). Perhaps even more surprising, recent evidence indicates that sometimes automatic processing may be superior to careful, conscious thought in terms of making excellent decisions (Galdi, Arcuri, & Gawronski, 2008).

A clear illustration of these advantages is provided by research conducted by Dijksterhuis and van Olden (2006). These social psychologists asked students to look at various posters and indicate the one they liked most. In one condition (immediate decision), the posters were all shown on a computer screen simultaneously, and students made their decision immediately. In another condition (conscious thought), the posters were shown one at a time for 90 seconds. After looking at the posters, the students were given paper and asked to list their thoughts and evaluations—to think carefully about the posters and their preferences. Finally, in a third condition (unconscious thought), participants worked on another task (solving anagrams) after seeing the posters, preventing them from consciously thinking about their preferences. Several minutes later, students indicated which poster they liked best.

All the participants then received a surprise: they were given their favorite poster to take home. Then, 3–5 weeks later they were telephoned and asked how satisfied they were with the poster they had received. They were also asked how much money they would want (in Euros) if they sold their poster. The researchers predicted that participants would actually be most satisfied with their choice in the unconscious condition, where they made the choice without an opportunity to think consciously about it. As you can see from Figure 2.10, this is precisely what happened. This result surprisingly suggests that participants actually made *better* decisions, in terms of satisfaction, when they chose on "automatic" than when they had a chance to think about the options carefully.

Why is this so? Perhaps the reason is that conscious thought has strict limits in terms of the amount of information it can handle. In other words, when we think actively about decisions, we may be unable to take account of all available information. In contrast, unconscious, automatic thought has much greater capacity. Similarly, when we think about decisions consciously, we may fail to weight the various dimensions or elements accurately. For instance, actively thinking about these dimensions may lead to confusion about which ones are the most important—causing us to second-guess ourselves. Unconscious, automatic processing may therefore reflect our real preferences more clearly. Whatever the precise reason, these findings, and those of many related studies (e.g., Ito, Chiao, Devine, Lorig, & Cacioppo, 2006), suggest that automatic processing offers important advantages beyond those of merely being quick and efficient. Despite the criticisms that have been leveled against this research methodology and the conclusion that unconscious decisions are better than those based on conscious thought (e.g., Newell & Shanks, 2014), there appears to be real drawbacks to relying solely on conscious thought in making decisions.

Figure 2.10 The Benefits of Automatic (Unconscious) Thought

Participants who were prevented from thinking consciously about their preferences for various posters (unconscious condition) were more satisfied with the choices they made than participants who could engage in careful, systematic thought (conscious) or participants who made their choice immediately after seeing the poster (immediate). These findings suggest that automatic processing offers more benefits than simply being quick and efficient.

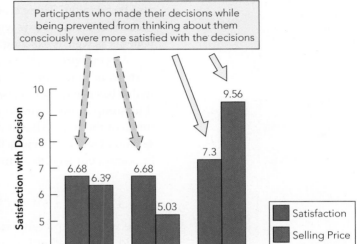

Key Points

- **Controlled processing** occurs in a systematic, logical, and highly effortful manner, whereas **automatic processing** occurs in a fast, intuitive, and relatively effortless manner.
- Considerable evidence indicates that automatic processing and controlled processing are distinctly different modes of social thought. In fact, different regions of the brain appear to be involved in these two types of processing, especially when evaluating various aspects of the social world.

- When schemas or other cognitive frameworks are activated (even without our conscious awareness), they strongly influence our behavior, triggering actions consistent with the frameworks and also preparing us to interact with the persons or groups who are the focus of those schemas.
- Automatic processing is clearly quick and efficient and may sometimes offer other advantages too—such as more satisfactory decisions.

2.4: Potential Sources of Error in Social Cognition: Why Total Rationality Is Rarer Than You Think

Objective **Evaluate the imperfections of the social cognition process**

Human beings are definitely not computers, and our thinking is not simply based on rational self-interest as economists have long assumed (Akerlof & Shiller, 2009). The judgments people make systematically deviate in a number of ways from perfect rationality. This is true for critical decisions such as choosing a career path or whom to marry, as well as making financial decisions about investment stocks or credit card use. Our actions often reflect overconfidence and optimism (Gärling, Kirchler, Lewis, & van Raaij, 2009).

While we can imagine being able to reason in a perfectly logical way, we know from our own experience that often we fall short of this goal. In our efforts to make sense of the social world, we are subject to a wide range of tendencies that, together, can lead us into serious error. We'll now consider how several of these tendencies affect social cognition. Before doing so, however, we should emphasize the following point: While these aspects of social thought do sometimes result in errors, they can also be adaptive. These tendencies often reduce the effort required for navigating the social world. As we saw with heuristic use—these tendencies supply us with tangible benefits as well as exacting important costs.

As you will see, there are many different ways in which our social thought departs from rationality. To acquaint you with a wide range of these effects, we'll start with a basic tendency that seems to occur in a wide range of situations and often produces important errors in our social thought: our tendency to be overly optimistic much of the time. After considering this far-reaching general tendency, we'll turn to several other ways in which social thought departs from rationality, ones that are also important but tend to occur in specific situations.

2.4.1: Our Powerful Tendency to Be Overly Optimistic

If we were completely rational in the ways we think about the social world, we would simply gather information, process it, and then use it to make judgments and decisions. Instead, in many respects, most people tend to "see the world through rose-colored glasses." This tendency is known as the **optimistic bias**—a powerful predisposition to overlook risks and expect things to turn out well. In fact, research findings indicate that most people believe they are *more* likely than others to experience positive events, and *less* likely to experience negative events (Shepperd, Carroll, & Sweeny, 2008). Our strong leaning toward optimism can be seen in many specific judgments. Most people believe that they are more likely than others to get a good job, have a happy marriage, and live to a ripe old age, but less likely to experience negative outcomes such as being fired, getting seriously ill, or getting divorced (Kruger & Burrus, 2004; Schwarzer, 1994).

Similarly, we often have greater confidence in our beliefs or judgments than is justified—an effect known as the **overconfidence bias**. Vallone, Griffin, Lin, and Ross (1990) illustrated how overconfident people can be in their predictions about themselves by asking students to indicate early in the academic year whether they would perform a number of actions (e.g., drop a course, move on or off campus). The students were also asked to indicate how confident they were in their predictions. The students were wrong a substantial proportion of the time. Even when they were 100 percent confident in their predictions they were wrong 15 percent of the time.

Ironically enough, people who are *least* competent in a domain are often the *most* likely to be overconfident of their judgments in that domain! Like many other types of judgments, we frequently have to assess our competence under conditions of uncertainty—where all the relevant information is not known. Consider just a few examples. Have we picked the best health insurance plan to meet our future needs? Are our retirement funds sufficiently diversified to weather even a rocky stock market? Is our new kitchen design optimal? Did the essays we wrote for college admission cover all the essential points?

Caputo and Dunning (2005) have pointed out that one critical reason that we may be overly confident of our judgments and actions in all these cases is because we often lack essential information. That is, we do not know enough to realize what we have missed. These researchers argue that overconfidence often stems from *errors of omission.* Suppose you were asked to list as many uses as possible for WD-40, an oil lubricant. You come up with, what you think is, an impressive list of 20 legitimate uses for it. Would you see yourself as competent at this task? Based on the research conducted by Caputo and Dunning (2005), people do confidently rate their abilities as high under these circumstances, but they should not. In the WD-40 example, you had no way of knowing about the other 1,980 legitimate uses for this product that you have missed! Indeed, when these researchers told their study participants about all the missed possible solutions, people's confidence in their ability dropped to levels more in line with objective measures of performance. So, one important reason we display overconfidence is that we lack the relevant feedback that would help moderate our confidence. As the cartoon in Figure 2.11 suggests, overconfidence may explain why entrepreneurs who start a new business believe that their chances of making it work are much higher than is actually true (Baron & Shane, 2007).

THE ROCKY PAST VERSUS THE GOLDEN FUTURE: OPTIMISM AT WORK   Think back over your life. Did it have good times and some bad? Now, try to imagine your future. How do you think it will unfold? If you are like most people, you may notice a difference in these descriptions. While most of us recognize that our past has been mixed in terms of "highs" and "lows," we tend to forecast a very golden future—one in which we will be quite happy, and few negative events will happen to us. In fact, research by Newby-Clark and Ross (2003) indicates that this tendency is so strong that it occurs even when people have just recalled negative episodes from their own pasts.

What accounts for this difference between past and future? When we think about the past, we can recall failures, unpleasant events, and other disappointments, but these unexpected possibilities are not salient when we think about our future. Instead, when we think about the future, we tend to concentrate on desirable goals, personal happiness, and doing things we have always wanted to do—such as traveling to exotic places. Since our thinking is dominated by these positive thoughts, we make highly optimistic predictions about the future. We tend to perceive it as indeed golden, at least in its promise or potential for us. In short, the optimistic bias seems to occur not just for specific tasks or situations, but for projections of our entire future as well.

Figure 2.11 Overconfidence in Action: Believing You'll Score Big Before You Have Started

Research indicates that business entrepreneurs frequently express greater confidence in their likelihood of succeeding than the objective odds would warrant.

"You asked for a loan of $50 million so you could open 800 pizza restaurants. How about you start with one and build from there?"

Perhaps people also feel optimistic about the future because it just feels good to do so. But, still, might there be hidden costs of being optimistic about ourselves and our future—particularly if we get there and find out our optimism was misplaced? Research by Sweeny and Shepperd (2010) has addressed this question. Students in a psychology class were asked to estimate the grade they would receive on their first exam and their emotional state was measured. Then, the students received their grade and their emotions were again measured.

Students who were more optimistic about the grade they would receive initially reported more positive emotions, suggesting that optimism does feel good. But what happened when the students learned whether their optimism was warranted or not (i.e., they learned their exam grade)? For those optimistic students who overestimated their exam scores, after they learned their actual score, they felt much worse than the realists or pessimists who did not overestimate. The good news is, 24 hours later, those negative emotions had dissipated. This means that even though being optimistic about our future outcomes can make us feel good, if the basis for it is disconfirmed we may feel bad—but fortunately—only temporarily!

WHEN OPTIMISM AFFECTS OUR ABILITY TO PLAN EFFECTIVELY   Another illustration of optimism at work is the **planning fallacy**—our tendency to believe that we can get more done in a given period of time than we actually can, or that a given job will take less time than it really will. We can see this aspect of the optimistic bias in announced schedules for public works (e.g., new roads, airports, bridges, stadiums) that have no chance of being met. Individuals, too, adopt unrealistically optimistic schedules (see Figure 2.12). If you have ever estimated that a project would take you a certain amount of time but then found that it took considerably longer, you are already familiar with this effect of the planning fallacy.

Why do we (repeatedly) fall prey to this particular kind of optimism? Social psychologists who have studied this tendency suggest that several factors play a

Figure 2.12 The Planning Fallacy: When Our "To-Do Lists" Are Unrealistic

The tendency to believe that the plans we construct are doable, that we can accomplish more than we actually can in a given period of time, or that nothing will interfere with the achievement of our goals reflects the planning fallacy in action. Most of us have pretty unrealistic "to-do lists" that rarely, if ever, get completed on schedule.

role (Buehler, Griffin, & Ross, 1994). When individuals make predictions about how long it will take them to complete a given task, they focus primarily on the future and how they will perform the task. This, in turn, prevents them from looking backward in time and remembering how long similar tasks took them in the past. As a result, one important "reality check" that might help them avoid being overly optimistic is removed. Yet, when given information about other people and their experiences, people's estimates often become more realistic (Shepperd, Waters, Weinstein, & Klein, 2015). It should help to consider past experiences with tasks that took longer than expected. But, people tend to attribute such outcomes to unusual circumstances and factors outside their control. As a result, they tend to overlook important potential obstacles that can't be easily foreseen (but invariably will arise) when predicting how long a task will take, falling prey to the planning fallacy again.

These cognitive factors are not the entire story, though. Additional findings suggest that another factor, *motivation* to complete a task, also plays an important role in the planning fallacy. When predicting, individuals often guess that what will happen is what they *want* to happen (Johnson & Sherman, 1990). In cases where they are strongly motivated to complete a task, people make overly optimistic predictions about when they will attain this desired state of affairs (Newby-Clark & Ross, 2003). It appears, then, that our estimates of when we will complete a task are indeed influenced by our hopes and desires. We want to finish on time, so we predict that we will.

Are some people more prone to the planning fallacy than others? As we just discussed, when people are focused on the goal of completing a task, rather than the steps involved in doing so, they are likely to make overly optimistic predictions for how much time it will take to do so. Weick and Guinote (2010) proposed that people in powerful positions are more likely to fall prey to the planning fallacy because they are focused on the goal of getting the task done, whereas people who occupy less powerful positions are more likely to be focused on *how* to get the task done—the steps needed to complete the job. The researchers tested this idea by having some participants think about an episode in their past when they held a position of relative power. Others were asked to think of an episode when they occupied a position of relative powerlessness. Subsequently, both groups of participants were asked to format a document using software that was complicated. But, before actually doing the task, they were asked to estimate how long it would take them to finish.

As shown in Figure 2.13, both groups of participants showed the planning fallacy. That is, both groups seriously underestimated the number of minutes they would need to complete the editing task. The actual performance time was the same for both groups. However, as researchers predicted, participants who first thought of themselves as occupying a position of power underestimated the time much more than did participants who thought of themselves as occupying a position of powerlessness. These results are consistent with the idea that power leads us to focus too narrowly on task completion, rather than the steps involved in getting there, which can lead us to seriously underestimate how long it will take to finish tasks.

Figure 2.13 Power and the Planning Fallacy

Both powerful and powerless people seriously underestimated how long it would take them to complete a complex word processing task, but those who thought of themselves occupying a powerful position mispredicted the time that would be needed most. These results are consistent with the idea that power leads us to focus too narrowly on task completion, rather than the steps involved in getting there, which can lead us to seriously underestimate how long it will take us to finish a task.

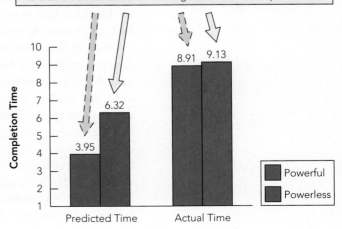

Those who thought of themselves in a powerful position underestimated how long it would take them to complete the task more than those thinking of themselves as powerless

2.4.2: Situation-Specific Sources of Error in Social Cognition: Counterfactual Thinking and Magical Thinking

The optimistic bias is very general in nature. As we've seen, it can be found in a wide range of social situations. Other important forms of bias in our social thought are more restricted in the sense that they tend to occur only in certain kinds of situations. We'll now examine two of these biases—counterfactual thinking and what is sometimes termed magical thinking.

COUNTERFACTUAL THINKING: IMAGINING "WHAT MIGHT HAVE BEEN" Suppose that you take an important exam. When you receive your score, it is a "C—"—a much lower grade than you had hoped. What thoughts will enter your mind as you consider your grade? If you are like most people, you may quickly begin to imagine "what might have been"—how you could have received a higher grade. "If only I had studied more, or come to class more often," you may think to yourself. And then, perhaps you may begin to formulate plans for actually doing better on the next test.

Such thoughts about "what might have been"—known in social psychology as **counterfactual thinking**—occur in a wide range of situations, not just ones in which we experience disappointments. Suppose you read an article in the newspaper about someone who left work at the normal time and was injured in an automobile accident in which another driver ran a stop sign. Certainly, you would feel sympathy for this person and would probably recommend some form of compensation.

Now imagine the same story with a slight difference. The same person was injured in the same kind of accident, but in this case, he left work early to run an errand. Since the accident is the same, you should rationally feel the same amount of sympathy for the victim. But in fact, you may not. Because he left work earlier than usual, it is easy to imagine him *not* doing so, thereby avoiding the accident. Or, suppose he took an unusual route home instead of his normal one. Would that make a difference in the sympathy you would feel? Research indicates the answer is yes—emotional responses differ depending on how easy it is to mentally undo the circumstances that preceded the event.

Because it is easier to undo in our minds taking the unusual route than the normal one, sympathy for the accident victim will also differ. In other words, counterfactual thoughts about what might have happened, instead of what did happen can influence your sympathy as well as your recommendations concerning compensation for the victim (Miller & McFarland, 1987). This difference in the intensity of the sympathy evoked has been observed even for highly tragic events, including cases of rape and the loss of a child in an auto accident (Branscombe, Owen, Garstka, & Coleman, 1996; Davis, Lehman, Wortman, Silver, & Thompson, 1995; Wolf, 2010).

Counterfactual thoughts seem to occur automatically in many situations. It seems easy to imagine that things might have turned out differently. Recent research has revealed that belief in free will, which is the opposite of determinism, encourages counterfactual thinking (Alquist, Ainsworth, Baumeister, Daly, & Stillman, 2015). In studies where participants' belief in free will was temporarily strengthened, more counterfactual alternatives were generated by the participants for hypothetical and actual past events. The same thing occurred in studies that measured people's endorsement of the free will concept. This research suggests that counterfactual thinking—imagining what might have happened instead of what did—can help people learn from mistakes and plan for the future. Believing that people have the power to act differently (i.e., believing in free will) facilitates this form of social thought. By imagining how we might have done better, we may come up with improved strategies and ways of using our effort more effectively.

Counterfactual thinking can have a wide range of effects—some are beneficial and some can be costly to the persons involved (Kray, Galinsky, & Wong, 2006). Depending on our focus, imagining counterfactuals for outcomes we receive can either boost or reduce our current mood. If individuals imagine *upward counterfactuals*—comparing their current outcomes with more favorable ones—the result may be strong feelings of dissatisfaction. For instance, Olympic athletes who win a silver medal experience such reactions because they can easily imagine winning a gold medal (Medvec, Madey, & Gilovich, 1995). Alternatively, if individuals compare their current outcomes with less favorable ones—"it might have been worse"—they may experience positive feelings (Nario-Redmond & Branscombe, 1996). Such reactions have been found among Olympic athletes who win bronze medals. They can easily imagine what it would be like to have not won any medal whatsoever. In summary, engaging in counterfactual thought can strongly influence our current moods and our willingness to gamble on obtaining alternative outcomes in the future (Petrocelli & Sherman, 2010).

In addition, it appears that particular types of counterfactual thinking can reduce the bitterness of negative outcomes. After tragic events, such as the death of a loved one, people often find solace in thinking, "Nothing more could be done; the death was inevitable." In other words, they adjust their view concerning the inevitability of the death to make it seem more certain and therefore unavoidable. In contrast, different counterfactual thoughts may increase their suffering. For example, "If only the illness had been diagnosed sooner . . ." or "If only we had gotten him to the hospital quicker. . . ." Assuming that negative events or disappointments were inevitable tends to make those events more bearable (Tykocinski, 2001). Therefore, our tendency to think not only about what is, but also about what *might* have been, can have far-reaching effects on many aspects of our social thought and behavior.

MAGICAL THINKING, TERROR MANAGEMENT, AND BELIEF IN THE SUPERNATURAL
Please answer truthfully:

> *If you are in class and don't want the professor to call on you, do you try to avoid thinking about being called on?*
>
> *Do you knock on wood, blow on dice before rolling them, carry a lucky charm, or feel you might be "tempting fate" if you don't watch your college team play during the playoffs?*
>
> *If someone offered you a piece of chocolate shaped like a cockroach or a snake, would you eat it?*

On the basis of purely rational considerations, your answers should be "no," "no," and "yes." But are those the answers you actually gave? Probably not. In fact, research findings indicate that human beings are quite susceptible to what has been termed **magical thinking** (Rozin & Nemeroff, 1990). Such thinking makes assumptions that don't hold up to rational scrutiny but that feel compelling nonetheless (Risen & Gilovich, 2007).

One principle of magical thinking assumes that one's thoughts can influence the physical world in a manner not governed by the laws of physics. For instance, if you think about being called on by your professor, it does not change the probability that you actually will be. Likewise, simply sticking pins in a doll, thinking about it as hurting your enemy, does not mean such "voodoo" really can harm another person. But, based on the *law of similarity*, which suggests that things that resemble one another share basic properties, it might be easy to think that sticking a doll that looks like an enemy can cause the same kind of harm to the real person. For the same reason, people won't eat a chocolate shaped like a cockroach even though they know, rationally, that its shape has nothing to do with its taste (see Figure 2.14).

People also seem to believe that they are "buying peace of mind" when they purchase insurance. That is, not only will they be covered if something does go wrong, but the very act of buying insurance will ensure nothing does go wrong. Research

Figure 2.14 Magical Thinking: When Rationality Is Absent

Would you eat the cakes shown here? Many people would not, even though they realize that the shape of the cake has nothing to do with its taste. This aspect of magical thinking illustrates the law of similarity—the perception of the cakes is affected because they have properties resembling other disgusting objects.

indicates that by turning down an insurance opportunity, people believe they are "tempting fate" and increasing the likelihood that disaster will strike (Tykocinski, 2008). In fact, the more uncertain a performance outcome is, the more people are likely to engage in superstitious behavior, such as carrying lucky items (Hamerman & Morewedge, 2015).

Surprising as it may seem, our thinking about many situations is frequently influenced by magical thinking. So, what is the basis of seemingly nonrational thinking? Some theorists have suggested that it is because we, as human beings, are uniquely aware of the fact that we will die. This, in turn, causes us to engage in what is known as **terror management**—efforts to come to terms with the certainty of death and its unsettling implications (Greenberg et al., 2003). One kind of thinking that helps with terror management is the belief that supernatural powers outside our understanding and control can influence our lives. Research indicates that when we are reminded of our own mortality, beliefs in the supernatural are strengthened (Norenzayan & Hansen, 2006). In short, when we come face to face with the certainty of our own deaths, we try to manage the strong reactions this produces. One way of doing this is to engage in thinking that is largely outside of what we consider to be rational thought.

So, the next time you are tempted to make fun of someone's superstitious belief (e.g., fear of the number 13 or fear of black cats crossing one's path), don't be too quick to laugh. Your own thinking is almost certainly *not* totally free from the kind of "magical" (i.e., nonrational) assumptions that seem to underlie a considerable portion of our social thought.

Key Points

- Social thought departs from rationality in a number of ways. People show a strong **optimistic bias**, expecting that they are more likely than others to experience positive outcomes but less likely than others to experience negative ones.
- People frequently exhibit an **overconfidence bias** when making predictions. Those who have the least competence

in a particular domain are most likely to be overly confident of their judgments in that domain. This tendency seems to be due to *errors of omission*, when we lack comparison information that would help moderate our confidence.
- People make overly optimistic predictions about how long it will take them to complete a given task, an effect known as the **planning fallacy**. This occurs repeatedly both

because we fail to consider obstacles we may encounter when predicting how long a task will take. Also, when we are strongly motivated to complete a task, we often fail to consider all the time-consuming steps necessary to do so.

- When individuals imagine "what might have been," they engage in **counterfactual thinking**. Such thought can reduce our sympathy for people who have experienced negative outcomes. But *upward counterfactuals* can also motivate us to perform better in the future, in hope of avoiding the outcome that did occur. Belief in free will encourages counterfactual thinking.

- There are important limits on our ability to think rationally about the social world. One involves **magical thinking**—assuming our thoughts can influence the physical world, or believing that our actions (e.g., not buying insurance) may "tempt fate" and increase the likelihood of negative events. Based on the similarity of two objects, we may believe that the properties of one object can pass to the other.

- One form of magical thinking—belief in the supernatural—may partly stem from **terror management**—our efforts to cope with the knowledge that we will die. Reminders of our own mortality strengthen supernatural beliefs.

2.5: Affect and Cognition: How Feelings Shape Thought and Thought Shapes Feelings

Objective   **Assess the interrelation of affect and cognition**

Think of a time in your life when you were in a very good mood—something good happened and you were feeling great joy. Now, in contrast, remember a time when you were in a very bad mood—something negative occurred and you were feeling down and blue. Like the emotion characters "Joy" and "Sadness" from Disney's film *Inside Out* (see Figure 2.15), was your thinking about the world different at these two times, when each emotion was in control of your consciousness? In other words, did

Figure 2.15 Emotions Can Color Our Experiences and Memories

As Disney's movie, *Inside Out*, illustrates, our experience and view of the world can be different depending on whether "Joy" or "Sadness" is at the controls. Memories of the past can be colored by which emotion we are feeling at the present time.

you remember your experiences and the other people who shared them in contrasting ways? In all likelihood you did, because a large body of research indicates there is a continuous and complex interplay between *affect*—our current moods or emotions—and *cognition*—various aspects of the ways in which we think, process, store, remember, and use information (e.g., Forgas, 2006; Isen & Labroo, 2003). The word *interplay* is not used lightly because existing evidence strongly suggests that the relationship between affect and cognition is very much a two-way street. Our emotions and moods strongly influence several aspects of cognition. Cognition, in turn, exerts strong effects on our emotions and moods (e.g., Baron, 2008; McDonald & Hirt, 1997). Let's take a closer look at the nature of these effects.

2.5.1: The Influence of Affect on Cognition

Perhaps it will seem obvious to you that our current moods can influence our perceptions of the world around us. When we are in a good mood (experiencing positive affect), we tend to perceive almost everything—situations, other people, ideas, even new inventions—in more positive terms than we do when we are in a negative mood (Blanchette & Richards, 2010; Clore, Schwarz, & Conway, 1993). Indeed, this effect is so strong and so pervasive, that we are even more likely to judge statements as true if we encounter them while in a positive mood than if we read or hear them while in a neutral or negative mood (Garcia-Marques, Mackie, Claypool, & Garcia-Marques, 2004). Positive moods can also encourage people to feel they understand the world better (Hicks, Cicero, Trent, Burton, & King, 2010). To illustrate this, these researchers presented ambiguous items to their participants: abstract art or Zen koans (riddles) such as "If a placebo has an effect, is it any less real than the real thing?" Then, the researchers asked each individual to explain the meaning of the item. Participants who were in a positive mood consistently reported a greater understanding of the ambiguous stimuli than participants who were feeling negative. This capability for understanding was particularly strong among participants who reported that they tend to use heuristics when making judgments.

Mood effects on perception also have important practical implications. For instance, consider their impact on job interviews—a context in which interviewers meet many people for the first time. A growing body of evidence indicates that even experienced interviewers cannot avoid being influenced by their own current moods. When interviewers are in a good mood, they assign higher ratings to interviewees than when they are in a bad mood (Robbins & DeNisi, 1994). Other research has illustrated that positive moods can make us less defensive and thereby less likely to blame a victim of assault, compared to negative moods (Goldenberg & Forgas, 2012).

Another way in which affect influences cognition involves its impact on memory. Two different, but related, kinds of effects seem to occur. One is known as **mood congruence effects**. This type refers to the fact that current moods strongly determine which information in a given situation is noticed and then entered into memory. In other words, your current mood serves as a kind of filter, primarily permitting information that is consistent with your moods to be stored in long-term memory.

In comparison, the effect known as **mood-dependent memory** reflects what specific information is *retrieved* from memory (Baddeley, 1990; Eich, 1995). When experiencing a particular current mood, people are more likely to remember information they acquired in the past while in a similar mood, as opposed to remembering information they acquired while in a different mood. Current moods, in other words, serve as a kind of *retrieval cue*, prompting recall of information consistent with past moods.

Here's an illustration of the difference between mood congruence effects and mood-dependent memory. Suppose you meet two people for the first time. You meet one when you are in a very good mood but you meet the other one when you are in a very bad mood. Because of mood congruence effects, you will probably notice and store in memory mainly positive information about the first person, but mainly negative information about the second person. Your mood when you meet these individuals determines what you notice and remember about them. Now, imagine that at a later time, you are in a good mood. Which person comes to mind? Probably the one you met while in a similar (good) mood. Here, your current mood serves to trigger memories of information you acquired (and stored in memory) when you were in a similar mood in the past.

Together, mood congruence and mood-dependent memory strongly influence the information we store in memory. Since this is the information we can later remember, the impact of affect on memory has important implications for many aspects of social thought and behavior. Figure 2.16 summarizes these mood and memory processes.

Our current moods also influence another important component of cognition—creativity. The results of several studies suggest that being in a happy mood can increase creativity by activating a wider range of ideas or associations. Creativity consists, in part, of combining such associations into new patterns (Isen, 2000). A meta-analysis that combined studies investigating the relationship between mood and creativity (Baas, De Dreu, & Nijstad, 2008) revealed that positive moods facilitate creativity most when they are relatively high in arousal (e.g., happiness) rather than low in arousal (e.g., relaxation).

Yet another way in which affect influences cognition involves the tendency to engage in heuristic processing. This type of thinking relies heavily on mental "shortcuts" (heuristics) and knowledge acquired through past experience. Heuristic processing has important implications for decision making and problem solving—activities we all perform frequently. Research findings indicate that persons experiencing positive affect are more likely to rely on previously acquired "rules of thumb" and previously gathered information when dealing with current problems or decisions. In other words, we are more likely to engage in heuristic thought when we're in a good mood than when we are experiencing negative affect (Mackie & Worth, 1989; Park & Banaji, 2000; Wegner & Petty, 1994).

Finally, we should mention that our current moods often influence our interpretations of the motives behind people's behavior. Positive affect tends to promote attributions of positive motives, while negative affect tends to encourage attributions of negative motives (Forgas, 2006). As we will describe in Chapter 3, our thoughts about the cause of others' behavior play an important role in many situations, so this is another way in which the interplay between affect and cognition can have important effects.

2.5.2: The Influence of Cognition on Affect

Most research on the relationship between affect and cognition has focused on how feelings influence thought. However, there is also strong evidence for the reverse—the impact of cognition on affect. One aspect of this relationship is described in the *two-factor theory* of emotion (Schachter, 1964). This theory suggests that we often don't know our own feelings or attitudes directly. Rather, since these internal reactions are somewhat ambiguous, we infer their nature from the external world—from the kinds of situations in which we experience these reactions. For example, if we experience increased arousal in the presence of an

Figure 2.16 The Effects of Mood on Memory

Our moods influence what we remember through two mechanisms: mood congruence effects, which refer to the fact that we are more likely to store or remember information consistent with our current mood, and mood-dependent memory, which refers to the fact that we tend to remember information consistent with our current moods.

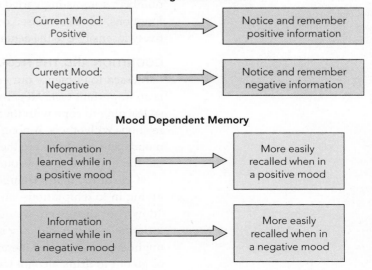

Mood Congruence Effects

| Current Mood: Positive | → | Notice and remember positive information |

| Current Mood: Negative | → | Notice and remember negative information |

Mood Dependent Memory

| Information learned while in a positive mood | → | More easily recalled when in a positive mood |

| Information learned while in a negative mood | → | More easily recalled when in a negative mood |

attractive person, we may conclude that we are in love. In contrast, if we experience increased arousal after being cut off in traffic by another driver, we may conclude that what we feel is anger. In this way, our thoughts can affect our feelings.

A second way in which cognition can influence emotions is by activating schemas containing a strong affective component. For example, if we categorize an individual as belonging to a group different than our own, we may experience a different emotional response than if we categorized that same individual as a member of our own group. Let's consider a research instance where people view others receiving a seemingly painful needle injection in the hand. When Caucasian participants were shown a dark-skinned hand being injected, they exhibited lower empathic reactions (indicated by reduced activity in the brain's pain areas) than when they were shown a Caucasian hand being injected (Avenanti, Sirigu, & Aglioti, 2010). The same results—in reverse—were observed for participants of African descent. Greater empathic pain reactions in the brain were observed when the hand was black compared to when it was white. These results indicate that how we think about others—and who we think those others are—tells us how we feel about such persons, and whether we "feel" their pain or not.

Another intriguing line of research suggests that factors that influence our cognition differ from factors that influence our emotions. Much research indicates that our **affective forecasts**—predictions of how we would feel about an event we have not experienced—are often inaccurate (Dunn & Laham, 2006). To the extent that our cognition (affective forecasts) is based on a different way of processing information compared to actual emotional experience, these two types of responses—forecasting and experiencing—should differ. Dunn and Ashton-James (2008) conducted a number of studies to investigate this idea. In one experiment, some participants were placed in the "experiencer role." They were given a news article about a deadly forest fire in Spain and were asked to report their actual emotions while reading about the tragedy. Another group of participants was placed in the "forecaster role." They were simply asked to predict how they would feel "*if* they read about a deadly forest fire in Spain." The scope of the tragedy was also varied. Some participants were told that five people were killed by the fire, while other participants were told that 10,000 people were killed.

The number of people killed affected how bad the forecasters expected to feel. In other words, the forecasters believed they would be responsive to the magnitude of the tragedy. In contrast, the number of people killed did *not* affect how those in the experiencer role actually reported feeling. Thus, those who were actually exposed to the tragic loss information did not differentiate their emotional response according to numbers. Because rational cognition is responsive to abstract symbols, including numbers, forecasting varied depending on the scale of the tragedy being considered. Emotions, which are based on concrete images and immediate experiences, were relatively insensitive to the actual numbers of people killed (scope of the tragedy).

COGNITION AND THE REGULATION OF AFFECTIVE STATES   Can our thoughts be harnessed to influence our emotional experience? Learning to regulate our emotions is an important task. Negative events and outcomes are an unavoidable part of life, so learning to cope with them is crucial for personal adjustment and for good social relations with others. Among the most important techniques we use for regulating our moods and emotions are the ones involving cognitive mechanisms. In other words, our thoughts can regulate our feelings.

One of the many techniques we use to improve our current mood is the act of giving in to temptation—an especially common coping mechanism. When we feel "down" or distressed, we often engage in activities that we know might be bad for us in the long run, but they make us feel better, at least temporarily. For instance, we might engage in "retail therapy" by going shopping, or we might eat fattening foods or go out to drink alcohol with our friends, as illustrated in Figure 2.17. Why do we

Figure 2.17 Activities Aimed at Regulating Our Negative Moods

When people are feeling down, many engage in activities designed to make them feel better—they go shopping, eat, consume alcohol, and so on. Research findings suggest that engaging in such actions can reflect a conscious strategy for regulating our emotions.

choose these actions even though we know full well that they can have an important "downside"? In the past, social psychologists assumed that people engaged in potentially detrimental actions because the emotional distress experienced reduced either our capacity or motivation to control our impulses. However, Tice et al. (2000) argue that cognitive factors play a role in such behavior. We yield to such temptations because they help us deal with strong negative feelings.

To test this prediction, Tice et al. (2000) first affected participants' moods by giving them stories to read in which they would imagine themselves as a hero or protagonist. One group of participants had an inspiring story in which they saved a child's life. The other group had a story in which they ran a red light and caused the death of a child. Then, participants were told that either their moods could change over time or their moods were "frozen" so could not change. Participants were next led to believe they would work on an intelligence test that would be graded. Before doing the test, they were given a 15-minute practice session to prepare. The experimenter then left them in a room containing test-related materials for practicing *and* distracters—games they could play.

The question was, would people in a bad mood spend more of the practice time with the distracters (procrastinating) than those in a good mood? More importantly, would this occur only in the condition where participants believed they could change their own moods? After all, there would be no point in playing with the distracters if participants believed their moods could not be altered. Tice et al. (2000) predicted that persons in a bad mood would procrastinate more, but only when they believed doing so would enhance their moods. The results offered clear support for this prediction. These findings indicate that the tendency to yield to temptation is a conscious choice, not a simple lapse in the ability to control our own impulses. What about situations when we are tempted to act dishonorably, such as cheating? In the special feature **"What Research Tells Us About...Why Not Controlling Ourselves Can Make Us Feel Good,"** we'll see why behaving unethically can sometimes evoke feelings of self-satisfaction.

2.5.3: Affect and Cognition: Social Neuroscience Evidence for Two Separate Systems

As you have seen, existing evidence indicates that affect and cognition are intimately linked—each one has the capability of influencing the other. However, we should also note that recent findings using neuroscience techniques (e.g., scanning of human

What Research Tells Us About...

Why Not Controlling Ourselves Can Make Us Feel Good

People often believe they would feel guilty if they engaged in unethical behavior. That is, our affective forecasts predict negative emotions in such cases. Anticipation of negative self-directed affect (expecting to feel bad) probably prevents many from engaging in forbidden temptations. How, then, do we explain the many well-known cases of people who have cheated "the system?" Examples include Lance Armstrong, the famous bicyclist who won numerous Tour de France races by using illegal performance-enhancing drugs, and swindlers such Frank Abagnale—made famous in the movie *Catch Me If You Can*—and Bernie Madoff. There are also famous tax evaders, incidents of workplace theft, and students cheating on exams, all of which involve unethical behavior without obvious or direct personal harm to another person. Is material gain (e.g., money, prestige, good grades) the only reason for cheating, or is there something else?

Fascinating research by Ruedy, Moore, Gino, and Schweitzer (2013) suggests that behaving unethically can boost positive affect under some circumstances. In their first study, these researchers described to the participants a situation where either the participants themselves or another person could dishonestly report the amount of work they accomplished and receive more money than was deserved, or they could behave honestly. As expected, participants predicted that they or another person who cheated in this way would both feel more

negative emotion than if either had behaved honestly. So, nobody *expects* that people who cheat will feel good after cheating.

What's much more interesting is what happened after people were actually given an opportunity to behave dishonestly. In one study, an accomplice of the experimenter either over-reported the participant's score (i.e., cheated on the participant's behalf) or reported the score correctly. In another study, participants either had an opportunity to "secretly peek" at the correct answers on an important test or had no such opportunity. In a final study, participants were asked to solve very difficult puzzles. Before reporting their score, some participants explicitly learned that the experimenters could not "check whether they had cheated"; other participants were not given this information.

What were the results? In all three studies, participants who cheated reported more positive affect and less negative affect than participants who did not cheat. In fact, in the last study, cheating participants, who believed that the experimenters could not detect whether cheating had occurred, felt the most self-satisfaction of all! This suggests that sometimes cheating can be emotionally rewarding, especially when people feel "they have gotten away with something." Interestingly enough, this result is not a possibility that people anticipate. Participants mispredicted how they and others would feel after cheating. Unless the participants had actually cheated, they did not seem to understand the emotional benefits that cheaters and swindlers might reap from their behavior.

brains as individuals perform various activities) indicate there may be two distinct systems involved in processing social information within the human brain (Spunt & Lieberman, 2013). One system is concerned with what could be termed "reason" (logical thought); its operation can be disrupted by cognitive load. The other system deals primarily with affect or emotion and is less sensitive to cognitive load. These two systems, although distinct in certain respects, interact in many ways during problem solving, decision making, and other important forms of cognition.

For instance, consider research that employs what is known as the "dictator" game. Two persons were told they can divide a given sum (e.g., $10) between them. One person can suggest an initial division and the second can accept or reject it. But, if the second person turns down the proposal, they both receive nothing. Since any division provides the second person with positive payoffs, total rationality (and classic economic theory) suggests that acceptance of any division offered is the most rational (and best) course of action. In fact, however, most people reject divisions that give them less than $3, and many reject divisions that offer them less than $5.

Magnetic resonance imaging scans of the brains of people playing this game reveal two different systems at work. When people receive offers they view as unfair, brain regions related both to reasoning (e.g., the dorsolateral prefrontal cortex) and to emotion (e.g., the limbic system) are active. The more activity in the emotion-processing regions, the greater the likelihood that individuals will reject the offers and act in ways that are contrary to their own economic interests (Sanfey, Rilling, Aronson, Nystrum, & Cohen, 2003). These findings, and those of many other studies, provide concrete evidence for the existence of two distinct systems (reason and emotion) that

Key Points

- *Affect* influences cognition in multiple ways. Our current moods can cause us to react positively or negatively to new stimuli, including other persons. The extent to which we think systematically or in a more automatic manner can influence memory through **mood-dependent memory** and **mood congruence effects**.

- When we are in a positive mood, we tend to think heuristically to a greater extent than when we are in a negative mood. Specifically, we show increased reliance on stereotypes and other mental shortcuts when we are in a positive mood.

- Cognition influences affect through our interpretation of emotion-provoking events and through the activation of schemas containing a strong affective component. When we observe another person experiencing pain, the level of empathetic response in our brains depends on how we categorize or feel about the other person.

- **Affective forecasts**—predictions of how we would feel about an event we have not experienced—are often

inaccurate because cognition and affect are based in different systems within the brain. Those in a forecasting role are sensitive to the numbers of people harmed, whereas those in an experience role are not. People forecast that cheating would make them feel more negative emotions than positive. However, evidence suggests that cheating can make people feel good; in effect, self-satisfaction can emerge from feeling "we got away with something."

- We employ several cognitive techniques to regulate our emotions or feelings. For instance, when distressed, we can consciously choose to engage in activities that, while damaging in the long run, make us feel better in the short run. Failure to control ourselves can, surprisingly, evoke positive feelings of satisfaction.

- Research in social neuroscience indicates that we may actually possess two distinct systems for processing social information—one concerned with logical thought and the other with affect or emotion.

interact in complex ways during decision making and other cognitive processes (Gabaix & Laibson, 2006; Naqvi, Shiv, & Bechara, 2006).

Overall, evidence from research using modern techniques for scanning brain activity during cognitive processes suggests that affect plays a fundamental role in human thought. In order to fully understand the complex ways in which we think about the social world and our place in it, we must take into account that certain aspects of our thought can also influence our feelings. Affect and cognition are not one-way streets; they are two-way streets with the potential of one influencing the other.

Summary and Review

Because we have limited cognitive capacity, we may attempt to reduce the effort we expend on **social cognition**—how we think about other persons and the social world. Given our limited capacity to process information, we often experience **information overload**. To cope with this condition, we use **heuristics**—simple rules of thumb for making decisions in a quick and relatively effortless manner. The **representativeness heuristic** suggests that the more similar an individual is to typical members of a given group (the **prototype**), the more likely she or he is to belong to that group. When using the representativeness heuristic, people tend to ignore base rates—frequencies of events or instances in the total population. Another heuristic is **availability**, which suggests that the easier it is to bring information to mind, the greater its impact on subsequent decisions or judgments. Use of the **availability heuristic** can lead us astray to the extent that vivid events are easier to bring

to mind, but they are not necessarily more frequent in occurrence. A third heuristic is **anchoring and adjustment**, which leads us to use a number or value as a starting point from which we then make adjustments. These adjustments often are not sufficient. The **portion size effect** is a good example of anchoring and inadequate adjustment. A fourth heuristic related to the status quo leads us to favor "old" over "new."

Schemas are a basic component of social cognition. These mental frameworks, formed through experience, help us to organize social information. Once formed, schemas exert powerful effects on what we notice (attention), enter into memory (encoding), and later remember (retrieval). More information that is consistent with schemas is remembered than information that is inconsistent with them. But inconsistent information is also strongly represented in memory. Schemas are often **primed**—activated by experiences, events, or stimuli. Once they are primed, schemas tend to show a strong **perseverance effect**—in spite of disconfirming information—until they are somehow expressed in thought or behavior. Such expression (known as **unpriming**) then reduces their effects. Schemas can also exert self-fulfilling effects, causing us to behave in ways that confirm them. **Metaphors**, which relate an abstract concept to another dissimilar one, can shape how we respond to the social world.

Controlled processing occurs in a systematic, logical, and highly effortful manner, whereas **automatic processing** occurs in a fast, intuitive, and relatively effortless manner. A large amount of evidence indicates that automatic processing and controlled processing are distinctly different modes of social thought. In fact, different regions of the brain appear to be involved in these two types of processing, especially when evaluating various aspects of the social world. When schemas or other cognitive frameworks are activated (even without our conscious awareness), they can influence our behavior, triggering actions consistent with the frameworks and also preparing us to interact with the persons or groups who are the focus of those schemas. Automatic processing is quick and efficient, offering other advantages such as increased satisfaction with our decisions. Decisions we must make under **conditions of uncertainty**—where the "correct" answer is difficult to know—often involve the use of heuristics—simple rules for drawing inferences in a rapid and efficient manner.

People show a strong **optimistic bias**, expecting positive events and outcomes and fewer negatives in many contexts. In addition, people tend to exhibit an **overconfidence bias** in their judgments and predictions about themselves. This occurs because people make errors of omission; they lack the comparison information that would allow them to know what factors they have not considered. One example of our optimism at work is the **planning fallacy**—our tendency to believe that a task will take less time than it really will. In many situations, individuals imagine "what might have been" instead of what was—**counterfactual thinking**. Such thought can affect our sympathy for people who have experienced negative outcomes. Counterfactual thinking seems to occur automatically in many situations. Upward counterfactuals can help improve learning by motivating us to avoid undesirable outcomes in the future, while downward counterfactuals (imagining how an event might have turned out worse) can be comforting.

There are important limits on our ability to think rationally about the social world. One involves **magical thinking**—thinking based on assumptions that don't hold up to rational scrutiny. For instance, we may believe that if two objects are in contact, properties can pass from one to the other. One form of magical thinking—belief in the supernatural—may partly stem from **terror management**—our efforts to cope with the knowledge that we will die.

Affect (our moods and emotions) influences cognition in multiple ways. Our current moods influence our perceptions of the world around us. The extent to which we think systematically or heuristically can influence memory through **mood congruence effects** and **mood-dependent memory**. Affect can also influence creativity and our interpretations of others' behavior. Cognition influences affect through our interpretation of emotion-provoking events and through the activation of schemas containing a strong affective component. In addition, we employ several cognitive techniques to regulate our emotions or feelings (e.g., consciously giving in to temptation to reduce negative feelings). Although affect and cognition are closely intertwined, social neuroscience research indicates that they involve distinct systems within the brain. People make **affective forecasts**—predictions of how they would feel about an event they have not experienced—using the cognitive system, but respond with the emotional system when experiencing those events.

Chapter 3
Social Perception
Seeking to Understand Others

Chapter Overview

Learning Objectives

3.1 Determine how the five basic nonverbal channels of communication help us judge emotional states

3.2 Explain how the process of attribution helps our understanding of others' behavior

3.3 Describe why initial information is important in forming perceptions of others

Social history contains many instances of liars—people who mislead others with statements about their own behavior or almost anything else. Consider a few of the more famous ones who deceived a huge number of people before they were finally caught. One example is Frank Abagnale, Jr. By the time he was 21, he had lied so convincingly that he persuaded others he was a lawyer, college professor, pediatrician, and airline pilot (see Figure 3.1). Another example, U.S. President Richard Nixon, claimed that he knew nothing about a burglary in the offices of his political opponents. He did this so convincingly that he was re-elected. When his lies were uncovered, however, he resigned from office. A more recent example is the Volkswagen scandal. The company knowingly used a specially designed software to provide false emissions data during testing. By engaging in this deception, it allowed the company to mask the environmental harm the cars were causing. With this lie exposed, Volkswagen was forced to do a massive recall of vehicles.

Figure 3.1 The Difficulties of Perceiving Others Accurately

Often, our efforts to understand others—to perceive them accurately—are unsuccessful because sometimes people try to conceal their motives and plans from us. The movie, *Catch Me If You Can*, illustrates how convincing some liars can be. In this film, an airline pilot was just one of the professions that Frank Abagnale, Jr. (played by Leonardo DiCaprio) impersonated.

Of course, not only famous people and big companies lie; we all experience lies by others in our daily lives. And, if we are totally honest, we must admit that we sometimes engage in deceptions ourselves. Often these are trivial and have few, if any, consequences. For instance, when a teenager is asked, "Did you do your homework?" he or she may answer "Yes . . ." even though this is not true. But still, although many lies may seem trivial, they appear to occur frequently. If lying is so common, why don't we easily recognize it for what it is? Why don't we see through the dishonesty in others' statements? Or, to put in other terms, why don't we always perceive others accurately—for what they are, rather than what we *think* they are? These puzzling questions are ones to which social psychologists have devoted much research attention.

Perceiving others accurately is important for effective interaction. It is essential to know what they are *really* like beneath the public mask presented to the world and determine whether they are being honest with us about their motives. If we can't successfully assess whether people are trying to mislead us or not, we may find it difficult to interact effectively and build good relationships with them. So how do we accomplish these tasks? Social psychologists have sought to address this question by studying what is termed **social perception**—the process through which we seek to know other people. This process involves understanding the ways we gather and analyze information about people.

Social perception is a key foundation of our social lives and the focus of this chapter. To convey the wealth of knowledge that social psychologists have gathered about this topic, we'll proceed as follows. First, we'll consider many of the nonverbal ways through which we learn about others including cues from their facial expressions, eye contact, body movements, postures, and touch. Second, we'll examine the process through which we attempt to understand the reasons behind others' behavior. This includes trying to discover *why* they acted as they did in a given situation, what goals they are seeking to achieve, and what intentions they have (Burrus & Roese, 2006). This is a crucial process because, as we'll soon see, the conclusions we reach about why others behave as they do can strongly influence our reactions to what they say and do—and even provide insights into why some people do horrible things. Third, we'll examine how we form first impressions of others and how we try to ensure that others form favorable impressions of us.

3.1: Nonverbal Communication: An Unspoken Language

Objective **Determine how the five basic nonverbal channels of communication help us judge emotional states**

Careful research reveals that social actions—our own and those of others—are often affected by temporary factors or causes. Changing moods, shifting emotions, fatigue, illness, drugs, and even hidden biological processes, such as the menstrual cycle, can all influence the ways in which we think and behave. No doubt we have all experienced instances when bad moods or physical problems have affected our interactions with others, perhaps resulting in lost tempers.

Because temporary states exert important effects on people's behavior and social thought, recognizing and understanding these conditions is often very useful. Sometimes, this is a relatively easy task—we ask others how they are feeling or what kind of mood they are in, and they tell us. At other times, however, people are unwilling to reveal their inner feelings (DePaulo et al., 2003; Forrest & Feldman, 2000). For example, negotiators often hide their reactions from their opponents. Also, salespersons frequently show more liking and friendliness toward potential customers than they really feel (see Figure 3.2).

Figure 3.2 Facial Expressions Are Not Always a Good Indicator of Underlying Emotions

Salespeople typically smile all the time, regardless of what they are feeling or thinking inside, because they realize the benefits of making others like them—more sales.

In situations when it is inappropriate or impossible to ask others how they are feeling, we can pay careful attention to *nonverbal cues* provided by changes in their facial expressions, eye contact, posture, body movements, and other expressive actions. In fact, such behavior is relatively *irrepressible*—difficult to control—so that even when others try to conceal their inner feelings from us, those emotions often "leak out" in many ways through nonverbal cues. Information conveyed by cues other than the content of spoken language, as well as our efforts to interpret it, is often described by the term **nonverbal communication** (Ko, Judd, & Blair, 2006). We'll now take a closer look at some basic ways this communication takes place.

3.1.1: Basic Channels of Nonverbal Communication

Most people tend to behave differently when experiencing different emotional states. But precisely how do differences in your inner states—emotions, feelings, and moods—show up in your behavior? This question relates to the basic channels through which nonverbal communication takes place. Research findings indicate there are five basic channels: facial expressions, eye contact, body movements, posture, and touching.

FACIAL EXPRESSIONS: CLUES TO OTHERS' EMOTIONS More than 2,000 years ago, the Roman orator Cicero made an interesting statement: "The face is a picture of the mind with the eyes as its interpreter." In other words, human feelings and emotions are often reflected in the face. Modern research suggests that Cicero was correct: We do learn much about others' current moods and feelings from their facial expressions. From a very early age, five different basic emotions are clearly represented on the human face: anger, fear, happiness, sadness, and disgust (Izard, 1991; Rozin, Lowery, & Ebert, 1994). Surprise has also been suggested as a basic emotion reflected clearly in facial expressions, but evidence is mixed, so surprise may not be a basic emotion or as clearly represented in facial expressions as other emotions (Reisenzein, Bordgen, Holtbernd, & Matz, 2006).

The fact that there are only five basic emotions represented on our faces, however, does *not* imply that human beings can show only a small number of facial expressions. On the contrary, emotions occur in many combinations, for example, joy together with sorrow and fear combined with anger. In addition, each of these reactions can vary greatly in strength. There may be only a small number of basic facial expressions, but the number of variations on these themes is immense (see Figure 3.3).

Now for another important question: Are facial expressions universal? In other words, if you traveled to a remote part of the world and visited a group of people who had never met an outsider before, would their facial expressions in various situations resemble your own? Would they smile in reaction to events that made them happy, frown when exposed to conditions that made them angry, and so on? Further, would you be able to recognize their emotional expressions as readily as ones shown by persons belonging to your own culture? Early research seemed to suggest that facial expressions are universal in both their use and recognition (Ekman & Friesen, 1975). Subsequent research has confirmed that happiness is indeed accurately recognized across cultures most of the time. Sadness and disgust are considerably less accurately recognized, although they are still correctly identified at above-chance levels. Fear is least likely to be accurately recognized, partly because it is often confused with surprise (Elfenbein & Ambady, 2002).

Certain facial expressions—smiles and frowns—are often seen as representing the basic underlying emotions of happiness and anger in many cultures (Shaver, Murdaya, & Fraley, 2001), although the overall pattern of findings is not entirely consistent (e.g., Russell, 1994; Carroll & Russell, 1996). Numerous studies have clearly shown that people are a great deal more accurate in recognizing the facial expressions of members of their own national group than facial expressions of members of another national group (Elfenbein & Ambady, 2002). Cultural differences also exist with respect to the precise meaning of various facial expressions, but unlike spoken languages, they do not seem to require as much in the way of translation.

CAN WE ACCURATELY RECOGNIZE OTHERS' FACIAL EXPRESSIONS?   Research findings indicate that we can recognize others' emotions from their facial expressions relatively well, but large individual differences exist in performing this task. Some people are better at recognizing facial expressions than others. In other words,

Figure 3.3 Facial Expressions: The Range Is Huge

Although only five basic emotions are represented in distinct facial expressions that can be recognized across various cultures, these emotions can occur in many combinations and in varying degrees. As a result, the number of unique facial expressions is almost limitless.

people differ in terms of what might be called "reading others" (Hall, Andrzejewski, Yopchick, 2009).

You might think that one reason that some individuals are successful at reading others is because they typically show emotions clearly on their own faces. Surprisingly, though, research findings related to this idea are mixed. A review of available evidence (Elfenbein & Eisenkraft, 2010) indicates that both reading and expressing emotions are related but only when individuals are *trying* to communicate their feelings to others. When these expressions occur spontaneously—for instance, an expression of joy when something wonderful suddenly happens—then being able to recognize others' facial expressions and displaying those cues clearly oneself are *not* related. To put it in other terms, people who express their emotions openly and easily are not necessarily accurate at recognizing the facial expressions of others. Accuracy appears to be tied to people's intentional focus on showing their own emotions in their facial expressions. Perhaps they gain greater insight into the nature of others' expressions by doing so and this helps them to recognize others' underlying feelings more accurately.

EYE CONTACT AS A NONVERBAL CUE   Have you ever had a conversation with someone who was wearing very dark or mirrored sunglasses? If so, you may have felt uncomfortable because you couldn't see the other person's eyes and therefore were uncertain about how she or he was reacting. Ancient poets often described the eyes as "windows to the soul." In one important sense, they were correct: We often learn much about others' feelings from their eyes. For example, we interpret a high level of gazing from another person as a sign of liking or friendliness (Kleinke, 1986). In contrast, if others avoid eye contact with us, we may conclude they are unfriendly, they don't like us, or they are simply shy.

While a high level of eye contact with others is usually interpreted as a sign of liking or positive feelings, there is one exception to this general rule. If another person gazes at us continuously and maintains eye contact regardless of what we do, she or he can be said to be **staring**. A stare is often interpreted as a sign of anger or hostility—as in a *cold stare*—and most people find this particular nonverbal cue disturbing (Ellsworth & Carlsmith, 1973). In fact, we may quickly terminate social interaction with someone who stares at us and may even leave the scene (Greenbaum & Rosenfield, 1978). This is one reason that experts on road rage—highly aggressive driving by motorists—recommend that drivers avoid extended eye contact with people who are disobeying traffic laws and rules of the road (Bushman, 1998). People who are already in a highly excitable state may interpret anything resembling a stare from another driver as an aggressive act and react accordingly. Staring can also be interpreted as simply "weird." In other words, we tend to regard people who stare as being rude or clueless about how to behave in social situations (Bond et al., 1992).

BODY LANGUAGE: GESTURES, POSTURE, AND MOVEMENTS   Try this simple demonstration for yourself:

> First, remember some incident that made you angry—the angrier the better. Think about it for a minute.
>
> Now, try to remember another incident, one that made you feel sad—again, the sadder the better.

As you were remembering, did you change your posture or move your hands, arms, or legs as your thoughts shifted from the first event memory to the second? There is a good chance that you did, because our current moods or emotions are often reflected in the positions, postures, and movements of our bodies. Together, these nonverbal behaviors are termed **body language**. As with facial expressions and eye contact, body language can also provide useful information about others.

Body language often reveals others' emotional states. Large numbers of movements—especially ones in which one part of the body does something to another part (touching, rubbing, scratching)—suggest emotional arousal. The greater the frequency of such behavior, the higher is the level of arousal or nervousness. Further, in many settings, "fidgeting" is also interpreted as a sign of lying. So you might want to avoid such squirming in social situations. Otherwise, the people around you may begin to wonder about you and your motives.

More specific information about others' feelings is often provided by gestures. These fall into several categories, but perhaps the most important are *emblems*—body movements that carry specific meanings in a given culture. Do you recognize the hand gestures shown in Figure 3.4? In the United States and several other countries, these movements have clear and definite meanings. However, in other cultures, they might have no meaning, or even a different meaning entirely. For this reason, it is wise to be careful about using gestures while traveling in cultures different from your own; you may offend the people around you without meaning to do so!

TOUCHING: WHAT IT TELLS US ABOUT PEOPLE   When I eat in restaurants, I am always very friendly toward the servers. I joke with them, smile, and say thank-you often. As a result, these people often pat me on the shoulder. In this particular situation, their touch likely indicates friendliness toward me and perhaps appreciation for my courteous treatment of them. But touching does not always reflect these kinds of feelings. In fact, the meaning of a touch depends on various factors: who does the touching (friend or stranger, male or female); the nature of the physical contact (brief or prolonged, gentle or rough, area of the body touched); and the context in which the touching takes place (business or social setting, doctor's office). Depending on the combination of these factors, touch can suggest friendliness, affection, sexual interest, dominance, caring, or aggression. Despite such complexities, existing evidence indicates that when touching is considered appropriate, it often elicits positive reactions in the person being touched (e.g., Alagna, Whitcher, & Fisher, 1979; Levav & Argo, 2010). But remember, it must be viewed as appropriate to evoke such reactions.

The handshake is one acceptable way that people in many different cultures touch strangers (although it is not the norm in many Asian societies where bowing is used as a greeting). "Pop psychology" and books on etiquette (e.g., Vanderbilt, 1957) suggest that handshakes reveal much about people's personalities. Research findings

---

Figure 3.4 Hand Gestures: Different Meanings in Different Countries

In the United States, both of these common hand gestures have a clear meaning. However, in some other countries they mean something entirely different. For example, you probably perceive a thumbs-up gesture as meaning "Well done!" or "That's great!" But in certain places, like the Middle East, it means "Sit on this!" or "Up yours!" Likewise, the OK sign means different things in different countries: "money" in Japan; "zero" in France; and in many other countries, such as Brazil, an offensive gesture symbolizing a body orifice.

(Chaplin, Phillips, Brown, Clanton, & Stein, 2000) confirm that the firmer, longer, and more vigorous others' handshakes are, the higher we rate them in terms of extraversion and openness to experience, and the more favorable our first impressions of them tend to be.

Other forms of touching, too, can sometimes be appropriate. For instance, Levav and Argo (2010) found that a light, comforting pat on the arm can induce feelings of security among both women and men—but only if the touching is performed by a woman. Such feelings of security, in turn, influence actual behavior. Individuals touched on the shoulder by a female experimenter actually showed greater risk taking in an investment task than those who were not touched, or people who were touched only through handshakes.

To summarize, touching can serve as another source of nonverbal communication. When touching is viewed as appropriate (e.g., the handshake in some cultures), it can elicit positive reactions. However, if it is viewed as inappropriate, the person doing the touching is usually perceived negatively.

3.1.2: Nonverbal Cues in Social Life

It is often suggested that "a picture is worth a thousand words" or "actions speak volumes." Applied to interpersonal communication, these sayings suggest that we can learn more from people's nonverbal cues than from their words. Although verbal communication—spoken and written words—is very important, in this section we'll examine ways that nonverbal cues are perhaps even more revealing than words.

PARALANGUAGE: HOW WE SPEAK Research findings indicate that we can often learn more from nonverbal cues that occur when people speak than from their words alone. *Paralanguage* is a type of nonverbal communication involving vocal effects other than speech, such as tone (an attitude or feeling conveyed through sound) and pitch (highness or lowness of sound). When we interact with others, they often express emotions through the quality or specific sound of their voices that is independent of the words they are using. For instance, someone may not overtly say that they are angry, but we can sometimes "hear it" in their voices. Their irritation and annoyance shows through tone, volume, and/or other sound-related aspects.

Is paralanguage a more accurate guide to people's emotions than their words? To investigate this question, Hawk, van Kleef, Fischer, and van der Schalk (2009) exposed research participants to recordings of another person expressing various emotions. Some participants received the spoken words themselves about emotions, while others were exposed to nonlinguistic cues that occurred as they spoke (e.g., screaming to show fear, laughing to show joy, snorting to show disgust). Other participants were exposed to various facial expressions reflecting the emotions, for instance, "clenched teeth" or "huge smile." Participants then used these cues to try to recognize the emotions represented. As Hawk and colleagues predicted, the sounds that occurred during speech (e.g., laughing, crying) and the facial expressions were more accurate guides to the emotions underlying people's statements than the spoken words themselves (e.g., "I'm feeling very happy"). In this case, the nonverbal cues truly did "speak volumes."

IS THERE REALLY A "LOOK OF LOVE?" Many song lyrics suggest that people show outward signs of affection nonverbally. For example, "The look of love is on your face . . ." and "Your eyes are the eyes of a woman in love. . . ." Most people would agree that love is outwardly visible, as shown in Figure 3.5. People in love tend to look at and touch each other differently than those not in love (e.g., holding hands in public, standing very close, putting an arm around the other). Research conducted by Gonzaga, Kelmer, Keltner, and Smith (2001) supports these informal observations by providing direct evidence that nonverbal cues can reflect love.

Figure 3.5 Love Reflected in Nonverbal Cues

Research findings confirm the belief that people in love reveal their feelings in their nonverbal cues, for instance, when they gaze lovingly into each other's eyes and hold hands.

These researchers recruited couples in romantic relationships to participate in a study of interactions between partners. Two weeks before the study began, participants were asked to fill out questionnaires that measured the degree to which they were in love. During the study, the couples discussed several questions relating to their relationship—ones that would evoke positive reactions (e.g., their first date) and others that would evoke thoughts of conflicts in their relationships (e.g., problems sharing work, problems related to spending quality time together). During these conversations, their behavior was videotaped. Afterward, several judges rated the extent to which the couples demonstrated nonverbal cues viewed as reflecting love—smiles, head nods, leaning toward one another, positive gestures (e.g., reaching out to the partner). The frequency of these nonverbal cues was then related to their reports of the degree to which they were in love. As expected, the stronger their reported love, the more frequently they showed these nonverbal cues. Moreover, this was true whether they were discussing topics likely to elicit positive emotions *or* negative emotions (i.e., conflict). In short, inner feelings of love were reflected in their overt nonverbal actions under both positive and negative conditions. This is another important way in which individuals communicate through their facial expressions, body movements, and gestures.

THE FACIAL FEEDBACK HYPOTHESIS A song from the musical *The King and I* says, "Whenever I feel afraid, I hold my head erect and whistle a happy tune. . . . The result of this deception is very strange to tell, for when I fool the people I fear, I fool myself as well." What these lyrics are saying, in essence, is that our actions—and especially, perhaps, our nonverbal behaviors—influence our feelings. In other words, not only do our emotions influence our nonverbal cues, the cues themselves influence our internal feelings (Duclos, Laird, Schneider, Sexter, Stern, & Van Lighten, 1989; McCanne & Anderson, 1987).

Many studies offer support for the *facial feedback hypothesis*—the view that facial expressions can actually trigger emotions. For instance, McCanne and Anderson (1987) asked female participants to imagine positive and negative events (e.g., inheriting a million dollars; losing a really close friendship). While imagining those events, they were told to either enhance or suppress two groups of facial muscles: the one that is active when we smile or view happy scenes, and the other that is active when we frown or view unhappy scenes. Measurements of electrical activity of both these sets of muscles indicated that after a few practice trials, most persons could carry out this task quite successfully. They could enhance or suppress muscle tension when told to do so and could do this without any visible change in their facial expressions.

After imagining each scene, participants rated their emotional experiences in terms of enjoyment or distress. If the facial feedback hypothesis is correct, those ratings should be affected by participants' efforts to enhance or suppress tension in the relevant muscles. If they enhanced activity in muscles associated with smiling, they should report more enjoyment of the positive events. If they suppressed such activity, they should report less enjoyment. Results offered clear support for these predictions. Participants reported less enjoyment of the positive events when they suppressed activity in the appropriate muscle and a tendency to report less distress to the negative events when they suppressed the muscle involved in frowning.

Convincing as these findings are that facial expressions trigger emotions, there is an important problem in interpreting the results. Instructions to enhance or inhibit certain muscles could have influenced participants' reports of their own emotional experiences. To get around such problems, more recent research (Davis, Senghas, Brandt, & Ochsner, 2010) used a very ingenious solution: Researchers compared the facial expressions and emotional reactions of two groups of people who received different types of antiwrinkle drug injections. Before these injections, both groups of participants were shown positive and negative video clips. On a scale of very negative to very positive, the participants rated how they felt after viewing each video clip. Eight days later, one group received injections of Botox®, a drug that paralyzes muscles involved in facial expressions. The other group received Restylane®, a drug that simply fills in wrinkles without paralyzing facial muscles. Fourteen to twenty-four days after receiving the injections, participants were again shown positive and negative video clips, and were asked to rate their feelings after each one.

The group that received Botox injections reported weaker emotional reactions to both types of video clips. That is, they reported weaker negative feelings after viewing the negative clips, and weaker positive feelings after viewing the positive clips (see Figure 3.6). These findings suggest that feedback from our facial muscles plays a role in shaping our emotional experiences. It seems to be the case that what we show on our face does influence what we experience on the "inside."

3.1.3: Recognizing Deception

If we're honest with ourselves, we've all been deceptive at one time or another, perhaps to avoid hurting others' feelings or to get ourselves out of "trouble" with a parent, friend, or professor. But lying, or more generally, deceptive communication, does occur more often than you think. Research findings indicate that most people tell at least one lie every day and some form of deception is used in almost 20 percent of people's social interactions (DePaulo & Kashy, 1998). Additional research indicates that a majority of strangers lie to each other at least once during a brief first encounter (Feldman, Forrest, & Happ, 2002; Tyler & Feldman, 2004).

HOW WELL DO WE RECOGNIZE DECEPTION?   Since lying appears to be frequent, you might think we should all be very familiar with it and able to recognize it when it occurs. However, in general, we rarely do little better than chance in determining whether others are lying or telling the truth (e.g., Ekman, 2001; Malone & DePaulo, 2001). One reason for this is we tend to perceive others as truthful and so we don't search for clues of deception (Ekman, 2001). Another reason is our desire to be polite, which makes us reluctant to discover or report deception by others. It is also the case that people differ in how they define lying. Some people report low frequencies of lying because they don't consider themselves trying to "intentionally mislead others" so

Figure 3.6 Evidence for the Facial Feedback Hypothesis

Participants who received injections of Botox, which paralyzes facial muscles, reported feeling less negative after viewing negative film clips, and less positive after viewing positive film clips, than participants who received Restylane, a drug that does not paralyze muscles.

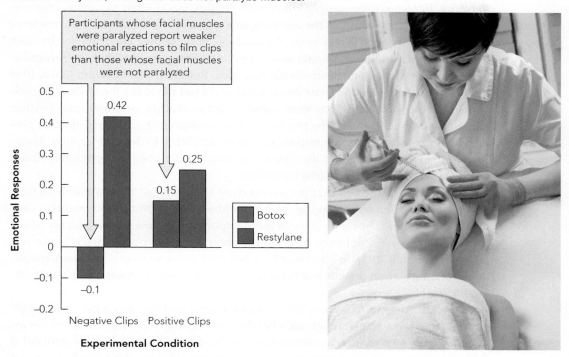

they do not perceive themselves as deceptive (Serota, Levine, & Boster, 2010). Using this more stringent definition of what a lie is, recent research finds that 60 percent of Americans report telling *no* lies on a given day and that most lies are actually being told by a small percentage of very prolific liars.

So, are some people better at recognizing lies than others? If most of us are not very good at accurately detecting deception in everyday life, perhaps there are trained experts who are very good at detecting lying. Ekman and O'Sullivan (1991) addressed this question by testing the accuracy of various types of law-enforcement personnel. Each participant was exposed to 10 one-minute videos of college-aged women, half of whom were lying about the feelings they were experiencing when watching a film and the other half were telling the truth. Accordingly, guessing by chance alone would produce a 50 percent accuracy rate. Surprisingly, of the professional groups tested, whose job experience ranged from 9 to 23 years, only one group—Secret Service agents—proved to be significantly above chance in accurately detecting deception (see Figure 3.7). Ekman and O'Sullivan suggested that members of the Secret Service may be more accurate than others because they spend their time scanning crowds and focusing on nonverbal behavior, whereas most people involved in law enforcement are focused on other dimensions of communication (i.e., what people say). Whatever the explanation, this research illustrates just how difficult it can be to detect deception, even for those who are expected to be able to do so as part of their job.

Figure 3.7 Are Experts Better Than Chance at Detecting Deception?

When asked to detect lying, various groups involved in some aspect of law enforcement did not exceed chance in accuracy. As shown in the graph, only Secret Service agents were significantly above chance in accurately detecting deception.

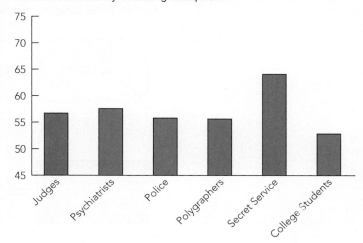

Our own moods can also influence our ability to recognize deception. Research indicates that people in a sad mood are better at recognizing deception than people in a happy mood (Reinhard & Schwarz, 2011). This may be because people experiencing negative feelings pay more attention to the content of a message—its words and meaning. In comparison, people who are in a happy mood often pay more attention to cues that are irrelevant to the meaning of a message, for instance, the attractiveness of the person who is delivering the message. Because they are distracted by cues unrelated to the message, people in a happy mood may be less likely to recognize deception in the message itself. To test this idea, Reinhard and Schwarz (2012) first induced a cheerful mood in some participants and a sad mood in others. Then, participants in both mood conditions were asked to judge whether messages from another student were true or false. The results of three experiments confirmed that, as predicted, our moods do play an important role in our ability to detect deception. Those who were in a negative mood were more successful at detecting deception than those who were in a positive mood (see Figure 3.8).

It has been suggested that people who are successful at lying are able to conceal their deception by managing their nonverbal cues. Existing evidence also suggests that another factor may be even more important: The nonverbal cues on which we tend to focus are not very informative about whether people are lying or not (Hartwig & Bond, 2011). In other words, when attempting to detect deception, people focus on information that are not valid indicators of whether others are lying or telling the truth.

Overall, we tend to believe others are engaging in deception when they fidget with objects, seem uncertain about what they are saying, and seem to have little interest in their own words. In comparison, we tend to judge others to be truthful if they show a pleasant facial expression, and seem genuinely involved in what they are saying. Although it has often been suggested that the way others look at us indicates whether they are lying or not, the evidence for this is weak. Whether people blink a lot while talking to us, avoid eye contact—or engage in a high level of it—doesn't seem to be related to whether they are, in fact, lying (DePaulo et al., 2003).

There are a few nonverbal cues that are moderately revealing of deception. However, these cues tend to go unnoticed because most people are not looking for them (e.g., Etcoff, Ekman, Magee, & Frank, 2000). These cues include **microexpressions**—fleeting

---

Figure 3.8 Moods Influence Our Ability to Recognize Deception

Research findings indicate that individuals in a sad mood are better at detecting deception than individuals in a happy mood. This is because a sad mood encourages careful attention to the content of a message and less attention to unrelated information. On the other hand, a happy mood encourages more attention to unrelated content and less attention to the message content, so its deceptive qualities are missed.

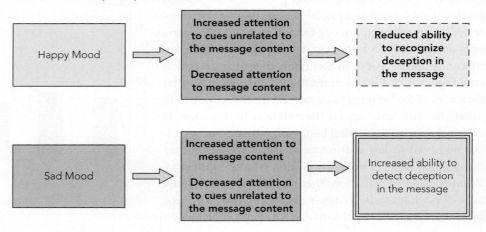

facial expressions lasting only a few tenths of a second. Such reactions appear on the face very quickly after an emotion-provoking event and are difficult to suppress. Another valid predictor of deception is *interchannel discrepancies*—for example, discrepancies between people's facial expressions and their body language. People who are lying often find it difficult to control all channels of communication at once. Lastly, *exaggerated facial expressions*—smiling more frequently than usual or showing an exaggerated level of interest in what we are saying—can reflect attempts to engage in deception.

In addition to these nonverbal cues, other signs of deception are sometimes present in nonverbal aspects of what people actually say. When people are lying, the pitch of their voices often rises. Similarly, they often take longer to respond to a question or are slower in describing events. People who are lying may tend to start sentences, stop them, and begin again. In other words, certain elements of **linguistic style**—aspects of speech apart from the meaning of words, such as pitch, speed, or pattern (rhythm)— are indications that a person may not be telling the truth.

In summary, through careful attention to nonverbal cues and various aspects of the way people speak (e.g., the pitch of their voices), we may be able to tell when others are lying. But to do so, we must exert a lot of cognitive effort. This includes trying to focus on nonverbal cues to which we typically don't pay attention. As a result, detecting deception accurately is very difficult, even for experts.

THE IMPORTANCE OF NONVERBAL CUES IN PROFESSIONAL SETTINGS   Nonverbal communication is clearly an important aspect of our efforts to understand others. Not only do we attempt to interpret what others are communicating based on their nonverbal cues in everyday social interactions, but we also do so in settings that have important consequences for us. For example, when we interact with medical professionals we may try to assess—based on their nonverbal behavior—whether they truly care about us or are merely "playing a role." Consider the last time you visited a doctor's office. Did you feel that she or he was really interested in your problems, or just wanted to finish as quickly as possible in order to move on to the next patient? What was it about the doctor's behavior that determined which of these judgments you formed?

Research findings provided by Dimatteo and Taranta (1979) indicate that nonverbal cues play a key role in doctor–patient relationships. These researchers asked patients to rate their doctors on the extent to which the doctors listened to them. Also, the doctors completed a measure of their own ability to accurately recognize others' facial expressions. The physicians who scored high on this facial recognition test received higher ratings from their patients than doctors who scored low. That is, doctors who could accurately "read" their patients' emotional reactions were perceived by their patients as really listening. Likewise, the higher the physicians scored on a test of their ability to communicate emotions to patients, the higher were their ratings from patients. In sum, the ability of doctors to both read and send nonverbal cues was an important factor in patient perceptions.

What specific aspect of a physician's nonverbal behavior affects patients? For people with serious illnesses, trust in their physician can be critical for reducing anxiety and willingness to follow treatment recommendations. To assess how eye contact and smiling affects the trust felt by patients, a video of an oncologist talking with breast cancer patients was presented. The video varied the extent that these two nonverbal cues were displayed (Hillen et al., 2015). Patients exposed to the doctor exhibiting more eye contact felt more trust. Likewise, the doctor who smiled more was perceived by patients as caring more.

Overall, the unspoken language of facial expressions, gestures, body movements, and other nonverbal cues not only play a role in everyday social life; they also influence outcomes far beyond informal situations. To learn how nonverbal cues affect impressions and performances during job interviews, see the feature, **"What Research Tells Us About…The Role of Nonverbal Cues in Job Interviews."**

What Research Tells Us About...

The Role of Nonverbal Cues in Job Interviews

While we might like to believe that the best job candidate—the person with the strongest qualifications—obtains the job, a large body of evidence indicates that many social factors, including aspects of the candidate's physical appearance, can play a role. Evidence also indicates that nonverbal cues displayed during interviews are important for making good impressions. For instance, in one study (Gifford, Ng, & Wilkinson, 1985), videotapes of actual job interviews were shown to professional interviewers—individuals who had several years' experience interviewing job applicants. These interviewers rated the applicants on their motivation and social skills—their ability to interact well with others. Nonverbal cues in the interviews were rated by trained judges.

Results indicated that several nonverbal cues—time talked, smiles, and gestures—were related to both judgments of applicants' motivation and their social skills. Applicants who rated high on these behaviors received higher ratings from the interviewers. So, does the most qualified candidate always get the job? It seems to depend on whether the candidate's nonverbal skills are included in the equation.

Might something as simple as posture affect interview performance? Research by Carney, Cuddy, and Yap (2010) suggests that it can. Feeling powerful is expressed nonverbally: occupying more space with a tall, strong posture. The opposite, low-power posture, is also visible: a hunched-over body that minimizes the space occupied. Not only does powerful versus nonpowerful posture influence the impression others form of us (see Figure 3.9); it can cause us to *feel* more powerful, which in turn can have an impact on our physiology and behavior. To test this possibility, Carney and colleagues instructed men and women how to assume a high- or low-power pose, which they were asked to maintain for a full minute. Participants were then given $2 and an opportunity to either gamble with it or keep

it. A saliva measure was also collected and later tested for the hormone testosterone.

Not only did participants report feeling more powerful in the high-power-posture condition compared to the low-power-posture condition, but the posture manipulation influenced increased risk taking (greater likelihood of gambling) and increase in testosterone. This research suggests that physical posture can help to mentally and physically prepare us for stressful situations by improving our confidence and ability to perform well in job interviews.

Figure 3.9 Nonverbal Cues Matter at Job Interviews

Research evidence indicates that a job applicant's nonverbal cues can influence evaluations and interview outcomes. Slouching like the person on the left will result in less success than the good posture and alertness of the person displayed on the right.

Key Points

- **Social perception** involves the processes through which we seek to understand other people. It plays a key role in social thought and behavior.
- In order to understand others' emotional states, we often rely on **nonverbal communication**—an unspoken language of facial expressions, eye contact, body movements, and touching.
- While facial expressions for all basic emotions may not be as universal as once believed, they do often provide useful information about others' emotional states.
- Although a high level of eye contact is usually interpreted as

a sign of positive feelings, **staring**—a continuous gaze—is often perceived as a sign of anger or hostility. Another type of nonverbal behavior is **body language**, which often reflects emotions through the positions, postures, and movements of our bodies. Likewise, touching, such as the way we shake hands, can reveal things about us.
- Many people express emotions through sounds independent of the words they speak. This type of nonverbal communication is called *paralanguage*—vocal effects other than speech, such as tone, volume, pitch, or rhythm.
- The *facial feedback hypothesis* suggests that we not

only show what we feel in our facial expressions; those expressions can also influence our own emotional states.

- We are generally not very accurate at recognizing deception for many reasons, such as our tendency to perceive others as truthful and our desire to be polite. As a result, we don't typically search for clues of deception. However, we are more successful at detecting liars when in a negative mood than in a positive mood.
- Noticing nonverbal cues such as **microexpressions**, interchannel discrepancies, and exaggerated facial expressions may be helpful in detecting deception but these cues tend to go unnoticed because most people are not looking for them. Sudden changes in **linguistic style**, such as the pitch or speed of speech, may also indicate deception.
- Nonverbal cues play a role in many important social situations—between doctors and their patients, as well as during job interviews. Posture in the form of power-posing can affect our confidence and actual performance in stressful situations.

3.2: Attribution: Understanding the Causes of Behavior

Objective   **Explain how the process of attribution helps our understanding of others' behavior**

Suppose you meet a very attractive person at a party. You'd like to see him or her again, so you ask, "Would you like to get together for a movie next week?" Your dreams of a wonderful romance are shattered when this person answers "No, sorry." Now you are left wondering *why* this person refused your invitation. Is it because the person doesn't like you? Or, is the person currently in a serious relationship and doesn't want to date anyone else? Maybe the person is so busy with other commitments that he or she has no spare time. You'd like to believe that this person wants to see you again, but is just too busy right now. Whichever inference you draw is likely to impact your self-esteem and will also influence what you do next. If you conclude that the person doesn't like you or is involved in a serious relationship, the chances are lower that you'll try to arrange another meeting than if you decide the person is currently just too busy.

This simple example illustrates an important fact about social perception: We often want to know why someone says or does certain things, and further, what kind of person they really are—what are their traits, motives, and goals? Social psychologists believe that our interest in such questions stems, in large part, from our basic desire to understand cause-and-effect relationships in the social world (Pittman, 1993; Van Overwalle, 1998). We don't simply want to know *how* others have acted—that's something we can readily observe. We also want to understand *why*, because that knowledge can help us understand them better and also help us predict their future actions. The process through which we seek such information and draw inferences is known as **attribution**. This process not only concerns our efforts to understand the causes behind others' behaviors, on some occasions, we also use it to understand the causes behind *our own* behavior. We'll now take a closer look at what social psychologists have learned about this important aspect of social perception (Graham & Folkes, 1990; Heider, 1958; Read & Miller, 1998).

3.2.1: Theories of Attribution: How We Attempt to Make Sense of the Social World

Because the attribution process is complex, many theories have been proposed to explain its operation—when, why, and how we do so. In this section, we will focus on two classic theories of attribution that continue to be especially influential. We'll also examine other factors related to causal attribution, including the effect of time, the ability to control or influence circumstances, the belief in fate versus personal choice, and the ways we interpret others' actions.

USING OTHERS' BEHAVIOR AS A GUIDE TO THEIR LASTING TRAITS   Jones and Davis's (1965) theory of **correspondent inference** asks how we use information about others' behavior as a basis for inferring their traits. In other words, the theory is concerned with how we decide, on the basis of others' overt actions, whether they possess specific traits or dispositions likely to be fairly stable over time. At first glance, this process might seem to be a simple task. Others' behavior provides us with a rich source on which to draw. So, if we observe behavior carefully, we should be able to learn a lot about people. Up to a point, this is true. The task is complicated, however, by the following fact: Individuals often act in certain ways not because doing so reflects their own preferences or traits, but rather because *external factors* leave them little choice. Suppose you go to restaurant and the receptionist who greets you smiles and acts in a friendly manner. Does this mean the receptionist is a friendly person who simply likes people? It's possible, but perhaps he or she is acting this way because that is what the job *requires*. Situations like this are common, so using others' behavior as a guide to their lasting traits or motives can be very misleading.

When are we likely to adjust our judgments about others' traits based on situational factors? According to the theory of correspondent inference (Jones & Davis, 1965; Jones & McGillis, 1976), we tend to focus on the types of actions that are most likely to prove informative. First, we are likely to consider behavior as corresponding a person's traits when the behavior seems freely chosen. In contrast, if behavior appears to be somehow forced on the person in question, we tend to see it as less indicative of that person's traits. Second, we pay careful attention to actions that show what Jones and Davis called **noncommon effects**—conditions that can be caused by one specific factor, but not by others. (Don't confuse this term with *uncommon* effects, which means infrequent effects.) Actions that produce noncommon effects are informative, because they rule out other possible causes and allow us to zero-in on a specific reason for another's behavior.

To illustrate the concept of noncommon effects, consider two different scenarios. Imagine that one of your friends just became engaged. His future spouse is very attractive, appears to love your friend, and has a warm personality. What can you learn about your friend from his decision to marry this person? Not so much. There are so many good reasons to select such a person that it is difficult to choose among them. In contrast, imagine that your friend's fiancé is very physically attractive, but she often treats him disrespectfully, and she has large student debts. Does the fact that your friend is marrying this woman tell you anything about him? Definitely. You can probably conclude that he cares more about physical beauty than being respected by his partner or having financial security.

As you can see from this example, we usually learn more about others from actions on their part that yield noncommon effects. This example also illustrates how expectations can affect the inferences we draw about another person's behavior. We usually expect a person to marry someone who obviously loves him or her. In this case, when your friend violates that expectancy by selecting a partner who appears not to act "normally," then we are more certain his decision reveals a great deal about him.

Finally, Jones and Davis suggest that we pay more attention to others' actions that are low in *social desirability*, than to actions that are high on this dimension. In other words, we learn more about others' traits from actions they perform that are somehow out of the ordinary, than from actions that are very much like those of most other people. For instance, if we see someone raise his or her hand to hit a small child or pet animal, we are likely to assume that behavior tells us something about the person's traits—in this case, that the person may be typically angry or aggressive (see Figure 3.10). On the other hand, if we see someone act in a socially desirable way—such as treating a child or pet gently—then we don't learn much that is unique about that person since most people would act in a similar manner.

In summary, according to the theory proposed by Jones and Davis, we are most likely to conclude that others' behavior reflects their stable traits (i.e., we are likely to

Figure 3.10 Unusual Behavior Often Tells Us a Lot About Others

When other people engage in unusual behavior—behavior different from that shown by most others, especially if socially undesirable—it often provides us with useful information for understanding their traits.

reach correspondent inferences between their behavior and their personal qualities), when their behavior (1) is freely chosen; (2) yields distinctive, noncommon effects; and (3) is low in social desirability or otherwise violates social norms.

KELLEY'S COVARIATION THEORY: HOW WE ANSWER "WHY" BEHAVIOR OCCURS   Consider the following events:

> *You arrange to meet someone at a restaurant, but she doesn't show up.*
> *You send several texts to a friend, but he never responds.*
> *You expect to receive a job promotion, but you don't receive it.*

In all these situations, you would probably wonder *why* these events occurred. Why didn't your acquaintance show up at the restaurant—did she forget, did she deliberately not come, or was there some other reason? Why did your friend fail to return your text messages—is he angry with you, is his cell phone not working, or is he just really busy? Why didn't you get the job promotion you wanted—is your boss disappointed in your performance, could you be the victim of some kind of discrimination, or did a combination of reasons influence the result?

In many situations, understanding the reason(s) "why" behind an event is the central attributional task we face. We want to know why other people acted as they did or why events turned out in a specific way. Such knowledge is crucial, for only if we understand the causes behind others' actions or events can we hope to make sense of the social world (and potentially prevent bad outcomes from happening in the future). Obviously, the potential number of specific causes behind others' behavior can be very large. To make the task more manageable, we often begin with a preliminary question: Did others' behavior stem mainly from *internal* causes (their own traits, motives, intentions), mainly from *external* causes (aspects of the social or physical world), or from a combination of the two? For example, you might wonder if the reason you didn't receive the promotion was that you really haven't worked very hard (an internal cause), your boss is unfair and biased against you (an external cause), or perhaps both were factors. How do we attempt to answer this question?

According to Kelley's *covariation theory* (Kelley, 1972; Kelley & Michela, 1980), in our attempts to answer the question "Why?" about others' behavior, we focus on three major types of information. First, we consider **consensus**—the extent to which other people react to a given stimulus or event in the same manner as the person we are evaluating. The higher the proportion of people who react in the same way, the higher is the consensus. Second, we consider **consistency**—the extent to which the person in question reacts to the stimulus or event in the same way on other occasions, over time. And third, we examine **distinctiveness**—the extent to which the person reacts in the same manner to other, different stimuli or events.

According to Kelley's theory, we are most likely to attribute another's behavior to *internal* causes under conditions in which consensus and distinctiveness are low, but consistency is high. In contrast, we are most likely to attribute another's behavior to *external* causes when consensus, consistency, and distinctiveness are all high. Finally, we usually attribute another's behavior to a combination of internal and external factors when consensus is low, but consistency and distinctiveness are high.

To illustrate these ideas, imagine that you see a server in a restaurant flirt with a customer. This behavior raises interesting questions. Why does the server act this way? Will you attribute the behavior to internal or external causes? Is the server simply someone who likes to flirt (an internal cause)? Or, is the customer extremely attractive—someone with whom many people flirt (an external cause)? According to Kelley's theory, your decision (as an observer of this scene) would depend on information relating to the three factors mentioned earlier. First, assume that the following conditions prevail: (1) You observe other servers flirting with this customer (consensus is high); (2) you have seen this server flirt with the same customer on other occasions (consistency is high); and (3) you have *not* seen this server flirt with other customers (distinctiveness is high). Under these conditions—high consensus, consistency, and distinctiveness—you would probably attribute the server's behavior to external causes. In other words, you would probably conclude that this customer is very attractive and that is why the server flirts with her.

Now, in contrast, assume these conditions exist: (1) No other servers flirt with the customer (consensus is low); (2) you have seen this server flirt with the same customer on other occasions (consistency is high); and (3) you have seen this server flirt with many other customers, too (distinctiveness is low). In this case, Kelley's theory suggests that you would attribute the server's behavior to internal causes—the server is simply a person who likes to flirt (see Figure 3.11). The basic assumptions of Kelley's theory have been confirmed in a wide range of social situations, so it seems to provide important insights into the nature of causal attributions. However, research on the theory also suggests the need for certain modifications or extensions, which we will now consider.

Figure 3.11 Kelley's Covariation Theory: An Example

Under the conditions shown in the top part of this figure, we would attribute the server's behavior to external causes—for example, the attractiveness of this customer. Under the conditions shown in the bottom part, however, we would attribute the server's behavior to internal causes—for instance, this person likes to flirt.

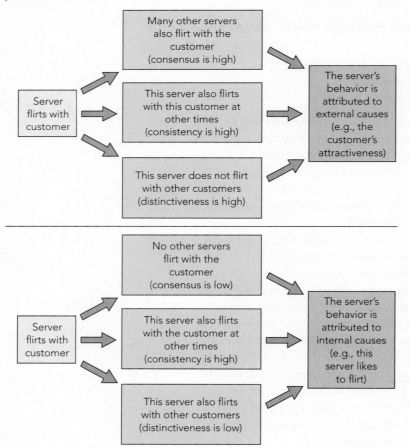

OTHER DIMENSIONS OF CAUSAL ATTRIBUTION   Although we are often very interested in knowing whether others' behaviors stem mainly from internal or external causes (i.e., something in the situation), this is not the entire story. In addition, we are concerned with two other questions: (1) Are the causal factors that influenced their behavior likely to be *stable* over time, or are those factors likely to change? (2) Are the factors *controllable*—can individuals change or influence them if they wish to do so (Weiner, 1993, 1995)? These aspects are independent of the internal–external dimension we just considered.

Some internal causes of behavior tend to be quite stable over time, such as personality traits and temperament (e.g., Miles & Carey, 1997). Other internal causes can, and often do, change greatly, for instance, motives, health, and fatigue. Similarly, some internal causes are controllable. For example, individuals can, if they wish, learn to hold their tempers in check. Other internal causes, such as chronic illnesses or disabilities, may be nearly impossible to control. The same is true for external causes of behavior: Some are stable over time (e.g., laws or social norms that define how we should behave in various situations), while others are not stable (e.g., encountering someone who is in a bad mood). A large body of evidence indicates that in trying to understand the causes behind others' behavior, we do take note of all three of these dimensions—internal–external, stable–unstable, and controllable–uncontrollable (Weiner, 1985, 1995).

FATE ATTRIBUTIONS VERSUS PERSONAL CHOICE   Attribution is also affected by whether we believe that events in our lives are "meant to be," or if we conclude that we play a role in causing those events to happen. For example, suppose something unexpected but important happens in your life: You win the lottery, or you break your leg just before a planned vacation and can't go. How do we account for such events? One interpretation is that events are due to our own actions: You broke your leg because you foolishly tried to reach something on a very high shelf while standing on a rickety chair. Another approach is attributing such events to *fate*—forces outside our understanding and control. In fate attributions, events occur because they are simply "destiny."

Both interpretations are possible, so what factors lead us to prefer one over the other? This intriguing question has been investigated in many studies (e.g., Burrus & Roese, 2006; Trope & Liberman, 2003), but some of the most interesting answers were provided by research conducted by Norenzayan and Lee (2010). These social psychologists suggested that belief in fate is related to two more basic beliefs: religious convictions concerning the existence of God, and a belief in complex causality—the idea that many causes influence events, and no one cause is essential. This idea also leads to the conclusion that unlikely events that occur are "meant to be." Since so many factors combine to lead to their occurrence, the presence or absence of one factor makes little difference—the events are "overdetermined."

To test these predictions, Norenzayan and Lee (2010) asked participants who identified themselves as Christians or as nonreligious, and who were of either European heritage or East Asian heritage, to read brief stories describing unexpected and improbable events. Participants were then asked to indicate the extent to which those events were due to fate or to chance. Here's an example: *It was 8:00 A.M. in the morning and the street was busy as usual. Kelly, on her way to school, stopped and reached down to tie her shoelace. While bent over, she found a little diamond ring lying right in front of her that couldn't have been spotted otherwise.*

As you can see in Figure 3.12, research results showed that people with strong religious beliefs were more likely to attribute unlikely events to fate (i.e., saw them as "meant to be") than nonreligious people. East Asians were more likely to do this too, because of their strong cultural beliefs concerning complex causality. In further studies, Norenazyan and Lee (2010) found that the belief in fate itself stemmed from the Christians' belief in God and the East Asians' belief in causal complexity.

Figure 3.12 How Do People Attribute Improbable Events?

Research findings indicate that improbable but important events are often attributed to fate rather than to personal actions. Religious persons who have a strong belief in God and people from cultures with strong beliefs in causal complexity (i.e., many factors combine to produce unlikely events) are most likely to attribute such events to fate and see as "meant to be."

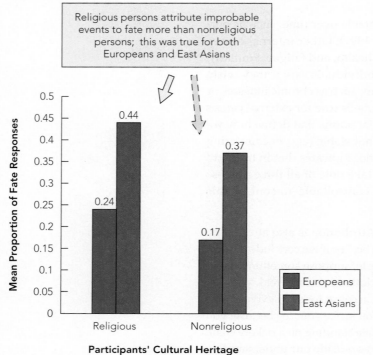

ACTION IDENTIFICATION AND THE ATTRIBUTION PROCESS

When we try to understand why others do what they do, including what goals they want to accomplish, we usually have a wide range of possible interpretations to choose from. Suppose you saw someone putting loose change into a jar. You could conclude, "She wants to avoid losing the change so she puts it into the jar." Alternatively, you could conclude, "She is trying to save money so she can contribute to her own education." The first conclusion is a concrete interpretation that focuses on the action itself. The second, in contrast, is more abstract, attributing intentions and goals to this person. The action is the same (putting change into a jar), but our interpretation of it—and why it occurs—is very different. The interpretation we place on an act—in terms of differing degrees of abstraction—is known as **action identification**.

Research findings indicate that action identification is a basic influence on the attributions we make. When we view others' actions concretely, involving little more than the actions themselves, we also tend to make few attributions about their intentions or higher-order cognition. When, instead, we view others' actions more abstractly, as having greater meaning, we attribute much greater mental activity to them. We see their actions not simply as produced by the present situation, but as reflecting much more—the person's goals, characteristics, and intentions—their *mind*, if you will. Research conducted by Kozak, Marsh, and Wegner (2006) provides strong support for this reasoning. Across several studies, they found that the more others' actions are interpreted at higher levels of abstraction (as reflecting more than the action itself), the more those people are also perceived as possessing complex motives, goals, and thought processes. So, where attribution is concerned, it is not simply *what* other people do that helps shape our perceptions of them; our interpretation of their actions is crucial, too.

3.2.2: Basic Sources of Error in Attribution

Although we generally do a good job of evaluating the social world, we are far from being perfectly accurate. In fact, our efforts to understand other people—and ourselves—are subject to several types of biases. Attribution "errors" can lead us to false conclusions about why others acted as they did and also influence our predictions of how they will act in the future.

CORRESPONDENCE BIAS: THE FUNDAMENTAL ATTRIBUTION ERROR

Imagine that you witness the following scene. A man arrives at a meeting 1 hour late. On entering, he drops his notes on the floor. While trying to pick them up, his glasses fall off and break. Later, he spills coffee all over his tie. How would you explain these events? The chances are good that you might conclude "This person is disorganized and clumsy." Are such attributions accurate? Perhaps, but it is also possible that the man was late because of unavoidable delays at the airport, he dropped his notes because they were printed on slick paper, and he spilled his coffee because the cup was too hot to hold. In this example, the inclination to overlook potential *external* causes of the man's behavior illustrates what Jones (1979) labeled the **correspondence bias**—the tendency to explain others' actions as stemming from (corresponding to) their dispositions, even in the presence of clear situational causes (e.g., Gilbert & Malone, 1995).

The correspondence bias has been observed so frequently (at least among people in Western nations) that social psychologists refer to it as the **fundamental attribution error**. In short, we tend to perceive others as acting as they do because they are "that kind of person," rather than because of the many external factors that may influence their behavior. This tendency occurs in a wide range of contexts, but appears to be strongest in situations where both consensus and distinctiveness are low, as predicted by Kelley's theory, and when we are trying to predict others' behavior in the far-off future rather than the immediate future (Nussbaum, Trope, & Liberman, 2003; Van Overwalle, 1998). Why? When we think of the far-off future, we tend to do so in abstract ways. This leads us to think about others in terms of their traits. As a result, we tend to overlook potential external causes of their behavior.

Even though this fundamental attribution error has been demonstrated in many studies and also strongly affected subsequent research aimed at understanding attribution processes, we now know that culture can modify this bias. For example, we know that people in Asian cultures are considerably less susceptible to making internal attributions for other people's behavior. Indeed, adults in India, when asked to explain why others had behaved either positively or negatively, favored situational explanations over internal attributions (Miller, 1984). Also, differences among Americans, based on their religion, have been observed (e.g., Li et al., 2012). For example, Protestants are more likely to make internal attributions than are Catholics.

THE STRENGTH OF THE CORRESPONDENCE BIAS   Suppose that you read a short essay written by another person on a controversial topic. On the basis of this essay, you would probably expect to get an idea where the writer stands with respect to this issue—is she "pro" or "anti"? So far, so good. But now assume that before reading the essay, you learned that the author had been *instructed* to write it so as to support a particular position—again, "pro" or "anti." From a purely rational perspective, you should realize that in this case, the essay may tell you *nothing* about the writer's true views. After all, she (or he) was merely following instructions. However, two social psychologists—Jones and Harris (1967)—challenged the idea that people would correct their inference about the writer even though they were aware of the situational constraint the writer faced. Instead, these researchers predicted that the fundamental attribution error is so strong, that most people would assume they can determine the writer's views from the essay—even when the person was *told* to write it in a particular way.

To test their reasoning, Jones and Harris asked research participants to read a short essay that either supported or opposed Fidel Castro's rule in Cuba (remember, the research was conducted in 1967). In one condition, participants were told that the essay writer had free choice as to what position to take. In another condition, they were told that the writer was instructed to create the essay in a pro-Castro or anti-Castro manner. After reading the essay, participants were asked to estimate the essay writer's true beliefs. Results were clear: Even in the condition where the writer had been instructed to take one specific position, American research participants assumed they could tell the writer's real views from the essay. In other words, they attributed the essay writer's actions to internal factors (her or his true beliefs), even though they knew this was not the case! Clearly, this research was a dramatic demonstration of the fundamental attribution error in action.

Subsequent research, also viewed as "classic" in the field, reached the same conclusions. For instance, in a revealing study by Nisbett, Caputo, Legbant, and Marecek (1973), participants were shown a series of 20 paired traits (e.g., quiet-talkative, lenient-firm) and were asked to decide which of those traits were true of themselves, their best friend, their father, a casual acquaintance, and Walter Cronkite (a famous newscaster at the time). The participants were also offered a third option: They could choose "depends on the situation." Results again offered strong evidence for the fundamental attribution error. Participants in the study chose "depends on the situation" much more often for themselves than for other people. In other words, they reported that their

Figure 3.13 The Fundamental Attribution Error in Action: Classic Evidence

Research participants were asked if certain traits were true of themselves and several other specific people. They also had the option of choosing the response "depends on the situation." Participants indicated that their own actions were strongly influenced by external (situational) causes, but the actions of other people were assumed to stem primarily from internal causes (people's traits).

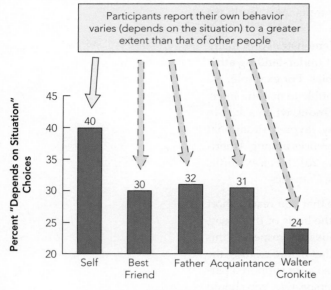

Target of Attributions

own behavior varied from situation to situation, but the behavior of others (their best friend, father, or even a famous news anchor) primarily reflected personal traits (see Figure 3.13).

CORRESPONDENCE BIAS IN E-MAIL Suppose you receive an e-mail message filled with spelling and grammatical errors. Would you assume that the person who sent the e-mail was in a big hurry, was lazy and careless, or perhaps doesn't know English very well? Would it make a difference if the message seemed rude, or if you knew something about the person's background? What role might the correspondence bias play in your interpretation?

To see if correspondence bias operates in e-mail communications, Vignovic and Thompson (2010) conducted a study in which employees of an organization received an e-mail message from a stranger. The message either indicated that the sender was from another culture or it did not provide such information. Also, the message was one of three types: It either had no spelling or grammatical errors, and was polite; contained spelling or grammatical errors, but was polite; or contained no spelling and grammatical errors, but was not polite (i.e., was terse and lacking in conversational tone). After receiving the message, participants rated the sender on a number of dimensions of personality.

If participants learned that the sender was from another culture, they did not down-rate this person in terms of conscientiousness, intelligence, and other characteristics. However, learning that the sender was from a different culture did *not* reduce the negative inferences drawn from a lack of politeness. This indicates that the correspondence bias operates in attributions about others based on e-mail, just as it does in attributions based on face-to-face contacts with them. Although the impact of this bias can be reduced when a clear, situational explanation for spelling and grammatical errors is known, it can still continue to strongly influence perceptions of others, even if we know about possible external causes of their actions.

WHY THE CORRESPONDENCE BIAS OCCURS Social psychologists have conducted many studies in order to find out why the correspondence bias occurs (e.g., Robins, Spranca, & Mendelsohn, 1996). One possibility has to do with whether we notice situational (external) causes or not. For instance, when we observe another person's behavior, we tend to focus on his or her actions. The context in which the person behaves, and hence the potential situational causes of his or her behavior, often fades into the background. As a result, dispositional (internal) causes are perceived (they are *salient*) whereas situational ones are not. In other words, the person we are observing is high in *perceptual salience* and is the focus of our attention, while situational factors that might also have influenced this person's behavior are less salient and so seem less important. Alternatively, we might notice such situational causes, but give them insufficient weight in our attributions.

Another explanation of why the correspondence bias occurs may be related to the general process we use when trying to understand others' behaviors. We tend to begin our evaluations by assuming that people's actions reflect their underlying characteristics. Then, we attempt to correct for any possible effects of the external world—the current situation. Such cognitive attempts at correction, however, are often insufficient—we don't make enough allowance for the impact of external factors (Gilbert & Malone, 1995).

Evidence for this two-step process—a quick, automatic reaction followed by a slower, more controlled correction—has been obtained in many studies (Chaiken &

Trope, 1999; Gilbert, 2002), so it seems to offer a compelling explanation for the correspondence bias (i.e., fundamental attribution error). In fact, it appears that most people are aware of this process. Most of us are aware of the fact that we start by assuming other people behave as they do because of internal causes (e.g., their personality, their true beliefs), but then correct this assumption, at least to a degree, by taking account of situational constraints. Perhaps even more interesting is our tendency to assume we adjust our attributions—take situational constraints into account—more than other people do. In other words, we perceive that we are less likely to fall victim to the correspondence bias than other people (Pronin, Lin, & Ross, 2002).

ACTOR–OBSERVER EFFECT: "YOU'RE CLUMSY; I SLIPPED."   Powerful as it is, the correspondence bias applies mainly to attributions we make about others. We don't tend to "overattribute" our own actions to internal causes. This fact helps explain another, closely related type of attributional bias known as the **actor–observer effect** (Jones & Nisbett, 1971). This effect is the tendency to attribute our own behavior to situational (external) causes, but the behavior of others to dispositional (internal) causes. For example, when we see another person trip and fall, we tend to attribute it to his or her clumsiness. If *we* trip, however, we are more likely to attribute our fall to situational causes, such as ice on the sidewalk.

The actor–observer effect occurs partly because we are usually quite aware of the many external factors affecting our own actions, but less aware of external factors when we focus on the actions of other people. Thus, we tend to perceive our own behavior as arising largely from situational causes, but the behavior of others as deriving mainly from their traits.

SELF-SERVING BIAS: "I'M GOOD; YOU'RE LUCKY."   Suppose you wrote and submitted a paper for a class. When you received it back, you found the following comment: "An outstanding paper—one of the best I've seen in years. A+" To what would you attribute this success? Probably, you would explain it in terms of internal causes—your high level of talent, the effort you invested in writing the paper, and so on. Now, in contrast, imagine that when you got the paper back, these comments were written on it: "Unsatisfactory paper—one of the worst I've seen in years" How would you interpret this outcome? The chances are good that you would be tempted to focus mainly on external (situational factors)—the difficulty of the task, your professor's unfairly harsh grading standards, the fact that you didn't have enough time to do a good job, and so on.

This tendency to attribute our own positive outcomes to internal causes but negative outcomes to external factors is known as the **self-serving bias**. Based on research, this bias appears to be both general in scope and powerful in its effects (Brown & Rogers, 1991; Miller & Ross, 1975). Several explanations have been suggested to account for this pervasive bias, but most fall into two categories: cognitive and motivational explanations. The cognitive model suggests that we attribute our own positive outcomes to internal causes, but negative ones to external causes, because we *expect* to succeed. For this reason, we have a tendency to attribute our positive outcomes to internal causes more than to external causes (Ross, 1977). In contrast, the motivational explanation suggests that the self-serving bias stems from our need to protect and enhance our self-esteem (Greenberg, Pyszczynski, & Solomon, 1986). While both cognitive and motivational factors play a role in the self-serving bias, research evidence has offered more support for the motivational view (e.g., Brown & Rogers, 1991).

Interestingly, the results of several studies indicate that the strength of the self-serving bias varies across cultures (Oettingen, 1995; Oettingen & Seligman, 1990). In particular, it is weaker in cultures, such as those in Asia, that place a greater emphasis on group outcomes and group harmony. By comparison, the self-serving bias is stronger in Western cultures, where individual accomplishments are emphasized and it is considered appropriate for winners to highly celebrate their victories. Consistent with this idea, Lee and Seligman (1997) found that Americans of European descent showed a larger self-serving bias than either Chinese Americans or mainland Chinese. Once again, we see that cultural factors often play an important role in many basic aspects of social thought.

Let's explore a related aspect of the self-serving bias in the following feature, **"What Research Tells Us About...Why Some People Conclude They Are Superior to Others."**

What Research Tells Us About...

Why Some People Conclude They Are Superior to Others

A very compelling example of the self-serving bias involves what is known as **hubris**—the strong tendency to hold exaggerated positive views about oneself (Hayward, Shepherd, & Griffin, 2006). Hubris, in the form of excessive confidence, is all too common. A person who exhibits hubris typically perceives the self as being solely responsible for positive outcomes. Indeed, our highly individualistic culture strongly encourages the belief that creative outcomes in science, music, art, and business are the product of the "special abilities" of individuals, while neglecting the critical role played by the "times" and the communities in which the creative outcomes emerged (Haslam, Adarves-Yorno, Postmes, & Jans, 2013). For instance, in each of these fields, prizes are typically awarded to individuals on the assumption that they alone produced the valued outcome. Yet, some scientists and rock stars alike do reference others' influences on them—noting the vital role of stimulating discussions, critical questions asked of them, and constructive feedback received while collaborating with others (John-Steiner, 2000).

Although some thinkers and inventors do at times acknowledge the role of the situation and of other people in their achievements, others do not. Ironically enough, their backgrounds and the institutions they emerge from may encourage the belief that they alone are responsible for their successes. This fosters the belief that their decisions could not possibly be wrong—that is, self-serving attributions. CEOs of giant corporations often experience hubris, which can even lead them to pay unwarranted premiums when acquiring other companies. For example, in a sample of 106 corporate acquisitions, Hayward and Hambrick (1997) assessed the CEOs' self-importance and the extent of recent prior media praise for the CEOs as predictors of shareholder wealth loss as a result of the acquisitions. These measures of CEO hubris were especially strong predictors of their firms' losses when there was a lack of external accountability. Steve Jobs (see Figure 3.14), co-founder and longtime CEO of Apple, Inc., was sometimes accused of hubris, a "media star" who seemed to underplay the important roles played by others in the firm's success.

Many researchers have noted that the theories and perspectives taught in MBA programs emphasize self-interest, which includes seeking maximal personal compensation over long-term organizational benefits (Bebchuk & Fried, 2005). Intriguing research by Miller and Xu (2015) also suggests that norms prevalent in some institutions are likely to foster the self-serving bias

in their members. Miller and Xu collected data using a sample of 444 American CEOs, all of whom had appeared on the cover of major business magazines. These researchers wanted to examine potential associations between CEOs who graduated from MBA programs (versus those who did not) and the extent to which those CEOs showed self-serving (versus firm-serving) behavior.

In the year following the CEOs' cover stories, Miller and Xu found that the CEOs' percentage of personal compensation rose more for the MBA graduates than for the non-MBAs. This occurred even though the performance of the MBA graduates' firms fell more sharply in subsequent years than the non-MBAs' companies. This research suggests that what these CEOs learned while in business school was an approach that emphasizes personal agency and self-confidence, which may not be conducive to long-term organizational success. Perhaps when such fame is achieved, outcomes are especially likely to be attributed by the CEOs to internal and stable causes; they see themselves as responsible for their firm's success and they also convince others that it was due to their lasting skills and talents.

Figure 3.14 Hubris: Why Some People—Often Those in High-Status Positions—Sometimes Conclude They Are Superior to Others

When individuals attribute their success solely to internal causes (e.g., their own talent or skill), they are exhibiting hubris—exaggerated positive views of themselves. Was this true for Steve Jobs, co-founder and longtime CEO of Apple, Inc.? Some observers believe that it was.

HOW WE EXPLAIN UNEXPECTED EVENTS   Everyone experiences unexpected negative events. For example, your computer's hard drive "dies" and you lose important files; you drop your cell phone and it breaks just when you need it; or your school's team loses an important game even though it was strongly favored to win. Often, we attribute events like these to external agencies: Your computer was defective, you dropped your cell phone because someone bumped into you, your school's team was robbed of a win by biased referees, and so on. In contrast, when positive events occur, we tend to attribute these outcomes to internal causes—our competence and talents. As the name of the self-serving bias suggests, we tend to attribute negative events to external causes, but positive ones to internal causes.

Research conducted by Morewedge (2009) illustrates our tendency to show the self-serving bias when explaining unfavorable outcomes. Participants played a two-player "ultimatum game" on a computer in which a "partner" was given $3.00 to divide in any way that partner wished. The study participant then decided to accept or decline the way the money was divided. Participants were not told whether they were playing against a real person or a computerized "partner." In one condition, the partner offered a very favorable division: $2.25 for the participant, but only $0.75 for the self. In another condition, the partner offered an equal division: $1.50 for each player. In a very unfavorable condition, the partner offered only $0.75 to the participant and kept $2.25 for the self.

After playing the game several times, participants were asked whether they thought the partner was a real person or a computer. Morewedge predicted that participants would be more likely to believe that the partner was human in the very unfavorable condition and most likely to believe the partner was a computer in the very favorable condition. The tendency to attribute negative events to external agents would lead participants to perceive the unfair division as the work of another person, not a mere machine. Results offered strong support for this prediction.

3.2.3: Applications of Attribution Theory: Interventions and Insights

Kurt Lewin, one of the founders of modern social psychology, often remarked "There's nothing as practical as a good theory." By this he meant that once we obtain scientific understanding of some aspect of social thought or behavior, we can, potentially, put this knowledge to practical use. Where attribution theory is concerned, this has definitely been the case. As basic knowledge about attribution has grown, so has the range of practical problems to which such information has been applied (Graham & Folkes, 1990; Miller & Rempel, 2004). As an example of such research, we'll examine how attribution theory has been applied to understanding depression, a mental health disorder. We'll also use attribution theory to gain insights on terrorism and people's explanations for their harm-doing.

ATTRIBUTION AND DEPRESSION   Depression is by far the most common psychological disorder. In fact, it has been estimated that almost half of all human beings experience depression symptoms at some time during their lives (e.g., Blazer, Kessler, McGonagle, & Swartz, 1994). Many factors play a role in depression, including what might be termed a *self-defeating* pattern of attributions. In contrast to most people, who show the self-serving bias described previously, depressed individuals tend to exhibit the opposite pattern. They attribute *negative* outcomes to lasting, internal causes such as their own traits or lack of ability, but attribute *positive* outcomes to temporary, external causes such as good luck or special assistance from others. As a result, these individuals perceive they have little or no control over what happens to them—they are simply being blown about by the winds of unpredictable fate. As depression deepens, the tendency to engage in this self-defeating pattern of attribution is strengthened.

Fortunately, several forms of therapy based on attribution theory have been developed and appear to be quite successful (Amirkhan, 1998; Cruwys, South, Greenaway, & Haslam, 2015; Robinson, Berman, & Neimeyer, 1990). These forms of therapy focus on helping depressed people to change their pattern of attributions—to take personal credit for successful outcomes, to stop blaming themselves for negative outcomes (especially ones they could not control), and to view at least some failures as the result of external factors.

ATTRIBUTION AND TERRORISM When the word *terrorism* is mentioned, many people tend to recall major events that happened closest to home, such as 9/11 (2001) when terrorists destroyed the World Trade Center in New York City and hit the Pentagon in Washington, D.C., killing thousands of people (see Figure 3.15). Another example occurred in 1995 when hundreds of people were killed by Timothy McVeigh and Terry Nichols, two Americans who blew up the Federal Building in Oklahoma City. But terrorism transcends national boundaries, occurring all over the world. It also takes many forms of harm-doing, including kidnappings, torture, and executions. How do terrorists who commit such atrocities explain what they do? Attribution theory offers some insights to how terrorists justify their actions.

Halverscheid and Witte (2008) analyzed the public speeches by members of Al Qaeda justifying terrorist acts they had committed between 2001 and 2004. (If these researchers were to repeat their study today, they would certainly include statements by ISIL, or ISIS, which has committed many atrocities in Syria and other parts of the Middle East). These speeches were specifically examined for statements that attributed the group's actions to various causes—in particular, efforts to do the most good for the largest number of people or efforts to "punish" enemies for violating basic human rights. Results indicated that Al Qaeda emphasized the idea that its actions were justified because of the harm done by their enemies—essentially, Western nations such as the United States—to Muslim populations. In short, they justified their actions by attributing them to external causes—they were simply responding to powerful and evil provocations from others.

In contrast, the United States justified its actions in Iraq and Afghanistan as deriving, at least in part, from internal causes—their desire to "do good" by removing a cruel

Figure 3.15 Insights to Terrorism: Attribution Theory Provides Some Clues

The 9/11 Memorial commemorates the thousands of people who were killed by terrorists on September 11, 2001. Terrorists often attribute their harmful actions to external causes, justifying their actions as serving a higher purpose or as punishment for those perceived to be "enemies."

dictator and trying to establish more stable and responsible governments. More generally, we know that people tend to make different attributions for their own groups than they do for other groups. In other words, they tend to perceive harm-doing by their own group as more justifiable than when the same behavior is committed by members of another group (Tarrant, Branscombe, Warner, & Weston, 2012).

In summary, basic principles of attribution theory help shed light on the reasons why terrorists feel justified in doing what they do—and also why powerful nations feel justified in using their military might to, ostensibly, contribute to human well-being. While these suggestions should be viewed as only tentative in nature—ones that rest on only a small amount of evidence—they illustrate the basic fact that attribution theory can provide insights for a wide range of situations and events.

Key Points

- To obtain information about others' traits, motives, and intentions, we often engage in **attribution**—efforts to understand *why* people have acted as they have.
- According to Jones and Davis's theory of **correspondent inference**, we attempt to infer others' traits from observing certain aspects of their behavior—especially behavior that is freely chosen, produces **noncommon effects**, and is low in social desirability.
- According to Kelley's *covariation theory*, we are interested in the question of whether others' behavior stems from *internal* causes (their traits, motives, intentions) or *external* causes (aspects of the social or physical world). To answer this question, we focus on information relating to **consensus**, **consistency**, and **distinctiveness**.
- Two other important dimensions of causal attribution relate to whether specific causes of behavior are seen as stable or unstable over time, and whether behavioral causes are controllable or not controllable.
- Another factor relating to attribution concerns the extent to which we ascribe events in our lives to fate—what was "meant to be"—or to personal causes. Individuals who believe strongly in the existence of God are more likely to attribute improbable but important events to "what was meant to be." This is also true of persons whose cultural heritage accepts complex causality for important events.
- When we interpret a person's action, the level of abstraction we use is called **action identification**. A low-level interpretation focuses on the action itself, whereas a high-level interpretation focuses on the intentions and goals of the person we are observing.
- Attribution is subject to many potential sources of bias. One of the most important of these is the **correspondence bias**—the tendency to explain others' actions as stemming from dispositions, even in the presence of situational causes. This bias has been observed so frequently that social psychologists refer to it as the **fundamental attribution error**.
- Two other attributional biases are the **actor–observer effect** (the tendency to attribute our own behavior to external, situational causes but the behavior of others to internal causes) and the **self-serving bias** (the tendency to attribute positive outcomes to internal causes but negative ones to external causes). The self-serving bias is especially strong for negative events, which are often attributed to external agents.
- A related aspect of the self-serving bias—**hubris**—is a form of exaggerated self-confidence. People who exhibit hubris often perceive themselves as being solely responsible for positive outcomes.
- Attribution theory has useful applications beyond our interpretations of day-to-day interactions with others. For example, identifying self-defeating patterns of attribution in depressed people led to new treatments for changing those patterns. Attribution theory also provides insights to the reasons why terrorists feel justified committing their harmful actions.

3.3: Impression Formation and Management: Combining Information About Others

Objective **Describe why initial information is important in forming perceptions of others**

When we meet another person for the first time, we are—quite literally—flooded with information. We can see, at a glance, how they look and dress, how they speak, and how they behave. Although the amount of information reaching us is large, we somehow manage to combine it into an initial *first impression* of this person—a mental representation that is the basis for our reactions to her or him. In this section, we'll explore how these impressions develop and what we do to maintain favorable impressions.

3.3.1: Impression Formation

Clearly, **impression formation**—how we develop our views of others—is an important aspect of social perception. This fact raises several critical questions: What, exactly, are first impressions? How are they formed—and how quickly? Are they accurate? We'll now examine what social psychologists have discovered about these and related issues. To do so, we'll begin with some classic research in the field, and then move on to more recent research and its findings.

FOUNDATIONAL RESEARCH ON FIRST IMPRESSIONS: CENTRAL AND PERIPHERAL TRAITS As we have already seen, some aspects of social perception, such as attribution, require lots of hard mental work. It's not always easy to draw inferences about others' motives or traits from their behavior. In contrast, forming first impressions seems to be relatively effortless. As Solomon Asch (1946), one of the founders of experimental social psychology, put it: "We look at a person and immediately a certain impression of his character forms itself in us. A glance, a few spoken words are sufficient to tell us a story about a highly complex matter . . ." (p. 258). How do we manage this to do this? How, in short, do we form impressions of others in the quick and seemingly effortless way that we often do? This is the question Asch set out to study.

At the time Asch conducted his research, social psychologists were heavily influenced by the work of *Gestalt psychologists*, specialists in the field of perception. A basic principle of Gestalt psychology is: "The whole is often greater than the sum of its parts." This means that what we perceive is often more than the sum of individual sensations. To illustrate this point for yourself, simply look at a painting. What you see is not individual strokes of paint on the canvas; rather, you perceive an integrated whole—for example, a portrait, a landscape, or a bowl of fruit. So as Gestalt psychologists suggested, each part of the world around us is interpreted, and understood, in terms of its relationships to other parts or stimuli—in effect, as a totality.

Asch applied these ideas to understanding impression formation, suggesting that we do not form impressions simply by adding together all of the traits we observe in other persons. Rather, we perceive these traits *in relation to one another*, so that the traits cease to exist individually and become, instead, part of an integrated, dynamic whole. To test these ideas, Asch came up with an ingenious approach. He gave individuals lists of traits supposedly possessed by a stranger, and then asked them to indicate their overall impressions of this person. For example, in one study, participants read one of the following two lists:

intelligent—skillful—industrious—warm—determined—practical—cautious

intelligent—skillful—industrious—cold—determined—practical—cautious

As you can see, the lists differ only with respect to two words: *warm* and *cold*. Thus, if people form impressions merely by adding together individual traits, or by averaging over the value assigned to each trait, the impressions formed by persons exposed to these two lists should not differ very much. However, this was *not* the case. Participants who read the list containing *warm* were much more likely to view the stranger as generous, happy, good-natured, sociable, popular, and altruistic than were people who read the list containing *cold*. The words *warm* and *cold*, Asch concluded, were *central traits*—ones that strongly shaped overall impressions of the stranger and colored the meaning of other adjectives in the lists. Asch obtained additional support for this view by substituting the words *polite* and *blunt* for *warm* and *cold*. When he did this, the two lists yielded highly similar impressions of the stranger. So, it appeared that *polite* and *blunt* were *not* central traits that colored the entire impressions of the stranger.

On the basis of many studies such as this one, Asch concluded that forming impressions of others involves more than simply combining individual traits. As he put it: "There is an attempt to form an impression of the *entire* person. . . . As soon as two or more traits are understood to belong to one person they cease to exist as isolated traits, and come into immediate . . . interaction. . . . The subject perceives not this *and* that quality, but the two entering into a particular relation. . . ." (1946, p. 284). While research on impression formation has become far more sophisticated since Asch's early work, many of his basic ideas about impression formation have exerted a lasting impact, and are still worthy of careful consideration today.

HOW QUICKLY AND ACCURATELY ARE FIRST IMPRESSIONS FORMED?   A growing body of research suggests that first impressions are often accurate. Many studies have reported that even working with what are known as **thin slices** of information about others—for instance, photos or short videos of them—perceivers' first impressions are reasonably accurate (e.g., Ambady, Bernieri, & Richeson, 2000; Borkenau, Mauer, Riemann, Spinath, & Angleitner, 2004). For example, "thin slices" of body movement information accurately predicted judges' perceptions of a speaker's extraversion (Koppensteiner, 2013).

People do better in forming first impressions of some characteristics than others (Gray, 2008), but overall, they can accomplish this task fairly well—very quickly and with better-than-chance accuracy. How quickly? In one study (Willis & Todorov, 2006), participants viewed faces of strangers for very brief periods of time: 1/10 of a second, half a second, or a second. Then, they rated the strangers on several traits: trustworthiness, competence, likeability, aggressiveness, and attractiveness. These impression ratings were compared with the ratings provided by another group of people who were allowed to examine photos of the same actors without any time constraints. The ratings of the two groups were very similar (i.e., they were highly correlated). In fact, correlations between the two sets of ratings (the ones done without any time limits and the ones completed at short exposure times) ranged from about .60 to about .75. So, first impressions can be formed very quickly and are slightly better than chance in terms of accuracy (see Figure 3.16).

Forming first impressions of others quickly is especially valuable if these impressions involve characteristics that can help us avoid danger. For example, threat—to the extent this characteristic shows on strangers' faces—would be especially valuable to detect as quickly as possible. Evidence reported by Bar, Neta, and Linz (2006) indicates that impressions of others' potential threat can be formed very fast. Participants were shown photos of faces with neutral expressions, but still differed in the extent to which they appeared threatening. These faces were shown for 26 milliseconds (.026 of a second), 39 milliseconds (.39 seconds), or 1,700 milliseconds (1.7 seconds). Participants then rated each face on a scale ranging from least threatening to most threatening. Results indicated that the ratings of faces shown for 39 milliseconds and 1,700 milliseconds correlated highly, but that these correlations were much lower for the 26 milliseconds condition. This suggests there are some limits to how quickly we can form first impressions of others—below .04 seconds, this task does not seem possible. But still, .04 seconds is an incredibly short period of time, so clearly we can get an overall idea of what others are like very, very quickly.

Another aspect of Bar and colleagues' research involved asking participants to rate others' intelligence, again from seeing their faces for 39 milliseconds or 1,700 milliseconds. In this case, there was no relationship between the ratings in the two conditions. This suggests that first impressions of others' intelligence are not formed as quickly as those for threat. Perhaps, since judgments of intelligence are not as important for our survival as judgments about threat, there may be no major advantage to

Figure 3.16 How Quickly Are First Impressions Formed?

Research findings indicate that first impressions of others are formed with lightning speed—in many cases, within a few seconds and sometimes in less than one second!

being able to form impressions of intelligence as quickly. In any case, this research raises an important question: What factors influence the extent to which first impressions are accurate? While there are no definite answers, the formation of first impressions depends on several factors such as the format in which information about others is encountered (face-to-face meetings, photos, videos of others), and the dimensions along which these ratings are made. In general, though, existing evidence suggests that our first impressions of others are more accurate than chance—that is, our impressions of others are somewhat related to their actual personalities, intelligence, and many other factors, but only slightly better than chance (Ames, Kammrath, Suppes, & Bolger, 2010).

CAN FIRST IMPRESSIONS BE CHANGED?   Given that our first impressions of others are not always accurate, then another important question is under what conditions are we likely to correct our impressions. Research results indicate that we can adjust or even reverse our first impressions of others, but only under certain conditions. Evidence for such adjustments has been obtained in several studies (Gawronski & Bodenhausen, 2006). Drawing on existing evidence (e.g., Cone & Ferguson, 2015), researchers have noted that first impressions can be changed by acquiring new information, or rejecting existing information. One of the most informative studies on changing first impressions was conducted by Mann and Ferguson (2015). They suggested that first impressions are often changed through a reinterpretation of previous information. Suppose you meet someone for the first time and acquire information that indicates the person is rude—he walked away from you in the middle of a conversation. Later, you learn that the person left because he was diabetic and needed insulin immediately. Under those conditions, you might reinterpret the information that led you to form your initial negative first impression.

To test this reasoning, Mann and Ferguson (2015) presented participants with information about a stranger named Francis who had broken into two houses. Some participants learned that he had done this to vandalize the homes. As a result, they formed negative first impressions of him. Later, they received information indicating that, in fact, he had broken into the homes to save people from a fire. The researchers predicted that this new information would lead the participants to reinterpret the initial information, so that now they would view his actions as positive. Indeed, the findings revealed that their impressions of Francis did change, becoming more positive.

In further studies, Mann and Ferguson found that only certain types of new information used for reinterpreting initial impressions produced positive changes. For example, in the case when participants learned that Francis had saved a child who had fallen onto subway tracks, the overall impression of him improved, but the new information did not totally offset the original, negative first impression. In other words, the information about saving a child, although positive, was not relevant to the initial information that Francis had broken into two houses (see Figure 3.17). Overall, Mann and Ferguson's (2015) research indicates that first impressions can be changed in several ways: by acquiring new information, rejecting previous information, or perhaps most effectively, reinterpreting information that produced the initial impression.

To summarize, research indicates that people can form first impressions of others on the basis of small amounts of information and these impressions show a better-than-chance level of accuracy. However, despite people being generally quite confident about the validity of their first impressions, such confidence and actual accuracy are unrelated to each other. So, should we trust our first impressions of others? The best answer seems to be we can to some extent, but we should do so with caution.

3.3.2: Impression Management

The desire to make a favorable impression on others is a strong one, so most of us do our best to "look good" to others when we meet them for the first time. Social psychologists use the term **impression management** or **self-presentation** to describe these efforts to make a good impression on others. The research results on this process suggest it is well worth our effort: people who engage in impression management successfully often gain important advantages in many situations (e.g., Sharp & Getz, 1996; Wayne & Liden, 1995). What tactics do people use to create favorable impressions on others, and which tactics work best? Is impression management related to subsequent behavior in social or work situations? Let's see what careful research has revealed about these intriguing questions.

Figure 3.17 Can First Impressions Be Changed?

Research findings indicate that first impressions can be changed, especially when the information that led to the initial first impression is reinterpreted on the basis of additional, relevant information.

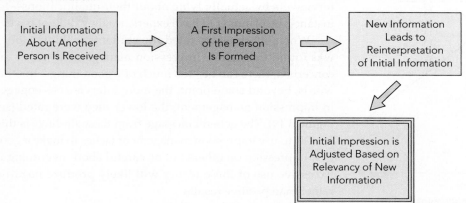

Figure 3.18 Self-enhancement—One Technique of Impression Management

In order to improve the impressions we make on others, many people (increasingly, men as well as women) use products claiming to enhance physical beauty and appeal to others.

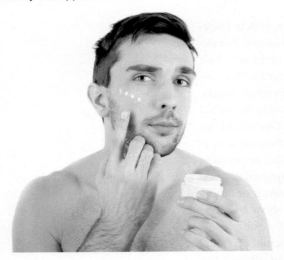

TACTICS FOR "LOOKING GOOD" TO OTHERS Although we use many different techniques for boosting our images, most of these tactics fall into two major categories: *self-enhancement* (efforts to increase our appeal to others) and *other-enhancement* (efforts to make the target person feel good in various ways). With respect to self-enhancement, specific strategies include efforts to boost one's appearance—either physical or professional. Physical appearance relates to the attractiveness and appeal of the individual, while professional appearance relates to personal grooming, appropriate dress, and personal hygiene. A meta-analysis of the many studies assessing the biasing effects of physical attractiveness on job-related outcomes revealed that it plays a substantial role and applies to both men and women (Hosoda, Stone-Romero, & Coats, 2003). The existence of extensive beauty aids and flourishing clothing industries suggests some ways in which people attempt to improve both aspects of their appearance and the first impressions they make on others (see Figure 3.18). Forms of other-enhancement include flattering others, expressing agreement with them, doing favors for others, and asking for their advice.

HOW WELL DO IMPRESSION MANAGEMENT TACTICS WORK?

Growing evidence, much of it from practical real-life situations, indicates that impression management tactics do not always work. Up to a point, efforts to "put our best foot forward" do result in positive first impressions (Barrick, Swider, & Stewart, 2010). But if others perceive we are trying to fool them, they may react negatively. Such effects are clearly visible in job interviews. For instance, Swider, Barrick, Harris, and Stoverink (2011) asked students who were studying to be accountants to participate in interviews conducted by graduate students. These graduate students were studying to become human resource experts—people who often conduct interviews to screen for the best job applicants.

Figure 3.19 Can People Engage in Too Much Impression Management?

Up to a point, efforts to make a good impression on others can succeed. However, when these efforts become obvious to the people toward whom they are directed, tactics can backfire and actually produce negative impressions.

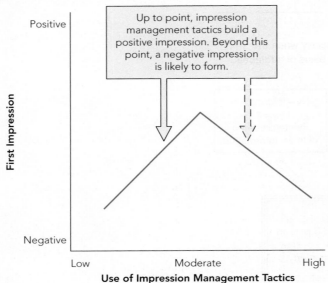

The interviews consisted of two parts. The first part was used to create rapport—friendly feelings—between the interviewers and interviewees. The second part was a very realistic job interview. After the interviews, the interviewees were asked to rate the extent to which they had used impression management tactics. Specifically, they rated the extent to which they tried to present themselves in a very positive way—as the perfect person for the job. Ratings indicated that some interviewees used impression management tactics to a moderate degree—they simply emphasized their qualifications. Others tried to boost the impressions made on the interviewers by actually lying about their qualifications—for instance, by claiming to have experience they did not have.

When interviewers rated the students seeking a job, it was found that where impression management tactics are concerned, there can be "too much of a good thing." In other words, beyond some point, the more interviewees engaged in impression management, the lower they were rated (see Figure 3.19). The general message from these findings is this: It's OK to use impression management tactics to make a good first impression on others but be careful about overdoing it. Excessive use of these tactics will likely produce negative rather than positive results.

Key Points

- Most people are concerned with making good *first impressions* on others because they believe those impressions will exert lasting, positive effects. Research on **impression formation** or **self-presentation**—the process through which we form our views of others—suggests that this is true.

- Asch's classic research on impression formation indicates that impressions of others involve more than simple summaries of their traits. Some traits (*central traits*) can influence the interpretation of other traits.

- First impressions are formed very quickly—within seconds or less—but speed does not necessarily equal accuracy. Although some studies show that even **thin slices** of information about others produce reasonably accurate perceptions, other studies indicate that first impressions are above chance in accuracy for only some attributes (e.g., threat).

- First impressions can be changed when new information is acquired. This occurs primarily when new information causes us to reinterpret the initial information, and the new information is relevant to the situation being judged.

- In order to make a good impression on others, individuals often engage in **impression management** or **self-presentation** tactics. Most techniques used for this purpose fall into two categories: *self-enhancement* (efforts to boost one's appeal to others) and *other-enhancement* (efforts to induce positive moods or reactions in others).

- Evidence indicates that impression management tactics can work, but only up to a point. If they are overdone, these tactics can be recognized for what they are, and generate negative rather than positive reactions from others.

Summary and Review

Social perception involves the processes through which we seek to understand other people. In order to understand others' emotional states, we often rely on **nonverbal communication**—an unspoken language of facial expressions, eye contact, body movements, and touching. While facial expressions for all basic emotions may not be as universal as once believed, they do often provide useful information. For instance, a high level of eye contact is usually interpreted as a sign of positive feelings, but a continuous gaze—**staring**—is often perceived as a sign of anger or hostility. **Body language** also reflects emotions through the positions, postures, and movements of our bodies. Even the way we shake hands can reveal things about us. In addition, people can express emotions through vocal effects, such as tone, volume, pitch, and rhythm. Not only do our emotions influence our nonverbal cues, the cues themselves may influence our internal feelings, as suggested by the facial feedback hypothesis.

A few nonverbal cues are moderately revealing of deception, such as **microexpressions** and interchannel discrepancies, but they tend to go unnoticed. Signs of deception are also sometimes present in **linguistic style**—aspects of people's speech apart from the words they say, such as a sudden rise in the pitch of the voice. Our own moods can influence our ability to recognize deception; we tend to be better at recognizing deception when we're in a sad mood than a happy mood. Nonverbal cues can have important repercussions in professional settings, affecting impressions and performances during job inter-

views and the level of trust that patients feel toward their doctors.

To obtain information about others' traits, motives, and intentions, we often engage in **attribution**—efforts to understand *why* people have acted as they have. According to Jones and Davis's theory of **correspondent inference**, we attempt to infer others' traits from observing certain aspects of their behavior—especially behavior that is freely chosen, produces **noncommon effects**, and is low in social desirability. According to Kelley's covariation theory, we are interested in whether others' behavior stems from internal or external causes, so we focus on information relating to **consensus**, **consistency**, and **distinctiveness**. Two other important dimensions of causal attribution relate to whether specific causes of behavior are stable or unstable over time, and whether behavioral causes are controllable or not controllable. When we interpret a person's action, the level of abstraction we use is called **action identification**.

One factor relating to attribution concerns the extent to which we ascribe events in our lives to fate—what was "meant to be"—or to personal causes. Individuals who believe strongly in the existence of God are more likely to attribute improbable but important events to "what was meant to be." This is also true of persons whose cultural heritage accepts complex causality for important events.

Attribution is subject to bias. **Correspondence bias (fundamental attribution error)** is the tendency to explain others' actions as stemming from dispositions, even in the presence of situational causes. Two other attributional errors are the **actor–observer effect** (the tendency to attribute our own behavior to external causes but that of others to internal causes) and the **self-serving bias** (the tendency to attribute positive outcomes to internal causes, but negative ones to external causes). The self-serving bias is especially strong for negative events, which we often attribute to external agents rather than aspects of ourselves. A related aspect of the self-serving bias is **hubris**. People who exhibit hubris often perceive themselves as being solely responsible for positive outcomes.

Most people are concerned with making good first impressions on others because they believe that these impressions will exert lasting, positive effects. Research on **impression formation**—the process through which we form our views of others—suggests that this is true. Asch's classic research on impression formation indicates that impressions of others involves more than simple summaries of their traits. Some traits (central traits such as warm and cold) can influence the interpretation of other traits.

First impressions are formed very quickly—within seconds or less—but speed does not necessarily equal accuracy. Although some studies show that even **thin slices** of information about others produce reasonably accurate perceptions, other research indicates that first impressions are above chance in accuracy for only some attributes (e.g., threat). Once they are formed, first impressions can be changed when new information is acquired. This occurs primarily when new information causes us to reinterpret the initial information, and the new information is relevant to the situation being judged.

In order to make a good impression on others, individuals often engage in **impression management** or **self-presentation**. Most techniques used for this purpose fall into two categories: self-enhancement (efforts to boost one's appeal others) and other-enhancement (efforts to induce positive moods or reactions in others). Evidence indicates that impression management tactics can work, but only up to a point. If they are overdone, these tactics can be recognized for what they are, and generate negative rather than positive reactions from others.

Chapter 4
The Self
Answering the Question "Who Am I?"

Chapter Overview

Learning Objectives

4.1 Compare the way we manage ourselves in different social situations to how others perceive us

4.2 Explain how we arrive at an understanding of our own selves

4.3 Use the personal-versus-social identity continuum to understand how different identities affect our behavior

4.4 Examine the health implications of being unrealistically optimistic about the self

4.5 Determine the factors that impact self-esteem

4.6 Analyze how prejudice and trying to conceal our identity impacts well-being

Facebook is an environment in which many interesting aspects of self and identity can be readily observed. By providing an important outlet for presenting ourselves to others, Facebook may even be regarded as a public forum for creating our identities. Like other social environments, Facebook can be used to carry on conversations with others, express political views, and indicate social preferences (e.g., favorite books, music, and movies). Perhaps without even realizing it, you may use Facebook as a place to document your personal growth. In other words, over time Facebook may reveal a sense of who you are through accumulated postings, including photos of yourself at different stages of life, important events you participated in, or more mundane matters such as the dinner you cooked and ate last night.

As the largest social networking site, Facebook meets the criteria for a genuine social environment (see Figure 4.1). But how do our interactions on Facebook differ from face-to-face interactions? Obviously, with Facebook we can connect with others almost anywhere and anytime. Another noticeable difference is the extra time you can take to compose what you communicate via Facebook. This includes your responses to others' posts, as well as what you share about yourself. Because we can choose to withhold

Figure 4.1 Online Interaction: It's There Wherever and Whenever You Want It

Facebook and other social media allow us to interact with others and present ourselves however we want.

some crucial information about ourselves when communicating on social media, we can attempt to craft how others see us. Generally, people tend to portray themselves in their profiles a little more positively than they are in reality (Toma & Carlson, 2015).

Most people are concerned with how they are perceived by others, whether in social media interactions or face to face. Your ability to control the image you present changes in a social media environment. For example, Facebook friends can post on your "timeline" unless you select the user setting that prevents this. What others post on your Facebook timeline can affect your ability to create the image you might prefer others to see. This could be more of an issue if you have friends who tag you in photos that might not show you in the most attractive light. Also consider that some things you share on Facebook can appear in search engine results, allowing potential employers and others to find information posted about you even if they aren't actually logged into Facebook.

The manner in which social networking sites allow the sharing of information can also impact other aspects of your life. For instance, on Facebook your privacy may be compromised in ways that allow marketers to target you. Whether you see this as a big problem or a minor inconvenience is determined by how much you value your privacy. Older people want to guard their privacy more than younger ones, who don't always care as much. If you don't take the time to get familiar with Facebook's data policy and adjust user privacy settings, then you shouldn't be surprised when you receive direct marketing, often with ads based on information you provided about yourself!

The nature of the self—including how we think and feel about ourselves—is an important research topic in social psychology. In this chapter, we will examine a number of related issues such as who is more accurate in predicting our behavior, ourselves or others who know us well, and how we develop self-knowledge. We will also investigate whether the self is a single, stable construct, or if "who we are" differs depending on the social context. In other words, do people experience themselves the same way all the time, or does their experience of themselves depend on what social comparison is evoked in different contexts? A critical aspect of this question is how different audiences and their treatment of us may influence the way we see and evaluate ourselves. We'll also explore whether one aspect of the self is more *true* or predictive of behavior than another. Next, we'll address questions related to self-esteem. What is it, how do we get it, and how do we lose it? How does changing the context—such as moving to a new country—affect our self-esteem? Are there group differences in the average level of self-esteem? Specifically, do men and women differ in their levels of self-esteem?

Finally, we'll look in depth at the ways people cope when their self is a target of prejudice. We'll consider the consequences of concealing one's identity, and what happens when people feel excluded or devalued because of their group membership. This includes the ways in which people's well-being and their performance of tasks can be affected by potential rejection based on their social identity.

4.1: Self-Presentation: Managing the Self in Different Social Contexts

Objective **Compare the way we manage ourselves in different social situations to how others perceive us**

William Shakespeare said long ago in his play *As You Like It*, "All the world's a stage, and all the men and women merely players." In social psychological terms, this means that all of us are faced with the task of presenting ourselves to a variety of audiences, and we may play different roles (be different selves) in different plays (in different contexts). As we've discussed, nowhere is the choice of how to present ourselves

Figure 4.2 Not All Aspects of Ourselves Are Equally Available When We Communicate Over the Internet

As shown in this cartoon, it may be easier to conceal important information about ourselves on the Internet than in face-to-face encounters.

"On the Internet, nobody knows you're a dog."

more obvious than on social networking sites, such as Facebook (see Figure 4.2). We can choose to reveal a lot about who we think we are—including photographic evidence of ourselves—or we can, to some extent, limit who has access to such information. How much can we really control what others learn about us and the inferences they draw based on that information? In fact, is it possible that others might know more about us—and be better at predicting our behavior—than we are ourselves?

4.1.1: Self–Other Accuracy in Predicting Our Behavior

There are many reasons for assuming that people know themselves better than anyone else does. After all, each of us has access to our internal mental states (e.g., feelings, thoughts, aspirations, and intentions), which others do not (Pronin & Kruger, 2007; Wilson & Dunn, 2004). For this reason alone, it seems intuitively obvious that we must know ourselves best—but is it true? Research evidence suggests that having access to our intentions, which observers do not have, is one reason why we are sometimes inaccurate about ourselves (Chambers, Epley, Savitsky, & Windschitl, 2008). Consider the following example. My friend Shirley is chronically late for *everything*. Frequently, she's more than a half hour late. I simply cannot count on her to be ready when I arrive to pick her up, or for her to arrive on time if we are meeting somewhere. Would she characterize herself that way? Probably not. But, you might ask, how could she *not* know this about herself? Well, it could be precisely because she knows her intentions—she means to be on time and knows the effort she puts into trying to achieve that goal. That information could lead her to believe she *actually* is mostly on time! So, in this instance, I might claim that I know her better than she knows herself because I can predict her behavior more accurately, at least in this domain.

Despite such examples, many people strongly believe that they know themselves better than others know them. Ironically, some of those same people claim they know certain *others* better than those others know themselves (Pronin, Kruger, Savitsky, & Ross, 2001). Part of the problem in determining who is most accurate—ourselves or others who are close to us—has been due to people reporting both their own perceptions and behaviors (see Figure 4.3). As you'll probably agree, behavioral self-reports are hardly an *objective* criterion for determining accuracy. Continuing with the example of Shirley, she'd likely admit to being occasionally late, but she would also say that she always tries hard to be on time. She might even recall a few instances when that was true. So how can the self–other accuracy problem be addressed?

Vazire and Mehl (2008) found a clever way to deal with the problem of collecting both self-perceptions and behavior frequencies from the same source. To develop a more objective index of how a person actually behaves on a daily basis, these researchers had participants wear a digital audio recorder with a microphone that recorded the ambient sounds of people's lives during waking hours. Recordings were automatically made approximately every 12.5 minutes for 4 days. Research assistants later coded the recorded sounds according to the categories shown in Table 4.1. Before

Figure 4.3 The Difficulty in Trying to Predict Ourselves

There is a basic problem in trying to predict ourselves: We are both the experiencer and the predictor. Others may be more accurate at predicting our behavior because they lack access to our intentions and are merely reporting on behavior frequency.

Table 4.1 Who Is More Accurate About Our Behavior: Self or Others?

Often, a close other's ratings and multiple others' ratings of research participants' behavioral frequencies (e.g., attending class) were more strongly related to actual behavioral frequencies than the participant's own self-ratings. So, sometimes we can predict our own behavior better than others can, but not always.

Behavior	Self	Aggregated Informants	Single Informant
With other people	.14	.36**	.30**
On the phone	.37**	.40**	.32**
Talking one-on-one	−.06	.25*	.22*
Talking in a group	.25*	.20*	.25*
Talking to same sex	.34**	.25*	.13
Talking to opposite sex	.31**	.32**	.18
Laughing	.23*	.25*	.13
Singing	.34**	.29**	.34**
Crying	.18	.16	.19
Arguing	.28**	−.05	.09
Listening to music	.40**	.34**	.26*
Watching TV	.55**	.39**	.36**
On the computer	.29**	.31**	.20
At work	.25*	.35**	.22*
Attending class	.07	.33**	.26*
Socializing	.18	.30**	.27*
Indoors	.16	.16	.20
Outdoors	.11	.05	.10
Commuting	.27**	.16	.14
At a coffee shop/bar/restaurant	.27**	.15	.24*

SOURCE: Based on research by Vazire & Mehl, 2008.

Level of statistical significance: $*p < .05$, $**p < .01$

the participants' actual behaviors were recorded, they provided self-ratings (predictions) concerning the frequency they expected to perform each behavior (more or less than the average person) on a daily basis. For every participant, the researchers also recruited three informants who knew the participant well (e.g., friends, parents, romantic partners). These informants provided the same type of ratings: They predicted the frequency the participant would engage in each behavior, using the same average person as comparison. As you can see in Table 4.1, sometimes the participants' own ratings were more strongly related to the frequency of their actual behavior. However, sometimes others' ratings of the participants were more strongly related to actual behavior. So, at times, other people do seem to "know" us better than we know ourselves.

Although people routinely show biases in their self-perceptions, to what extent are they aware they might be biased? Bollich, Rogers, and Vazire (2015) attempted to answer this difficult question in the following way. Participants were asked to rate themselves on 10 desirable traits (e.g., extraverted, warm, dependable, intelligent, funny, and physically attractive). The researchers then e-mailed several of each participant's peers to have them rate the person on those same traits. Four days later, participants were asked to indicate whether they had been biased (e.g., more favorable or more unfavorable) when they previously provided trait ratings about themselves.

Virtually everyone reported they had been biased—either positively or negatively—on at least one trait they had previously rated. Further, most of the perceived bias was indicated by people who admitted they may have been "overly positive" about themselves. When people's own self-perceptions were correlated with those of their peers' perceptions of them, little correspondence was found. However, when people's own ratings and their perceived bias were correlated, a strong relationship was obtained. So, we appear not to be so accurate about ourselves (at least according to our peers). But we tend to recognize when we've rated ourselves too highly on positive traits when later given the chance to consider our bias.

4.1.2: Self-Presentation Tactics

What methods do we use when we are trying to affect the impression that others form of us? First of all, people often try to ensure that others form impressions of them based on their most favorable self-aspects; that is, they engage in **self-promotion**. If we want others to think we're smart, we can emphasize our intelligence "credentials"—grades obtained, awards won, and degrees sought. If we want others to conclude we are fun, we can tell jokes, or talk about the great parties we've attended or hosted. As Figure 4.4 suggests, sometimes these tactics work. If we say we're really good at something, people will often believe us. Self-promotion may even help convince ourselves that what we say is true!

Considerable research from a **self-verification perspective**—the processes we use to lead others to agree with our own self-views—suggests that negotiation occurs in attempts to get others to agree with our self-claims (Swann, 2005). For example, while trading self-relevant information with a potential roommate, you might stress the student part of your self-concept. That is, you would probably emphasize your good study habits and pride in your good grades and underplay your fun-loving qualities. This potential roommate might even note that "You don't sound like you're very interested in having fun here at college." To gain that person's agreement with your most central self-perception—serious student—you may even be willing to entertain a negative assessment of your fun quotient, as long as the other person is willing to go along with your self-assessment of the dimension most critical to you. In

---

Figure 4.4 Self-Promotion: Convincing Others We Are as Good as We Claim

By claiming we are good at something—promoting ourselves—we can often get others to believe us.

this instance, it may be especially useful for you to downplay your own partying skills so that the other person can achieve distinctiveness on this dimension. Indeed, in this interaction, the potential roommate might wish to emphasize his or her party side. Through this sort of self-presentational exchange process, you may "buy" the roommate's self-assessment as a party type, to the extent that it helps you to "sell" your own self-assessment as an excellent student.

According to the self-verification view, we may still wish to have other people—particularly those closest to us—see us as we see ourselves, even if it means potentially receiving information that is negative about ourselves (Swann & Bosson, 2010). Suppose you are certain that you lack athletic ability, are shy, or lack math skills. Even though these attributes might be seen as relatively negative compared to their alternatives—athletic star, extroverted, or math whiz—you might prefer to have people see you consistent with how you see yourself. Research has revealed that, when given a choice, we prefer to be with other people who verify our views about ourselves rather than with those who fail to verify our dearly held self-views—even if those are not so flattering (Chen, Chen, & Shaw, 2004). However, there are real limits to this effect. As Swann and Bosson (2010) note, people who fear they are low in physical attractiveness do not appreciate close others who verify this self-view!

We can also choose to create a favorable self-presentation by conveying our positive regard for others. It is most assuredly true that we like to feel that others respect us, and we really like those who convey this to us (Tyler & Blader, 2000). To achieve this end, you can present yourself to others as someone who particularly values or respects them. In general, when we want to make a good impression on others, it can be useful to employ **ingratiation** tactics. Although, as suggested in the cartoon shown in Figure 4.5, it is possible to overdo it. For the most part, though, we can make others like us by praising them. This is generally quite effective unless people suspect our sincerity (Vonk, 1999). To achieve the same effect as ingratiation, we can be **self-deprecating**—imply that we are not as good as the other person, by communicating admiration or by simply lowering an audience's expectations of our abilities.

Self-presentations are not always completely honest. They are at times strategic, and as discussed in Chapter 3, sometimes deceptive. Research indicates that college students report telling lies to other people about twice a day (Kashy & DePaulo, 1996)—frequently to help protect the other person but sometimes to advance their own interests. Consistent with the former possibility, people who tell more lies tend to be more popular. In a study addressing the honesty of self-presentations on the Internet, Ellison, Heino, and Gibbs (2006) concluded that people often attempt to balance the desire to present an authentic sense of self with some "self-deceptive white lies." That is, people's profiles online reflect, to some degree, their "ideal self" rather than their "actual self." Thus, as shown in Figure 4.6, there can be a discrepancy between how we might like to see ourselves and what we are actually like. However, the extent of to which people self-enhance on Facebook (versus other online networking sites) is somewhat limited because people are aware that their Facebook friends know them offline and might realize when they are not telling the truth (Wilson, Gosling, & Graham, 2012).

Figure 4.5 Ingratiation: Presenting Ourselves as Respecting Others

We can usually get others to like us by using ingratiation tactics, such as communicating our respect for them. However, ingratiation can backfire if we are perceived as being insincere or excessive.

"A simple 'Thank You' would suffice."

Figure 4.6 Discrepancy Between Our Ideal and Actual Selves

People's online profiles on many networking sites may be closer to their ideal selves than to their actual selves.

Key Points

- Facebook is an important medium through which we present ourselves to others. Like offline communication, people attempt to portray themselves on Facebook a little more positively than they are in reality.
- Even though we have access to information (intentions, goals) that others do not, that information itself may bias our own behavioral self-reports. Research that independently recorded people's actual behavior revealed that sometimes others can predict our own behavior better than we can, but sometimes the reverse is true.
- We can choose various self-presentational strategies—including **self-promotion**, **self-deprecation**, and

ingratiation tactics—as means of making a positive impression on others. We can also agree with others' preferred self-presentations so that they will in turn agree with our own self-views, as a means of achieving **self-verification**.
- Sometimes we are less than perfectly honest with other people, and this is often rewarded with greater popularity. On many social networking sites, we tend to present ourselves in terms of our "ideal" self rather than our "actual" self, although this discrepancy is relatively small on Facebook because we know our friends there offline first.

Figure 4.7 Self-Help Books Recommend Introspection

Many popular books imply that the route to self-knowledge lies in introspection, but recent research reveals that such self-reflection can be misleading. Depending on the nature of the factors that are actually driving our behavior, introspection may misdirect us about why we respond as we do.

4.2: Self-Knowledge: Determining Who We Are

Objective **Explain how we arrive at an understanding of our own selves**

We now turn to some of the ways we use to gain self-knowledge. One straightforward method is to try to directly analyze ourselves. Another method is to try to see ourselves as we think others see us—to take an observer's perspective on the self. We will first consider the consequences of both these approaches, and then explore what social psychological research says about how to know ourselves better.

4.2.1: Introspection: Looking Inward to Discover the Causes of Our Own Behavior

People often assume that **introspection**—privately thinking about the factors that made us who we are—is a useful way to learn about the self. In a host of self-help books that sell millions of copies per year (see Figure 4.7), we are told time and again that the best way to get to know ourselves is by looking inward. Indeed, many people in our society believe that the more we introspect—particularly the more we examine the reasons why we act as we do—the greater the self-understanding we will achieve. Is this really the best way to arrive at an accurate understanding of ourselves?

First of all, considerable social psychological research has revealed that we do not always know or have conscious access to the reasons for our actions. However, we can certainly generate—after the fact—what might seem to be logical theories of why we acted as we did (Nisbett & Wilson, 1977). Because we often genuinely don't know why we feel a particular way, generating reasons (which might be inaccurate) could cause us to arrive at false conclusions. In a series of introspection studies, Wilson and Kraft (1993) illustrated how this effect can happen. Participants were asked to describe their feelings about a wide range of topics, from "why I feel as I do about my romantic partner" to "why I like one type of jam over another." After introspecting about the reasons for their feelings, people changed their attitudes, at least temporarily, to match their stated reasons. As you might imagine, this can lead to incorrect inferences because the original feelings—based on other factors entirely—are still there. So, thinking about reasons for our actions can misdirect our quest for self-knowledge when our behavior is really driven by our feelings.

Another way in which introspection might be rather misleading to us is when we attempt to predict our future feelings in response to some event, what researchers call "affective forecasting." Try imagining how you would feel living in a new city, being fired from your job, or living with another person for many years. When we are not in these specific circumstances, we might not be able to accurately predict how we would respond when we are in them, and this applies to both positive and negative future circumstances.

Why is it we have so much difficulty predicting our future responses? When we think about something terrible happening to us and try to predict how we would feel 1 year after the event, we are likely to focus exclusively on the awfulness of that event and neglect all the other factors that will almost certainly contribute to our happiness level as the year progresses (Gilbert & Wilson, 2000). Consequently, people tend to predict that they would feel much worse than they actually would when the future arrives. Likewise, for positive events, if we focus on only that great future event, we will mispredict our happiness as being considerably higher than the actual moderate feelings that are likely 1 year later. In the case of predicting our responses to such positive events in the future, miscalculation would occur because we are unlikely to consider the daily hassles we are also likely to experience in the future, and those would most definitely moderate how we actually feel.

Let's consider another important way in which introspection can lead us astray. Think now about whether spending money on a gift for someone else or spending that same amount of money on something for yourself would make you happier. If you are like most people, you are likely to think that buying something cool for yourself would make you happier than using your money to buy something for someone else. But, yet, recent research has revealed exactly the opposite—that spending money on others makes us happier than spending money on ourselves! In a nationally representative sample of Americans, Dunn, Aknin, and Norton (2008) asked respondents to rate how happy they were and to indicate how much of their monthly income they spend on expenses and gifts for themselves versus gifts for others and donations to charity. Overall, of course, people spent more on themselves than on others, but the important question is which actually predicts respondents' happiness? These researchers found that personal spending was unrelated to happiness, but that more spending on others predicted greater happiness. This was true regardless of people's level of annual income—so whether you are rich or poor, there seems to be a happiness bonus for giving to others that has been observed across very different cultures (Aknin et al., 2013).

But, you might say, this was a correlational study and therefore we can't be sure that spending on others causally drove respondents' happiness. So, Dunn et al. (2008) performed a simple but telling experiment. They had psychology students rate their happiness in the morning and then they were given either $5 or $20 that they had to spend by 5 P.M. that same day. Half of the participants were told to spend that money on a personal bill or gift for themselves, while the other half were told to spend the money on a charitable donation or gift for someone else. Which group was happier at the end of the day?

Regardless of the amount of money they were given to spend, participants reported significantly greater happiness when they spent their windfall on others compared to those who spent it on themselves. This experiment provides clear evidence that how we choose to spend our money is more important for our happiness—and in a counterintuitive direction—than is how much money we make. However, new participants who were asked to simply estimate which condition would bring them greater happiness overwhelmingly thought that spending the money on themselves would make them happier than would spending it on others. And, those who simply estimated how they would feel reported that receiving $20 would bring greater happiness than receiving the $5. But, neither of these self-predictions turned out to be true! What this means is that we often don't know how events will affect us and simply introspecting about it will not help us learn how events actually do affect our emotions and behavior.

4.2.2: The Self from the Observer's Standpoint

As we saw in an earlier section of this chapter, sometimes other people are more accurate in predicting our behavior than we are. So, one way that we can attempt to learn about ourselves is by taking an "observer" perspective on own past. Because actors and observers differ in their focus of attention, and observers are less likely to be swayed by knowing our intentions and so forth, they could potentially have greater insight into when we will behave as we have done in the past. In contrast, as actors, we direct our attention outwardly, and tend to attribute behavior more to situational causes (e.g., it was the traffic that made me late, or the phone rang just as I was going out). Observers, though, focus their attention directly on the actor, and they tend to attribute more dispositional causes for the same behavior (see Chapter 3 for more on actor-observer differences). Therefore, if we take an observer's perspective on ourselves, we should be more likely to characterize ourselves in dispositional or trait terms. Pronin and Ross (2006) found this to be true when people were asked to describe themselves as they were 5 years ago or as they are today. The self in the present was seen as varying with different situations and was characterized less frequently in terms of general dispositions or traits than was the past self. As shown in Figure 4.8, this was the case regardless of the actual age of the participants (and therefore the length of their pasts). Both middle-aged and college-aged participants saw themselves in terms of consistent traits (as observers tend to) when they were describing themselves in the past compared to when they were describing their present selves.

How might considering ourselves from an observer's perspective change the way we characterize ourselves and therefore provide self-insight? Pronin and Ross (2006) used different types of acting techniques as a method for examining how considering ourselves from an observer's perspective changes how we characterize ourselves. The participants were divided into two groups and given "acting" instructions using one of two methods. In the "method-acting" condition, they were told that the goal was to "feel as if you *are* this other person." In the "standard-acting" condition, they were told that the goal was to "put on a performance so that you *appear* to others as though you are this person." After practicing various scenes using their assigned method, the participants were then told to enact a family dinner when they were 14 years old. In this case, everyone played their past self from one of two perspectives: One group was told to play their past self from the perspective of someone experiencing it, and the other group was told to play their past self as if they were an outside observer. Again, the number of consistent dispositions or traits used to describe their 14-year-old self was the central measure of interest: Did taking an observer stance on the self lead to greater trait consistency perceptions of the self? The answer was a clear yes. Those who performed with the method-actor technique were more actor-like and perceived themselves as more variable, whereas those who played themselves from a more "observer-acting" perspective perceived themselves in terms of consistent traits. So, when we try to

Figure 4.8 Selves Across Time: Taking an Observer's Perspective on One's Past Self

In both college students and middle-aged people, the past self is described in more trait terms—as observers do—compared to the present self.

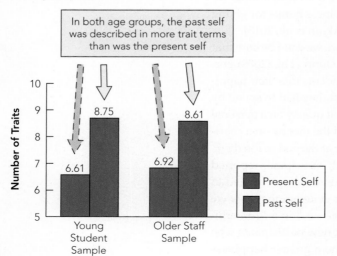

learn about the self from the vantage point of another, we are more likely to see ourselves as observers do—in terms of consistent behavioral tendencies. So, one way to gain self-insight is to try to see ourselves as others do, and consider the possibility that they are more right than we are!

But, is all introspection inevitably misleading? No. It depends on *what* we introspect about. When the behavior in question is actually based on a conscious decision-making process—and is not based on unconscious emotional factors—thinking about those reasons might well lead to accurate self-judgments. On the other hand, when we fail to take into account factors that really do influence how we feel (e.g., giving to others can make us happy), introspection is unlikely to lead to accurate self-inferences. So, while looking inward can be helpful, it may lead us astray under plenty of circumstances. When asked, people can easily generate reasons for why they do what they do, but those reasons may be based on self-theories about the causes of behavior, and, as we saw with the effects of spending money on ourselves versus others, those theories may not be correct! By relying on such theories, we may remain unaware of the real reasons, for example, emotional factors, that cause our behavior. It is also the case that most of us may not have very good theories about how thinking about emotional events will affect us. For example, research (Koo, Algoe, Wilson, & Gilbert, 2008) has revealed that rather than thinking about positive outcomes that have happened to us, if instead we think about how those same positive outcomes might *not* have happened to us at all, we will feel happier. So, it is fair to say that gaining insight into one's own emotions, motivations, and behaviors can be tricky indeed.

Key Points

- One common method by which we attempt to gain self-knowledge is through **introspection**—looking inwardly to assess and understand why we do what we do.
- When it comes to self-queries about why we acted as we did, mistaken results can occur if we do not have conscious access to the factors that actually influenced our responses, although after the fact we can and do construct explanations that seem plausible to us.
- When it comes to predicting how we might feel in the future, we fail to take into account other events that

will moderate how we will feel besides the extreme and isolated event being judged.
- Most people believe that spending money on themselves will make them happier than spending the same amount on others. But, research demonstrates that the opposite is true. What this means is we often don't know how our actions will affect us and introspecting about it won't help.
- One way self-reflection can be helpful is to take an observer's stand point on our behavior. Doing so leads us to see ourselves in more trait-like consistent terms, as observers tend do.

4.3: Personal Identity Versus Social Identity

Objective   **Use the personal-versus-social identity continuum to understand how different identities affect our behavior**

According to **social identity theory** (Tajfel & Turner, 1986), we can perceive ourselves differently at any given moment in time, depending on where we are on the **personal-versus-social identity continuum**. At the personal end of this continuum, we think of ourselves primarily as individuals. At the social end, we think of ourselves as members of specific social groups. We do not experience all aspects of our self-concept simultaneously; where we place ourselves on this continuum at any given moment will influence how we think about ourselves. This momentary **salience**—the part of our identity that is the focus of our attention—can affect much in terms of how we perceive ourselves, and respond to others.

When our personal identity is salient and we think of ourselves as unique individuals, this results in self-descriptions that emphasize how we differ from other individuals. For example, you might describe yourself as fun when thinking of yourself at the personal identity level—to emphasize your self-perception as having more of this attribute than other individuals you are using as the comparison. Personal identity self-description can be thought of as an **intragroup comparison**—involving comparisons with other individuals who share our group membership. For this reason, when describing the personal self, which group is the referent can affect the content of our self-descriptions (Oakes, Haslam, & Turner, 1994; Reynolds et al., 2010). Consider how you might characterize yourself if you were asked to describe how you are different from others. You could describe yourself as particularly liberal if you were comparing yourself to your parents, but if you were indicating how you are different from other college students you might say that you are rather conservative. The point is that even for personal identity, the content we generate to describe ourselves depends on some comparison, and this can result in us thinking about and describing ourselves differently—in this example as either liberal or conservative—depending on the comparative context.

At the social identity end of the continuum, perceiving ourselves as members of a group means we emphasize what we share with other group members. We describe ourselves in terms of the attributes that differentiate our group from another comparison group. Descriptions of the self at the social identity level are **intergroup comparisons** in nature—they involve contrasts between groups. For example, when your social identity as a fraternity or sorority group member is salient, you may ascribe traits to yourself that you share with other members of your group. Attributes of athleticism and self-motivation might, for example, differentiate your group from other fraternities or sororities that you see as being more studious and scholarly than your group. For many people, their gender group is another important social identity and, when salient, can affect self-perceptions. So, if you are female and your gender is salient, you might perceive the attributes that you believe you share with other women (e.g., warm and caring) and that you perceive as differentiating women from men as self-descriptive. Likewise, if you are male, when gender is salient, you might think of yourself (i.e., self-stereotype) in terms of attributes that are believed to characterize men and that differentiate them from women (e.g., independent, strong).

What's important to note here is that when you think of yourself as an individual, the content of your self-description is likely to differ from when you are thinking of yourself as a member of a category that you share with others. Of course, most of us are members of a variety of different groups (e.g., gender, occupation, age, sexual orientation, nationality, sports teams), but all of these will not be salient at the same time, and they may differ considerably in how important they are to us. But, when a particular social identity is salient, people are likely to act in ways that reflect that aspect of their self-concept. So a number of situational factors may alter how we define ourselves, and the actions that stem from those self-definitions will differ accordingly. Figure 4.9 summarizes the processes involved and consequences of experiencing the self in personal rather than social identity terms.

Because, at any given time, we can define ourselves differently, this means we have many "selves." Can we say that one of these is the "true" self—either the personal self or any one of a person's potential social identities? Not really. All of these could be correct portraits of the self and accurately predict behavior, depending on the context and comparison dimension (Oakes & Reynolds, 1997; Reynolds et al., 2010). Note, too, how some ways of thinking about ourselves could even imply behaviors that are opposite to those that would result from other self-descriptions (e.g., fun versus scholarly; liberal versus conservative).

Figure 4.9 The Personal-Versus-Social Identity Continuum

Depending on whether we define ourselves in terms of our personal or social identity, self-content will be the result of an intragroup or intergroup comparison. Our identity experience will be either as an individual or as a member of a social group.

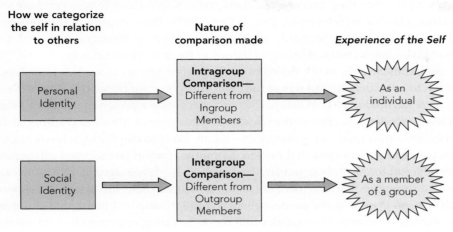

Despite such potential variability in self-definition, most of us manage to maintain a coherent image of ourselves, while recognizing that we may define ourselves and behave differently in different situations. This can occur either because the domains in which we see ourselves as inconsistent are deemed to be relatively unimportant, or they simply are not salient when we think of ourselves in terms of any particular identity (Patrick, Neighbors, & Knee, 2004). We'll have more to say below on how people manage conflict among the different aspects of the self.

4.3.1: Who I Think I Am Depends on the Social Context

People do describe themselves differently depending on whether the question they are asked implies a specific situation or is more open-ended. This effect was illustrated by Mendoza-Denton, Ayduk, Mischel, Shoda, and Testa (2001). In their study, participants were given one of two different types of sentence completion tasks. When the prompt was open-ended, such as "I am a(n) . . . person," self-definition as an individual is implied. In this condition, participants' responses were primarily trait-like and global (e.g., "I am an ambitious person"). When, however, the prompt implied particular settings, "I am a(n) . . . when . . . " then the responses were more contingent on the situation considered by the participant (e.g., "I am an ambitious person when a professor provides me with a challenge").

People also differ across time and place in the extent to which they emphasize the personal self and its uniqueness from others. For example, a recent analysis of the names given to the 325 million American babies born between 1880 and 2007 indicates that parents have increasingly, across time, given their children less common names, with this trend escalating particularly after 1980 (Twenge, Abebe, & Campbell, 2010). Presumably, it is easier to—and there's a greater expectancy that you will—differentiate yourself from others when you have a unique name that you do not share with them. This shift away from common given names, which was observed across all ethnic groups, has been reflected in an increasing emphasis on individualism across this century, with Americans increasingly endorsing individualistic traits for themselves (Twenge, Konrath, Foster, Campbell, & Bushman, 2008).

How might the social context serve to cue social identities that differentially emphasize the personal self and individualism? Research has revealed that bilingual

Asian students living in Hong Kong answer the question, "Who am I?" when it is asked in English in terms of personal traits that differentiate them from others, reflecting an individualistic self-construal. However, when they are asked the same question in Chinese, these bilingual students describe themselves in terms of group memberships that they share with others, reflecting a more interdependent self-construal (Trafimow, Silverman, Fan, & Law, 1997). Thus, important differences in self-descriptions emerge primarily when a particular group identity is activated, as it was in this example, when thinking of the self in English versus Chinese.

Such context shifts in self-definition can influence how we categorize ourselves in relation to other people, and this in turn, can affect how we respond to others (Ryan, David, & Reynolds, 2004). When participants categorize a person in need as a fellow university student—so that person is seen as a member of the same category as the participant—then men and women were equally likely to display high levels of care-oriented responses toward that person. In contrast, when participants categorized themselves in terms of their gender, then women displayed significantly more care-oriented responses than did men. In fact, men reduced their care-oriented responses to the person in need in the gender salient condition compared to the shared university-identity condition. Thus gender differences in caring responses toward another individual depend on gender being a salient category. Of course, gender is a powerful social category that is likely to be activated a great deal of the time (Fiske & Stevens, 1993). This means it is likely to influence perceptions of the self and our responses to others with some frequency.

Not only must gender be salient for gender differences in **self-construal** or how we characterize ourselves to emerge, but research (Guimond et al., 2007) has also revealed that how we perceive ourselves depends on which gender group is the comparison. In a five-nation study, these investigators found that only when men and women were asked to compare themselves to members of the other gender group (an intergroup comparison was made) did they display the expected gender difference in rated self-insecurity. That is, when women compared themselves to men they said they were insecure, and when men compared themselves to women they said they were not insecure. In this case, people saw themselves as consistent with their own gender group's stereotype. However as shown in Figure 4.10, when the same self-judgments were made in an intragroup group context—where women compared their standing on this trait to other women and men compared their standing to other men—no gender differences in perceived insecurity of the self were found. So, how we see ourselves—in terms of what traits we have—depends on the comparison we use when assessing ourselves.

WHEN AND WHY SOME ASPECTS OF THE SELF ARE MORE SALIENT THAN OTHERS.   What determines which aspect of the self will be most influential at any given moment? This is an important question precisely because the self-aspect that is salient can have a major impact on our self-perceptions and behavior.

First, one aspect of the self might be especially relevant to a particular context (e.g., thinking of ourselves as fun when at a party but as hard working when we are at work). Second, features of the context can make one aspect of the self highly distinctive, with that aspect of identity forming the basis of self-perception. Suppose an office has only one woman among several men. In this context, the woman's gender distinguishes her from her colleagues and is therefore likely to be frequently salient. Thus the lone woman is particularly likely to feel "like a

Figure 4.10 Measuring Gendered Self-Perceptions Around the World

In a cross-cultural study of 950 participants from five nations (France, Belgium, Malaysia, The Netherlands, and USA), gender differences in perceiving the self as insecure were present *only* when people compared themselves to members of the other gender group; no significant gender difference was found when the self was compared to members of their own gender group.

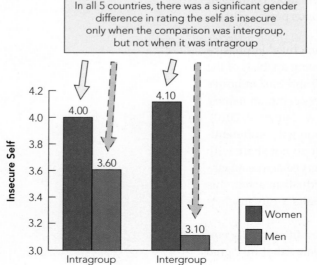

woman," and she may be treated based on the stereotype of that group (Fuegen & Biernat, 2002; Yoder & Berendsen, 2001). Similarly, African American students at predominantly Caucasian universities where other minority group members are rare are likely to think of themselves in terms of their race (Pollak & Niemann, 1998; Postmes & Branscombe, 2002).

Third, some people may be more ready to categorize themselves in terms of a particular personal trait (e.g., intelligence) or social identity (e.g., gender) because of its importance to the self. People who are highly identified with their national group (e.g., Americans) are more reactive to threat to that identity than are people who are less identified (Branscombe & Wann, 1994).

Fourth, other people, including how they refer to us linguistically, can cue us to think of ourselves in personal-versus-social identity terms. Aspects of the self-concept that are referred to as nouns (e.g., woman, student) are particularly likely to activate social identities (Simon, 2004). Nouns suggest discrete categories, which trigger perceptions of members of those categories as sharing a fundamental nature or essence that is different from members of other categories (Lickel, Hamilton, & Sherman, 2001). In contrast, aspects of the self that are referred to with either adjectives or verbs (e.g., athletic, taller, extremely supportive) reference perceived differences between people within a category (Turner & Onorato, 1999) and are especially likely to elicit self-perceptions at the personal identity level.

EMOTIONAL CONSEQUENCES WHEN CHOICES ARE MADE BY DIFFERENT SELVES. Have you ever had the experience of buying something new and later, after getting it home, you think, "What on earth was I thinking when I selected that?" Well, you are not alone! Research by LeBoeuf, Shafir, and Bayuk (2010) has illuminated this postconsumer regret process, explaining it in terms of different salient selves at the time the purchase is made and when you later experience it. Let's see how this process could play out with your student identity.

While most students come to college to develop their intellectual skills, this stage of life also involves developing the social side of oneself. To test whether the salience of these differing aspects of an identity affects the choices we make, LeBoeuf et al. (2010) first made one of these aspects of the student identity salient by asking participants to take a survey about world issues (the "Scholar" identity condition) or about campus socializing (the "Socialite" condition). Participants were then given an opportunity to choose from different consumer items—magazines in this study. When the scholar aspect of their identity was salient, the students chose more scholarly publications (e.g., *The Economist, Wall Street Journal*), but selected more social publications (e.g., *Cosmopolitan, Sports Illustrated*) in the Socialite condition. In a subsequent study, the same pattern of results was obtained when Chinese Americans first thought of themselves in terms of their Chinese identity ("think of your favorite Chinese holiday") or their American identity ("think of your favorite American holiday). In this case, those whose American self-aspect was salient chose cars that were more unique in color, whereas those whose Chinese self-aspect was salient chose more traditional car colors. These studies illustrate that the aspect of ourselves that is salient can affect our consumer choices.

But, what about the issue of satisfaction (or regret) over the choices we have already made? Does the degree of satisfaction we experience depend on there being a match between the self-aspect that is salient when the choice is made and the self-aspect that is salient when the choice is experienced or evaluated? To answer this question, LeBoeuf et al. (2010) again made their participants' student identity—either the scholarly or socializing aspect—salient. This was again done simply by giving participants a survey about "world issues" to activate the scholarly self, or a survey about "campus life" to activate the socialite self. At this point, participants were asked to choose a film to watch. Once the film choice was made, but before watching the film clip, their original or the other self-aspect was made salient—students were reminded of their scholarly self by asking about their interest in attending graduate school or their socialite self by asking about their interest in various university sports teams.

As can be seen in Figure 4.11, participants who watched the film that they chose when the same identity aspect was salient, enjoyed the experience, liked the film, and did not regret their choice, whereas those whose identities in each time period were inconsistent with each other did not enjoy the experience, disliked the film more, and regretted their choice. These findings indicate that our choices and experiences stemming from them can depend on which aspect of our selves is salient, and they go some way toward explaining that question we have to occasionally ask ourselves—"what was I thinking when I selected that option?"

4.3.2: Who I Am Depends on Others' Treatment

How others treat us, and how we believe they will treat us in the future, have important implications for how we think about ourselves. When it comes to the self, no one is truly an island. If we expect that others will reject us because of some aspect of ourselves, there are a few response options available to us (Tajfel, 1978). To the extent that it is possible to change an aspect of ourselves and avoid being rejected, we could potentially choose to do that. In fact, we could choose to only change that particular feature when we anticipate being in the presence of others who will reject us because of it. In other words, for some aspects of ourselves, we can attempt to hide them from disapproving others. For example, the U.S. military policy of "don't ask, don't tell" implied there are group identities we can choose to reveal or not. However this option will be practically impossible for some social identities. We can't easily hide or change our race, gender, or age. In some cases, even if we could alter the part of the self that brings rejection, we may rebel against those rejecting us by making that feature even more self-defining. That is, we may emphasize that feature as a method of contrasting ourselves from those who reject us—in effect, we

---

Figure 4.11 When Choices Are Made by Different Salient Selves

Participants who made film choices when one aspect of their identity was salient, but another aspect of their identity was salient at the time they experienced the film, were less positive about the experience than when the identities matched at both time periods. Because identity salience can fluctuate, this is one reason why we can come to regret choices that looked good to us earlier.

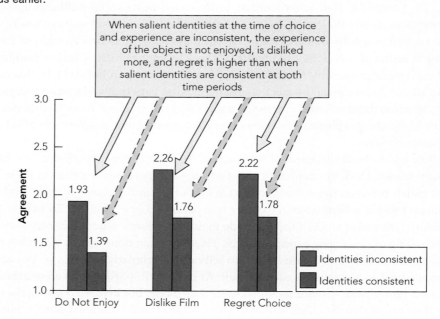

can publicly communicate that we value something different than those who might judge us negatively because of it.

This point was illustrated in research conducted by Jetten, Branscombe, Schmitt, and Spears (2001). These researchers studied young people who elect to get body piercings in visible parts of the body other than earlobes (e.g., navel, tongue, eyebrow), a practice that has gained in popularity. How we dress and alter our bodies can be conceptualized as important identity markers—ways of communicating to the world who we are. Although some identity markers may bring acceptance into peer groups, they may be perceived by other groups as weird or antinormative. Today, getting body piercings and tattoos may be comparable to the wearing of blue jeans and men having long hair in the 1960s. These identity markers were the visible indicator of a "hippie" identity, reflecting a self-perception as a rebel against the establishment. Like their 1960s counterparts, today's young people who opt for visible body piercings and tattoos may be engaged in a similar form of rebel identity construction.

People who get such visible markings often know that they are likely to be discriminated against because of them. This expectation can lead to stronger self-definition in terms of a social identity that is actively rejecting the dominant culture's standards of beauty. An expectation of rejection and devaluation on the part of the culture as a whole can result in increasingly strong identification with a newly forming cultural group. Those with body piercings who were led to expect rejection from the mainstream, identified more strongly with other people who have body piercings than did those who were led to expect acceptance from the mainstream (Jetten et al., 2001). As Figure 4.12 illustrates, people with lots of body piercings and tattoos seem to be communicating that "we are different from the mainstream." If the practice of getting body piercings ultimately becomes diffused throughout the culture—as happened when everyone started wearing blue jeans—then those who are attempting to convey their collective difference from the mainstream may be compelled to become increasingly more extreme to achieve the same identity end. For more information about the importance of group identities for psychological well-being, see our special feature, **"What Research Tells Us About…The Importance of Belonging and Group Ties."**

Figure 4.12 Claiming an Identity That Is "Nonmainstream"

Many forms of body adornment and body modification are visual indicators of how we see ourselves—our identities. These people may be conveying to the "mainstream" that they are not one of them, and that they want to "fit in" with their peer group.

What Research Tells Us About...

The Importance of Belonging and Group Ties

Feeling that you belong, by being part of groups that you value is critical for psychological and physical health. For example, research following adolescents from age 13 through adulthood (ages 25–27) has found that being close with one's peer "pack" in adolescence predicts greater overall physical health across time, even when controlling for a variety of factors associated with health (Allen, Uchino, & Hafen, 2015). Indeed, feeling you don't belong with your peer group is associated with abnormal patterns of brain activation (elevated amygdala responses), a clear marker of stress (Berns et al., 2005) that is referred to as "the pain of independence."

Are the benefits of group ties for health limited to those who are young? Recent research with elderly adults (age 60 and older) provides evidence of their importance for cognitive health—measures assessing memory and intellectual ability—and emotional health in terms of lowering anxiety (Gleibs et al., 2011; Haslam, Cruwys, Milne, Kan, & Haslam, 2016). In fact, interventions among depressed older adults show that joining groups can reduce the incidence of depression relapse. Using a large nationally representative sample of British adults, Cruwys et al. (2013) showed that people who were depressed and who belonged to no groups had a 41 percent likelihood of relapse over a 4-year period. If, however, they joined one group their risk of depression relapse was reduced by 24 percent and if they joined three groups their relapse risk dropped by 63 percent.

Does belonging to and feeling you belong to social groups—by promoting positive social identities—have implications for people's self-esteem? Is it primarily group memberships that people identify with that are psychologically important to them—because they define the self—that have the power to boost self-esteem? A series of recent studies with respondents from around the world indicate that this is the case. Among adolescents in both Germany and Israel, having multiple social identifications (e.g., as students, with their family group, with their nation) was positively related to level of personal self-esteem (Benish-Weisman, Daniel, Schiefer, Mollering, & Knafo-Noam, 2015). Moreover, it was social identification that increased self-esteem across time, rather than people with higher self-esteem increasingly valuing their group memberships.

In a series of studies using a wide variety of groups—British school children, residents in a homeless shelter in Australia, elderly persons in China—it was found that the number of group memberships that are important to those respondents predicted their level of self-satisfaction (Jetten et al., 2015). To test whether it is merely having more interpersonal friendships rather than more important group memberships that predict personal self-esteem, these researchers undertook a complete **social network analysis**—where the number of friendship ties between all members of a school population were calculated. How well connected each boy in the network was to others through friendship ties was compared to how many important groups each student belonged to in terms of their ability to predict the boys' level of personal self-esteem. The number of important group memberships predicted self-esteem, while the number of interpersonal ties in the network made no additional contribution. This suggests that it is group memberships that provide people with meaning and the basis for self-definition, which builds personal self-esteem.

Among university students, many do form strong identification with and value their university sports teams, their gender group, and national identity. Jetten et al. (2015) found that among American students personal self-esteem was greater as they highly identified with more of those groups. As Figure 4.13 reveals, not feeling highly identified with any of those groups was associated with lower self-esteem, while increasingly identifying with more of them resulted in higher self-esteem. By locating the self in the greater social world, defining the self in terms of these valued groups provides a basis for feeling good about the self as a worthy individual.

Figure 4.13 Personal Self-Esteem Is Higher When More Groups Are Highly Identified With

American university students who highly identified with more of their social groups such as their gender, university sports team, and nationality reported increasingly greater personal self-esteem.

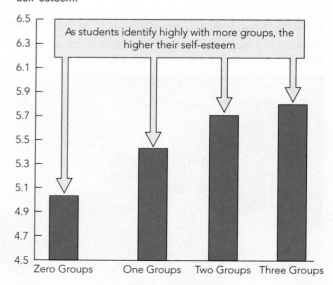

4.3.3: The Self Across Time: Past and Future Selves

Sometimes people think about the ways they have developed and changed across time. Studies of **autobiographical memory** (Wilson & Ross, 2001) have revealed that by strategically comparing our present selves with our past selves, we can feel good about ourselves by perceiving improvement over time. To illustrate this, Ross and Wilson (2003) performed a series of studies in which they asked people to describe a "past self"—either a self that was perceived to be far in the past or one that was more recent. Criticism of the "distant" past self was greater than the self that was perceived as "nearer" to the present. These researchers argued that by derogating our distant past selves, we can feel like we have really grown (i.e., are better now). In contrast, when people feel close in time to some self-failure, the current self is seen less positively than when that same failure is seen as far in the distant past. Consistent with this self-protective idea, when people are asked to write about two memorable life experiences—one in which they were blameworthy and one in which they were praiseworthy—people generated more recent praiseworthy events but described blameworthy events that are further in their past (Escobedo & Adolphs, 2010).

What about self comparisons in the other direction—are there emotional consequences of thinking about future **possible selves**? Thinking about a positively valued possible self can inspire people to forego current activities that are enjoyable but will not help, or might even hinder, bringing about this improved future self (Markus & Nurius, 1986). In this instance, we may forego immediately enjoyable activities to achieve the goal of becoming our desired possible self.

Think about what may be required to attain a valued future self or add a new identity. You may have to give up fun time in order to attain the status of being a college graduate, complete years of schooling and long internships to become a doctor, or put in many grueling hours in law school and study for state bar exams to become a lawyer. Lockwood and Kunda (1999) found that **role models**—other people we wish to imitate or be like—can inspire us to invest in such long-term achievements, but we must see the possible self that the role model represents as being potentially attainable. Receiving parental support for hoped-for future possible academic selves can also help us believe we can attain it (Zhu, Tse, Cheung, & Oyserman, 2014). The image of a possible future self has been found to influence people's motivation to study harder, give up smoking, or invest in parenting classes, when a new and improved self is imagined as likely to result from such changes. We may suffer in the present as long as we believe a more desired future possible self is achievable. The photo in Figure 4.14 shows the joy that can be experienced when a new identity—as a college graduate—is attained.

People also consider how to avoid negative and feared future possible selves, for example, when we are making New Year's resolutions. Polivy and Herman (2000) suggest that envisioning the self-changes required to avoid these outcomes can induce feelings of control and optimism, but failing to keep those resolutions is a common experience and repeated failures can lead to unhappiness. When people feel they want to change but cannot succeed in doing so, they may be tempted to reduce this uncomfortable state of self-awareness by distracting themselves—either in mundane ways such as getting lost in a novel or in more damaging ways such as consuming heavy amounts of alcohol (Baumeister, 1991).

4.3.4: Why Self-Control Can Be Difficult to Achieve

People often want to change themselves by, for example, quitting smoking, going on a diet, or studying more effectively—but they may find it difficult to stick with such long-range goals. Instead, people often succumb to the lure of an immediate reward and break with their prior commitment. In other words, we fail to control ourselves in some meaningful way.

Figure 4.14 Will You Be Celebrating Your New College Graduate Self Soon?

Achieving some possible selves can be hard work, but well worth the effort!

How does the way we think about ourselves affect our success in endeavors that require **self-control**—refraining from actions we might enjoy more—but performing actions we prefer not to if they help us move toward key goals? How difficult is it to maintain our resolve and stick to long-term goals, even though short-term outcomes might be more immediately gratifying? Some researchers have suggested that the act of controlling ourselves is taxing and makes exercising subsequent self-control more difficult. Vohs and Heatherton (2000) have claimed that we have a limited ability to regulate ourselves, and if we use our control resources on unimportant tasks, there will be less available for the important ones. People who are first required to control themselves in some way (e.g., not think about a particular topic, engage in two tasks simultaneously, or control their emotional expression), do less well on later self-control tasks than those who have not had to recently control themselves.

Consider Vohs and Heatherton's study of chronic dieters who have a long history of attempting to resist temptation in the interests of achieving long-term weight loss. When these participants were first placed close to a dish of appealing candy, their ability to self-regulate on a second task was reduced—so they ate more ice cream than those who did not have to first control themselves. So, not only is controlling ourselves sometimes difficult to do in the first place, but after doing so successfully, it can impair our ability to do so again. This means that having to make choices between desirable items (e.g., among consumer goods when shopping)—because you have to stay on a budget—can reduce our ability to engage in self-control at a later time (Vohs et al., 2014).

To the extent that self-control is a finite resource, **ego depletion**—the diminished capacity to exert subsequent self-control after previously doing so—might be expected in many domains requiring self-regulation. A meta-analysis of studies in which ego depletion has occurred (due to effort to exert self-control on a prior task) reports effects on a wide variety of outcomes (Hagger, Wood, Stiff, & Chatzisarantis, 2010). Prior efforts to exert self-control had negative consequences for subsequent self-control efforts including greater subjective fatigue, perceived difficulty of achieving self-control, and lowered blood glucose levels. Ego depletion was least likely to impair subsequent self-control when the initial control effort was shorter rather than longer, when participants had received training in self-regulation, and a rest period occurs between the initial and subsequent self-control tasks. Self-control can also be increased by thinking abstractly about our goals (Fujita & Han, 2009); that is, we have to remind ourselves of our overall goals and plan (e.g., desire to lose weight) rather than the details of what we are doing right now (e.g., not diving into that chocolate cake). To sum up, the ability to control our selves—either to avoid doing what we no longer want to do or staying focused and doing more of what we do want—can be increased, but it appears to take practice, and many factors can undermine development of this skill!

Key Points

- **Social identity theory** indicates that we can think about ourselves differently depending on which aspect of self is salient along the **personal versus social identity continuum**. At the personal end of this continuum, we think of ourselves primarily as individuals. At the social end, we think of ourselves as members of specific social groups. The **salience** of these different aspects of the self can vary with the social context. When the personal self is salient, our behavior is based on **intragroup** contrasts—comparisons with other ingroup members. When the social self is salient, behavior reflects **intergroup** comparisons (contrast with the outgroup). People have multiple social identities, each of which could have rather different implications for behavior, depending on which is activated in a particular context.
- The context that we find ourselves in can alter the aspect of the self that is salient. Gender differences in **self-construal** will be exhibited most when our gender group identity is salient, and they may be absent entirely when another group identity is salient. For example, gender differences in perceived insecurity of the self across five different nations are observed when the self is compared to members of the other gender group but not when the self is compared to members of one's own gender group.
- Several different factors can influence what aspect of the self is salient and influential for our behavior: When the context makes one aspect particularly relevant, when the context makes one distinct from others, when one is of greater importance to us, and others' treatment of us or language use.
- We can regret or be unsatisfied with choices we make when a different self-aspect is salient when we consume the goods compared to when they were selected.

- One response to perceived rejection by others is to emphasize the aspect of one's identity that differentiates the self from those rejecting us. To create a self-perception as a rebel one can take on a feature that differentiates members of one's peer group from the mainstream.
- Feeling that you belong, by being part of groups that you value is critical for psychological and physical health. **Social network analysis**—where ties among all members of a population are assessed—has revealed that what is important for students' well-being is not the number of friends they have but how many groups they belong to that they perceive as important.
- **Autobiographical memory** concerns how we think about ourselves across time. This can be influenced by our motivation to protect ourselves such that we see a negative self as more distant than a positive self. **Possible selves** or those we might become too have motivational properties; they can lead us to forgo immediate rewards in order to become a desired future self. **Role models** can inspire us toward long-term achievements, but we must see that possible self as attainable.
- Groups provide meaning to us and are a basis for self-definition. Images of future possible selves can inspire us to make difficult changes in the present to achieve this more desirable self. **Self-control** has been conceptualized as a limited resource and **ego depletion** following efforts to self-regulate can make it more difficult to exert self-control subsequently. Self-control is most likely to be achieved when we focus on our abstract goals rather than the details of what we are doing right now.

4.4: Social Comparison: How We Evaluate Ourselves

Objective Examine the health implications of being unrealistically optimistic about the self

How do we evaluate ourselves and decide whether we're good or bad in various domains, what our best and worst traits are, and how likable we are to others? Social psychologists believe that all human judgment is relative to some comparison standard (Kahneman & Miller, 1986). So, how we think and feel about ourselves will depend on the standard of comparison we use. To take a simple example, if you compare your ability to complete a puzzle to a child's ability to solve it, you'll probably feel pretty good about your ability. This would represent a **downward social comparison**—where your own performance is compared with someone who is less capable than yourself. On the other hand, if you compare your performance on the same task to a puzzle expert you might not fare so well and not feel so good about yourself. This is the nature of **upward social comparisons**, which tend to be threatening to our self-image. Clearly, being able to evaluate ourselves positively depends on choosing the right standard of comparison!

You might be wondering why we compare ourselves to other people. Festinger's (1954) **social comparison theory** suggests that we compare ourselves to others because for many domains and attributes, there is no objective yardstick to evaluate ourselves against; other people are therefore highly informative. Are we brilliant or average? Charming or not charming? We can't tell by looking into a mirror or introspecting, but perhaps we can acquire useful information about these and many other questions by comparing ourselves to other people. Indeed, feeling uncertain about ourselves is one of the central conditions that lead people to engage in social comparison and otherwise assess the extent to which we are meeting cultural norms (Wood, 1989; van den Bos, 2009).

To whom do we compare ourselves, or how do we decide what standard of comparison to use? It depends on our motive for the comparison. Do we want an accurate assessment of ourselves, or do we want to simply feel good about ourselves? In general, the desire to see ourselves positively appears to be more powerful than either the desire to accurately assess ourselves or to verify strongly held beliefs about ourselves (Sedikides & Gregg, 2003). But, suppose, for the moment, that we really do want an accurate assessment. Festinger (1954) originally suggested we can gauge our abilities most accurately by comparing our performance with someone who is similar to us. But what determines similarity? Do we base it on age, gender, nationality, occupation, year in school, or something else entirely? In general, similarity tends to be based on broad social categories, such as gender, race, age, or experience in a particular task domain (Goethals & Darley, 1977; Wood, 1989).

Often, by using comparisons with others who share a social category with us, we can judge ourselves more positively than when we compare ourselves with others who are members of a different social category (especially if that category is more advantaged than our own). This is partly because there are different performance expectations for members of different categories in particular domains (e.g., children versus adults, men versus women). To the extent that the context encourages us to categorize ourselves as a member of a category with relatively low expectations in a particular domain, we will be able to conclude that we measure up rather well. For example, a woman could console herself by thinking that her salary is "pretty good for a woman," while she would feel considerably worse if she compared her salary to that of men, who on average, are paid more (Reskin & Padavic, 1994; Vasquez, 2001). Self-judgments are often less negative when the standards of our ingroup are used (Biernat, Eidelman, & Fuegen, 2002). Indeed, such ingroup comparisons may protect members of disadvantaged groups from painful social comparisons with members of more advantaged groups (Crocker & Major, 1989; Major, 1994).

Some suggest that the goal of perceiving the self positively is the "master motive" of human beings (Baumeister, 1998). How we achieve the generally positive self-perception that most of us have of ourselves depends on how we categorize ourselves in relation to comparison others (Wood & Wilson, 2003). Such self-categorization influences how particular comparisons affect us by influencing the *meaning* of the comparison. Two influential perspectives on the self—the **self-evaluation maintenance model** and **social identity theory**—both build on Festinger's (1954) original social comparison theory to describe the consequences of social comparison in different contexts.

Self-evaluation maintenance (Tesser, 1988) applies when we categorize the self at the personal level, and we compare ourselves as an individual to another individual. Social identity theory (Tajfel & Turner, 1986) applies when we categorize ourselves at the group level (e.g., as a woman), and the comparison other is categorized as sharing the same category as ourselves. When the context encourages comparison at the group level, the same other person will be responded to differently than when the context suggests a comparison between individuals. For example, another member of our gender group who performs poorly might be embarrassing to our gender identity when we categorize ourselves as also belonging to that group. In contrast, that same poor performing ingroup member could be flattering if we were to compare ourselves personally to that other individual.

Let's consider first what happens in an interpersonal comparison context. When someone with whom you compare yourself outperforms you in an area that is important to you, you may be motivated to distance yourself from the person because this information evokes a relatively painful interpersonal comparison. After all, this other person has done better than you have on something that matters to you. Conversely, when you compare yourself to another person who performs even worse than you, then you will be more likely to align yourself with that other person because the comparison is positive. By performing worse than you, this person makes you look good by comparison. Such psychological movement toward and away from a comparison other who performs better or worse than us illustrates an important means by which positive self-evaluations are maintained when our personal identities are salient.

So, will we always dislike others who do better than us? No—it depends on how we categorize ourselves in relation to the other. According to social identity theory, we are motivated to perceive our groups positively, and this should especially be the case for those who most strongly value a particular social identity. Other people, when categorized as a member of the same group as ourselves, can help make our group more positive when they perform well. Therefore when we think of ourselves at the social identity level, say in terms of a sports team, then a strong performing teammate will enhance our group's identity instead of threatening it.

Therefore, either disliking or liking of the same high performing other person can occur, depending on whether you think of that person as another individual or as someone who shares your group identity. The other's excellent performance has negative implications for you when you compare yourself to her or him as an individual, but positive implications for you when you compare members of your group to those of another group.

To test this idea that different responses to a person can occur, Schmitt, Silvia, and Branscombe (2000) first selected participants for whom the performance dimension was relevant to the self; that is, they selected participants who said that being creative was important to them. Responses to another person who performs better or equally poorly as the self should depend on how you categorize yourself—at the individual level or at the social identity level. As shown in Figure 4.15, when participants believed their performance as an individual would be compared to the other person, they liked the poor performing target more than the high performing target who represented a threat to their positive personal self-image. In contrast, when participants categorized themselves in terms of the gender group that they shared with that person and the expected comparison was intergroup in nature (between women and men), then the high performing other woman was evaluated more positively than the similar-to-self poor performing other. Why? Because this talented person made the participants' group—women—look good. Because different contexts can induce us to categorize ourselves as an individual or as a member of a group, it has important implications for the effects that upward and downward social comparisons will have on self-evaluation.

Figure 4.15 How Much Do We Like Another Who Performs Better or Worse Than the Self?

Research indicates that liking depends on whether the context is interpersonal, where the personal self is at stake, or intergroup, with the social self at stake. As illustrated here, a low performing other is liked best in an interpersonal context and a high performing other is liked best in an intergroup context.

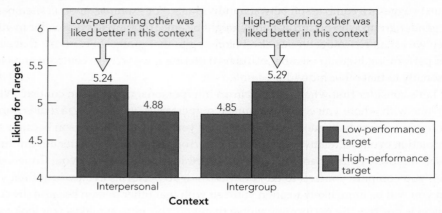

4.4.1: Self-Serving Biases and Unrealistic Optimism

Most people want to feel positively about themselves, and there are a number of strategies that can be used to ensure we see ourselves favorably much of the time. Many of us show the **above average effect**—we think we are better than the average person on almost every dimension imaginable (Alicke, Vredenburg, Hiatt, & Govorun, 2001; Klar, 2002). Even people who are known to be objectively low on certain traits show self-enhancement! For example, people convicted of violence and theft-related crimes rate themselves as better than the average community member in terms of morality, kindness to others, generosity, trustworthiness, and honesty (Sedikides, Meek, Alicke, & Taylor, 2014). These and other findings make clear that people's tendency to see themselves as better than others (in terms of both their traits and abilities) is motivated; indeed the extent to which people do so predicts increases in self-esteem across time (Zuckerman & O'Loughlin, 2006).

Even when we are directly provided with negative social feedback that contradicts our typically rosy view of ourselves, people show evidence of forgetting such instances and emphasizing information that supports their favored positive self-perceptions (Sanitioso & Wlodarski, 2004). Likewise, information that might imply we are responsible for negative outcomes is assessed critically, and our ability to refute such arguments appears to be rather remarkable (Greenwald, 2002).

In contrast to our resistance to accepting responsibility for negative outcomes, we easily accept information that suggests we are responsible for our successes. Not only do people show self-serving biases for their personal outcomes, but they do so also for their group's achievements. Fans of sports teams often believe that their presence and cheering was responsible for their team's success (Wann & Branscombe, 1993). It turns out that, on the whole, we are unrealistically optimistic, and this has implications for our mental and physical health. A classic paper by Taylor and Brown (1988) documented the many forms of positive illusions that people hold. By illusion, we do not mean grandiose beliefs about the self—as might be found in some forms of psychopathology. Rather, "unrealistic optimism," for example, involves seeing our own chances for success in life as *slightly higher* than our peers' chances. Of course, it cannot be true that all of us have higher likelihoods of successful life outcomes than our peers—we are not living in Garrison Keillor's Lake Wobegon, so we can't all be "above average."

Sorrentino and colleagues (2005) showed such optimism was not limited to North Americans, but is also found among the Japanese. In fact, such optimism is on the rise among Americans. For example, expectations among high school students that they will obtain a graduate degree rose to 50 percent by 2006, a number that is dramatically higher than the actual percentage that will do so (Twenge & Campbell, 2008). In a more mundane realm, Taylor (1989) notes that people's daily things-to-do lists are a "poignant example" of the unrealistic optimism phenomenon. We routinely fail to get even half of what's on our list accomplished (that's certainly true for my life!), but we repeat the same behavior day after day, oblivious to how unrealistic our plans are and continuing to expect to get everything on our list done.

Taylor and Brown (1988) documented the connection between positive illusions and contentment, confidence, and feelings of personal control. People who believe they can finish their to-do lists are more likely to proceed with feelings of self-efficacy and higher motivation than people who are more realistic. Thus higher motivation and greater persistence are associated with unrealistic optimism—and these lead to higher levels of performance on average and greater feelings of satisfaction.

But, surely, you might wonder, isn't there a downside? Poor decisions must end up producing bad consequences when reality doesn't match up to those expectations. Despite the many reasons you might generate for why unrealistic optimism could be dangerous or unwise, research has consistently found that unrealistic optimism appears to be generally adaptive (Armor & Taylor, 2002).

Key Points

- Social comparison is a central means by which we evaluate ourselves. **Downward social comparison** refers to instances in which we compare to someone of lesser ability than ourselves. Such comparisons can be flattering.
- **Upward social comparisons**, in contrast, refer to instances in which we compare to someone who outperforms us in areas central to the self. **Social comparison theory** suggests people often compare their abilities to others who are similar to them in terms of broad social categories such as gender, race, age or experience with a task.
- We often find people who outperform us to be threatening when we compare ourselves to them as individuals, but they are viewed more positively when we categorize ourselves and them together as members of the same group.
- Social comparison theory spawned two perspectives on the consequences of negative or upward social comparisons for the self—the **self-evaluation maintenance model** and **social identity theory**. When we categorize at the individual level, we distance from a better performing other, but when we categorize at the social identity level, we distance from that same poor performing other.
- Most people show unrealistic optimism when it comes to their outcomes relative to others and exhibit the **above average effect**—where we think we are better than most others on many dimensions. These positive illusions have been linked with various adaptive outcomes.

4.5: Self-Esteem: Attitudes Toward Ourselves

Objective   **Determine the factors that impact self-esteem**

For the most part, **self-esteem** has been conceptualized by social psychologists as the overall attitude people hold toward themselves. What kind of attitude do you have toward yourself—is it positive or negative? Is your attitude toward yourself stable, or do you think your self-esteem varies across time and settings? Evidence concerning the average level of self-esteem in American high school students suggests that it has been gradually increasing over time (Twenge & Campbell, 2008). Relative to students in the 1970s, high school students in 2006 report on average liking themselves considerably more.

But, are there points at which self-esteem changes for most everyone? How about the self-esteem of students who attend university? New research following students over the 4 years of college indicates that self-esteem drops during the first year, substantially for most students (Chung et al., 2014). This drop during the first year is followed by an increase in self-esteem that continues through the end of college. This post-first year increase is a function of performance: Those who get better grades in college tend to increase in self-esteem across time more than those who receive worse grades. Further, students are fairly accurate in their perceptions of whether their self-esteem changed across the college years—and about which direction. So, as you will see, while self-esteem is often thought of as, and measured, like a stable trait, it can and does change in response to life events.

4.5.1: The Measurement of Self-Esteem

The most common method of measuring personal self-esteem as an overall assessment of self-evaluation is with the 10-item Rosenberg (1965) scale. As shown in Figure 4.16, the items on this scale are quite transparent. On this measure, people are asked to rate their own explicit attitude toward themselves. Given that most people can guess what is being assessed with these items, it is not surprising that scores on this scale correlate very highly with responses to the single item, "I have high self-esteem" (Robins, Hendin, & Trzesniewski, 2001). There are also more specific measures of self-esteem that are used to assess self-esteem in particular domains, such as academics, personal relationships, appearance, and athletics, with scores on these more specific types of self-esteem being predicted by performance indicators in those domains (Swann, Chang-Schneider, & McClarty, 2007).

As Figure 4.17 illustrates, people's self-esteem is often visibly responsive to life events. When we reflect on our achievements, self-esteem increases and focusing on our failures typically hurts self-esteem (Sedikides, Wildschut, Arndt, & Routledge, 2008). For example, when people are reminded of the ways they fall short of their ideals, self-esteem decreases (Eisenstadt & Leippe, 1994). When people with low self-esteem receive negative feedback, their self-esteem suffers further declines (DeHart & Pelham, 2007). Being ostracized, excluded, or ignored by other people can be psychologically painful and cause reductions in self-esteem (DeWall et al., 2010; Williams, 2001).

Several research groups have attempted to measure self-esteem with greater subtlety (Greenwald & Farnham, 2000). Self-esteem scores based on explicit measures such as the Rosenberg scale could be biased by self-presentation concerns. Responses also might be guided by norms—for example, people may report high levels of

---

Figure 4.16 Measuring Self-Esteem: The Rosenberg Scale

Each of the items with an asterisk is reverse-scored, and then an average of all 10 items is computed so that higher numbers indicate greater self-esteem.

1. I feel that I am a person of worth, at least on an equal basis with others.
2. I feel that I have a number of good qualities.
3. All in all, I am inclined to feel that I am a failure.*
4. I am able to do things as well as most other people.
5. I feel I do not have much to be proud of.*
6. I take a positive attitude toward myself.
7. On the whole, I am satisfied with myself.
8. I wish I could have more respect for myself.*
9. I certainly feel useless at times.*
10. At times I think I am no good at all.*

Figure 4.17 Self-Esteem: Attitudes Toward the Self

One's self-esteem, or attitude about oneself, can range from very positive to very negative. At least temporarily, the individuals shown here would seem to be expressing very negative and very positive attitudes about themselves.

think that is "normal" and what others do. To bypass such strategic concerns, researchers have developed a number of [self-est]eem implicitly by assessing automatic associations between [positive and] negative concepts. The most common of the **implicit self-**[esteem measures tapp]ing self-feelings of which we are not consciously aware is the [Implicit Association T]est (Greenwald & Nosek, 2008; Ranganath, Smith, & Nosek, [2008). These] two types of measures of self-esteem—implicit and ex-[plicit—are uncor]related with each other, which is consistent with the assump-[tion that they are cap]turing different processes. An important question is whether [implicit self-esteem ch]anges with the circumstances, as we know explicit self-esteem [does. In one study,] Dijksterhuis (2004) used the logic of classical conditioning [to determ]ine whether implicit self-esteem can be improved without the [participant's conscio]us awareness. After repeatedly pairing representations of the self (I, ___, ___) with positive trait terms (e.g., nice, smart, warm) that were presented subliminally (too quickly for participants to consciously recognize them), implicit self-esteem was found to be significantly higher for these participants than for those in a control group who were not exposed to such self-positive trait pairings. Furthermore, this subliminal conditioning procedure prevented participants from suffering a self-esteem reduction when they were later given negative false feedback about their intelligence. Therefore, and consistent with research on explicit self-esteem (studies using the Rosenberg scale) that shows people with high self-esteem are less vulnerable to threat following a failure experience, this subliminal training procedure appears to provide similar self-protection at the implicit level when faced with a threat to the self.

Consistent with this analysis concerning nonconscious influences on self-esteem, DeHart, Pelham, and Tennen (2006) found that young adults whose parents were consistently nurturing of them reported higher implicit self-esteem than those whose parents were less nurturing. Conversely, young adults whose parents were overprotective of them showed lower implicit self-esteem than those whose parents displayed trust in them during their teenage years. Such implicit messages—based on our experiences with our parents—may lay the foundation for implicit associations between the self and positive attributes, or the self and negative attributes.

Figure 4.18 Classic Advice: You Can Do Anything Through Positive Thinking!

This book by Norman Vincent Peale has been a big seller for more than 50 years, but perhaps the effects of practicing such positive self-talk are more complex than originally supposed.

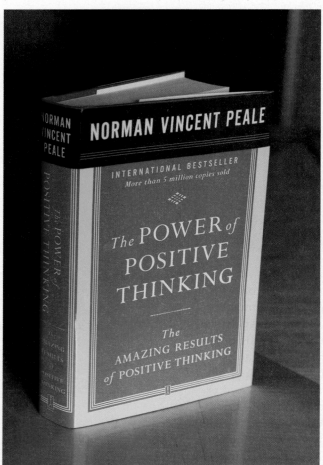

Much in American culture encourages people to think positively about themselves. When you are facing a big challenge, do you follow the advice that Norman Vincent Peale offered in his (1952) book *The Power of Positive Thinking* (see Figure 4.18)? The advice was simple enough—"tell yourself that you can do anything, and you will"; "tell yourself that you're great, and you will be." Who practices this advice? And, does doing so work?

To address these questions, Wood, Perunovic, and Lee (2009) first simply asked college students when and how often they use positive self-talk (e.g., "I will win"; "I will beat this illness"). Only 3 percent of their sample said they "never" do this, while 8 percent said they do so "almost daily," with the majority somewhere in between. As might be expected, their participants were most likely to say they use positive self-talk before undertaking a challenge (e.g., before an exam or before giving a presentation). Wood et al. (2009) suggested that for people with high self-esteem, such self-talk represents a confirmation of their already positive self-views. But for people with low self-esteem, positive self-talk might simply serve to remind them that they might not measure up. These researchers had high and low self-esteem people focus on how "I am a lovable person" and other statements of that sort. After this task, participants' happiness with themselves was assessed. For those low in self-esteem, this treatment did not appear to work; they remained less happy with themselves than high self-esteem people. So, positive self-talk may not be as beneficial as once believed—at least among those who need it most.

4.5.2: How Migration Affects Self-Esteem

Each year millions of students leave their home state or country to attend university elsewhere. You might be one of them. How does such a move affect psychological well-being, including self-esteem? Research examining the well-being of domestic and international students who have moved within or to the United States finds that adjustment among international students initially is lower than that of domestic students but that both groups improve over a 6-month period (Hechanova-Alampay, Beehr, Christiansen, & Van Horn, 2002). Improvements in well-being were due to two factors: increasing *self-efficacy*—the sense that one is capable of getting things done, and *social support*—both from those at home and positive interactions with peers at the new location. Other research with international students has found that self-esteem improves to the extent that they form a new minority identity shared with others who have also undergone the same migration experience—that of "International Student" (Schmitt, Spears, & Branscombe, 2002). Developing this new identity is particularly important for the well-being of students who, after arriving in the United States, perceive themselves as discriminated against because they are "foreigners."

Is the self-esteem of students affected when they move to a location where their ethnic group is the majority or to one where their ethnic group is a minority? Recent research has addressed this question with Asian and European American students who moved from California to Hawaii (Xu, Farver, & Pauker, 2015). In their home state of California, European Americans are the numeric majority and Asian Americans the minority, while this is reversed in Hawaii with Asian Americans the numeric majority and European Americans the minority. How is the self-esteem of these two ethnic groups affected by this numeric change? European Americans' self-esteem levels were lower after their first year in Hawaii where their ethnic group was a minority, suggesting that the change from majority to minority may have challenged their views about themselves. In contrast, for Asian Americans, although their ethnic identity became less salient by the move from a minority to majority context, their self-esteem was unchanged.

People also migrate from one country to another not just for a few years as a student, but with the goal of permanently relocating, often becoming citizens of the new country. Indeed, there has been an ongoing mass migration of people from Syria and other locations in the Middle East and North Africa into Europe over the past several years. As shown in Figure 4.19, both adults and children brave treacherous travels on the sea to reach safety. It will no doubt take considerable time for their well-being to improve, given the trauma many have already experienced. But, what are the well-being consequences of immigrating to another country—not as refugees who are fleeing from terrifying conditions, but when this migration is freely chosen? Despite the millions of people who immigrate to another country every year, little research has examined the self-esteem of immigrants both before and after doing so. One valuable study that did so (Lonnqvist, Leikas, Mahonen, & Jasinskaja-Lahti, 2015) found that immigrants from Russia to Finland showed reductions in self-esteem from preimmigration to 3 years postimmigration. Like the student migrants discussed previously, these immigrants had higher self-esteem to the extent that they experienced high social support and high self-efficacy. This research reveals that changing circumstances—even when those are chosen—can have implications for our self-esteem.

Figure 4.19 Syrian Refugees Struggling to Survive: The Humanitarian Crisis

Research indicates that migration—even when freely chosen—can present difficulties for well-being. However, the current crisis and mass migration from Syria and other Middle Eastern locations entails considerable trauma.

4.5.3: Do Women and Men Differ in Their Level of Self-Esteem?

Who do you think, on average, has higher or lower self-esteem—women or men? Many people might guess that men have higher self-esteem overall than women. Why would that be? To the extent that self-esteem is affected by how important others see us and the treatment we receive from them (Mead, 1934), then we might expect that women will have lower self-esteem overall compared to men. Because women have historically occupied lower status social positions and are frequently targets of prejudice, these could have negative consequences for their self-esteem. Self-esteem in girls and women may reflect their devalued status in the larger society, with many feeling that they just cannot measure up to societal standards.

In a 14-nation study, Williams and Best (1990) assessed the self-concepts of women and men. In nations such as India and Malaysia, where women are expected to remain in the home in their roles as wives and mothers, women had the most negative self-concepts. In contrast, in nations such as England and Finland, where women are more active in the labor force and the status difference between women and men is less, members of each gender tend to perceive themselves equally favorably. This research suggests that when women are excluded from important life arenas, they will have worse self-concepts than men. Longitudinal research with employed women in the United States too finds that women in jobs in which gender discrimination is most frequent exhibit increasingly poorer well-being (Pavalko, Mossakowski, & Hamilton, 2003). Harm to women—as a function of employment in a discriminatory work environment—was observed over time in comparison to their health status before such employment began.

A meta-analysis comparing the global self-esteem of women and men in 226 samples collected in the United States and Canada from 1982 to 1992 likewise found that men have reliably higher self-esteem than women (Major, Barr, Zubek, & Babey, 1999). Although the size of the effect obtained across all these studies was not large, as Prentice and Miller (1992) point out, sometimes small differences between groups can be quite impressive. Precisely because there are substantial differences within each gender group in level of self-esteem, being able to detect reliable group differences in self-esteem both within and across nations is remarkable. Major et al. (1999) found that the self-esteem difference between men and women was less among those in the professional class and greatest among those in the middle and lower classes. Again, those women who have attained culturally desirable positions suffer less self-esteem loss than those who are more likely to experience the greatest devaluation. Indeed, recent longitudinal research has noted that the substantial gender difference in self-esteem that they observed during the adult working years begins to decline at about 65 years of age, with the gender groups converging in old age (Orth, Trzesniewski, & Robins, 2010).

So, is the common sense notion that overall self-esteem suffers for groups that are devalued in a given society correct after all? The research findings offer a straight forward answer for gender: Yes. Likewise, for many other devalued groups, perceiving discrimination has a significant negative effect on a variety of indicators of health (Pascoe & Smart Richman, 2009). How badly self-esteem suffers depends on how much discrimination and devaluation the group that is the subject of such treatment experiences (Hansen & Sassenberg, 2006). In the special feature, **"What Research Tells Us About...Perceived Discrimination and Self-Esteem,"** we'll see that the negative effects of discrimination on self-esteem, and other forms of well-being, differ depending on what group is the target. All devalued groups do not suffer to the same extent.

What Research Tells Us About...

Perceived Discrimination and Self-Esteem

What are the emotional consequences of perceiving oneself as a target of discrimination? This question has been addressed in many investigations—both in correlational studies that assess this relationship in a wide variety of groups around the world, and in experiments that permit causal inferences about the effects of different types of attributions made for an identical negative outcome.

Why should we expect that perceiving oneself as a target of discrimination will negatively affect well-being? First of all, discrimination is often experienced as a form of exclusion, frequently from important life domains (i.e., good jobs, better housing). Second, discrimination conveys devaluing and disrespect within society more broadly, and we know that inclusion and feeling valued are important conditions for humans to thrive. Third, perceiving discrimination threatens feelings of control and can create a sense of powerlessness—it communicates that you will not have the same opportunities for success in life as others. For all these reasons, the self-esteem and well-being costs more generally should be especially negative when discrimination is seen as pervasive across time and occurring in many contexts. Of course this is more likely to be true for disadvantaged groups than advantaged groups, so perceiving discrimination should be more harmful for disadvantaged groups than advantaged groups.

A meta-analysis that has integrated the results of hundreds of studies involving 144,246 people found that perceived discrimination is negative for all sorts of indicators of psychological well-being, including self-esteem (Schmitt, Branscombe, Postmes, & Garcia, 2014). As you might have expected, the effect is significantly more negative for disadvantaged groups compared to advantaged groups. Many different types of disadvantaged groups were studied and the effect of perceived discrimination on their self-esteem was more negative for some than others. Can you guess for which forms of discrimination—racism, sexism, sexual orientation, physical illness or disability, mental illness, HIV+, or weight—self-esteem might be more negative? Table 4.2 presents the standardized effect sizes (which are correlations, weighted by sample size) across studies for the relationship found between perceived discrimination and self-esteem, as well as other indicators of psychological distress.

Shown here are the standardized effect sizes (correlations, weighted by sample size) across a variety of studies conducted. For all of these groups, the effect of perceived discrimination on self-esteem and other indicators of psychological distress is significant and negative. That means the more members of these groups perceive discrimination, the worse their well-being. However, as you can see, for some groups the relationship was much more strongly negative than for others.

The harm to well-being of perceived discrimination shown here may reflect in part the negative effect of experiencing discrimination—the worse treatment received—rather than the perception of one's outcomes being due to discrimination. To separate the effects of *objective encounters* with discrimination from the *subjective interpretation* of the cause of that experience, experiments that control actual discrimination by giving everyone the same treatment and then varies the interpretation people give to it permits us to learn the causal effect of perceiving our negative outcomes as stemming from discrimination. There are two types of experiments that have been done to address this issue, and as you'll see they result in dramatically different effects. Let's see how they are done and what we've learned from them.

Suppose you receive negative feedback from another person about your job interview performance, or otherwise receive some undesirable treatment. It is possible to make several different types of attributions for such unfavorable outcomes. Research investigating this issue can vary aspects of the situation to make discrimination plausible—because the interviewer is prejudiced against your racial group, or make it seem like you lacked the needed ability so not passing the interview would be seen as deserved. Neither of these attributions (to discrimination or personal deservingness) is particularly great for self-esteem. Both reflect something about you that is stable and difficult to change (your group membership and your ability). Based on a meta-analysis of experiments concerning single outcomes like this, across 54 samples there was no overall negative effect of attributing the negative outcome to discrimination versus personal deservingness (Schmitt et al., 2014).

The second type of experiment that has been conducted, however, revealed different results. In these studies, the negative outcome always happens too, but perceptions of how widespread discrimination is more generally have been manipulated. That is, if the person treating you badly is thought to be like many other interviewers you might encounter (e.g., they are all sexist), then discrimination may be seen as pervasive, but if the interviewer you encountered is the only one who is sexist, then discrimination against your group may be seen as a relatively rare occurrence. For these studies, there was a substantial negative effect on a variety of indicators of well-being of attributing one's negative outcome to discrimination when it conveyed a message that discrimination is pervasive. Such instances communicate that your identity is not valued and you can expect more outcomes like this, which is why it causes significant harm to well-being. What is fundamentally important for whether psychological well-being will be harmed is how likely it is that you can expect to encounter discriminatory treatment in the future. Such an interpretation of negative outcomes is more likely for disadvantaged than advantaged groups, explaining why harm to well-being is greater for the former than the latter.

Table 4.2 The Relationship Between Perceived Discrimination and Psychological Well-Being

Type of Discrimination	Self-Esteem	Psychological Distress
Racism	−.13	−.25
Sexism	−.09	−.22
Sexual Orientation	−.17	−.29
Physical Illness/Disability	−.54	−.39
Mental Illness	−.31	−.29
Weight	−.21	−.38
HIV+	−.24	−.34
Other (age, unemployment)	−.21	−.30

Key Points

- **Self-esteem** is our overall attitude toward ourselves. Self-esteem is most frequently measured with explicit items that directly assess our perceived level of self-esteem. Other *implicit* measures of self-esteem assess how strong the positive or negative association between ourselves and stimuli associated with us are, including trait terms. People may not be aware of their **implicit self-esteem**.

- Self-esteem is responsive to life experiences, and more specific forms of self-esteem depend on how we perform in those domains. Even implicit self-esteem can change with circumstances.

- People often engage in positive self-talk, especially when preparing for a challenge. Research has found that such positive self-talk in low self-esteem people is not effective in improving feelings about themselves.

- Migration—either to attend university elsewhere or to immigrate to another country—can initially have a negative effect on self-esteem. Over time, however, self-esteem may improve, particularly when they receive social support and feel self-efficacy.

- There is a small but reliable gender difference in self-esteem. Women's self-esteem is worse than men's to the extent that they live in a nation with more exclusion of women from public life compared to women who live in a nation with higher labor force participation by women. Among those U.S. women who work in occupations in which discrimination is frequent and pervasive, lower self-esteem is more prevalent than among women in occupations in which discrimination is encountered less often.

- Meta-analysis reveals that perceived discrimination is more harmful for the self-esteem of disadvantaged groups than advantaged groups. Experiments that vary the perception that discrimination against one's group is pervasive rather than rare reveal a negative causal effect of seeing discrimination as pervasive so difficult to avoid.

4.6: The Self as a Target of Prejudice

Objective **Analyze how prejudice and trying to conceal our identity impacts well-being**

Although the experience of not getting what you want is generally negative, how you explain such undesirable outcomes has important implications for how people feel about themselves, and by extension, how people cope. As you saw in the prior section, attributions affect the meaning derived from events; as a result, some attributions for a negative outcome are more psychologically harmful than others and undermine self-esteem (Weiner, 1985). We now consider the consequences of concealing or not concealing one's identity for a person's self-esteem, and then turn to the behavioral consequences of perceiving the self as a target of prejudice.

4.6.1: Concealing Our Identity: How Well-Being Can Suffer

For some identities that we might possess, negative treatment is widely and routinely experienced. For example, gay men and lesbians often face violence because of their sexual orientation, those with mental and physical disabilities may experience public shaming, as do people who are overweight, and employment and other forms of discrimination are frequent among those who are HIV infected or have other chronic health conditions such as traumatic brain injury. For some of these identities, people may be tempted to hide, or not reveal, "who they are" in order to avoid such prejudicial treatment (Pachankis, 2007). But choosing not to reveal, or repeatedly having to decide to do so or not, can be a substantial burden in its own right (Quinn & Chaudoir, 2009). In addition, while discrimination personally may be avoided with this strategy, awareness of societal devaluation of one's group will not be. To the extent that harm to well-being is a result of this broader perception, people with concealable stigmatized identities might exhibit lower self-esteem and greater psychological distress than those with stigmatized identities that are not readily concealed. A meta-analysis examining the effects of concealability of a stigmatized identity has revealed more negative effects on well-being compared to identities such as gender and race that are not concealable (Schmitt et al., 2014). In fact, the long-term consequences of hiding one's sexual identity was poignantly revealed in a study of HIV infected gay men. These men were more likely to acquire other infections and died earlier than those with the same physical condition but who did not hide their sexual orientation (Cole, Kemeny, Taylor, & Visscher, 1996). Avoiding discrimination with successful concealment can come at quite a cost—negative health and well-being stemming from loneliness and not being able to connect with others like oneself.

Suppose you were to interact with someone who you knew did not like your academic major and actually preferred to interact with someone from another major. If you were induced to hide your major when interacting with this person, would you feel you might not be "true to yourself" and instead be "inauthentic" compared to if you revealed your identity—even knowing it would be disliked? This is precisely the situation that Newheiser and Barreto (2014) created in order to examine the interactional consequences of hiding one's true identity. As shown in Figure 4.20, participants in this experiment who hid their stigmatized identity did report worrying more that they wouldn't be able to be themselves and felt more inauthentic compared to participants who revealed their disliked identity. Moreover, after actually interacting with the other person, observers who were blind to what condition participants had been in perceived the individuals who hid their identity as disclosing less about themselves and perceived the overall interaction as less positive than when the individuals had revealed their true identity. This suggests that while we may hide a stigmatized identity to belong, doing so may actually heighten our sense that we don't belong and set us up for awkward social interactions.

Figure 4.20 To Hide Who You Are, or Be the Real You?

When a stigmatized identity was hidden, participants who did so felt greater authenticity concerns about themselves than those who were not induced to hide their identity. Observers of their interaction with another person saw the "hiding" others as disclosing less about themselves and had a less positive impression of the interaction than when the "true" identity had been revealed.

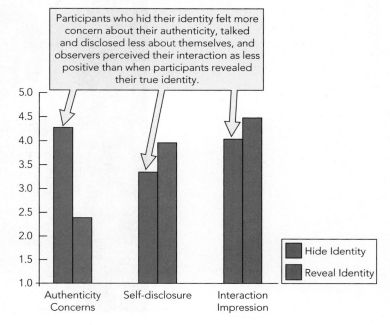

4.6.2: Overcoming the Effects of Stereotype Threat

Perceiving the self as a target of prejudice not only harms psychological well-being, it can also interfere with people's ability to acquire new skills. Several studies have found that when people fear that others will discover their devalued group membership, as might be the case for concealable stigmas, such fear can negatively affect people's ability to learn and can affect task performance (Frable, Blackstone, & Scherbaum, 1990; Lord & Saenz, 1985; Schmader, 2010).

How might these performance deficits in those with a stigmatized self be prevented? Research suggests that a critical issue is the extent to which people can affirm themselves in other ways. Martens, Johns, Greenberg, and Schimel (2006) examined whether first having people affirm their most valued attribute, perhaps a talent for art or another accomplishment, would eliminate cognitive deficits in those who were later reminded of their stigmatized group membership; this was exactly what they found. Thus, it is the extent to which a negative stereotype may define a person's entire worth that leads to underperformance, and re-affirming the individual's worth can provide protection. Another important way that underperformance effects may be overcome includes making salient the stereotype-defying accomplishments of an important role model who shares one's stigmatized group membership. In a test of whether the election of Barack Obama as U.S. president could have a beneficial effect on African Americans' verbal test performance, Marx, Ko and Friedman (2009) gave a random selection of Americans a difficult verbal test before and immediately after exposure to these accomplishments. While the test performance of Caucasian and Af-

Figure 4.21 Stereotype-Defying Accomplishments of Another Who Shares One's Stigmatized Identity Improves Test Performance

Making salient the achievements of a famous fellow ingroup member improved verbal test scores in a random sample of African Americans.

rican Americans before Obama received the Democratic nomination differed (with African Americans scoring less well than Caucasians), after exposure to the achievements of this famous fellow ingroup member, African Americans' performance on this difficult verbal test improved; in fact, following Barack Obama's election, no racial difference in test performance was observed. So, making salient the stereotype-defying accomplishments of another person who shares one's stigmatized group, as shown in Figure 4.21, can powerfully counter vulnerability to performance deficits.

Stereotype threat, which is a particular kind of social identity threat, occurs when people believe they might be judged in light of a negative stereotype about their social identity or that they may inadvertently act in some way to confirm a negative stereotype of their group (Logel et al., 2009; Steele, 1997; Steele, Spencer, & Aronson, 2002). When people value their ability in a certain domain (e.g., math), but it is one in which their group is stereotyped as performing poorly (e.g., women), stereotype threat can occur. When those who are vulnerable to this threat are reminded in either an overt or subtle way that the stereotype might apply to them, then performance in that domain can be undermined. Consider the experience of the women engineering students studied by Logel et al. (2009). When these women were exposed to a sexist man, their subsequent performance on a math test was undermined, although their performance on an English test was unaffected. Interacting with the sexist man made their identity as women salient, and while trying to counteract this threat by suppressing thoughts of gender stereotypes, they inadvertently confirmed the stereotype about women's poor math ability.

Such stereotype threat effects are fairly difficult to control. For example, simply telling women before they take a math test that men do better on math than women do (Spencer, Steele, & Quinn, 1999) or having African Americans indicate their race before taking a difficult verbal test (Steele & Aronson, 1995) is sufficient to evoke stereotype threat and hurt their performance. Indeed, because women are negatively stereotyped as being worse at math than men, women tend to perform more poorly when they simply take a difficult math test in the presence of men, whereas they tend to perform better when the same test is taken only in the presence of other women (Inzlicht & Ben-Zeev, 2000).

Consider the dilemma of women who have taken a lot of math classes and who perceive math to be an important aspect of their self-concept. What if they also value their identity as women? When they find themselves exposed to information that suggests there are reliable sex differences in math ability, with men doing better than women, these women are likely to experience threat. How then do they manage to cope with such threat, without simultaneously distancing from either the math domain or their group as a whole? Pronin, Steele, and Ross (2004) found that high-math-identified women distanced themselves only from gender stereotypic dimensions that are deemed to be incompatible with math success (e.g., leaving work to raise children, being flirtatious) but they did not do so for gender stereotypic dimensions deemed to be irrelevant to math success (e.g., being empathic, being fashion conscious). Only in the stereotype threat condition did this reduced identification occur, suggesting it was a motivated process designed to alleviate the threat experienced.

Why do stereotype threat-based performance decrements occur? Some researchers suggest that anxiety is evoked in women, African Americans, and Latinos when their group membership is portrayed as predictive of poor performance (Osborne, 2001). Some studies have, however, failed to find increased self-reported anxiety among stigmatized group members experiencing stereotype threat (Aronson et al., 1999). This could be because members of stigmatized groups are reluctant to admit their feelings of anxiety, or it may be that they do not actually realize they are feeling anxious so they cannot accurately report those feelings.

Research that has examined nonverbal measures of anxiety illustrates how anxiety does play a crucial role in stereotype threat effects. In a clever test of the hypothesis that anxiety causes stereotype threat performance deficits, Bosson, Haymovitz, and Pinel (2004) first either reminded or did not remind gay and straight participants of their category membership before videotaping their interactions with young children in a nursery school. Participants were first asked to indicate their sexual orientation on a form just before they interacted with the children. After this subtle reminder that their sexual orientation group is stereotyped as one that is dangerous to children, the gay participants' childcare skills (as rated by judges unaware of the hypotheses and procedure) suffered compared to when they were not so reminded of their category membership and its associated stereotype. This same group membership reminder had no effect on the straight participants, because there is no associated stereotype of danger to children. Consequently, straight participants were not at risk of potentially confirming a negative stereotype in the performance situation they faced.

Was increased anxiety in the gay men the cause of the reduction in their rated childcare skills? On standard self-report measures of anxiety and evaluation apprehension, the answer would seem to be no—Bosson, Haymovitz, & Pinel, (2004) did not obtain differences in these self-reports as a function of either sexual orientation or stereotype threat condition. Importantly, however, independent judges' ratings of nonverbal anxiety—as indicated by various behaviors indicating discomfort during the interaction with the children—were affected by sexual orientation and stereotype threat. Among the gay men who were reminded of their category membership, their anxiety was discernible in their nonverbal behavior compared to the gay men who were not experiencing stereotype threat. That is, although the gay men experiencing stereotype threat did not rate themselves as more anxious, they were visibly more fidgety; they averted their eyes more, and otherwise exhibited signs of discomfort more than gay men not experiencing stereotype threat. And, this nonverbal anxiety disrupted their interactions with the children. However among heterosexual men, reminders of their category membership tended to result in fewer nonverbal symptoms of anxiety compared to when their category was not made relevant.

Is it only for groups that are historically devalued in the culture as a whole that stereotype threat effects have been observed? No. Such effects occur with men, who are not a devalued group as a whole but who are stereotyped as being less emotional than women (Leyens, Désert, Croizet, & Darcis, 2000). When men were reminded of

Key Points

- People with some identities receive negative treatment and this may tempt them to "hide" who they are. Concealing a stigmatized identity may help people avoid overt forms of discrimination, but awareness of societal devaluation is still likely. Concealable stigmatized identities have more negative effects on well-being compared to stigmatized identities that are not concealable.

- Hiding an identity that you anticipate being disliked by another can lead to feelings of inauthenticity and less positive social interactions.

- The fear of confirming others' negative stereotypes about one's group identity can disrupt performance. Affirming another aspect of the self or exposure to a stereotype-defying role model who shares one's stigma can result in improved performance.

- **Stereotype threat** effects occur in capable people in a domain they value. They have been observed in historically

devalued group members (African Americans, women) and in dominant groups (Caucasians, men) when they believe they might negatively compare on an important dimension with members of another group.

- Stereotype threat effects are difficult to control, and they can be induced easily. Simply requiring people to indicate their group membership before taking a test in a domain in which they are vulnerable is enough to undermine performance.

- When people experience stereotype threat, they can distance themselves from the negative part of the stereotype about one's group.

- Anxiety appears to be one mechanism by which stereotype threat effects occur. However self-report measures of anxiety often fail to reveal its importance, although nonverbal indicators of anxiety do predict performance disruption.

the stereotype concerning their emotional deficits, their performance on a task requiring them to identify emotions suffered. In an even more dramatic way, Stone, Lynch, Sjomeling, and Darley (1999) illustrated a similar point. In their research, Caucasian men who expected to be compared to African American men performed more poorly on an athletic performance task when they believed it reflected "natural athletic ability." The reverse occurred when Caucasian men believed the exact same task reflected "sports intelligence," which is a dimension on which they expect to excel as compared with African American men. Likewise, although there is no stereotype that Caucasians perform poorly on math, when they are threatened by a potentially negative comparison to Asians who are stereotyped as performing better than Caucasians, then they show math performance deficiencies (Aronson et al., 1999). Thus expecting to do poorly in comparison to another group can undermine performance, even in members of historically advantaged groups. While we will examine related issues on the effects of stereotyping on its targets in Chapter 6, the research we have reviewed here on stereotype threat effects illustrates the importance of group membership for the experience of threat to the self, and how such threat can easily disrupt performance.

Summary and Review

Sometimes close others can be better at predicting our behavior than we ourselves are. That is because observers and actors attend to different behavioral features. Sometimes people put information about themselves on Facebook that is a little more positive than they really are. When people are asked if their self-descriptions might be biased, the more positive their ratings were, initially, the more they perceived the possibility of bias.

We face many audiences and how we present ourselves to others can vary. We might attempt to engage in **self-promotion**—present our most favorable self-aspects—on some occasions and on others we may be motivated to present ourselves in ways that induce others to agree with our own self-views. That is, we may engage in **self-verification**, even if it means having others agree with the negative qualities we believe we possess. We may also create a favorable self-presentation by using **ingratiation** tactics that convey respect for others, or occasionally **self-depreciate** to communicate admiration for the other by comparison.

Self-knowledge is sought through two primary methods—introspection and considering ourselves from others' vantage point. Introspection is tricky because we often don't have conscious access to the emotional factors that affect our behavioral choices, or to what actually brings us happiness. We also may have difficulty predicting how we will feel in the future because we neglect to consider other events that will also occur besides the focal ones considered. When we think of ourselves by taking an observer's perspective, we see the self in more trait terms and less responsive to situations, as observers do.

How we think about ourselves varies depending on where we are on **personal-versus-social identity contin-uum** at any given moment in time. At the personal identity level we can think of ourselves in terms of attributes that differentiate ourselves from other individuals, and therefore will be based on **intragroup comparison**. At the social identity level, perceptions of ourselves are based on attributes that are shared with other group members; perception of the self at the social identity level stems from **intergroup comparison** processes.

Self-definitions can vary across situations, with each being valid predictors of behavior in those settings. How we conceptualize ourselves can also depend on how others expect us to be and how we believe they will treat us. Across time, Americans have increasingly come to define themselves in terms of individualistic traits. Context shifts that change whether or not we define ourselves in terms of our gender can result in gender differences in self-construal appearing or disappearing. What aspect of the self is influential at any moment in time depends on: context, distinctiveness of the attribute, importance of the identity, and how others refer to us.

Different aspects of the self may be salient when a selection is made and when it is experienced or consumed. Dissatisfaction and regret are higher when the self-aspects are inconsistent with each other when the choice is made and when it is experienced. When other people reject us because of some aspect of our identity, people often rebel against those doing the rejecting and make that feature even more self-defining. Today, people who get body piercings and tattoos are attempting to communicate their difference from the "mainstream."

Other future **possible selves**, besides who we are currently, can motivate us to attempt self-change. Role models can represent future possible selves that we can attain.

When people compare their present self to their past self, the further in the past that self is the more we downgrade it relative to our present self. This approach to **autobiographical memory** allows us to feel good about our current self. Dreaded possible selves can lead us to give up certain behaviors (e.g., smoking), while desired possible selves can lead us to work long hours to attain them.

Self-control is necessary if we are to forego immediate pleasures in exchange for long-term goals. How the self is construed affects our ability to resist temptation. Self-control may be a resource that can be temporarily used up—**ego depletion**—which makes it more difficult to self-regulate. Subsequent self-control can be more difficult when the initial control effort was longer, when no rest period is given, or when people lack training in self-regulation.

How we feel about ourselves can be assessed directly and explicitly, or with more implicit or indirect methods. Both explicit and implicit measures of **self-esteem** are responsive to life events. Positive self-talk (thinking about how "I'm a lovable person") is not necessarily beneficial for low self-esteem people.

Social comparison is a vital means by which we judge ourselves. **Upward social comparisons** at the personal level can be painful, and **downward social comparisons** at this level of identity can be comforting. The reverse is true when ones social identity is salient—we dislike another ingroup member who performs poorly but respond positively to an ingroup member who performs better than us because that person makes our group look good.

Most people show self-serving biases, such as the **above average effect**, where we see ourselves more positively (and less negatively) than we see most other people. We consistently hold positive illusions about ourselves and are unrealistically optimistic about our ability to avoid negative outcomes. Americans' optimistic expectations for themselves have been rising. Such unrealistic optimism is, however, predictive of positive mental and physical health.

When we migrate from one state or country to another, psychological well-being is often affected. Initially, students who migrate show lower self-esteem, but improvements over time are a function of self-efficacy and social support. Women do, on average, have lower self-esteem than men. This is particularly the case in nations where women do not participate in the labor force, and in the United States among middle-class and lower-class women who work in environments in which gender-based devaluation is most frequent.

There are emotional costs of perceiving oneself as a target of discrimination. A meta-analysis of the hundreds of studies assessing perceived discrimination and self-esteem showed that it is more negative for disadvantaged groups than advantaged groups. Experiments have revealed that when the self is seen as a target of pervasive discrimination, it is more harmful for self-esteem than when it is seen as reflecting an isolated outcome.

For some socially devalued identities, people may attempt to hide or not reveal it to avoid prejudicial treatment. People with concealable stigmatized identities have lower self-esteem than people whose stigmatized identities cannot be concealed. Hiding an important identity can make people feel inauthentic and decrease forms of self-disclosure that makes interaction more positive.

Stereotype threat effects can occur in historically devalued groups when they are simply reminded of their group membership and fear they might confirm negative stereotypes about their group. Stereotype threat can undermine performance in dominant group members as well, when they fear a negative comparison with members of another group that is expected to outperform them. This undermining of performance only occurs on dimensions relevant to the stereotype. Stereotype threat performance decrements can be prevented by (1) affirming the self in another way, (2) exposure to a stereotype-defying role model, and (3) distancing from aspects of the stereotype that are incompatible with high performance. Anxiety, at least nonverbal indicators of it, plays a role in the emergence of stereotype threat-based performance deficits. Members of any group can be vulnerable to performing less favorably when a salient comparison group is expected to perform better at a task. Stereotype threat research reveals how our group memberships can affect our self-concepts and performance on tasks we care deeply about.

Chapter 5
Attitudes
Evaluating and Responding to the Social World

Chapter Overview

Learning Objectives

5.1 Identify the learning processes through which our attitudes are formed

5.2 Examine the link between attitudes and behavior and the factors that affect their relationship

5.3 Explain the two processes through which attitudes guide behavior

5.4 Indicate the factors that determine whether persuasion attempts to alter our attitudes will be effective

5.5 Examine the methods that help people resist skilled attempts to persuade us

5.6 Evaluate the effects of cognitive dissonance on attitude change

What are your beliefs about climate change? How were those beliefs formed? Are some views particularly credible—because of the source's expertise—and likely to influence you more than others? According to the Intergovernmental Panel on Climate Change (2014), human activity has increased carbon emissions in the planet's atmosphere, which have now reached unprecedented levels. As a result, global warming is on the rise and increased extreme weather events (e.g., droughts, rising sea levels, wildfires, and heat waves) can be expected.

While virtually all climate scientists (98 percent) agree that human-caused climate change is indeed happening, there is much less certainty about this among members of the general public. Is this "belief gap" simply a matter of the public not being adequately informed, or are there psychological factors that predict how people perceive this complex environmental issue? The Pew Research Center reports that, as of August 2014, 50 percent of the U.S. population believes that the earth is getting warmer because of human activity. Endorsement of this belief varies quite a bit by age: Among those 65 years and over only 31 percent agree, while 60 percent of those aged 18–29 do. Belief in climate change also differs by level of education: Only 44 percent of those with high school education agree, while 60 percent of those with a college degree do. We also know that beyond education and age, there is an important role of self-interest in the attitudes people form about climate change and the intensity with which those are held. That is, people who live on coastlines (around the world) are more concerned about climate change and the expected rise in sea levels than are people who are less proximal and therefore expect to have less direct experience with the consequences (Milfont, Evans, Sibley, Ries, & Cunningham, 2014). Similarly, having experienced deviations from local normal temperatures—in terms of either heat or cold—is associated with increased concern about climate change (Brooks, Oxley, Vedlitz, Zahran, & Lindsey, 2014).

Is how you feel about climate change—and what should be done to mitigate or adapt to it—more strongly influenced by scientists' statements on the matter, or are you more influenced by politicians' statements—and does which party those politicians are affiliated with matter? Let's consider how attitudes toward climate change in the United States vary as a function of political party affiliation. Representative surveys of U.S. adults reveal substantial differences in views on climate change by political affiliation. While 71 percent of Democrats (and Independents who lean Democratic) believe human activity is causing climate change, only 27 percent of Republicans (and Independents who lean Republican) do so (Pew Research Center, 2015). Because our identities—who we are—shape our beliefs about the world, willingness to take action to combat climate change or any other collective risk we might face is likely to differ for those aligned with different political groups.

Figure 5.1 How Are Attitudes Toward Climate Change Formed?

Do our beliefs about climate change depend on our experience with abnormal weather events, or the perceived likelihood that we will be affected (i.e., living near a coast so that rising sea levels are a worry)? Are our beliefs about this issue shaped by the norms of important groups that we belong to?

Is it possible that because the consequences of climate change are so severe and frightening that many people are tempted to look away or ignore the issue altogether? U.S. President Obama stated (*New York Times*, 2014) that "Climate change is one of the most significant long-term challenges that this country and the planet faces . . . and the fact of climate change is not something we can afford to deny. The trick is to find that fine line between making people feel the problem is urgent, but not insoluble." Is it possible that too much fear will indeed fail to persuade and instead undermine people's willingness to accept the "climate change is occurring" message? Are some of the likely effects of climate change, shown in Figure 5.1, sufficiently frightening that large numbers of us simply dismiss the message?

In this chapter we will explore the factors that shape the attitudes we hold, and address the key question of whether our attitudes are simply a product of rational thought. We will consider how other people affect the attitudes we form, and what happens when we react against their attempts to influence us. How people respond to explicit attempts to persuade them is a complicated issue involving several different processes. We consider when, for example, people closely scrutinize the arguments presented in a message and are guided by communicator credibility, and when we might be motivated by other factors (see Figure 5.2 for an amusing take on this issue). We will also address the important issue of when and how we manage to persuade ourselves—why our behavior can lead us to change our attitudes. Along the way we will consider whether all attitudes are equal, or if some attitudes are more strongly linked to behavior than others. Lastly, we will examine the process by which our attitudes guide our behavior.

Social psychologists use the term **attitude** to refer to people's *evaluation* of almost any aspect of the world (e.g., Albarracin, Johnson, & Zanna, 2005; Olson & Kendrick, 2008). People can have favorable or unfavorable reactions to issues such as climate change, objects, a specific person, or entire social groups. Some attitudes appear to be quite stable and resistant to change, while others may be unstable and show considerable variability depending on the situation (Schwarz & Bohner, 2001). We may hold some attitudes with great certainty, while our attitudes toward other objects or issues may be relatively unclear or uncertain (Tormala & Rucker, 2007).

Do you have strong attitudes toward gun control, abortion, and same-sex marriage, or do you feel somewhat uncertain about what position to hold on these issues? What is your attitude toward the legalization of marijuana, an issue currently on the agenda of many state legislatures and about which public opinion has shifted considerably over the last decade? Like attitudes toward climate change, is your

Figure 5.2 The Prospect of Climate Change Induces Fear in Many

Public opinion polls in 2014 indicate that there is a major political divide among Americans on whether human-induced climate change is real or not, with a much larger percentage of Democrats agreeing compared to Republicans. As suggested here, scientists report that climate change is taking place, but the public on the whole is less certain, making politicians leery about openly endorsing such a frightening possibility.

attitude toward marijuana likely to depend on your age, education level, political affiliation, or whether you have used it or not (see Figure 5.3)? Does it matter whether you think other people see its use as acceptable or not? What role does consensus—the extent to which we see others as sharing our attitudes—have on the attitudes we hold? When others with whom we identify appear to strongly endorse an attitude position, it leads us to want to be more similar to them and results in the expression of more attitude certainty as well (Clarkson, Tormala, Rucker, & Dugan, 2013).

The study of attitudes is central to the field of social psychology because attitudes are capable of coloring virtually every aspect of our experience. Even when we do not have strong attitudes toward a specific issue, related values can influence what attitudes we form. Let's consider public attitudes toward another scientific issue, specifically the use of human embryonic stem cells. Research findings indicate that attitudes toward such novel issues are shaped by long-term values—religious beliefs, for example, predict the formation of these new attitudes—rather than the extent to which the public possesses scientific knowledge on the topic (Ho, Brossard, & Scheufele, 2008). As we saw in Chapter 2, the tendency to evaluate stimuli as positive or negative—something we favor or are against—appears to be an initial step in our efforts to make sense out of the world. Responding to a stimulus in terms of our attitudes—on an immediately evaluative basis—produces different brain wave activity than when a response is made on a nonevaluative basis (Crites & Cacioppo, 1996). Our brains operate differently depending on whether we are engaged in rapid evaluative perception or a more thoughtful examination of our world.

While many attitudes are **explicit attitudes**—conscious and reportable—others may be **implicit attitudes**—less controllable and potentially not consciously accessible to us. Consider the explicit versus implicit attitudes distinction as it applies to racial attitudes. Many "color-blind" or self-perceived egalitarian Americans will

Figure 5.3 Marijuana Attitudes: To Support Legalization or Not

As of 2014, 23 U.S. states have legalized or decriminalized possession of marijuana for medical or recreational purposes. What factors are likely to influence people's attitudes toward this substance?

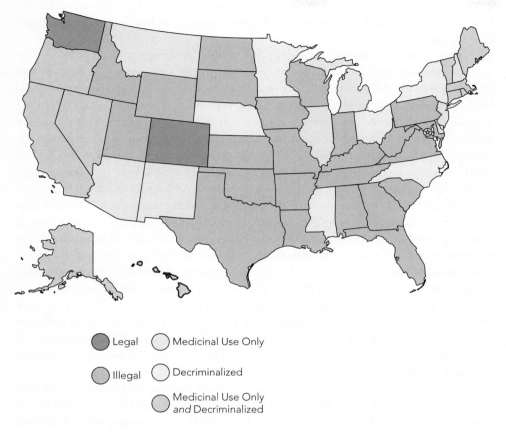

- ● Legal
- ● Illegal
- ○ Medicinal Use Only
- ○ Decriminalized
- ○ Medicinal Use Only *and* Decriminalized

report positive explicit attitudes toward African Americans. However, they may also display negative involuntary evaluative reactions toward African Americans—implicit attitudes—because it is almost impossible to grow up in the United States without acquiring such negative racial associations (Fazio & Olson, 2003). Such implicit attitudes have consequences for important outcomes such as juror decision making when the defendant is African American (Goff, Eberhardt, Williams, & Jackson, 2008).

While social psychologists can learn people's attitudes about many objects from their conscious reports of the thoughts and feelings they have about them, another approach is required if we want to learn someone's implicit attitudes—that is, attitudes they may be either unwilling or unable to report. A method for assessing these is the *Implicit Association Test* (IAT) (Greenwald, McGhee, & Schwarz, 1998). The IAT is based on the fact that we may associate various social objects more or less readily with positive or negative descriptive words. When there is a close association between a social group—say, Canadians—and some evaluative word such as "polite," one's reaction in identifying this connection is faster than if the social object was paired with a word that one did not readily associate with Canadians, perhaps "rude." Quicker reactions to positive objects and one social group over another can reflect differential valuing of that group. Consider the gender gap in wages that continues to exist today. Might it be that this is due, in part, to the valued attribute of "money" being automatically associated with men versus women? Research by Williams, Paluck, and Spencer-Rodgers (2010) using the IAT obtained evidence that male references (e.g., man, son, husband) were automatically associated with wealth-related terms (e.g., rich, cash, paycheck) as indicated by faster response latencies to those pairings than with female references (e.g., mother, aunt, daughter). If you would like to see how assessment of implicit attitudes is done, the website http://implicit.harvard.edu/implicit offers a wide-ranging set of IATs about groups that you can take and receive feedback concerning your implicit attitudes about those groups.

Before doing so, though, consider one warning: Although the IAT is viewed by some investigators as an important way to "get inside your head," a criticism that has been leveled at this test is that it really assesses commonly known connections between social groups and various attributes, even though the respondent might not actually endorse the validity of those connections. That is, one might be fully aware of a common negative stereotype regarding a particular social group, but not personally concur with that negative belief. Consider the possibility raised by Arkes and Tetlock (2004). Because well-known African American leaders are likely to have knowledge of the negative stereotypic attributes associated with African Americans, they might "fail" the IAT! That is, this measure might suggest such persons hold negative attitudes toward their own group, African Americans. Because implicit measures may be assessing familiarity with the culture rather than an individual's *actual* attitudes, the meaning of IAT scores remains controversial (Gawronski, LeBel, & Peters, 2007). Moreover, research has revealed that the IAT is susceptible to deliberate faking (Fiedler, Messner, & Bluemke, 2006) and that people are often aware of and surprisingly accurate in predicting their IAT responses (Hahn, Judd, Hirsh, & Blair, 2014). Despite these ambiguities, a review of research comparing implicit and explicit attitudes indicates that they reflect distinct evaluations of the world around us, and implicit attitudes can predict some behaviors better than explicit attitude measures (Greenwald, Poehlman, Uhlmann, & Banaji, 2009).

Social psychologists view attitudes as important because they often *do* influence our behavior. This is especially likely to be true when attitudes are strong and accessible (Bizer, Tormala, Rucker, & Petty, 2006; Fazio, 2000). What is your attitude toward Kim Kardashian, Sadie Robertson, Tyler Posey, Amy Schumer, Blake Shelton, and Janel Parrish? If positive, you may enjoy following their activities on Twitter, Facebook, or Instagram, as shown in Figure 5.4. Do you like reality TV? If so, we might predict that you probably watch *Keeping up with the Kardashians*, *The Voice*, *Dancing*

Figure 5.4 Attitudes Toward Celebrities Predict Behaviors Reflecting Interest in Their Lives

When people hold positive attitudes toward particular celebrities (from left to right: Sadie Robertson, Janel Parrish, and Tyler Posey), they are likely to enjoy hearing about events in their lives, follow their postings on Twitter or Facebook, and generally attend to information about them.

with the Stars, Deadliest Catch, or *Duck Dynasty.* If instead you prefer dramas, perhaps you watch *Pretty Little Liars* or *Teen Wolf.*

Attitudes can also affect important behavioral choices that have long-term consequences, so it is important to understand how they influence decision making. Suppose you receive an e-mail from your student health services office encouraging you to get the flu shot this fall in order to avoid potentially catching the flu? What factors are likely to influence your choice to do so or not? Because people differ in the extent to which they give weight to future consequences, this might affect how information about getting vaccinated is processed and therefore attitude-based decisions. Morison, Cozzolino, and Orbell (2010) proposed the model shown in Figure 5.5 where considering future consequences can lead to more positive thoughts about a message concerning a vaccine's benefits and risks, and these thoughts should predict attitudes toward the vaccine.

To test their model, these investigators first assessed parents' tendencies to consider future consequences of their decisions, and then gave them balanced information concerning the benefits and risks of having their daughters vaccinated for the human papilloma virus (which causes cervical cancer in women). After reading the information about the virus and vaccine, parents listed their thoughts about it, which were later coded as positive or negative. Then, attitudes toward the vaccine were measured, as was anticipated regret if they did not have their daughter vaccinated and she gets the virus in the future. Finally, the parents' agreement to have their daughter vaccinated was assessed. Results supported the model: Parents who think more about future consequences of their actions generated more positive thoughts (relative to negative thoughts) about the vaccination, which in turn predicted more positive attitudes toward the vaccine and greater anticipated regret of not doing so—both of which fed into choosing to have their daughter vaccinated. So, sometimes attitudes are formed on the basis of careful consideration of the information and, once those attitudes are formed, they can predict behavior in important domains such as medical decision making.

In this chapter, we will consider many influences on *attitude formation.* After doing so, we'll address in-depth a question we have already raised: When do attitudes influence behavior and, importantly, when do they not? Then, we'll turn to the important question of how attitudes are changed—the process of *persuasion.* We'll also examine some reasons *why* attitudes are often resistant to change. Finally, we'll consider the intriguing fact that on some occasions our own actions shape our attitudes rather than vice versa. The process that underlies such effects is known as *cognitive dissonance,* and it has fascinating implications not just for attitude change, but for many aspects of social behavior as well.

Figure 5.5 Factors That Influence Attitudes and Medical Decision Making

People who consider the future consequences of their actions reported more positive than negative thoughts about a vaccine after reading balanced information about its potential benefits and risks, and this predicted their attitudes about the vaccine and the extent to which regret for not acting was anticipated—which then predicted the decision to agree to receiving the vaccination.

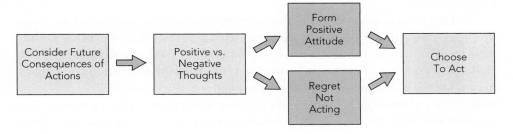

5.1: Attitude Formation: How Attitudes Develop

Objective **Identify the learning processes through which our attitudes are formed**

How do you feel about each of the following: tattoos on people's bodies, the TV programs *Game of Thrones* and *Grey's Anatomy*, sushi, the police, Toyotas, graffiti, cats, and Country music? Most people have attitudes about each of these. Did you acquire them as a result of your own experiences with each, from other people with whom you have had personal contact, or through exposure via the media? Are your attitudes toward these objects held with great certainty, or are they flexible and likely to change as conditions do? One important means by which our attitudes are formed is through the process of **social learning**. In other words, many of our views are acquired by interacting with others, or simply observing their behavior. Such learning occurs through several processes that are outlined in the following subsections.

5.1.1: Classical Conditioning: Learning Based on Association

It is a basic principle of psychology that when a stimulus that is capable of evoking a response—the *unconditioned stimulus*—regularly precedes another neutral stimulus, the one that occurs first can become a signal for the second—the *conditioned stimulus*. Advertisers have considerable expertise in using this principle to create positive attitudes toward their products. To use this method for creating attitudes, you need to know what your potential audience already responds positively toward (to use as the unconditioned stimulus). If you are marketing a new beer, and your target audience is young adult males, you might safely assume that attractive young women will produce a positive response. Then, you pair the product repeatedly (the formerly neutral or conditioned stimulus—say, your beer logo) with images of attractive women and, before long, positive attitudes will be formed toward your new beer! Of course, for other target audiences, another unconditioned stimulus might be successfully paired with the new beer logo to achieve the same result. As shown in Figure 5.6, Budweiser and many other manufacturers have used this principle to beneficially affect sales of its product.

Classical conditioning can affect attitudes via two pathways: the direct and indirect route (Sweldens, van Osselaer, & Janiszewski, 2010). The more generally effective and typical method used—*the direct route*—can be seen in the Budweiser advertisement. That is, positive stimuli (e.g., images of *different* women) are repeatedly paired with the product, with the aim being to directly transfer the affect felt about the women to the brand. However, by pairing a *specific* celebrity endorser who is already liked by the target audience with a brand, a memory link between the two can be established. With this indirect route, the idea is that by repeatedly presenting that specific celebrity with the product, then whenever that celebrity is thought of, the product too will come to mind. Think now about Michael Jordan; does Nike come to mind more rapidly for you? For this indirect conditioning process to work, people need not be aware that this memory link is being formed, but they do need to feel positively toward the unconditioned stimulus—that is, that particular celebrity (Stahl, Unkelbach, & Corneille, 2009).

Not only can classical conditioning contribute to shaping our attitudes—it can do so even though we are not aware of the stimuli that serve as the basis for this kind of conditioning. For instance, in one experiment (Walsh & Kiviniemi, 2014), students saw photos of apples and bananas. While these photos were shown, other photos known to induce either positive or negative feelings were exposed for very brief periods of time—so brief that participants were not aware of their presence. Participants who were nonconsciously exposed to photos that induced positive feelings (e.g., baby animals) were later more likely to select fruit as a snack than participants

Figure 5.6 Classical Conditioning of Attitudes—The Direct Route

Initially people may be neutral toward a product label. However, after repeatedly pairing the product's logo with an "unconditioned stimulus" of various attractive women to the targeted group of young males, then seeing the beer logo may come to elicit positive attitudes on its own.

who had been exposed to photos that nonconsciously induce negative feelings (e.g., junk cars) or those who had been exposed to neutral images (e.g., baskets). Even though participants were not aware that they had been exposed to the second group of photos, because they were presented very briefly, the photos did significantly influence participants' fruit eating, and this was not the result of conscious changes in beliefs about the nutritional benefits of eating fruit. The repeated pairing of fruits with positive images created affective associations that affected subsequent behavioral choices. These findings suggest that attitudes can be influenced by **subliminal conditioning**—classical conditioning that occurs in the absence of conscious awareness of the stimuli involved.

Indeed, **mere exposure**—having seen an object before, but too rapidly to remember having seen it—can result in attitude formation (Bornstein & D'Agostino, 1992). We know that this is a case of subliminal conditioning because patients with advanced Alzheimer's disease—who therefore cannot remember seeing the stimuli—show evidence of having formed new attitudes as a result of mere exposure (Winograd, Goldstein, Monarch, Peluso, & Goldman, 1999). It is also the case that even when we can remember being exposed to information, its mere repetition creates a sense of familiarity and results in more positive attitudes. Moons, Mackie, and Garcia-Marques (2009) refer to this as the *illusion of truth effect*. The studies by these researchers revealed that more positive attitudes developed following exposure to *either* weak or strong arguments—when little detailed message processing occurred. Although this has substantial implications for the likely impact of advertising on the attitudes we form—as a result of merely hearing the message repeated—it is good to know that this effect *can* be overcome when people are motivated and able to process the message extensively.

Once formed, such attitudes can influence behavior—even when those attitudes are inconsistent with how we are explicitly expected to behave. Consider the child whose attitudes toward an ethnic or religious group such as Arabs or Muslims have been classically conditioned to be negative, and who later are placed in a classroom where such negative attitudes are non-normative (i.e., they are deemed unacceptable).

Figure 5.7 Feelings of Threat Can Result in Prejudice, Even When Norms Are Anti discriminatory

In this study, an antidiscrimination norm against showing prejudice toward foreigners was only effective at reducing favoritism toward members of their own group when people were feeling little threat. But when threat is present, an explicit antidiscrimination norm is not effective—people continue to discriminate by showing favoritism toward their own group members.

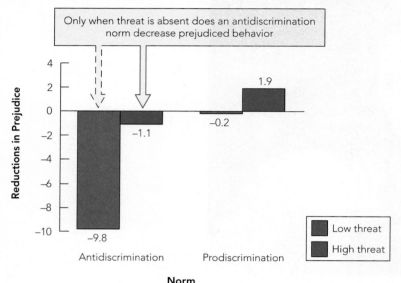

Research conducted in Switzerland by Falomir-Pichastor, Munoz-Rojas, Invernizzi, and Mugny (2004) has revealed that, as shown in Figure 5.7, when norms are antidiscriminatory, if feelings of threat from that "outsider" group are low, then prejudice can be reduced. When, however, feelings of threat are high, then the child is likely to continue to show prejudice even when the norms are antidiscriminatory. This research illustrates that attempts to change negative attitudes using explicit norms may only be effective when threat is absent.

5.1.2: Instrumental Conditioning: Rewards for the "Right" Views

When we asked you earlier to think about your attitudes toward marijuana, some of you may have thought immediately "Oh, that's wrong!" This is because most children have been repeatedly praised or rewarded by their parents and teachers ("just say no" programs) for stating such views. As a result, individuals learn which views are seen as the "correct" attitudes to hold—because of the rewards received for voicing those attitudes by the people they identify with and want to be accepted by. This is consistent with the huge gulf in attitudes toward Climate Change held by Republicans and Democrats in the United States. Attitudes that are followed by positive outcomes (e.g., praise) tend to be strengthened and are likely to be repeated, whereas attitudes that are followed by negative outcomes (e.g., punishment) are weakened and their likelihood of being expressed again is reduced. Thus, another way in which attitudes are acquired is through the process of **instrumental conditioning**—differential rewards and punishments. Sometimes the conditioning process is rather subtle, with the reward being psychological acceptance—by rewarding children with smiles, approval, or hugs for stating the "right" views. Because of this form of conditioning, until the teen years—when peer influences become especially strong—most children express political, religious, and social views that are highly similar to those of their parents and other family members (Oskamp & Schultz, 2005).

What happens when we find ourselves in a new context where our prior attitudes may or may not be supported? Part of the college experience involves leaving behind our families and high school friends and entering new **social networks**—sets of individuals with whom we interact on a regular basis (Eaton, Majka, & Visser, 2008). The new networks (e.g., new sorority or fraternity) we find ourselves in may contain individuals who share our attitudes toward important social issues, or they may be composed of individuals holding different attitudes toward those issues. Do new attitudes form as we enter new social networks—in part, to garner rewards from agreeing with others who are newly important to us?

To investigate this issue, Levitan and Visser (2009) assessed the political attitudes of students at the University of Chicago when they arrived on campus and then determined over the course of the next 2 months the networks the students became part of, and how close the students felt toward each new network member. This allowed the researchers to determine the influence of these new peers on students' political attitudes. Those students who entered networks with more diverse attitudes toward affirmative action exhibited greater change in their attitudes over the 2-month period. These results suggest that entering new social networks can be quite influential—particularly when they introduce us to new strong arguments not previously encountered (Levitan & Visser, 2008). The desire to fit in with others and be rewarded for holding similar attitudes can be a powerful motivator of attitude formation and change.

It is also the case that people may be consciously aware that different groups they are members of will reward (or punish) them for expressing support for particular attitude positions. Rather than being influenced to change our attitudes, we may find ourselves expressing one view on a topic to one audience and another view to a different audience. Indeed, such potentially incompatible audiences tend to remain physically separated (e.g., your parents and your friends on campus). For this reason, as suggested in Figure 5.8, we are unlikely to be caught expressing different attitudes to audiences in different networks!

One way that social psychologists study the extent to which our reported attitudes depend on the expected audience is by varying who we believe will learn our attitude position. For example, people seeking membership in a fraternity or sorority (e.g., pledges) express different attitudes about other fraternities and sororities depending on whether they believe their attitudes will remain private or they think that the powerful members of the group who will be controlling their admittance will learn of the attitude position they advocated (Noel, Wann, & Branscombe, 1995). When those who are attempting to gain membership in an organization believe that other members will learn of "their attitudes," they derogate other fraternities or sororities as a means of communicating to decision makers that the particular organization they want to be admitted to is seen as the most desirable. Yet, when they believe their attitude responses will be private, they do not derogate other fraternities or sororities. Thus, our attitude expression can depend on the rewards we have received in the past and those we expect to receive in the future for expressing particular attitudes.

Figure 5.8 Expressing Different Attitudes to Different Audiences

People often tailor their attitudes to match those of their audience. When interacting with different people in our social network, or when the context changes and those we interact with changes, our attitudes can shift.

5.1.3: Observational Learning: Learning by Exposure to Others

A third means by which attitudes are formed can operate even when direct rewards for acquiring or expressing those attitudes are absent. This process is **observational learning**, and it occurs when individuals acquire attitudes or behaviors simply by observing others (Bandura, 1997). For example, people acquire attitudes toward many topics and objects by exposure to advertising—where we see "people like us" acting positively or negatively toward different kinds of objects or issues.

Why do people often adopt the attitudes that they hear others express, or acquire the behaviors they observe in others? One answer involves the mechanism of **social comparison**—our tendency to compare ourselves with others in order to determine whether our view of social reality is correct or not (Festinger, 1954). That is, to the extent that our views agree with those of others, we tend to conclude that our ideas and attitudes are accurate; after all, if others hold the same views, these views *must* be right! But are we equally likely to adopt all others' attitudes, or does it depend on our relationship to those others?

People often adjust their attitudes so as to hold views closer to those of others who they value and identify with—their **reference groups**. For example, Terry and Hogg (1996) found that the adoption of favorable attitudes toward wearing sunscreen depended on the extent to which the respondents identified with the group advocating this change. As a result of observing the attitudes held by others who we identify with, new attitudes can be formed.

Consider how this could affect the attitudes you form toward a new social group with whom you have personally had no contact. Imagine that you heard someone you like and respect expressing negative views toward this group. Would this influence your attitudes? While it might be tempting to say "Absolutely not!" research findings indicate that hearing others whom we see as similar to ourselves state negative views about a group can lead us to adopt similar attitudes—without ever meeting members of that group (e.g., Maio, Esses, & Bell, 1994; Terry, Hogg, & Duck, 1999). In such cases, attitudes are being shaped by our own desire to be similar to people we like. Now imagine that you heard someone you dislike and see as dissimilar to yourself expressing negative views toward this group. In this case, you might be less influenced by this person's attitude position. People are not troubled by disagreement with, and in fact expect to hold different attitudes from, people whom they categorize as different from themselves; it is, however, uncomfortable to differ on important attitudes from people who we see as similar to ourselves and therefore with whom we expect to agree (Turner, 1991).

Not only are people differentially influenced by others' attitude positions depending on how much they identify with those others, they also *expect* to be influenced by other people's attitude positions differentially depending on how much they identify with those others. When a message concerning safe sex and AIDS prevention was created for university students, those who identified with their university's student group believed that they would be personally influenced by the position advocated in the message, whereas those who were low in identification with their university's student group did not expect to be personally influenced by the message (Duck, Hogg, & Terry, 1999). Thus, when we identify with a group, we expect to be influenced by those others and, in fact, are likely to take on the attitudes that are perceived to be normative for that group.

Consider whether the identity relevance of a message concerning a new product might influence the attitude you form. To address this question, Fleming and Petty (2000) first selected students to participate who were either high or low in identification with their gender group. Then, they introduced a new snack product

Figure 5.9 Attitude Formation Among Those Who Are Highly Identified with Their Gender Group

Men formed more positive attitudes toward the new product when they thought other men liked it, but women formed more positive attitudes toward the product when they thought other women liked it.

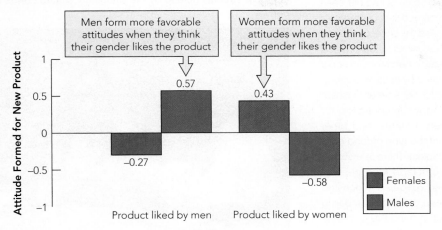

("Snickerdoodles") to men and women as either "women's favorite snack food" or "men's favorite snack food." As Figure 5.9 illustrates, among those who were highly identified with their gender group, a more favorable attitude toward this product was formed when the message was framed in terms of their own group liking that food. In contrast, among those low in identification with their gender group, no differences in the attitudes formed toward the new food were found as a function of which gender was said to favor that food. These findings indicate that the attitudes we form are indeed influenced by our identification with groups and our perception of what attitudes are held by members of those groups.

For more on the surprising role that modeling plays in our attitudes toward foods—what and how much we should eat—see the special section, **"What Research Tells Us About…Social Modeling and Eating."**

What Research Tells Us About…

Social Modeling and Eating

What, when, and how much we eat is profoundly affected by other people. Not only do we typically eat in the presence of others (e.g., dinner with our families), but we learn early in life what foods are acceptable for people like us to eat (e.g., pork is prohibited by some religions) and which potential foods are perceived as disgusting (e.g., worms, dogs, snakes, and cockroaches in North America). In fact, we may form negative attitudes toward some previously eaten and acceptable foods, based on newly acquired political beliefs (e.g., becoming vegetarian and subsequently refusing to eat meat).

Social norms can influence our beliefs not just of what are appropriate foods to eat, but also *how much* we should consume. Obesity and weight loss both have been linked to the social networks we belong to (Pachucki, Jacques, & Christakis, 2011). In-

deed, across studies that have manipulated food intake norms—information that others in one's group believe high-caloric intake is normative or that low-caloric intake is—there is evidence that the choices and actual quantity of food eaten is affected (Robinson, Thomas, Aveyard, & Higgs, 2014). When eating with others, we tend to mimic our companions eating behavior—a clear social modeling effect. Such mimicry is thought to reflect ingratiation, or the desire to be accepted by those others.

Research conducted by Robinson, Tobias, Shaw, Freeman, and Higgs (2011) confirmed the role of social acceptance needs in matching the eating of another person. These investigators first made half of their participants feel socially accepted—so their need to match the other person's eating would be lower—and the other half were assigned to a control condition where social acceptance needs were not addressed. Then, the participants were asked to play four games of "Hangman" with an accomplice of the experimenters who ate a set number of pieces of popcorn that was prominently displayed during the game playing. As was expected, participants whose need for acceptance had not been satisfied (those in the control condition), matched the accomplice's eating more closely than those whose need for acceptance had been satisfied. This suggests that regardless of our actual physical hunger state, social modeling of others' eating behavior can occur as a means of feeling closer to and accepted by another person.

A meta-analysis that combined over 69 studies assessing the effect of social models on eating, while controlling for participants' body weight, gender, dieting status, and other relevant factors, found that regardless of the type of food consumed (e.g., cookies, fruits, and vegetables), there is a strong modeling effect where people match others in food quantity intake (Cruwys, Bevelander, & Hermans, 2015). As suggested by Figure 5.10, it could be useful to keep the social modeling effects on eating attitudes and behavior in mind the next time you meet a friend for dinner. Social modeling effects are known to be especially likely when others are categorized as "like the self." When out with friends, I know that I've ordered a dessert when they have, despite my conscious belief that I shouldn't!

Figure 5.10 Modeling Others' Eating

Attitudes toward food, and intake quantity, are influenced by other people, especially people we feel similar to because we are most strongly guided by the seemingly shared norms they convey.

Key Points

- **Attitudes** can reflect evaluations of any aspect of the world, and thereby color our perceptions.
- Attitudes can be **explicit**—conscious and easy to report—or **implicit**—which implies they are potentially not consciously accessible. The *Implicit Association Test* is often used to assess whether the associations people have between a group or object are positive or negative.
- Attitudes are acquired from other persons through **social learning** processes. Such learning can involve classical conditioning, instrumental conditioning, or observational learning. Attitudes toward new topics can be shaped by the groups we belong to and value (i.e., our **reference groups**).
- Attitudes can be classically conditioned even without our awareness—via **subliminal conditioning** and **mere exposure**.
- Attitudes that are acquired through **instrumen-**

tal conditioning stem from differential rewards and punishments for adopting particular views. Attitudes can shift as people enter new **social networks** composed of individuals who hold differing attitudes.
- Because we compare ourselves with others to determine whether our view of social reality is correct or not, we are often influenced by the attitudes that others hold. As a result of the process of **social comparison**, people tend to adopt the attitude position of those they see as similar to themselves but not of those seen as dissimilar.
- When we identify with a group, we expect to be influenced by messages that are aimed at our group. We do not expect to be influenced when we do not identify with the group to which the attitude-relevant message is aimed. Attitudes about food and eating intake reflect modeling of others we perceive to be like ourselves.

5.2: When and Why Do Attitudes Influence Behavior?

Objective   **Examine the link between attitudes and behavior and the factors that affect their relationship**

So far we have considered how attitudes are formed. But we haven't addressed another important question: Do attitudes predict behavior? This question was first addressed more than 70 years ago in a classic study by LaPiere (1934). To determine whether people with negative attitudes toward a specific social group would in fact act in line with their attitudes, he spent 2 years traveling around the United States with a young Chinese couple. Along the way, they stopped at 184 restaurants and 66 hotels and motels. In the majority of the cases, they were treated courteously; in fact, they were refused service only once. After their travels were completed, LaPiere wrote to all the businesses where he and the Chinese couple had stayed or dined, asking whether they would or would not offer service to Chinese visitors. The results were startling: 92 percent of the restaurants and 91 percent of the hotels that responded said "No to Chinese customers!"

These results seemed to indicate that there is often a sizeable gap between attitudes and behavior—that is, what a person says and what that person actually does when confronted with the object of that attitude may be quite different. Does this mean that attitudes don't predict behavior? Not necessarily. To understand why attitudes might not straightforwardly predict behavior, we need to recognize that there are various norms that can affect the likelihood of discriminatory behavior. So even the most prejudiced people will not always act on their attitudes—when there are strong situational pressures to do otherwise. Likewise, there are social conditions under which people who do not think of themselves as prejudiced may find themselves discriminating against others based on their group membership. Let's consider now how the social context can affect the link between attitudes and behavior.

5.2.1: Role of the Social Context in the Link Between Attitudes and Behavior

You have probably experienced a gap between your own attitudes and behavior on many occasions—this is because the social context can directly affect the attitude–behavior connection. For instance, what would you say if one of your friends shows you a new tattoo of which he or she is proud and asks for your opinion? Would you state that you do *not* like it, if that was your view? The chances are quite good that you would try to avoid hurting your friend's feelings so you might even say you *like* it even though your attitude is negative. In such cases, we are clearly aware of our conscious choice not to act on our "true" attitude. As this example illustrates, depending on the degree to which the action has social consequences or not, attitudes may be differentially related to behavior. In contrast to your attitude–behavior inconsistency in responding to your friend's tattoo, your attitude might be a very good predictor of whether *you* would get a tattoo or not.

Because of the important role that the social context plays in determining when attitudes and behavior will be related, recent research has focused on the factors that determine *when* consistency can be expected, as well as the issue of *how* attitudes influence behavior. Several factors determine the extent to which attitudes and behavior correspond, with aspects of the situation influencing the extent to which attitudes determine behavior. In addition, features of the attitudes themselves are also important—for example, how *certain* you are of your own attitude. Attitudes that we hold with greater certainty are more strongly linked to behavior (Tormala & Petty, 2004) compared to attitudes about which we feel some uncertainty. Indeed, when people are induced to think that their attitudes are stable across time, they feel more certain about those attitudes and are more likely to act on them (Petrocelli, Clarkson, Tormala, & Hendrix, 2010). It is well known that older people are often more certain of their attitudes than are young people. Recent research suggests that this is partly due to older people placing greater value on "standing firm" or being resolute in the attitude positions they adopt, and for this reason they tend to show greater attitude–behavior consistency compared to younger people (Eaton, Visser, Krosnick, & Anand, 2009).

Have you ever been worried about what others would think of you if you expressed your "true" attitude toward an issue? If so, you will understand the dilemma that Stanford University students experienced in a study conducted by Miller and Morrison (2009). The private attitudes of those students toward heavy alcohol consumption were relatively negative. But, they believed that other students' attitudes toward heavy alcohol consumption were more positive than their own (an instance of **pluralistic ignorance**, where we erroneously believe others have attitudes different than ourselves). When these students were randomly assigned to receive information about other Stanford students' alcohol attitudes—that they held either more positive or more negative attitudes than their own—the students differed in how comfortable they felt expressing their attitude about alcohol use with another Stanford student and their likelihood of choosing alcohol policies as a topic for discussion. The students expressed greater comfort discussing campus drinking and chose that topic for discussion more often when they thought other students' attitudes were more pro-alcohol than their own, but they were less willing to do so when they learned other students' attitudes were more negative than their own. This pattern of wanting to express attitudes in the direction of the perceived campus norm but not when our attitudes go against the norm was especially strong for students who highly identified with their student group.

5.2.2: Strength of Attitudes

Consider the following situation: A large company markets a dangerous product to the public for decades, while internally sharing memos about the addictiveness of the product and how to manipulate that addictiveness. Along the way, an executive of the company has serious moral qualms about the rightness of these actions. Eventually, the concerned employee tips off the news media about these practices and an investigation is begun. The "whistle-blower" is eventually found out and is even sued by his former employer (although the lawsuit that was initiated against him is ultimately dropped).

You may recognize the person and company being described here because these events were ultimately made into a movie, *The Insider*. It was Jeffrey Wigand who blew the whistle on the practices of the tobacco industry in general and his former employer in particular—Brown & Williamson. Why might people take such drastic and potentially risky action (i.e., informing on their employer)? The answer is clear: Such persons are passionately committed to the notion that corporations must be honest, especially when there is the potential for damage to the public. Attitudes like these—that are based on moral convictions—can give rise to intense emotion and strongly predict behavior (Mullen & Skitka, 2006). In other words, whether attitudes will predict sustained and potentially costly behavior depends on the strength of the attitudes. Let's consider why attitude strength has this effect.

The term *strength* captures the *extremity* of an attitude (how strong the emotional reaction is), the degree of *certainty* with which an attitude is held (the sense that you know what your attitude is and the feeling that it is the correct position to hold), as well as the extent to which the attitude is based on *personal experience* with the attitude object. These three factors can affect attitude *accessibility* (how easily the attitude comes to mind in various situations), which ultimately determines the extent to which attitudes drive our behavior (Fazio, Ledbetter, & Towles-Schwen, 2000). As shown in Figure 5.11, all of these components of attitude strength are interrelated, and each plays a role in the likelihood that attitudes will be accessible and affect behavior (Petty & Krosnick, 1995). We'll now take a closer look at each of these important factors.

5.2.3: Attitude Extremity: Role of Vested Interests

Let's consider first attitude *extremity*—the extent to which an individual feels strongly—in one direction or the other—about an issue (Visser, Bizer, & Krosnick, 2006). One of the key determinants of this is what social psychologists term *vested interest*—the

Figure 5.11 How Attitude Strength Influences Attitude–Behavior Consistency

Attitudes that are extreme, certain, and formed on the basis of personal experience with the attitude object tend to be strong attitudes, which are more likely to be accessible when a behavioral response is made. Greater attitude–behavior consistency is found when attitudes are strong rather than weak.

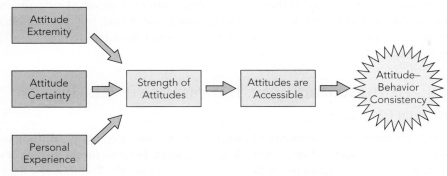

extent to which the attitude is relevant to the concerns of the individual who holds it. This typically amounts to whether the object or issue might have important consequences for this person. The results of many studies indicate that the greater such vested interest, the stronger the impact of the attitude on behavior (Crano, 1995; Visser, Krosnick, & Simmons, 2003). For example, when students at a large university were telephoned and asked if they would participate in a campaign *against* increasing the legal age for drinking alcohol from 18 to 21, their responses depended on whether they would be affected by the policy change or not (Sivacek & Crano, 1982). Students who would be affected by this new law—those younger than 21—have a stronger stake in this issue than those who would not be affected by the law because they were already 21 or would reach this age before the law took effect. Thus, it was predicted that those in the first group—whose interests were at stake—would be much more likely to join a rally against the proposed policy change than those in the second group. This is exactly what happened: While more than 47 percent of those with high vested interest agreed to take part in the campaign, only 12 percent of those in the low vested interest group did so.

Not only do people with a vested interest behave in a way that supports their cause, they are likely to elaborate on arguments that favor their position. By doing so, attitude-consistent thoughts come to mind when an issue is made salient. For example, Haugtvedt and Wegener (1994) found that when participants were asked to consider a nuclear power plant being built in their own state (high personal relevance) they developed more counterarguments against the plan than when the power plant might be potentially built in a distant state (low personal relevance). Thus, attitudes based on vested interest are more likely to be thought about carefully, be resistant to change, and be an accessible guide for behavior.

Research findings indicate that vested interests are particularly likely to affect judgments and behavior in the immediate context, whereas abstract values are more likely to when the judgment or behavior is in the distant future (Hunt, Kim, Borgida, & Chaiken, 2010). The issue these researchers tackled was one that has long puzzled those interested in voting and that Frank (2004) addressed in his book *What's the Matter with Kansas?* That is, when do people vote their economic self-interests and when do they "apparently act against their economic self-interests" and, instead, vote in favor of value-based proposals?

To test when vested interests are paramount and when they may play a lesser role in behavior, students' material interests were pitted against their egalitarian values. White American students were given a proposal that they believed would be enacted at their university either immediately or in the distant future. It would involve raising tuition by 10 percent in order to restore funds used for recruiting minority students that had been cut. Participants in the immediate condition who would experience the increase *opposed* the proposal, particularly when their own financial strain was high. In effect, they acted on their economic self-interests. In contrast, participants in the distant condition *favored* the proposal to the extent that they had egalitarian social attitudes. This research suggests that vested material interests do affect attitudes and voting when the policy is framed as having an immediate impact, but that for policies framed as having an impact only in the future, people favored and voted based on their values.

5.2.4: Attitude Certainty: Importance of Clarity and Correctness

Research has identified two important components of attitude certainty: **attitude clarity**—being clear about what one's attitude is—and **attitude correctness**—feeling one's attitude is the valid or proper one to hold. Research by Petrocelli, Tormala, and Rucker (2007) provides evidence for the distinction between these two components of attitude certainty by showing how different factors affect them.

To accomplish this task, Petrocelli and colleagues (2007) first determined that their participants felt negatively about a specific attitude issue: requiring students to carry identification cards with them at all times. Then, in order to manipulate the perception of *consensus* concerning their attitude position, half of the participants were given feedback that most other students (89 percent) agreed with their attitude toward the identification card issue, while the other half were told that most other students disagreed (only 11 percent agreed) with them. Although attitude clarity was equivalent in both the high and low consensus conditions, perceived correctness was greater when consensus was high (the 89 percent condition) rather than low (only 11 percent). When a person learns that others share one's attitudes, it acts as justification for that attitude and thereby increases certainty.

Clarity, the other component of attitude certainty, reflects a lack of ambivalence about an attitude issue. The more often you are asked to report on your attitude, the more it will facilitate clarity and thereby certainty. Repeatedly stating your attitude appears to "work" by increasing your subjective sense that you really *do* know how you feel about an object or issue. When Petrocelli et al. (2007) had their participants express their attitudes toward gun control either several times or only once, attitude certainty differed. Those in the "more expressions" condition had greater certainty about their attitudes toward gun control than those in the "single expression" condition.

What happens when both the clarity and correctness components are varied simultaneously? Returning to the identity card example, Petrocelli et al. (2007) gave students with negative attitudes toward the policy manipulations that were designed to affect both correctness (consensus) and clarity (repeated expression). The students were then given a persuasive message with strong arguments in favor of the policy but against their initial attitudes—why the policy would enhance student safety. More attitude change resulted in the low-clarity than the high-clarity condition (single versus repeated expression), and more attitude change occurred in the low-correctness versus the high-correctness condition (low versus high consensus). Both components of attitude certainty, when they are high, can increase resistance to a persuasive message—each independently contributing to resistance to persuasion.

The social context too is important in assessing the relative effects of attitude clarity and correctness. High clarity will be more predictive of behavior in private, but not public contexts—where correctness concerns are likely to be greater. Moreover, when people's attitudes are attacked, successfully resisting those attacks may well increase perceptions of attitude certainty because mounting and expressing counterarguments will increase perceptions of attitude correctness. In terms of attitude–behavior consistency, an attitude that is high on *both* clarity and correctness is most likely to reliably predict behavior in public and in private.

5.2.5: Role of Personal Experience

Depending on how attitudes are formed initially, the link between attitudes and behavior can differ. Considerable evidence indicates that attitudes formed on the basis of direct experience with the object about which we hold a particular attitude can exert stronger effects on behavior than ones formed indirectly. This is because attitudes formed on the basis of direct experience are likely to be stronger and be more likely to come to mind in the presence of the attitude object (Tormala, Petty, & Brinol, 2002). Similarly, attitudes based on personal relevance are more likely to be elaborated on in terms of supporting arguments, and this makes them resistant to change (Wegener, Petty, Smoak, & Fabrigar, 2004). Consider the difference between having a friend tell you that a particular car model, "Brand X," is a lemon versus having experienced some failures with this brand yourself. When looking at new models of "Brand X," would your friend's opinion even come to mind? Maybe not. Would your own experiences come to mind? Very likely. Thus, when you have direct experience with an attitude object it is likely to be quite personally relevant and strong, and your attitude toward it is likely to predict your behavior in the future.

Personal experience is one way to create involvement with an issue, and people who are more involved with an issue and whose values are linked with that issue are more likely to act on their attitudes (Blankenship & Wegener, 2008). For example, when students were asked to consider a novel issue—whether a fictitious country, Tashkentistan, should be allowed to join the European Union—in light of a value of importance to them (e.g., freedom) or in light of a value of little importance (e.g., unity), they spent more time thinking about and elaborating on the message when it involved important values compared to when it did not. This elaboration resulted in stronger attitudes, which in turn guides behavior even in contexts where those attitudes are under attack.

In sum, existing evidence suggests that attitudes really *do* affect behavior (Eagly & Chaiken, 1993; Petty & Krosnick, 1995). However, the strength of this link is strongly determined by a number of factors. First of all, situational constraints may not permit us to overtly express our attitudes. Second, attitude extremity, which is a function of whether we have a vested interest in the issue or not, influences whether our attitudes translate into behavior, and this is particularly likely when a message is framed as having an immediate impact rather than one far in the future. Third,

Key Points

- Attitudes toward a group, issue, or object do not always directly predict behavior. Rather, there are situational constraints and norms that affect our willingness to express our true attitudes. Concerns about what others, especially those with whom we identify, may think of us can limit the extent to which our attitudes and behavior are consistent.
- People sometimes show **pluralistic ignorance**—erroneously believing that others have different attitudes than themselves. This can limit the extent to which their attitudes are expressed in public.

- Strong attitudes are ones we are committed to, and we typically have moral values to support them. For this reason, they are more likely to be accessible at the time we take action and are particularly likely to influence behavior.
- Attitude strength subsumes several factors: *extremity*, *certainty*, and *degree of personal experience*. Those attitudes that are more extreme, certain (both in terms of **attitude clarity** and perceived **attitude correctness**), and based on personal experience or important values are more likely to be accessible and guide behavior than are less extreme, unclear, and indirectly formed attitudes.

attitudes that are clear and experienced as correct are more likely to affect behavior than are those that lack clarity or that we are uncertain about their correctness. Fourth, whether we have personal experience with the attitude object or perceive it as relevant to our important values can affect the accessibility of the attitude, and attitudes that are more accessible are more likely to determine behavior compared to those that are not accessible.

5.3: How Do Attitudes Guide Behavior?

Objective **Explain the two processes through which attitudes guide behavior**

When it comes to the question of *how* attitudes guide behavior, it should come as no surprise that researchers have found that there is more than one basic mechanism through which attitudes shape behavior. We will first consider behaviors that are driven by attitudes based on reasoned thought, and then examine the role of attitudes in more spontaneous behavioral responses.

5.3.1: Attitudes Arrived at Through Reasoned Thought

In some situations we give careful, deliberate thought to our attitudes and their implications for our behavior. Insight into the nature of this process is provided by the **theory of reasoned action**, which was later refined and termed the **theory of planned behavior** (Ajzen & Fishbein, 1980). This theoretical view starts with the notion that the decision to engage in a particular behavior is the result of a rational process. Various behavioral options are considered, the consequences or outcomes of each are evaluated, and a decision is reached to act or not to act. That decision is then reflected in *behavioral intentions,* which are often good predictors of whether we will act on our attitudes in a given situation (Ajzen, 1987). Indeed, for a number of behavioral domains—from condom use to engaging in regular exercise—intentions are moderately correlated with behavior (Albarracin, Johnson, Fishbein, & Muellerleile, 2001).

Recent research has made it clear that the intention–behavior relationship is even stronger when people have formed a plan for how and when they will translate their intentions into behavior (Barz et al., 2014; Frye & Lord, 2009). Suppose that you form the intention to go to the gym to work out. If you develop a plan for *how* you will translate your intention into actual behavior—beginning with setting your alarm, preparing your exercise clothes, and so forth—you will be more likely to succeed at doing so. In my own case, because I formed the intention to walk three mornings a week, I made a commitment to do so with my next-door neighbor. The reason that this is a particularly effective **implementation plan** is that I no longer have to assess whether I *really* want to go out today—in the cold, rain, or whatever, or rely on having my attitude toward getting more exercise be accessible at that time of the morning. As Gollwitzer (1999) has noted, such a plan to implement our intentions is very effective because it involves delegating control of one's behavior to the situation—in my case, my alarm clock beeping and, if that hasn't worked, my neighbor ringing my doorbell!

But, how do you form an intention to change some aspect of your behavior? According to the theory, intentions are determined by two factors: *Attitudes toward the behavior*—people's positive or negative evaluations of performing the behavior (whether they think it will yield positive or negative consequences), and *subjective norms*—people's perceptions of whether others will approve or disapprove of this behavior. A third factor, *Perceived behavioral control*—people's appraisals of their ability to perform the behavior—was subsequently added to the theory (Ajzen, 1991). Perhaps a specific example will help illustrate the nature of these ideas.

Suppose an adolescent male is considering joining Facebook. Will he actually take action, and go through the process of joining up on the website? First, the answer will depend on his intentions, which will be strongly influenced by his attitude toward

Facebook. His decision of whether to join or not will also be based on perceived norms and the extent to which he feels able to execute the decision. If the teen believes that becoming a member will be relatively painless and it will make him look more sociable (he has positive attitudes toward the behavior), he also believes that people whose opinions he values will approve of this action (subjective norms), and that he can readily do it (he knows how to access Facebook, upload some photos, and he believes he can control how much of his private data are exposed), his intentions to carry out this action may be quite strong. On the other hand, if he believes that joining Facebook might be dangerous because of the exposure of private data, joining might not really lead to more interaction with friends, or his friends will disapprove, then his intention to join will be relatively weak. His intentions are more likely to translate into behavior if he formulates a plan for when and how to join (e.g., "On Friday when I get done with school, I'll log on to Facebook and join up"). Of course, even the best of intentions can be thwarted by situational factors (e.g., an emergency that he has to attend to comes up on Friday), but, in general, intentions are an important predictor of behavior.

Reasoned action and planned behavior ideas have been used to predict behavior in many settings, with considerable success. Indeed, research suggests that these theories are useful for predicting such divergent behaviors as soldiers' conduct on the battlefront (Ajzen & Fishbein, 2005) and whether individuals drive a vehicle after they have consumed alcohol (MacDonald, Zanna, & Fong, 1995).

5.3.2: Attitudes and Spontaneous Behavioral Reactions

Our ability to predict behavior in situations where people have the time and opportunity to reflect carefully on various possible actions that they might undertake is quite good. However, in many situations, people have to act quickly and their reactions are more spontaneous. Suppose another driver cuts in front of you on the highway without signaling. In such cases, attitudes seem to influence behavior in a more direct and seemingly automatic manner, with intentions playing a less important role. According to Fazio's attitude-to-behavior process model (Fazio, 1990; Fazio & Roskos-Ewoldsen, 1994), some event activates our attitude; that attitude, once activated, influences how we perceive the attitude object. At the same time, our knowledge about what's appropriate in a given situation (our knowledge of various social norms) is also activated. Together, the attitude and the previously stored information about what's appropriate or expected shape our *definition* of the event. This perception, in turn, influences our behavior. Let's consider a concrete example.

Imagine that someone cuts into your traffic lane as you are driving (see Figure 5.12). This event triggers your attitude toward people who engage in such discourteous

---

Figure 5.12 Spontaneous Attitude-to-Behavior Process Effects

According to the attitude-to-behavior process view, events trigger our attitudes and, simultaneously, the appropriate norms for how people should or typically do behave in a given situation. In this case, being cut off in traffic by another driver triggers our attitudes toward such persons and our knowledge that this action is atypical. This interpretation, in turn, determines how we behave. Thus, attitudes are an important factor in shaping our overt behavior.

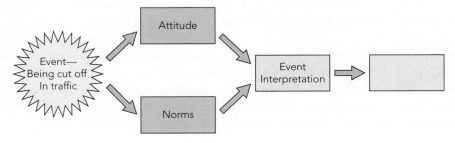

Key Points

- Several factors affect the strength of the relationship between attitudes and behavior; some of these relate to the situation in which the attitudes are activated, and some to aspects of the attitudes themselves.
- Having an **implementation plan**—specific actions that indicate how to translate our intentions into behavior is very effective because it involves delegating control of one's behavior to the situation.
- According to the **theory of reasoned action** and **theory of planned behavior**, attitudes influence behavior through

two different mechanisms. When we can give careful thought to our attitudes, *intentions* derived from our attitudes, *norms*, and *perceived control over the behavior*, all predict behavior.

- The **attitude-to-behavior process model** suggests that attitudes can be automatically activated and influence behavior by shaping interpretation of the situation, which in turn dictates behavior.

behavior, and, at the same time, your understanding of how people should behave on expressways. As a result, you perceive this action as non-normative, which influences your interpretation of and your response to that event. You might think, "Who does this person think she/he is? What nerve!" or, perhaps your response is more situational, "Gee, this person must be in a big hurry." Whichever of these interpretations of the event is made, it will shape the individual's behavior. Several studies provide support for this perspective on how attitudes can influence behavior by affecting the interpretation given to the situation.

In short, attitudes affect our behavior through at least two mechanisms, and these operate under somewhat contrasting conditions. When we have time to engage in careful, reasoned thought, we can weigh all the alternatives and decide how we will act. Under the hectic conditions of everyday life, however, we often don't have time for this kind of deliberate weighing of alternatives, and often people's responses appear to be much faster than such deliberate thought processes can account for. In such cases, our attitudes seem to spontaneously shape our perceptions of various events—often with very little conscious cognitive processing—and thereby affects our immediate behavioral reactions (e.g., Bargh & Chartrand, 2000; Dovidio, Brigham, Johnson, & Gaertner, 1996). To the extent that a person repeatedly performs a specific behavior—and a habit is formed—that person's responses may become relatively automatic whenever that same situation is encountered (Wood, Quinn, & Kashy, 2002).

5.4: The Science of Persuasion: How Attitudes Are Changed

Objective **Indicate the factors that determine whether persuasion attempts to alter our attitudes will be effective**

How many times in the last few days has someone tried to change your attitudes about something or other? If you stop and think for a moment, you may be surprised at the answer, for it is clear that each day we are literally bombarded with such attempts, some of which are illustrated in Figure 5.13. Billboards, television commercials, magazine ads, telemarketers, pop-up ads on your computer, and even our friends—the list of potential "would-be persuaders" seems almost endless. To what extent are such attempts at **persuasion**—efforts to change our attitudes through the use of various kinds of messages—successful? And what factors determine if they succeed or fail? Social psychologists have studied these issues for decades, and as we'll soon see, their efforts have yielded important insights into the cognitive processes that play a role in persuasion (e.g., Petty, Wheeler, & Tormala, 2003; Wegener & Carlston, 2005).

Figure 5.13 Persuasion: A Part of Daily Life

Each day we are bombarded with dozens of messages designed to change our attitudes or our behavior. Clearly, if they weren't effective at least some of the time, advertisers would not pay the sums that they do for these opportunities to try and persuade us to buy what they are promoting.

5.4.1: Persuasion: Communicators, Messages, and Audiences

Early research efforts aimed at understanding persuasion involved the study of the following elements: Some *source* directs some type of *message* to some person or group of persons (the *audience*). Persuasion research conducted by Hovland, Janis, and Kelley (1953) focused on these key elements, asking: "*Who* says *what* to *whom* with what effect?" This approach yielded a number of important findings, with the following being the most consistently obtained.

- Communicators who are *credible*—who seem to know what they are talking about or who are expert with respect to the topics or issues they are presenting—are more persuasive than those who are seen as lacking expertise. For instance, in a famous study on this topic, Hovland and Weiss (1951) asked participants to read communications dealing with various issues (e.g., atomic submarines, the future of movie theaters—remember, this was back in 1950). The supposed source of these messages was varied so as to be high or low in credibility. For instance, for atomic submarines, a highly credible source was the famous scientist J. Robert Oppenheimer, while the low-credibility source was *Pravda*, the newspaper of the Communist party in the Soviet Union (notice how the credible source was an in-group member, but the low credible source for these American participants was an out-group source). Participants expressed their attitudes toward these issues a week before the experiment, and then immediately after receiving the communications. Those who were told that the source of the messages they read was a highly credible in-group member showed significantly greater attitude change than those who thought the message was from the out-group, which lacked trustworthiness and credibility. Members of our own group are typically seen as more credible and therefore are likely to influence us more than those with whom we do not share a group membership and with whom we might even *expect* to disagree (Turner, 1991).

- Communicators can, though, lose their credibility and therefore their ability to persuade. One means by which credibility can be undermined is if you learn that a communicator has a personal stake (financial or otherwise) in persuading you to adopt a particular position. Consequently, communicators are seen as most credible and, therefore persuasive, when they are perceived as arguing against their self-interests (Eagly, Chaiken, & Wood, 1981).

- Communicators who are physically attractive are more persuasive than communicators who are not attractive (Hovland & Weiss, 1951). Frequently, advertisers who use attractive models are attempting to suggest to us that if we buy their product, we too will be perceived as attractive. Another way that communicators can be seen as attractive is via their perceived likeability (Eagly & Chaiken, 1993). We are more likely to be persuaded by a communicator we like than one we dislike. This is one reason that famous sports figures such as LeBron James, musicians such as Beyoncé Knowles, actresses such as Jennifer Aniston, and actors such as Brad Pitt are selected as spokespersons for various products (see Figure 5.14)—we already like them so are more readily persuaded by them.

- Communicators who we feel we know already—that is, those in our own social networks—are also likely to be persuasive. When opinions, including recommendations and general product information, are provided in an informal person-to-person manner, it is referred to as word-of-mouth marketing (Katz & Lazarsfeld, 1955). If you have ever told someone about a good restaurant or movie or made some other type of product recommendation, you've engaged in word-of-mouth marketing. People we know and already like will be especially influential, in part because we see them as trustworthy and as having the same interests as ourselves.

- In what has come to be called eWOM (electronic word-of-mouth), Facebook, Twitter, and the other Internet forums have become means by which the transmission of word-of-mouth communications is accomplished. When tracking a conversation on Facebook or just browsing through your daily "news feed," information about which of your friends "like" a particular product is readily available. Marketers know such "recommendations" from friends will be highly persuasive. Cheung, Luo, Sia, and Chen (2009) found that credibility in the online context is a major concern so recommendation ratings from "friends" are particularly important in determining whether consumers will be persuaded to act by purchasing. As Harris and Dennis (2011) indicate, Facebook alone has a membership of 500 million worldwide, and the average user has 130 "Friends." People are spending more

---

Figure 5.14 Attractiveness in Persuasion: Can the Same Person Persuade Us to Buy Different Types of Products?

Research reveals that we are more persuaded by someone we view as attractive and like. In fact, actors such as Brad Pitt shown here are selected to be spokesperson for many different products—both those that are beauty relevant (perfume) and those that are not (watches).

time on Facebook than other sites combined and, increasingly, many of our commercial transactions and retail decisions now occur within that site.

- Messages that do not appear to be designed to change our attitudes are often more successful than those that seem to be designed to achieve this goal (Walster & Festinger, 1962). Indeed, a meta-analysis of the existing research on this issue indicates that forewarning does typically lessen the extent to which attitude change occurs (Benoit, 1998). So, simply knowing that a sales pitch is coming your way can undermine its persuasiveness.

- One approach to persuasion that has received considerable research attention is the effect of **fear appeals**—messages that are intended to arouse fear in the recipient. When the message is sufficiently fear arousing that people genuinely feel threatened, they are likely to argue against the threat, or else dismiss its applicability to themselves (Liberman & Chaiken, 1992; Taylor & Shepperd, 1998). Indeed, there is evidence using neuroscience methods, where event-related brain potentials are assessed, that when people are exposed to a highly threatening health message, they allocate their attention away when the message *is* self-relevant (Kessels, Ruiter, Wouters, & Jansma, 2014).

Yet, as Figure 5.15 illustrates, gruesome fear-based ads have been used in an attempt to frighten people about future consequences if they fail to change their behavior. Despite the long-standing use of such fear-based messages, a meta-analysis of studies examining the role of fear in persuasion finds that they are not generally effective at changing people's behaviors (de Hoog, Stroebe, & de Wit, 2007).

Might inducing more moderate levels of fear work better? There is some evidence that this is the case—but it needs to be paired with specific methods of behavioral change that will allow the negative consequences to be avoided (Petty, 1995). If people do not know how to change, or do not believe that they can succeed in doing so, fear tends to induce avoidance and defensive responses.

Research findings (Broemer, 2004) suggest that health messages of various sorts are *more* effective if they are framed in a positive manner (e.g., how to attain good health) rather than in a negative manner (e.g., risks and undesirable consequences of particular behaviors). Consider how message framing and perceived risk of having a serious outcome befall the self can affect persuasion following exposure to a message designed to encourage low income ethnic minority women to be tested for HIV (Apanovitch, McCarthy, & Salovey, 2003). Those women who perceived themselves as unlikely to test positive for HIV were more likely to be persuaded to be tested (and they actually got tested) when the message was framed in terms of the gains to be

---

Figure 5.15 Using Fear to Encourage Change

Many messages use frightening images in an attempt to "scare people" into changing their attitudes and behavior, including the sorts of warnings illustrated here that are aimed at getting people to stop smoking or behave in environmentally friendly ways to mitigate climate change.

had by doing so (e.g., "The peace of mind you'll get or you won't have to worry that you could spread the virus") than when the message was framed in terms of potential losses they would otherwise experience (e.g., "You won't have peace of mind or you could spread the virus unknowingly to those you care about"). Positive framing can be effective in inducing change—especially when individuals fail to perceive themselves as especially at risk.

Early research on persuasion certainly provided important insights into the factors that influence persuasion. What this work did *not* do, however, was offer a comprehensive account of *how* persuasion occurs. For instance, why, precisely, are highly credible or attractive communicators more effective in changing attitudes than less credible or attractive ones? Why might positive message framing (rather than negative, fear-based) produce more attitude change? In recent years, social psychologists have recognized that to answer such questions, it is necessary to carefully examine the cognitive processes that underlie persuasion—in other words, what goes on in people's minds while they listen to a persuasive message. It is to this highly sophisticated work that we turn next.

5.4.2: The Cognitive Processes Underlying Persuasion

What happens when you are exposed to a persuasive message—for instance, when you watch a television commercial or see ads pop up on your screen as you surf the Internet? Your first answer might be something like "I think about what's being said," and in a sense, that's correct. But as we saw in Chapter 2 people often do the least amount of cognitive work that they can in a given situation. Indeed, people may *want* to avoid listening to such commercial messages (and thanks to DVDs and Netflix, people can skip commercials with those formats entirely). But when you are subjected to a message, the central issue—the one that seems to provide the key to understanding the entire process of persuasion—is really, "How do we process (absorb, interpret, evaluate) the information contained in such messages?" The answer that has emerged from hundreds of separate studies is that basically, we can process persuasive messages in two distinct ways.

SYSTEMATIC VERSUS HEURISTIC PROCESSING The first type of processing we can employ is known as **systematic processing** or the **central route to persuasion**, and it involves careful consideration of message content and the ideas it contains. Such processing requires effort, and it absorbs much of our information-processing capacity. The second approach, known as **heuristic processing** or the **peripheral route to persuasion**, involves the use of mental shortcuts such as the belief that "experts' statements can be trusted," or the idea that "if it makes me feel good, I'm in favor of it." This kind of processing requires less effort and allows us to react to persuasive messages in an automatic manner. It occurs in response to cues in the message or situation that evoke various mental shortcuts (e.g., beautiful models evoke the "What's beautiful is good and worth listening to" heuristic).

When do we engage in each of these two distinct modes of thought? Modern theories of persuasion such as the **elaboration-likelihood model** (**ELM**; e.g., Petty & Cacioppo, 1986; Petty, Cacioppo, Strathman, & Priester, 2005) and the **heuristic-systematic model** (e.g., Chaiken, Liberman, & Eagly, 1989; Eagly & Chaiken, 1998) provide the following answer. We engage in the most effortful and systematic processing when our motivation and capacity to process information relating to the persuasive message is high. This type of processing occurs if we have a lot of knowledge about the topic, we have a lot of time to engage in careful thought, the issue is sufficiently important to us, or we believe it is essential to form an accurate view (Maheswaran & Chaiken, 1991; Petty & Cacioppo, 1986).

In contrast, we engage in the type of processing that requires less effort (heuristic processing) when we lack the capacity or time to process more carefully (we must make up our minds very quickly or we have little knowledge about the issue) or when our motivation to perform such cognitive work is low (the issue is unimportant to us or has little potential effect on us). Advertisers, politicians, salespersons, and others wishing to change our attitudes prefer to push us into the heuristic mode of processing because, for reasons described later, it is often easier to change our attitudes when we think in this mode than when we engage in more careful and systematic processing. Strong arguments in favor of the position being advocated are not needed when people do not process those arguments very carefully! The two routes to persuasion suggested by the ELM model are shown in Figure 5.16.

What role might consuming a drug like caffeine have on persuasion? The central route to persuasion works when people attend to a message and systematically process its contents. Given that caffeine intake should increase people's ability to systematically process the contents of a message, if people have the opportunity to focus on a persuasive message without being distracted, they should be persuaded more after consuming caffeine than after not consuming it. In contrast, when people are highly distracted, it should prevent them from systematically processing the message—and if caffeine works via the central route—distraction should lessen the extent to which they are persuaded.

Research findings have supported these ideas: In low-distraction conditions, those who have consumed caffeine agree more with the message (they are persuaded away from their original opinion) than those who received a caffeine-free placebo. In contrast, when people are distracted and systematic processing of the message content is impossible, there is no difference in the attitudes of those who consumed caffeine and those who did not (Martin, Hamilton, McKimmie, Terry, & Martin, 2007). It is the increased thinking about the message when people are not distracted that can result in increased persuasion in caffeine drinkers. So, as shown in Figure 5.17, be prepared to think carefully about the messages you are exposed to when you get your next "caffeine fix"!

The discovery of these two contrasting modes of processing—systematic versus heuristic—has provided an important key to understanding when and how persuasion

---

Figure 5.16 The ELM Model: A Cognitive Theory of Persuasion

According to the elaboration-likelihood model (ELM), persuasion can occur in one of two ways. First, we can be persuaded by systematically processing the information contained in the persuasive messages (the central route), or second, by use of heuristics or mental shortcuts (the peripheral route). Systematic processing occurs when the message is important to us and we have the cognitive resources available to think about it carefully. Heuristic processing is most likely when the message is not important to us or we do not have the cognitive resources (or time) to engage in careful thought.

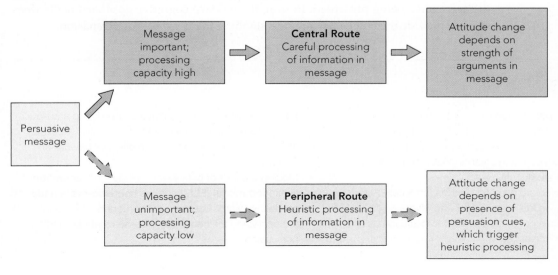

Figure 5.17 Drinking Beverages Containing Caffeine Can Increase Persuasion

Are these people, after getting a "dose" of caffeine, more likely to be persuaded by the messages they receive—than people who have not consumed caffeine? Yes, to the extent that the message is systematically processed.

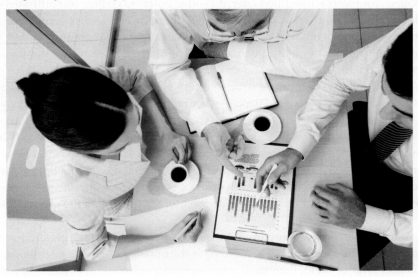

occurs. For instance, when persuasive messages are not interesting or relevant to individuals, the degree of persuasion they produce is *not* strongly influenced by the strength of the arguments these messages contain. When such messages are highly relevant to individuals, however, they are much more successful in inducing persuasion when the arguments they contain *are* strong and convincing. Can you see why this so? According to modern theories such as the ELM that consider these dual pathways, when relevance is low, individuals tend to process messages through the heuristic mode, using various mental shortcuts. Thus, argument strength has little impact. In contrast, when relevance is high, they process persuasive messages more systematically and in this mode, argument strength *is* important (e.g., Petty & Cacioppo, 1986).

Similarly, the systematic versus heuristic distinction helps explain why people can be more easily persuaded when they are distracted than when they are not. Under these conditions, the capacity to process the information in a persuasive message is limited, so people adopt the heuristic mode of thought. If the message contains cues that will induce heuristic processing (e.g., communicators who are attractive or seemingly expert), persuasion may occur because people respond to these cues and not to the arguments being presented. In sum, the modern cognitive approach really does seem to provide the crucial key to understanding many aspects of persuasion.

Key Points

- Early research on **persuasion**—efforts to change attitudes through the use of messages—focused primarily on characteristics of the *communicator* (e.g., expertise, attractiveness), *message* (e.g., fear appeals), and *audience* (e.g., friends who are like us).
- Communicators who are deemed credible, physically attractive, people we like already, and who offer a message that seems not to be designed to persuade us usually are most persuasive.

- **Fear appeals**—messages that are intended to arouse fear—if too frightening tend not to be effective. Positively framed messages are often more effective persuasion devices.
- Modern theories of persuasion include the **elaboration-likelihood model (ELM)** and the **heuristic-systematic model**. Research based on these models has sought to understand the cognitive processes that play a role in persuasion.

- Persuasive messages can be processed in two distinct ways: through **systematic processing** or **central route to persuasion**, which involves careful attention to message content, or through **heuristic processing** or **peripheral route to persuasion**, which involves the use of mental shortcuts (e.g., "experts are usually right").
- Argument strength only affects persuasion when more systematic processing is engaged, whereas peripheral cues such as features of the communicator's attractiveness or expertise only affect persuasion when more heuristic processing occurs.
- Substances such as caffeine can affect persuasion because of their effects on systematic processing of the information in a message.

5.5: Resisting Persuasion Attempts

Objective   **Examine the methods that help people resist skilled attempts to persuade us**

As we have been discussing, people can be persuaded to change their attitudes and behavior—either because they think systematically about a compelling message, or because they are influenced by more peripheral cues. Why then might people sometimes be a "tough sell" where efforts to change attitudes are concerned? The answer involves several factors that, together, enhance our ability to resist even highly skilled efforts at persuasion.

5.5.1: Reactance: Protecting Our Personal Freedom

Few of us like being told what to do, but in a sense that is precisely what advertisers and other would-be persuaders do. You have probably experienced another individual who increasingly pressures you to change your attitude on some issue. In both of these instances, whether "public" persuaders or private ones, you are on the receiving end of threats to your freedom to decide for yourself. As a result, you may experience a growing level of annoyance and resentment. The final outcome: Not only do you resist their persuasion attempts, but you may actually lean over backward to adopt views *opposite* to those the would-be persuader wants you to adopt. Such behavior is an example of what social psychologists call **reactance**—a negative reaction to efforts by others to reduce our freedom by getting us to believe or do what *they* want (Brehm, 1966). Research indicates that in such situations, we do often change our attitudes and behavior in the opposite direction from what we are being urged to believe or to do. Indeed, when we are feeling reactance, strong arguments in favor of attitude change can increase opposition compared to moderate or weak arguments (Fuegen & Brehm, 2004).

The existence of reactance is one reason that hard-sell attempts at persuasion often fail. When individuals perceive such appeals as direct threats to their personal freedom (or their image of being an independent person), they are strongly motivated to resist. This process was illustrated by recent research among college students who were presented with a persuasive message concerning an extra assignment by an instructor using forceful language or not (Ball & Goodboy, 2014). Greater dissent and challenge behavior toward the instructor emerged in the forceful language condition, which reflected students' experience of threat and attempts to restore their freedom after experiencing reactance.

5.5.2: Forewarning: Prior Knowledge of Persuasive Intent

When we watch television, we fully expect there to be commercials, and we know full well that these messages are designed to persuade us to purchase various products. Similarly, we know that when we listen to a political speech that the person delivering it is attempting to persuade us to vote for him or her. Does the fact that we know in advance about the persuasive intent behind such messages help us to resist them? Research on the effects of such advance knowledge—known as **forewarning**—indicates that it does (e.g., Cialdini & Petty, 1981; Johnson, 1994). When we know that a speech or written appeal is designed to alter our views, we are often less likely to be affected by it than when we do not possess such knowledge. Why? Because forewarning influences several cognitive processes that play an important role in persuasion.

First, forewarning provides us with more opportunity to formulate *counterarguments*—those that refute the message—and that can lessen the message's impact. In addition, forewarning provides us with more time to recall relevant information that may prove useful in refuting the persuasive message. Wood and Quinn (2003) found that forewarning was generally effective at increasing resistance, and that simply *expecting* to receive a persuasive message (without actually even receiving it) can influence attitudes in a resistant direction. In many cases, then, forewarned is indeed forearmed where persuasion is concerned. But what if you are distracted between the time of the warning and receipt of the message—to such an extent that it prevents you from forming counterarguments? Research has revealed that forewarning does not prevent persuasion when people are distracted; in this case, people are no more likely to resist the message than those not forewarned of the upcoming persuasive appeal.

There are instances where forewarnings can encourage attitude shifts toward the position being advocated in a message, but this effect appears to be a temporary response to people's desire to defend their view of themselves as not gullible or easily influenced (Quinn & Wood, 2004). In this case, because people make the attitude shift before they receive the persuasive appeal, they can convince themselves that they were not in fact influenced at all! Furthermore, in such cases, distraction after forewarning has been received—which presumably would inhibit thought—has no effect on the extent to which attitudes are changed in the direction of the expected message. In this type of forewarning situation, people appear to be using a simple heuristic (e.g., I'll look stupid if I don't agree with what this expert says) and change their attitudes before they even receive the message.

5.5.3: Selective Avoidance of Persuasion Attempts

Still another way in which we resist attempts at persuasion is through **selective avoidance**, a tendency to direct our attention away from information that challenges our existing attitudes. Television viewing provides a clear illustration of the effects of selective avoidance. People do not simply sit in front of the television passively absorbing whatever the media decides to dish out. Instead, they channel-surf, mute the commercials, record their favorite programs, or simply cognitively "tune out" when confronted with information contrary to their views. The opposite effect occurs as well. When we encounter information that *supports* our views, we tend to give it our full attention. Such tendencies to ignore information that contradicts our attitudes, while actively attending to information consistent with them, constitute two sides of what social psychologists term *selective exposure*. Such selectivity in what we make the focus of our attention helps ensure that many of our attitudes remain largely intact for long periods of time.

5.5.4: Actively Defending Our Attitudes: Counterarguing Against the Competition

Ignoring or screening out information incongruent with our current views is certainly one way of resisting persuasion. But growing evidence suggests that in addition to this kind of passive defense of our attitudes, we also use a more active strategy as well: We actively counterargue against views that are contrary to our own (Eagly,

Chen, Chaiken, & Shaw-Barnes, 1999). By doing so, it makes the opposing views more memorable than they would be otherwise, but it reduces their impact on our attitudes.

Eagly, Kulesa, Brannon, Shaw, and Hutson-Comeaux (2000) identified students as either "pro-choice" or "pro-life" in their attitudes toward abortion. These students were then exposed to persuasive messages that were either consistent with their attitudes or were contrary to their views. After hearing the messages, participants reported their attitudes toward abortion, the strength of their attitudes, and listed all the arguments in the message they could recall (a measure of memory). In addition, they listed the thoughts they had while listening to the message; this provided information on the extent to which they counterargued against the message when it was contrary to their own views.

The results indicated that the counterattitudinal message and the proattitudinal message were equally memorable. However, participants reported thinking more systematically about the counterattitudinal message, and reported having more oppositional thoughts about it—a clear sign that they were indeed counterarguing against this message. In contrast, they reported more supportive thoughts in response to the proattitudinal message. Therefore, one reason we are so good at resisting persuasion is that we not only ignore information that is inconsistent with our current views, but we also carefully process counterattitudinal input and argue actively against it. In this way, exposure to arguments opposed to our attitudes can serve to strengthen the views we already hold, making us more resistant to subsequent efforts to change them.

5.5.5: Individual Differences in Resistance to Persuasion

People differ in their vulnerability to persuasion (Brinol, Rucker, Tormala, & Petty, 2004). Some people may be resistant because they are motivated to engage in counterarguing; they therefore would agree with items such as "When someone challenges my beliefs, I enjoy disputing what they have to say." On the other hand, some people are relatively resistant to persuasion because they attempt to bolster their own beliefs when they encounter counterattitudinal messages. Those individuals would be likely to agree with items such as "When someone gives me a point of view that conflicts with my attitudes, I like to think about why my views are right for me." To determine whether scores on these two measures of resistance to persuasion were in fact predictive of attitude change, Brinol et al. (2004) measured these self-beliefs and then gave participants an advertisement for "Brown's Department Store." These researchers found that scores on both these measures assessing different approaches to resisting persuasion predicted successful resistance to the message in the advertisement. Furthermore, the types of thoughts people have when they are confronted with a counterattitudinal message are predicted by their preference for resisting persuasion by either counterarguing or bolstering their initial attitude position. So, apparently people do know something about how they deal with attempts to persuade them, and they use their favored techniques quite effectively!

5.5.6: Ego-Depletion Can Undermine Resistance

As we just described, your ability to resist persuasion can result from successful counterarguing against a persuasive message or consciously considering why your initial attitude is better than the position you are being asked to adopt. Factors that make either of these strategies more difficult—because they undermine our ability to engage in **self-regulation**—could certainly undermine our ability to resist persuasion. To the extent that people have a limited capacity to self-regulate (i.e., to engage their willpower in controlling their own thinking), prior expenditure of these limited resources could leave us vulnerable to persuasion. For example, when people are tired,

Figure 5.18 Evidence That Ego-Depletion Can Make Weak Ideas Persuasive

When people were not ego-depleted, they differentiated between weak and strong arguments, and were only persuaded by strong arguments. In contrast, when people were suffering from ego-depletion, they failed to differentiate between strong and weak arguments, and were therefore equally persuaded by both.

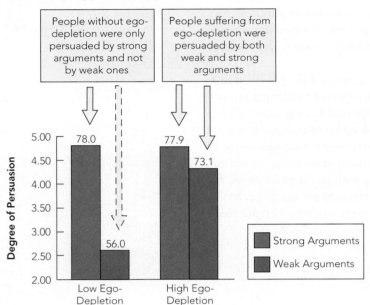

have failed to self-regulate on a prior task, or otherwise are in a state of **ego-depletion**, they may simply acquiesce when confronted with a counterattitudinal message—that is, they will show attitude change.

To assess this process, Wheeler, Brinol, and Hermann (2007) gave participants an easy or difficult first task, with the difficult task being designed to deplete their self-regulation resources. Subsequently, participants were given a weak or strong (well-argued) message in favor of mandatory comprehensive examinations for graduation—a topic these students were initially strongly against. Did ego-depletion result in people being more persuaded by bad (weak) arguments? The answer, as shown in Figure 5.18, was a resounding yes. The weak arguments were unpersuasive among those who were not ego-depleted, but they were just as persuasive to those who were ego-depleted as were the strong arguments. Examination of the participants' thoughts in response to the message verified that the nondepleted participants had more favorable thoughts about the message when the arguments were strong compared to when they were weak. In contrast, the thoughts of the ego-depleted participants were equally as favorable in the strong and weak arguments case.

Recent research has confirmed too that those who have resisted a persuasive message have less ability to subsequently exert self-control (Burkley, 2008; Vohs et al., 2008; Wang, Novemsky, Dhar, & Baumeister, 2010). So not only does prior resistance deplete our self-control, which results in greater vulnerability to persuasion, but when we are depleted, we may find it more difficult to resist would-be persuaders' weak messages. Furthermore, when people are attempting to persuade others, they are more likely to be dishonest when their capacity to exert control has been depleted (Mead, Baumeister, Gino, Schweitzer, & Ariely, 2009). This research suggests that we need to beware of communicators who are the most tired when they are attempting to persuade us—for they may be strongly tempted to color the truth in ways that favor them over us.

Key Points

- Several factors contribute to our ability to *resist persuasion*. One such factor is **reactance**—negative reactions to efforts by others to reduce or limit our personal freedom, which can produce increased opposition to the message content.
- Resistance to persuasion is often increased by **forewarning**—the knowledge that someone will be trying to changes our attitudes—and by **selective avoidance**—the tendency to avoid exposure to information that contradicts our views.
- When we are exposed to persuasive messages that are contrary to our existing views, we actively counterargue

against them. This is a critical means by which our resistance to persuasion is increased.
- There are also individual differences in the ability to resist persuasion. Those include consciously counterarguing against messages we receive and bolstering our initial attitude position when confronted with a counterattitudinal message.
- **Ego-depletion** from exerting effort on another task can undermine our ability to **self-regulate** and resist persuasion. When ego-depleted, people are equally likely to be persuaded by both strong and weak messages. As persuaders, the ego-depleted are also less likely to be honest.

5.6: Cognitive Dissonance: What Is It and How Do We Manage It?

Objective   **Evaluate the effects of cognitive dissonance on attitude change**

When we first introduced the question of whether, and to what extent, attitudes and behavior are linked, we noted that in many situations, there can be a sizable gap between what we feel on the inside (positive or negative reactions to some object or issue) and what we show on the outside. For instance, I have a neighbor who recently purchased a huge SUV. I have strong negative attitudes toward such giant vehicles because they get very low gas mileage, add to pollution, and block my view while driving. But when my neighbor asked how I liked her new vehicle, I hesitated and then said "Nice, very nice," with as much enthusiasm as I could muster. She is a very good neighbor who looks after my cats when I'm away, and I did not want to offend her. But I certainly felt uncomfortable when I uttered those words. Why? Because in this situation I was aware that my behavior was *not* consistent with my attitudes and this is an uncomfortable state to be in. Social psychologists term my reaction **cognitive dissonance**—an unpleasant state that occurs when we notice that our attitudes and our behavior are inconsistent. As you will see, when we cannot justify our attitude-inconsistent behavior, we may end up changing our own attitudes.

Any time you become aware of saying what you don't really believe (e.g., praise something you don't actually like "just to be polite"), make a difficult decision that requires you to reject an alternative you find attractive, or discover that something you've invested effort or money in is not as good as you expected, you are likely to experience dissonance. In all these situations, there is a gap between your attitudes and your actions, and such gaps tend to make us uncomfortable. In fact, research has revealed that the discomfort associated with dissonance is reflected in elevated activity in the left front regions of our brain (Harmon-Jones, Harmon-Jones, Fearn, Sigelman, & Johnson, 2008). Most important from the present perspective, cognitive dissonance can sometimes lead us to change our own attitudes—to shift them so that they *are* consistent with our overt behavior, even in the absence of any strong external pressure to do so.

5.6.1: Dissonance and Attitude Change: The Effects of Induced Compliance

We can engage in attitude-discrepant behavior for many reasons, and some of these are more compelling than others. When will our attitudes change more: When there are "good" reasons for engaging in attitude-discrepant behavior or when we lack justification for doing so? Cognitive dissonance theory predicts that dissonance will be stronger when we have *few* reasons for engaging in attitude-discrepant behavior. When we have little justification and therefore cannot explain away our actions to ourselves, dissonance can be quite intense.

In the first test of this idea, participants initially engaged in an extremely boring series of tasks—turning pegs in a board full of holes (Festinger & Carlsmith, 1959). After the task was over, the experimenter made an unusual request: He told participants that his assistant had not shown up that day and asked if the participant would "fill in" by greeting the next participant and telling that person that the task to be performed was an *interesting* one. Half of these participants were told that they would be paid $20 if they would tell this fib to the waiting participant, and the other half were told that they would receive $1 for doing so. After doing the "favor" of telling the person waiting this fib about the experiment—the participants were asked to report their own attitudes toward the boring task (i.e., rate how interesting the task was).

The participants who were paid $20 rated the task as *less* interesting than participants who were paid $1. When you were paid $20, you would have had a justification for lying, but not so much when you were paid $1 to tell that same lie. So, when there is *insufficient justification* for your behavior, a situation that was truer in the $1 condition (than the $20) of the experiment, there is a greater need to reduce your dissonance. So, what do people do to reduce their greater dissonance in the $1 condition? They change the cognition that is causing the problem! Since, in this example, you can't change the lie you told (i.e., deny your behavior), you can decide it wasn't really a lie at all by "making" the boring task more interesting and reporting your attitude as being more positive in the $1 condition than in the $20 condition.

As Figure 5.19 illustrates, cognitive dissonance theory predicts that it will be easier to change individuals' attitudes by offering them *just enough* to get them to engage in attitude-discrepant behavior. Social psychologists sometimes refer to this surprising prediction as the **less-leads-to-more effect**—less reasons or rewards for an action often leads to greater attitude change—and it has been confirmed in many studies (Harmon-Jones, 2000; Leippe & Eisenstadt, 1994). The more money or other rewards that are offered to people for them to behave in an attitude-discrepant way provides a justification for their actions and can undermine the likelihood that attitude change will occur. Small rewards lead to greater attitude change primarily when people believe that they were personally responsible for both the chosen course of action and any negative effects it produced. However, if ordered by an authority to do a particular behavior that is inconsistent with our personal attitudes, we may not feel responsible for what happens and therefore not experience dissonance.

5.6.2: Alternative Strategies for Resolving Dissonance

As we have described, dissonance theory began with a very reasonable idea: People find inconsistency between their attitudes and actions uncomfortable. But is changing our attitudes the only method by which we can resolve dissonance? No, we can also alter our behavior so it is more consistent with our attitudes—for example, we could resolve to only buy organic products *in the future* and not change our "green environmental attitudes" after we've made some non-environmental-friendly purchase.

Figure 5.19 Why Smaller Inducements Often Lead to More Attitude Change After Attitude-Discrepant Behavior

When individuals have strong reasons for engaging in attitude-discrepant behavior, they experience relatively weak dissonance and do not change their attitudes. In contrast, when they have little apparent justification for engaging in the attitude-discrepant behavior, they will experience stronger dissonance and greater pressure to change their attitudes. The result—less justification leads to more dissonance and more change following attitude-discrepant behavior.

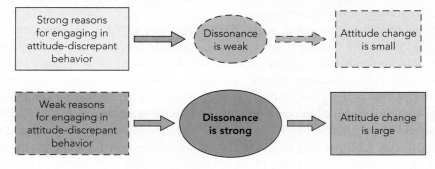

Another option for managing dissonance when inconsistency is salient involves deciding that the inconsistency actually doesn't matter! In other words, we can engage in *trivialization*—concluding that either the attitudes or behaviors in question are not important so any inconsistency between them is of no importance (Simon, Greenberg, & Brehm, 1995).

Each of these strategies can be viewed as *direct* methods of dissonance reduction: They focus on the attitude–behavior discrepancy that is causing the dissonance. Research by Steele and his colleagues (e.g., Steele & Lui, 1983; Steele, 1988) indicates that dissonance can also be reduced via *indirect* means. That is, although the basic discrepancy between the attitude and behavior is left intact, the unpleasant or negative feelings generated by dissonance can be still reduced by, for example, consuming alcohol. Adoption of indirect tactics to reduce dissonance is most likely when the attitude–behavior discrepancy involves *important* attitudes or self-beliefs (so trivialization isn't feasible). Under these conditions, individuals experiencing dissonance may not focus so much on reducing the gap between their attitudes and behavior, but instead on other methods that will allow them to feel good about themselves despite the gap (Steele, Spencer, & Lynch, 1993).

Specifically, people can engage in **self-affirmation**—restoring positive self-evaluations that are threatened by the dissonance (Elliot & Devine, 1994; Tesser, Martin, & Cornell, 1996). This can be accomplished by focusing on positive self-attributes—good things about oneself. For instance, when I experienced dissonance as a result of saying nice things about my neighbor's new SUV, even though I am strongly against such vehicles, I could remind myself that I am a considerate person. By contemplating positive aspects of the self, it can help to reduce the discomfort produced by my failure to act in a way that was consistent with my pro-environmental (and anti-SUV) attitudes. However we choose to reduce dissonance—through indirect tactics or direct strategies that are aimed at reducing the attitude–behavior discrepancy—we all find strategies to help us deal with the discomfort that comes from being aware of discrepancies between our attitudes and behavior.

5.6.3: When Dissonance Is a Tool for Beneficial Changes in Behavior

- People who don't wear seat belts are much more likely to die in accidents than those who do . . .

- People who smoke are much more likely to suffer from lung cancer and heart disease than those who don't . . .

- People who engage in unprotected sex are much more likely than those who engage in safe sex to contract dangerous diseases, as well as have unplanned pregnancies . . .

Most of us know these statements are true, and our attitudes are generally favorable toward using seat belts, quitting smoking, and engaging in safe sex (Carey, Morrison-Beedy, & Johnson, 1997). Despite having positive attitudes, they are often *not* translated into overt actions: Some people continue to drive without seat belts, to smoke, and to have unprotected sex. To address these major social problems, perhaps what is needed is not so much a change in attitudes as shifts in overt behavior. Can dissonance be used to promote beneficial behavioral changes? A growing body of evidence suggests that it can (Batson, Kobrynowicz, Dinnerstein, Kampf, & Wilson, 1997; Gibbons, Eggleston, & Benthin, 1997), especially when it is used to generate feelings of **hypocrisy**—publicly advocating some attitude, and then making salient to the person that they have acted in a way that is inconsistent with their own attitudes. Such feelings might be sufficiently intense that only actions that reduce dissonance directly, by inducing behavioral change, may be effective. These predictions concerning the possibility of dissonance-induced *behavior change* have been tested in several studies.

Stone, Wiegand, Cooper, and Aronson (1997) asked participants to prepare a speech advocating the use of condoms (safe sex) to avoid contracting AIDS. Next, participants were asked to think of reasons why they themselves hadn't used condoms in the past (*personal reasons*) or reasons that people in general sometimes fail to use condoms (*normative reasons* not involving their own behavior). The researchers predicted that dissonance would be maximized in the personal reasons condition, where participants had to come face-to-face with their own hypocrisy. Then, all persons in the study were given a choice between a direct means of reducing dissonance—purchasing condoms at a reduced price, or an indirect means of reducing dissonance—making a donation to a program designed to aid homeless persons (see Figure 5.20). The results indicated that when participants had been asked to focus on the reasons why they didn't engage in safe sex in the past, an overwhelming majority chose to purchase condoms, suggesting that their behavior in the future will be different—the direct route to dissonance reduction. In contrast, when asked to think about reasons why people in general didn't engage in safe sex, more actually chose the indirect route to dissonance reduction—a donation to aid the homeless project—and didn't change their behavior.

These findings suggest that using dissonance to make our own hypocrisy salient can indeed be a powerful tool for changing our behavior in desirable ways. For maximum effectiveness, however, such procedures must involve several elements: People must publicly advocate the desired behaviors (e.g., using condoms), they need to be induced to think about their *own* behavioral failures in the past, and they must be given access to direct means for reducing their dissonance (i.e., a method for changing their behavior). When these conditions are met, dissonance can bring about beneficial changes in behavior. To understand more about how culture can modify dissonance and other attitude processes, see the special section, **"What Research Tells Us About... Culture and Attitude Processes."**

Figure 5.20 Indirect Route to Dissonance Reduction

When individuals are made to confront their own hypocrisy, most choose to reduce their dissonance through direct means (by changing their behavior). However, when individuals are asked to think about reasons why people in general do not act according to their beliefs, many choose to reduce dissonance via an indirect route such as donating to charity. Doing so allows people to feel better about themselves, even though their own behavior does not change.

What Research Tells Us About...

Culture and Attitude Processes

Cultures differ dramatically in the extent to which people are expected to act in ways that are consistent with prevailing social norms—a tendency known as cultural "**tightness versus looseness**" (Gelfand et al., 2011). In cultures such as the United States, which is a relatively loose one, because there is a lower emphasis on self-regulation and fewer situational constraints on behavior, personal attitudes are fairly good guides for behavior. In contrast, in cultures such as India and Pakistan, which are relatively tight cultures, personal attitudes are less strongly linked to behavior; instead, everyday behaviors are more likely to be dictated by duty to others and social norms.

New theorizing about attitudes suggests that existing approaches, such as those described in this chapter, reflect Western philosophical views that conceptualize attitudes as "personal preferences" and, consequently, do not match findings from research in other cultural contexts where perceived normative appropriateness is crucial for predicting behavior (Riemer, Shavitt, Koo, & Markus, 2014). For example, in Japan and China, people's personal environmental attitudes are not good predictors of their purchasing "green products," although in the United States they are. In these non-Western contexts, people's choices are fundamentally shaped by the social context and beliefs about what others expect of them. As a result, providing information about the choices that others are making (i.e., that they are purchasing "green") will be most effective in non-Western contexts.

Based on Riemer et al.'s (2014) review of cross-cultural research on attitudes and behavior, all of the following illustrate differences that have been observed between Western and non-Western contexts:

- Beliefs about whether personal attitudes and behavior *should* be consistent or not, and whether they *should* differ across time.
- The extent to which cognitive dissonance is experienced when attitudes and behavior are inconsistent.
- Having strong and clear attitudes is less important for effective functioning in non-Western context than in Western contexts.
- Being influenced by what others expect when making choices "feels" right in non-Western contexts, but is seen as a struggle for personal control in Western contexts.
- Successful persuasive advertisements in Western contexts often emphasize personal uniqueness, whereas they are likely to emphasize being appropriate for one's social position in non-Western contexts.
- Degree to which attitude expression is stable or more malleable according to the context.
- Whether people who "do it their way" are considered good and normal, or immature and unwise for not considering the consequences of their actions for others.

As this summary reveals, many attitude processes do indeed differ when closely examined in Western compared to non-Western contexts. Accordingly, how we attempt to change attitudes—particularly those of relevance around the globe such as climate change, and what to do about it, which we described in the opening of this chapter—may require different approaches in Western and non-Western settings.

Key Points

- **Cognitive dissonance** is an aversive state that occurs when we notice discrepancies between our attitudes and our behavior. Experiencing dissonance produces increased left frontal cortical activity and attitude change.
- Dissonance often occurs in situations involving *forced compliance*, in which we are minimally induced by external factors to say or do things that are inconsistent with our attitudes.
- Dissonance can lead to attitude change when we have reasons that are barely sufficient to get us to engage in attitude-discrepant behavior. Stronger reasons (or larger rewards) produce *less* attitude change: This is sometimes referred to as the **less-leads-to-more effect**.

- Dissonance can be reduced directly (e.g., changing our attitudes) or with other methods for dealing with dissonance including *trivialization*, and *indirect* methods such as **self-affirmation** on some other dimension.
- Dissonance induced through **hypocrisy**—inducing individuals to advocate certain attitudes or behaviors and then reminding them that their own behavior has not always been consistent with these attitudes—can be a powerful tool for inducing beneficial changes in behavior.
- Cultures differ in their **tightness versus looseness**. In tight cultures there is a greater expectation that people conform to important social norms than in loose cultures.

Summary and Review

Attitudes are evaluations that can color our experience of virtually any aspect of the world. Often, attitudes are **explicit**—so consciously accessible and easy to report. But attitudes can also be **implicit**, and therefore not consciously accessible or controllable. Attitudes are often acquired from other persons through **social learning**. Such learning can involve **classical conditioning**, **instrumental conditioning**, or **observational learning**. In fact, attitudes can be formed via **subliminal conditioning**—which occurs in the absence of conscious awareness of the stimuli involved—and **mere exposure**.

Attitudes are also formed on the basis of **social comparison**—our tendency to compare ourselves with others to determine whether our view of social reality is or is not correct. In order to be similar to others we like, we accept the attitudes that they hold, to the extent that we identify with that group. As we move into new **social networks**, attitudes can shift rapidly as a means of fitting in when those networks consist of people holding differing attitudes.

Several factors affect the strength of the relationship between attitudes and behavior.

Situational constraints may prevent us from expressing our attitudes overtly—including concerns about what others may think of us. People often show **pluralistic ignorance**—erroneously believing that others have different attitudes than we do, which can limit our willingness to express our attitudes in public. Several aspects of attitudes themselves also moderate the attitude–behavior link. These include factors related to attitude strength: including the *extremity* of our attitude position, the *certainty* with which our attitudes are held, and whether we have *personal experience* with the attitude object. All of these factors can make our attitudes more accessible, and therefore likely to guide our behavior.

Attitudes can influence behavior through two different mechanisms. According to the **theory of reasoned action** and **theory of planned behavior**, when we can give careful thought to our attitudes, *intentions* derived from our attitudes strongly predict behavior. According to the **attitude-to-behavior process model**, in situations where our behavior is more spontaneous and we do not engage in such deliberate thought, attitudes influence behavior by shaping our perception and interpretation of the situation.

Early research on **persuasion**—efforts to change attitudes through the use of messages—focused primarily on the *source*, the *message*, and the *audience*. More recent research has sought to understand the cognitive processes that play a role in persuasion. Such research suggests that we process persuasive messages in two distinct ways: through **systematic processing**, which involves careful attention to message content, or through **heuristic processing**, which involves the use of mental shortcuts (e.g., "experts are usually right"). Consuming caffeine increases the extent to which people are persuaded by increasing their ability to systematically process the message contents.

Several factors contribute to people's ability to *resist persuasion*. One such factor is **reactance**—negative reactions to efforts by others to reduce or limit our personal freedom. When people feel reactance, they often change their attitudes in the *opposite* direction from that advocated. This is one reason that the "hard-sell" can be counterproductive. Resistance to persuasion is often increased by **forewarning**—the knowledge that someone is trying to changes our attitudes. This typically gives us a chance to counterargue against the expected persuasive appeal, and thereby resist the message content when it is presented. Forewarning does not prevent persuasion though when people are distracted and therefore unable to expend effort refuting the message in advance.

People also maintain their current attitudes by **selective avoidance**—the tendency to overlook or disregard information that contradicts our existing views. Likewise, people give close attention to information that supports their views, and by means of *selective exposure* will actively seek out information that is consistent with their existing attitudes.

When exposed to information that is inconsistent with our views, we can actively counterargue against it. The more people have oppositional thoughts when exposed to a counterattitudinal message, the more they are able to resist being persuaded by it. In a sense, people provide their own defense against persuasion attempts. People also differ in their vulnerability to persuasion. Some people are aware that they use counterarguing and others know they attempt to bolster their original views when they encounter persuasion situations.

Our ability to resist persuasion can depend on our own psychological state—whether we are **ego-depleted** or not. When ego-depleted, people experience greater difficulty **self-regulating**, which undermines resistance to persuasion. When people are ego-depleted, they do not differentiate between messages with strong and weak arguments and are equally persuaded by both. In contrast, when ego-depletion is low, people are not persuaded by weak arguments, only by strong arguments.

Cognitive dissonance is an unpleasant state that occurs when we notice discrepancies between our attitudes and our behavior. Dissonance is aversive and attempts to resolve it are reflected in increased cortical activity. Festinger and Carlsmith's (1959) classic study illustrated that dissonance is stronger when we have little justification for our attitude-inconsistent behavior. In contrast, stronger reasons (or larger rewards) can produce *less* attitude change—the **less-leads-to-more effect**—because the person feels justified in their attitude-inconsistent behavior in that case.

Dissonance often occurs in situations involving *forced compliance*—ones in which we are induced by external factors to say or do things that are inconsistent with our attitudes. In such situations, attitude change is maximal when we have reasons that are barely sufficient to get us to engage in attitude-discrepant behavior. Other means of coping with dissonance, besides changing our attitudes, include *trivialization* or concluding that the inconsistency is unimportant. Dissonance can also be dealt with by use of *indirect* strategies; that is, to the extent that the self can be *affirmed* by focusing on some other positive feature of the self, then dissonance can be reduced without changing one's attitudes. Dissonance that is induced by making us aware of our own **hypocrisy** can result in behavioral changes.

Many attitude processes appear to differ in Western compared to non-Western cultural settings. Because cultures differ dramatically in the extent to which people are expected to act in ways that are consistent with prevailing social norms—a tendency known as cultural **tightness versus looseness**—behavior that is driven by personal attitudes or social norms also differs.

Chapter 6
Causes and Cures of Stereotyping, Prejudice, and Discrimination

Chapter Overview

Learning Objectives

6.1 Examine how inequality is perceived by different groups

6.2 Evaluate how people form and use stereotypes

6.3 Recall the factors leading to prejudice against specific groups

6.4 Explain how subtle forms of discrimination are the manifestations of prejudice

6.5 Outline ways of reducing prejudice

On August 9, 2014, Michael Brown and a friend were stopped by Ferguson, Missouri, police officer Darren Wilson while walking down the street. Although eyewitness testimony differs on what happened next, the altercation between the unarmed 18-year-old Brown, a black man, and the 28-year-old Wilson, a white police officer, resulted in Brown being fatally shot six times. Following his death, residents gathered outside the Ferguson police department to protest this police shooting, holding signs such as those shown in Figure 6.1 that read "Black Lives Matter" and "Hands Up: Don't Shoot." The protests in Ferguson, and subsequently in other cities across the United States, garnered considerable media attention, placing race relations and police tactics at the forefront of news and public discussion.

Figure 6.1 Do Black and White Americans Perceive Tragic Events Involving Police Actions Differently?

As these images suggest, Black Americans perceive the Ferguson, Missouri, events as reflecting racism, especially in terms of police treatment. National opinion polls after the incident revealed that the majority (80 percent) of African Americans perceive the shooting as raising important issues about race relations, while many (47 percent) white Americans believe such racial issues are receiving more attention than they deserve.

Why were these residents of Ferguson and other cities so upset over Michael Brown's death? Why did so many people feel a strong connection to the protesters, supporting them and their cause through social media outlets such as Facebook and Twitter? While any loss of life may be viewed as tragic, what made this case so important that hundreds of people would come together and collectively voice their anger and sadness for such a long period of time? Before trying to answer these questions, let's first look at the protests themselves.

During the Ferguson protests, the actions of both protesters and police became hot button issues. Some felt that the protesters were using the death of Michael Brown as an excuse to loot and vandalize local businesses. Others argued that this was a peaceful movement akin to the civil rights rallies of the 1960s and aimed only at generating change in how the police deal with black citizens. In fact, many prominent citizens including local Alderman Antonio French and U.S. Senator Claire McCaskill joined the protest to show their support.

In contrast to this perception of peaceful protest, the police response indicated they viewed the situation differently. Using military tactics and equipment, the police of Ferguson, as shown in Figure 6.2, reacted as if the protesters represented a violent threat to the safety and security of local businesses and townspeople. To suppress the protests, the Ferguson police department utilized tear gas, rubber bullets, smoke grenades, and the presence of heavy weapons to try to control and dissolve the protests. Senator McCaskill herself reported being subjected to tear gas from officers while she sat quietly with a group of young Ferguson protesters. Alderman Antonio French related how he was pulled from his car, handcuffed, and detained overnight for being present at the protest. Both politicians related how they were just two of the many citizens treated as if they were violent insurgents by police. Police officers were also documented arresting journalists and confiscating their filming equipment during the protests, citing their participation in an unlawful assembly as cause.

The police actions in Ferguson came under close scrutiny by national and international groups alike, with many citizens, politicians, police officers, and human rights advocates admonishing the Ferguson police for what they viewed as an inappropriate escalation of conflict and the violation of the protesters human rights that resulted in greater acts of violence. There is a considerable divide in views surrounding this incident and its implications for race relations. According to a Pew Research Center poll, 70 percent of black Americans say the police are doing a "poor job" treating racial groups fairly, while only 25 percent of white Americans agree with this assessment. Why do black and white Americans differ so much in their interpretation of the shooting of Michael Brown and the police response to the protests that followed? How can two groups have such differing perceptions of the same situation? In this chapter we will examine social psychological research that can help us answer these and other questions by considering how the groups we belong to can shape our interpretation and reaction to situations involving race, gender, nationality, and other social categories.

At some time or other, everyone comes face to face with **prejudice**—negative emotional responses or dislike based on group membership. Such experience with prejudice can come about either because we are the target of it, we observe others' prejudicial treatment of members of another group such as African Americans as we discussed in the opening example, or when we recognize

Figure 6.2 Facing Police Attempts to Disolve the Ferguson, Missouri, Protests

In response to reports of vandalizing and looting, military-style policing directed at the protestors produced a wide public opinion racial divide. Black Americans on the whole felt the police went too far in their response, while only a minority of white Americans felt the same.

prejudice in ourselves and realize our actions toward some groups are less positive compared to how we respond to members of our own group. As you will see in this chapter, the *roots* of prejudice can be found in the cognitive and emotional processes that social psychologists have measured with reference to a variety of different social groups.

Prejudice may be perceived by its perpetrators (and, sometimes, even its victims) as legitimate and justified (Crandall, Eshleman, & O'Brien, 2002; Effron & Knowles, 2015; Jetten, Schmitt, Branscombe, Garza, & Mewse, 2011) or it can be seen as entirely illegitimate and something that individuals should actively strive to eliminate (Maddux, Barden, Brewer, & Petty, 2005; Monteith, Ashburn-Nardo, Voils, & Czopp, 2002). Furthermore, prejudice and discriminatory treatment can be blatant or it can be relatively subtle (Barreto & Ellemers, 2015). Indeed, all forms of **discrimination**—differential treatment based on group membership—are not perceived by its perpetrators, and responded to by its targets, in the same way.

In this chapter, we begin by considering how our own group membership affects perceptions of social outcomes. As you saw in the opening, white and black Americans often respond differently to issues concerning racial treatment on the part of the police, particularly the shooting of young black men. Social psychological research has confirmed that there is a good reason for this. Using meta-analysis as a means of summarizing the results of 42 experiments, the evidence indicates that white participants are substantially faster to shoot unarmed black targets than white targets in a speeded laboratory "shooting" task (Mekawi & Bresin, 2015).

Likewise, when we examine the nature of **stereotyping**—beliefs about what members of a social group are like—and consider how it is related to discrimination, we will need to address the role of the perceiver's group membership. In the section on stereotyping, we will particularly emphasize gender stereotyping, in part because its role in our own lives is easy to recognize—we all have a stake in gender relations. Although there is a high degree of interpersonal contact between men and women, which tends to be absent in many other cases including racial and religious groups (Jackman, 1994), gender-based discrimination continues to affect a substantial proportion of the population, particularly in the workplace. We will next turn to perspectives on the origins and nature of prejudice, and address why it so persistent across time and social groups. Lastly, we will explore various strategies that have been used to successfully change stereotypes and reduce prejudice.

6.1: How Members of Different Groups Perceive Inequality

Objective   **Examine how inequality is perceived by different groups**

Whether discrimination is perceived to be legitimate or not and the extent to which progress toward its reduction has been made depends on whether one is a member of the group experiencing or perpetrating the discrimination. For example, white and black Americans show substantial differences in how much discrimination and racial inequality they perceive to be present in employment wages (Miron, Warner, & Branscombe, 2011). Furthermore, whites perceive less racism in many everyday events than do blacks (Johnson, Simmons, Trawalter, Ferguson, & Reed, 2003). This pattern is found in many groups that differ in status—with high-status groups perceiving the status differential that favors them as less than members of low-status groups (Exline & Lobel, 1999). In terms of perceptions of how much progress has been made in moving toward equality, national surveys consistently find that white respondents perceive there to have been "a lot of progress," whereas black respondents are more likely to perceive that there has been "not much progress." Is one group correct in their perceptions and the other group incorrect? How are we to account for such different subjective perceptions of the same events and outcomes?

An important step in accounting for these differing perceptions involves consideration of the different meanings and implications derived from any potential change in the status relations between the groups. According to Kahneman and Tversky's (1984) prospect theory (for which the 2002 Nobel Prize in economics was awarded), people are **risk averse**—they tend to weigh possible losses more heavily than equivalent potential gains. To take a monetary example, the possibility of losing a dollar is subjectively more negative than the possibility of gaining a dollar is positive.

How might this idea apply to perceptions of social changes that could result in greater racial equality? Let's assume that whites will perceive greater equality from the standpoint of a potential "loss" for their group—compared to their historically privileged position. Whites will therefore respond to additional movement toward equality more negatively, and suppose that more change has already occurred, than will blacks. In contrast, if we assume that blacks are likely to see greater equality as a potential "gain" for them—compared to their historically disadvantaged position—then change toward increased equality will be experienced as a positive. But, if a "possible loss" evokes more intense emotion than a "possible gain," then increased equality should be more negative for whites than the same increased equality is positive for blacks. Research has revealed that white Americans who are highly identified with their racial group do respond negatively—with increased racism—when their race-based privileges are questioned (Branscombe, Schmitt, & Schiffhauer, 2007).

Even a cursory look at racist websites and other sources such as those shown in Figure 6.3 reveals that they often frame existing race relations as "white people are losing ground." This is, of course, not unlike how the Nazis and other anti-Semitic groups (again, all too easily found on the Internet) framed German losses (and Jewish gains). Indeed, considerable evidence indicates that hate crimes increase as minorities are perceived as gaining political power (Dancygier & Green, 2010).

Although hate group members are *not* typical white Americans, perhaps this tendency to see social change as a zero-sum outcome in which "we are losing" plays a role in explaining the discrepancies that are observed between minority and majority perceptions of inequality. To test this explanation, Eibach and Keegan (2006) had white and nonwhite participants create a graph—in one of three forms—depicting change in the racial composition of students in U.S. universities from 1960 to the present. In the "Minority gains and white losses" case, the percentages they were asked to insert showed the percent of whites going down, and the exact same percentage increase in favor of minorities. In a "white losses only" case, the graphs that students were asked to draw simply showed a reduction in the percentage of whites, and in the "Minorities gain only" case they simply showed an increase in the percentage of minorities at American universities.

In both conditions where "white losses" were included, white participants saw race relations in a more "zero-sum" fashion than when "Minority gains" alone were considered. What impact did this have on judged progress toward equality? When participants focused on "white losses," there were racial group differences in judged progress—mirroring the consistently obtained national survey findings. White participants perceived greater progress toward equality

Figure 6.3 Hate Groups on the Internet

Hate groups incite concerns about their own group by claiming theirs is "losing ground" and that the targeted group is illegitimately gaining. Hate is then seen as justified in order to protect their group.

for minorities than did nonwhite participants. However, when only "Minority gains" were considered, whites perceived less progress toward equality; in fact, in that case, their perceptions were not different than the nonwhite participants. So, the "racial divide" in public perceptions of events would appear to stem in part from whites' framing social change as involving losses for their own group.

It is worth considering whether a similar tendency to frame affirmative action as a loss of white privilege or as a gain for minorities can account for racial differences in support for that social change policy too (Crosby, 2004). Research reveals that when whites expect that affirmative action procedures will negatively affect white Americans' chances to obtain jobs and promotions—by focusing on possible losses their own racial group could experience—whites oppose affirmative action policies, regardless of what impact it might have on minority groups (Lowery, Unzueta, Goff, & Knowles, 2006). Similarly, among white South Africans, support for affirmative action for black Africans depends on the extent to which they are perceived as a threat to white South Africans' high-status jobs and access to good housing (Durrheim et al., 2009).

Has the election of Barack Obama to the U.S. Presidency changed these racial dynamics in perceptions of progress and support for policies that are aimed at addressing racial inequality such as affirmative action? Clearly, the election of Barack Obama was one dramatic example of how much race relations in the United States have changed since the 1954 U.S. Supreme Court decision *Brown v. Topeka Board of Education*, which made racial segregation in public institutions such as schools illegal. However, as shown in Figure 6.4, research has revealed that pre- to postelection white Americans came to believe that there is *less* need for further racial progress and *less* support for social policies aimed at increasing equality (Kaiser, Drury, Spalding, Cheryan, & O'Brien, 2009). As we will discuss later in this chapter, the presence of "token" (numerically infrequent) minorities or women in highly visible positions can lead majority group members to believe that not only has substantial change occurred, but that there is less need for further social change. For other surprising findings concerning why people might misperceive the amount of inequality that exists, see the special section **"What Research Tells Us About...Biases in Our Beliefs About Inequality."**

Figure 6.4 Perceptions of Racial Progress and Need for Future Progress Was Affected by the Election of Barack Obama

Ironically, the election of Barack Obama, the first African American as U.S. President, reduced the perceived need among white Americans for further progress toward racial equality and support for policies to achieve that goal.

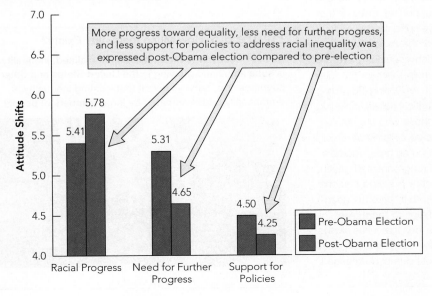

What Research Tells Us About...

Biases in Our Beliefs About Inequality

How would you answer the question: "How much wealth inequality exists in the United States?" And is it too little, too much, or just the right amount? Given the "Occupy Wall Street" and other similar movements around the world (see Figure 6.5), it might seem that many believe the existing (and growing) inequality in the United States is too great. Such concern about rising inequality may stem from the multiple social ills, including reduced psychological well-being, that such inequality is linked with (see Wilkinson & Pickett, 2010). Indeed, increasing inequality is associated with decreased tolerance for ethnic diversity (Corneo & Neher, 2014) and increased prejudice toward minorities (Andersen & Fetner, 2008).

When social psychologists asked a representative sample of Americans these two questions about wealth inequality (Norton & Ariely, 2011), they found that how much inequality exists was dramatically underestimated and that the majority of their respondents felt it *should be even less than they erroneously believed it was*! That is, when asked how much wealth the richest 20 percent of Americans possess, respondents estimated that it was 59 percent of the nation's total wealth. In actuality, the top 20 percent in the United States owns 84 percent of the wealth. When asked about how much the top 20 percent should ideally own, respondents believed it should be just 32 percent (which is closer to Sweden, a well-known low-inequality nation, than the United States). Similar underestimates of existing wealth inequality have been obtained in Australia, a nation with somewhat less inequality than the United States (Norton, Neal, Govan, Ariely, & Holland, 2014). In both of these nations, though, people's actual desire to live in a more equal society did not differ much as a function of their political orientation (e.g., Democrat vs. Republican), despite the fact that beliefs about the causes of poverty do differ according to political ideology (Guimond & de la Sablonniere, 2015).

So what accounts for these widespread misperceptions concerning how much inequality exists? And, if people really knew how much inequality actually does exist, would we see more people seeking change—and supporting policies that would bring about such change—than we currently do?

First, with respect to the question of the misperception of how much wealth inequality exists, in rich countries there are a number of widely shared beliefs that help maintain the idea such differential outcomes are actually just. As Dorling (2015) has documented, people subscribe to a few critical beliefs, including the idea that "prejudice is normal," with those who are not "us" being seen as not deserving. This helps us collectively remain remarkably unaware of how inequality based on group membership is transmitted across generations—through inherited wealth. A second widely shared set of beliefs—that pursuing personal self-interest at the expense of others (i.e., that "greed is good") because it is efficient (creates growth)—helps to "normalize" inequality, especially when coupled with the idea that it has always been this way (even though it is historically relatively recent) and therefore such "natural" social arrangements cannot be changed.

Unfortunately, other mechanisms help to mask how much inequality (and prejudice) exists and how it is maintained. Because we live out our lives in relatively segregated contexts (e.g., neighborhoods, schools, and employment), and we judge the nature of the world based on the experiences of our family, friends, coworkers and neighbors who are placed similarly to ourselves, we may fail to see the amount of inequality that actually exists. That is, by comparing ourselves with other similarly wealthy or similarly poor people, we may fail to see the substantial differences that truly exist. If vast differences in wealth are not perceived, there will be little support for redistribution of it.

Consider recent research involving both American and New Zealand citizens conducted by Dawtry, Sutton, and Sibley (2015) that illustrates this process. Respondents were first asked to estimate the annual household income for their personal social contacts that they have face-to-face interaction with. They then did the same household income estimation task for their entire nation, and indicated how fair and satisfied they were with that income distribution. Lastly, respondents indicated whether they supported redistribution of wealth through taxes on the rich and welfare benefits for the poor (i.e., means of reducing inequality). Regardless of respondents' political orientation, the perceived national income distribution closely reflected respondents' own household income and members of their personal social circle. People who are wealthier and whose contacts are also, estimated that the rest of their nation was too (i.e., they failed to see inequality). As a result of perceiving the population as a whole as wealthy, like one's own group, the economic status quo was seen as fair and wealth redistribution policies were opposed. So, misperception concerning the extent of wealth inequality that exists is based on our own social placement and assuming that the experience of others is similar to those in our own social circle.

Figure 6.5 How Much Inequality Exists?

As the Occupy Wall Street movement claimed, inequality is substantial and growing in the United States and other countries. Yet, surveys reveal that existing inequality is dramatically underestimated by large numbers of people.

Key Points

- **Prejudice**—**negative** emotional responses toward members of a group, **stereotyping**—beliefs about what members of a group are like, and **discrimination**—differential treatment—can be based on many different category memberships including age, race, marital status, gender, religion, and sexual orientation.

- All forms of differential treatment based on group membership are *not* perceived and responded to in the same way. There is a substantial "racial divide" in the perception of the legitimacy of police treatment. Black Americans report that the police do not treat racial groups fairly, while few white Americans agree with this view.

- Prospect theory argues that people are **risk averse**—and they therefore weigh possible losses more heavily than equivalent potential gains.

- When change is seen as a potential loss, those who are privileged respond more negatively to further change and suppose greater change toward equality has already occurred compared to those who do not see it as a loss for them.

- Social groups differ in the value they accord "equality." When equality is framed as a loss for whites, they perceive that more progress has already occurred and they are less supportive of affirmative action. Perceived threat to the dominant group's economic well-being lowers support for affirmative action.

- The election of Barack Obama, which was indeed unimaginable only a few decades earlier, had the effect of increasing white Americans' perceptions that substantial racial progress has been made, and also decreased the perceived need for policies aimed at creating greater racial equality.

- People substantially underestimate the extent to which inequality exists, while they report desiring greater equality. Widely shared beliefs (e.g., prejudice is normal; greed is good) help to support existing inequality, as does basing our perceptions of the nation on our own personal social circle.

6.2: The Nature and Origins of Stereotyping

Objective   **Evaluate how people form and use stereotypes**

In everyday conversation, the terms *stereotyping, prejudice,* and *discrimination* are often used interchangeably. However, social psychologists have traditionally drawn a distinction between them by building on the more general attitude concept (see Chapter 5). That is, **stereotypes** are considered the cognitive component of attitudes toward a social group—specifically, beliefs about what a particular group is like. Prejudice is considered the affective component, or the feelings we have about a particular group. Discrimination concerns the behavioral component, or differential actions taken toward members of specific social groups.

According to this attitude approach, some groups are characterized by negative stereotypes and this leads to a general feeling of hostility (although, as we will see, there might actually be other types of emotions underlying prejudice toward different groups), which then results in a *conscious intention* to discriminate against members of the targeted group. As we describe recent research in this chapter, ask yourself the following question, which researchers are increasingly raising: "How well does the prevailing attitude approach to stereotyping, prejudice, and discrimination capture the phenomena of interest?" (Adams, Biernat, Branscombe, Crandall, & Wrightsman, 2008). Are there questions and findings the attitude approach cannot address or account for? Are stereotypes about social groups always negative beliefs—for example, do we typically stereotype groups of which we are members in negative terms? Is prejudice always reflected in exclusion and hostility? Could there be such a thing as "benevolent prejudice"? Can discrimination occur without any conscious intention to do so? These are all issues that we will consider in this chapter.

6.2.1: Stereotyping: Beliefs About Social Groups

Stereotypes about groups are the beliefs and expectations that we have concerning what members of those groups are like. Stereotypes can include more than just traits; physical appearance, abilities, and behaviors are all common components of stereotypic expectancies (Deaux & LaFrance, 1998; Zhang, Schmader, & Forbes, 2009). The traits thought to distinguish between one group and another can be either positive or negative; they can be accurate or inaccurate, and may be either agreed with or rejected by members of the stereotyped group.

Gender stereotypes—beliefs concerning the characteristics of women and men—consist of both positive and negative traits (see Table 6.1). Stereotypes of each gender are typically the converse of one another. For instance, on the positive side of the gender stereotype for women, they are viewed as being kind, nurturant, and considerate. On the negative side, they are viewed as being dependent, weak, and overly emotional. Thus, our collective portrait of women is that they are high on warmth but low on competence (Fiske, Cuddy, Glick, & Xu, 2002). Indeed, perceptions of women are similar on these two dimensions to other groups (e.g., the elderly) who are seen as relatively low in status and nonthreatening (Eagly, 1987; Stewart, Vassar, Sanchez, & David, 2000).

Men too are assumed to have both positive and negative stereotypic traits (e.g., they are viewed as decisive, assertive, and accomplished, but also as aggressive, insensitive, and arrogant). Such a portrait—being perceived as high on competence but low on communal attributes—reflects men's relatively high status (e.g., the category "rich people" is perceived similarly on these two dimensions; Cikara & Fiske, 2009). Interestingly, because of the strong emphasis on warmth in the stereotype for women, people tend to feel somewhat more positively about women on the whole compared to men—a finding described by Eagly and Mladinic (1994) as the "women are wonderful" effect.

Despite this greater perceived likeability, women face a key problem: The traits they supposedly possess tend to be viewed as less appropriate for high-status positions than the traits presumed to be possessed by men. Women's traits make them seem appropriate for "support roles" rather than "leadership roles" (Eagly & Sczesny, 2009). Although dramatic change has occurred in the extent to which women participate in the labor force—from 20 percent in 1900 to 59 percent in 2005 (U.S. Census Bureau, 2007)—the vast majority of working women in the United States and other nations are in occupations that bring less status and monetary compensation than comparably skilled male-dominated occupations (Tomaskovic-Devey et al., 2006).

STEREOTYPES AND THE "GLASS CEILING" Although there are clear organizational benefits of gender diversity in upper management in terms of developing new markets

Table 6.1 Traits Stereotypically Associated with Women and Men

As this list of stereotypic traits implies, women are seen as "nicer and warm," whereas men are seen as more "competent and independent."

Female Traits	Male Traits
Warm	Competent
Emotional	Stable
Kind/polite	Tough/coarse
Sensitive	Self-confident
Follower	Leader
Weak	Strong
Friendly	Accomplished
Fashionable	Nonconformist
Gentle	Aggressive

SOURCE: Based on: Deaux & Kite, 1993; Eagly & Mladinic, 1994.

and other forms of innovation (Ellemers, 2014), women continue to be underrepresented in the corporate world. Only 16 percent of corporate officers in the United States are women, and only about 1 percent of CEO positions in Fortune 500 companies are occupied by women (Catalyst, 2009; U.S. Bureau of Labor Statistics, 2006). In other occupations, more progress can be seen. Although the political power structure remains heavily male dominated, women have been seeking elected office in record numbers (Center for American Women and Politics, 2010). In terms of high-level judicial appointments, in addition to Ruth Bader Ginsburg, with the appointment of Sonia Sotomayor in 2009 and Elena Kagan in 2010, the U.S. Supreme Court now has its highest representation of women—33 percent. In science and health care, the percentage of women has grown too, although the gender wage gap continues to be substantial (Shen, 2013).

Despite the gains for women in these important institutions, in corporate settings, while women are making it into middle management they are infrequently found in the higher echelons. This situation, where women find it difficult to advance, may be indicative of a **glass ceiling**—a final barrier that prevents women, as a group, from reaching top positions in the workplace. Several studies have confirmed that a "think manager—think male" bias exists and can help explain how the glass ceiling is maintained (Bruckmüller & Branscombe, 2010; Schein, 2001). Because the stereotypic attributes of a "typical manager" overlap considerably with the "typical man" and share fewer attributes with the "typical woman," this leads to a perceived "lack of fit" of women for positions of organizational leadership (Eagly & Sczesny, 2009; Heilman, 2001). The cartoon in Figure 6.6 provides an amusing illustration of how the perceived lack of fit of those newly entering the field and the group membership of typical leaders of the past may be perceived.

So is it just a matter of being perceived as "leadership material"? Not necessarily. Even when women do break through the glass ceiling, they experience less favorable outcomes in their careers because of their gender than do men (Heilman & Okimoto, 2007; Stroh, Langlands, & Simpson, 2004). For example, when women serve as leaders, they tend to receive lower evaluations from subordinates than males, even when

Figure 6.6 Progress Toward Gender Equality Is an Ongoing Process

As this cartoon illustrates, women's (or the dragon's) presence in male-dominated professions (the knights' domain) represents a "good start," but there might seem to be some fit issues between the old membership and the new leadership.

"To begin with, I would like to express my sincere thanks and deep appreciation for the opportunity to meet with you. While there are still profound differences between us, I think the very fact of my presence here today is a major breakthrough."

they act similarly (Eagly, Makhijani, & Klonsky, 1992; Lyness & Heilman, 2006). Indeed, those women who have been successful in competitive, male-dominated work environments are most likely to report experiencing gender discrimination compared to those in gender stereotypic occupations (Ellemers, 2014; Redersdorff, Martinot, & Branscombe, 2004), and they are especially likely to be evaluated negatively when their leadership style is task-focused or authoritarian (Eagly & Karau, 2002).

In other words, when women violate stereotypic expectancies concerning warmth and nurturance, and instead act according to the prototype of a leader, particularly in masculine domains, they are likely to face hostility and rejection (Bowles, 2013; Glick & Rudman, 2010). Violations of stereotype-based expectancies by women in the workplace appear to evoke threat in some men, particularly among those inclined to sexually harass (Maass, Cadinu, & Galdi, 2013). Indeed, both women and men seem to be aware of the consequences of appearing to violate gender stereotypic expectancies. Because of fear of the social punishments that are likely following such violations, when told that they were highly successful on a knowledge test typical of the other gender group, participants were more likely to lie about which test they performed well on and to hide their success from others (Rudman & Fairchild, 2004). These results suggest that it takes a lot of courage to attempt to defy gender stereotypes!

GENDER STEREOTYPES AND THE "GLASS CLIFF" When, then, are women most likely to gain access to high-status positions—or break through the glass ceiling? Michelle Ryan and Alex Haslam offered the intriguing hypothesis that times of crisis may be "prime time" for women's advancement. There are a host of individual examples that might seem to confirm the idea that women achieve leadership positions when "things are going downhill." Here are a few examples: Shortly after Sunoco Oil's shares fell by 52 percent in 2008, Lynn Laverty Elsenhans was appointed CEO. Kate Swann was appointed CEO of the bookseller, W.H. Smith following a substantial share price drop that required massive job cuts. And, not to leave out the political leadership realm, Johanna Siguroardottir was appointed the first female Prime Minister of Iceland shortly after that country's economy collapsed. To investigate whether these examples are merely coincidental or represent a real phenomenon, in an intriguing series of studies, Ryan and Haslam (2005, 2007) provided evidence that women are indeed more likely to gain admittance to valued leadership positions when a crisis has occurred, the leadership position is more precarious, and there is greater risk of failure—what they refer to as the **glass cliff effect**.

In their first archival studies, they analyzed large companies on the London Stock Exchange, assessing their performance before new members were appointed to the board of directors. Ryan and Haslam (2005) found that companies that had experienced consistently poor stock performance in the months preceding the appointment were more likely to appoint a woman to their boards, whereas those that were performing well in the period before the appointment were unlikely to do so.

To ensure that "bad corporate performance history" was the cause of women being selected for these positions, in a series of experiments using different respondent populations (e.g., students, managers), these researchers found that when people were presented with an equally qualified male and female candidate, the female was selected significantly more often when the position was risky and the male candidate was selected more often when the situation was not risky (Ryan, Haslam, Hersby, Kulich, & Wilson-Kovacs, 2009). Table 6.2 provides a summary of the contexts studied and findings obtained. What these findings imply is that when men's stereotypic leadership attributes appear not to be working because the organization that has been historically led by men is on a downhill trend, then women with their presumed stereotypic communal attributes are seen as suitable for leadership (Bruckmüller & Branscombe, 2010; Bruckmüller, Ryan, Rink, & Haslam, 2014).

CONSEQUENCES OF TOKEN WOMEN IN HIGH PLACES Does the success of those individual women who do break through the glass ceiling in politics (e.g., see Figure 6.7)

Table 6.2 Are Women Most Likely to Be Appointed to Leadership Positions Under Risky Conditions?

Research reveals that women are more likely to be selected for precarious leadership positions, whereas men are more likely to be selected when there are "good prospects" of success.

As shown in this table, research reveals that women are consistently more likely to be selected compared to men for precarious leadership positions, whereas men are more likely to be selected when there are "good prospects" of success.

Conditions under which women have been found to be placed on "the glass cliff": respondents were provided with information about two equally qualified candidates and they favor selecting the woman over the man when:
- The organizational unit to be managed is in crisis, rather than when it is running smoothly
- Financial director for large company is to be hired when the company is on a downward trajectory versus an upward trajectory
- An attorney is appointed to a legal case that is doomed to fail, rather than when it has a good chance of success
- A director for a music festival is selected when it is declining in popularity, rather than when it is increasing in popularity
- A political candidate is selected to run when the election is unwinnable versus certain to win
- CEO hired for a supermarket chain that is losing money and closing stores versus making money and opening new stores

SOURCE: Based on research summarized in Ryan, Haslam, Hersby, Kulich, and Wilson-Kovacs (2009).

make discrimination seem less plausible as an explanation for other women's relative lack of success? To the extent that such numerically infrequent high-status women is taken as evidence that gender no longer matters, people may infer that the relative infrequency of women in high places is due to their lacking the necessary qualities or motivation to succeed. For this reason, the success of a few women may obscure the structural nature of the disadvantages that women on the whole still face. Thus, the presence of a few successful women can lead those who do not achieve similar success to believe that they "lack the merit" needed to succeed (Castilla & Benard, 2010; Schmitt, Ellemers, & Branscombe, 2003).

A number of laboratory experiments have confirmed that **tokenism**—where only a few members of a previously excluded group are admitted—can be a highly effective strategy for deterring collective protest in disadvantaged groups. For instance,

Figure 6.7 Do Visible High-Status Women Lead Us to Believe That Discrimination Is a Thing of the Past?

Hillary Clinton, contender for the U.S. Presidency in 2016, and other female leaders including Janet Yellen, Chair of the Federal Reserve, may suggest to ordinary women and men that group membership is no longer an important impediment for getting ahead.

allowing even a small percentage (e.g., 2 percent) of low-status group members to advance into a higher-status group deters collective resistance and leads disadvantaged group members to favor individual attempts to overcome barriers (Lalonde & Silverman, 1994; Wright, Taylor, & Moghaddam, 1990).

What effect does exposure to visible tokens have on women and men who are observers? Might it make ordinary women and men complacent with regard to the ongoing barriers that women as a group face, and result in beliefs that help to maintain the status quo? Research has explored the consequences of exposure to token practices within an organization (Danaher & Branscombe, 2010). In one experiment, university women were first told that Boards of Regents govern universities in the United States. They were then told that the composition of the board at their university had been stable over the past 10 years and they were given a list of 10 fictitious names of people on the board. In the "open" condition, five of the names were female; in the "token" condition, only one name was female; in the "closed" condition, no female names were present, so all 10 board member names were male. The women were then asked to imagine that a seat on their Board of Regents had been vacated and that they were offered the newly opened seat. From this perspective, participants were asked to indicate the extent to which they would identify with the organization, and they completed a measure assessing their beliefs about meritocracy (e.g., "All people have equal opportunity to succeed").

In both the open and token conditions, women reported believing in meritocracy more than in the closed condition. Likewise, in both the open and token conditions, the participants reported greater identification with the organization than in the closed condition. This means that token conditions—to the same degree as when there is equal gender representation—encourages women to maintain their faith that they can move up and engenders allegiance to organizations where they are substantially underrepresented. In a subsequent experiment, both men and women were asked to imagine serving as an employee in an organization whose hiring policies resulted in 50 percent of employees being women (open), 10 percent were women (token), or only 2 percent were women (virtually closed). The open condition was seen as more fair to women and the closed condition was seen as more fair to men, but the token condition was perceived by both genders as *equally fair for women and men*. Token practices, therefore, appear to serve to maintain the status quo by making women's token representation in organizational settings appear fair.

There are other negative consequences of tokenism, especially when the subsequent performance and well-being of the people occupying those positions are considered. First, people who are hired as token representatives of their groups are perceived quite negatively by other members of the organization (Fuegen & Biernat, 2002; Yoder & Berendsen, 2001). In a sense then, such tokens are "set up" to be marginalized by their coworkers. Job applicants who are identified as "affirmative action hirees" are perceived as less competent by people reviewing their files than applicants who are *not* identified in this manner (Heilman, Block, & Lucas, 1992). Second, as shown in Figure 6.8, when Brown, Charnsangavej, Keough, Newman, and Rentfrow (2000) told some women that they were selected to lead a group because "there was a quota for their gender," the women's performance in that role was undermined compared to when the women were led to believe that their qualifications as well as their gender played a role in their selection.

In whatever form it occurs, research indicates that *tokenism* can have at least two negative effects. First, it lets prejudiced people

Figure 6.8 Believing You Are Selected Strictly Based on Gender Leads to Underperformance

When women were told that they were selected because of a quota, their leadership performance was reduced compared to when they believed their qualifications also played a role in their selection, or when no information was given about why they were made leader.

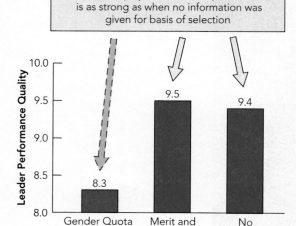

Only when selected solely on the basis of their gender does leadership performance decline. When merit played a role also, performance is as strong as when no information was given for basis of selection

off the hook; they can point to the token as public proof that they are not really bigoted, and the presence of a token helps to maintain perceptions that the existing system is fair—even among members of the disadvantaged group. Second, it can be damaging to the self-esteem and confidence of the targets of prejudice, including those few people who are selected as tokens.

RESPONSES TO THOSE WHO SPEAK OUT ABOUT DISCRIMINATION   What happens when tokens or other targets of discrimination complain about their treatment? Complaining about unjust circumstances can serve a useful function (Kowalski, 1996). It draws people's attention to unfairness, which can ultimately bring about improvement. But, complaining can be also construed as attempting to escape personal responsibility and that is one reason that observers might be suspicious of it.

To test this idea, Kaiser and Miller (2001) told participants about an African American student who attributed his negative grade on an essay to racial discrimination (the "complaint" condition), or that he accepted responsibility for his bad outcome (the "I'm responsible" condition). Regardless of whether the white perceivers in the study thought the bad grade was due to discrimination or not, they evaluated the student more negatively in the "complaint" condition than in the "I'm responsible" condition. Thus, even when we as observers think that another person's negative outcome is not that person's fault, we have a negative impression when that individual does not accept responsibility for the outcome and instead attributes it (accurately) to discrimination!

Moreover, members of the complainer's own ingroup may disapprove of discrimination claimers, when they believe it could suggest to outgroup members that the ingroup is given to unjustified griping (Garcia, Horstman Reser, Amo, Redersdorff, & Branscombe, 2005). Only when the complainer's ingroup believes that the complaint is appropriate because the discrimination is serious and that complaining is likely to improve the situation of the group as a whole are they likely to support a fellow ingroup member who complains about discriminatory treatment (Garcia, Schmitt, Branscombe, & Ellemers, 2010).

Perhaps actual business managers would be concerned about fairness in their own organizations and therefore be responsive to people who claim to have experienced racial discrimination. To assess this possibility, Kaiser et al. (2013) randomly assigned white business managers to first consider what their company does to increase diversity or to a control condition where they considered what their company does to increase environmental sustainability. These managers were then presented with a detailed case file documenting racial discrimination, which they were to consider as though it occurred in their own company. The managers who had first thought about their diversity efforts, perceived the discrimination claim as less legitimate, less of a cause for concern, and importantly, reported being less willing to support the employee filing the discrimination claim compared to managers who had not thought about their diversity efforts. These researchers point out that organizations with diversity structures in place could create the "illusion of fairness" and, ironically, undermine majority group members sensitivity to actual discrimination against minorities and ultimately produce more negative responses to minorities who do claim discrimination.

6.2.2: Is Stereotyping Absent If Members of Different Groups Are Rated the Same?

Most of us would be quick to answer this question with a definite "Yes," but we would be wrong! Biernat's (2012) work on **shifting standards** indicates that although the same evaluation ratings can be given to members of different groups, stereotypes may have influenced those ratings. Furthermore, those identical evaluation ratings given to members of different groups will *not* necessarily translate into the same behavioral expectations for the people rated—suggesting that stereotyping has occurred.

How does this work? People can use different standards—but the same words—to describe different objects. For example, I may say that I have a large cat and a small car, but I don't mean that my large cat is anywhere near the size of my small car! When I use the word *large* to describe both a car and a cat, I am using different comparisons ("large as cats go" and "small compared to other cars").

Likewise, for judgments of people, I may use the same sort of language to describe two basketball players whom I believe will actually perform quite differently. Consider the two basketball players shown in Figure 6.9. I might refer to the 10-year-old basketball player as "great," but that does not mean the same thing as when I say my favorite NBA player is "great." The 10-year-old is excellent *in comparison to other child players*, whereas the NBA player is excellent *in comparison to other professional players*. Terms such as *good–bad* and *small–large* can mask our use of different standards or comparisons—in this case, age. But other standards are available—standards that will always mean the same thing no matter what is being referred to. That is, when rating a basketball player, I might use a standard such as "percentage of free throws made"; such a standard is the same no matter who (the 10-year-old or the NBA player) is attempting to sink those shots from the free-throw line. These standards are referred to as **objective scales**, because the meaning is the same no matter who they are applied to, whereas standards that can take on different meanings, depending on who they are applied to, are called **subjective scales**. Because people shift the meaning with subjective standards and language, it allows for real stereotyping effects to be present, *even when the same rating is given to two quite different targets*.

How might this play out when a person has to evaluate a male and a female to decide which should be promoted to management? If the evaluator believes that males have more competence in management than females, although both the female and male candidates are rated "good" on business success likelihood, that "good" rating will translate into different things on measures whose meaning is the same no matter who is rated. So when asked to rate the male and female applicants on their potential

---

Figure 6.9 Does It Mean the Same Thing When Different People Are Rated the Same?

We might give both the young player on the left and the NBA player on the right a "6" on a 1 to 6 ("very poor to very good") subjective rating scale. But the "6" rating for the boy might translate into low expectations for his ability to consistently sink baskets, whereas the "6" for the professional player would translate into high expectations for sinking baskets (percentage of shots sunk being an objective scale with a constant meaning no matter who it is applied to).

sales capabilities in dollars they will sell per year, the male may be rated higher on this objective measure than the female applicant. Thus, the use of subjective rating scales can conceal the presence of stereotypical judgments, whereas use of objective scales tends to expose them. Numerous studies have supported the process where "same" ratings on subjective scales do not mean "equal" on objective scales, or the absence of stereotyping. In fact, the more people show evidence of using shifting race-based standards, the more they behaviorally discriminate against black job candidates (Biernat, Collins, Katzarska-Miller, & Thompson, 2009).

6.2.3: Can We Be Victims of Stereotyping and Not Even Recognize It: The Case of Single People

Do people always recognize when they stereotype themselves and others? Or, are there circumstances in which we might largely concur with widely held stereotypes—even ones that reflect poorly on ourselves? DePaulo (2006) points out one intriguing instance of this in her research on **singlism**—the negative stereotyping and discrimination that is directed toward people who are single. In a study of over 1,000 undergraduates, DePaulo and Morris (2006) measured how single and married people are characterized. As shown in Table 6.3, the attributes these primarily single participants used to describe "singles" are fairly negative, particularly in contrast to how they described "married" people. And, the differences in the descriptions spontaneously used to describe these groups was often quite substantial: 50 percent of the time, married people were described as kind, giving, and caring, but those attributes were applied to single people only 2 percent of the time. Furthermore, this difference in how married and single people are stereotyped is even greater when the targets are described as over 40 years old compared to when they were said to be 25 years of age. In fact, people who *choose* to be single are perceived as lonelier, less sociable, and more miserable than those who are not single by choice (Slonim, Gur-Yaish, & Katz, 2015).

Although single people currently represent more than 40 percent of American adults (U.S. Census Bureau, 2007), there is no shortage of evidence of discrimination against them (DePaulo & Morris, 2006). When asked to indicate who they would prefer to rent property to, people overwhelmingly chose a married couple (70 percent) over a single man (12 percent) or single woman (18 percent). There are also a variety of legal privileges that come with married status: employer-subsidized health benefits for spouses, discounts on auto insurance, club memberships, and travel, as well as tax and Social Security benefits. So, why is this inequality not salient (and protested) by its victims? One reason is that single people fail to realize it. When singles are asked if they are members of any groups that might be targets of discrimination, DePaulo and Morris (2006) found that only 4 percent spontaneously mention "single" as such a category. When asked directly if singles might be stigmatized, only 30 percent of

Table 6.3 Traits Stereotypically Associated with Single and Married People

As this list of stereotypic traits illustrates, single people are stereotyped in largely negative terms, whereas those who are married are characterized in terms of more positive attributes.

Traits of Single People	Traits of Married People
Immature	Mature
Insecure	Stable
Self-centered	Kind
Unhappy	Happy
ugly	Honest
Lonely	Loving
Independent	Giving

SOURCE: Compiled based on DePaulo and Morris (2006).

singles say that could be the case! In contrast, almost *all* members of other stigmatized groups, including those based on race, weight, and sexual orientation, agree they could be discriminated against.

So, a lack of awareness of the negative stereotyping and discrimination they face does appear to be part of the explanation for why singles themselves fail to acknowledge singlism. But might it also be a case in which people (even its victims) feel that such discrimination is legitimate? When Morris, Sinclair, and DePaulo (2007) asked whether a landlord who refused to rent a property to various categories of people—African Americans, women, homosexuals, or obese people—had stereotyped and engaged in discrimination, participants agreed that was the case, but *not* when the person who was refused the rental was single. These results support the idea that discrimination against single people is seen—by both single and married people—as more legitimate than any of these other forms of discrimination. As we will discuss in the next section on prejudice, there are groups who we seem to feel it is justified to feel prejudice toward. (Although it may not be typical for members of those groups to agree!)

DePaulo and Morris (2006) suggest that negative stereotyping and discrimination against singles serve to protect and glorify an important social institution—marriage—and this is a central reason that it is so widespread and heavily legitimized. Singles, by definition, challenge the existing belief system that finding and marrying one's soulmate is crucial to having a meaningful life. By derogating those who challenge that idea, we can all believe in vital cultural "myths." Consider how just knowing that the people shown in Figure 6.10 have chosen to be single or are part of a couple can change what inferences we might make about what they are likely to be like.

6.2.4: Why Do People Form and Use Stereotypes?

Stereotypes often function as **schemas**, which as we saw in Chapter 2 are cognitive frameworks for organizing, interpreting, and recalling information. So, categorizing people according to their group membership can be efficient for human beings who may invest little cognitive effort in many situations. Thus, one important reason people hold stereotypes is that doing so can conserve the cognitive effort that may be used for other tasks (Bodenhausen, 1993; Macrae, Milne, & Bodenhausen, 1994). According to this view, we rely on our stereotypes when responding to others because it is easy.

But *which* stereotype are we most likely to use—if people can be categorized in terms of several different group memberships? Consider the person shown in Figure 6.11. Are we most likely to stereotype her as a woman, Asian American, or waitress? Both ethnicity and gender are categories that people frequently employ, but given the restaurant context and our interaction with her as a customer, research suggests that people would be most likely to stereotype her in terms of her occupation (Yzerbyt & Demoulin, 2010). Indeed, as you will see later in this chapter, stereotypes can serve important motivational

Figure 6.10 How Does Being Single or Part of a Couple Influence Perceptions of People?

Do the single people in Panels A and B seem more self-centered and less well-adjusted compared to when we see them as part of a couple as shown in Panel C? Research suggests this is the case.

purposes; in addition to providing us with a sense that we can predict others' behavior, they can help us feel positive about our own group identity in comparison to other social groups. For now though, let's consider what the cognitive miser perspective suggests in terms of how stereotypes are used.

STEREOTYPES: HOW THEY OPERATE   Consider the following groups: gun owners, Mexican Americans, professors, U.S. soldiers, homeless people, Russians, and dog lovers. Suppose you were asked to list the traits most characteristic of each. You would probably not find this a difficult task. Most people can easily construct a list for each group and they could probably do so even for groups with whom they have had limited contact. Stereotypes provide us with information about the typical traits possessed by people belonging to these groups and, once activated, these traits seem to come automatically to mind (Bodenhausen & Hugenberg, 2009). It is this fact that explains the ease with which you can construct such lists, even though you may not have had much direct experience with those groups.

Figure 6.11 What Stereotype Is Most Likely to Be Applied to Predict This Person's Behavior?

Even though ethnicity and gender are basic categories that are readily employed, given the context, we may be particularly likely to perceive this person in terms of her occupational role.

Stereotypes act as theories, guiding what we attend to, and exerting strong effects on how we process social information (Yzerbyt, Rocher, & Schradron, 1997). Information relevant to an activated stereotype is often processed more quickly, and remembered better, than information unrelated to it (Krieglmeyer & Sherman, 2012; Macrae, Bodenhausen, Milne, & Ford, 1997). Similarly, stereotypes lead us to pay attention to specific types of information—usually, information consistent with our stereotypes.

When we encounter someone who belongs to a group about whom we have a stereotype, and this person does not seem to fit the stereotype (e.g., a highly intelligent and cultivated person who is also a member of a low-status occupational group), we do not necessarily alter our stereotype about what is typical of members of that group. Rather, we place such people into a special category or **subtype** consisting of people who do not confirm the schema or stereotype (Queller & Smith, 2002; Richards & Hewstone, 2001). Subtyping acts to protect the stereotype of the group as a whole (Park, Wolsko, & Judd, 2001). When the disconfirming target is seen as not typical of the group as a whole, stereotypes are not revised.

DO STEREOTYPES EVER CHANGE?   If stereotypes are automatically activated and we interpret information in ways that allow us to maintain our stereotypes, this raises the question: Do stereotypes ever change? Many theorists have suggested that stereotyping will be stable as long as the nature of the relationship that exists between those groups is stable (e.g., Eagly, 1987; Oakes, Haslam, & Turner, 1994; Pettigrew, 1981; Tajfel, 1981). That is, because we construct stereotypes that reflect how we see members of different groups actually behaving, stereotype change should occur when the relations between the groups change (so the behaviors we observe change accordingly).

In an interesting demonstration of this process, Dasgupta and Asgari (2004) assessed women students' gender stereotypes in their first year and again in their second year in college. The students in this study were attending either a women's college where by their second year they had repeated exposure to women faculty behaving in nontraditional ways or they were attending a coeducational college where they had considerably less exposure to women faculty. As expected, agreement with gender stereotypes was significantly reduced among the students attending a women's college compared to those attending a coeducational college, and the extent of the stereotype change that occurred was predicted by the number of women faculty the students had exposure to in a classroom setting.

Key Points

- **Stereotypes** are beliefs about what members of a particular group are like. **Prejudice** is the feelings component of our reactions toward particular groups, and **discrimination** is differential behavior that is directed toward members of specific groups.

- **Gender stereotypes**—beliefs about the different attributes that males and females possess—act as **schemas** for interpreting their actions and outcomes. Women are stereotyped as high on warmth, but low on competence, while men are stereotyped as low on warmth, but high on competence.

- A **glass ceiling** exists such that women encounter more barriers than men in their careers, and as a result find it difficult to move into top positions. Women are especially likely to be affected in the workplace by the "think manager–think male" bias.

- Women who violate stereotypic expectancies, especially on the warmth dimension, are likely to face hostility. Defying gender stereotypes can be difficult for both women and men.

- Women are most likely to be appointed to leadership positions when a crisis has occurred, the position is more precarious, and there is a greater risk of failure, which has been referred to as the **glass cliff effect**. When men's stereotypic attributes appear to have led the organization downhill, then women's presumed stereotypic communal attributes are seen as suitable in a new leader.

- **Tokenism**—the hiring or acceptance of only a few members of a particular group has two effects: It maintains perceptions that the system is not discriminatory and it harms how tokens are perceived by others and can

undermine performance when they believe their appointment to leadership positions was without regard to their merit. Exposure to token conditions can maintain people's perceptions of fairness and their belief in meritocracy.

- Publicly claiming discrimination as a cause of one's outcomes can produce negative responses by both outgroup and ingroup members, albeit for different reasons. Managers who have considered their diversity efforts are the least supportive of those who complain about racial discrimination.

- Stereotypes can influence behavior even in the absence of different **subjective scale** ratings. When **objective scale** measures are employed, where **shifting standards** cannot occur and the meaning of the response is constant, the effect of stereotypes can be observed.

- In the case of **singlism**—negative stereotyping and discrimination directed toward people who are single—both single and married people show the effect. Singlism may stem from the targets being unaware of the discrimination they face, or because they too see it as legitimate to be biased against their group.

- Stereotypes lead us to attend to information that is consistent with them and to construe inconsistent information in ways that allow us to maintain our stereotypes. When a person's actions are strongly stereotype discrepant, we **subtype** that person as a special case that proves the rule and do not change our stereotypes.

- Stereotypes change as the relations between the groups are altered. Those who are exposed to women in nontraditional roles show reductions in gender stereotyping.

6.3: Prejudice: Feelings Toward Social Groups

Objective   **Recall the factors leading to prejudice against specific groups**

Prejudice has been traditionally considered the feeling component of attitudes toward social groups. It reflects a negative response to another person based solely on that person's membership in a particular group—which Gordon Allport, in his 1954 book *The Nature of Prejudice*, referred to as "antipathy" that is generalized to the group as a whole. In that sense, prejudice is *not* personal—it is an affective reaction toward the category. In other words, a person who is prejudiced toward some social group is predisposed to evaluate its members negatively *because* they belong to that group. **Discrimination** has been traditionally defined as less favorable treatment or negative actions directed toward members of disliked groups (Pettigrew, 2007). Whether prejudice will be expressed in overt discrimination or not will depend on the perceived norms or acceptability of doing so (Crandall et al., 2002; Jetten, Spears, & Manstead, 1997). Indeed, as you will see in the final section of this chapter, changing the perceived norms for treatment of a particular group is sufficient to alter prejudice expression.

Research has illustrated that individuals who score higher on measures of prejudice toward a particular group do tend to process information about that group differently than individuals who score lower on measures of prejudice. For example, information relating to the targets of the prejudice is given more attention than information not relating to them (Hugenberg & Bodenhausen, 2003). Indeed, those who are high in prejudice toward a particular social group are very concerned with learning the group membership of a person (when that is ambiguous). This is because they believe the groups have underlying **essences**—often some biologically based feature that distinguishes that group from other groups, which can serve as justification for their differential treatment (Yzerbyt, Corneille, & Estrada, 2001). As a result of consistently categorizing people in terms of their group membership, one's feelings about that group are legitimized, which results in discrimination (Talaska, Fiske, & Chaiken, 2008).

As an attitude, prejudice is the negative feelings experienced when in the presence of, or merely think about, members of the groups that are disliked (Brewer & Brown, 1998). However, some theorists have suggested that all prejudices are *not* the same—or at least they are not based on the same type of negative feelings. According to this view, we may not be able to speak of "prejudice" as a *generic* negative emotional response at all. Instead, we may need to distinguish between prejudices that are associated with specific intergroup emotions including fear, anger, envy, guilt, or disgust (Glick, 2002; Mackie & Smith, 2002). As depicted in Figure 6.12, even when the level of prejudice toward different groups (i.e., overall negative feelings toward that group) is similar, distinct emotions can form the primary basis of prejudicial responses. For example, these respondents' primary emotional response toward Native Americans was pity, but their primary emotional response toward gay men was disgust (Cottrell & Neuberg, 2005).

Figure 6.12 Different Social Groups Evoke Different Emotions

Even when the overall level of prejudice toward different groups is similar, quite different emotional profiles may be evoked. This has important implications for how prejudice toward different groups might best be changed.

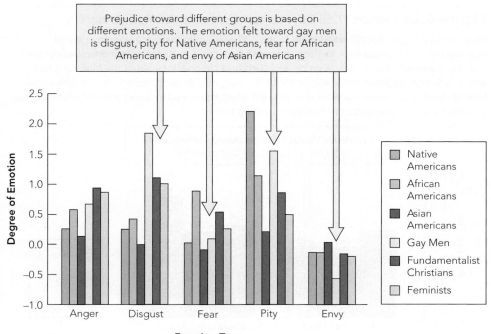

Depending on *what* emotion underlies prejudice toward a particular group, the discriminatory actions that might be expected could be rather different. For example, when people's prejudice primarily reflects anger, then they may attempt to directly harm the outgroup (Mackie, Devos, & Smith, 2000). In contrast, prejudice based on pity or guilt might lead to avoidance of the outgroup because of the distress their plight evokes (Miron, Branscombe, & Schmitt, 2006). According to this perspective, prejudice reduction efforts may need to tackle the specific intergroup emotion that prejudice toward a group is based on. For example, to the extent that fear is reduced when prejudice is based on that emotion, then discrimination may also be reduced (Miller, Smith, & Mackie, 2004).

Research also suggests that inducing some negative emotions can directly lead to discrimination (DeSteno, Dasgupta, Bartlett, & Cajdric, 2004). In two experiments, these researchers found that after experiencing anger, but not sadness or a neutral state, more negative attitudes toward an outgroup was expressed. In these studies, participants were first assigned to **minimal groups**—they were falsely told that they *belong* to a social group that was created in the context of the study. Once participants were categorized as belonging to one group rather than another, they were given an emotion-inducing writing task (e.g., to write in detail about when they felt very angry, very sad, or neutral in the past). Finally, participants were asked to evaluate other members of their ingroup (e.g., those wearing the same color wristband) or the outgroup (e.g., those wearing another color wristband).

As shown in Figure 6.13, reaction times to associate positive or negative evaluation words with the ingroup and outgroup differed depending on the type of negative emotion participants experienced. When feeling angry, they more rapidly associated the outgroup with negative evaluations and the ingroup with positive evaluations, whereas it took longer to learn to associate the outgroup with positive evaluations and the ingroup with negative evaluations. When either feeling sad or neutral, in contrast, no difference in time to associate each group with positive or negative evaluations was obtained. This suggests that even **incidental feelings** of anger—those caused by factors other than the outgroup per se (in this case, the writing task)—can generate automatic prejudice toward members of groups to which we do not belong.

Figure 6.13 Prejudice Can Develop from Incidental Feelings of Anger

When feeling angry, people take longer to learn to associate positive evaluations about members of an outgroup than to learn to associate positive evaluations with members of their ingroup. Likewise, it takes longer to develop negative associations about the ingroup when angry, although negative associations about the outgroup develop rapidly. These differences in time to develop associations were only present when anger was induced and not when sadness or a neutral mood preceded the evaluation pairing task.

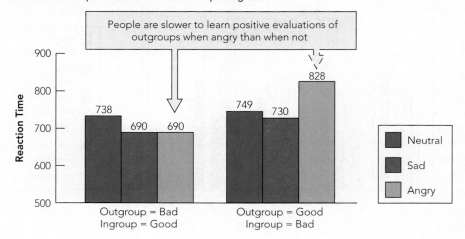

As you can see, such **implicit associations**— between group membership and evaluative responses—can be triggered in a seemingly automatic manner as a result of ingroup and outgroup categorization. The important point about such implicit prejudice is this: We may not be aware of it, although our judgments and decisions about other people and how we interact with them can be influenced. Consider the decisions made by white participants in a simple video game about whether to shoot or not shoot either black or white targets who were armed or unarmed (Correll, Urland, & Ito, 2006). Overall, participants were quicker in deciding to shoot armed black targets than armed white targets, and they were faster in deciding not to shoot unarmed whites compared to unarmed blacks. Those who had stronger implicit associations between blacks and violence were especially likely to show these decision biases. In fact, such automatic prejudice effects are particularly difficult to inhibit following alcohol consumption (Bartholow, Dickter, & Sestir, 2006).

Before turning to a discussion of the many ways that prejudice can be expressed in overt behavior, we will first address an important question: What motives might affect the extent to which prejudice is felt? What psychological benefits might people get from expressing prejudice toward particular groups?

6.3.1: The Origins of Prejudice: Contrasting Perspectives

Several important perspectives have been developed to answer the question: "Where does prejudice come from, and why does it persist?" The most general response to this question has focused on perceived **threat**—be it either material or symbolic—to a valued ingroup (Esses, Jackson, & Bennett-AbuAyyash, 2010). We will first consider how perceptions of threat to self-esteem and group interests are critical for prejudice. Then we will contemplate how competition for scarce resources can increase prejudice. At the end of this section, we will examine whether categorizing the self as a member of a group, and others as members of a different group, is a sufficient condition for prejudice to occur. Based on a cross-cultural study of 186 different societies, it is clear that the more important loyalty to one's own ingroup is, the greater the support there is for prejudice toward outgroups (Cohen, Montoya, & Insko, 2006). So feelings about one's own group are related to prejudice toward outgroups.

THREATS TO SELF-ESTEEM   It is certainly true that prejudice cannot be understood unless threat—and how it affects people—is taken into account. People want to see their own group positively (Tajfel & Turner, 1986), which in practice means more positively than some other group. When an event threatens people's perceptions of their group's value, they may retaliate by derogating the source of the threat. It is also the case that perceiving a threat to our group can lead us to identify more with our ingroup. Several studies, using reminders of the terrorist attacks of September 11, 2001, as the threatening event, have found increases in identification with the nation (Landau et al., 2004).

Does the event that threatens one's group identity need to involve possible death, or is it sufficient that it simply implies your group is not as positive as you would like to see it, for prejudice responses to occur? To test this idea, American college students, who differed in the extent to which they placed value on their identity as Americans, were shown one of two 6-minute videos based on the movie *Rocky IV* (Branscombe & Wann, 1994). In one clip, Rocky (an American boxer played by Sylvester Stallone) won the match against Ivan (a Russian contender). This version was not threatening, for it supports Americans' positive views of their group as winners. In the other clip, Rocky loses the fight to Ivan, the Russian. This version was threatening, particularly to those who highly value their identity as Americans, and it lowered feelings of self-esteem based on group membership. The question is, Can exposure to such a minor threat to identity in the laboratory result in prejudice? The answer obtained was yes—those who were highly identified as Americans and who saw the threatening Rocky "as loser" film clip showed increased prejudice toward Russians and advocated they be kept out of the United States in the future. In fact, the more these participants negatively evaluated Russians, the more their self-esteem based on their group membership subsequently increased.

This research suggests that holding prejudiced views of an outgroup allows group members to bolster their own group's image, particularly when it has been threatened. By "putting down" members of another group, we can affirm our own group's comparative value—and such prejudice is most strongly expressed when threat is experienced. The important role of such perceived threat to one's group has been demonstrated in a wide variety of group contexts: whites' prejudice toward black Americans (Stephan et al., 2002), prejudice toward various immigrant groups (Esses, Jackson, Nolan, & Armstrong, 1999; Stephan, Renfro, Esses, Stephan, & Martin, 2005), Catholics and Protestants in Northern Ireland (Tausch, Hewstone, Kenworthy, & Cairns, 2007), and men's prejudice and sabotaging actions toward women they perceive as "moving in" on males' traditional territory (Netchaeva, Kouchaki, & Sheppard, 2015; Rudman & Fairchild, 2004). Evidence for this process, illustrated in Figure 6.14, has been obtained in numerous studies.

Overall, then, advantaged groups exhibit prejudice toward outgroups most strongly when they are experiencing a threat to their group's image and interests. Because of the critical role that perceived threat can play in maintaining and escalating prejudice, research has addressed how such threat may be reduced. Simply reminding people who value their ingroup identity—as Democrats or Republicans—that they share a more inclusive identity (American) with the other group can lower perceived threat and prejudice (Riek, Mania, Gaertner, McDonald, & Lamoreaux, 2010). We will return to this technique, known as *recategorization*, in our discussion of procedures for reducing prejudice.

COMPETITION FOR RESOURCES AS A SOURCE OF PREJUDICE   It is sad but true that the things people want most—good jobs, nice homes—are in short supply. Quite frequently, these are **zero-sum outcomes**—if one group gets them, the other group cannot. Consider the conflict between the Israelis and Palestinians, which has been ongoing since the creation of the state of Israel in 1948. Both want to control Jerusalem. This sort of conflict over desirable territory has been considered within **realistic conflict theory** to be a major cause of prejudice (Bobo, 1983). The theory further suggests that as competition escalates, the members of the groups involved will come to view each other in increasingly negative terms. They may label each other as "enemies," view their own group as morally superior, draw the boundaries between themselves and their opponents more firmly, and, under extreme conditions, come to see the opposing group as not even human (Bar-Tal, 2003).

While competition can intensify conflict, as you will see, it may not be the *most basic cause* of conflict between groups. A classic study by Sherif, Harvey, White, Hood,

---

Figure 6.14 Prejudice Persists When It Serves Our Group's Interests

When self-esteem is threatened, people are most likely to derogate the groups representing the threat. Indeed, doing so helps to boost or restore threatened self-esteem. Via this mechanism, groups can maintain their dominant position.

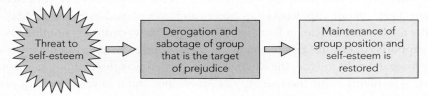

and Sherif (1961) with middle-class well-adjusted boys illustrates the process. The boys were brought to a summer camp called *Robber's Cave*, where they were randomly assigned to two different groups, but because their cabins were well separated they were unaware of the existence of the other group. Initially, the boys in each cabin enjoyed hiking, swimming, and other sports, and they rapidly developed strong attachments to their group—choosing names for themselves (*Rattlers* and *Eagles*) and making up flags with their groups' symbols on them. In the second phase of the study, the groups were brought together and they began a series of competitions. They were told that the winning team would receive a trophy and various desirable prizes; since both groups of boys wanted the prizes badly, the stage was set for intense competition.

As the boys competed, the tension between the groups rose. At first it was limited to verbal taunts, but soon escalated into direct acts—such as when the Rattlers broke into the Eagles' cabin, overturning beds and generally wreaking havoc. The two groups voiced increasingly negative views of each other, while heaping praise on their own group. In short, strong prejudice developed.

In the final phase, competition was eliminated, but that alone did not reduce the negative reactions toward the other group. Only when conditions were altered so that the groups found it necessary to work together to reach **superordinate goals**—ones they both desired but neither group could achieve alone—did dramatic change occur. The boys worked cooperatively together to restore their water supply (secretly sabotaged by the researchers), combined funds to rent a movie, and jointly repaired a broken-down truck so they could all go into town to get ice cream. The tensions between the groups gradually decreased, and many cross-group friendships developed.

Despite what Sherif's research showed about factors that can intensify and reduce intergroup conflict, what he did *not* show is whether competition is *necessary* for prejudice to develop. In fact, prior to the introduction of the competition, the *mere knowledge* of the other group was sufficient to generate name-calling between the two groups of boys. Perhaps simply being a member of a group and identifying with it is sufficient for prejudice to emerge. This is the idea that Tajfel and Turner (1986) developed further in their social identity theory, which we turn to next.

COGNITIVE EFFECTS OF SOCIAL CATEGORIZATION: THE US-VS.-THEM EFFECT "How is genocide possible?" This was a question that preoccupied Henri Tajfel throughout his life, in part because he was a Jew who had lived through the Nazi Holocaust. Unlike some who believed that the source of such intergroup violence lay in irrationality, Tajfel (1982) believed that there were important cognitive processes involved. He argued that a history of conflict, personal animosity, individual self-interest or competition were not *necessary* to create group behavior. Perhaps, as with boys in Sherif's study, if people were merely categorized into different groups, then you would see the beginnings of ingroup loyalty and outgroup discrimination. Indeed, he was searching for a "baseline" condition where prejudice would be lacking, when he stumbled onto the most basic condition needed to create prejudice.

Tajfel, Billig, Bundy, and Flament (1971) originated a paradigm for studying intergroup behavior in which participants were categorized into groups on some trivial basis. He had participants view a set of pictures—as shown in Figure 6.15—by the artists Klee and Kandinsky. In all instances, participants were assigned to one group or the other randomly, but were told that it was based on whether they had shared a preference for Klee or Kandinsky paintings. Each group that was created on this minimal basis had no history, no contact among its members, no leader—that is, nothing whatsoever that would cause it to be a real "group."

The task of the participants was simply to allocate points or money, between two other participants—one of whom was presented as an ingroup member and one of whom was an outgroup member. Participants on average awarded members of their own group more than members of the other group. Furthermore, when participants

Figure 6.15 Social Categorization: Ingroups and Outgroups

In Panel A, the artist Paul Klee's work is shown, and a Kandinsky painting is shown in Panel B. A "minimal" categorization can be created by telling participants that they share a preference for one artist over the other.

could choose to allocate more money in *absolute terms* to members of their own group, they chose to allocate smaller absolute amounts *if* that would also mean allocating *relatively* less to members of the other group, suggesting that the participants were attempting to maximize the difference between the rewards given to the two groups. The results of these experiments were shocking at the time, because they illustrated how people could be divided into distinct categories on almost any basis, and doing so could result in different perceptions of, and actions toward, *us* (members of their own group) versus *them* (members of the other group).

Once the social world is divided into "us" and "them," it takes on emotional significance. Some differences are granted social importance and have meaning for our identities (Oakes et al., 1994). People in the "us" category are viewed in more favorable terms, while those in the "them" category are perceived more negatively. Indeed, it may be widely *expected* that some groups should be disliked, while prejudice toward other groups is seen as not justified (Crandall et al., 2002). For example, college students who were asked to rate the extent to which it was appropriate or legitimate to express prejudice toward 105 different social groups did so easily. The top-10 groups it is acceptable to display prejudice toward, and the 10 for whom it is least legitimate to express prejudice against, are shown in Table 6.4.

How, precisely, does social categorization result in prejudice? **Social identity theory** suggests that individuals seek to feel positively about the groups to which they belong, and part of our self-esteem is derived from our social group memberships (Tajfel & Turner, 1986). Since people who are identified with their group are most likely to express favoritism toward their own group and a corresponding bias against outgroups, valuing our own group will have predictable consequences for prejudice. Can extreme valuing of our own group, what has been called feeling "fused with our group," affect willingness to engage in extreme actions to benefit and protect it?

Recent research has addressed this precise question (Swann, Jetten, Gómez, Whitehouse, & Bastian, 2012). These researchers first assess **identity fusion**—the extent to which a person sees the self and their group as overlapping. The idea is that people who see themselves as fused with their nation yoke their personal agency to their group and see its outcomes as like their own. Therefore, when given an opportunity to protect their group they will be more willing to do so than those who do not

Table 6.4 Who Do We Believe It Is OK or Not OK to Express Prejudice Toward?

The "top 10" list on the left indicates what groups college students perceive it to be acceptable and legitimate to feel prejudice toward. The "top 10" list on the right indicates what groups they perceive it to be unacceptable and illegitimate to feel prejudice toward. How do you think these lists would differ for people living in other regions of the United States besides the Midwest? How might they differ for people who are members of different ethnic groups?

Prejudice Legitimized	Prejudice Seen as Illegitimate
Rapists	Blind people
Child abusers	Women homemakers
Child molesters	People who are deaf
Wife beaters	People who are mentally impaired
Terrorists	Family men
Racists	Farmers
Ku Klux Klan members	Male nurses
Drunk drivers	Librarians
Nazi party members	Bowling league members
Pregnant women who drink alcohol	Dog owners

SOURCE: Based on data provided by Crandall, Eshleman, and O'Brien (2002).

yoke themselves to their group. In a series of studies, fused and nonfused students were asked how they would respond to a moral dilemma. The dilemma they were confronted with has been referred to as the "trolley problem." People are asked to imagine a runaway trolley that is about to kill five of their ingroup members, unless the participant jumps from a bridge onto the trolley's path, thereby re-directing the trolley away from the others. Participants have to choose between letting the trolley crush five of their fellow ingroup members, or sacrificing themselves to save the five ingroup members (who were strangers to them). As you can see in Figure 6.16,

Figure 6.16 Identity Fusion: Willingness to Die for One's Group

People who are "fused" see themselves as completely overlapping with their group. A greater percentage of those who were fused with their national group, Spain, were willing to sacrifice themselves to save ingroup members than were people who were not fused.

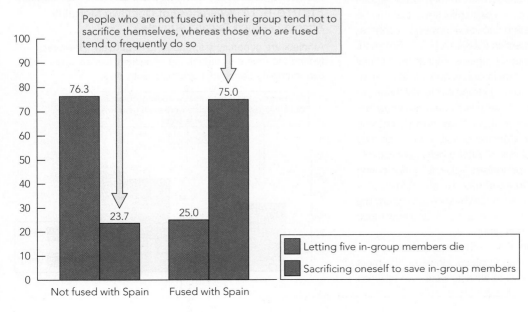

75 percent of those who were fused with Spain chose to sacrifice themselves to save five other Spaniards, whereas only 24 percent of those who were not fused chose to do so.

When a person's identity is fused with a group, it appears to create a willingness to undertake extreme forms of self-sacrifice to protect the group. This research provides us with insight into how emotional responses to others and extreme behavior can be influenced by people's relationship to their group (fused or not fused) and how we categorize those who are at risk ("us" or "them"). For another perspective on how prejudice toward outgroups can stem from our own concerns—in this case **existential threat**—which stems from anxiety based on awareness of our own mortality, see the special section **"What Research Tells Us About...The Role of Existential Threat in Prejudice."**

What Research Tells Us About...

The Role of Existential Threat in Prejudice

Prejudice toward atheists is widespread in the United States and elsewhere; in fact, it is explicitly and more strongly endorsed than prejudice toward almost any other group including Muslims, ethnic minorities, and gay people (Franks & Scherr, 2014). American Christians are most likely to say they would *not* vote for an atheist for public office, perceive atheists as untrustworthy, and report feeling fear and disgust in response to this category. Why does the lack of belief in God elicit such intense prejudice? Atheists are likely to represent a threat to widely shared ingroup values and for this reason can be seen as threatening the existing social order that provides meaning.

How might people's own *existential anxiety*—arising from awareness of our own mortality—affect prejudice toward atheists? Might such prejudice be especially high when our own mortality is salient, which brings questions of existential meaning to mind? Guided by **terror management theory,** which argues that awareness of death can evoke existential terror that can be reduced by adhering to prevailing cultural worldviews, recent research has addressed this question (Cook, Cohen, & Solomon, 2015). Given that the existence of atheists implies the cultural worldview of those who do believe in God is questionable, atheists are likely to be experienced as a strong existential threat. To test this straightforward idea, these researchers randomly assigned college students to think about "their own death" (the mortality salient condition) or a control condition in which they were to think about "a painful event." After a delay, participants were asked about their feelings toward "Atheists" (people who do not believe in God) or "Quakers" (people who adhere to a small Christian organization), how much distance they would like to maintain between themselves and that group, and how much they would trust members of that group.

As you can see in Figure 6.17, Atheists were, overall, responded to more negatively than Quakers. However, the most extreme negative responses toward atheists were evoked when

participants' own mortality had been made salient. This same pattern of results was obtained for social distancing and distrust: When death was salient, participants wanted greater distance from atheists and distrusted them more than in the pain control condition. A subsequent study illustrated too that thinking about atheism made thoughts of death more accessible (like the morality salient condition) than in the control condition.

This research suggests that our own existential concerns can elicit prejudice toward a group that is seen as a fundamental threat to our cultural worldview that is adhered to as a means of protecting us from the terror of our own mortality. Indeed, the mere existence of atheists seems to arouse concerns about mortality.

Figure 6.17 Awareness of Our Own Mortality Affects Feelings Toward Atheists

Atheists are generally responded to negatively. However, feeling thermometer ratings are especially low so when our own mortality concerns have been activated.

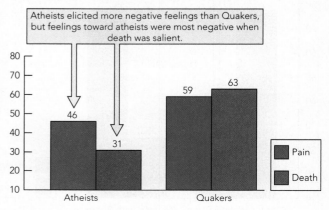

Key Points

- **Discrimination** refers to the unfavorable treatment or negative actions directed toward members of disliked groups, which are believed to have **essences** that make them inferior to other groups. Whether discrimination will be expressed or not depends on the perceived norms or acceptability of doing so.
- Research indicates that prejudice may reflect more specific underlying emotional responses toward different outgroups including fear, anger, guilt, pity, and disgust. Different behaviors are likely, depending on the emotional basis of the prejudice. Even **incidental feelings** caused by factors other than the outgroup can result in prejudice.
- **Implicit associations**—links between group membership and evaluations—can be triggered automatically from categorizing others as ingroup or outgroup members.
- Prejudice persists because derogating outgroups can protect our self-esteem. **Threat** to our group's interests can motivate prejudice, and perceived competition between groups for resources can escalate conflict.
- The Robber's Cave study of two groups of boys at a summer camp who had been in conflict showed that **superordinate goals** transformed **zero-sum outcomes** where only one group could get the desired outcome into shared outcomes that could only be obtained if the groups worked together. This reduced the conflict between the groups.
- According to **social identity theory**, prejudice is derived from our tendency to divide the world into "us" and "them" and to view our own group more favorably than various outgroups. This is true even when the groups are formed on a **minimal** or trivial basis.
- People may feel it is legitimate to display prejudice toward some groups, but it is seen as highly illegitimate to express prejudice toward other groups.
- People who are fused with their group are particularly likely to say they would sacrifice their own life to save other ingroup members. Emotional responses to others and extreme behavior can be influenced by people's relationship to their group (**identity fusion**) and how others are categorized ("us" or "them").
- **Terror management theory** argues that awareness of our own mortality can evoke **existential threat** that can be reduced by adhering to our cultural worldview. Because atheists represent an existential threat, they are especially likely to be responded to negatively when our mortality is salient.

6.4: Discrimination: Prejudice in Action

Objective **Explain how subtle forms of discrimination are the manifestations of prejudice**

Attitudes, as we noted in Chapter 5, are not always reflected in overt actions, and prejudice is no exception to this. In many cases, people with negative attitudes toward various groups cannot express their views directly. Laws, social pressure, fear of retaliation—all serve to deter them from putting their prejudiced views into practice. For these reasons, blatant forms of **discrimination**—negative actions toward the objects of racial, ethnic, and gender prejudice—have decreased in recent years in the United States and many other countries (Devine, Plant, & Blair, 2001; Swim & Campbell, 2001). Thus, actions such as restricting members of various groups to certain seats on buses or in movie theaters, barring them from public schools—all common in the past—have vanished. This is not to suggest that extreme expressions of prejudice do not occur. On the contrary, dramatic instances of "hate crimes"—crimes based on racial, ethnic, and other types of prejudice—do occur. Despite such extreme incidents, prejudice, in general, often finds expression in much more subtle forms of behavior. We turn now to these *subtle* or *disguised* forms of discrimination.

6.4.1: Modern Racism: More Subtle, but Just as Harmful

At one time, many people felt no qualms about expressing openly racist beliefs (Sears, 2008). Now, few Americans agree with such antiblack sentiments. Does this mean that racism is on the wane? Many social psychologists believe that "old-fashioned racism," encompassing blatant feelings of superiority, has been replaced by more subtle forms, which they term **modern racism** (McConahay, 1986; Swim, Aikin, Hall, & Hunter, 1995).

What is such racism like? It can involve concealing prejudice from others in public settings, but expressing bigoted attitudes when it is safe to do so; for instance, in the company of friends known to share these views. Indeed, peers' prejudiced attitudes are one of the best predictors of one's own prejudiced attitudes (Poteat & Spanierman, 2010). It might also involve attributing various bigoted views to sources other than prejudice, whenever another explanation for potentially biased behavior is feasible. It could also involve attempting to appear "color blind" and refusing to acknowledge race as a means of suggesting one is not racist.

In an interesting demonstration of this strategy (Norton, Sommers, Apfelbaum, Pura, & Ariely, 2006), white participants who were concerned about appearing racist were placed in a setting where they had to describe another individual to either a black or white partner. When their partner in this game was black, participants were reluctant to use race as a descriptive term—even when it was highly diagnostic of the person they were asked to describe (e.g., the only black person in a group of whites). In contrast, when their partner was white, the same person the participant was to describe was referred to in terms of his or her race. Precisely because many people want to conceal their racist attitudes—both from others and from themselves—and "failing to even notice race" might seem to be one way of doing so, social psychologists have had to develop unobtrusive means of studying such attitudes. Let's take a look at how such prejudice can be detected.

MEASURING IMPLICIT RACIAL ATTITUDES: FINDING A "BONA FIDE PIPELINE" The most straightforward approach to measuring prejudice is to simply ask people to express their views toward various racial or ethnic groups. But many people are not willing to admit to holding prejudiced views, so alternative ways of assessment have been developed. In recent years, as we discussed in Chapter 5, social psychologists have recognized that many attitudes people hold are **implicit**—they exist and can influence behavior, but the people holding them may not be aware of their impact. In fact, in some cases, they might vigorously deny that they have such views and instead proclaim their "color blindness" (Dovidio, Gaertner, & Kawakami, 2010; Greenwald & Banaji, 1995). How then can such subtle forms of prejudice be measured? Several different methods have been developed (Kawakami & Dovidio, 2001), but most are based on **priming**—where exposure to certain stimuli or events "prime" information held in memory, making it easier to bring to mind, or more available to influence our current reactions.

One technique that makes use of priming to study implicit or automatically activated racial attitudes is known as the **bona fide pipeline** (Banaji & Hardin, 1996; Towles-Schwen & Fazio, 2001). With this procedure, participants see various adjectives and are asked to indicate whether they have a "good" or "bad" meaning by pushing one of two buttons. Before seeing each adjective, however, they are briefly exposed to faces of people belonging to various racial groups (blacks, whites, Asians, Latinos). It is reasoned that implicit racial attitudes will be revealed by how quickly participants respond to the words that have a negative meaning. In contrast, participants will respond more slowly to words with a positive meaning after being primed with the faces of those same minority group members, because the positive meaning is inconsistent with the negative attitude elicited by the priming stimulus.

Research findings using this procedure indicate that people do indeed have implicit racial attitudes that are automatically elicited, and that such automatically elicited attitudes can, in turn, influence important forms of behavior such as decisions concerning others and the degree of friendliness that is expressed in interactions with them (Fazio & Hilden, 2001; Towles-Schwen & Fazio, 2001). The important point to note is this: Despite the fact that blatant forms of racism and sexism have decreased, automatic prejudice is very much alive and, through more subtle kinds of reactions, continues to affect behavior.

HOW PREJUDICED PEOPLE MAINTAIN AN "UNPREJUDICED" SELF-IMAGE   Despite the evidence of ongoing racial inequality, as well as widespread existence of subtle and implicit prejudice, many white Americans believe they are unprejudiced (Feagin & Vera, 1995; Saucier, 2002). So, given the strong evidence that racial prejudice is still with us (Dovidio et al., 2010), how do people who harbor prejudice come to perceive themselves as unprejudiced?

Recent research suggests that it is through social comparison with extreme images of bigots that many people who are prejudiced can perceive themselves as not matching that prototype (O'Brien et al., 2010). In a series of studies, these researchers exposed participants to words or images reflecting extreme bigotry, such as those shown in Figure 6.18. In each case, participants exposed to the bigotry primes rated themselves as more unprejudiced than participants exposed to race-neutral materials. In fact, when the possibility that they might be revealed as harboring racism was suggested, participants expressed greater interest in viewing extreme racist materials than participants who were not threatened with the possibility that their own racism might be revealed.

WHEN WE CONFRONT WHAT OUR GROUP HAS DONE TO ANOTHER GROUP   People want to think of the groups that they belong to and identify with as being good and moral. In recent years, particularly with the release of photographs of American soldiers humiliating Muslim detainees and torturing them at Abu Ghraib prison in Iraq and elsewhere, research has considered the question of how people respond when they learn about the prejudicial actions of their own group. Do we perceive such harmful actions as torture, or as justifiable? In a representative sample of American adults, Crandall, Eidelman, Skitka, and Morgan (2009) described such practices of torture against detainees as either part of the status quo, having been used for more than 40 years, or as new and something their group had never done previously. They found

Figure 6.18 Extreme Representations of Racists Help Many Maintain the View That They Are Unprejudiced

Exposure to extreme images or even just the labels of these groups (e.g., KKK) relative to a control condition in which these images are absent increases white American students' perception that they are unprejudiced. This is because these racist groups set an extreme comparison, which college students do not match.

that torture was seen as more justifiable when described as a long-standing practice compared to when it was described as something new. Torture is also seen as more moral when our own group is said to have committed it than when another group is said to have acted in the same way (Tarrant, Branscombe, Warner, & Weston, 2012).

Exposure to how one's group has acted in a prejudiced fashion toward other groups can evoke defenses in order to avoid the aversive feelings of **collective guilt**—an emotional response that people can experience when they perceive their group as responsible for illegitimate wrongdoings (Branscombe & Miron, 2004). When the ingroup's responsibility for the harmful actions cannot be denied, people can "blame the victims" for its occurrence by suggesting that they deserved the outcomes they received. Derogation of victims helps perpetrators to feel less burdened when faced with their harm doing (Bandura, 1990). At its most extreme, the victims can even be excluded from the category "human" entirely so they are seen as not deserving humane treatment at all, which will permit any harm done to them to be seen as justified (Bar-Tal, 2003). As Aquino, Reed, Thau, and Freeman (2006) illustrate in their research, dehumanization of the victims helps to justify our group's actions as having served a "righteous purpose"—that of retaliating against our enemy's "evil." **Moral disengagement**—no longer seeing sanctioning as necessary for perpetrating harm—makes it "okay" for our military personnel to maltreat prisoners, if doing so can be seen as somehow protecting the ingroup (Bandura, 1999).

There are other ways that people can deal with their group's harm-doing—such as motivated forgetting. Sahdra and Ross (2007) have shown that people's memory for harmful behaviors committed by their ingroup is not equivalent to their memory of instances where their ingroup was victimized by another group. In their research, Sikh and Hindu Canadians were asked about their memories concerning events that were committed in India by Sikhs and Hindus, in which each group had targeted innocent and unarmed members of the other group for violent acts. When asked to recall three incidents from the 1980s (a period of heavy intergroup violence), participants were less likely to remember incidents in which their own group had been perpetrators of violence than incidents in which their group members were the victims of violence. Individuals who were more highly identified with their ingroup recalled the fewest instances of ingroup harm-doing to others. Members of both the groups involved in this religious conflict tailored their memories so that events in which their group perpetrated harm against others were more difficult to bring to mind than events in which the other group victimized their group. Thus, people have available to them a variety of motivated mental strategies that help them maintain a favorable view of their ingroup, despite its prejudicial treatment of others (Sharvit, Brambilla, Babush, & Colucci, 2015).

Key Points

- Blatant racial discrimination has decreased, but more subtle forms such as modern racism persist.
- Those high in modern racism may want to hide their prejudice. The **bona fide pipeline** is based on the assumption that people are unaware of their prejudices, but they can be revealed with **implicit** measures. **Priming** or making a category accessible for which the individual has negative attitudes will result in faster responses to words with negative meanings.
- People can maintain the view that they are unprejudiced by comparing themselves to extreme bigots.

- When we are exposed to instances in which members of our own group have behaved in a prejudicial fashion, we can avoid feeling **collective guilt** to the extent that we can conclude the harmful acts were legitimate because it is a long-standing practice, the people harmed do not warrant concern, or doing so serves the ingroup's higher goals. People also show evidence of motivated forgetting of their own group's harm doing. Such **moral disengagement** can also involve justifying the harm committed by their own group or dehumanizing the victims.

6.5: Why Prejudice Is Not Inevitable: Techniques for Countering Its Effects

Objective   **Outline ways of reducing prejudice**

Prejudice, in some form, appears to be an all-too-common aspect of life in most societies (Sidanius & Pratto, 1999). Does this mean that it is inevitable? As we explained in this chapter, prejudice certainly has some clear properties (e.g., it will escalate under competition, when others are categorized as the outgroup). Yet, under the right conditions, prejudice toward particular groups can be reduced. We turn now to some of the techniques that social psychologists have developed in their attempts to reduce prejudice.

6.5.1: On Learning Not to Hate

According to the **social learning view**, children acquire negative attitudes toward various social groups because they hear such views expressed by significant others, and because they are directly rewarded (with love, praise, and approval) for adopting these views. The more white participants' parents are prejudiced, and the less positive participants' own interactions with minority group members are; the more discriminatory their behavior when interacting with African Americans (Towles-Schwen & Fazio, 2001). Indeed, the degree to which parents' racial attitudes and their children's are related depends on the extent to which children identify with their parents. Children who care about making their parents proud of them show the greatest parental influence. In a sample of fourth and fifth graders, it was found that parental and children's racial attitudes were positively related *only* among children with relatively high identification with their parents (Sinclair, Dunn, & Lowery, 2005).

But people continue to be socialized in terms of ethnic attitudes well beyond childhood. What are the consequences of joining institutions that subtly support either diversity or prejudice toward particular outgroups? Guimond (2000) investigated this issue among Canadian military personnel. He found that English Canadians became significantly more prejudiced toward specific outgroups (e.g., French Canadians, immigrants, and civilians) and internalized justifications for the economic gap between their own group and these outgroups as they progressed through the 4-year officer training program. Further, he found that the more they identified with the military; the more they showed increases in prejudice over time. It would seem therefore that institutions, which can be molded to value diversity or prejudice, can exert considerable influence on the adults who identify with them.

6.5.2: The Potential Benefits of Contact

Can racial prejudice be reduced by increasing the degree of contact between different groups? The idea that it can do so is known as the **contact hypothesis** and there are several good reasons for predicting that such a strategy can be effective (Pettigrew, 1997). Increased contact between people from different groups can lead to a growing recognition of similarities between them—which can change the categorizations that people employ. As we saw earlier, those who are categorized as "us" are responded to more positively than those categorized as "them." Increased contact, or merely having knowledge that other members of our group have such contact with outgroup members, can signal that the norms of the group are not so "antioutgroup" as individuals might initially have believed. The existence of cross-group friendships suggests that members of the outgroup do not necessarily dislike members of our ingroup, and this knowledge can reduce intergroup anxiety.

Consider, for example, the situation of Catholics and Protestants in Northern Ireland. Members of these groups live in highly segregated housing districts, and contact between the members of the two groups is often perceived negatively. Social psychologists (Paolini, Hewstone, Cairns, & Voci, 2004) have found that direct contact between members of these two religious groups, as well as indirect contact (via knowledge of other ingroup members' friendships with outgroup members) can reduce prejudice by reducing anxiety about future encounters with outgroup members.

Other research has likewise suggested that among linguistic groups throughout Europe, positive contact that is seen as reflective of increased cooperation between the groups can change norms so that group equality is favored and, thereby, reduce prejudice (Van Dick et al., 2004). Moreover, the beneficial effects of such cross-group friendships can readily spread to other people who have not themselves experienced such contacts: simply knowing about them can be enough.

In a series of studies involving heterosexuals who were friends with a gay man, Vonofakou, Hewstone, and Voci (2007) found that degree of perceived closeness with the friend and the extent to which the gay friend was seen as typical of that group predicted lower prejudice toward gay men as a whole. Perceived closeness lessened anxiety about interacting with gay people, and perceiving the friend as typical ensured that the friend was not subtyped as different from other members of the group—optimal conditions for generalization of contact and stereotype change.

6.5.3: Recategorization: Changing the Boundaries

Think back to your high school days. Imagine that your school's football team was playing an important game against a rival school from a nearby town. In this case, you would certainly view your own school as "us" and the other school as "them." But now imagine that the other school's team won, and went on to play against a team from another state in a national tournament. *Now* how would you view them? The chances are good that under these conditions, you would view the other school's team (the team you lost to) as "us"; after all, they now represent *your* state. And of course, if a team from a state other than your own was playing against teams from other countries, you might then view them as "us" relative to the "foreign team."

Situations like this, in which we shift the boundary between "us" and "them," are quite common in everyday life, and they raise an interesting question: Can such shifts—or **recategorizations** as they are termed by social psychologists—be used to reduce prejudice? The **common ingroup identity model** suggests that it can (Gaertner, Rust, Dovidio, Bachman, & Anastasio, 1994; Riek et al., 2010). To the extent that individuals who belong to different social groups come to view themselves as members of a *single social entity,* their attitudes toward each other become more positive. So, while "us" and "them" categorical distinctions can produce prejudice, as we learned earlier in this chapter, when "them" becomes "us," prejudice should be eliminated.

How can we induce people who belong to different groups to perceive themselves as members of a single group? As Sherif et al. (1961), observed at the *Robber's Cave* boys camp that we discussed earlier, when individuals belonging to initially distinct groups work together toward *shared* or *superordinate* goals, they come to perceive themselves as a single social entity. This causes feelings of hostility toward the former outgroup—toward "them"—to fade away. Such effects have been demonstrated in several studies (Gaertner, Mann, Murrell, & Dovidio, 1989; Gaertner, Mann, Dovidio, Murrell, & Pomare, 1990), in both the laboratory and the field. When *recategorization* is successfully induced, it has proven to be a useful technique for reducing prejudice toward those who were previously categorized as outgroup members.

The power of shifting to a more inclusive category for reductions in negative feelings toward an outgroup has been shown even among groups with a long history, including one group's brutality toward another. Consider how Jews in the present are likely to feel about Germans, given the Holocaust history. Although that conflict has long been terminated, to the extent that the victim group continues to categorize Jews and Germans as separate and distinct groups, contemporary Germans are likely to be responded to with prejudice—even though they were not alive during the time of the Nazi atrocities against the Jews. In a strong test of the recategorization hypothesis, Jewish Americans were induced to either think about Jews and Germans as separate groups, or to categorize them as members of a single and maximally inclusive group—that of humans (Wohl & Branscombe, 2005). Following this manipulation, Jewish participants were asked to indicate the extent to which they were willing to forgive Germans for the past. In the condition, where Germans and Jews were thought about as separate groups, participants reported less forgiveness of Germans compared to when the two groups were included in one social category—that of humans. Including members of an outgroup in the same category as the ingroup has important consequences for prejudice reduction and willingness to have social contact—even with members of an "old enemy" group.

6.5.4: The Benefits of Guilt for Prejudice Reduction

When people are confronted with instances in which they have personally behaved in a prejudiced fashion, it can lead to feelings of guilt for having violated one's personal standards (Monteith, Devine, & Zuwerink, 1993; Plant & Devine, 1998). But what about when a person is a member of a group that has a history of being prejudiced toward another group—might that person feel "guilt by association," even if that person has not personally behaved in a prejudiced fashion? Considerable research has now revealed that people can feel **collective guilt** based on the actions of other members of their group (Branscombe, 2004). Can such feelings of collective guilt be used as a means of reducing racism?

In a set of studies, Powell, Branscombe, and Schmitt (2005) found evidence that feeling collective guilt can reduce racism. First, these researchers recognized that the difference between two groups can be framed either in terms of the disadvantages experienced by one group *or* the advantages experienced by the other. Therefore, in one condition, white participants were asked to write down all the advantages they receive because of their race. In the other condition, participants were asked to write down all the disadvantages that blacks receive because of their race. This simply varied how the existing racial inequality was framed. As expected, the white advantage framing resulted in significantly more collective guilt than did the black disadvantage framing. Furthermore, as shown in Figure 6.19, the more collective guilt was experienced in the white advantage condition, the lower subsequent racism, whereas the black disadvantage framing did not have this effect. Reflecting on racial inequality can be an effective means of lowering racism, to the extent that the problem is seen as one involving the ingroup as beneficiary. Indeed, when perceptions of inequality as stemming from white advantage are combined with a sense of efficacy to bring about social change, feeling collective guilt can lead to antidiscrimination behavior (Stewart, Latu, Branscombe, & Denney, 2010).

6.5.5: Can We Learn to "Just Say No" to Stereotyping and Biased Attributions?

Throughout this chapter, we have noted that the tendency to think about others in terms of their group membership is a key factor in the occurrence of prejudice. As described earlier, individuals acquire stereotypes by learning to associate certain characteristics (e.g., negative traits such as "hostile" or "dangerous") with various racial or ethnic groups; once such automatic associations are formed, members of these groups can serve as primes for racial or ethnic stereotypes, which are then automatically

Figure 6.19 Collective Guilt Can Reduce Racism

The same inequality between groups can be framed as either reflecting the advantages of one group or the disadvantages of the other. Having white Americans think about inequality as white advantage led to increased feelings of collective guilt, and this, in turn, resulted in lowered racism. A little collective guilt then may have social benefits.

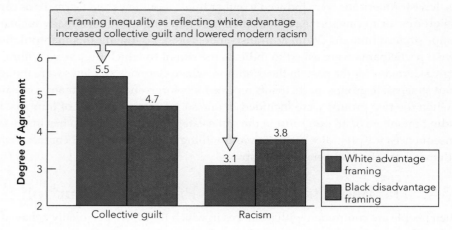

activated. Can individuals actively break the "stereotype habit" by saying "no" to the stereotypic traits they associate with a specific group? Kawakami, Dovidio, Moll, Hermsen, and Russin (2000) reasoned that people can learn to not rely on stereotypes they already possess.

To test this idea, the researchers conducted several studies where participants' stereotypic associations were first assessed. After this, participants were divided into two groups. In one group—those in the *stereotype maintaining* condition—participants were instructed to respond "yes" when they were presented with a photograph of a white person and a white stereotype word (e.g., *ambitious* or *uptight*) or a photograph of a black person and a black stereotype word (e.g., *athletic* or *poor*). They were told to respond "no" to stereotype-inconsistent word-picture pairings (e.g., a word consistent with the stereotype for whites, but paired with a photo of a black individual). Those in a second group, the *stereotype negation* condition, were told to respond "no" when presented with a photo of a white person and a word consistent with this stereotype or a photo of a black person and a word consistent with the stereotype for blacks. On the other hand, they were told to respond "yes" to stereotype-inconsistent pairings of words and pictures. In other words, they practiced negating their own implicit racial stereotypes. Participants in both groups performed these procedures several hundred times.

The results were clear. Reliance on stereotypes can be reduced through the process of repeatedly saying "no" to them. Prior to negation training, participants categorized white faces more quickly than black faces after seeing white stereotype words, but black faces more quickly after seeing black stereotype words. After negation training designed to weaken these implicit stereotypes, however, these differences disappeared. Although we do not yet know how reduced stereotype activation influences actual interactions with group members, the possibility that people can learn to say "no" to racial and ethnic stereotypes, with practice in doing so, is encouraging.

Can the same practice in making nonstereotypic attributions for negative outgroup behavior be taught and thereby reduce stereotyping? As we discussed in Chapter 3, people display the *fundamental attribution error*, and when applied to groups we see negative behaviors on the part of outgroup members as due to their internal qualities and positive behaviors by outgroup members as situationally (i.e., externally) caused. Research by Stewart, Latu, Kawakami, and Myers (2010) indicates that by repeatedly pairing external attributions for negative behavior with black faces compared to trials with the neutral task, implicit racial stereotyping can be reduced. Following such attributional training, the speed of responding to black faces with negative attributes did not differ from the speed of responding to white faces paired with those negative attributes.

6.5.6: Social Influence as a Means of Reducing Prejudice

Providing people with evidence that their own group *likes* members of another group that is typically the target of prejudice can sometimes serve to weaken such negative reactions (Pettigrew, 1997; Wright, Aron, McLaughlin-Volpe, & Ropp, 1997). In contrast, when stereotypic beliefs are said to be endorsed by the individual's ingroup and that individual's membership in that group is salient, then the ingroup's beliefs are more predictive of prejudice than are the individual's personal beliefs about the outgroup (Haslam & Wilson, 2000; Poteat & Spanierman, 2010). This suggests that stereotypes that we believe to be widely shared within our own group play a critical role in the expression of prejudice.

Evidence that social influence processes can be used to reduce prejudice was offered by Stangor, Sechrist, and Jost (2001). White students were first asked to estimate the percentage of African Americans possessing various stereotypical traits. After completing these estimates, participants were given information suggesting that other students in their university disagreed with their ratings. In one condition (favorable feedback) they learned that other students held more favorable views of African Americans than they did (i.e., the other students estimated a higher incidence of positive traits and a lower incidence of negative traits than they did). In another condition (unfavorable feedback), they learned that other students held less favorable views of African Americans than they did (i.e., these people estimated a higher incidence of negative traits and a lower incidence of positive traits). After receiving this information, participants again estimated the percentage of African Americans possessing positive and negative traits. Participants' racial attitudes were indeed affected by social influence. Endorsement of negative stereotypes increased in the unfavorable feedback condition, while endorsement of such stereotypes decreased in the favorable feedback condition.

Together, these findings indicate that racial attitudes certainly do not exist in a social vacuum; on the contrary, the attitudes that individuals hold are influenced not only by their early experience but also by current peer members of their group. The moral is clear: If people can be induced to believe that their prejudiced views are "out of line" with those of most other people—especially those they respect—they may well change those views toward a less prejudiced position.

Key Points

- Social psychologists believe that stereotyping and prejudice are not inevitable; a variety of reduction techniques have been successfully employed.
- According to the **social learning view**, children acquire prejudiced attitudes from their parents, and this is especially the case for children who strongly identify with their parents. Participating in institutions and having peers that justify discrimination help to maintain prejudiced attitudes.

- The **contact hypothesis** suggests that bringing previously segregated groups into contact can reduce prejudice, especially when the contact is with outgroup members who are seen as typical of their group, the contact is seen as important, it results in cross-group friendships, and anxiety about interacting with outgroup members is reduced.
- As suggested by the **common ingroup identity model**, prejudice can also be reduced through

recategorizations—shifting the boundary between "us" and "them" to include former outgroups in the "us" category. This is the case even for long-standing enemy groups when the maximal category—humans—is used.

- Emotional techniques for reducing prejudice are also effective. People with egalitarian standards can feel guilty when they violate those beliefs and personally behave in a prejudicial fashion. People can also feel **collective guilt** for their group's prejudiced actions. By framing inequality as due to the ingroup's advantages, collective guilt can be induced and this in turn can reduce racism, and increase antidiscrimination behavior when people feel able to make a difference.

- Reductions in prejudiced responses can also be accomplished by training individuals to say "no" to associations between stereotypes and specific social groups or by training them to make situational attributions for negative outgroup behavior.
- Social influence plays an important role in both the maintenance and reduction of prejudice. We want to hold beliefs that we see as normative of our group; providing individuals with evidence suggesting that members of their group hold less prejudiced views than they previously believed can reduce prejudice.

Summary and Review

Discriminatory treatment can be based on many different types of category memberships—from those that are temporary and based on "minimal" criteria, to long-term group memberships such as ethnicity, gender, religion, and sexual orientation. Discrimination based on all these types of group memberships are not perceived and responded to in the same way; some forms of discrimination are seen as legitimate, while others are seen as illegitimate.

Members of different groups are likely to perceive discrimination and the relations between those groups rather differently. When changes to the existing relations between racial groups are assessed, whites see more progress toward equality than do blacks. Research suggests that this is partly due to whites perceiving change and equality as a potential loss for them, whereas blacks perceive the same increases in egalitarianism as gains. People are **risk averse** with potential losses having greater psychological impact than potential gains.

Gender stereotypes are beliefs about the different attributes that males and females possess. Women are stereotyped as high on warmth dimensions but low on competence, while men are viewed as possessing the reverse combination of traits. The **glass ceiling** effect is when qualified women have disproportionate difficulty attaining high-level positions. Women are most likely to be sabotaged when men are experiencing threat and women behave in a stereotype-inconsistent manner. Stereotypes lead us to attend to information that is consistent with them, and to construe inconsistent information in ways that allow us to maintain our stereotypes. Women are more likely to be appointed to leadership positions following a crisis and when there is greater risk of failure—the **glass cliff effect.**

Tokenism—the hiring or acceptance of only a few members of a particular group—has two effects: It maintains perceptions that the system is not discriminatory (belief in meritocracy) and it can harm how tokens are perceived by others. Those who complain about discrimination risk negative evaluations.

Stereotypes can influence behavior even in the absence of different **subjective scale** evaluations of men and women. When **objective scale** measures are employed, where **shifting standards** cannot be used and the meaning of the response is constant, women are likely to receive worse outcomes than men.

Singlism is negative stereotyping and discrimination directed toward people who are single. Both those who are single and those who are married show this bias, which may arise either because it is seen by them as legitimate or because they lack an awareness of the bias.

Stereotypes are resistant to change, but they are revised as the relations between the groups are altered. Women who are repeatedly exposed to women faculty behaving in nontraditional roles show less agreement with gender stereotypes.

Prejudice can be considered an attitude (usually negative) toward members of a social group. It can be triggered in a seemingly automatic manner and can be implicit in nature. Prejudice may reflect more specific underlying emotional responses to different outgroups including fear, anger, guilt, pity, envy, and disgust.

According to **social identity theory**, prejudice is derived from our tendency to divide the world into "us" and "them" and to view our own group more favorably than various outgroups. Prejudice persists because disparaging outgroups can protect our self-esteem. **Threat** to our group's interests can motivate prejudice, and perceived competition between groups for resources can escalate conflict. Prejudice toward atheists, according to **terror management theory,** reflects our own existential anxiety so is especially likely to be high when our mortality is salient.

While blatant **discrimination** has clearly decreased, more subtle forms such as **modern racism** persist. The **bona fide pipeline** uses implicit measures to assess prejudices that people may be unaware they have. People can maintain an unprejudiced self-image by comparing themselves to those with extremely bigoted attitudes.

When we are exposed to instances where members of our own group have behaved in a prejudicial fashion we can feel **collective guilt** to the extent that we do not engage in strategies that allow us to conclude our group's harmful acts were legitimate. People also show evidence of "motivated forgetting," where instances of our group's harm doing toward others are more difficult to recall than are instances in which our group was harmed by an enemy outgroup.

Social psychologists have found that prejudice can be reduced by several techniques. One technique involves **direct contact** between members of different groups.

Particularly when an outgroup member is seen as typical of their group, the contact is viewed as important, and it results in cross-group friendships, then prejudice can be reduced. Simply knowing that members of one's own group have formed friendships with members of an outgroup may be sufficient to reduce prejudice.

As suggested by the **common ingroup identity model,** prejudice can also be reduced through recategorization—shifting the boundary between "us" and "them" so as to include former outgroups in the "us" category. This is the case even for long-standing enemy groups when the more inclusive category is that of "human."

Prejudice reduction can also be accomplished by training individuals to say "no" to associations between stereotypes and specific social groups, and to make situational attributions for negative outgroup behaviors. Emotions can be used to motivate others to be nonprejudiced; feeling collective guilt can result in reductions in racism when the ingroup is focused on as a cause of existing racial inequality. Providing individuals with evidence suggesting that one's ingroup has less prejudiced views than oneself too can be used to effectively reduce prejudice.

Chapter 7
Liking, Love, and Other Close Relationships

Chapter Overview

Learning Objectives

7.1   Describe the psychological factors that cause us to like others

7.2   Explain how frequency of exposure and physical attractiveness enhance interpersonal attraction

7.3   List the factors that lead individuals to like or dislike each other

7.4   Describe three main types of close relationships formed by people

People clearly differ in how much they are liked. Some are liked by almost everyone they meet. Others elicit the opposite reaction—people dislike them and try to avoid contact with them. Let's consider the dramatic example of a graduate student; we'll call him David.

David clearly had charisma—a magnetic appeal that drew people to him. Women liked him, men liked him, students and faculty both liked him—virtually everyone he met fell under his "spell." People liked him so much that they were more than willing to give him lots of help. As a result, graduate school was a breeze for David. He was successful at almost every academic task, and his teacher ratings from students were also very positive. In fact, everyone on the faculty agreed that he was the best student they had seen in many years. Love, too, easily came his way—women almost lined up to date him because of his charming ways.

Why was David so likable? A combination of factors played a role. He had exceptional social skills. For instance, everyone with whom he interacted formed the impression that he was deeply interested in them and what they were doing. He did this by subtly calling attention to similarities between himself and others, and expressing a strong liking for others. David also had a very pleasant appearance, although he was not especially good looking. To put it simply, people liked to be around him.

Sadly, there was a dark side to David's charm. It gradually became clear that he was exploiting another student who loved him dearly. She did almost all of his work while he concentrated on being charming. Similarly, David's academic mentor, who virtually viewed him as an adopted son, did everything he could to advance David's career. This included providing truly positive recommendations to prospective employers on David's behalf. As a result of this help—and David's own "smooth" performance during job interviews—he had many offers. David chose a very attractive job—the best available at the time.

But then, something really strange happened. During a routine review of David's credentials by his employer, it was discovered that he never received his PhD! Why? When he got tired of standing in line to file the final forms and could not persuade the others present to let him skip to the front, he simply left. Once the missing degree was discovered, he was fired. But again, because of his charm, he was given another year to complete the necessary paperwork, after which he could resume his job. Although David did complete his degree, he essentially disappeared from sight a year later. Where he went remains a mystery. But everyone who knew him is sure that wherever he is, and whatever he is doing, he is using his strong personal appeal for his own benefit.

As illustrated by this story, we don't merely interact with others; we also form relationships with them. Some of these are insignificant and short-lived, such as a relationship with a waiter or a salesperson in a store. Others play a truly crucial role in our lives and last for years or even decades, as seen in Figure 7.1. It's important to note, though, that relationships with others don't fall into two neat categories—short term and trivial, or long term and important. Rather, they vary greatly along these

Figure 7.1 Relationships with Others: From Short-Lived and Trivial to Long Term and Important

During our lives, we form many relationships with others. Some of these are temporary and relatively unimportant—for instance, a short-term relationship with a waiter in a restaurant. In contrast, other relationships last for years, or even decades, and play an important role in our lives.

dimensions. For example, a relationship with a lab partner might be short term but very important to us during its existence.

In this chapter, we will focus on relationships that are relatively lasting and important. To do so, we will examine what we know about liking, love, and other close relationships. The earlier story about David involved all three of these relationship types. We will begin by examining the foundations of liking and its effects. In David's case, many people often went out of their way to do things for him because he was so well liked. Social psychologists often refer to liking by the term *interpersonal attraction*—why people like or dislike each other. But this term should not be confused with *physical attractiveness*, which is only one factor in liking others. To avoid confusion on this point, we will refer to *liking* instead of *interpersonal attraction* throughout the chapter.

Next, we will turn to love and examine its meaning, emergence, and effects. The powerful feelings of love can take several different forms including romantic love, love of a parent for her or his children, and the love of a couple who have been together for decades. Love can move someone to self-sacrifice for another person. Recall the female graduate student who loved David so much that she was willing to do his work, even though her actions put her own success at risk.

Finally, we will focus on other kinds of close relationships—those between friends or family members. Remember David's relationship with the professor who was his mentor, who liked him so much that he did everything possible to advance David's career? This was certainly an important relationship for both of them, but much more temporary than the professor expected.

7.1: Internal Sources of Liking Others: The Role of Needs and Emotions

Objective Describe the psychological factors that cause us to like others

When most people think about liking or disliking others, they tend to focus on factors relating to these individuals: Are they similar or dissimilar to us in important ways? Do we find them physically attractive? Are they pleasant and fun to be with or unpleasant and annoying? As you will soon see, these factors do indeed play a powerful role in attraction. However, our initial feelings of liking or disliking others also stem from internal sources—our basic needs, motives, and emotions. We will begin by focusing on those sources of attraction.

7.1.1: The Importance of Affiliation in Human Existence: The Need to Belong

Much of our life is spent interacting with other people. This tendency to affiliate (i.e., associate with them) seems to have a neurobiological basis (Rowe, 1996). In fact, the **need for affiliation** with others and to be accepted by them may be just as basic to our psychological well-being as hunger and thirst are to our physical well-being (Baumeister & Leary, 1995; Koole, Greenberg, & Pyszczynski, 2006). From an evolutionary perspective, this makes perfect sense. Cooperating with other people almost certainly increased our ancestors' success in obtaining food and surviving danger. As a result, a strong desire to affiliate with others seems to be a basic characteristic of our species. Human infants, for instance, are apparently born with the motivation and ability to seek contact with their interpersonal world. Even newborns tend to look toward faces in preference to other stimuli (Mondloch et al., 1999).

INDIVIDUAL DIFFERENCES IN THE NEED TO AFFILIATE   Although the need to affiliate with others appears to be very basic among human beings, people differ greatly in the strength of this tendency. These differences, whether based on genetics or experience, constitute a relatively stable trait (or disposition). Basically, we tend to seek the amount of social contact that is optimal for us, preferring to be alone some of the time and in social situations some of the time (O'Connor & Rosenblood, 1996).

When their affiliation needs are not met, how do people react? When, for example, other people ignore you, what is the experience like? Most people find it highly unpleasant, as shown in Figure 7.2. Being "left out" by others hurts—it leaves people with the sense that they have lost control and makes them feel both sad and angry because they simply don't belong (Buckley, Winkel, & Leary, 2004). In addition, social exclusion leads to increased sensitivity to interpersonal information (Gardner, Pickett,

---

Figure 7.2 Affiliation Needs Are Not Always Met

Almost everyone has a need to affiliate with others—to form relationships with people and interact with them. If these needs are not met, people who are excluded may experience feelings of rejection and strong sadness.

& Brewer, 2000) and actually results in less effective cognitive functioning (Baumeister, Twenge, & Nuss, 2002).

ARE THERE PEOPLE WHO DON'T NEED OTHER PEOPLE? Decades of research by social psychologists indicate that the need to affiliate with others is both strong and general (e.g., Baumeister & Twenge, 2003; Koole, Greenberg, & Pyszczynski, 2006). However, there are some people who claim to have little or no need for emotional attachments to others, and who, in fact, tend to avoid close relationships (e.g., Collins & Feeney, 2000). Are such people really an exception to the general rule that human beings have a strong need to affiliate? This is a difficult question to answer because such people strongly proclaim they do not have these needs. However, research by social psychologists indicates that even people who *claim* to have little or no need for affiliation do, at least to some extent (e.g., Carvallo & Gabriel, 2006). True—they may have less need for human emotional attachments than most other people, but even they show increased self-esteem and improved moods when they find out they are accepted by others—the people they claim not to need.

In short, all human beings—even people who claim otherwise—have a need to feel connected to others. In fact, the need for affiliation is a very basic aspect of the social side of life. Some people may conceal this need under a mask of seeming indifference, but the need is still there. Differences between individuals exist in the level of need or the *attachment style*—the ways in which we form emotional bonds and regulate our emotions in close relationships. (More details on specific attachment styles and their effects on social relationships are provided later in this chapter.)

Research by Gillath and his colleagues (e.g., Gillath et al., 2005, 2006) indicates that attachment styles exert strong effects on both our thinking about others and our relationships with them. In turn, these effects influence important aspects of our behavior, such as the tendency to seek others' support or engage in *self-disclosure*—revealing our innermost thoughts and feelings. Individual differences in attachment style can even be measured at the level of brain functioning. For instance, the more intensely individuals fear rejection and abandonment by others (*attachment anxiety*), the more activity is seen in parts of the brain linked to emotion. This brain activation occurs when they think about negative outcomes in relationships, such as conflict, breakups, or the death of partners (Gillath et al., 2005). In sum, attachment style clearly plays an important role in our relationships with others and in the cognitive and neural processes that underlie these relationships.

SITUATIONAL INFLUENCES ON THE NEED TO AFFILIATE While people differ with respect to their need to affiliate with others, external events can temporarily boost or reduce this need. When people are reminded of their own mortality, for example, a common response is the desire to affiliate with others (Wisman & Koole, 2003). Similarly, after highly disturbing events such as natural disasters, many people experience an increased desire to affiliate with others—primarily to obtain help and comfort and reduce negative feelings (Benjamin, 1998; Byrne, 1991).

One basic reason for responding to stress with friendliness and affiliation was first identified by Schachter (1959). His early work revealed that participants in an experiment who were expecting to receive an electric shock preferred to spend time with others facing the same unpleasant prospect rather than being alone. Those in the control group, not expecting an unpleasant electric shock, preferred to be alone or didn't care whether they were with others or not. One conclusion from this line of research was that "misery doesn't just love any kind of company, it loves only miserable company" (Schachter, 1959, p. 24).

Why should real-life threats and anxiety-inducing laboratory manipulations arouse the need to affiliate? Why should frightened, anxious people want to interact with other frightened, anxious people? One answer is that such affiliation provides the opportunity for *social comparison*. People want to be with others—even strangers—

to communicate about what is going on, to compare their perceptions, and to make decisions about what to do. Arousing situations lead us to seek "cognitive clarity" (to know what is happening) and "emotional clarity" (Gump & Kulik, 1997; Kulik, Mahler, & Moore, 1996). In other words, contact with other humans that is likely to include both conversations and hugs can be a real source of comfort.

7.1.2: The Role of Affect: Do Our Moods Play a Role in Liking Others?

As we have seen in other chapters, positive and negative affect (moods and emotions) are complex: They vary in intensity (valence) and arousal (low to high), and perhaps other dimensions as well. But despite this complexity, one basic principle has emerged over and over again in careful research: A positive affect, regardless of its source, often leads to positive evaluations of other people—the feeling of liking them. Likewise, a negative affect often leads to negative evaluations—disliking them (Byrne, 1997; Dovidio, Gaertner, Isen, & Lowrance, 1995). These effects occur in two different ways: directly and indirectly.

When another person says or does something that makes you feel good or bad, these feelings have a *direct effect* on how much you like that person. It's not surprising that you like someone who makes you feel good and dislike someone who makes you feel bad (Ben-Porath, 2002; Reich, Zautra, & Potter, 2001). More unexpected are the indirect effects of emotions or feelings on attraction—sometimes known as the *associated effect*. In this case, liking or disliking someone you meet is influenced by unrelated events or people in your life. The other person is simply present at the same time your emotional state is aroused by something or someone else. Even though the individual is not in any way responsible for what you are feeling, you nevertheless tend to evaluate him or her more positively when you are feeling good and more negatively when you are feeling bad. For example, if you meet a stranger shortly after you receive a low grade on an exam, you will tend to like that person less than if you had received a high grade.

These associated (or indirect) influences of affective states on attraction have been demonstrated in many experiments involving emotional states based on a variety of diverse external causes. Examples include the following: subliminal presentations of pleasant versus unpleasant pictures—for example, kittens versus snakes (Krosnick, Betz, Jussim, & Lynn, 1992); the presence of background music that college students perceived as pleasant versus unpleasant—for example, rock and roll versus classical jazz (May & Hamilton, 1980); and even the positive versus negative mood states that the research participants reported before the experiment began (Berry & Hansen, 1996).

Why do the indirect effects caused by our emotions have such a big impact on liking and disliking? Classical conditioning, a basic form of learning, discussed in Chapter 5, plays an important role. When a neutral stimulus (e.g., another person we are meeting for the first time) is paired with a positive stimulus (something that makes us feel good), it is evaluated more positively than a neutral stimulus that has been paired with a negative stimulus (something that makes us feel bad), even when we are not aware that such pairings occurred (Olson & Fazio, 2001). We might even deny that these stimuli have any effect at all on whether we like or dislike a stranger.

Advertisers and others who want to influence us seem to be well aware of this basic conditioning process. They often seek to generate positive feelings and emotions among the people they want to sway. Then, they associate these emotions with the products—or political candidates—they want to promote. The goal is to make us like whatever (or whoever) is being "sold" by linking it with positive feelings. This can be accomplished by using highly attractive models in ads and commercials for products or by associating the products with happy times and pleasant experiences (see Figure 7.3). Political candidates use the same basic principle by associating themselves

Figure 7.3 Associating Products with Positive Affect—a Key Technique Used in Advertising

Many advertisements attempt to associate a particular product with positive feelings in order to increase people's liking for the item being promoted. In many instances, this involves showing people who are demonstrating extreme happiness or pleasure while using the product or simply being in its presence.

with happy celebrations. For example, they often arrange to have truly committed supporters present at political rallies so they will be seen surrounded by cheering crowds. Again, the goal is to increase liking by associating the candidates with positive feelings.

How effective are such attempts to increase our liking for various items or people by influencing our moods (affect)? Research findings (e.g., Pentony, 1995) indicate that irrelevant affective states—ones induced by factors unrelated to the candidates, products, or items being sold—can indeed influence our liking for them, and hence our overt actions (our votes, our purchase decisions). Keep this point in mind the next time you are exposed to any kind of message that is clearly designed to elicit positive or negative feelings. The ultimate goal may be to persuade or influence you, not merely to make you feel good.

Key Points

- *Interpersonal attraction* refers to the evaluations we make of other people—the positive and negative attitudes we form about them.
- All human beings have a **need for affiliation**, the motivation to interact with other people in a cooperative way. The strength of this need differs among individuals and across situations. Even people who claim they do not have this need show evidence that they do.
- Positive and negative affect (moods and emotions) influence attraction both directly and indirectly. A *direct*

effect occurs when a person is responsible for arousing an emotion in us. An *associated effect*, or indirect effect, occurs when the source of our emotional trigger is elsewhere—an unrelated event or person—and the person currently present is simply associated with that emotion.
- The indirect (associated) effects of emotion are used by advertisers and politicians who understand that associating products and candidates with positive feelings can influence our purchasing and voting decisions.

7.2: External Sources of Attraction: The Effects of Proximity, Familiarity, and Physical Beauty

Objective **Explain how frequency of exposure and physical attractiveness enhance interpersonal attraction**

Whether or not two specific people ever come in contact with each other is often determined by accidental, unplanned aspects of where they live, work, or play. For example, two students assigned to adjoining classroom seats are more likely to interact with each other than if their seats were several rows apart. Once **proximity** (physical nearness to others) brings about contact, additional factors play an important role. One of these is outward appearance—others' **physical attractiveness**. Another is the extent to which the two people find that they are similar in various ways.

7.2.1: The Power of Proximity: Unplanned Contacts

More than 8 billion people now live on our planet, but you will probably interact with only a relatively small number of them during your lifetime. In the absence of some kind of contact, you obviously can't become acquainted with other people or have any basis on which to decide whether you like or dislike them. In a sense, proximity is needed before feelings of attraction can develop. Actually, that was true in the past, but now *social networks* and other electronic media make it possible for people to interact and form initial feelings of liking or disliking without direct face-to-face contact. Ultimately, of course, physical nearness must occur for close relationships to develop beyond the "virtual world." Some would argue that this isn't true. They feel friendships formed on Facebook, for instance, are as real—and often as strong—as friendships formed on the basis of direct, personal contact. Even though physical proximity may no longer be a requirement for interpersonal attraction, it's worthwhile to take a look at classic research on the role of proximity in liking (or disliking) others.

WHY DOES PROXIMITY MATTER? REPEATED EXPOSURE IS THE KEY Picture yourself in a large lecture class on the first day of school. Let's say that you don't see anyone you know and the instructor has assigned students to seats alphabetically. At first, this roomful of strangers is a confusing blur of unfamiliar faces. Once you find your assigned seat, you probably notice the person sitting on your right and the one on your left, but you may or may not speak to one another. By the second or third day of class, however, you recognize your "neighbors" when you see them and may even say, "Hi." In the weeks that follow, you may have bits of conversation about the class or about something that is happening on campus. If you see either of these two individuals at some other location, there is mutual recognition and you are increasingly likely to interact. After all, it feels good to see a familiar face.

Numerous early studies in the United States and in Europe revealed that students are most likely to become acquainted if they are seated in adjoining chairs (Byrne, 1961a; Maisonneuve, Palmade, & Fourment, 1952; Segal, 1974). In addition to proximity in the classroom, investigations conducted throughout the 20th century indicated that people who live or work in close proximity are likely to become acquainted, form friendships, and even marry one another (Bossard, 1932; Festinger, Schachter, & Back, 1950).

Why does proximity influence our level of attraction to something—a person, object, or almost anything else? The answer appears to lie in the **repeated exposure effect** (Zajonc, 1965). Apparently, the more often we are exposed to a new stimulus—such as a new person, a new idea, or a new product—the more favorable our evaluation of it tends to become. This effect is subtle—we may not be aware of it—but it is both powerful and general (i.e., it occurs in a wide range of situations). Research findings indicate that it occurs for people, places, words, objects—almost everything. Moreover, this effect is present very early in life. Infants tend to smile more at a photograph of someone they have seen before but not at a photograph of someone they are seeing for the first time (Brooks-Gunn & Lewis, 1981). In short, the more familiar we are with almost anything, the more we tend to like it because we've been exposed to it over and over.

A very clear demonstration of the repeated exposure effect is provided by a study conducted in a classroom setting (Moreland & Beach, 1992). In a college course, one female assistant attended class 15 times during the semester, a second assistant attended class 10 times, a third attended 5 times, and a fourth did not attend the class at all. None of the assistants interacted with the other class members. At the end of the semester, the students were shown slides of the four assistants and asked to indicate how much they liked each one. Results indicated that the more times a particular assistant attended class, the more she was liked. In this and many other experiments, repeated exposure was found to have a positive effect on attraction.

Zajonc (2001) explains the effect of repeated exposure by suggesting that we ordinarily respond with at least mild discomfort when we encounter anyone or anything new and unfamiliar. As we become more familiar with another person, for example, such feelings decrease and may be replaced by positive ones. Research conducted by Reis, Maniaci, Caprariello, Eastwick, and Finkel (2011) provides evidence that increasing familiarity does indeed lead to positive reactions. In this study, pairs of individuals met and discussed several topics. "What is something you have always wanted to do but probably never will be able to do?" "What is one thing about yourself that most people would consider surprising?" The pairs discussed two, four, or six topics. Then, they rated their partners' attractiveness. As the researchers predicted, the greater the number of topics discussed, the higher the ratings.

In a follow-up study (Reis et al., 2011), students engaged in unstructured Internet chats with a stranger. They engaged in these chats (which lasted 10–15 minutes each) two, four, six, or eight times. As in the previous study, the more times participants interacted with the strangers, the higher was their reported attraction to those partners. Why did this effect occur? Reis et al. (2011) obtained additional information. Based on participant feedback, increased interaction led to feelings that their partners were more responsive and they knew their partners better. As a result, they felt more comfortable interacting with their partners. So, frequency of exposure to another person generates increased familiarity with that person. In turn, familiarity leads to positive reactions toward the individual (see Figure 7.4).

There is one important exception to the equation of "increased contact = greater liking." When initial reactions to another person are negative, repeated contact leads to reduced rather than increased attraction. This is not surprising. Who wants to be around people they find irritating or annoying? Also, repeated meetings tend to strengthen these negative reactions (Swap, 1977). Aside from this pattern, the more we interact with others, the more we tend to like them.

Figure 7.4 Increased Exposure to Another Person Increases Liking for That Person

Research findings indicate that the more often we are exposed to or interact with another person, the more we like that person. The reason seems to be that we feel more comfortable with her or him and feel that he or she is more responsive to us.

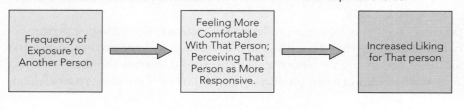

THE EFFECTS OF SOCIAL MEDIA ON PROXIMITY AND REPEATED EXPOSURE We do not have to be exposed to another person directly, or be near them physically, to like them or develop relationships with them. This can happen through social media, too. In a sense, modern technology has altered the effects of proximity and frequency of exposure—at least in the way that these factors involve physical dimensions of being near another person and actually meeting them often. To better understand the impact of social media on proximity and attraction, let's consider research insights on both positive and negative aspects of using Facebook.

In some research, frequent use of Facebook has been found to result in mild depression for many users. For instance, Kross et al. (2013) found that the more time people spent on Facebook, the lower was their subjective well-being—how happy they felt about their lives. On the other hand, direct (off-line) social contact had the opposite effect: the more it occurred, the higher was individuals' subjective well-being. In a recent review of this research, Blease (2015) concluded that Facebook users most susceptible to mild depression are the ones with a large number of Facebook friends, who spend a large amount of time reading friends' updates, and the extent to which those updates bragged about their friends' recent accomplishments or positive experiences. Blease (2015) further suggested that depressive effects stem from the fact that using Facebook is a solitary activity that provides individuals with an opportunity to compare themselves with others. The greater the number of "friends" with whom they can compare themselves, and the more favorably those friends present themselves, the sadder the comparisons make them feel. So, it's important to keep in mind that even though social media can help people form relationships with others, they may also have negative effects on users.

Other research by Manago, Taylor, and Greenfield (2012) indicates that using Facebook status updates, which encourages emotional disclosure to other people in users' social networks, can lead to a greater sense of satisfaction and social support. College students in this study were asked to complete an online survey about their relationships. As they answered the questions, they were instructed to methodically sample their Facebook contacts' pages and look at those contacts' Facebook profiles. Results of this study confirmed that using Facebook can increase the size and scope of users' social networks by expanding the number of acquaintances with whom they shared interests. To a smaller degree, using Facebook helped increase the number of people with whom they had close relationships, and even the number of relationships with strangers.

Large social networks on Facebook, in turn, led participants in the research to estimate that their own public status updates were viewed by a larger number of their Facebook contacts. These status updates were used to share emotional thoughts and feelings—a factor that can increase emotional disclosure and social intimacy with others. Findings by Manago and colleagues (2012) indicate that the larger the users' social networks, the higher were users' life satisfaction and perceived levels of social support. These findings suggest that social media sites, such as Facebook, can play a valuable role in an increasingly digital world by helping individuals to satisfy their basic need to affiliate with others and form permanent relationships with them. So, overall, social media can exert positive as well as negative effects on users.

7.2.2: Physical Beauty: Its Role in Interpersonal Attraction

"Love at first sight," "struck with a lightning bolt"—different cultures have different phrases, but they all refer to the fact that sometimes just seeing someone for the first time can be the basis for powerful feelings of attraction toward that person. Although we are warned repeatedly against being too susceptible to others' physical charms, it is all too clear that physical appearance often plays a powerful role in interpersonal attraction and influences many aspects of social behavior (e.g., Vogel, Kutzner, Fiedler, & Freytag, 2010). How strong are these effects? Why do they occur? What is physical attractiveness? Do we believe that "what is beautiful is good"—that attractive people possess many desirable characteristics aside from their physical beauty? And, if we are in a relationship, do we perceive our partner accurately, or perhaps, as more attractive than other people do? These are the questions we will now examine.

BEAUTY MAY BE ONLY SKIN DEEP, BUT WE PAY A LOT OF ATTENTION TO IT   You've probably heard the saying "Beauty is only skin deep." It warns us to avoid assigning too much importance to how people look. But existing evidence indicates that even if we want to, we can't really follow this advice because physical appearance is a powerful factor in our liking for others (Collins & Zebrowitz, 1995; Perlini & Hansen, 2001). Both in experiments and in the real world, physical appearance impacts many types of interpersonal evaluations. For instance, attractive defendants are found guilty by judges and juries less often than unattractive ones (e.g., Downs & Lyons, 1991). Furthermore, attractive people are judged to be healthier, more intelligent, and more trustworthy. They are also viewed as possessing desirable social characteristics—such as kindness, generosity, and warmth—to a greater extent than less attractive people (Lemay, Clark, & Greenberg, 2010). People even respond more positively to attractive infants than to unattractive ones (Karraker & Stern, 1990). As we will see in our later discussions of romantic relationships, physical appearance also plays an important role in mate selection.

THE "WHAT IS BEAUTIFUL IS GOOD" EFFECT   Why are attractive people generally viewed as possessing desirable characteristics (such as intelligence, good health, kindness, and generosity) to a greater extent than those who are less attractive? One possibility, first suggested by Dion, Berscheid, and Walster (1972) is related to *stereotyping*—making assumptions about social groups in terms of the traits they are believed to share. Most of us possess a very positive stereotype for people who are highly good looking—a physical attractiveness stereotype. Evidence for this interpretation has been obtained in many studies (Snyder, Tanke, & Berscheid, 1977; Langlois et al., 2000), and has been the most widely accepted view for many years. Reason tells us that if we do possess a favorable stereotype for physically attractive people, then this cognitive framework will strongly shape how we perceive and think about them.

Another interpretation for the "what is beautiful is good" effect has been suggested by Lemay, Clark, and Greenberg (2010). They propose that three steps are involved. First, we desire to form relationships with attractive people. Second, this desire leads us to perceive them as interpersonally responsive in return—as kinder, more outgoing, and socially warmer than less attractive people. In other words, we project our own desire to form relationships with these people onto them. It is this projection that generates very positive perceptions of them.

To test this theory, Lemay and colleagues performed several studies. In one, participants first viewed photos of strangers rated very high or below average in physical attractiveness (8.5 and higher or 5.0 and below on a 10-point scale). Then, they rated their own desire to form relationships with both attractive and unattractive people, and the extent to which they believed those people desired to form relationships with others (their need to affiliate). In addition, participants rated the target people's interpersonal traits—the extent to which they were perceived as kind, generous, extraverted, warm, and so on.

It was predicted that attractive people would be viewed as higher in the need for affiliation than those lower in attractiveness, and would also be rated more favorably in terms of various interpersonal traits. Most important, it was predicted that these effects

Figure 7.5 The "What Is Beautiful Is Good" Effect: Why It Occurs

We tend to perceive physically beautiful people as also having other desirable characteristics (such as kindness, generosity, and warmth). Our own desire to form relationships with these people leads us to project similar feelings onto them. As a result, we tend to perceive them very positively—even on dimensions having nothing directly to do with physical beauty.

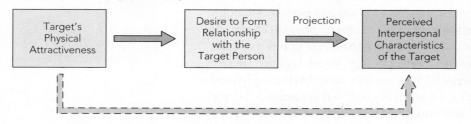

would be mediated by participants' level of desire to form relationships with the attractive and unattractive strangers. The research offered support for this suggestion, indicating that it was the projection of their own desire to get to know the attractive strangers that led participants to perceive those strangers in favorable terms (see Figure 7.5).

How accurate are the beliefs that physically beautiful people are also more socially poised, kind, outgoing, and so on, than less attractive people? Despite widespread acceptance of these beliefs, most of them appear to be incorrect (Feingold, 1992; Kenealy, Gleeson, Frude, & Shaw, 1991). For instance, dishonest people, such as swindlers, can be good looking (and often are). On the other hand, many people who do not look like glamorous movie stars—for instance, Bill Gates or Warren Buffet—are often intelligent, interesting, kind, and generous.

Sometimes the "what is beautiful is good" effect is accurate. For example, attractiveness is associated with popularity, good interpersonal skills, and high self-esteem (Diener, Wolsic, & Fujita, 1995; Johnstone, Frame, & Bouman, 1992). Perhaps this is so because very attractive people spend their lives being liked and treated well by other people who are responding to their appearance (Zebrowitz, Collins, & Dutta, 1998). However, people who are very attractive to others are usually aware that they are pretty or handsome (Marcus & Miller, 2003). They may try to use this characteristic for their own advantage—for instance, in persuading or influencing others (Vogel, Kutzner, Fiedler, & Freytag, 2010), as illustrated in Figure 7.6. But whether people use their physical attractiveness for "good" or for "evil" is independent of the attractiveness itself. So our tendency to evaluate them positively on other dimensions appears to rest on shaky grounds.

WHAT MAKES A PERSON PHYSICALLY ATTRACTIVE?   Researchers assume that there must be some underlying basis for physical attractiveness because there is

---

Figure 7.6 Beautiful People Are Not Necessarily Good

Shown here are the stars of "American Hustle," a movie about people scamming other people. Sydney Prosser (played by Amy Adams) is one of the characters in this film who uses her good looks to her benefit. Like many real-life confidence artists who are highly attractive, this helps her take advantage of others who falsely assume that what is beautiful is also good.

surprisingly good agreement about attractiveness both within and between cultures (Cunningham, Roberts, Wu, Barbee, & Druen, 1995; Fink & Penton-Voak, 2002; Marcus & Miller, 2003). Despite general agreement about who is and who is not attractive, it is not easy to identify the precise cues that determine these judgments. To discover what these factors are, social psychologists have used two quite different procedures.

One approach is to identify a group of individuals who are rated as attractive and then determine what the people have in common. Cunningham (1986) asked male undergraduates to rate photographs of young women. The women who were judged to be most attractive fell into one of two groups, as shown in Figure 7.7. Some had "childlike features" consisting of large, widely spaced eyes and a small nose and chin. Women like Meg Ryan and Amy Adams fit this category and are considered "cute" (Johnston & Oliver-Rodriguez, 1997). The other category of attractive women had mature features with prominent cheekbones, high eyebrows, large pupils, and a big smile; Angelina Jolie and Kim Kardashian are examples. These same two general facial types are found among fashion models, and they are commonly seen among white, African American, Hispanic, and Asian women (Ashmore, Solomon, & Longo, 1996). Although there is less evidence on this point, the same general categories seem to exist for men. Being highly attractive can mean looking "cute" or "boyish," or mature and masculine.

A second approach to determining what is attractive was taken by Langlois and Roggman (1990). They used computer digitizing to combine multiple facial photographs into a photo of one face. The image in each photo was divided into microscopic squares, and each square was translated into a number that represented a specific shade. Then the numbers were averaged across two or more pictures, and the result was translated back into a composite image.

Figure 7.7 Two Types of Attractive Women: Cute or Mature

The study of physical attractiveness has identified two types of women who are rated most attractive. One category is considered cute—childlike features, large widely spaced eyes, with a small nose and chin—for example, Meg Ryan. The other category of attractiveness is the mature look—prominent cheekbones, high eyebrows, large pupils, and a big smile—for example, Kim Kardashian.

You might reasonably guess that a face created by averaging would be rated as average in attractiveness. Instead, composite faces were rated as *more* attractive than most of the individual faces used to make the composite (Langlois, Roggman, & Musselman, 1994; Rhodes & Tremewan, 1996). In addition, the more faces that were averaged, the more beautiful was the resulting face. As shown in Figure 7.8, when you combine as many as 32 faces, "you end up with a face that is pretty darned attractive" (Judith Langlois, as quoted in Lemley, 2000, p. 47).

Why should composite faces be especially attractive? It is possible that each person's schema of women and of men is created in our cognitions in much the same way that the averaged face is created. That is, we form such schemas on the basis of our experiences with many different images, so a composite face is closer to that schema than is any specific face. If this is an accurate analysis, a composite of other kinds of images should also constitute the most attractive alternative. In a sense, we create our own composite faces on the basis of our own experience. Faces that most closely match that composite are perceived as attractive. This helps explain why we each have our own perceptions of what is, and what is not, attractive. Personal exposure to other faces is unique for each of us. However, sometimes the physical appearances of two people in a relationship are so different from one another that we can't help but wonder what attracted them to each other. This topic is explored in the special feature, **"What Research Tells Us About…Dramatic Differences in Appearance Between Partners: Is Love Really Blind?"**

Figure 7.8 Averaging Multiple Faces Results in an Attractive Face

When computer images of several different faces are combined to form a composite, the resulting average face is seen as more attractive than the individual faces that were averaged. As the number of faces contributing to the average increases, the attractiveness of the composite increases.

2 Faces

4 Faces

8 Faces

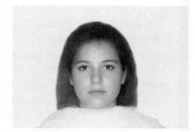
16 Faces

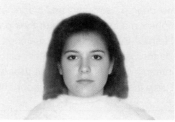
32 Faces

RED REALLY IS SEXY—AND ATTRACTIVE When archaeologists open Egyptian tombs that have been sealed for thousands of years, they often find cosmetics. Among these cosmetics are red lipstick and red rouge. In fact, in many ancient cultures, as well as many modern ones, the color red has been associated with increased attractiveness, at least for women (see Figure 7.10). This belief is also evident in literature, as in Nathaniel Hawthorn's classic story *The Scarlet Letter*. This color is also associated with famous "red light districts" throughout the world.

Interestingly, outside our own species, many primate females display red on their genitals, chest, or face during ovulation—when they are, at least from a reproductive point of view, at their sexiest. These observations have led social psychologists to suggest that perhaps the color red *does* have special significance and can increase women's attractiveness to men. In a sense, then, beauty is generated not only by the face or body, but may involve other, seemingly peripheral environmental cues.

Evidence that red raises the attractiveness of women has been reported by Elliot and Niesta (2008). These social psychologists performed several studies in which both male and female participants saw photos of strangers who were either standing against a red background or one of a different color (white, gray, or green). The strangers either wore a red or blue shirt. Research participants rated the attractiveness and sexual appeal of the people in the photos. When photos of the female strangers were shown against a red background, male participants assigned much higher ratings of attractiveness to the

What Research Tells Us About...

Dramatic Differences in Appearance Between Partners: Is Love Really Blind?

As you probably know from your own experience, individuals differ greatly in what they find to be physically attractive in others. As a result, some couples seem to be completely mismatched. For example, a very tall woman chooses a very short man, or a young person chooses a partner who is very much older. Or, people choose others who come from very different backgrounds than themselves. Did you ever see the movie My Big Fat Greek Wedding? In it, two people from very different ethnic groups fall in love, and this creates humorous situations as their two families struggle to understand and cope with these differences.

Such situations often lead us to ask "What does he or she see in his or her partner?" Why do couples form who seem mismatched? (See Figure 7.9 for an example.) Does this simply reflect individual differences in preferences, or is it because each person's strong attraction to their partner leads them to perceive this person as more beautiful than other people? Studies indicate that the answer is somewhat complex.

Research reported by Solomon and Vazire (2014) suggests that couples do tend to perceive their partners as more attractive than other people do. However, they are aware of this tendency at least to some degree. Solomon and Vazire expressed the essence of this phenomenon in the title of their paper, "You are so beautiful . . . to me." So seemingly mismatched couples form because each partner is, in a sense, at least partially "blinded" by their strong attraction to each other, but they recognize their differences and view them as relatively unimportant.

Figure 7.9 Why Do Couples Form Who Seem Mismatched?

When couples form in which the partners are vastly different from one another in physical appearance, it may be because the partners perceive each other as more attractive than outside observers do. Each partner may be partially "blinded" by their strong attraction to each other, but they recognize their differences and view them as relatively unimportant.

Figure 7.10 Does the Color Red Enhance Women's Physical Attractiveness?

Many cultures—both ancient and modern—accept the view that red on the lips and the face, and perhaps in clothing too, can enhance women's physical appeal. Recent research by social psychologists suggests that there may be a sizable grain of truth in this belief.

strangers than when the same women were shown against a white background. For women participants, however, the background color or shirt color did not make a significant difference in the perceived attractiveness of the male strangers. So, as Elliot and Niesta (2008) suggest, red is indeed romantic and carries a special meaning in the language of love—or at least when it comes to men's attraction.

OTHER ASPECTS OF APPEARANCE THAT INFLUENCE ATTRACTION When we meet someone for the first time, we usually know very quickly whether our reactions to them are positive or negative. Aside from physical beauty, what influences these reactions? One factor is physique or body build. Although the stereotypes associated with different body builds are often misleading or just plain wrong, many people tend to associate a round body build with an easygoing disposition, relaxed personality, and a lack of personal discipline. A firm and muscular body, in contrast, is assumed to indicate good health with high energy and vigor. A thin

Figure 7.11 Weight Versus Attractiveness: Promoting Size Acceptance

Obesity is on the rise in the United States and elsewhere. Since many people (but not all) view being overweight as unattractive, heavy people sometimes experience bullying and discrimination. However, organizations such as NAAFA seek to help counter this type of negative behavior.

and angular body is perceived as a sign of intelligence and perhaps an introspective personality (Gardner & Tuckerman, 1994).

Another factor that influences physical attractiveness is the extent to which a person is overweight. A growing proportion of many countries' populations are overweight, which is generally viewed negatively. It is important to note, though, that in several cultures being overweight is considered *highly* attractive, for instance, in some African nations. In one country—Mauritania—young women are actively encouraged to eat to gain weight, in order to increase their attractiveness. In the United States, several groups, such as the National Association to Advance Fat Acceptance (NAAFA), have made it their goal to end size discrimination (see Figure 7.11). Yet, in most societies beings overweight still tends to detract from a person's attractiveness, which, in turn, can have negative effects on many aspects of life, from dating to careers (e.g., Crandall & Martinez, 1996).

Key Points

- The initial contact between two people is often based on **proximity**—nearness to each other in physical space. Proximity to others leads to more frequent interaction, which in turn often produces familiarity and increased attraction (the **repeated exposure effect**).
- *Social networks* make it possible for people to interact and form initial feelings of liking or disliking without physical proximity. Use of social media sites can result in both positive and negative effects. On one hand, excessive comparison of ourselves to others may harm well-being if we perceive our friends as more successful than we are. On the other hand, a large social network can lead to a greater sense of social support, particularly when communications involve the sharing of emotional thoughts and feelings with others.

- Attraction toward others is often strongly influenced by their observable characteristics, especially their **physical attractiveness**. Research also offers support for the "love is blind" suggestion: Partners in romantic relationships tend to perceive each other as more attractive than people outside the relationship.
- We often assume that "what is beautiful is good," apparently because we want to form relationships with attractive people. As a result, we may project positive interpersonal traits onto them.
- Red does indeed appear to be "sexy" and enhances women's attractiveness, as many cultures have believed throughout recorded history.
- In addition to attractiveness, physique (body build) and weight are other observable characteristics that influence initial interpersonal evaluations.

7.3: Sources of Liking Based on Social Interaction

Objective   **List the factors that lead individuals to like or dislike each other**

Although proximity, repeated exposure, others' physical appearance, and our own need for affiliation can exert powerful effects on interpersonal attraction, these factors are far from the entire story. Additional variables that strongly affect attraction emerge only as we interact with others, communicate with them, and acquire more information about them. Among these, two sources of liking have been found to be the most influential: our degree of *similarity* to others and the extent to which they like us. In addition, we will examine sources of liking related to social skills, personality traits, and gender differences.

7.3.1: Similarity: Birds of a Feather Actually Do Flock Together

Writing about friendship more than 2,000 years ago, Aristotle (330 BC/1932) suggested that similarity is often the basis for this important kind of relationship. Empirical evidence for this view—known as the *similarity hypothesis*—was not available until many centuries later, when Sir Francis Galton (1870/1952) obtained correlational data on married couples. His findings indicated that spouses did in fact resemble one another in many respects. In the first half of the 20th century, additional correlational studies continued to find that friends and spouses expressed a greater than chance degree of similarity (e.g., Hunt, 1935). Because the research was correlational in nature, though, these findings could have meant that similarity leads to liking, or, that liking leads to similarity—people who like each other become more similar over time.

In a study considered a true "classic" of social psychology, Newcomb (1956) found that similar attitudes *predicted* subsequent liking between students. In his research, he reasoned that if attitudes were measured before people had met, and it was found later that the more similar their attitudes the more they liked each other, it could be concluded that similarity produced their attraction. To test this hypothesis, he studied transfer students—ones who had not met each other before coming to the university. He measured their attitudes about issues via mail—such as family, religion, public affairs, and race relations—before the students reached campus. Then, their liking for one another was assessed weekly after they came to campus.

Results indicated that the more similar the students were initially, the more they liked each other by the end of the semester. This was strong evidence that similarity produced attraction rather than vice versa. Newcomb's initial findings were confirmed in many later studies (Byrne, 1961a; Schachter, 1951). Just as Aristotle and others had suggested, research findings tend to confirm the similarity hypothesis: The more similar two people are to each other, the more they tend to like each other.

This conclusion probably seems reasonable, but what about the idea that "opposites attract?" Don't we sometimes find people attractive who are very different from ourselves? As we noted previously, informal evidence suggests that this might be so. In early research on this topic, the proposed attraction of opposites was often phrased in terms of *complementarities*—differences that, when combined, help to make the individual parts work well together (i.e., complement each other). For instance, it was suggested that dominant individuals would be attracted to submissive ones, talkative people to quiet ones, sadists to masochists, and so on. The idea was that such complementary characteristics would be mutually reinforcing (i.e., beneficial to both people in the relationships) and hence a good basis for attraction.

Surprisingly, direct tests of these propositions failed to support complementarity as a determinant of attraction, even with respect to dominance and submissiveness (Palmer & Byrne, 1970). With respect to attitudes, values, personality characteristics, bad habits, intellectual ability, income level, and even minor preferences (such as choosing the right-hand aisle versus the left-hand aisle in a movie theater), similarity was found to result in attraction (Byrne, 1971). So, overall, there is little if any evidence for the suggestion that opposites attract. Of course, there can be exceptions to this general rule, but attraction seems to derive much more strongly from similarity than complementarity.

One such exception occurs in male–female interactions in which one person engages in dominant behavior and the other responds in a submissive fashion (Markey, Funder, & Ozer, 2003; Sadler & Woody, 2003). This specific kind of complementarity leads to greater attraction than when the second person copies the first person (i.e., is also dominant; Tiedens & Fragale, 2003). With respect to other kinds of interaction (e.g., a person who is verbally withdrawn and unresponsive interacting with someone who is verbally expressive and critical), opposite styles not only fail to attract but are quite incompatible. These situations are more likely to lead to rejection and avoidance than liking and attraction (Swann, Rentfrow, & Gosling, 2003). Overall, then, the evidence is both strong and consistent: Similarity—not complementarity (opposites)—seems to be the basis for attraction across many kinds of situations and many kinds of relationships.

SIMILARITY–DISSIMILARITY EFFECT: A CONSISTENT PREDICTOR OF ATTRACTION   Based on the discussion of affect earlier in this chapter, it's easy to see how similarity tends to arouse positive feelings and dissimilarity tends to arouse negative feelings—the **similarity–dissimilarity effect**. Much of the early work on this effect focused on **attitude similarity**, the extent to which two individuals share the same ways of thinking or feeling toward something or another person. However, the meaning of attitude similarity was generally expanded to include not only similarity of attitudes, but also of beliefs, values, and interests.

The initial laboratory experiments on attitude similarity consisted of two steps. First, the attitudes of the participants were assessed. Second, these individuals were exposed to the attitudes, beliefs, values, and interests of a stranger and asked to evaluate that person (Byrne, 1961b). The results were straightforward: People consistently indicated that they liked strangers similar to themselves much better than they liked dissimilar ones. Not only they did liked people who were similar to themselves, they also judged them to be more intelligent, better informed, more moral, and better adjusted than people who were dissimilar to them.

Many such investigations, with a variety of populations, procedures, and topics, revealed that people respond to the similarity–dissimilarity effect in a surprisingly precise way. Attraction is determined by the **proportion of similarity**. That is, when the number of topics on which two people express similar views is divided by the total number of topics on which they have communicated, the resulting proportion can be inserted in a simple formula that allows us to predict attraction (Byrne & Nelson, 1965). The higher the proportion of similarity, the greater the liking. No one knows exactly how people process attitudinal information to produce that outcome. It appears that people automatically engage in some kind of cognitive addition and division, manipulating the units of positive and negative affect they experience.

The effect of attitude similarity on attraction is a strong one. It holds true regardless of the number of topics on which people express their views and regardless of how important or trivial the topics may be. It holds equally true for males and females, regardless of age, educational, or cultural differences (Byrne, 1971). The general level of attraction may vary and the total impact of proportion may vary, based on dispositional factors, but the basic proportion effect remains true (Kwan, 1998; Monteil & Michinov, 2000; Singh & Teoh, 1999).

Beyond attitudes and values, many kinds of situations involving the similarity–dissimilarity effect have been investigated. In each instance, people prefer others who are similar to themselves rather than those who are dissimilar. Examples include the similarity–dissimilarity effect with respect to smoking marijuana (Eisenman, 1985), religious practices, self-concept (Klohnen & Luo, 2003), being a "morning person" versus an "evening person" (Watts, 1982), and finding the same jokes amusing (Cann, Calhoun, & Banks, 1997). One of the most interesting areas of research on the effects of similarity involves **physical attractiveness**, so let's take a closer look at that work.

DO WE SEEK SIMILARITY EVEN WITH RESPECT TO PHYSICAL ATTRACTIVE-NESS?   Suppose you had a magic potion you could use to make anyone you wish fall in love with you. What kind of romantic partner would you choose? Would you choose a person you find incredibly physically attractive? Many people say they would, but if they paused for a moment, they might realize that such a person would also be extremely attractive to many others. This poses risks: The chosen partner might like or love you now but may be strongly tempted to leave you for someone new since she or he has a large number of choices. In short, you might not remain "number one" for very long.

Because of these potential problems, it appears that we tend to choose partners who are similar to ourselves in physical attractiveness, even though we'd prefer very attractive ones (known as the **matching hypothesis**). This view was first proposed by Berscheid, Dion, Walster, and Walster (1971), who found that couples who were similar in physical attractiveness were more likely to continue dating than those who were very different from each other. Although the findings of other studies offered support for this view, some evidence indicated that people don't always choose their "match" in appearance; they sometimes try to obtain the most attractive partners available (e.g., Kalick & Hamilton, 1986).

In more recent research, van Straaten, Holland, Finkenauer, Hollenstein, and Engels (2010) reported findings that offer strong support for the matching hypothesis. These researchers had male and female strangers interact briefly in a study supposedly concerned with student preferences in daily life. During the videotaped interactions, the attractiveness of the two participants was rated by observers. In addition, the observers rated the extent to which each partner engaged in efforts to make a favorable impression on the other person. Finally, each participant also rated his or her interest in dating the stranger.

If the matching hypothesis is accurate, then we should expect that participants would invest more effort in trying to impress their partners when they were similar in attractiveness than when they were different. Results confirmed these predictions for the men: They invested more effort in building a relationship with the stranger when they were more similar to that person in attractiveness than when they were different. This result occurred even though the men were very interested in dating the extremely attractive participants. (Remember, according to the matching hypothesis, we *prefer* very attractive partners but focus on obtaining ones who match our own level of attractiveness.) For the women, however, the same pattern did *not* emerge (see Figure 7.12). This was not surprising because women are generally much less willing to express overt interest in a potential romantic partner than men. So the women did not engage in strong efforts to impress their partners regardless of whether they were similar to those people or not.

Overall, these findings suggest that although we may daydream about incredibly attractive romantic partners, we focus most of our effort on obtaining ones who closely match our own level of attractiveness. This may not lead to the fulfillment of our fantasies but does provide the basis for relationships that are mutually desired and have a better chance to survive and prosper.

DO EVEN TRIVIAL SIMILARITIES GENERATE ATTRACTION?

Do you think that if you have the same first letter in your name as another person you will like him or her more than if you do not? What about having the same number on a sweater as another person? Would you find this person more attractive than if the number were different? Before you laugh, consider the following possibility: Perhaps our positive feelings about ourselves—for instance, toward our own names—spill over into increased attraction toward others who share these seemingly trivial characteristics. This effect is known as *implicit egotism*, meaning that positive associations with something about ourselves do indeed increase attraction toward others who share whatever these are—our names, the number of our home address, or almost anything else.

Research by Pelham, Carvallo, and Jones (2005) provides convincing evidence for the effects of implicit egotism. They examined records of marriages that took place in several states over a very long period—from 1823 to1965. By chance alone, some of the people marrying would have last names with the same first letter, estimated to be 6.55 percent. The actual proportion was higher: 7.51 percent. The same pattern occurred when they varied the apparent trivial similarity between individuals (e.g., they had the same or different numbers on jerseys they wore). Even this similarity increased attraction. These findings, and those of other studies (Montoya, Horton, & Kirchner, 2008), underscore the importance of similarity as a basis for attraction. Its effects are strong and can occur even when we are not paying careful attention.

WHY DO WE LIKE OTHERS WHO ARE SIMILAR TO OURSELVES BUT DISLIKE THOSE WHO ARE DIFFERENT? To ask the same question in a slightly different way, *why* does similarity elicit positive affect (i.e., feelings) while dissimilarity elicits negative affect? The oldest explanation—**balance theory**—was proposed independently by Newcomb (1961) and Heider (1958). This framework suggests that people naturally organize their likes and dislikes in a symmetrical way (Hummert, Crockett, & Kemper, 1990).

When two people like each other and discover they are similar in some specific respect, this constitutes a state of *balance*, which is emotionally pleasant. When two people like each other but later find out they are dissimilar in some specific respect, the result is *imbalance*, which is emotionally *un*pleasant. In a state of imbalance, individuals strive to restore balance by inducing one of them to change and thus create similarity. Balance is also maintained by underestimating or ignoring the dissimilarity or by simply deciding to dislike one another. Whenever two people dislike one another,

Figure 7.12 Evidence for the Matching Hypothesis

Participants in the study illustrated here were observed interacting with an opposite-sex stranger. Men invested more effort in trying to form relationships when they were more similar to their partners in physical attractiveness than when they were very different. The same pattern did not emerge for women; they were more reluctant to engage in overt relationship-building actions regardless of similarity. (Only data for men are shown.)

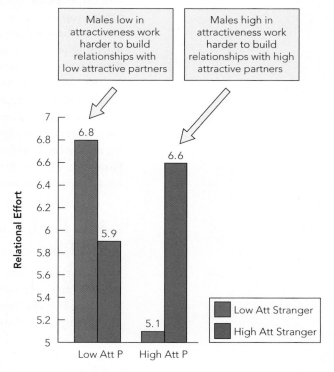

their relationship involves *nonbalance.* This is not especially pleasant or unpleasant because each individual is indifferent about the other person's similarities or dissimilarities.

The aspects of balance theory are helpful but they do not deal with the question of why similarity should matter in the first place. Why should you care if someone differs from you with respect to musical preferences, belief in God, or anything else? One answer is provided by Festinger's (1954) **social comparison theory**. Briefly stated, you compare your attitudes and beliefs with those of others because the only way you can evaluate the accuracy of your views and their "normality" is by finding that other people agree with you. This is not a perfect way to determine the truth, but it is often the best we can do. For example, if you are the *only one* who believes that global warming is happening so quickly that the seas will flood many coastlines next year, the odds are that you are incorrect.

No one wants to be in the position of being "wrong," so we turn to others to obtain *consensual validation*—evidence that they share our views. When you learn that someone else holds the same attitudes and beliefs that you do, it feels good because such information suggests that you have sound judgment, are in contact with reality, and so on. Dissimilarity suggests the opposite, and that creates negative feelings. However, dissimilarity that comes from outgroup members is less uncomfortable for us because we expect them to be different from ourselves (Haslam, 2004).

7.3.2: Reciprocal Liking or Disliking: Liking Those Who Like Us

Most everyone wants to be liked. Not only do we enjoy being evaluated positively, we welcome such input even when we know it is simply undeserved flattery. To an outside observer, false flattery may be perceived for what it is—inaccurate. But to the person being flattered, it is likely to appear accurate, even if it's not completely honest (Gordon, 1996; Vonk, 1998, 2002). Only if flattery is totally obvious does it sometimes fail.

Research findings offer strong support for the powerful effects of reciprocal liking and disliking (e.g., Condon & Crano, 1988). Overall, it appears that the rule of reciprocity—acting toward others in the way they have acted toward us—operates with respect to attraction, too. In general, we tend to like those who express liking toward us, and dislike those who express dislike for us (e.g., Condon & Crano, 1988).

7.3.3: Social Skills: Liking People Who Are Good at Interacting with Others

Do your recall David, the graduate student described at the beginning of this chapter? He was incredibly likable. Virtually everyone with whom he interacted liked him and sought further contact with him. David had a very high level of what social psychologists call **social skills**—a combination of aptitudes that help individuals who possess them to interact effectively with others. In turn, this increases people's liking of them (Rubin, Bukowski, & Laursen, 2011).

Social skills have been found to be an important "plus" in a wide range of settings—from politics and legal proceedings to forming romantic relationships. For instance, in the courtroom, defendants high in social skills are declared innocent more often than those lower in such skills (or, if they are convicted, they tend to receive lesser sentences). Individuals high in social skills often receive more promotions and larger raises wherever they work. Likewise, doctors who are high in social skills are more popular with patients and therefore more effective in getting patients to follow

Figure 7.13 Social Skills: An Important Source of Interpersonal Liking

Social skills are combined aptitudes that help people interact effectively with others. These skills have beneficial effects for the people who demonstrate them. For example, doctors with a good "bedside manner" are generally well-liked and therefore more successful in getting patients to follow their advice.

their advice (see Figure 7.13). And of course, people high in social skills have more success in romance. They attract more partners and have a wider range of choice among them (e.g., Kotsou, Nelis, Grégoire, & Mikolajczak, 2011).

So what, precisely, are these valuable social skills? Here is a brief overview that includes the social skills studied primarily by social psychologists as well as closely related skills studied by organizational psychologists who investigate their impact in work settings (e.g., Ferris, et al., 2007).

- *Social astuteness (social perception)*: The capacity to perceive and understand others (their traits, feelings, and intentions) accurately. People high on this dimension recognize the subtleties of interpersonal interactions, a skill that helps them develop effective, positive relationships with others.

- *Interpersonal influence: The ability to change others' attitudes or behavior by using a variety of techniques—for example, persuasion and subtle techniques such as the "foot in the door" tactic (starting with a small request and then escalating to a larger one).*

- *Social adaptability: The capacity to adapt to a wide range of social situations and to interact effectively with a wide range of people.*

- *Expressiveness*: The ability to show emotions openly, in a form others can readily perceive.

Clearly, David (the graduate student) possessed these skills to a high degree. He could "read" other people accurately—quickly gaining insight into their major traits. David was highly successful in influencing others by using several techniques that encouraged people to like him. He was also very adaptable—a social chameleon. That is, he could adjust his personal style to whatever situation he faced. In short, David was very interpersonally appealing to other people.

In David's case, he used his social skills for his own personal advantage. However, social skills are not necessarily used to manipulate or take advantage of others. For instance, a professor with a high degree of social skills may be more effective in motivating students to come to class, and as a result they learn more. Regardless of how social skills are used, however, they play an important role in the liking of others.

7.3.4: Personality and Liking: Why People with Certain Traits Are More Attractive Than Others

When we interact with other people—especially those we don't already know—we can observe some of their characteristics as the interaction unfolds. As you've learned, first impressions can be formed very quickly. These impressions can range from quite accurate to very inaccurate. One major theory of personality, known as the "Big Five," suggests there are five broad aspects of personality: openness—being imaginative, seeking new ideas, and pursuing new experiences; conscientiousness—being organized, neat, and "on time" with respect to deadlines and meetings; agreeableness—approaching others with trust and cooperation; extraversion—the strong tendency to be outgoing, expressive, warm, and energetic; and emotional stability—the degree to which people do not have very large swings in mood over time (e.g., Barrick & Mount, 1991). Interestingly, some of these characteristics are apparent almost immediately—after just a few minutes (e.g., Zhao & Seibert, 2006). People high in agreeableness and extraversion are viewed as rather likable; they receive higher ratings of interpersonal attractiveness from others (Zhao & Seibert, 2006).

Another, and perhaps less desirable aspect of personality, is known as **narcissism** (e.g., Morf & Rhodewalt, 2011). People high in narcissism have inflated views of themselves—an extreme and unjustified high self-esteem. People with a high level of narcissism focus mostly on themselves while largely ignoring the needs and feelings of others. They resemble Narcissus, a figure in Greek mythology who admired his own reflection in a pond so intensely that he drowned pursuing it. Overall, narcissists communicate the belief that they are superior and should be admired by others. When people interact with narcissists repeatedly, these behaviors make them unlikable.

Surprisingly, narcissists may actually seem very likable at first. Why? On the basis of previous research, Back, Schmukle, and Egloff (2011) tested the possibility that narcissists are initially liked because they are seen as charming, extraverted, more open, and even more competent than other people. In one study, the researchers asked a group of students to step forward, one at a time, to introduce themselves. Later, students rated the degree of the others' narcissism and indicated how much they'd like to get to know the other students. In short, the researchers measured both likableness and potential popularity. Results indicated that the higher students scored in terms of narcissism, the higher were their ratings on both likability and popularity dimensions.

Further evidence was derived from analysis of the videotapes made as each student introduced herself or himself. These analyses indicated that several different factors contributed to narcissists' high ratings by other students. Students with higher narcissism ratings showed charming facial expressions, humor, and self-assurance—all likeable attributes. So in summary, it does appear that narcissists seem likable at first. It is only later, after people get to know them better, that their negative behaviors tip the balance toward dislike (see Figure 7.14).

Figure 7.14 Narcissism: From Initial Liking to Later Disliking

People high in narcissism have inflated views of themselves—extreme, unjustified self-esteem. At first, they appear charming and are liked by others. Later, as their true personality is recognized, they are strongly disliked.

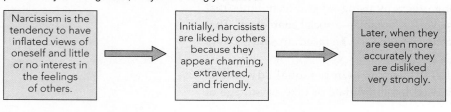

7.3.5: What Do We Desire in Others? Gender Differences and Changes over Stages of a Relationship

In this chapter so far, we have focused on the factors that lead individuals to like or dislike each other. Now, consider a different but closely related question: What do people desire in others? Suppose you could design the perfect person for a particular kind of relationship—a romantic interest, a work-group member, someone to play sports with. What characteristics would you want these people to have? That question has been addressed by social psychologists. Research indicates that the question "What do we desire in our ideal partner?" is, perhaps, too general. The characteristics we seek and prefer in others may change depending on our gender and the stage or length of our relationship with them. That is, the traits we look for when we're just getting acquainted with someone can change after we form an actual relationship, or after that relationship has existed for months, years, or even decades. In this section, we will consider gender differences mainly within the context of romantic relationships because that has been the primary focus of much of this research.

To begin, it's important to identify characteristics that both women and men uniformly find desirable in others. Many studies have investigated this issue, but one of the most revealing was conducted by Cottrell, Neuberg, and Li (2007). These researchers began by asking undergraduate students to "create an ideal person" by rating 31 positive characteristics in terms of how important each was for their ideal person to have. Included among the characteristics were trustworthiness, cooperativeness, agreeableness (kind, interpersonally warm), extraversion (outgoing, sociable), emotional stability, physical health, and physical attractiveness. Results indicated that trustworthiness and cooperativeness were seen as the most important traits, followed by agreeableness and extraversion. These initial findings indicated that overall, there are indeed characteristics that most people desire in others. The research did not, however, address another question: Do the desired characteristics vary with different types of relationships? In other words, do we desire different traits in friends, workpartners, lovers, friends, or employees?

To find out, the researchers asked male and female students to imagine creating ideal members of several different groups and relationships—work project team members, final exam study group members, golf team members, sorority members, fraternity members, close friends, and employees. For each group or relationship, students rated the extent to which 75 different traits were important for the ideal person to possess, as shown in Table 7.1. Across all seven relationships, trustworthiness and cooperativeness were rated as most important. Agreeableness followed closely, as

Table 7.1 What Do We Desire in Others? It Depends on the Context

As shown here, several traits (trustworthiness, cooperativeness, agreeableness) are viewed as important in "ideal partners" across many different kinds of relationships (project teams, employees, friends, etc.). The importance of other traits, however, varies with the kind of relationship in question. For instance, attractiveness is important in a sorority member, but not in a project team or study group member. (High ratings for various traits are shown in italic and indicate that the traits in question were rated as very important by research participants.)

Trait	Project Team	Study Group	Golf Team	Sorority	Fraternity	Close Friend	Employee
Trustwothiness	7.35	6.87	7.74	7.45	7.33	7.68	7.78
Cooperativeness	6.39	5.93	5.70	6.51	6.29	6.79	6.28
Agreeableness	6.36	5.65	5.38	6.99	6.50	7.14	6.76
Attractiveness	2.84	2.68	3.17	6.36	5.24	4.73	3.74
Intelligence	7.67	7.74	5.52	6.04	5.97	6.51	7.39
Humor	5.17	4.48	5.02	6.61	6.92	7.53	5.49
Wealth	3.43	2.17	3.70	4.82	4.92	3.94	4.45

SOURCE: Based on data from Cottrell et al., 2006.

did extraversion. As you might expect, though, other traits were viewed as more or less important depending on the kind of relationship participants had with the imaginary "ideal" person. For instance, intelligence was rated as very important for project teams and study groups, but much less important for fraternity or sorority members. Similarly, humor was rated as very important for close friends, but less important for employees, project team members, and study group members.

Overall, the results pointed to two major conclusions. First, there are several traits (trustworthiness, cooperativeness, agreeableness, and extraversion) that we value in everyone—no matter what kind of relationship we have with them. Second, we value other traits differentially—that is, to a greater or lesser degree—depending on the kind of relationship we have with the other person.

Now, what about differences based on gender? Do women and men desire different qualities in potential romantic partners? It is widely believed that men focus more on physical attractiveness than women. Thus, men's ideal romantic partner would be attractive, as attractive as they can obtain. Women, too, are interested in physical attractiveness, but they weigh this variable as somewhat less important than other characteristics.

Women assign greater importance to traits related to forming stable relationships, such as a partner's potential future earnings. Although financial support might seem unrelated to romance, sociobiological theory (role of our genes in social behavior) suggests that women tend to seek mates—at least long-term ones—who could potentially support them and their children. This view is reflected in *parental investment theory* (Bjorklund & Kipp, 1996) which says that the one who invests and risks the most in reproduction—usually the female—will be the most particular when selecting a mate. Women, even today, tend to invest more time and energy in child rearing duties than do men. At present, of course, some women in relationships also provide equal financial resources as men. But in spite of the growth in women's financial independence, a recent meta-analysis of hundreds of studies on gender differences in ideal romantic partners suggests there may still be some gender differences (although small) related to financial support (Eastwick, Luchies, Finkel, & Hunt, 2014).

Another factor that plays a role in our concept of an ideal romantic partner is the stage of a relationship. Before a relationship forms, physical attractiveness may predict the choice of a romantic partner. As the relationship develops, the effect of physical attractiveness decreases. The partners get to know each other better and include other factors (e.g., intelligence and stability) in the equation. Later, though, the impact of physical attractiveness may increase slightly. Why? Is it because the partners begin to entertain the idea that they could do even better if they sought a new relationship? This is pure speculation, but as we will see later in the chapter, jealousy and infidelity may play a factor.

To summarize, the characteristics we desire in those with whom we form relationships appears to vary according to factors such as the type of relationship, our gender, and the stage of the relationship. Available evidence indicates that the answer to the question "What do we want in an ideal partner?" seems to be "It depends."

Key Points

- One of the many factors determining attraction toward another person is *similarity* to that individual in terms of attitudes, beliefs, values, and interests.
- Despite the continuing popularity of the idea that opposites attract (*complementarity*), that rarely seems to be true in the real world.

- The **similarity–dissimilarity effect** is seen when people respond positively to indications that another person is similar to them and negatively to indications that another person is dissimilar from themselves. The extent to which two individuals share the same ways of thinking or feeling is called **attitude similarity**. The

- larger the **proportion of similarity**, the greater the attraction.
- Most research supports the **matching hypothesis**—the view that we tend to choose romantic partners who are similar to ourselves in terms of physical attractiveness, even though we might prefer to have more attractive ones.
- Even seemingly trivial similarities, such as sharing the same first letter of a name or having the same number on a jersey, can increase our attraction to other individuals—an effect known as *implicit egotism*.
- **Balance theory** offers an explanation for why we like others who are similar to ourselves and dislike those who are different. *Balance* (liking plus agreement) results in a positive emotional state. *Imbalance* (liking plus disagreement) results in a negative state and a desire to restore balance. *Nonbalance* (disliking plus either agreement or disagreement) leads to indifference.
- People compare their attitudes and beliefs with others' views as a means of self-evaluation when there is no objective "yardstick" available. That is, they engage in **social comparison**. We turn to others to obtain *consensual validation*, evidence that they share our views.
- Other factors that influence our liking for others are their **social skills**, how much they like us, and certain aspects of their personality such as **narcissism**. We may like narcissistic people at first because of their outgoing ways, but liking usually turns to dislike after we get to know them better.
- Of the "big five" broad aspects of personality (openness, conscientiousness, agreeableness, extraversion, and emotional stability), people high is agreeableness and extraversion receive higher ratings of interpersonal attractiveness.
- The traits we desire in other people typically vary depending on the type of relationship, the stage (or length) of the relationship, and our gender.

7.4: Close Relationships: Foundations of Social Life

Objective   **Describe three main types of close relationships formed by people**

In a sense, interpersonal attraction is the beginning of many relationships. If we have a choice, we tend to spend time with people we like, and to develop friendships, romances, or other long-term relationships with them. In other cases, of course, relationships are not voluntary in this way. We have long-term relationships with family members (our parents, siblings, grandparents, and other relatives) which exist from birth and continue throughout life—sometimes whether we like it or not. And still other relationships are related to our jobs, careers, or education. Most people have coworkers and bosses, some of whom they like and others whom they'd prefer to avoid. Regardless of whether relationships are formed voluntarily or are the result of birth or external constraints (where we work), they certainly play a crucial role in the social side of life.

Social psychologists are fully aware of the central role of relationships in our lives, and have turned growing attention to understanding basic questions about those relationships. How and why are they formed? How do they develop? What functions do they serve? And, how and why do they sometimes end in unhappy or personally devastating ways, such as divorce, conflict, or even physical violence? This section provides an overview of social psychology research results on these and related questions (e.g., Arriaga, Reed, Goodfriend, & Agnew, 2006). We will start by examining the close relationships between romantic partners. Later, we will discuss other types of relationships that also play a major role in our lives—families and close friendships.

7.4.1: Romantic Relationships and the (Partially Solved) Mystery of Love

"I love you." Those are perhaps the most dramatic and emotion-filled words one person can say to another. **Love** is far beyond mere attraction—it suggests a much stronger, and often much more lasting, relationship. But what, precisely, is love? From a general standpoint, we could say that love is a combination of emotions, cognitions, and behaviors that play a crucial role in close relationships. As with terms such as *justice* and *loyalty*, we believe that we can recognize love when we see it. But we also often realize that love is hard to define and may mean different things to different people or have different meanings within different kinds of relationships.

In a sense, love is somewhat mysterious. Social psychologists have long sought to solve the mystery of love, and in their research have addressed many questions: What is love? Where or how did it originate? What role does it play in romantic relationships? How does it develop? Does love grow gradually out of existing relationships, or does it occur suddenly, such as "love at first sight," or both ways? Even though these are complex questions, careful research has provided at least partial answers to them. Be ready for some surprises, though, because the findings of carefully conducted research have sometimes provided answers that are very different from the thoughts provided by poets, philosophers, or popular singers. We will begin with a discussion of the nature, origin, and components of love and then focus on love's role in romantic relationships.

LOVE: ITS BASIC NATURE   Love is certainly one of the most popular topics in songs, movies, and novels. Most people would agree that it plays a key role in our lives and our personal happiness. Love is a familiar experience in many, but not all, cultures, and recent polls indicate that almost three out of four Americans say they are currently "in love." In part, love is an emotional reaction that seems as basic as sadness, happiness, and fear (Shaver, Morgan, & Wu, 1996). In fact, love may actually be good for you in terms of psychological adjustment. Research by social psychologists indicates that falling in love leads to an increase in self-efficacy and self-esteem—an important ingredient in psychological health and happiness.

Surprisingly, social psychologists did not attempt to study love systematically until the 1970s when one of them (Rubin, 1970) developed a measure for romantic love. Others (Berscheid & Hatfield, 1974) proposed a psychological theory of love. Since then, love has been a major topic of interest for social psychologists. As a result of such research, we now know, fairly clearly, what love is *not*. It is not merely a close friendship extended to physical intimacy, and it involves more than merely being romantically or sexually interested in another person. The specific details appear to vary from culture to culture (Beall & Sternberg, 1995), but the experience we call love appears to be a relatively universal one (Hatfield & Rapson, 1993).

WHAT IS THE ORIGIN OF LOVE?   No one—including social psychologists—knows for sure where the essence of love originated. One possibility is that love is simply a pleasant fantasy that people share at certain times of life—much like a belief in Santa Claus or the Tooth Fairy when we are children. Another explanation involves our ancient ancestors. In order to survive, it was necessary for early humans to reproduce successfully; their numbers were small so this was truly crucial. Buss (1994) suggests that reproductive success would be more likely if heterosexual pairs were erotically attracted to one another, and if they were willing to invest time and effort in feeding and protecting any offspring they produced. In essence, two basic features of love—desire and commitment—grew out of out of conditions that made love an important adaptation for our species (Rensberger, 1993).

COMPONENTS OF LOVE.   Sternberg's (1986) **triangular model of love** (shown in Figure 7.15) is one important framework for understanding the various components of love. This theory suggests that each love relationship is made up of three basic components that are present in varying degrees in different couples (Aron & Westbay, 1996). One component is **intimacy**—the closeness two people feel and the strength of the bond that holds them together. Partners high in intimacy are concerned with each other's welfare and happiness. They value, like, count on, and understand one another.

A second component in Sternberg's theory is **passion**, based on romance, physical attraction, and sexuality—the sexual motives and sexual excitement associated with a couple's relationship. The third component, **decision/commitment**, represents cognitive factors such as the decision to love and be with a person, plus a commitment to

Figure 7.15 Sternberg's Triangular Model of Love

Sternberg suggests that love has three basic components: intimacy, passion, and decision/commitment. For a given couple, love can be based on any one of these three components, on a combination of any two of them, or on all three. These various possibilities yield seven types of relationships, including the ideal (consummate love) that consists of all three basic components equally represented.

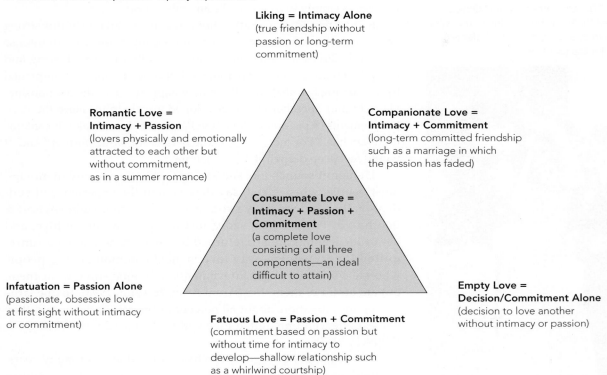

Liking = Intimacy Alone
(true friendship without passion or long-term commitment)

Romantic Love = Intimacy + Passion
(lovers physically and emotionally attracted to each other but without commitment, as in a summer romance)

Companionate Love = Intimacy + Commitment
(long-term committed friendship such as a marriage in which the passion has faded)

Consummate Love = Intimacy + Passion + Commitment
(a complete love consisting of all three components—an ideal difficult to attain)

Infatuation = Passion Alone
(passionate, obsessive love at first sight without intimacy or commitment)

Fatuous Love = Passion + Commitment
(commitment based on passion but without time for intimacy to develop—shallow relationship such as a whirlwind courtship)

Empty Love = Decision/Commitment Alone
(decision to love another without intimacy or passion)

maintain the relationship on a permanent or long-term basis. When all three angles of the triangle are equally strong and balanced, the result is what Sternberg describes as **consummate love**. He suggests that consummate love is the ideal form but often difficult to attain or maintain.

COMPANIONATE LOVE   In Sternberg's model, companionate love is a combination of intimacy plus commitment. This type of love is based on a very close relationship in which two people have a great deal in common, care about each other's well-being, and express mutual liking and respect (Caspi & Herbener, 1990). Hatfield (1988) describes this type of love as the "affection we feel for those with whom our lives are deeply entwined." Perhaps companionate love is not as exciting as relationships with a high level of passion, but it does serve as a foundation for lasting, committed relationships—for instance, marriages that last many years.

THE ROLE OF PASSIONATE LOVE IN ROMANTIC RELATIONSHIPS   In 1989, Aron and his colleagues pointed out that many people fall in love, but no one ever seems to have "fallen in friendship." Falling in love sometimes begins as a sudden, overwhelming, surging, all-consuming positive reaction to another person—a reaction that feels as if it's beyond control. This emotional and often unrealistic response is called **passionate love**. Many Hollywood films reflect a theme of passionate love. For instance, in the classic film "The Godfather," when Michael Corleone sees Apollonia Vitelli for the first time, he is immediately "hit with the thunderbolt," as described by his companions (see Figure 7.16).

Is sexual attraction an essential component of passionate love? Meyers and Berscheid (1997) propose that it is. But sexual attraction is not sufficient in and of itself for concluding that we are in love with another person. You can be sexually attracted to

Figure 7.16 Love at First Sight

Many people say they've experienced love at first sight—overwhelming attraction to another person on first meeting this person, or merely seeing her or him. Such an experience was shown clearly in the classic film "The Godfather," when Michael Corleone (played by Al Pacino) and his future wife, Apollonia Vitelli (played by Simonetta Stefanelli), see each other for the first time.

someone without being in love, but you aren't likely to be in love in the absence of sexual attraction (Walster et al., 2000). Surveys indicate that college students agree (Regan, 1998). For many people, love makes sex more acceptable, and sexual activity tends to be romanticized (Baumeister, 2005). That's why it is more acceptable for two people to "make love" than simply to copulate like animals in heat.

In addition to sexual attraction, passionate love includes strong emotional arousal, the desire to be physically close, and an intense need to be loved as much as you love the other person. Loving and being loved are positive experiences, but they are often accompanied by a recurring fear that something may happen to end the relationship. Hatfield and Sprecher (1986) developed a scale to measure the various elements of passionate love (the Passionate Love Scale). It contains items such as "For me, _____ is the perfect romantic partner" and "I would feel deep despair if _____ left me."

Though it sounds like something that happens only in movies, most people, when asked, say they've had the experience of suddenly falling in love with a stranger—love at first sight (Averill & Boothroyd, 1977). Often, sadly, just one person falls in love, and her or his feelings are not returned by the partner, known as **unrequited love**. Such one-way love is most common among people who are conflicted about attachments to others—they want them, but are afraid of them, too (Aron, Aron, & Allen, 1998). In one large survey investigation, about 60 percent of the respondents said they had experienced unrequited love within the past 2 years (Bringle & Winnick, 1992).

Two social psychologists who have studied love for many years, Hatfield and Walster (1981), suggest that passionate love requires the presence of three basic factors. First, you must have a concept of passionate love—a basic idea of what it is—and believe that it exists (Sternberg, 1986). Second, an appropriate love object must be present. "Appropriate" tends to mean a physically attractive person of the opposite sex who is not currently married, although this differs between cultures and in various groups within a culture. Third, you must be in a state of physiological arousal (sexual excitement, fear, anxiety, or whatever) that can then be interpreted as the emotion of love (Dutton & Aron, 1974; Istvan, Griffitt, & Weidner, 1983). Together, these three conditions set the stage for falling passionately in love.

Being in love is not all "roses." It can be threatened, or even destroyed, by two important factors: jealousy and infidelity. We will discuss both in the special feature, **"What Research Tells Us About…Two Factors That May Destroy Love—Jealousy and Infidelity."**

7.4.2: What Do We Seek in Romantic Partners?

As described earlier, physical beauty and also youth have been found to be among the most important characteristics people generally seek in a potential romantic partner. Evolutionary psychology suggests why this would be so. These characteristics are associated with reproductive potential. Young people and ones we find attractive are generally healthier and fitter than older people or ones who are not attractive. So both women and men might well be expected to prefer romantic partners who show these characteristics. In general, that's true, but existing evidence indicates that even today, these qualities count more heavily for men than women. In other words, women's physical appeal and youth play a stronger role in men's preferences than men's physical appeal and youth play in women's choice of romantic partners (Scutt, Manning, Whitehouse, Leinster, & Massey, 1997). But the situation is really more complex than this, as we will now explore.

Consider what your ideal mate would be like. Would you want the same qualities in such a person regardless of your goals and social circumstances? Perhaps not. For example, Eagly, Eastwick, and Johannesen-Schmidt (2009) predicted that if individuals planned to pursue a career outside the home, they might seek a mate with the skills necessary to be a homemaker. Likewise, if people anticipated being a homemaker, they might prefer a mate who is likely to be a good provider. In other words,

What Research Tells Us About...

Two Factors That May Destroy Love—Jealousy and Infidelity

Jealousy has often been described as "the green-eyed monster" and with good reason. Feelings of *jealousy*—concerns that a romantic partner or other person about whom we care deeply might, or has already, transferred their affection or loyalty to another—are deeply distressing. Research by Chan, Tong, Tan, and Koh (2013) indicates that jealousy is indeed a negative experience. Participants in the research were first asked to think about a situation in which they felt jealous. Then they were asked to taste two different products. Later, the participants were asked to think about a time when they experienced love and then were given the same two products to taste. The products were rated more bitter after the participants focused on feelings of jealousy than after they thought about an experience of love. In fact, when thinking about love, they rated the products as sweeter.

Jealousy can occur in many situations—whenever a valued relationship with another person is threatened by a rival (e.g., DeSteno, 2004). However, jealousy seems to exert its strong and most dangerous effects with respect to romantic relationships, when one partner becomes interested in a rival (Harris, 2003). Statistics indicate that jealousy is a major factor in a large proportion of homicides against women; they are most likely to be murdered by jealous current or former partners (U.S. Department of Justice, 2003).

Why, more precisely, does jealousy occur? Growing evidence indicates we experience jealousy largely because anticipated or actual social rejection threatens our self-esteem. However, this threatened self-esteem may be experienced somewhat differently by women and men. Some evidence indicates that men experience greater jealousy over their partner's sexual attraction to another person, while women experience greater jealousy over their partner's emotional attraction to another person (e.g., Buss, Larsen, Westen, & Semmelroth, 1992). Regardless, when jealousy occurs strongly, it can cause love to decline or even vanish entirely.

Another factor that generates jealousy and can have devastating effects on a relationship is *infidelity*: a partner's betrayal through intimate relations with others (i.e., cheating or adultery). Infidelity is the most frequent reason for divorce (Previti & Amato,

2003). It also has negative effects on mental and physical health by increasing depression (Gordon, Baucom, & Snyder, 2004).

Although infidelity is not restricted to one gender, culture, or socioeconomic level, when it occurs among powerful people—such as politicians, military leaders, and high-level executives—it receives widespread attention (see Figure 7.17). This leads to an intriguing question: Is there a link between power and infidelity? That is, do powerful people engage in this behavior more frequently than less powerful people? Research by Lammers, Stoker, Jordan, Pollman, and Stapel (2011) indicates that they do.

In their research, Lammers et al. (2011) asked more than 1,500 employed people to respond to a questionnaire in which they indicated their intentions to engage in infidelity. If they had already been unfaithful, they noted how often this behavior had occurred. The participants also provided information on their level of power within the organizations where they worked—how high they were in status. Finally, participants completed items that measured their confidence in their own attractiveness, their ability to attract another partner, their closeness to their current partner, and the degree of risk that being unfaithful would involve.

Results indicated the more power individuals had, the greater their infidelity—in terms of actual incidents as well as intended ones. Moreover, these results appeared to be due primarily to their confidence. In other words, a high level of power led individuals to feel confident about their ability to engage in infidelity. This, in turn, actually increased the likelihood of such behavior. Even though power certainly offers many advantages, helping to maintain love in a committed relationship is not one of them.

The costs of infidelity can be substantial. Evidence reported by Lehmiller (2009) indicates that people engaged in secret romances often experienced stress as they attempted to conceal those relationships from their partners. Not surprisingly, they also experienced reduced closeness with their partners. As Lehmiller notes (2009, p. 1465): "The costs associated with maintaining a secret romance tend to outweigh any benefits derived from the sense of mystery or excitement thought to accompany such relationships."

Figure 7.17 Infidelity Can Lead to Devastating Consequences

When President Bill Clinton's affair with a White House intern—Monica Lewinski—was revealed, public reaction was very negative, partly because it seemed possible that he used the prestige of his office to begin this affair. During a lengthy investigation, Congress charged President Clinton with lying under oath to a federal grand jury and obstructing justice. Even though President Clinton was eventually acquitted of those charges, the country (and no doubt his family) went through significant turmoil because of his affair.

the social roles people expect to play in life would be an important factor in determining what they sought in a possible future mate. Eagly and colleagues reasoned that social roles would be more important than gender, although some differences between women and men might still exist.

To study these possibilities, they asked male and female participants to imagine that in the future, they are married with children, and they are either the primary provider for their family or the primary homemaker. Participants were then asked to indicate the extent to which various mate characteristics would be important to them, from irrelevant to indispensable. Several of these characteristics related to being a good provider (ambition, industriousness), while others related to being a good homemaker (desire to have a home and children; good cook and housekeeper).

Results indicated that the role individuals expected to play did influence the skills or traits they would find important in a mate. For both men and women, when participants expected to be a provider, they rated homemaker skills in their potential mate as more important than provider-related skills. When they expected to be a homemaker, however, they rated provider skills in potential mates as more important than homemaker skills (see Figure 7.18). In other words, they sought someone with whom they could readily divide key tasks or responsibilities. In addition, some gender differences were observed. Regardless of the role they expected to play themselves, women valued good provider skills more highly than did men. In addition, women also expressed a preference for mates older than themselves, while men expressed a preference for younger ones.

7.4.3: Relationships with Family Members: Our First—and Most Lasting—Close Relationships

In the 1950s and 1960s, television shows presented "perfect" families, at least as defined at that time. These families had a mother, father, and children, all of whom loved each other and got along pretty well, despite minor disagreements or arguments. Also, extended family—grandparents, aunts, uncles, and cousins—was portrayed as sharing the family experience, freely providing support and advice for their relatives.

Family structure has changed a lot since that earlier time, as illustrated by television shows such as "Modern Family" (see Figure 7.19). But one fact is clear: Relationships with family members are still important. They certainly change as we mature and move through different phases of life, but they remain a constant foundation of our social existence.

RELATIONSHIPS WITH PARENTS Parent–child interactions are of basic importance because this is usually one's first contact with another person. We come into the world ready to interact with other humans (Dissanayake, 2000), but the specific characteristics of those interactions differ from person to person and from family to family. It is those details that seem to have important implications for our later interpersonal behavior.

Figure 7.18 Future Roles and Mate Preference

For both women and men, the characteristics they sought in a potential mate varied in terms of the social role they expected to play—primary provider or primary homemaker. When participants expected to be a homemaker, they valued provider skills and traits more highly than homemaker skills and traits, while when they expected to be a provider, they valued homemaker skills more highly. So anticipated future roles strongly affect what we seek in a potential mate.

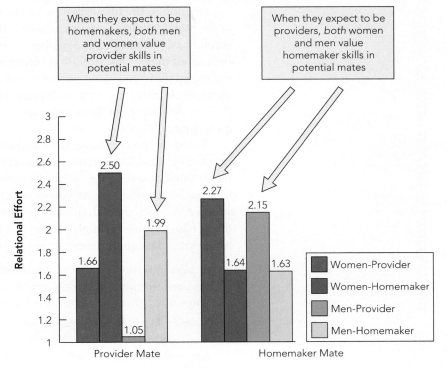

Figure 7.19 Families Portrayed on Television: "Ideal" Versus "Real Life"

During the 1950s and 1960s, many popular TV programs showed families that were virtually perfect: wise, sensitive parents and loving, respectful children. Today's TV shows tend to reflect more realism, for as you know, many real-life families don't live up to this ideal picture.

Social psychologists have studied early relationships between parents and children to see how events during childhood shape our social relationships throughout life. For example, on the basis of careful studies of mothers and infants, Bowlby (1969, 1973) developed the concept of **attachment style**—the degree of security an individual feels in interpersonal relationships. Infants, Bowlby suggests, acquire two basic attitudes during their earliest interactions with an adult. The first is an attitude about self, *self-esteem*. The behavior and the emotional reactions of the caregiver (parent) provide information to the infant that he or she is a valued, important, loved individual or, at the other extreme, someone who is without value, unimportant, and unloved. The second basic attitude concerns other people and involves general expectancies and beliefs about them. This attitude is **interpersonal trust** and is based largely on whether the caregiver is perceived by the infant as trustworthy, dependable, and reliable or as relatively untrustworthy, undependable, and unreliable. Research findings suggest that we develop these basic attitudes about self and about others long before we acquire language skills.

Based on the two basic attitudes, infants, children, adolescents, and adults can be roughly classified as having a particular style involving relationships with others. If you think of self-esteem as one dimension and interpersonal trust as another, then four possible patterns exist: one in which an individual is high on both dimensions, another in which the individual is low on both dimensions, and two others in which the person involved is high on one and low on the other. These four contrasting attachment styles can be described as follows:

- A person with a **secure attachment style** is high in both self-esteem and trust. Secure individuals are best able to form lasting, committed, satisfying relationships throughout life (Shaver & Brennan, 1992).

- *Someone low in both self-esteem and interpersonal trust has a **fearful-avoidant attachment style**. Fearful-avoidant individuals tend to not form close relationships or tend to have unhappy ones (Tidwell, Reis, & Shaver, 1996).*

- *Low self-esteem combined with high interpersonal trust produces a **preoccupied attachment style**. Individuals showing this pattern of attachment want closeness (sometimes excessively so), and they readily form relationships. They cling to others but expect to be rejected eventually because they believe themselves to be unworthy (Lopez et al., 1997; Whiffen, Aube, Thompson, & Campbell, 2000).*

- Finally, those with a *dismissing attachment style* are high in self-esteem and low in interpersonal trust. This combination leads people to believe that they are very deserving of good relationships. But because these individuals don't trust others, they fear genuine closeness. They are the kind of people who say they don't want or need close relationships with others (Carvallo & Gabriel, 2006).

These contrasting styles of attachment can strongly shape the relationships that individuals have with others. For instance, people with a secure attachment style are more likely to have positive long-term relationships, while those with a fearful-avoidant style often avoid such relationships or have ones that fail—often very badly.

Attachment styles, although formed early in life, are *not* set in stone; they can be changed by life experiences. For instance, someone with a secure attachment style could experience a painful relationship breakup that reduces—at least temporarily—his or her self-esteem, and undercut feelings of security. However, attachment styles tend to be stable over long periods of time (Klohnen & Bera, 1998) and, for that reason, can have strong implications for a wide range of life outcomes. For example, adolescents with an insecure attachment style often do worse in school than adolescents with secure attachment styles, form fewer friendships, and often turn into "outsiders." Such people also experience higher levels of stress when they have conflicts within relationships (Previti & Amato, 2003). Perhaps worst of all, those with insecure attachment (and especially a fearful-avoidant style) are more likely to commit suicide (Orbach et al., 2007).

RELATIONSHIPS WITH OTHER ADULT FAMILY MEMBERS.   Besides the mother and father (or other initial caregiver), other adult family members may interact with infants and young children. For instance, grandparents, aunts, and uncles can also have strong effects on a child's development and later social behavior (Lin & Harwood, 2003; Maio, Fincham, & Lycett, 2000). Because these people differ in personality characteristics, children can be influenced in a variety of ways (Clark, Kochanska, & Ready, 2000). For example, the negative effects of having a withdrawn, unreliable mother can be partly offset by the presence of an outgoing, dependable grandfather. Every interaction is potentially important as a young person is developing attitudes about the meaning and value of such factors as trust, affection, self-worth, competition, and humor (O'Leary, 1995). When an older person plays games with a youngster, learning involves not only the game itself, but also how people interact in a social situation, follow a set of rules, behave honestly or cheat, and how they deal with disagreements. All of this affects the way the child interacts with other adults and with peers (Lindsey, Mize, & Pettit, 1997).

RELATIONSHIPS WITH SIBLINGS   Sibling interactions contribute to what we learn about interpersonal behavior (Dunn, 1992). Among elementary school children, those without siblings are found to be liked less by their classmates. Children with no siblings also tend to be either more aggressive or more victimized by aggressors than those with siblings. This is presumably because having brothers or sisters provides useful interpersonal learning experiences (Kitzmann, Cohen, & Lockwood, 2002).

Sibling relationships, unlike those between parent and child, often combine feelings of affection, hostility, and rivalry (Boer, Westenberg, McHale, Updegraff, & Stocker, 1997). A familiar theme in sibling quarrels is some version of "Mom always liked you best" or "They always did more for you than me." Parents, it seems, seldom admit that they feel any such favoritism. Most of us have experienced (or observed in others) multiple examples of sibling rivalry. It's not uncommon to hear adults complain about events involving competition between siblings. However, according to Boer and associates (1997), most siblings get along fairly well. There are certainly exceptions to this rule, but in general, sibling rivalry is far surpassed by the shared memories and affection that siblings feel for one another (see Figure 7.20).

7.4.4: Friendships: Relationships Beyond the Family

Beginning in early childhood, most of us establish casual friendships with peers who share common interests. These relationships generally begin on the basis of proximity. For example, we may have shared the same class in school, lived in the same neighborhood, or met as a result of parental friendships. Such relationships are maintained in part by mutual interests and by positive rather than negative experiences together, sometimes developing into much stronger social ties.

CLOSE FRIENDSHIPS   Many childhood friendships simply fade away. But sometimes a relationship begun in early childhood or adolescence can mature into a close friendship that involves increasingly mature types of interaction. Such friendships can survive for decades—even for an entire life. These long-term friendships have several important characteristics. For example, many people tend to engage in self-enhancing behavior (such as bragging) when interacting with a wide range of others, but they exhibit modesty when interacting with their long-term friends (Tice et al., 1995). Close friends are less likely to lie to one another, unless the lie is designed to make the friend feel better (DePaulo & Kashy, 1998). And friends begin to speak of "we" and "us" rather than "she and I" or "he and I" (Fitzsimons & Kay, 2004).

Figure 7.20 Rivalry Between Siblings

In many families, siblings get along very well (as those shown here). In other cases, rivalry is very strong. For example, Olivia de Havilland and her sister Joan Fontaine were two famous actresses in the past who strongly competed with each other—even for the same Oscar award.

Once a close friendship is established, the two individuals spend increasing amounts of time together, interacting in varied situations, self-disclosing, and providing mutual emotional support (Laurenceau, Barrett, & Pietromonaco, 1998; Matsushima & Shiomi, 2002). A close friend is valued for his or her generosity, sensitivity, and honesty—someone with whom you can relax and be yourself (Urbanski, 1992). But cultural differences exist with respect to friendship, too. For instance, Japanese college students describe a "best friend" as someone in a give-and-take relationship, a person with whom it is easy to get along, who does not brag, and is considerate and not short-tempered (Maeda & Ritchie, 2003). American students describe close friends in a similar way, except they also value friends who are spontaneous and active.

GENDER AND FRIENDSHIPS   How do women and men differ when it comes to relationships with friends? Although such differences tend to be small, they do exist. Women tend to place greater emphasis on intimacy—expecting to share and discuss emotions and experiences with their friends and receive emotional support from them. In contrast, men tend to form friendships on the basis of activities—playing sports, working on joint projects, sharing hobbies (Fredrickson, 1995). For example, if a man is playing baseball with friends and falls, skinning his knee, his male friends may shout, "Get off the field—you are stopping the game." In contrast, his female friends might be more likely to rush over to see if he needs help.

IS SIMILARITY THE BASIS FOR FRIENDSHIP?   Earlier, we noted that similarity is an important basis for interpersonal attraction. The more similar people are in any of many different ways (attitudes, personality, interests, and values), the more they tend to like one another. Is this also a basis for friendship? To find out, Selfhout, Denissen, Branje, and Meeus (2009) conducted research with individuals who were becoming acquainted and forming friendships. These research participants were freshmen at a European university. During orientation sessions, they completed a questionnaire on several key aspects of personality (the "Big Five" dimensions—e.g., extraversion, agreeableness, openness, conscientiousness, and emotional stability). In terms of these definitions, they rated both themselves and other students they had recently met. Then, they completed similar questionnaires once a month for several months. This provided information both on *actual similarity* between participants in the study and on their *perceived similarity*—how similar they perceived themselves to be. In addition, ratings by peers were included. Finally, students also provided information on their developing friendships—the extent to which they were friends with other participants in the study.

The key question was, would actual similarity or perceived similarity be a better predictor of friendship formation? Although many previous studies suggest that actual similarity should play a key role, other research indicates that determining actual similarity takes a long time and is often an uncertain process. Perceived similarity, however, can develop almost immediately and exert its effects from the very start of a relationship. Results offered support for this alternative prediction. In fact, actual similarity did not predict who became friends; instead perceived similarity predicted this outcome very well. For people who are just beginning to get acquainted, perception appears to be more important than underlying reality, in terms of friendship formation.

Key Points

- From a general standpoint, **love** is a combination of emotions, cognitions, and behaviors that play a crucial role in close relationships. Although love is hard to define, most would agree that it goes far beyond mere sexual or romantic attraction.

- The reproductive success of our ancient ancestors was enhanced not only by sexual attraction between males and females but also by bonding between mates and between parents and their offspring.

- Sternberg's **triangular model of love** includes three components of love: **passion** (physical attraction and sexual excitement), **intimacy** (emotional closeness), and **decision/commitment** (a cognitive decision to love and to be committed to a relationship). When all three angles of the triangle are equally strong and balanced, the result is **consummate love**.

- **Passionate love**—a sudden, overwhelming emotional response to another person—is just one kind of love. Companionate love resembles a very close friendship that includes caring, mutual liking, and respect. **Unrequited love** is love felt by one person for another who does not feel love in return.

- *Jealousy* is a powerful emotion that research indicates is often triggered by threats to our self-esteem—threats arising when we fear that someone we love or care about will desert us for a rival. One factor that produces very strong jealousy is *infidelity* (adultery) on the part of the partner—either imagined or real. Secret relationships may be enticing, but the costs of forming them are high.

- The traits we desire in a romantic partner are influenced by gender preferences and by the future roles we expect our partner and our self to occupy.

- Our first relationships are within the family where we acquire an **attachment style,** the degree of security experienced in the context of these relationships. The two main components of an attachment style are based on the levels of *self-esteem* and **interpersonal trust**.

- Attachment styles developed in the family influence the nature of other relationships, such as romantic partnerships and friendships. As a result, attachment styles play an important role in many life outcomes. The four main attachment styles are **secure** (high in both self-esteem and interpersonal trust), **fearful-avoidant** (low in both self-esteem and interpersonal trust), **preoccupied** (low self-esteem and high interpersonal trust), and **dismissing** (high self-esteem and low interpersonal trust).

- In addition to our parents, interactions with siblings and other relatives (grandparents, aunts, uncles, cousins) are important for the development of attitudes related to trust, affection, self-worth, competition, and humor.

- Friendships outside of the family often begin in childhood or adolescence and are initially based on proximity and parental friendships. With increasing maturity, it becomes possible to form close friendships that involve spending more time together, interacting in many different situations, providing mutual social support, and engaging in self-disclosure.

- Some gender-related differences tend to exist in the formation of friendships. Women tend to place a greater emphasis on intimacy (sharing emotions and experiences) whereas men tend to form friendships based on activities (playing sports or working on projects).

- Although *actual similarity* between individuals is an important factor in interpersonal attraction, research findings indicate that *perceived similarity* plays a more important role in the early stages of friendship, when individuals are first becoming acquainted.

Summary and Review

Interpersonal attraction refers to the evaluations we make of other people—the positive and negative attitudes we form about them. Human beings have a strong **need for affiliation**, the motivation to interact with other people in a cooperative way. The strength of this need differs among individuals and across situations, but even people who claim they do not have it show evidence that they do.

Positive and negative affect influence attraction both directly and indirectly. Direct effects occur when another person is responsible for arousing positive emotions or feelings. Indirect effects occur when the emotion comes from another source, and another person is simply associated with its presence. The indirect (associated) effects of emotion are applied by advertisers and political tacticians who understand that associating products and candidates with positive feelings can influence our purchasing and voting decisions.

The initial contact between two people is very often based on **proximity**—nearness to each other in physical space. Proximity leads to **repeated exposure effect** and that, in turn, often produces familiarity and increased attraction. Social networks make it possible for people to interact and form initial feelings of liking or disliking without physical proximity, but using social media sites has the potential for both positive and negative side effects.

Attraction toward others is often strongly influenced by their observable characteristics, especially their **physical attractiveness**. Research also offers support for the "love is blind" suggestion: Partners in romantic relationships tend to perceive each other as more attractive than people outside the relationships. In addition to physical attractiveness, other observable characteristics that influence interpersonal evaluations include physique (body build), weight, and even the color red. Because we often assume that "what is beautiful is good," we may project positive interpersonal traits onto people we find attractive.

One of the many factors determining attraction toward another person is similarity to that individual in terms of the way we think and feel (**attitude similarity**); our beliefs, values, and interests; and many other similarities—even trivial ones such as the same first letter in a name. The **similarity–dissimilarity effect**, when people respond positively to those who are similar to them and negatively to those who are dissimilar, is a consistent predictor of attraction. The larger the **proportion of similarity**, the greater the attraction. Evidence also supports the **matching hypothesis**—the view that we tend to choose romantic partners who are similar to ourselves in terms of physical attractiveness, even though we might prefer to have more attractive ones.

Theoretical perspectives, such as the **balance theory** and the **social comparison theory**, offer explanations for the powerful effects of similarity on attraction. Other factors that influence how much we like or dislike others are their **social skills**, how much they like us, and certain aspects of

their personality—for instance, **narcissism**. Of the "big five" broad aspects of personality, people high in agreeableness and extraversion receive higher ratings of interpersonal attractiveness. However, the traits we desire in other people can vary depending on the type of relationship, the stage (or length) of the relationship, and our gender.

Love is a combination of emotions, cognitions, and behaviors that play a crucial role in close relationships. The reproductive success of our ancient ancestors was enhanced by not only by sexual attraction between males and females, but also by bonding between mates and between parents and their offspring. There are multiple components of love including **passion**, **intimacy**, and **decision/commitment**, as illustrated in Sternberg's **triangular model of love**. This framework for understanding love suggests that when these components are equally strong and balanced, the result is **consummate love**. Another type of love, **companionate love**, is based on friendship, mutual attraction, shared interests, respect, and concern for one another's welfare.

In romantic attraction, a person may experience an intense emotional response to another person called **passionate love**. However, if this love is unrealistic it may become **unrequited love**—when love is felt by one person for another who does not feel love in return. The traits we seek in a romantic partner are often influenced by gender preferences and by the future roles we expect our partner and our self to occupy. Two factors that can destroy romantic love are jealousy and infidelity (adultery). Jealousy is a powerful emotion often triggered by threats to our self-esteem—when we fear that someone we love or care about will desert us for a rival. Research findings indicate that powerful people, such as politicians or top executives, are more likely to engage in infidelity than less powerful people.

Our first relationships are within the family where we acquire an **attachment style** based on levels of self-esteem and **interpersonal trust** in the context of these relationships. These attachment styles (**secure, fearful-avoidant, preoccupied**, and **dismissing**) influence the nature of other relationships, thereby playing an important role in many life outcomes. In addition to our parents, interactions with siblings and other relatives (grandparents, aunts, uncles, and cousins) are important for the development of attitudes related to trust, affection, self-worth, competition, and humor.

Friendships outside the family begin in childhood or adolescence and are initially based simply on factors of proximity or parental friendships. Some gender-related differences tend to exist in the formation of friendships, and similarity is also a strong factor. Research findings indicate that perceived similarity plays a more important role than actual similarity when individuals are first becoming acquainted. Over time, it becomes possible to form **close friendships** that involve interacting in many different situations, providing mutual social support, and engaging in self-disclosure.

Chapter 8
Social Influence
Changing Others' Behavior

Chapter Overview

Learning Objectives

8.1 Describe the factors that influence conformity

8.2 Describe the six basic principles of compliance and how they function

8.3 Analyze the role of authority in inducing obedience

8.4 Describe several forms of unintentional social influence

Be honest: Do you ever text while driving? Statistics indicate that many people (especially young drivers) do. And if you text while driving, do you believe that it's safe—that you can handle it without any risk? If you think texting behind the wheel is safe, please think again: Evidence indicates that it is not. For instance, almost 25 percent of all traffic accidents in the United States involve texting while driving (or other forms of distraction) and more than 300,000 people are injured—many seriously—in these accidents. And consider this: Texting while driving is six times more likely to cause an accident than driving drunk! Recognizing the seriousness of this problem, many public service organizations have launched campaigns to increase awareness of the dangers of driving while texting, and it appears that these campaigns have been successful: Not only have they raised awareness of this problem, they have also encouraged state governments to adopt laws making it illegal to text while driving. And in those states, the number of accidents involving texting has in fact decreased. Ads emphasizing the dangers of texting behind the wheel have been very creative—and persuasive. For example, see the ad in Figure 8.1.

And now, a different story. In 2008, Bernie Madoff—a man who is perhaps the biggest swindler of all time—was arrested by federal authorities. Perhaps you have

Figure 8.1 Text While You Drive—If You Want to Die Young!

In recent years, campaigns have been launched to make drivers (especially young ones) aware of the dangers of texting while driving. Here is one ad that has been used for this purpose.

heard of him because he cheated hundreds of individuals, and even large charitable organizations, out of more than $65 billion. He did this by running a giant Ponzi scheme—a swindle in which investors are lured into pouring their money into a company that offers high rates of return—for example, 15 percent a year when government bonds are paying 2 percent. What happens then is this: The first investors do indeed receive these returns, but *not* because the person running the Ponzi scheme has made outstanding investments; rather, early investors are paid with money from *later* investors! In short, the people who invest initially do well, but those who invest later on—especially near the end of the swindle—lose everything as the scheme collapses. But how, you might wonder, could Bernie Madoff convince hundreds of people—many of whom were highly sophisticated about financial matters—to invest their money in his phony company? The answer is complex, but involves the fact that he used techniques that, together, made individuals almost desperate to invest! For instance, he made every new investor feel as though he was doing them a favor by taking their money. Also, he hinted that soon, no more funds would be accepted. And he relied on word of mouth—investors who received large profits told their friends and family about this "opportunity"—which led a growing number of people to want a piece of this financial "pie." The final result was the same as for all Ponzi schemes: Ultimately, there was not enough money from new investors to pay the previous ones, and the whole structure collapsed. Bernie Madoff was convicted of numerous crimes and sentenced to many years in prison. But he was not sorry for what he did; in fact he blamed investors for being stupid enough to fall for his swindle!

Why do we begin with these two seemingly unrelated stories? Simply to call your attention to the central role of **social influence**—efforts by one or more people to change the behavior, attitudes, or feelings of one or more others (Cialdini, 2000, 2006). As you'll see in this chapter, social influence is indeed a very powerful force—it often succeeds in changing the behavior of the people toward whom it is directed. The examples discussed earlier, however, call attention to another important point: Social influence, itself, is neither good nor bad. It can be used to manipulate others for selfish outcomes, as illustrated by Bernie Madoff, or to produce positive social effects, as in "don't text while driving" campaigns. Regardless of the goal of social influence, the methods used can vary greatly, ranging from convincing the target people that doing what the influencer wants is the "right" thing to do, to a wide range of tactics for convincing them to say "yes" to personal requests. Whatever the goals or methods used, though, social influence always involves efforts by one or more people to induce some kind of change in others. Efforts to change others' attitudes through persuasion was discussed in detail in Chapter 5, so here we will focus on social influence focused on changing others' behavior.

Specifically, we'll examine what social psychologists have learned about three major forms of influence. The first is **conformity**, which involves efforts to change others' behavior through norms about how to behave in a given situation. These **norms**—can be formal, as in speed limits, rules for playing games or informal, as in the general rule "Don't stare at people on an elevator."

A second kind of social influence involves efforts to change others' behavior through direct requests—a process known as **compliance** (or seeking compliance). Many techniques for getting the target people to say "Yes" exist, and we examine several of these (Cialdini, 2006; Sparrowe, Soetjipto, & Kraimer, 2006). Yet another form of social influence involves following direct orders or commands from others, a process known as **obedience**.

We'll also discuss what is, in some ways, the most intriguing form of social influence—influence that occurs when other people change our behavior without intending to do so (e.g., Fitzsimons & Bargh, 2003). We'll refer to such effects as **unintentional social influence**, and will describe several different forms in which it can occur.

8.1: Conformity: How Groups—and Norms—Influence Our Behavior

Objective **Describe the factors that influence conformity**

- *During an exam, another student's cell phone begins to ring loudly. What does this person do?*
- *You are driving on a street when you see and hear an ambulance approaching from behind. What do you do?*
- *In a supermarket, a new checkout line suddenly opens, right next to a checkout with a long line of shoppers. Who gets to go first in that new line?*

In each of these situations, the people involved could, potentially, behave in many different ways. But probably, you can predict with great certainty what most will do. The student with the loud cell phone will silence it quickly. When you hear an ambulance, you will pull over to the right and perhaps stop completely until it passes. The checkout line is a little trickier. People near the front of the long checkout line should get to be first in the new line—but this might not happen. Someone from the back of the long line might beat them to it. In contexts where norms are clearer, greater conformity by most people can be expected compared to contexts like this where norms are less clear about what action is the "correct" one.

The fact that we can predict others' behavior (and our own) with confidence in these and many other situations illustrates the powerful and general effects of pressures toward **conformity**—doing what we are *expected* to do in a given situation. Conformity, in other words, refers to pressures to behave in ways consistent with rules indicating how we should, or ought to, behave. These rules—whether subtle or obvious—are known as *social norms*, and they can exert powerful effects on our behavior. The uncertainty you might experience in the checkout line situation stems from the fact that the norms in that situation are not very clear: When a new checkout opens, should people in the front or the back of the line should go first?

In some instances, social norms are stated explicitly and are quite detailed. For instance, many governments function through written constitutions and laws; baseball and other games have very specific rules; and signs in many public places (e.g., along highways, in parks, at airports) describe expected behavior in considerable detail (e.g., *Speed Limit 60 mph; Keep Off the Grass; No Parking*). In other situations, norms may be rather implicit, and in fact, may have developed in a totally informal manner. For instance, we all recognize such unstated rules as "don't talk loudly on your cell phone in locations where this will intrude on other people," and "Try to look your best when going on a job interview." Regardless of whether social norms are explicit or implicit, formal or informal, though, one fact is clear: Most people follow them most of the time. For instance, virtually everyone regardless of personal political beliefs stands when the national anthem of their country is played at sports events or other public gatherings. Similarly, few people visit restaurants without leaving a tip for the server. In fact, so powerful is this informal social norm that most people leave a tip of around 15 percent or more regardless of the quality of the service they have received (Azar, 2007).

At first glance, this strong tendency toward conformity—toward going along with society's or a group's expectations about how we should behave in various situations—may seem objectionable. After all, it does place restrictions on personal freedom. Actually, though, there is a strong basis for so much conformity: Without it, we would quickly find ourselves facing utter chaos. Imagine what would happen outside movie theaters, stadiums, or at supermarket checkout counters if people did *not* obey the norm "Form a line and wait your turn." In some countries, this norm does not exist and instead it is "Push your way to the front," which could make people used to the "form a line" norm indignant. And consider the danger to both drivers and pedestrians if there were no clear and widely followed traffic regulations. In some countries these are lacking or routinely ignored. Basically, when people don't follow existing social norms, their actions are unpredictable—and sometimes, that can be dangerous (see Figure 8.2).

Another reason people conform is, simply, to "look good" to others—to indicate that they are "good citizens," and are following the rules—whatever these are in a specific time and place. But again, be honest: How much do *you* conform? Do you usually do what you are "supposed" to do, or do you, challenge the rules and follow your own desires? Whatever your answer, please see the following special section to learn what social psychologists have discovered about this issue.

Given the importance and frequency of conformity, it is surprising that it received relatively little attention in social psychology until the 1950s. At that time, Solomon Asch (1951), whose research on impression formation we considered in Chapter 3, carried out a series of experiments on conformity that yielded dramatic results.

8.1.1: Social Pressure: The Irresistible Force?

Suppose that just before an important math exam, you discover that your answer to a homework problem—a problem of the type that will be on the test—is different from that obtained by one of your friends. How would you react? Probably with some concern. Now imagine that you learn that a second person's answer, too, is different from yours. To make matters worse, it agrees with the answer reported by the first person. How would you feel now? The chances are good that your anxiety will increase. Next, you discover that a third person agrees with the other two. At this point, you know that you are in big trouble. Which answer should you accept? Yours or the one obtained by these three other people?

Life is filled with such dilemmas—instances in which we discover that our own judgments, actions, or conclusions are different from those reached by other people.

Figure 8.2 Conformity: It Makes Life More Predictable

When norms telling people how to behave don't exist—or are largely ignored—chaos can develop. Countries in which traffic regulations are taken lightly provide a clear illustration of this fact—and of why conformity can sometimes be very useful.

Figure 8.3 Asch's Line Judgment Task

Participants in Asch's research were asked to report their judgments on problems such as this one. Their task was to indicate which of the comparison lines (1, 2, or 3) best matched the standard line in length. To study conformity, he had participants make these judgments out loud, only after hearing the answers of several other people—all of whom were Asch's assistants. On certain critical trials the assistants all gave wrong answers. This exposed participants to strong pressures toward conformity.

Standard Line

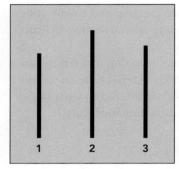

Comparison Lines

What do we do in such situations? Important insights into our behavior were provided by studies conducted by Solomon Asch (1951, 1955).

Asch created a compelling social dilemma for his participants whose task was ostensibly to simply respond to a series of perceptual problems such as the one in Figure 8.3. On each of the problems, participants were to indicate which of three comparison lines matched a standard line in length. Several other people (usually six to eight) were also present during the session, but unknown to the real participant, all were assistants of the experimenter. On certain occasions known as *critical trials* (12 out of the 18 problems) the accomplices offered answers that were clearly wrong: They unanimously chose the wrong line as a match for the standard line. Moreover, they stated their answers *before* the real participants responded. Thus, on these critical trials, the people in Asch's study faced precisely the type of dilemma described earlier. Should they go along with the other individuals present or stick to their own judgments? The judgments seemed to be very simple ones, so the fact that other people agreed on an answer different from the one the participants preferred was truly puzzling. Results were clear: A large majority of the participants in Asch's research chose conformity. Across several different studies, fully 76 percent of those tested went along with the group's false answers at least once; and overall, they voiced agreement with these errors 37 percent of the time. In contrast, only 5 percent of the participants in a control group, who responded to the same problems alone, made such errors.

Of course, there were large individual differences in this respect. Almost 25 percent of the participants *never* yielded to the group pressure. (We'll have more to say about such people soon.) At the other extreme, some individuals went along with the majority nearly all the time. When Asch questioned them, some of these people stated: "I am wrong, they are right"; they had little confidence in their own judgments. Most, however, said they felt that the other people present were suffering from an optical illusion or were merely sheep following the responses of the first person. Yet, when it was their turn, these people, too, went along with the group. They knew that the others were wrong (or at least, *probably* wrong), but they couldn't bring themselves to publicly disagree with them.

In further studies, Asch (1959, 1956) investigated the effects of shattering the group's unanimity by having one of the accomplices break with the others. In one study, this person gave the correct answer, becoming an "ally" of the real participant; in another study, he chose an answer in between the one given by the group and the correct one; and in a third, he chose the answer that was even more incorrect than that chosen by the majority. In the latter two conditions, in other words, he broke from the group but still disagreed with the real participant. Results indicated that conformity was reduced under all three conditions. However, somewhat surprisingly, this reduction was greatest when the dissenting assistant expressed views even more extreme (and wrong) than the majority. Together, these findings suggest that it is the unanimity of the group that is crucial; once it is broken, no matter how, resisting group pressure becomes much easier.

There's one more aspect of Asch's research that is important to mention. In later studies, he repeated his basic procedure, but with one important change: Instead of stating their answers out loud, participants wrote them down on a piece of paper. (See special feature **"What Research Tells Us About . . . How Much We Really Conform"**)

What Research Tells Us About...

How Much We Really Conform

For many of us, the term "conformity" has a negative sound: Others may go along with the crowd but *we* don't like to think of ourselves as doing so. We are independent spirits and ignore norms whenever we wish. But is this true? Despite independence being a strong American value (Markus & Kitayama, 1991), evidence gathered by social psychologists suggests that perhaps, we think we are more independent than we really are.

In fact, conformity is a fact of social life. We tend to wear the same styles of clothing as our friends, listen to the same kinds of music, see the same movies, read the same books and visit many of the same websites on the internet. Why? Because overall, we feel much more comfortable when we are similar to others we value than when we are different from them. So, contrary to our beliefs about ourselves, we often conform to a greater degree than we think. In other words, although we tend to see ourselves as standing out from crowd, this may be a self-enhancing illusion. Evidence pointing to this conclusion is provided by many classic experiments, several of which we'll review. In these studies, people who are exposed to the actions of others (and the implicit norms these establish) often do go along with these rules—even when they deny doing so.

Evidence for the fact that people believe they are less susceptible to conformity pressure than other people is provided by research conducted by Pronin, Berger, and Molouki (2007). They reasoned that people underestimate the impact of social influence on their own actions because in trying to understand these actions, people tend to focus on internal information rather than on their overt actions. As in the *actor–observer* difference (discussed in Chapter 3), we each know much more about our own thoughts and feelings than we do about the thoughts and feelings of others, so when we estimate how much oneself and others are influenced by conformity pressure, we tend to conclude that it is less important in shaping *our* actions than those of other people. For instance, we "know" that we choose to dress in popular styles because we like them—not because others are wearing them. When making the same judgment about other people, though, we assume that they are blindly following fashion, without necessarily liking it. Pronin and colleagues call this the **introspection illusion**, to refer to the fact that often, conformity occurs nonconsciously, and so escapes our introspection (or notice).

To test this reasoning, they conducted several studies. In one, participants read a series of recommendations about student life and learned that these recommendations had been endorsed or not endorsed by a group of fellow students. They then voted on each proposal themselves, indicating whether they supported it or did not support it. This provided a measure of their conformity to the panel's recommendations. Students then rated the extent to which they believed the panel's recommendations had influenced their own behavior, and also the behavior (i.e., voting) of another student, whose answers they

were shown. The stranger agreed with the panel on precisely the same number of recommendations as did the students, so they actually showed equal conformity. But when they rated how much they and the other person had conformed, results were clear: Participants in the study rated the other person as being more influenced than they themselves were (see Figure 8.4). In contrast, they viewed themselves as being more influenced than the other person by the contents of each proposal rather than the panel's recommendations.

In short, it appears that although we show conformity in many contexts—and for good reason—we underestimate the extent to which others' actions influence us. We should add that this is true particularly in individualistic cultures such as the United States; in such cultures, people prefer to think of themselves as unique people who set their own course through life. But in more collectivist societies, such as Japan, conforming has no negative implications attached to it, and as a result, people may be more willing to admit that they conform, because doing so is seen as a good thing.

Figure 8.4 The Illusion That We Are Less Influenced by Conformity Than Others

Participants reported that they were less influenced by conformity to a group's judgments than was another person (a stranger). In fact, they actually conformed as much as this person did—whose ratings on various issues were designed to conform precisely the same as each participant. Still, despite this objective fact, they perceived the other person as showing more conformity.

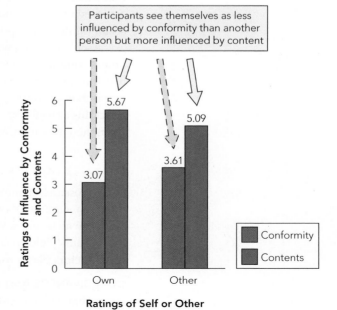

As you might guess, conformity dropped sharply because the participants didn't have to display the fact that they disagreed to the other people present. This finding points to the importance of distinguishing between *public conformity*—doing or saying what others around us say or do, and *private acceptance*—actually coming to feel or think as others do. Often, it appears, we follow social norms overtly, but don't actually change our private views (Maass & Clark, 1984). This distinction between public conformity and private acceptance is an important one, and we'll refer to it at several points in this book.

8.1.2: How Social Norms Emerge

A clear illustration of private acceptance of social influence was provided many years ago by another founder of social psychology—Muzafer Sherif (1937). Sherif was interested in several questions, but among these, two were most important: (1) How do norms develop in social groups? (2) How strong is their influence on behavior once those norms emerge? To examine these issues, he used a very interesting situation. When placed in completely dark room and exposed to a single, stationary point of light, most people perceive the light as moving about. This is because in the dark room, there are no clear cues to distance or location. The perceived movement of the point of light is known as the autokinetic phenomenon.

Sherif (1937) realized that he could use this situation to study the emergence of social norms. This is so because there is considerable ambiguity about how much the light is moving and different people perceive it as moving different distances. Thus, when placed in this setting with several others and asked to report how much they perceive the light to be moving, they influence one another and soon converge on a particular amount of movement; that agreement, in a sense, constitutes a group norm. If the same individuals are then placed in the situation alone, they continue to give estimates of the light's movement consistent with the group norm, so clearly, the effect of such norms once formed can persist. This suggests that these effects reflect changes in what participants actually believe—*private acceptance* or commitment; after all, they continue to be influenced by the group norm even if they are no longer in the group!

Sherif's findings help explain why social norms develop in many situations—especially ambiguous ones. We have a strong desire to be "correct"—to behave in an appropriate manner—and behaving consistent with social norms help us attain that goal. This is one key foundation of social influence; another is the desire to be accepted by others and liked by them. Together, these two factors virtually assure that social influence is a powerful force—one that can often strongly affect our behavior.

Asch's research was the catalyst for much research in social psychology, as many others sought to determine the processes underlying conformity and to identify factors that influence it (e.g., Crutchfield, 1955; Deutsch & Gerard, 1955). Indeed, such research is continuing today, and is adding to our understanding of the factors that affect this crucial form of social influence (e.g., Bond & Smith, 1996; Lonnqvist, Leikas, Paunonen, Nissinen, & Verkasalo, 2006).

8.1.3: Factors Affecting Conformity

Asch's research demonstrated the existence of powerful pressures toward conformity, but even a moment's reflection suggests that conformity does not occur to the same degree in all settings. Why? In other words, what factors determine the extent to which individuals yield to conformity pressure or resist it? Research findings suggest that many factors play a role; here, we'll examine those that appear to be most important.

COHESIVENESS AND CONFORMITY: BEING INFLUENCED BY THOSE WE LIKE One factor that strongly influences our tendency to conform—to go along with whatever norms are operating in a given situation—is **cohesiveness**—the extent to which we are attracted to a particular social group and want to belong to it (Turner, 1991). The greater cohesiveness is the more we tend to follow the norms (i.e., rules) of the group. This is hardly surprising: The more we value being a member of a group and want to be accepted by the other members, the more we want to avoid doing anything that will separate us from them. So, prestigious fraternities and sororities can often extract very high levels of conformity from would-be members who are very eager to join these highly selective groups. Similarly, acting and looking like others is often a good way to win their approval. So, in very basic terms, the more we like other people and want to belong to the same group as they do, and the more we are uncertain of winning their acceptance, the more we tend to conform (Crandall, 1988; Latané & L'Herrou, 1996; Noel, Wann, & Branscombe, 1995). In other words, cohesiveness and the desire to be accepted can be viewed as factors that intensify the tendency to conform (see Figure 8.5).

CONFORMITY AND GROUP SIZE: WHY MORE EXERTS GREATER SOCIAL PRESSURE Another factor that produces conformity is the size of the group that is exerting influence. Asch (1956) and other early researchers (Gerard, Wilhelmy, & Conolley, 1968) found that conformity increases with group size, but only up to about three or four members; beyond that point, it appears to level off. However, later research has found that conformity tends to increase with group size up to eight group members and beyond (e.g., Bond & Smith, 1996). In short, the larger the group—the greater the number of people who behave in some specific way—the greater our tendency to conform, and "do as they do."

CONFORMITY AND STATUS WITHIN A GROUP In many contexts, group members differ with respect to status, and one important source of such differences is seniority: Senior members feel less pressure to conform. Junior members of the group, in contrast, experience strong pressures to go along; after all, their position is not assured and one way of gaining status is to conform to the group's established norms or rules. Evidence for such effects has been reported by Jetten, Hornsey, and Adarves-Yorno (2006). These researchers found that, for instance, seniors at a university rated themselves lower in a measure of conformity (e.g., "I am easily influenced by other students") than sophomores and juniors. Moreover, senior (high-status) persons viewed others as more conforming than themselves. Indeed, the researchers found similar effects among social psychology professors: Those who were junior (they had few years as a professor) reported a stronger tendency to conform than those who were more senior. Together, these studies suggest that although pressures to conform are strong in many settings, high status gives people an "out"—while others have to conform, *they* do not.

Figure 8.5 Cohesiveness: A Magnifier of Conformity Pressure

The more strongly we are attracted to a group to which we belong or would like to belong, the more likely we are to conform to the norms of this group, especially if we feel less uncertain about our acceptance by the group. For instance, "pledges" hoping to join popular sororities or fraternities tend to show high levels of conformity to the norms of these groups.

DESCRIPTIVE AND INJUNCTIVE SOCIAL NORMS: HOW NORMS AFFECT BEHAVIOR

Social norms, as we have already seen, can be formal or informal in nature—as different as rules printed on large signs and informal guidelines such as "Don't leave your shopping cart in the middle of the parking lot outside a supermarket." This is not the only way in which norms differ, however. Another important distinction is that between **descriptive norms** and **injunctive norms** (Cialdini, Kallgren, & Reno, 1991; Reno, Cialdini, & Kallgren, 1993). Descriptive norms are ones that simply describe what most people do in a given situation. They influence behavior by informing us about what is generally seen as effective or appropriate in that situation. In contrast, injunctive norms specify how people *ought* to be behave—what is approved or disapproved behavior in a given situation. For instance, there is a strong injunctive norm against cheating on exams—such behavior is considered to be ethically wrong. The fact that some students disobey this norm does not change the moral expectation that they should obey it.

Both kinds of norms can exert strong effects upon our behavior (e.g., Brown, 1998). But *when*, precisely, are such norms most likely to be obeyed? One answer is provided by **normative focus theory** (Cialdini, Reno, & Kallgren, 1990). This theory suggests that norms will influence behavior only to the extent that they are *salient* (i.e., relevant, significant) to the people involved at the time the behavior occurs. In other words, people will obey injunctive norms only when they think about them and see them as applying to themselves and their actions. This prediction has been verified in many different studies (Reno, Cialdini, & Kallgren, 1993; Kallgren, Reno, & Cialdini, 2000), so it seems to be a general principle that even injunctive norms—which can be very powerful—influence our actions mainly when we recognize them and believe that they apply to us personally. This is one reason why people sometimes ignore even clear and strong injunctive norms. One example of ignoring injunctive norms is provided by people who own very expensive cars and park them so that they take up two spots. Clearly, by doing so, they are violating the strong injunctive norm indicating that each driver should occupy only one spot (see Figure 8.6).

Figure 8.6 Ignoring Injunctive Norms: Doing What We Want Instead of What We Are Supposed to Do

People who own very expensive cars often try to protect them by taking up two parking spots. This violates the strong injunctive norm indicating that we should park between the lines of a single spot.

8.1.4: Social Foundations of Conformity: Why We Often Choose to "Go Along"

As we have just seen, several factors determine whether and to what extent conformity occurs. Yet, this does not alter the essential point: Conformity is a basic fact of social life. Most people conform to the norms of their groups most of the time. Why is this so? Why do people often choose to go along with these social rules instead of resisting them? The answer seems to involve two powerful motives possessed by all human beings: the desire to be liked or accepted by others and the desire to be right—to have accurate understanding of the social world (Deutsch & Gerard, 1955; Insko, 1985)—plus cognitive processes that lead us to view conformity as fully justified after it has occurred (e.g., Buehler & Griffin, 1994).

NORMATIVE SOCIAL INFLUENCE: THE DESIRE TO BE LIKED   How can we get others to like us? This is one of the eternal puzzles of social life and many tactics can prove effective in this regard. One of the most successful of these is to appear to be as similar to others as possible. From our earliest days, we learn that agreeing with the people around us, and behaving as they do, causes them to like us. Parents, teachers, friends, and others heap praise and approval on us for showing such similarity (recall our discussion of attitude formation in Chapter 5). One important reason we conform, therefore, is this: We have learned that doing so can help us win the approval and acceptance we crave. This source of conformity is known as **normative social influence**, since it involves altering our behavior to meet others' expectations.

THE DESIRE TO BE RIGHT: INFORMATIONAL SOCIAL INFLUENCE   If you want to know your weight, you can step onto a scale. If you want to know the dimensions of a room, you can measure them directly. But how can you establish the accuracy of your own political or social views, or decide which hairstyle suits you best? There are no simple physical tests or measuring devices for answering these questions. Yet we want to be correct about such matters, too. The solution to this dilemma is obvious: To answer such questions, we refer to other people. We use their opinions and actions as guides for our own. Such reliance on others, in turn, is often a powerful source of the tendency to conform. Other people's actions and opinions define social reality for us, and we use them as a guide for our own actions and opinions. This basis for conformity is known as **informational social influence**, since it is based on our tendency to depend on others as a source of information about many aspects of the social world.

Research evidence suggests that because our motivation to be correct or accurate is very strong, informational social influence is a powerful source of conformity. However, as you might expect, this is more likely to be true in situations where we are highly uncertain about what is "correct" or "accurate" than in situations where we have more confidence in our own ability to make such decisions (Baron, Vandello, & Brunsman, 1996). Of course, this depends on "who we are" and whose norms are salient. We won't think out-groups are "correct" as much as in-groups (Turner, 1991).

8.1.5: The Downside of Conformity

Earlier, we noted that the tendency to conform—to obey social norms—can produce positive effects. The fact that most people comply with most social norms most of the time introduces a large measure of predictability into social relations: We know how we and others are expected to behave, and can proceed on the assumption that these expectations will be met. Other motorists will drive on the correct side of the street (whatever that is in one's own society), and stop for red lights; people waiting for service in a store will form a line and wait their turn. But as we have already noted, there is definitely a downside to conformity, too. In fact, recent research by social psychologists suggests that pressures to conform, and our tendency to surrender to such pressures, can sometimes result in very harmful effects. In fact, we'll now discuss what is perhaps the most dramatic research illustrating such effects—a famous study by Philip Zimbardo, which showed, among other things, the powerful impact of norms concerning various social roles.

Do good people ever do bad things? The answer, of course, is "Yes." History is filled with atrocities performed by people who, most of the time, were good neighbors, parents, and friends, and who often showed kindness and concern for others in their daily lives. Yet, under some conditions, they seem to surrender all these positive qualities and engage in actions that most of us would find inexcusable. The key question for social psychologists is: Why? What makes good people turn bad—at least sometimes? There is no single answer, and later in this chapter, we'll discuss *obedience*—a form of social influence that sometimes induces good people to do bad things. But now, we'll focus on the answer provided by one very famous study in social psychology, Zimbardo's prison study. Here's how this famous study took place.

> Imagine that one Sunday afternoon you hear a loud knock on your door. When you go to answer, you find yourself face to face with several police officers. Without any explanation, they arrest you and take you downtown to be photographed, fingerprinted, and "booked." (Participants did know that they had volunteered to take part in social psychological research, but still, these events were still surprising for many of them.) Next, you are blindfolded and driven to a prison whose location you can only guess. Once there, you are stripped of all your clothes and are forced to dress in an uncomfortable, loose-fitting gown and a tight nylon cap. All of your personal possessions are removed and you are given an I.D. number instead of a name. Then you are locked in an empty cell containing only the bare necessities. All guards in the prison wear identical uniforms and reflecting sunglasses. And they carry clubs, whistles, and other signs of their authority.
>
> As a prisoner, you are expected to obey a long set of rules under threat of severe punishment. You must remain silent during rest periods and after lights are turned out each night. You must address other prisoners only by their I.D. numbers and your guards as "Mr. Correctional Officer." And you must ask their permission to do anything—from reading and writing to going to the bathroom.

How would you react to such conditions? Would you obey? Rebel? Become angry? Depressed? Resentful? And what if you were a guard instead of a prisoner? Would you treat prisoners with respect or would you seek to humiliate them if you were told to do so? These are the questions Zimbardo and his colleagues investigated in the famous Stanford Prison Study. It was conducted in the basement of the Stanford University psychology building, and all guards and prisoners were paid volunteers. In fact, whether a volunteer became a guard or a prisoner was determined at random.

The main purpose of the study was to determine whether participants would come to behave like real guards and real prisoners—whether they would, in a sense, conform to the norms established for these respective roles. The answer was clear: They did. The prisoners were rebellious at first, but then became increasingly passive and depressed. And the guards grew increasingly brutal and sadistic. They harassed the prisoners, forced them to make fun of one another, and assigned them to difficult, senseless tasks. The guards were encouraged to dehumanize the prisoners, thereby coming to perceive them as inferior to themselves. In fact, these changes in behavior were so dramatic that it was necessary to stop the study after only 6 days; initial plans called for it to last 2 weeks.

So, what do we learn from this striking and thought-provoking research? Philip Zimbardo, who planned the research and served as "Prison Warden," contends that it drives home a key point about human behavior: It is the *situations* in which people find themselves—not their personal traits—that largely determine their behavior. Yes, people do differ in many ways; but place them in a powerful situation like this one, and such differences tend to disappear. Zimbardo (2007) suggests that it is this tendency to yield to situational pressures—including conformity to role-based norms—that is responsible for much evil behavior. As he puts it: " . . . we all like to think that the line between good and evil is impermeable—that people who do terrible things . . . are on the other side of the line—and we could never get over there . . . . My work began by saying no, that line is permeable. The reason some people are on the good side of the line is that they've never been fully tested . . . ." In other words, according to Zimbardo, placed in the wrong kind of situation, virtually all of us—even those who have always been good, upstanding citizens—might commit atrocities.

Zimbardo leaves some room for personal heroism: He recognizes that some people seem able to resist even powerful situational or conformity pressures (and we'll soon present research that explains why). Indeed, there are many historical examples of people who have resisted under the most difficult circumstances (e.g., Nelson Mandela, see Haslam & Reicher, 2012). But most of us, Zimbardo contends, cannot—situations are often stronger than our ability to resist and remain true to our values. As we'll soon see, though, several factors can reduce the "press" of the situation on us, allowing us to resist the pressure to conform (e.g., Galinsky, Magee, Gruenfeld, Whitson, & Liljenquist, 2008). Evidence that is provided by research involving another dramatic prison study (this time conducted jointly by social psychologists and the BBC; Reicher & Haslam, 2006). In this research, volunteers were, again, placed in a kind of "prison" and were randomly assigned to be either guards or prisoners. And once more, the guards were given means to enforce their authority over the prisoners (e.g., they could place disobedient prisoners in an isolation cell as punishment). Overall, then, although the BBC prison study was similar in many respects to Zimbardo's famous study, important differences did exist.

For instance, in the Reicher and Haslam study it was explained to the guards and prisoners that they had been chosen for these roles on the basis of extensive psychological tests (all volunteers were actually assessed by trained psychologists prior to their selection as participants in the study). Further, it was explained that in the initial days of the study the guards could "promote" prisoners they selected to become guards, and in fact, one prisoner *was* promoted to become a guard. After this event, however, it was made clear that guards would remain guards and prisoners would remain prisoners, so no chance of further changes existed. Then, 3 days later, both guards and prisoners were told that careful observations indicated that in fact, no differences existed between the two groups. However, since it would be impractical to change the roles now, they would remain unchanged for the rest of the study. In a sense, this removed any legitimacy of assignments to these roles.

These differences turned out to have dramatic effects on the results. In contrast to the findings of the Stanford Prison Study, guards and prisoners in the BBC research did *not* passively accept their roles. Rather, the guards actually rejected their power over the prisoners while the prisoners, in contrast, identified closely with one another and took action to gain equal power. They succeeded, and for a time, the "prison" adopted a democratic structure in which guards and prisoners had relatively equal rights (see Figure 8.7). When this new structure seemed to fail, however, both groups moved toward acceptance of a rigidly authoritarian approach in which the prisoners surrendered almost totally and no longer offered any resistance to their inequality.

These findings point to an important conclusion: Social norms and the social structure from which they arise do not necessarily produce acceptance of inequalities. On the contrary, whether individuals go along with roles (and norms) that impose inequality depends on the extent to which the people involved identify with these roles; if their identification with the existing structure is low, they may resist and seek social

Figure 8.7 Conformity: Sometimes, It Leads Good People to Do Evil Things—But Not Always!

In a recent study that replicated Zimbardo's famous Stanford prison experiment, volunteers were also placed in a simulated "prison" and played the roles of prisoners and guards. Initially, they showed behavior consistent with these roles, but soon the guards rejected the norms of their assigned roles, and the prisoners formed a cohesive collective identity and rebelled against the existing power structure.

change rather than simply resign themselves to their disadvantaged fate. As noted by one social psychologist (Turner, 2006), this is why social change occurs: People decide to challenge an existing social structure rather than accept it, as happened in the 1950s and 1960s in the civil rights movement in the United States, the women's movement of the 1970s and 1980s, and the "Arab Spring" which started in 2010, and continued till 2012. Large numbers of people challenged the "status quo," and the result was major social change.

In sum, although the power of social norms and social roles to induce conformity is strong, as we'll note in a later discussion of obedience, it is not invincible. Sometimes, under the right conditions, individuals challenge existing social orders and the rules they impose, and actively seek social change. As Turner (2006, p. 45) puts it, social psychologists realize that social structures are not set in stone; on the contrary, " . . . the future is created in the social present" and change as well as stability is a common aspect of the social side of life.

8.1.6: Reasons for Nonconformity: Why We Sometimes Choose "Not to Go Along"

Our discussion so far may have left you with the impression that pressures toward conformity are so strong that they are all but impossible to resist. But as Reicher and Haslam's (2006) BBC prison study illustrated, this is simply not the case. Individuals—or groups of individuals—*do* sometimes resist conformity pressure. This was certainly true in Asch's research where, as you may recall, most of the participants yielded to social pressure, but only part of the time. On many occasions, they stuck to their guns even in the face of a unanimous majority that disagreed with them. If you want other illustrations of resistance to conformity pressures, just look around you: You will find that while most people adhere to social norms most of the time, some do not. And most people do not go along with *all* social norms; rather, they pick and choose, conforming to most but rejecting at least a few. For instance, some people choose to hold and express unpopular political or social views, and continue to do so even in the face of strong pressure to conform. So, conformity pressures are not irresistible. What accounts for our ability to resist them? Many factors play a role, but we'll focus on those identified in recent research as ones that seem to tip the balance away from conformity and toward independent thought and action.

THE ACTOR–OBSERVER EFFECT REVISITED: ITS ROLE IN RESISTING PRESSURES TO CONFORM   Recall the actor–observer effect discussed in Chapter 3. It refers to the fact that we tend to attribute our own behavior to external causes (i.e., the situation we face), but the actions of others to internal causes, such as their personality. Is this effect relevant to conformity? Research by Dong, Dai, and Wyer (2014) suggests that it is. These researchers studied **synchronous behavior**—behavior in which individuals match their actions to those of others. For instance, members of a choir sing in unison, members of an orchestra may all play the same notes, and soldiers march in step with one another (see Figure 8.8). Such behavior may stem from feelings of connectedness to a group—the people involved match their actions to others in the group to which they belong. Doing so may then induce stronger tendencies to conform.

The actor–observer effect enters the picture in the following way: We may either be engaged in synchronous behavior ourselves, or simply observe others doing it. As actors, we experience the pressures to conform arising from group membership, but as observers, we do not, and may, instead become sensitive to restrictions that synchronous behavior exerts on our personal freedom. Dong et al. (2014) reason further that as a result, observers may experience **reactance**—the feeling that our personal freedom is being restricted, and that we should resist strong pressure to conform to maintain our individuality. In other words, whether we choose to "conform" in situations requiring synchronous behavior, or resist such pressures depends, in part, on whether we are participating in such actions or merely observing them. In five studies, Dong and colleagues found evidence that actors are more likely to conform when they are focused on the goals they hope to achieve (e.g., giving a great performance when they are part of a choir or orchestra) while observers may be less aware of these goals, and so focus on the freedom of action given up by the people they watch, who are behaving in the precisely the same manner. This may induce strong feelings of reactance and the belief in observers that—I would never do that—"I want to be an

Figure 8.8 Reactions to Synchronous Behavior: Different for Actors and Observers

Recent research indicates that in some settings, individuals experience strong pressures to do exactly what others are doing. However people who observe such actions do not experience such pressures.

individual, not part of a faceless, conforming group." As a result, their tendency to conform in this similar situation would be reduced. So in a sense, observing conforming behavior by others helps people who observe such behavior to resist the pressure to "go along."

POWER AS A SHIELD AGAINST CONFORMITY Power . . . the very word conjures up images of people who are in charge—political leaders, generals, heads of corporations. Such people often seem to enjoy more freedoms than the rest of us: *They* make the rules and they can shape situations rather than be molded by them. Does this also make them immune—or at least resistant—to social influence? Several social psychologists have suggested that it does. For instance, Keltner, Gruenfeld, and Anderson (2003) have noted that the restrictions that often influence the thought, expression, and behavior of most people do not seem to apply to the powerful. There are several reasons why this might be so.

First, powerful people are less dependent on others for obtaining social resources. As a result, they may not pay much attention to threats from others or efforts to constrain their actions in some way. Second, they may be less likely to take the perspective of other people (Galinsky, Magee, Inesi, & Gruenfeld, 2006), and so be less influenced by them. Instead, their thoughts and actions are more directly shaped by their own internal states; in other words, there might be a closer correspondence between their traits and preferences and what they think or do than is true for most people. Overall, then, situational information might have less influence on the attitudes, intentions, and actions of powerful people.

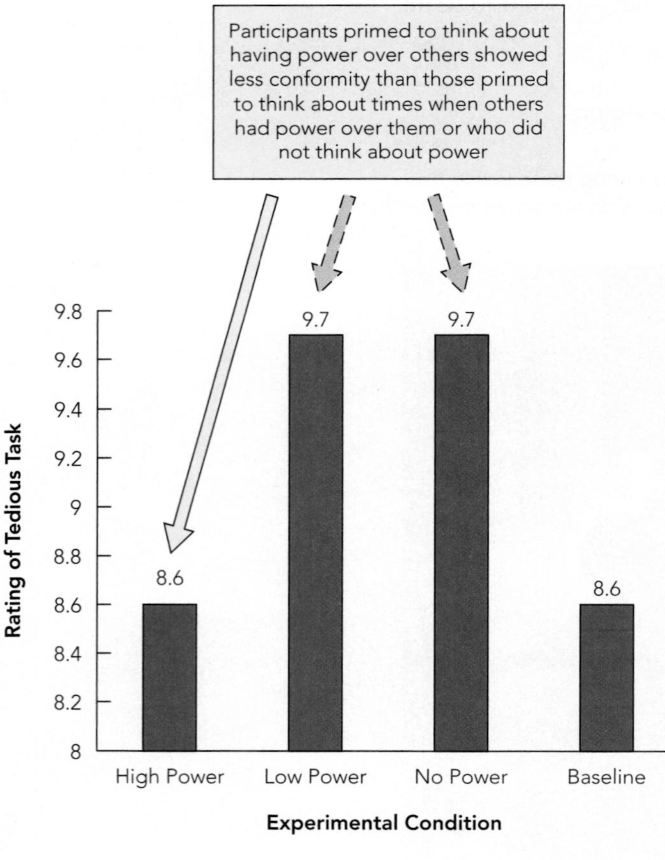

Research conducted by Galinsky et al. (2008) indicates that people who possessed power, or were merely primed to think about it, were in fact less likely to show conformity to the actions or judgments of others than people lower in power. In one study, for instance, participants were asked to think either about a situation in which they had power over someone (high power) or a situation in which someone else had power over *them* (low power). In a third condition they did not think about power. Following these conditions, they performed a tedious word construction task—one that most people do not find interesting or enjoyable. Then, they were asked to rate this task. Before doing so, however, they learned that 10 other students rated it very high on both dimensions. (In a control, baseline condition, they did not receive this information.)

It was predicted that the people who were primed to think about a time when they had power over others would rate the task less favorably than those who thought about times when others had power over them—in other words, their feelings of power would affect the extent to which they were influenced by the judgments of other people. In contrast, those not asked to think about power would be influenced by others' opinions and therefore rate the task more favorably. As you can see from Figure 8.9, this is precisely what happened. People in the high power group did rate the task as less enjoyable and interesting than those in the low power group. In fact,

Figure 8.9 Power Reduces Conformity

Participants asked to remember times when they had power over others (high power) were less influenced by ratings of a tedious task supposedly provided by other students than participants who thought about times when others had power over them (low power) or who did not think about power. (In the baseline conditions, participants didn't think about power.)

Participants primed to think about having power over others showed less conformity than those primed to think about times when others had power over them or who did not think about power they rated it as low as those who received no bogus ratings supposedly provided by other students. In sum, power seems to free those who possess it from situational control, and to make them relatively resistant to the conformity pressures that strongly influence most of us much of the time. And in fact, we sometimes admire powerful people who ignore the rules and view their independent actions as further proof that they are somehow deserving of the power they possess.

THE DESIRE TO BE UNIQUE AND NONCONFORMITY Most people believe that they conform less than others, as the research of Pronin and colleagues (2007) showed. In a sense, this is far from surprising, because we all want to believe that we are unique individuals (see Snyder & Fromkin, 1980). Yes, we may generally dress, speak, and act like others most of the time, but in some respects, we still want to be unique. Could this desire be a factor in resisting conformity pressure? Two social psychologists—Imhoff and Erb (2009)—have obtained evidence indicating that, as other researchers suggested, it is. They reasoned that people have a need for uniqueness and that when it is threatened (when they feel their uniqueness is at risk)—they will actively resist conformity pressures to restore their sense of uniqueness.

To test this prediction, participants completed a questionnaire that, supposedly, assessed several key personality traits. They then either provided feedback indicating either that the participant was "exactly average" on these traits, or offered no feedback. The first group, of course, experienced a threat to their uniqueness, so they were expected to be motivated to resist pressures to conform. Conformity was measured in terms of the extent to which they went along with what were supposedly majority opinions about the desirability of a nearby lake as a good spot for a vacation. For half of the participants, a majority of other people endorsed the lake, while for the remainder, they rated it lower. What would participants now do? If raising their uniqueness motivation resulted in less conformity, those who had learned they were "just average" on key personality traits would be less likely to go along with the majority than those who had not received this bogus information. Results shown in Figure 8.10 supported this prediction. When the motive to be somewhat unique was threatened, individuals did respond by showing nonconformity—they refused to endorse the views supported by a majority of other people.

THE BENEFITS OF NONCONFORMING Imagine that you go to a very expensive and exclusive store. How would you dress? Many people would assume that they should look their best because it is what shoppers in such stores are *supposed* to do. But imagine that you decided to dress casually— wear jeans and sneakers. What would happen? Would the clerks in the store ignore you or even be rude? Or would they perceive your casual dress as a sign of high status—that you are so successful or even famous you don't have to conform—norms are for others, not for you. Research by Bellezza, Gino, and Keinan (2014) predicted that the second outcome would occur— people who dress casually would be perceived more favorably than those who conform.

To test this reasoning, they conducted several studies. In one, salespersons in these stores (e.g., Armani, Burberry, Christian Dior) were asked to imagine that a shopper entered dressed either very casually—in gym clothes—or dressed in a much more elegant clothes; the salespersons then rated the status of these shoppers. As the researchers predicted, those who were casually dressed were seen as higher status

Figure 8.10 Asserting Uniqueness— One Way of Resisting Pressures to Conform

Research findings indicate that in order to resist strong pressure to conform people sometimes act in ways that emphasize their own uniqueness.

than those who were dressed in a way shoppers were expected to dress. In another study, a professor was described to students as dressing informally—in a T-shirt—or more formally, in a coat and tie. As expected, the students rated the casually dressed professor as higher in status. In a third study, they had students rated a professor who actually taught a class on negotiations dress dressed in a professional manner, or wearing red sneakers. Once again the "rebel" professor was rated higher in status. They explain these findings, as shown in Figure 8.11, as follows: Nonconforming individuals are seen as high in personal autonomy—they "do their own thing"—while those who conform are seen as lower in autonomy, and these perceptions translate into perceiving the nonconformists as higher in status.

In sum, many factors contribute to nonconformity, so its occurrence is definitely not an accident; nor does it always stem from Shakespeare's advice "To thine own self be true." Just as conformity stems from a variety of causes and motives, so too does independence. Therefore, while conformity is often a safe, convenient, and useful approach to social life, there is lots of room for independence and individuality, too.

8.1.7: Minority Influence: Does the Majority Always Rule?

As we noted earlier, individuals can, and often do, resist group pressure. Lone dissenters or small minorities can dig in their heels and refuse to go along. Yet there is more going on in such situations than just resistance; in addition, there are instances in which people—minorities within the larger group—actually turn the tables on the majority and *exert* rather than merely *receive* social influence. History provides many examples of such events. Giants of science, such as Galileo, Pasteur, and Freud, faced virtually unanimous majorities who initially rejected their views. Yet, over time, they overcame such resistance and won widespread acceptance for their theories.

More recent examples of minorities influencing majorities are provided by the successes of environmentalists who are very concerned about climate change. Initially, such people were viewed as holding strange ideas and being worried about nothing. Gradually, however, they succeeded in changing the attitudes of the majority so that today, many of their views are widely accepted. As a result, views regarding burning fossil fuels such as coal for

Figure 8.11 Failing to Conform Sometimes Is Equal to Higher Status

A series of intriguing studies found that when people don't conform, they are viewed as having high status. The reason is that people who don't conform are seen as having greater autonomy, allowing them to behave however they choose in almost any situation.

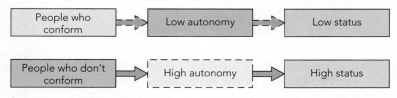

energy have become more negative, and positive views about hybrid cars (ones that run partly on gas and partly on electricity, see Figure 8.12) have become widespread.

But when, precisely, do minorities succeed in influencing majorities? Research findings suggest that they are most likely to do so under certain conditions (Moscovici, 1985). First, the members of such groups must be *consistent* in their opposition to majority opinions. If they waiver, or seem to be divided, their impact is reduced. Second, members of the minority must avoid appearing to be rigid and dogmatic (Mugny, 1975). A minority that merely repeats the same position over and over again is less persuasive than one that demonstrates a degree of flexibility. Third, the general social context in which a minority operates is important. If a minority argues for a position that is consistent with current social trends (e.g., conservative views at a time of growing conservatism), its chances of influencing the majority are greater than if it argues for a position out of step with such trends. Of course, even when these conditions are met, minorities face a tough uphill fight. But both history and research findings (Haslam & Reicher, 2012; Kenworthy & Miller, 2001) indicate that they can sometimes prevail. For instance, only a minority of the people living in the United States were in favor of gaining independence from Britain when the Revolutionary War began; but that minority did prevail and found a new nation that has served as a model for many others over the intervening centuries.

Figure 8.12 The Popularity of Hybrid Cars—A Result of Concern About Global Warming

When scientists first warned about global warming, many people were skeptical. Gradually, the minority who held these views convinced others of the accuracy of their views, and became a majority.

Key Points

- **Social influence**—the many ways in which people produce changes in others—in their behavior, attitudes, or beliefs—is a common part of life.
- Most people behave in accordance with *social norms* most of the time; in other words, they show strong tendencies toward **conformity**. Yet, they underestimate the degree to which they conform.
- Conformity was first systematically studied by Asch, whose classic research indicated that many people will yield to social pressure from a unanimous group. Many factors determine whether, and to what extent, conformity occurs. These include **cohesiveness**—degree of attraction felt by an individual toward some group, group size, and type of social norm operating in that situation—**descriptive** or **injunctive norms**.
- Norms tend to influence our behavior primarily when they are salient and seen as relevant to us.
- Two important motives underlie our tendency to conform: the desire to be liked by others and the desire to be right or accurate. These two motives are reflected in two distinct types of social influence: **normative** and **informational social influence**.
- Several factors encourage *nonconformity*—refusing to "go along" with the group. These include status within a group, power, and the desire to be unique.

- The effects of social influence are powerful and pervasive, but tend to be magnified in situations where we are uncertain about our own judgments of what is correct.
- When we are engaged in **synchronous behavior**—coordinated with others—ourselves, we experience pressures to conform. But as observers, we may instead become sensitive to restrictions that synchronous behavior exerts on personal freedom and experience **reactance**—and resist strong pressure to conform.
- Pressures to conform often produce harmful effects and cause even good people to perform harmful actions. This was dramatically illustrated by Zimbardo's famous prison study. The BBC prison study revealed that the extent to which this occurs depends on whether people identified with the role they were assigned; when they did not, conformity was less likely.
- Under some conditions, minorities can induce even large majorities to change their attitudes or behavior. This is most likely when the minority is consistent, but not seen as dogmatic.

8.2: Compliance: To Ask—Sometimes—Is to Receive

Objective   **Describe the six basic principles of compliance and how they function**

Suppose that you wanted someone to do something for you; how would you go about getting this person to agree? If you think about this question for a moment, you'll quickly realize that you have many tactics for gaining **compliance**—for getting others to say "yes" to your requests. What are these techniques and which ones work best? These are among the questions we'll now consider. Before doing so, however, we'll introduce a basic framework for understanding the nature of these techniques and why they often work.

8.2.1: The Underlying Principles of Compliance

Some years ago, Robert Cialdini, a well-known social psychologist, decided that the best way to find out about compliance was to study what he termed *compliance professionals*—people whose success (financial or otherwise) depends on their ability to get others to say "Yes." Who are such people? They include salespeople, advertisers, political lobbyists, fund-raisers, con artists, professional negotiators, and many others. Cialdini's technique for learning from these people was simple: He temporarily concealed his true identity and took jobs in various settings where gaining compliance is a way of life. In other words, he worked in advertising, direct (door-to-door) sales, fund-raising, and other compliance-focused fields. On the basis of these first-hand experiences, he concluded that although techniques for gaining compliance take many different forms, they all rest to some degree on six basic principles (Cialdini, 1994, 2008):

- *Friendship/liking*: In general, we are more willing to comply with requests from friends or from people we like than with requests from strangers or people we don't like.
- *Commitment/consistency*: Once we have committed ourselves to a position or action, we are more willing to comply with requests for behaviors that are consistent with this position or action than with requests that are inconsistent with it.
- *Scarcity*: In general, we value, and try to secure, outcomes or objects that are scarce or decreasing in availability. As a result, we are more likely to comply with requests that focus on scarcity than ones that make no reference to this issue.
- *Reciprocity*: We are generally more willing to comply with a request from someone who has previously provided a favor or concession to us than to someone who has not. In other words, we feel obligated to pay people back in some way for what they have done for us.
- *Social validation*: We are generally more willing to comply with a request for some action if this action is consistent with what we believe people similar to ourselves are doing (or thinking). We want to be correct, and one way to do so is to act and think like others.
- *Authority*: In general, we are more willing to comply with requests from someone who holds legitimate authority—or simply appears to do so.

According to Cialdini (2008), these basic principles underlie many techniques used by professionals—and ourselves—for gaining compliance from others. We'll now examine techniques based on these principles, plus a few others as well.

8.2.2: Tactics Based on Friendship or Liking

We've already considered several techniques for increasing compliance through liking in our discussion of *impression management* (Chapter 3)—various procedures for making a good impression on others. While this can be an end in itself, impression management techniques are often used for purposes of *ingratiation*—getting others to like us so that they will be more willing to agree to our requests (Jones, 1964; Liden & Mitchell, 1988).

What ingratiation techniques work best? A review of existing studies on this topic (Gordon, 1996) suggests that *flattery*—praising others in some manner—is one of the best. Another is known as *self-promotion*—informing others about our past accomplishments or positive characteristics ("I'm really very organized"; or "I'm really easy to get along with"; Bolino & Turnley, 1999). Other techniques that seem to work are improving one's own appearance, emitting many positive nonverbal cues, and doing small favors for the target people (Gordon, 1996; Wayne & Liden, 1995). Since we described many of these tactics in detail in Chapter 3, we won't repeat that information here. Suffice it to say that many of the tactics used for purposes of impression management are also successful means of increasing compliance.

Still another method for increasing others' liking of us—and thus increasing the chances that they will agree to requests we make—involves what has been termed *incidental similarity*—calling attention to small and slightly surprising similarities between them and ourselves. In several recent studies, Burger and his colleagues (Burger, Messian, Patel, del Pardo, and Anderson, 2004) found that people were more likely to agree to a small request (make a donation to charity) from a stranger when this person appeared to have the same first name or birthday as they did than when the requester was not similar to them in these ways. Apparently, these trivial forms of similarity enhance liking by creating a feeling of affiliation with the requester and so increases the tendency to comply with this person's requests.

8.2.3: Tactics Based on Commitment or Consistency

When you visit the food court of your local shopping mall, are you ever approached by people offering you free samples of food? If so, why do they do this? The answer is simple: They know that once you have accepted this small free gift, you will be more willing to buy something from the restaurant they represent. This is the basic idea behind an approach for gaining compliance known as the **foot-in-the-door technique**. Basically, it involves presenting target people with a small request—something so trivial that it is hard for them to refuse ("Accept this free sample") and then following up with a larger request—the one desired all along. The results of many studies indicate that this tactic works—it succeeds in inducing increased compliance (Beaman, Cole, Preston, Klentz, & Steblay, 1983; Freedman & Fraser, 1966). The foot-in-the-door technique rests on the principle of *consistency*: Once we have said "yes" to the small request, we are more likely to say "yes" to subsequent and larger ones because refusing these would be inconsistent with our previous behavior. For instance, I once had a friend who lived next door to a neighbor who had a young child. One day, the neighbor asked my friend if she would let her child stay in her apartment for a few minutes while she went to a nearby store for an item she needed for dinner. My friend agreed, and then, gradually, the size of the neighbor's requests increased: "Will you let her (she was a little girl) stay with you for an hour, while I go to the doctor?" Ultimately, requests became so large ("Can you let her stay with you all day . . . ") that my friend had to refuse—but it was hard to do since she had agreed to the smaller requests; she was the victim of the foot-in-the door effect.

The foot-in-the-door technique is not the only tactic based on the consistency/commitment principle, however. Another is the **lowball procedure**. In this technique, which is often used by automobile salespersons, a very good deal is offered to a customer. After the customer accepts, however, something happens that makes it necessary for the salesperson to change the deal and make it less advantageous for the customer—for example, the sales manager rejects the deal. The totally rational response for customers, of course, is to walk away. Yet, often they agree to the changes and accept the less desirable arrangement (Cialdini, Cacioppo, Bassett, & Miller, 1978). In instances such as this, an initial commitment seems to make it more difficult for individuals to say "no," even though the conditions which led them to say "yes" in the first place have now been changed (see Figure 8.13).

Clear evidence for the importance of an initial commitment in the success of the lowball technique is provided by research conducted by Burger and Cornelius (2003). These researchers phoned students living in dorms and asked them if they would contribute $5.00 to a scholarship fund for underprivileged students. In the lowball condition, she indicated that people who contributed would receive a coupon for a free smoothie at a local juice bar. Then, if the participant agreed to make a donation, she told them that she had just run out of coupons and couldn't offer them this incentive. She then asked if they would still contribute. In another condition (the interrupt condition), she made the initial request but before the participants could answer yes or no, interrupted them and indicated that there were no more coupons for people who donated. In other words, this was just like the lowball condition, except that participants had no opportunity to make an initial commitment to donating to the fund. Finally, in a third (control) condition, participants were asked to donate $5.00 with no mention of any coupons for a free drink. Results indicated that more people in the lowball condition agreed to make a donation than in either of the other two conditions.

These results indicate that the lowball procedure does indeed rest on the principles of commitment: Only when individuals are permitted to make an initial public commitment—when they say "yes" to the initial offer—does it work. Having made this initial commitment, they feel compelled to stick with it, even though the conditions that lead them to say "yes" in the first place no longer exist. Truly, this is a subtle yet powerful technique for gaining compliance.

Figure 8.13 The Lowball Technique in Action

In the lowball technique the target person agrees to what seems to be a very "good deal," and then, once they do, the person seeking compliance makes this "deal" less attractive. Yet, having made an initial commitment many people still say "yes." Automobile salespersons often use this technique, with the result that customers pay more for the car than they would if they refused.

Yet one more tactic based on the principle of consistency or commitment is known as **the lure effect** (Guéguen, Joule, & Marchand, 2011). In this technique the intended target of a request is first asked to agree to do something he or she finds appealing—for instance, complete a brief questionnaire for a fairly generous compensation—perhaps $10.00 for 10 minutes of their time. Then, once they agreed, targets were told that they were not needed to complete the questionnaire but would, instead, perform a very a boring task—copying letters from one page to another. Rationally, they should have refused: The "deal" had been changed. But in fact, a large proportion of the participants agreed to continue. In a sense is something like "bait and switch," and is related to the lowball procedure, because again, once individuals have agreed to a request for doing something they would enjoy, they feel committed to agreeing to a request for doing something they do not expect to enjoy.

8.2.4: Tactics Based on Reciprocity

Reciprocity is a basic rule of social life: We usually "do unto others as they have done unto us." If they have done a favor for us, therefore, we feel that we should be willing to do one for them in return. While this is viewed by most people as being fair and just, the principle of reciprocity also serves as the basis for several techniques for gaining compliance. One of these is, on the face of it, the opposite of the foot-in-the-door technique. Instead of beginning with a small request and then escalating to a larger one, people seeking compliance sometimes start with a very large request and then, after this is rejected, shift to a smaller request—the one they wanted all along. This tactic is known as the **door-in-the-face technique** (because the first refusal seems to slam the door in the face of the requester), and several studies indicate that it can be quite effective. For example, in one well-known experiment, Cialdini and his colleagues (1975) stopped college students on the street and presented a huge request: Would the students serve as unpaid counselors for juvenile delinquents 2 hours a week for the next 2 *years*? As you can guess, no one agreed. When the experimenters then scaled down their request to a much smaller one—would the same students take a group of delinquents on a 2-hour trip to the zoo—fully 50 percent agreed. In contrast, less than 17 percent of those in a control group agreed to this smaller request when it was presented cold rather than after the larger request.

Figure 8.14 The Door-in-the-Face on the Internet

People who visited a website concerned with helping children injured by mines in war zones who received a very large request they refused (door-in-the-door condition), later were more likely to visit a page on which they could make a donation to the children or actually begin the process of donating than those who never received the large request (control).

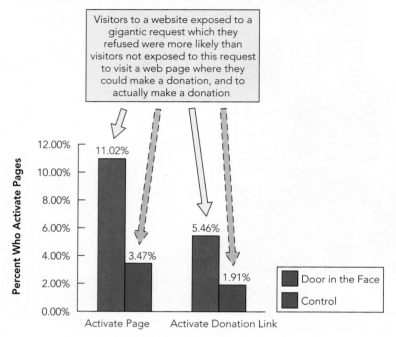

Research findings indicate that this tactic works on the Internet, as well as in face-to-face situations. Guéguen (2003) set up a website supposedly to help children who are the victims of mines in war zones. More than 3,600 people were contacted and invited to visit the site, and 1,607 actually did. Once there, they received either a very large request (the door-in-the-face condition): Would they volunteer 2–3 hours per week for the next 6 months to increase awareness of this problem? In contrast, those in a control group were simply invited to visit a page where they could make a donation to help the children. It was expected that very few people would agree with the large request—only two did. The key question was: Would more people who had received and refused the first request visit the donation site and actually begin the process of making a donation? As you can see in Figure 8.14, this is precisely what happened. Higher percentages of the door-in-the-face group than in the control group went to the donation page and activated the link to make a donation. So, clearly, this tactic can work in cyberspace as well as in person.

A related procedure for gaining compliance is known as the **that's-not-all technique**. Here, an initial request is followed, before the target person can say "yes" or "no," by something that sweetens the deal—a small extra incentive from the people using this tactic (e.g., a reduction in price, "throwing in" something additional for the same price). For example, television commercials for various products frequently offer something extra to induce viewers to pick up the phone and place an order. Several studies confirm informal observations suggesting that the *that's-not-all technique* really works (Burger, 1986). One reason that this tactic succeeds is because it is based on the principle of reciprocity: People on the receiving end of this approach view the "extra" thrown in by the other side as an added concession, and so feel obligated to make a concession themselves. The result: They are more likely to say "yes."

8.2.5: Tactics Based on Scarcity

Most of us have encountered "Going Out of Business Sales" or "End of Season Sales." Do they work? The answer is yes, because they are based on a general rule of life: Things that are scarce, rare, or in "Going Out of Business Sales" will soon disappear. Such sales are especially effective when they indicate that the deadline for their end is close—an effect known as the **deadline technique**.

Do these techniques for gaining compliance based on scarcity also work in other contexts? See the following section, **"What Research Tells Us About…Using Scarcity to Gain Compliance"**, for some answers. We'll address how well compliance tactics work in general in the next section.

8.2.6: Do Compliance Tactics Work?

Clearly, there are many different tactics for gaining compliance—for changing others' behavior in ways we desire. A large body of evidence indicates that often they are successful. But, surprisingly, research findings reported by Flynn and Lake (2008) indicate that we tend to underestimate their effectiveness. These researchers asked participants

What Research Tells Us About...

Using Scarcity to Gain Compliance

You probably know from your own experience that techniques for gaining compliance can succeed in many different settings, for instance, in getting someone to do a favor for you or to convince you to buy something. But there are other contexts in which these tactics are applied too, and perhaps one you haven't thought about is in obtaining the job you want. This might involve flattery—making positive statements about the person interviewing you for this job or the company offering it. But techniques involving scarcity may also work in this context—if used well. It works like this: During an interview, you indicate that you are considering several different jobs and have been offered one already. In this way, you suggest that other employers view you as an attractive candidate. Further, you might also hint that you have to make a decision very soon. This information can put pressure on the interviewer to say "yes"—to offer you the job,

after all, you may soon be unavailable. Research findings indicate that this tactic—which is based on scarcity—does work.

The scarcity principle for gaining compliance can also be applied in a very different context: romance. Do such tactics work in this important aspect of social life, too? Again, they have been found to be effective and take the form of **playing hard to get.** What this technique involves is causing the person you really want as a partner to believe that many other people find you attractive, so it may be difficult to win your affections because there's competition (Walster, Walster, Piliavin, & Schmidt, 1973). Although the "playing hard to get" technique does not always work—sometimes it discourages potential partners rather than fans their passion—it is sometimes effective and is another tactic based on convincing others that what they want is scarce and hard to obtain.

to estimate the likelihood that others would agree to their request—for instance to let them borrow the target person's cell phone, or to make a small donation to a charitable organization they represented. Overall, the people making the request underestimated compliance with their requests—by 50 percent. In other words, they thought they would have to ask twice as many people to help them as they actually did.

Why do we underestimate our success in getting others to say "yes?" Flynn and Lake (2008) found that this is due to the fact that people making requests focus on the costs of saying "yes"—the time and discomfort it will cause if the target person agrees—while people who are on the receiving side of such requests focus, instead, on the social costs of saying "no." Refusing a request from another person, especially if it is relatively small may put the refuser in a negative light: They may appear to be selfish, unfeeling, or even rude. Such concerns can deter them from refusing, and people seeking compliance tend to overlook these. (See Figure 8.15 for a summary of these suggestions.) In short, winning compliance is more complex than you might initially have thought, but it may also be easier to than you think.

Figure 8.15 Why We Underestimate Our Likelihood of Success in Gaining Compliance

Research findings indicate that people tend to underestimate the extent to which their efforts to gain compliance will succeed. This seems to be because when making a request, we focus on the costs to the target person of saying "yes." In contrast, the people we want to influence tend to focus on the costs of saying "no"—for instance, as appearing to be selfish or uncaring.

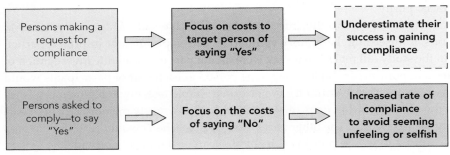

Key Points

- Individuals use many different tactics for gaining **compliance**—getting others to say yes to various requests. Many of these rely on basic principles well known to social psychologists.
- Three widely used tactics, the **foot-in-the-door technique**, the **lowball procedure**, and **the lure effect**, rest on the principle of commitment/consistency. In contrast, the **door-in-the-face** and **that's-not-all techniques** rest on the principle of reciprocity.

- **Playing hard to get** and the **deadline technique** are based on the principle of scarcity—something that is perceived as scarce or hard to obtain is valuable. Scarcity, one tactic for gaining compliance, can help individuals to get a job.
- People making requests tend to underestimate the likelihood that others will comply, perhaps because they ignore the social "costs" of refusal on the part of the target people.

8.3: Obedience to Authority: Would You Harm Someone If Ordered to Do So?

Objective   Analyze the role of authority in inducing obedience

Have you ever been ordered to do something you didn't want to do by someone with authority over you—a teacher, your boss, your parents? If so, you are already familiar with another major type of social influence—**obedience**—in which one person directly orders one or more others to behave in specific ways. Obedience is less frequent than conformity or compliance because even people who possess authority and could use it often prefer to exert influence in less obvious ways—through requests rather than direct orders (Yukl & Falbe, 1991). Still, obedience is far from rare, and occurs in many settings, ranging from schools through military bases. Obedience to the commands of people who possess authority is far from surprising; they usually have effective means for enforcing their orders. More unexpected is the fact that often, people lacking in such power can also induce high levels of submission from others. The clearest and most dramatic evidence for such effects was reported by Stanley Milgram in a series of famous but still controversial studies (Milgram, 1963, 1965a, 1974).

8.3.1: Obedience in the Laboratory

In his research, Milgram wished to find out whether individuals would obey commands from a relatively powerless stranger requiring them to inflict what seemed to be considerable pain on another person—a totally innocent stranger. Milgram's interest in this topic derived from tragic events in which seemingly normal, law-abiding people actually obeyed such directives. For example, during World War II, troops in the German army frequently obeyed commands to torture and murder unarmed civilians. In fact, the Nazis established horrible but highly efficient death camps designed to eradicate Jews, Gypsies, and other groups they felt were inferior or a threat to their own "racial purity."

In an effort to gain insights into the nature of such events, Milgram designed an ingenious, if unsettling, laboratory simulation. The experimenter informed participants in the study (all males) that they were taking part in a scientific investigation of the effects of punishment on learning. One person in each pair of participants would serve as a "learner" and would try to perform a simple task involving memory (supplying the second word in pairs of words they had previously memorized after hearing only the first word). The other participant, the "teacher," would read these words to the learner, and would punish errors by the learner (failures to provide the second word in each pair) through electric shock. These shocks would be delivered by means of the equipment shown in Figure 8.16, and as you can see from the photo, this device contained thirty numbered switches ranging from "15 volts" (the first) through "450 volts" (the 30th).

The two people present—a real participant and a research assistant—then drew slips of paper from a hat to determine who would play each role; as you can guess, the drawing was rigged so that the real participant always became the teacher. The teacher was then told to deliver a shock to the learner each time he made an error on the task. Moreover—and this is crucial—teachers were told to increase the strength of the shock each time the learner made an error. This meant that if the learner made many errors, he would soon be receiving strong jolts of electricity. It's important to note that this information was false: In reality, the assistant (the learner) never received any shocks during the experiment. The only real shock ever used was a mild pulse from button number three to convince participants that the equipment was real.

During the session, the learner (following prearranged instructions) made many errors. Thus, participants soon found themselves facing a dilemma: Should they continue punishing this person with what seemed to be increasingly painful shocks? Or should they refuse? If they hesitated, the experimenter pressured them to continue with a graded series "prods": "Please continue"; "The experiment requires that you continue"; "It is absolutely essential that you continue"; and "You have no other choice; you *must* go on."

Since participants were all volunteers and were paid in advance, you might predict that most would quickly refuse the experimenter's orders. In reality, though, *fully 65 percent showed total obedience*—they proceeded through the entire series to the final 450 volt level. Many participants, of course, protested and asked that the session should be ended. When ordered to proceed, however, a majority yielded to the experimenter's influence and continued to obey. Indeed, they continued doing so even when the victim pounded on the wall as if in protest over the painful shocks (at the 300-volt level), and then no longer responded, as if he had passed out. The experimenter told participants to treat failures to answer as errors; so from this point on, many participants believed that they were delivering dangerous shocks to someone who might already be unconscious!

In further experiments, Milgram (1965b, 1974) found that similar results could be obtained even under conditions that might be expected to reduce obedience.

Figure 8.16 Studying Obedience in the Laboratory

The left photo shows the apparatus Stanley Milgram used in his famous experiments on destructive obedience. The right photo shows the experimenter (right front) and a participant (rear) attaching electrodes to the learner's (accomplice's) wrist.

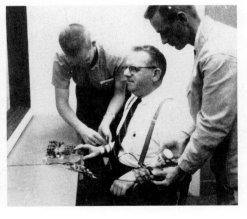

When the study was moved from its original location on the campus of Yale University to a run-down office building in a nearby city, participants' level of obedience remained virtually unchanged. Similarly, a large proportion continued to obey even when the accomplice complained about the painfulness of the shocks and begged to be released. Most surprising of all, about 30 percent obeyed even when they were required to grasp the victim's hand and force it down upon a metal shock plate. That these chilling results are not restricted to a single culture is indicated by the fact that similar findings were soon reported in several different countries (e.g., Jordan, Germany, Australia) and with children as well as adults (Kilham & Mann, 1974; Shanab & Yanya, 1977). Thus, Milgram's findings seemed to be alarmingly general in scope.

Psychologists and the public both found Milgram's results as highly disturbing. His studies seemed to suggest that ordinary people are willing, although with some reluctance, to harm an innocent stranger if ordered to do so by someone in authority—in a sense, echoing the theme stated by Zimbardo in his famous "Prison Study" and more recent work (Zimbardo, 2007).

At this point, you might be tempted to conclude: "OK, in 1960 people obeyed a man in a white laboratory coat. But today, people are much more sophisticated, so they would never hold still for this kind of thing. They'd just refuse to play the game." That's a comforting thought, but in fact, one social psychologist (Burger, 2009), replicated Milgram's research just recently. He made a few changes to protect participants from the extreme stress Milgram's procedures generated. For instance, he screened them to make sure that they had no medical problem that would make them especially susceptible to the harmful effects of stress. In addition, if they agreed to continue after the learner protested (150 volts), he stopped the study, thus avoiding further stress for the participants. Burger reasoned that he could do this because almost all of participants in Milgram's original research who continued past 150 volts went all the way to the end of the series. In addition, both females and males participated in the research; in Milgram's studies, only males took part.

In a recent replication of Milgram's famous research, high proportions of both men and women obeyed the experimenter's commands to deliver shocks to an innocent victim. They continued even after the victim asked to stop the study (150 volts), and even if they saw another person (a model) refuse to obey.

What were the results? Almost identical to those found by Milgram 45 years earlier. As you can see in Figure 8.17, a very high proportion (66.7 percent for men, 72.7 percent for women) continued past the 150 volts level—the point at which the victim protested and said he wanted to stop the experiment. In Milgram's study, the comparable figure was slightly higher. Further, when procedures were used in which an assistant of the experimenter refused to continue, this did not increase participant's willingness to stop: Fully 54.5 percent of men and 68.4 percent of women continued despite seeing another person refuse to obey.

So what do these results tell us? That the pressures to obey in a situation like the one Milgram created are difficult to resist—so difficult, that many people yield to them, even if this means harming another person who has done nothing to harm them. What are these pressures and what factors lie behind this tendency to obey in such situations? That's the question we'll consider next.

Figure 8.17 Obedience: Still a Powerful Form of Social Influence

In a recent replication of Milgram's famous research, high proportions of both men and women obeyed the experimenters commands to deliver shocks to an innocent victim. They continued even after the victim asked to stop the study (150 volts), and even if they saw another person (a model) refuse to obey.

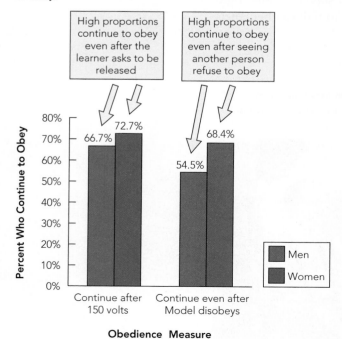

Obedience Measure

8.3.2: Why Destructive Obedience Occurs

As we noted earlier, one reason why Milgram's results are so disturbing is that they seem to parallel many real-life events involving atrocities against innocent victims such as the murder of millions of Jews and other people by the Nazis, the genocide advocated by the Hutu government in Rwanda in which 800,000 Tutsis were killed in less than 3 months in 1994, and the massacre of more than 1 million Armenians by Turkish troops in the early years of the 20th century. To repeat the question we raised earlier: Why does such destructive obedience occur? Since the participants in such tragedies and Milgram's studies were not "abnormal" we need to ask if perhaps they believed in what they were doing—the importance of the tasks or stated goals. As Haslam, Reicher, and Birney (2014) report in a recent analogue of these studies, the extent to which participants identified with the goals of the scientific enterprise predicted the extent to which they continued delivering shocks. Might such "identification with the cause" be critical to understanding the participants in these experiments—and many people in these tragic situations outside the laboratory? Believing in the larger purpose does appear to make people willing to yield to this form of social influence?

Social psychologists have identified several additional factors that seem to play a role, and together, these combine to make most people unable to resist such situational pressures (Burger, 2014). First, in many situations, the people in authority relieve those who obey of the responsibility for their own actions. "I was only carrying out orders" is the defense many offer after obeying harsh or cruel commands. In life situations, this transfer of responsibility may be implicit; the person in charge (e.g., the military or police officer) is assumed to have the responsibility for what happens. This seems to be what happened in the tragic events at Abu Ghraib prison camp in Iraq, when United States soldiers—both men and women—were filmed abusing and torturing prisoners. The soldiers' defense was "I was only following orders . . . I was told to do this and a good soldier always obeys." In Milgram's experiments, this transfer of responsibility was explicit. Participants were told at the start that the experimenter (the authority figure), not they, would be responsible for the learner's well-being. In view of this fact, it is not surprising that many obeyed: After all, they were completely off the hook.

Second, people in authority often possess visible badges or signs of their status. They wear special uniforms or insignia, have special titles, and so on. These serve to remind many individuals of the social norm "Obey the persons in charge." This is a powerful norm, and when confronted with it, most people find it difficult to disobey. After all, we do not want to do the wrong thing, and obeying the commands of those who are in charge usually helps us avoid such errors. In Milgram's study, the experimenter wore a white lab coat, which suggested that he was a doctor or someone with authority. So it's not surprising that so many participants obeyed the commands this person issued (Bushman, 1988; Darley, 1995).

A third reason for obedience in many situations where the targets of such influence might otherwise resist involves the gradual escalation of the authority figure's orders. Initial commands may call for relatively mild actions, such as merely arresting people. Only later do orders come to require behavior that is dangerous or objectionable (see Staub, 1989). For example, police or military personnel may at first be ordered only to question or threaten potential victims. Gradually, demands are increased to the point where these personnel are commanded to beat, torture, or even murder unarmed civilians. In a sense, people in authority use the foot-in-the-door technique, asking for small actions first but ever-larger ones later. In a similar manner, participants in Milgram's research were first required to deliver only mild and harmless shocks to the victim. Only as the sessions continued did the intensity of these "punishments" rise to potentially harmful levels.

Figure 8.18 Obedience to Authority: Why It Often Occurs

As shown here, several factors combine to make it all too easy to obey orders from people in authority—even if these commands involve harming others and violating our own ethical or moral standards.

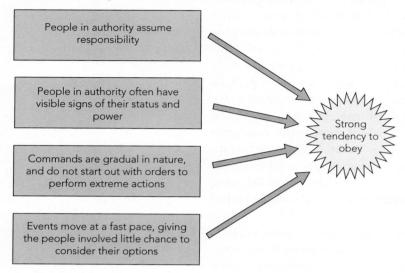

Finally, events in many situations involving destructive obedience move very quickly: Demonstrations turn into riots, arrests into mass beatings or murder, quite suddenly. The fast pace of such events gives participants little time for reflection or systematic thought: People are ordered to obey and—almost automatically—they do so. Such conditions prevailed in Milgram's research; within a few minutes of entering the laboratory, participants found themselves faced with commands to deliver strong electric shocks to the learner. This fast pace, too, may tend to increase obedience.

In sum, the high levels of obedience generated in Milgram's studies are not as mysterious as they may seem. A social psychological analysis of the conditions existing both in Milgram's studies and in many real-life situations identifies several factors that, together, may make it very difficult for individuals to resist the commands they receive (these are summarized in Figure 8.18). The consequences, of course, can be truly tragic for innocent and often defenseless victims.

8.3.3: Resisting the Effects of Destructive Obedience

Now that we have considered some of the factors responsible for the strong tendency to obey sources of authority, we will turn to a related question: How can this type of social influence be resisted? Several strategies may be helpful in this respect.

First, individuals exposed to commands from authority figures can be reminded that they—not the authorities—are responsible for any harm produced. Under these conditions, sharp reductions in the tendency to obey have been observed (e.g., Hamilton, 1978; Kilham & Mann, 1974).

Second, individuals can be provided with a clear indication that beyond some point, total submission to destructive commands is inappropriate. One procedure that can be effective in this regard involves exposing individuals to the actions of *disobedient models*—people who refuse to obey an authority figure's commands. Research findings indicate that such models can reduce unquestioning obedience (e.g., Rochat & Modigliani, 1995)—although as Burger (2009) reported, not always.

Third, individuals may find it easier to resist influence from authority figures if they question the expertise and motives of these figures. This is particularly the case when "identification with the authority's cause" is crucial to obedience (see Haslam, Reicher, & Birney, 2014). What motives lie behind their commands—socially beneficial goals or selfish gains? Dictators always claim that their brutal orders reflect their undying concern for their fellow citizens and are in their best interest, but to the extent large numbers of people question these motives, the power of such dictators can be eroded and perhaps, ultimately, be swept away.

Finally, simply knowing about the power of authority figures to command obedience may be helpful in itself. Some research findings (Sherman, 1980) suggest that when individuals learn about the results of this social psychological research, they often recognize these as important (Richard, Bond, & Stokes-Zoota, 2001), and sometimes change their behavior to take into account this new knowledge. With respect to destructive obedience, there is some hope that knowing about this process can enhance individuals' resolve to resist. To the extent this is so, then even exposure to findings as disturbing as those reported by Milgram can have positive social value.

The power of authority figures to command obedience is certainly great, but it is not irresistible. Under appropriate conditions, it *can* be countered or reduced. As in many other areas of life, there is a choice. Deciding to resist the commands of people in authority can, of course, be highly dangerous: They usually control most of the weapons, the army, and the police. Yet, history is filled with instances in which the authority of powerful and entrenched regimes has been resisted by courageous people who ultimately triumphed, despite the long odds against them (see Turner, 2006). The lesson is clear: Power is never permanent, and ultimately, victory often goes to those who stand for freedom and a different view of the world rather than to those who wish to control the lives of their fellow human beings.

Key Points

- **Obedience** is a form of social influence in which one person orders one or more others to do something, and they do so. It is, in a sense, the most direct form of social influence.
- Research by Stanley Milgram indicates that many people readily obey orders from a relatively powerless source of authority, even if these orders require them to harm another innocent person. The extent to which people identify with the authority figures and their cause predicts the extent to which they obey. Such *destructive obedience*, which plays a role in many real-life atrocities, stems from several factors. These include: The shifting of responsibil-

ity to the authority figure; outward signs of authority which remind many people of the norm "obey those in authority"; a gradual escalation of the scope of the commands given (related to the foot-in-the-door technique); and the rapid pace with which such situations proceed.
- Several factors can help to reduce the occurrence of destructive obedience. These include reminding individuals that they share in the responsibility for any harm produced, reminding them that beyond some point, obedience is inappropriate, calling the motives of authority figures into question, and informing the general public of the findings of social psychological research on this topic.

8.4: Unintentional Social Influence: How Others Change Our Behavior Even When They Are Not Trying to Do So

Objective   **Describe several forms of unintentional social influence**

Although conformity, compliance, and obedience are distinct forms of social influence, they all have one basic feature in common: All involve *intentional efforts* by one or more people to change the behavior and thoughts of other people. Even conformity, which might seem to differ from the compliance and obedience in this respect, involves the intention to influence others: For instance, groups—and society as a whole—generally want their members to follow the rules (i.e., norms), and put pressure (subtle or direct) on them to do so. But, is all social influence intentional? Do individuals sometimes influence others without overtly intending to do so? Research findings indicate that such **unintentional social influence** is actually quite common. We'll now describe several ways in which it can—and often does—occur.

8.4.1: Emotional Contagion

Suppose one of your good friends suddenly enters the room. She is overflowing with joy—happy, smiling, and bubbling with enthusiasm. You ask her to explain why she's feeling so great, but even before she does so, do you think you would "catch her mood"—would you begin to feel a little boost in your own emotions, so that you, too, start to feel happy? Probably you have had experiences like this one because it is clear that often we are influenced by others' moods or emotions. And if you have ever cried while watching someone in a movie shows sadness, or experienced joy when a character in a film or play shows happiness, you know about these kinds of reactions from firsthand experience.

Social psychologists refer to such effects (through which moods spread from one person to another) as *social contagion*, and view it as another, and very basic, form of social influence. The fact that moods or emotions are indeed "catching" is clear; but why does this occur? What mechanisms permit one person's moods to influence those of another, even if this person is not intending to produce such effects?

Initial research on this topic (e.g., Hatfield, Cacioppo, & Rapson, 1994), emphasized a very basic process: When we observe emotions in others, we tend to physically match their feelings. If they are happy, we begin to smile; if they are sad, we may frown. These effects occur automatically, and the result is that we come to feel what the other person is feeling. Certainly, this is correct to some extent. But it doesn't explain another interesting and important fact: Sometimes when we observe emotions in others we don't experience what they are feeling, but instead experience something very different. For instance, if you witness joy on the part of a team that has just defeated your own school's team, you will probably not feel happy. On the contrary, you may feel disappointment or even anger at their happy reactions. The German language has a specific word for this kind of reaction—*Schadenfreude*—which means taking pleasure in others' misfortunes or disappointments. Have you ever experienced such feelings? Unless you are a complete saint, you probably have; when others triumph over us, we are supposed to be "good losers," but it is sometimes easier to recommend such graciousness than to achieve it.

The fact that we sometimes experience the same emotions as others and sometimes ones quite different from theirs suggests that the situation is not simply one of "automatic mimicry." Rather, cognition, too must be involved. We not only notice others' emotions, but also interpret them. For instance, Parkinson and Simons (2009) suggest that sometimes, we interpret others' reactions as a source of information about how we should feel. For instance, if they are showing lots of anxiety and excitement while making a decision, we conclude that the decision is very important, and may begin to feel similar reactions. This is very different from a direct effect in which we observe their reactions and feel the same emotion automatically. The researchers obtained evidence supporting this proposal from a diary study in which participants reported on their own feelings, and those of another person who was important in their life (e.g., a partner or spouse), while making various decisions. Findings indicated that the reactions of the other person generated automatic emotional reactions and influenced appraisals of the situation (and these feelings) too.

In addition, other research (Epstude & Mussweiler, 2009) indicates that similarity to other people showing emotion is important in determining our own reactions. If we perceive ourselves as similar to them, then through social comparison processes, we tend to experience the emotions they are showing. If we perceive ourselves as dissimilar to them, then, we may experience countercontagion—emotions different from or even opposite to theirs.

To test these predictions, the researchers conducted a study in which participants were first induced to think about similarity or dissimilarity. (This was accomplished by having them examine some pictures, and describe either similarities or dissimilarities between them). Then, they listened to an audiotape in which an actor of their own gender read a passage; the actor was either in a slightly happy or slightly sad mood. Finally, participants rated their own mood. It was predicted that when primed to think about similarity, participants would perceive the actor as similar to themselves, and report being happier after hearing the happy actor than the sad one. When primed to think about dissimilarity, however, the opposite would be true. Results confirmed both predictions.

Overall, then, it is clear that our own feelings and emotions are often influenced by those of other people and that, moreover, this occurs even if they do not intend to affect us in this way. **Emotional contagion**, then, is a very basic and pervasive form of social influence, and one that may well play an important role in the social side of life. Recent research indicates that there is a neural mechanism in our brains that may underlie our reactions to others' emotions. This mechanism involves *mirror neurons*. These are neurons that respond as strongly when we observe another person's actions or expressions of emotion, as when we perform these actions and experience these emotions ourselves (Iacoboni, 2009). We'll discuss their effects further in Chapter 9.

8.4.2: Symbolic Social Influence

Have you been in a situation where you were about to do something, and before you did, asked yourself: "How would my parents, friends, or significant other feel about this? How would they react if I went ahead?" In such cases, the mere thought of the reactions of other people may have strong effect on our actions and our attitudes. Social psychologists refer to this as **symbolic social influence** and in such situations, once again, others influence us without trying to do so. Of course, they might attempt to exert such influence if they were present, but since they are not, it is our mental representations of others—what they want or prefer, our relationships with them, how we think they would evaluate us or our current actions—that influence us. For example, in one well-known study—which triggered initial interest in this topic—Baldwin, Carrell, and Lopez (1990) found that graduate students evaluated their own research ideas more negatively after being exposed, subliminally, to the face of their scowling department chair. In other words, although the chair's face was shown for so short a period of time that the graduate students were not aware of having seen him, his negative facial expression exerted significant effects on their evaluations of their own work anyway.

How can the psychological presence of others in our thoughts influence our behavior and thought? Two mechanisms seem to be involved, and both may involve goals—objectives we wish to attain. First, to the extent other people are present in our thoughts (and even if we are not aware that they are), this may trigger relational schemas—mental representations of people with whom we have relationships, and of these relationships themselves. When these relational schemas are triggered, goals relevant to them may be activated, too. For instance, if we think of a friend, the goal of being helpful may be activated; if we think of our mother or father, the goal of making them proud of us may be triggered. These goals, in turn, may affect our thoughts about ourselves, our behavior, and our evaluations of others. For instance, if the goal of helping others is triggered, then we may become more helpful. If the goal of being physically attractive is activated, we may refuse that delicious dessert when it is offered.

Second, the psychological presence of others may trigger goals with which that person is associated—goals they want us to achieve. This, in turn, can affect our performance on various tasks and our commitment to reaching these goals, among other things (e.g., Shah, 2003). For instance, if we have thoughts about our father, we know that he wants us to do well in school, our commitment to this goal may be increased and we may work harder to attain it—especially if we feel very close to him. In other words, to the extent that others are psychologically present in our thoughts, the nature of our relationships with them, goals we seek in these relationships, or goals these people themselves want us to attain, can all be stimulated, and these ideas and knowledge structures, in turn, can strongly affect our behavior.

While many different studies have reported such effects, research conducted on this topic by Fitzsimons and Bargh (2003) is especially revealing. In one such study, people at an airport were approached and asked to think either of a good friend, or someone with whom they worked. Then, they were asked to write down the initials of the person of whom they were thinking and to answer a series of questions about that person (e.g., describe his or her appearance; how long they had known that person and his or her age). Finally, participants were asked if they would be willing to help the researcher by answering a longer set of questions. It was predicted that those who thought about a friend would be more willing to help because thinking about a friend would trigger the goal of helping—something we often do for friends. This is precisely what happened: More people who thought about a friend than a coworker were willing to help. Note that they were not asked to help their friend; rather, they were asked to assist a stranger—the researcher. But still, thoughts of the friend affected their current behavior.

Findings such as these, and those reported in a growing number of other studies (Shah, 2003) suggest that we can be strongly influenced by other people when they are not physically present on the scene and trying to affect us, as long as they are psychologically present (in our thoughts).

8.4.3: Modeling: Learning from Observing Others

Whenever a plumber or electrician comes to my house, I follow this person around, watching what they do, and asking questions if they tell me that's OK. I do this simply because I want to learn from these people, who are experts in their field. Because I've done this often, the result is that now I can fix lots of things myself that I couldn't before. This kind of influence is known as *modeling,* or *observational learning,* and it refers to situations in which we learn from observing others and then do what they did (see Figure 8.19). Another term for this process is *imitation,* which has a negative ring to it—no one wants to be accused of imitating others, but imitation confers all the benefits of modeling and observational learning.

Modeling is a very general process—children learn from their parents and from teachers, individuals trying to acquire skills ranging from plumbing, playing a musical instrument, and even to how to conduct a scientific experiment—learn from others who already possess these skills. Modeling also occurs in many situations in which we are not sure how to behave—there are no clear rules for what is the appropriate way to act. In such situations, we rely on the actions of others as a guide to what we should do. This kind of influence is very strong: Research findings indicate that individuals

---

Figure 8.19 Observational Learning in Action

When electricians, plumbers or other skilled professionals come to my house, I follow them around watching what they do in order to learn from them. Like the person shown above, I am engaging in observational learning.

will match their own actions to those of others with respect to everything from expressions of their opinions to even aggression and helping. As we'll see in Chapter 10, individuals exposed to highly aggressive actions on the part of others—for instance, in violent video games or movies—show an increase in their own tendencies to aggress against others. In an analysis of the results of many studies concerning this topic (e.g., Anderson et al., 2010), they found that exposure to such games increases not only overt aggression, but also aggressive thoughts among the people who play them, and that this is true in many different countries. In short, modeling can produce either beneficial or harmful effects, depending on the actions on the part of others that individuals observe (see Figure 8.19).

Key Points

- Other people can influence us even when they do not intend to do—through **unintentional social influence**.
- Such influence takes several different forms. One is **emotional contagion**, instances in which our own emotions are influenced by those of others even when those individuals do not intend to produce such effects.

- Another is known as **symbolic social influence** and occurs when our thoughts about others influence our actions or thoughts even if they are not present.
- A third form of unintentional social influence is *modeling*, which we learn from observing the actions of others, or use them as a guide to our own behavior in situations where it is not clear how we should behave.

Summary and Review

Social influence—the many ways in which people produce changes in others—in their behavior, attitudes, or beliefs—is a common part of life. Most people behave in accordance with *social norms* most of the time; in other words, they show strong tendencies toward **conformity**. Conformity was first systematically studied by Solomon Asch, whose classic research indicated that people will yield to social pressure from a unanimous group. Many factors determine whether, and to what extent, conformity occurs. These include **cohesiveness**—degree of attraction felt by an individual toward some group, *group size*, and type of social norm operating in that situation—*descriptive* or *injunctive*. Norms tend to influence our behavior primarily when they are relevant to us. Two important motives underlie our tendency to conform: The desire to be liked by others and the desire to be right or accurate. These two motives are reflected in two distinct types of social influence: *normative* and *informational*.

Emotional contagion occurs when one or more people are influenced by the emotions of one or more others. Such contagion can lead to similarity or opposite emotional reactions on the part of the people involved depending on, for instance, the extent to which we feel similar to them.

Several factors encourage *nonconformity*—refusing to "go along" with the group, the effects of social influence are powerful and pervasive, but tend to be magnified in

situations where we are uncertain about our own judgments of what is correct They can be reduced by several conditions such as high status, power, and the desire to be unique. Resisting conformity pressure can provide benefits to the people who resist—for instance, they are perceived as being higher in status than those who conform. The effects of conformity pressures are often very strong, and even induce good people to perform bad actions. This was dramatically illustrated by Zimbardo's famous prison study.

Individuals use many different tactics for gaining **compliance**—getting others to say yes to various requests. Many of these techniques rest on basic principles well known to social psychologists. Two widely used tactics, the **foot-in-the-door technique** and the **lowball procedure** rely on the principle of commitment or consistency. In contrast, the **door-in-the-face** and **that's-not-all techniques** rely on the principle of reciprocity. **Playing hard to get** and the **deadline technique** are based on the principle of scarcity—where what is scarce or hard to obtain is seen as valuable.

Obedience is a form of social influence in which one person orders one or more others to do something, and they do so. It is, in a sense, the most direct form of social influence. Research by Stanley Milgram indicates that many people readily obey orders from a relatively powerless source of authority, even if these orders require them to do harm, to the extent that they identify with the authority's goals. A recent replication of this study reported results very similar to those obtained by Milgram. Such *destructive obedience*, which plays a role in many real-life atrocities, stems from several factors. These include the shifting of responsibility to the authority figure; outward signs of authority which remind many people of the norm "obey those in authority"; a gradual escalation of the scope of the commands given (related to the foot-in-the-door technique); and the rapid pace with which such situations proceed.

Several factors can help to reduce the occurrence of destructive obedience. These include reminding individuals that they share in the responsibility for any harm produced, reminding them that beyond some point obedience is inappropriate, calling the motives of authority figures into question, and informing the general public of the findings of social psychological research on this topic.

Other people can influence us even when they are not trying to do this. Such **unintentional social influence** takes several different forms. One is emotional contagion, instances in which our own emotions are influenced by those of others even when they do not intend to produce such effects. Another is known as **symbolic social influence** and occurs when our thoughts about others influence our actions or thoughts even if they are not present.

A third form of unintentional social influence is modeling, which we learn from observing the actions of others, or use them as a guide to our own behavior in situations where it is not clear how we should behave.

Chapter 9
Prosocial Behavior
Helping Others

Chapter Overview

Learning Objectives

9.1 Assess the factors that lead people to help others

9.2 Identify factors that influence whether bystanders will offer help in emergency situations

9.3 Determine the factors that increase or decrease people's willingness to help others

9.4 Relate crowdfunding to the factors influencing prosocial behavior

9.5 Describe the relationship between prosocial behavior and antisocial behavior

One sunny day in Ames, Iowa, Chris Ihle was returning from lunch. He had just parked his motorcycle when he noticed a car parked on the tracks at a railroad crossing. Looking up, he saw a train approaching—and fast! He ran to the car and shouted at the two people inside to move immediately, but the driver sat frozen at the wheel, and neither he nor his passenger replied. Thinking fast, Chris shouted to the driver to put the car in neutral and then tried to push it forward from behind. When it didn't move, he ran to the front and tried to push it back. This time, it did move and he managed to get it off the track, just as the train rushed by—it missed the car by a few inches. So his act of heroism saved the two people in the car, 84-year-old Marion Papich and his 78-year-old wife, Jean—from what was certain to be serious injury, or even death. Truly, he was a hero who risked his own life to help two strangers . . . and succeeded.

Around the globe, more than 3 billion people cook their meals and heat their homes with small stoves; these stoves burn many kinds of fuel—wood, charcoal, waste from farm land—but all of them are dangerous, both to the people who use them and to entire planet. These stoves are highly inefficient—they require a large amount of fuel to make a small amount of heat. They emit dangerous fumes, soot, and many other pollutants. And while you might think that these amounts are small, remember that they are probably more than a billion of them in use! The result: Together they account for more than 12 percent of all greenhouse gases released into the atmosphere (Global Alliance for Safe Cookstoves). Further, the pollution they emit is as harmful to the people exposed to it, since the stoves are often used in very small enclosures. And perhaps even worse, many thousands of children are burned by these hot stoves every year. Clearly, this is a major social and environmental problem, but can anything be done to relieve it? A group of engineers believed that it could and founded a company—Aprovecho—which means "make the best use of" in Spanish. Their goal was to build a better, safer, and more efficient cookstove and provide it to hundreds of millions of people at a price they could afford—a price that would provide no profits for the company or its founders, but would help solve this serious problem. More recently, this task has been carried forward by the Global Alliance for Clean Cookstoves, with the same goal and again, without making any profit. One of the stoves they developed is shown in Figure 9.1, and

Figure 9.1 Prosocial Behavior Can Help One Person—or Many Millions

Prosocial actions can be focused on helping one or a few other people, but can also benefit millions of people. A dramatic instance of this is provided by efforts to develop cooking stoves that are more efficient—and safer—than the ones that exist today. The scientists working on this task are doing so without any pay or other compensation. Thus, they are showing prosocial behavior.

it—and others that burn different kinds of fuel—has been provided (at the lowest price possible) to more than 100 million people, who benefit greatly from these products.

At first glance, these stories might seem totally unrelated; in terms of the events they describe, they are different. But, in fact, there is an underlying theme that connects them: They illustrate what social psychologists describe as **prosocial behavior**—actions by individuals that help others, often, with no immediate benefit to the helpers. Chris Ihle certainly helped the couple in the car, saving them from certain harm. Likewise, efforts to supply hundreds of millions of people with safer and more efficient cookstoves certainly help them, and the entire planet, too. So, prosocial behavior takes many different forms and can be focused on a few people, or on helping huge numbers in various ways.

In one sense, prosocial behavior is somewhat mysterious: Why should the people who engage in it risk their own safety, well-being, and time to help others who cannot reciprocate (at least immediately or overtly) such help? The answer, as uncovered by social psychologists, is that there are many motives behind such behavior, and many factors that increase, or decrease, its occurrence.

In this chapter, we will examine many aspects of prosocial behavior. We will start by describing the motives from which it springs. Then, since dramatic instances in which people help others occur in emergency situations (as it did in the situation involving the car stuck on the railroad track), we will focus attention on helping in such situations, because they provide important insights into the nature of prosocial behavior. After that, we will examine several factors that influence the occurrence of prosocial actions—both external factors relating to the situations in which it occurs and personal characteristics that influence the likelihood that specific people will, or will not, provide help when it is needed. We will also focus attention on an especially intriguing question: How do people who receive help respond to it? Will it be with gratitude, or, perhaps with embarrassment, or even resentment over receiving such assistance?

9.1: Why People Help: Motives for Prosocial Behavior

Objective   **Assess the factors that lead people to help others**

Why do people help others? Before addressing the specific factors that increase or decrease the tendency to engage in such actions, we will first focus on a key question: What motives underlie the tendency to help others? As we will see soon, many factors play a role in determining whether, and to what extent, specific people engage in such actions. Several aspects of the situation are important, and a number of personal (i.e., dispositional) factors are also influential. We will focus on these factors in later discussions.

9.1.1: Empathy-Altruism: It Feels Good to Help Others

One explanation of prosocial behavior involves **empathy**—the capacity to be able to experience others' emotional states, feel sympathetic toward them, and take their perspective (e.g., Eisenberg et al., 1999; Hodges, Kiel, Kramer, Veach, & Villaneuva, 2010). In other words, we help others because we vicariously experience any unpleasant feelings they are experiencing and want to help bring their negative feelings to an end, and one way of doing so is to help them in some way. This is unselfish because it leads us to offer help for no extrinsic reason, but it is also selfish, in one sense, since the behavior of assisting others helps us, too: It can make us feel better. Reflecting these basic observations, Batson, Duncan, Ackerman, Buckley, and Birch offered the **empathy-altruism hypothesis**, which suggests that at least some prosocial acts are motivated solely by the desire to help someone in need. Such motivation can be sufficiently strong that the helper is willing to engage in unpleasant, dangerous, and even life-threatening activities. Compassion for other people may outweigh all other considerations (Goetz, Keltner, & Simon-Thomas, 2010).

In fact, research findings indicate that empathy consists of three distinct components: an emotional aspect (*emotional empathy*, which involves sharing the feelings and emotions of others), a cognitive component, which involves perceiving others' thoughts and feelings accurately (*empathic accuracy*), and a third aspect, known as *empathic concern*, which involves feelings of concern for another's well-being (e.g., Gleason, Jensen-Campbell, & Ickes, 2009). This distinction is important, because it appears that the three components are related to different aspects of prosocial behavior, and have different long-term effects. For instance, consider the effects of empathic accuracy. This appears to play a key role in social adjustment—the extent to which we get along well with others.

In an informative study on this topic, Gleason and colleagues (2009) hypothesized that the higher adolescents are in empathic accuracy—that is, the better their skill in what has been termed "everyday mind-reading" (accurately understanding what others are thinking and feeling), the better their social adjustment: The more friends, they will have, the more they will be liked by their peers, the better the quality of their friendships, and the less they will be victims of bullying or social exclusion. Basically, the researchers reasoned that empathic accuracy would help the students respond appropriately to others; this in turn would lead to better relationships, and better adjustment (see Figure 9.2). Empathic accuracy was assessed by showing the participants in the study a videotape in which a student interacted with a teacher. The tape was stopped at specific points, and participants wrote down what they thought the other people were thinking or feeling; accuracy was assessed by comparing their responses to what the people in the tape reported actually thinking and feeling.

Results indicated that the higher students were in empathic accuracy, the better their social adjustment in terms of all the dimensions listed earlier (number of friends, peer acceptance, etc.). In short, a high level of empathic accuracy—clear understanding of others' feelings and thoughts—contributed strongly to their ability to get along well with others. Of course, we should add that it is possible that people who get along well with others become more empathetic, perhaps as a result of pleasant interactions with lots of other people. We mention this possibility not because we think it is more likely to be accurate, but mainly to remind you that establishing causality is always a difficult and tricky task, even in excellent research like this.

MIRROR NEURONS: A BIOLOGICAL FOUNDATION FOR EMPATHY—AND HELPING OTHERS

Research on the role of empathy in prosocial behavior raises an intriguing question: Is our ability to experience what others are experiencing somehow "built into" our brains, so that it happens automatically? The answer, provided by more than a decade of research, is that, in fact, there are areas of our brain specialized for just this function—to allow us to feel what others are feeling. This system is described by the term *mirror neurons*. The role of mirror neurons in empathy is supported by several

Figure 9.2 Empathic Accuracy: An Important Aspect in Social Adjustment

Recent research indicates that empathic accuracy—the ability to accurately understand others' feelings and thoughts (sometimes termed *everyday mind-reading*) plays an important role in social adjustment. Adolescents who are high in this skill have more friends and greater acceptance from their peers, and are victimized less by others than adolescents who are low in this skill. In contrast, those low in empathic accuracy tend to develop problems of social adjustment.

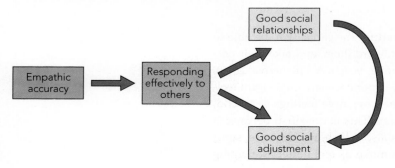

different lines of research (e.g., Baird, Scheffer, & Wilson, 2011). First, studies have investigated the relationship between individuals' self-reported capacity to experience empathy and activity in brain regions identified as including motor neurons. Findings (e.g., Pfeifer, Iacoboni, Mazziotta, & Dapretto, 2007) indicate that the higher an individual's capacity to experience empathy, the greater the activity in these regions when, for example, they observe another person in pain.

Other investigations have focused on what is known as autism spectrum disorder, a psychological disorder involving deficits in social communication and social interaction across multiple contexts. People with this disorder are characterized by reduced capacity to experience empathy. While research results have not been entirely consistent, they suggest, overall, that individuals with this disorder show reduced activity in the mirror neuron system, which implies this system underlies the occurrence of empathy. Additional research (Montgomery, Seeherman, & Haxby, 2009) has found that mirror neurons are active when individuals observe others' emotional expressions, but are *not* active when they observe facial movements unrelated to emotions—for instance, chewing or sneezing. This suggests that motor neurons are "tuned" to others' emotional experiences—and, thus, to empathy.

Finally, it has been found that compassion training—providing individuals with practice experiencing compassion or empathy toward others—increases activity in mirror neuron regions (Weng et al., 2013). In sum, there does indeed appear to be a neural foundation in our brains for empathy—in other words, for our human capacity to share others' pain—and joy.

Before concluding this discussion of empathy and its effects, we should add that after reviewing available evidence, Zaki (2014) concluded that several factors encourage empathy—positive affect, the desire to affiliate with others, and social desirability—the desire to "look good" to others by doing the right or approved thing in a given situation. However, empathy can be discouraged, by other factors, such as others' suffering (which can be too painful to watch), and the costs of experiencing empathy. In short, empathy toward others is far from an automatic reaction—it is more likely to occur under some circumstances than others.

9.1.2: Negative-State Relief: Helping Can Reduce Unpleasant Feelings

Another possible motive for helping others is, in a sense, the mirror image of empathy: Instead of helping because we care about the welfare of another person (empathic concern), understand their feelings (empathic accuracy), and share them (emotional empathy), we help because such actions allow us to reduce our own negative emotions. In other words, we do a good thing in order to stop feeling bad. The knowledge that others are suffering, or more generally, witnessing those in need can be distressing. To decrease this distress in ourselves, we help others.

This explanation of prosocial behavior is known as the **negative-state relief model** (Cialdini, Baumann, & Kenrick, 1981). Research indicates that it doesn't matter whether the bystander's negative emotions were aroused by something unrelated to the emergency or by the emergency itself. That is, you could be upset about receiving a bad grade or about seeing that a stranger has been injured. In either instance, you engage in a prosocial act primarily as a way to improve your own negative mood (Dietrich & Berkowitz, 1997; Fultz, Schaller, & Cialdini, 1988). In this kind of situation, unhappiness leads to prosocial behavior, and empathy is not a necessary component (Cialdini et al., 1987).

9.1.3: Empathic Joy: Feeling Good by Helping Others

How do you feel when you do a favor for someone you know or even a stranger? If you are like most people, such actions enhance your mood—you experience positive feelings. For instance, when I have lots of items in my shopping cart at the grocery store, and the person behind me in line has only two or three, I often say "Please, go ahead of me." Usually they smile and thank me—and as a result I get a small boost in positive feelings. Such situations illustrate another source of prosocial behavior: the **empathic joy hypothesis** (Smith, Keating, & Stotland, 1989). This view suggests that helpers enjoy the positive reactions shown by others whom they help. For instance, do you recall how good it felt seeing someone you care about smile and show pleasure when you gave them a gift? That is an example of empathic joy.

An important implication of this idea is that it is crucial for the person who helps to know that his or her actions had a positive impact on the victim. If helping were based entirely on emotional empathy or empathic concern, feedback about its effects would be irrelevant since we know that we "did good" and that should be enough. But it would not guarantee the occurrence of empathic joy. To test that prediction, Smith, Keating, and Stotland (1989) asked participants to watch a videotape in which a female student said she might drop out of college because she felt isolated and distressed. She was described as either similar to the participant (high empathy) or dissimilar (low empathy). After participants watched the tape, they were given the opportunity to offer helpful advice. Some were told they would receive feedback about the effectiveness of their advice while others were told that they would not be able to learn what the student eventually decided to do. It was found that empathy alone was not enough to produce a prosocial response. Rather, participants were helpful only if there was high empathy and they also received feedback about their action's impact on the victim.

Very impressive evidence for the importance of the rewards of helping others is provided by a study that was conducted in 136 different countries. In an initial study, the researchers (Aknin et al., 2013) had 200,000 people in all these different countries indicate whether they had donated money to charity during the past month and to complete a brief measure of their subjective well-being—the degree to which they were satisfied with their lives. The researchers predicted that there would be a positive correlation between these two variables, thus suggesting that helping others produced positive feelings in donors around the world. There was some variation in the strength of this relationship, suggesting that these findings reflect what is known as a *functional relationship*—it exists in all countries but in varying degrees, rather than an *accessible relationship*—which means that it appears everywhere with little or no variation. In other words, the link between helping others and feeling positive emotions exists everywhere, but it is stronger in some cultures than others. In additional research, Aknin et al. (2013) asked individuals in different countries that differ greatly in wealth (Canada, Uganda, and India) to recall a past instance in which they had spent money on themselves or others. They also responded to a brief measure of their happiness after doing so. Results indicated that participants in each country reported feeling happier after spending on another person than after spending on themselves. In short, overall, the findings support the general proposal that one reason individuals engage in prosocial behavior is that doing so makes them feel happier (see Figure 9.3).

9.1.4: Competitive Altruism: Why Nice People Sometimes Finish First

The three theoretical models described so far suggest that the affective state of the person engaging in a prosocial act is a crucial element. All three formulations rest on the assumption that people engage in helpful behavior either because they want to reduce others' negative feelings or because doing so helps *them* feel better—it counters negative moods or feelings. This general idea is carried one step further by another perspective on prosocial behavior—the **competitive altruism** approach.

Figure 9.3 The Joy of Helping Others Around the World

Research findings indicate that around the globe people who engage in prosocial behavior report feeling happier. The positive effects of helping seem to be universal among human beings and can be found in many different cultures.

This view suggests that one important reason that people help others is that doing so boosts their own status and reputation and, in this way, ultimately brings them large benefits, ones that more than offset the costs of engaging in prosocial actions.

Why might helping others confer status? Because often, helping others is costly, and this suggests to other people that the individuals engaging in such behavior have desirable personal qualities; they are definitely the kind of people a group—or society—wants to have around. For the people who engage in prosocial actions, too, the gains may be substantial. High status confers many advantages, and people who engage in prosocial behavior may be well compensated for their kind and considerate actions. For instance, as you probably know, many people who donate large amounts of money to universities are treated like stars when they visit their alma mater, and they may have entire buildings named after them. Research findings confirm that the motive to experience a boost in social status does lie behind many acts of prosocial behavior—especially ones that bring public recognition (e.g., Flynn, Reagans, Amanatullah, & Ames, 2006). So, overall, this appears to be an important motive for helping others.

9.1.5: Kin Selection Theory

A very different approach to understanding prosocial behavior is offered by **kin selection theory** (Cialdini, Brown, Lewis, Luce, & Neuberg, 1997; Pinker, 1998). From an evolutionary perspective, a key goal for all organisms—including us—is getting our genes into the next generation. Support for this general prediction has been obtained in many studies suggesting that in general we are more likely to help others to whom we are closely related than people to whom we are not related (Neyer & Lang, 2003). For example, Burnstein, Crandall, and Kitayama (1994) conducted a series of studies in which participants were asked whom they would choose to help in an emergency. As predicted on the basis of genetic similarity, participants were more likely to say they would help a close relative than either a distant relative or a nonrelative.

Figure 9.4 Why Alums Sometimes Make Huge Gifts to Their Colleges

Competitive Altruism in Action

According to the competitive altruism theory, people sometimes engage in prosocial behavior because doing so provides them with large gains in status. This kind of outcome is visible on many university campuses, where buildings or entire schools are named after people who make large donations. T. Boone Pickens (shown here in the center), is a graduate of Oklahoma State University, and recently donated $100,000,000 to the university. But please note: We don't mean to imply that this was his only or primary reason for making such a large donation. In fact, we're sure it derived largely from his deep commitment to Oklahoma State University and his personal kindness.

Furthermore, and consistent with kin selection theory, they were more likely to help young relatives, who have many years of reproductive life ahead of them, than older ones. So, given a choice between a female relative young enough to reproduce and a female relative past menopause, help would go to the younger individual.

Overall, then, there is considerable support for kin selection theory. There is one basic problem, though: We don't just help biological relatives; instead, often, we *do* help people who are unrelated to us. Why do we do so? According to kin selection theory, this would not be useful or adaptive behavior since it would not help us transmit our genes to future generations. One answer is provided by *reciprocal altruism theory*—a view suggesting that we may be willing to help people unrelated to us because helping is usually reciprocated: If we help them, they help us, so we do ultimately benefit, and our chances of survival could then be indirectly increased (Korsgaard, Meglino, Lester, & Jeong, 2010).

9.1.6: Defensive Helping: Helping Outgroups to Reduce Their Threat to Our Ingroup

As we saw in our discussion of prejudice (Chapter 6), people often divide the social world into two categories: their own ingroup and outgroups. Furthermore, they often perceive their own group as distinctive from other groups, and superior in several ways. Sometimes, however, outgroups achieve successes that threaten the supposed superiority of one's own group. Can that provide a motive for helping? Recent research suggests that it can, because one way of removing the threat posed by outgroups is to help them—especially in ways that make them seem dependent on such help, and therefore as incompetent or inadequate (Stürmer & Snyder, 2010). In other words, sometimes people help others—especially people who do not belong to their own ingroup—as a means of defusing status threats from them. Such actions are known as **defensive helping** because they are performed not primarily to help the recipients, but rather to "put them down" in subtle ways and so reduce their threat to the ingroup's status. In such cases, helping does not stem from empathy or positive reactions to the joy or happiness it induces among recipients, but, rather, from a more selfish motive: protecting the distinctiveness and status of one's own group.

Evidence for precisely such effects has been reported by Nadler, Harpaz-Gorodeisky, and Ben-David (2009). They told students at one school that students at another school scored either substantially higher than students at their own school on a test of cognitive abilities (this posed a high threat to the superiority of their own group), while students at a third school scored about the same as students at their school (this was low threat to their own group's superiority). When given a chance to help students at these two schools, participants offered more help to the high-threat school, presumably as a way of reducing the status threat from this rival institution.

Findings such as these emphasize the fact that helping others can stem from many different motives. Like many forms of social behavior, then, prosocial actions are complex not only in the forms they take and the factors that affect them, but with respect to the underlying motives from which they spring. Whatever the precise causes of such behavior, though it is clear that helping is an important and fairly common part of the social side of life—one with many beneficial effects both for helpers and those who receive assistance.

Key Points

- Several different motives may underlie prosocial behavior. The **empathy-altruism hypothesis** proposes that, because of empathy, we help those in need because we experience empathic concern for them.
- **Empathy** actually consists of three distinct components— emotional empathy, empathic accuracy, and empathic concern. All three components can serve as a basis for helping others.
- The **negative-state relief model** proposes that people help other people in order to relieve and make less negative their own emotional discomfort.
- The **empathic joy hypothesis** suggests that helping stems from the positive reactions recipients show when they receive help (e.g., gifts), and the positive feelings this, in turn, induces in helpers.

- Recent evidence indicates that people around the world experience positive feelings (affect) when they engage in prosocial behavior.
- The **competitive altruism theory** suggests that we help others as a means of increasing our own status and reputation—and so benefit from helping in important ways.
- **Kin selection theory** suggests that we help others who are related to us because this increases the likelihood that our genes will be transmitted to future generations.
- Another motive for helping behavior is that of reducing the threat posed by outgroups to one's own ingroup; this is known as **defensive helping**.

9.2: Responding to an Emergency: Will Bystanders Help?

Objective   Identify factors that influence whether bystanders will offer help in emergency situations

When an emergency arises, people often rush forward to provide help—as was true in the train incident described at the start of this chapter. But we also often learn from situations in which witnesses to an emergency stand around and do nothing; they take no action while victims suffer or perhaps even die. What can explain such dramatic differences in people's behavior? Let's see what social psychologists have discovered about this important question.

9.2.1: Helping in Emergencies: Apathy—or Action?

Consider the following situation. You are walking across an icy street; lose your footing as you step up on the curb, and fall, injuring your knee. Because of your pain and the slickness of the ice, you find that you can't get back on your feet. Suppose (1) the area is relatively deserted, and only one person is close enough to witness your accident or (2) the area is crowded, and a dozen people can see what happened. Common sense suggests that the more bystanders that are present, the more likely you are to be helped. In the first situation, you are forced to depend on the assistance of just one individual and that person's decision to help or not to help you. In the second situation, with 12 witnesses, there would seem to be a much greater chance that at least one of them (and quite possibly more) will be motivated to behave in a prosocial way. So, is there really safety in numbers? The more witnesses present at an emergency, the more likely the victims are to receive help? Reasonable as this may sound, research by social psychologists suggests that it may be wrong—dead wrong!

The reasons why it may be incorrect were first suggested by John Darley and Bibb Latané, two social psychologists who thought long and hard about this issue after learning of a famous murder in New York City. In this tragic crime, a young woman (Kitty Genovese) was assaulted by a man in a location where many people could see and hear what was going on; all they had to do was look out of their apartment windows. Yet, despite the fact that the attacker continued to assault the victim for many minutes, and even left and then returned to continue the assault later, *not a single person reported the crime to the police.* When news of this tragic crime hit the media, there was much speculation about the widespread selfishness and indifference of people in general or, at least, of people living in big cities. Darley and Latané, however, raised a more basic question: Common sense suggests that the greater the number of witnesses to an emergency (or in this case, a crime), the more likely it is that someone will help. So why wasn't this the case in the tragic murder of Kitty Genovese? In their efforts to answer this question, Darley and Latané developed several possible explanations and then tested them in research that is truly a "classic" of social psychology. Their ideas—and the research it generated—have had a lasting impact on the field. Let's take a closer look at this work.

9.2.2: Is There Safety in Numbers? Sometimes, but Not Always

In their attempts to understand why no one came to Kitty Genovese's aid—or even phoned the police—Darley and Latané considered many possible explanations. The one that seemed to them to be most promising, however, was very straightforward: Perhaps no one helped because *all the witnesses assumed that someone else would do it*! In other words, all the people who saw or heard what was happening believed that it was OK for them to do nothing because others would take care of the situation. Darley and Latané referred to this as **diffusion of responsibility** and suggested that according to this principle, the greater the number of strangers who witness an emergency, the *less* likely are the victims to receive help. After all, the greater the number of potential helpers, the less responsible any one individual will feel, and the more each will assume that "someone else will do it." We should add, however, that if the person needing help appears to be a member of one's own ingroup, they are more likely to get help (Levine, Prosser, Evans, & Reicher, 2005).

To test this reasoning, they performed an ingenious but disturbing experiment in which male college students were exposed to an apparent—but fictitious—emergency. During an experiment, a fellow student apparently had a seizure, began to choke, and was clearly in need of help. The participants interacted by means of an intercom, and it was arranged that some believed they were the only person aware of the emergency, one of two bystanders, or one of five bystanders. Helpfulness was measured in terms of (1) the percentage of participants in each experimental group who attempted to help and (2) the time that passed before the help began.

Darley and Latané's predictions about diffusion of responsibility were correct. The more bystanders participants believed were present, the lower the percentage who made a prosocial response (offered help to the apparent victim; see Figure 9.5) and the longer they waited before responding. Applying this to the example of a fall on the ice described earlier, you would be more likely to be helped if you fell with only one witness present than if 12 witnesses were present.

Over the years, additional research on prosocial behavior has identified a great many other factors that determine how people respond to an emergency. For instance, Kunstman and Plant (2009) suggest that the race of the victim and the helper may play a role, with black victims less likely to receive help from white bystanders, especially if they are high in *aversive racism* (negative emotional reactions to people of a certain race). We will discuss evidence concerning the reasons that people *don't* help in a later section, but it is important to note at this point that group membership of the potential helpers and the person in need can play a critical role in whether help is received. Overall, however, the bystander effect is clearly an important basic discovery concerning the social side of life with respect to helping between strangers, and one that common sense would not have predicted.

Figure 9.5 Diffusion of Responsibility and Helping in Emergencies

The greater the number of witnesses to a staged emergency, the less likely they were to help the apparent victim. This illustrates the powerful inhibiting effect of diffusion of responsibility in such situations.

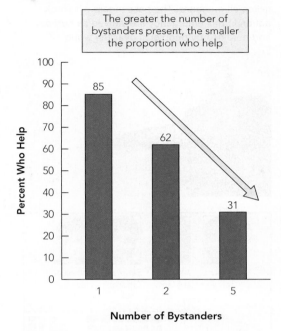

9.2.3: Key Steps in Deciding to Help—Or Not

As the study of prosocial behavior expanded beyond the initial concern with the number of bystanders, Latané and Darley (1970) proposed that the likelihood of a person engaging in prosocial actions is determined by a series of decisions that must be made quickly in the context of emergency situations. Indeed, such decisions *must* be made quickly, or, in many cases, it will be too late. (Recall how quickly Chris Ihle decided to try to push the car stalled on the train tracks to safety.)

Any one of us can sit back and decide instantly what bystanders should do. The witnesses to the assault on Kitty Genovese should either have called the police immediately or perhaps even intervened directly by shouting at the attacker or attempting to stop the attack. Indeed, on September 11, 2001, the passengers on one of the hijacked planes apparently responded jointly, thus preventing the terrorists from accomplishing their goal of crashing into the U.S. Capitol (see Figure 9.6). Why did they do so? Perhaps, as Levine and colleagues (2005) note, because they could see each other and interact directly. In contrast, when bystanders fail to help in emergency situations, as in the ones used by Darley and Latané, they can't interact directly, and this seems to be an important basis for their failure to act.

In a similar manner, the students in the laboratory experiment conducted by Darley and Latané (1968) should have rushed out of the cubicle to help their fellow student who was, apparently, having a medical emergency. Why didn't they do so? One answer is that when we are suddenly and unexpectedly faced with an emergency, the situation is often hard to interpret. Before acting, we must first figure out what, if anything is going on, and what we should do about it. This requires a series of decisions, and at each step—and for each decision—many factors determine the likelihood that

Figure 9.6 When Bystanders Do React to an Emergency: United Flight 93

Passengers on United Airlines Flight 93 took action in an emergency: They overpowered the four hijackers who tried to seize the plane and crash it into a public building in Washington. Instead, it crashed in a rural area of Pennsylvania, killing all on board. The passengers who took action in this emergency are viewed as heroes and heroines by people all over the world.

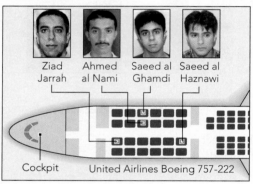

Ziad Jarrah   Ahmed al Nami   Saeed al Ghamdi   Saeed al Haznawi

Cockpit   United Airlines Boeing 757-222

we will fail to help. Here's a summary of the decisions involved, and the factors that play a role in each one.

1. *Noticing, or failing to notice, that something unusual is happening.* An emergency is obviously something that occurs unexpectedly, and there is no sure way to anticipate that it will take place or to plan how best to respond. We are ordinarily doing something else and thinking about other things when we hear a scream outside our window, observe that a fellow student is coughing and unable to speak, or observe that some of the other passengers on our airplane are holding weapons in their hands. If we are asleep, deep in thought, concentrating on something else, we may simply fail to notice that something unusual is happening. The passengers on Flight 93 saw the weapons of the hijackers and learned from the captain that the plane was being taken over by these people. In addition, they used their cell phones to learn of the other attacks (e.g., on the World Trade Center), so they knew that something terrible was occurring, and this made it easier for them to take action.

2. *Correctly interpreting an event as an emergency.* Even after we pay attention to an event, we often have only limited and incomplete information as to what exactly is happening. Most of the time, whatever catches our attention does not turn out to be an emergency and so does not require immediate action. Whenever potential helpers are not completely sure about what is going on, they tend to hold back and wait for further information. After all, responding as if an emergency is occurring when one is not can lead to considerable embarrassment. It's quite possible that in the early morning when Kitty Genovese was murdered, her neighbors could not clearly see what was happening, even though they heard the screams and knew that a man and a woman were having a dispute. It could have just been a loud argument between a woman and her boyfriend. Or, perhaps the couple was just joking with each other. Either of these two possibilities is actually more likely to be true than the fact that a stranger was stabbing a woman to death. With ambiguous information as to whether one is witnessing a serious problem or something trivial, most people are inclined to accept the latter, and take no action (Wilson & Petruska, 1984).

This suggests that the presence of multiple witnesses may inhibit helping not only because of the diffusion of responsibility, but also because it is embarrassing to misinterpret a situation and to act inappropriately. Making such a serious mistake in front of several strangers might lead them to think you are overreacting in a stupid way. And when people are uncertain about what's happening they tend to hold back and do nothing.

This tendency for an individual surrounded by a group of strangers to hesitate and do nothing is based on what is known as **pluralistic ignorance.** Because none of the bystanders knows for sure what is happening, each depends on the others to provide cues. Each individual is less likely to respond if the others fail to respond. Latané and Darley (1968) provided a dramatic demonstration of just how far people will go to avoid making a possibly ridiculous response to what may or may not be an emergency. They placed students in a room alone or with two other students and asked them to fill out questionnaires. After several minutes had passed, the experimenters secretly pumped smoke into the research room through a vent. When a participant was working there alone, most

(75 percent) stopped what they were doing when the smoke appeared and left the room to report the problem. When three people were in the room, however, only 38 percent reacted to the smoke. Even after it became so thick that it was difficult to see, 62 percent continued to work on the questionnaire and failed to make any response to the smoke-filled room. The presence of other people clearly inhibits responsiveness. It is as if risking death is preferable to making a fool of oneself.

This inhibiting effect is much less if the group consists of friends rather than strangers, because friends are likely to communicate with one another about what is going on (Rutkowski, Gruder, & Romer, 1983). The same is true of people in small towns who are likely to know one another as opposed to big cities where most people are strangers (Levine, Prosser, Evans, & Reicher, 2005). Also, and not surprisingly, any anxiety about the reactions of others and thus the fear of doing the wrong thing is reduced by alcohol. As a result, people who have been drinking show an increased tendency to be helpful (Steele, 1988)—another finding that is rather counterintuitive.

3. *Deciding that it is your responsibility to provide help.* In many instances, the responsibility for helping is clear. Firefighters are the ones to do something about a blazing building, police officers take charge when cars collide, and medical personnel deal with injuries and illnesses (see Figure 9.7). If responsibility is not clear, people assume that anyone in a leadership role must take responsibility—for instance, adults with children, professors with students. As we have pointed out earlier, when there is only *one* bystander, he or she usually takes charge because there is no alternative.

4. *Deciding that you have the knowledge and/or skills to act.* Even if a bystander progresses as far as Step 3 and assumes responsibility, a prosocial response cannot occur unless the person knows *how* to be helpful. Some emergencies are sufficiently simple that almost everyone has the necessary skills to help. If someone slips on the ice, most bystanders are able to help that person get up. On the other hand, if you see someone parked on the side of the road, peering under the hood of the car, you can't be of direct help unless you know something about cars and how they function. The best you can do is offer to call for assistance.

Figure 9.7 Responsibility for Others' Health and Safety and Helping

People who hold certain jobs—such as those on Emergency Medical Teams—take responsibility for helping others in a wide range of emergency situations, for instance, at the scene of a serious accident.

When emergencies require special skills, usually only a portion of the bystanders are able to help. For example, only good swimmers can assist a person who is drowning. With a medical emergency, a registered nurse is more likely to be helpful than a history professor (Cramer, McMaster, Bartell, & Dragma, 1988).

5. *Making the final decision to provide help.* Even if a bystander passes the first four steps in the decision process, help does not occur unless he or she makes the ultimate decision to engage in a helpful act. Helping at this final point can be inhibited by fears (often realistic ones) about potential negative consequences. In effect, potential helpers engage in "cognitive algebra" as they weigh the positive versus the negative aspects of helping (Fritzsche, Finkelstein, & Penner, 2000). As we will note in a later discussion, the rewards for being helpful are primarily provided by the emotions and beliefs of the helper, but there are a great many varieties of potential costs. For example, if you intervened in the Kitty Genovese attack, you might be stabbed yourself. You might slip while helping a person who has fallen on the ice. Or a person might be asking for assistance simply as a trick leading to robbery or worse (Byrne, 2001).

In sum, deciding to help in an emergency situation is not a simple, straightforward decision. Rather, it involves a number of steps or decisions, and only if all of these decisions are positive does actual helping occur. (Figure 9.8 summarizes these steps.)

Figure 9.8 Five Steps on the Path to Helping in Emergencies

As shown here, deciding to actually offer help to the victims of emergencies depends on five steps. Only if these steps or decisions are positive does actual helping occur.

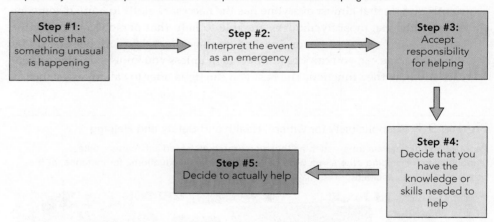

Key Points

- When an emergency arises and someone is in need of help, a bystander may or may not respond in a prosocial way—responses can range from apathy (and doing nothing) to heroism. In part because of **diffusion of responsibility**, the more bystanders present as witnesses to an emergency, the less likely each of them is to provide help and the greater the delay before help occurs (the *bystander effect*). This is true for helping between strangers, but is less likely to occur for helping among people who belong to same groups. **Pluralistic ignorance** can prevent any one person in a group of strangers from acting, as each of them

waits for cues from the others to decide on appropriate action.

- When faced with an emergency, a bystander's tendency to help or not help depends in part on decisions made at five crucial steps. First, it is necessary for the bystander to pay attention and be aware that an unusual event is occurring.
- Second, the bystander must correctly interpret the situation as an emergency.
- Third, the bystander must assume responsibility to provide help. Fourth, the bystander must have the required knowledge and skills to be able to act. In a final step, the bystander must decide to take action.

9.3: Factors That Increase or Decrease the Tendency to Help

Objective **Determine the factors that increase or decrease people's willingness to help others**

As we noted earlier, interest in prosocial behavior by social psychologists was first inspired by the question, "Why do bystanders at an emergency sometimes help and sometimes fail to do anything?" We have already considered one important factor to emerge from research on this question—the number of bystanders present. But clearly, individuals engage in prosocial behavior in a wide range of situations—not just those involving emergencies. We will now examine factors that either encourage or discourage prosocial behavior in many different settings. These can be external—involving the situations in which prosocial behavior occurs—or internal—relating to the personal characteristics and feelings of potential helpers.

9.3.1: Factors That Increase Prosocial Behavior

Are all people who need help equally likely to receive it? Or are some more likely to get assistance than others? And if so, why? Research findings offer intriguing insights into these and related questions.

HELPING PEOPLE SIMILAR TO OURSELVES It is obvious that most people are very likely to help family members and friends when they need assistance, so most of the research we will now discuss focuses on providing help to strangers. The situation is less clear-cut when strangers are involved. Suppose that you observe what seems to be an emergency, and the victim is a stranger. If this person is similar to you with respect to age, nationality, or some other factor, are you more likely to help than you would be if the victim were very different from yourself—for instance, much older, or a member of a group different from your own? The answer provided by careful research is "yes"—we are indeed more likely to help people who are similar to ourselves than people who are dissimilar (Hayden, Jackson, & Guydish, 1984; Shaw, Borough, & Fink, 1994). Research findings (Hodges and colleagues, 2010) indicate that part of the answer may involve the fact that similarity to others increases our empathic concern for them, and our understanding of what they are experiencing. In other words, we can empathize more readily with people similar to ourselves than those who are dissimilar because we can put ourselves in their place, and imagine what they are experiencing.

EXPOSURE TO PROSOCIAL MODELS—LIVE OR ELECTRONIC In an emergency, we know that the presence of bystanders who fail to respond inhibits helpfulness. It is equally true, however, that the presence of a helpful bystander provides a strong *social model*, and the result is an increase in helping behavior among the remaining bystanders. An example of such modeling is provided by a field experiment in which a young woman (a research assistant) with a flat tire parked her car just off the road. Motorists were much more inclined to stop and help this woman if they had previously driven past a staged scene in which another woman with car trouble was observed receiving assistance (Bryan & Test, 1967). Even the symbolic presence of one or more helping models can increase prosocial behavior. Have you ever visited a museum and then, on the way out, passed by a large glass case asking for donations? Often, the museums will place money in the case (including a few bills of large denominations—$10s or $20s)—in an effort to increase donations. And the tactic works: Many people passing the case think "Others have donated, so perhaps I should too" and then they actually reach into their pockets or purses for a donation (see Figure 9.9).

PLAYING PROSOCIAL VIDEO GAMES It is not only live, in-the-flesh, social models who behave in a prosocial manner that can increase our own tendency to do so—even

Figure 9.9 Prosocial Behavior Is . . . Contagious!

When people see another person behaving in a prosocial manner, their own tendency to perform such helpful actions is increased—a very positive result of the modeling effects we described in Chapter 7.

models shown electronically can have the same effects. This is demonstrated by the influence of exposure to prosocial behavior in video games. Many of these games, as we will see in Chapter 10, are aggressive in nature. But some video games, in contrast, involve prosocial actions: Characters in the game help and support one another. Does playing such games increase the tendency to engage in similar actions? Several theoretical frameworks (Bushman & Anderson, 2002; Gentile & Gentile, 2008) suggest that there are important reasons why this might be the case. For instance, playing prosocial video games might prime prosocial thoughts and schemas—cognitive frameworks related to helping others. Repeated exposure to such games can, over time, generate attitudes favorable to prosocial actions, emotions consistent with them (e.g., positive feelings associated with helping others), and other lasting changes in the ways in which individuals think that facilitate prosocial actions.

That such effects actually occur and are both strong and lasting in nature is indicated by a growing body of recent research. For instance, in a series of studies by Greitmeyer and Osswald (2010), participants played either prosocial (e.g., Lemmings), aggressive (e.g., Lamers), or neutral (Tetris) video games. Then, they were exposed to a situation in which they could engage in spontaneous helping: The experimenter spilled a cup of pencils on the floor. As expected, a higher proportion of those who had played the prosocial video games (57 percent) helped pick up the pencils, while lower proportions of those who had played the neutral game (33 percent) or the aggressive game (28 percent) helped.

In a follow-up study, participants played either prosocial or neutral video games and were again presented with an opportunity to help another person; in this case, though, helping involved intervening when a male assistant harassed a female experimenter. Again, a higher proportion who had played the prosocial video game intervened (56 percent), versus only 22 percent who had played the neutral game. Finally, to obtain evidence concerning the underlying mechanisms through which prosocial video games increase helping, the researchers conducted another study in which participants indicated what they had been thinking about while playing the video games. As predicted, those who played the prosocial game reported more thoughts about helping others than those who played the neutral game. So, consistent with these theoretical models, playing prosocial video games influenced actual helping by influencing participants' thoughts.

Similar confirming evidence has been reported in other studies (e.g., Gentile et al., 2009), including a longitudinal study in which the amount of time participants played prosocial video games was related to their helping of others several months later. As expected, the more they played prosocial games, the more likely they were to report engaging in such actions as "helping a person who was in trouble" months later. These findings indicate that playing prosocial video games produces not merely short-term effects, but ones of a more lasting nature.

In sum, video games—which have often been criticized as having negative effects on the people who play them—appear to be neutral in and of themselves. Depending on their content, they can facilitate either harmful, aggressive actions (see Chapter 10) or beneficial, prosocial ones. Clearly, it is the nature of the games— not the games themselves—that is crucial with respect to the social side of life.

FEELINGS THAT REDUCE OUR FOCUS ON OURSELVES Have you ever been somewhere that you experienced feelings of awe—for example, while peering into the Grand Canyon? Looking at Niagara Falls? In such situations, the feelings of awe we experience often lead us to realize how small and perhaps insignificant we are; such feelings occur in settings such as, Yellowstone National Park and Redwood forests, in which the trees have lasted for centuries and are truly majestic in appearance. Do such feelings have any relationship to prosocial behavior? Several social psychologists (Piff, Dietze, Feinberg, Stancato, & Keltner, 2015) reasoned that it does. They suggest that when we experience awe, our concern with ourselves and our worries—which can seem petty in the face of such feelings—can increase our tendency to help others. Past research has demonstrated such effects indirectly. For instance, Campbell, Bonacci, Shelton, Exline, and Bushman (2004) found that individuals who felt reduced self-importance were more likely donate to a good cause and were even less selfish in their personal relationships with others.

In research directly focused on the effects of feelings of awe on prosocial behaviour, Piff, Dietze, Feinberg, Stancato, and Keltner (2015) conducted a study in which participants were actually taken to a grove of giant trees and looked up at them for 1 minute or, at a nearby tall building (see Figure 9.10). It was expected that those who looked at the trees—which were truly impressive—would experience awe, but those who looked at a tall but ordinary building, would not. Participants in both groups then saw a minor accident in which the experimenter dropped a large number of pens. If awe increases prosocial behavior, those who saw the trees should help the experimenter more (i.e., pick up more pens for this person) than those who looked at the building. This is precisely what happened. So, awe—because it shifts our attention away from ourselves and our own concerns—does seem to increase the tendency to engage in prosocial behavior.

SOCIAL CLASS: DO PEOPLE WHO HAVE LESS GIVE MORE? At first glance, it seems reasonable to suggest

Figure 9.10 The Experience of Awe: Its Effects on Prosocial Behavior

When individuals experience awe—for instance, when they look at the Redwood forest—they tend to focus less on themselves and their own concerns. That, in turn, increases their tendency to help others who need assistance.

that the more resources people have—for instance, the more money at their disposal—the more generous they will be, that is the more likely they are to engage in prosocial behavior. However, there are several reasons for predicting that precisely the opposite will occur: The less financial resources people have, the more generous they will be. This may be so because people of lower socioeconomic class (i.e., those with less wealth and less education), often feel more dependent on others—they need them to survive. Further, people of lower socioeconomic background often report that they have less control over their lives and what happens to them which, in turn, leads them to form stronger connections to others who face the same situation. People higher in socioeconomic status and who have greater financial resources at their disposal, in contrast, often experience greater feelings of control, and so have lower needs to affiliate with others who are facing the same situation as themselves.

To test the prediction that people lower in socioeconomic status would actually show greater prosocial behavior than those higher in status, Piff, Kraus, Cote, Cheng, and Keltner (2010) conducted several studies. In one, participants played what is known as the "dictator game." In this game, one person is told that they can divide 10 points between themselves and a partner who can then either accept this division or reject it, but cannot change it. A measure of prosocial behavior is provided by the number of points participants assign to their partner. Participants also completed a measure of their own perceived social class, by indicating their own position on a drawing of a 10-rung ladder, ranging from very low income, education, and occupation on the bottom, to very high on the top. As predicted, results indicated that the lower their perceived socioeconomic status, the larger the number of points they gave to their partner.

In follow-up research, Piff et al. (2010) found that these results stemmed, at least in part, from differences in compassion for others: Individuals lower in socioeconomic status expressed greater compassion for others than individuals higher in socioeconomic status. In other words, believing that it is important to help others who need it and to take care of those who are vulnerable to harm underlies the negative link between socioeconomic status and kindness (see Figure 9.11). For another—and surprising—factor that increases prosocial behavior, see the section that follows.

9.3.2: Factors That Reduce Helping

There are many situations in which helping others could occur—and would be very valuable—yet it does not. This raises an important question—why don't they help, especially if they have resources or ability to do so? The answer involves several factors that tend to reduce the occurrence of prosocial behavior.

SOCIAL EXCLUSION: BEING "LEFT OUT" HURTS—AND MAY REDUCE THE TENDENCY TO HELP OTHERS As we noted earlier, prosocial behavior is more likely to be directed toward people we perceive as similar to ourselves rather than those we

---

Figure 9.11 Are Poorer People Actually More Helpful Than Those Who Are Richer?

Research indicates that there is a negative relationship between socioeconomic status and prosocial behavior. People lower in such status—and lower in income—are actually more likely to help others than people higher in such status and income. This difference exists because those lower in socioeconomic status have more compassion for others.

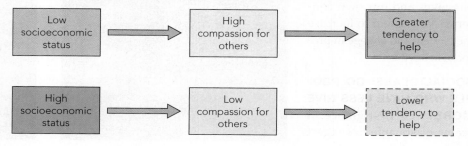

What Research Tells Us About...

Paying It Forward: Helping Others Because We Have Been Helped

Several years ago, I was driving and came to a bridge that charges a $1.00 toll. I pulled a dollar bill out of my wallet and was ready to pay the toll when—much to my surprise—the toll collector said: "You don't have to pay—the driver ahead of you paid your toll." I was truly surprised: Why would a total stranger pay for me? I had never experienced anything like it before. But now, I realize that such actions are far from rare: They are instances in which people do what's called *pay it forward*. Recently, social psychologists have focused their attention on this kind of prosocial behavior that occurs when one person—often a total stranger—helps another, who then instead of reciprocating to the person who helped them, helps someone else. Social psychologists have uncovered many interesting facts about this unusual form of prosocial behavior (Gray, Ward, & Norton, 2014).

A series of studies conducted by Jung, Nelson, Gneezy, and Gneezy (2014) are especially intriguing. These researchers studied "paying it forward" in several different contexts. In one, they obtained the cooperation of a museum. Visitors were then exposed to one of two conditions: a pay-what-you-wish condition (visitors could pay for their admission with any amount they wished) or pay-it-forward condition in which they were told that this was a pay-what-you wish day but that someone else had already paid their admission. The visitors in this group were also told that they could pay for someone else's admission if they wished. The key question was, having been helped by a stranger, would they now pay more for this person's admission? In other words, being the recipient of prosocial behavior from a stranger, would they now pay more for that person's admission (remember, this was a "pay what you wish day"). Results were clear: They did; those in the pay-what-you wish condition who had not been helped by a stranger paid $2.19 for admission. In the pay-forward condition where they had been helped by a stranger, they paid $3.07. So it was clear that a pay-it-forward effect occurred (see Figure 9.12).

Jung and colleagues repeated this research in an entirely different setting—a coffee house. Here, they were told that they could pay what they wished for their coffee, but that someone else had already paid for theirs. Also, they were told that

they could now pay for someone else's coffee—pay-it-forward. Again, they paid more for the coffee when someone else had paid for theirs.

Why do such effects occur—why are people more willing to help a stranger who has not helped them after being helped by a different stranger? One possibility is that people feel pressure to behave in a similar prosocial way as the stranger. Another is that receiving help from a stranger leads them to think about others' generosity, and to overestimate it. Whatever the explanation, it is clear that pay-it-forward illustrates that many different factors can influence our tendency to engage in prosocial behavior—and that some of them are very surprising.

Figure 9.12 Paying It Forward: Helping Others Because Someone Has Helped Us

When a stranger provides unexpected help to another person, the recipient often reciprocates such prosocial behavior by helping another person—not the one who helped them.

view as dissimilar. This suggests that prosocial behavior rests, at least to some degree, on a sense of community—the idea that we belong to, or fit into, a group in which the other members are like ourselves. What happens, then, if we are excluded from this group—or perceive that we no longer belong? Social psychologists refer to such situations as **social exclusion**, and have found that it has negative effects on the people excluded in several ways—it undermines their self-esteem, leads them to feel isolated, and less satisfied with their lives (see Figure 9.13). In addition, recent evidence indicates that social exclusion reduces the tendency of the excluded people to help others. This may occur for several reasons: Reduced feelings of empathy—especially toward the people who have rejected them, a tendency to see these people as hurtful or aggressive, seeking to harm the people who excluded them (Schonert-Reichl, 1999),

Figure 9.13 Being Excluded . . . Hurts

Research findings indicate that when individuals are excluded from a group to which they want to belong, their tendency to help others is reduced. This may be so for several reasons—excluded people feel less empathy toward others and they tend to see the people who rejected them as hurtful or aggressive.

and strong negative affect. Together, these perceptions and emotions may reduce the tendency to help others.

To test this possibility, Twenge, Baumeister, DeWall, Ciarocco, and Bartels (2007) conducted research in which participants were told that on the basis of a personality test, that they were likely to have many rewarding relationships with others in the years ahead, while others were told that they would be likely to end up alone in later life. A third, control group, was told that they were likely to have accidents in the years ahead. All three groups were given a payment for participating in the study, and then an opportunity to donate all or part of this to a Student Emergency Fund. It was predicted that those who were told that they were likely to be excluded in later life would donate less, and in fact, this is precisely what happened. In others words, feeling that they would be rejected by other people in the future, resulted in less willingness to help others now—even before such exclusion. The basic point, then, is that when people feel outside a group or community, don't expect them to offer to help to others within the group or community—they are, in a sense, disconnected from the potential recipients of help.

DARKNESS: FEELINGS OF ANONYMITY REDUCE THE TENDENCY TO HELP OTHERS Darkness has often been linked to disinhibited behavior—under 'cover' of darkness, people often engage in actions they would be reluctant to perform in broad day light. Why? One reason is that they feel anonymous: Others can't see them or evaluate their actions. If prosocial behavior sometimes occurs because it can be observed by others and is believed likely to win their approval, then darkness should reduce or eliminate this motive. In other words, people would be less likely to help others, or engage in other forms of prosocial behavior, in the presence of darkness—or merely when they believe that conditions provide them with anonymity.

Classic studies in social psychology on what is known as *deindividuation*—a reduced state of self-awareness that encourages impulsive behavior (see Chapter 11 for discussion of this research) indicates that when people feel anonymous, they may perform actions they would not perform under other conditions. However, it may not be merely feelings of anonymity that are operating: When people are part of a large crowd, they are more likely to obey the norms of that group, and do what others are doing (Postmes & Spears, 1998), so this may be an important factor in such situations. But does darkness itself encourage such feelings of anonymity and willingness to ignore social norms (see Figure 9.14)? Evidence reported by Zhong, Bohns, and Gino (2010) suggest that it can.

In an ingenious study, these researchers placed participants in a slightly darkened room, or in a room with bright lighting, and had them perform a task involving finding two numbers in matrixes of numbers that added up to 10. They were told that if they performed very well, they could receive an extra $10. Participants recorded their own scores, but unbeknownst to them these could then be compared with their actual scores. Zhong and colleagues predicted that participants would be more likely to exaggerate their scores (i.e., to be dishonest) in a dark room than a bright one, and in fact this is what happened. Fully 50 percent of the participants who performed the task in the dark room overstated their performance, while only 24.4 percent of those in the bright room did. Their performance itself was not different from that of people who performed in a bright room, so it appeared that darkness did in fact reduce their tendency to obey strong social norms against such behavior—that is, against being dishonest or cheating.

Although Zhong and colleagues did not collect data on prosocial behavior, their findings indicate that darkness may enhance the tendency to ignore a wide range of social norms. One such norm states: "We should help others in need of assistance." So, by extension, darkness—and the anonymity it produces—might lead to situations in which individuals feel little motivation to help others—after all, they can't be identified as the source of prosocial behavior. Similar findings were obtained when room lighting was not varied, but participants either wore or did not wear dark sunglasses which, presumably, would give them feelings of anonymity. In this study, those wearing the glasses were more likely to act in a selfish manner, taking more of an available prize for themselves, and giving less to their partners.

Figure 9.14 Does Darkness—and the Anonymity It Provides—Reduce Prosocial Behavior—and Perhaps, Increase Aggression?

Research findings indicate that conditions that increase anonymity—including darkness—can encourage harmful actions ranging from dishonesty to looting or even harming others. Of course, engaging in such behaviors would be incompatible with prosocial behavior.

PUTTING AN ECONOMIC VALUE ON OUR TIME REDUCES PROSOCIAL BEHAVIOR

As we have seen in this chapter, many factors can influence the tendency to help others in various ways. Emotional factors certainly play a role (empathy, current moods, feelings of awe), and cognitive factors (our accuracy in perceiving others' feelings and so in understanding their need for help), too, are important. An additional cognitive factor might be the extent to which we think about helping others in terms of the economic costs to us: Time used in helping others can't be used for other activities, including ones that generate income. To the extent that we think about helping in this way (e.g., the economic costs of volunteering our time), we may be less likely to engage in prosocial behavior.

Two researchers, DeVoe and Pfeffer (2010), have recently suggested that when people think about the economic value of their time, they may be less likely to volunteer it to help others. Certain professions, of course, train their members to think

What Research Tells Us About...

How People React to Being Helped

Throughout this chapter, we have implicitly assumed that prosocial behavior is a good thing; and why not? Helping others who need assistance and showing generosity are very positive actions. Thus, we have focused on factors that promote or deter prosocial behavior. But, what about the recipients of such assistance—do they always react positively to it? Your first answer might well be "Of course!" but think again: Have you ever received a gift you really didn't want, but had to pretend to like (see Figure 9.15)? Or has someone offered you help when you believed that you really didn't need it, which made you feel that the person offering it did not feel you were capable or competent? If so, you already know that prosocial actions do not always generate positive reactions; in fact, sometimes, they produce the opposite effects.

Evidence that this is so has been provided by many studies. The research indicates, first, that sometimes, being helped can threaten our self-esteem. As mentioned earlier, when we do not believe that we really *need* help, but it is still offered, or even forced upon us, reactions to it can be quite negative (DePaulo Brown, Ishii, & Fisher, 1981). A clear example of such effects occurs when a parent offers help to a teenager who protests loudly that "I'd rather do it myself!"

Another reason why prosocial actions may produce negative reactions in the person being helped occurs when the helper communicates a sense of superiority: "I'm helping you because I know so much more or have so much more than you do." Fortunately, such reactions can be reduced when recipients of help perceive that the people offering it sincerely care about them and their well-being.

But now, let's turn the situation around: Suppose you have offered help to another person and they have accepted it. What do you now expect? Often, people expect some indication of gratitude. If you don't receive it, will you be more or less likely to help this person in the future? Clearly, you will be less likely to help—after all, it's only fair for the recipient to say "Thank you." In contrast, if they do express their gratitude, your willingness to help them in the future might increase.

What is it about expressions of gratitude that increases prosocial behavior? Research conducted by Grant and Gino

(2010) provides an answer. They reasoned that when helpers are thanked by the people they assist, this boosts the helper's self-worth—the extent to which they feel valued and appreciated. To test this idea, they conducted a study in which participants were asked to edit a job application letter for another student. Then, they met the person they supposedly helped (actually, an accomplice of the experimenter) and had a brief conversation with her. The recipient of their help then either thanked them for their help, or did not. Their willingness to help this person was then measured by the amount of time they then spent editing a second letter. As expected, this was greater when they had been thanked than when they had not.

Overall, then, it seems that reactions to *being* helped can be positive or negative, and that reactions to *providing* help, too, can vary in this way. So by all means, help others who need your assistance—but recognize that such actions can sometimes be a mixed blessing.

Figure 9.15 Do the Recipients of Prosocial Behavior Always React Positively?

Although the recipients of prosocial actions often respond with gratitude and other positive feelings, sometimes—as shown here—they do not!

in just these ways. While physicians bill patients according to the procedures they perform, attorneys (and other professionals such as accountants) bill in terms of their time. In fact, many attorneys bill in tenths of an hour—for each 6-minute period they use in working on clients' cases. Does this make them less likely to engage in prosocial behavior? Findings reported by DeVoe and Pfeffer indicate that it does.

In one study, third-year law students, who had not yet practiced billing for their time, were asked to complete a questionnaire concerning their willingness to volunteer their time to organizations they cared about. Then, 5 months later, after graduating and taking jobs, they completed the same survey. Results indicated that as the researchers predicted, the now-practicing attorneys expressed less willingness to volunteer their time than they had as law students. In fact, later, when they were actually practicing law and billing for the time they invested in a case, they were asked how much time they were willing to volunteer to assist with various worthy causes. Results indicated that those in the billing condition, who focused on time and its use, expected to spend fewer hours on volunteer work than law students who had not yet engaged in such billing. These findings have been confirmed in other research, so it appears that to the extent we attach economic value to our time, we may be less likely to donate it to helping others (LeBoeuf, Shafir, & Bayuk, 2005). The milk of human kindness, it appears, dries up when it is measured precisely in tenths of an hour. But what happens when we *are* the beneficiary of such kindness? Do we always react in a positive way? For an answer to this question, please see the special feature, **"What Research Tells Us About...How People React to Being Helped."**

Key Points

- We are more likely to help others who are similar to ourselves than others who are dissimilar. This leads to lower tendencies to help people outside our own social groups.
- Helping is increased by exposure to prosocial models; it can also be increased by playing prosocial video games.
- Prosocial video games increase subsequent helping by priming prosocial thoughts, building cognitive frameworks related to helping.
- People higher in socioeconomic status are less likely to help others than are people lower in socioeconomic status.

- When a stranger has helped us, by "paying it forward," we are more likely to reciprocate by helping someone else.
- Several factors can discourage helping: after experiencing **social exclusion** or perceive that we no longer belong, when we feel anonymous (under cover of darkness), and when we place an economic value on our time.
- People who receive help from others do not always react positively in part, because it threatens their self-esteem.
- Expressions of gratitude from the recipients of help increases prosocial behavior, by enhancing helpers' feelings of self-worth.

9.4: Crowdfunding: A New Type of Prosocial Behavior

Objective   **Relate crowdfunding to the factors influencing prosocial behavior**

Suppose you were approached by a total stranger who asked you to donate funds so that she could start a new business. You would not own part of it because of your contribution, and she would never return your money. If you answered: "No way!" think again. In recent years, many internet sites have been established precisely for this reason: to help entrepreneurs obtain the funds they need to start a new business. Among these are sites such as Kickstarter, Fundraiser, and GoFundMe. In general, these sites present short videos by entrepreneurs in which they describe their products or services, and ask people who watch the video to contribute funds so that they can move ahead.

How successful are such efforts? Unbelievably so! For instance, one such project involved a new video game called Space Combat, which received more than $65 million from contributors. Most requests for funds, of course, are much smaller—entrepreneurs ask donors to contribute $5,000 or $10,000. Many of these fail, but many others succeed. This is known as **crowdfunding**—a process in which entrepreneurs use the money contributed to set up and then run their companies. Since contributors will receive virtually nothing in return (perhaps a T-shirt or other small "reward" for their help), this is clearly a form of prosocial behavior—and one that has grown hugely in recent years.

Crowdfunding sites carefully screen the projects entrepreneurs submit, and include safeguards to insure that the people who request funds really use them for the purposes they describe. The overall effects are very positive: Entrepreneurs acquire the funds they need to get started, and as you probably know, the companies they start often provide jobs and contribute to economic growth. So clearly, this is a form of prosocial behavior that benefits not just the entrepreneurs, but their communities too. Why do people contribute? It has been suggested that they do because they believe the products or services are good ones, and simply want to help the entrepreneurs to make them available. Whatever their reasons, it appears that crowdfunding is here to stay.

9.4.1: Emotion and Prosocial Behavior: Mood, Feelings of Elevation, and Helping

Suppose you want to ask another person for a favor; when would you do this? When she or he is in a very good mood or when she or he is in a very sad or angry mood? The answer is obvious: Most people know that other people—and they themselves—are more likely to engage in prosocial behavior when in a good mood than a bad mood. But research findings indicate that the situation is a bit more complicated than that.

POSITIVE EMOTIONS AND PROSOCIAL BEHAVIOR Many ingenious studies have been performed to investigate the potential link between good moods and helping. In general, this research indicates that people are more willing to help a stranger when their mood has been elevated by some recent experience—for instance, listening to a comedian (Wilson, 1981), finding money in the coin return slot of a public telephone (Isen & Levin, 1972), spending time outdoors on a pleasant day (Cunningham, 1979), or receiving a small unexpected gift (Isen, 1970). Even a pleasant fragrance in the air can increase prosocial behavior (Baron, 1990; Baron & Thomley, 1994)—something department stores know very well. That's why they often pump pleasant smells into the air in the hope that this will increase purchases by customers.

Under certain specific circumstances, however, a positive mood can *decrease* the probability of responding in a prosocial way (Isen, 1984). This is because being in a good mood can lead us to interpret various situations—especially emergencies—as not really serious. And even if it is clear that an emergency exists, people in a good mood sometimes help less than those in a neutral mood if helping involves actions that are difficult (Rosenhan, Salovey, & Hargis, 1981) or will detract from their current good mood.

NEGATIVE EMOTIONS AND PROSOCIAL BEHAVIOR If positive moods increase helping, do negative moods reduce such behavior? Some research findings offer support for this view (Amato, 1986). As is true of positive emotions, though, specific circumstances can strongly influence or even reverse this general trend. For example, if the act of helping others generates positive feelings, people in a bad mood may actually be more likely to help than those in a neutral or even positive mood because they want to make themselves feel better, and helping others can help them accomplish this goal (Cialdini, Kenrick, & Baumann, 1982). This is consistent with the negative-state relief model described earlier. A negative mood or emotion is most likely to increase prosocial behavior if the negative feelings are not too intense, if the emergency is clear-cut rather than ambiguous, and if the act of helping is interesting and satisfying rather than dull and unrewarding (Cunningham, Shaffer, Barbee, Wolff, & Kelley, 1990).

FEELINGS OF ELATION AND HELPING OTHERS When we see another person engaging in a kind or helpful act, this can have a strong effect on our emotions. In particular, it can trigger feelings of *elation*—it can make us feel inspired, uplifted, and optimistic about human nature. Does it also increase our tendency to engage in prosocial behavior? Recent evidence indicates that it does. Schnall, Roper, and Fessler (2010) conducted a series of studies in which participants were exposed either to an elevating video showing prosocial actions by others, a neutral video (about the ocean), or a video showing a funny comedian (mirth condition). The mirth condition was included as a control for the possibility that the effects of seeing other people behave in a prosocial manner merely increase positive affect, and as we noted earlier, positive moods do often increase helping in and of themselves.

After watching one of these videos, participants in the research had an opportunity act in a prosocial manner. In one study, for instance, they were asked if they would help the experimenter by completing a questionnaire described as boring. The measure of helping was how many minutes participants volunteered. It was predicted that those exposed to a video designed to induce feelings of elevation (feelings of being uplifted, inspired, etc.) would volunteer more time, and as you can see in Figure 9.16 this is precisely what happened. In fact, participants who viewed the elevating video volunteered about twice as much time as those in the other two conditions. The fact that the mirth condition (exposure to a funny comedian) did not increase helping indicates that feelings of elevation do indeed involve more than merely positive affect. The moral of such research is clear, and fits well with research on the effects of playing prosocial video games. The tendency to perform prosocial actions can be increased by exposure to others engaging in such actions. Kindness, in short, is "contagious" and can be encouraged by witnessing it in the actions of others.

Figure 9.16 Feelings of Elevation and Helping

Individuals exposed to a videotape designed to induce feelings of elevation (feelings of being uplifted, inspired) later engaged in more helping than those exposed to a humorous tape or scenes of the ocean.

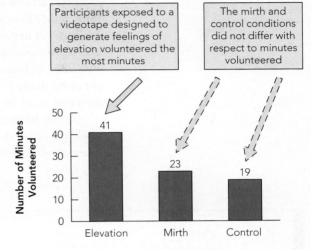

9.4.2: Gender and Prosocial Behavior: Do Women and Men Differ?

Suppose you wanted someone to help you cope with a distressing situation—one that has caused you to experience very intense, negative emotions. Would you seek—and expect—more help from women or men? In another context, suppose that you were seeking someone who would be willing to offer help to a stranger but doing so would expose the helper to considerable danger—for instance, rescuing someone from a burning building or from the ocean where they appeared to be drowning. Who would you expect to be more likely to perform this task, men or women? Many people would answer "women" to the first situation and "men" to the second. This suggests that, in fact, we don't expect women and men to differ in terms of their overall willingness to engage in prosocial behavior; rather, such differences may emerge only in specific situations.

A large body of research (e.g., Eagly, 2009) provides support for this suggestion: Women are more helpful than men in some contexts, and men are helpful than women in other contexts. These differences are consistent with gender roles or stereotypes which suggest that women are more likely to be friendly, unselfish, and concerned with others, while men tend to be masterful, assertive, competitive, and dominant. These gender stereotypes indicate, overall, that women are more communal than men—they connect with others and bond with them in close interpersonal relationships. In contrast, men are expected to be more agentic—they tend to connect not in close relationships, but rather, with collectives—that is, relatively large groups. For instance, women form close relationships with their friends—relationships in which they offer each other emotional support. Although men, too, form friendships, they are often focused on activities—people with whom they play tennis or golf, or with whom they discuss investments.

The implications of these differences is that women are more likely to engage in prosocial actions when these involve people with whom they have personal relationships rather than with strangers, while men may be just as likely to help a stranger as a friend. For instance, research findings indicate that men are more likely than women to receive awards for heroism—helping others when doing so involves risking their own lives. In fact, more than 90 percent of such awards go to men. In contrast, women are more likely to receive awards for helping organizations in their communities—ones that focus on assisting specific individuals in need of assistance.

So, are women or men higher in their tendency to engage in prosocial behavior? The answer is: This is the wrong question; instead we should ask, "When—in what situations—do such differences exist?"

Key Points

- Receiving help does not always generate positive reactions in the recipients. In fact, under some conditions, they are more likely to experience feelings of resentment and unwanted obligations to the helper.
- An important factor determining how recipients react to help is the motivation underlying such behavior. If it seems to stem from internal motives (e.g., a genuine desire to help), positive feelings and reactions may result. If, instead, it stems from external motives (i.e., the helper felt obligated to extend assistance), reactions tends to be far less favorable.
- Similar effects occur among helpers, too: They react more positively to helping others when the recipients express gratitude.

- **Crowdfunding**, a new form of prosocial behavior, allows individuals to make financial contributions to entrepreneurs, to help them start new companies. The contributors receive nothing in return for their help.
- Women and men do not differ in prosocial behavior overall, but women are more likely to engage in prosocial actions when these involve people with whom they personal relationships than with strangers, while men may be just as likely to help a stranger as a friend.

9.5: Final Thoughts: Are Prosocial Behavior and Aggression Opposites?

Objective   **Describe the relationship between prosocial behavior and antisocial behavior**

Helping and hurting: At first glance, they certainly seem to be opposites. Rushing to the aid of victims in emergencies, donating to charity, volunteering to help the wildlife harmed by the oil spill in the Gulf of Mexico, giving directions to people who are lost—these and countless other helpful actions seem in many ways the opposite of *aggression*, which social psychologists generally define as intentional efforts to harm others in some way (see Chapter 10). But are helping and aggression really opposites? If you stopped one hundred people at random, and asked them to place helping and aggression along a line, almost all of them would place these forms of social behavior at opposite sides.

But get ready for a surprise: Social psychologists have thought long and hard about this issue and reached the conclusion that in many ways, prosocial behavior and aggression are not opposites. In fact, they overlap much more than you might expect. First, consider the motives underlying such actions. The motivation for helping, you might assume is simply to do something beneficial for the recipient; the motivation for aggression, in contrast, is to do something to harm the recipient in some way. But look a bit more closely: As we have seen in this chapter, people sometimes engage in prosocial actions not primarily to help the recipients, but rather, to boost their own status and to gain a positive reputation. Their motivation, in short, is not necessarily to do something beneficial for the recipients. Certainly, that motive does exist in the form of empathy-based helping; but it is often not the primary motivation responsible for helpful actions toward others.

Now consider aggression: Is the motivation behind such behavior always to harm the victim in some way? Consider the following situation: A sports coach, dissatisfied with the effort an athlete is investing in practice and angry at this person, orders the athlete to take "ten laps around the field" and then also confines the athlete to her or his room that evening: no parties or getting together with friends. Do these actions—which might seem to be aggressive (at least potentially from the recipient's point of view)—stem from a motive to harm the athlete? Not necessarily. The coach takes these actions to help the athlete improve—or at least, become more motivated. We could offer many other examples, but the main point is clear: The motives behind prosocial behavior and aggression sometimes overlap and can't be easily separated. In this respect, certainly, they are not polar opposites.

Now, consider, the specific actions involved in prosocial behavior and aggression. These, you might guess, are direct opposites. Prosocial actions help the recipients in some way, while aggressive actions harm them, so they involve very different kind of actions. Perhaps. But now imagine the following scene: A young woman takes a sharp needle and uses it to puncture the skin of another person, who cries out in pain. Is she behaving aggressively? Maybe yes, maybe no. What if she is placing a tattoo on the supposed "victim's" body—one she has requested and paid for in advance? So while these actions might appear to be aggressive, they may actually have little or nothing to do with harming the "victim." Not all aggressive and prosocial actions overlap in this sense, but some do and this suggests that these two aspects of social behavior are *not* direct opposites.

Finally, consider the *effects* of aggression and prosocial behavior. By definition, aggression produces harm and prosocial actions produce benefits, but again, not always. For instance, consider someone who uses a very sharp knife to cut into the body of another person. Is this aggression? On the surface it may appear to be. But what if the person performing this action is a skilled surgeon, trying to save the other person's life? The short-term effects might seem harmful (the "victim" bleeds profusely), but the long-term effects are actually beneficial: The patient's health is restored. Similarly, prosocial actions can seem beneficial in the short term, but harm the recipient in the long-term. Help we don't request or want can undermine our self-esteem and confidence, so short-term benefits can soon turn into long-term harm.

Finally, we should mention the fact that research findings (e.g., Hawley, Card, & Little, 2007) indicate that aggression and prosocial behavior are sometimes used by the same people to gain popularity and status. Specifically, such research indicates that individuals who behave aggressively can be highly attractive to others—rather than merely alarming—if they combine such actions with prosocial ones. Such people are seen as tough and assertive, but also as possessing social skills that allow them to be charming and helpful; and they know when to "turn" their tough sides on and off. Hawley and her colleagues describe this as "the allure of mean friends" (the appeal of people who are indeed aggressive, but also have other skills that help them to attain important goals) and have found that this combination of toughness and prosocial action is seductive, and far from rare.

As you can see, then, the question of whether helping and aggression are opposites is far more complex than first meets the eye. The motives from which these forms of behavior spring, the behaviors themselves, and effects they produce are complex and overlap much more than you at might initially guess. And that's not really surprising because all social behavior is complex; generally, it stems from many different motives, takes a wide range of forms, and produces many different effects. So yes, indeed, helping and hurting are very different in several respects but not, perhaps, as different as common sense suggests.

Summary and Review

Several different motives may underlie **prosocial behavior**. The **empathy-altruism hypothesis** proposes that, because of empathy, we help those in need because we experience empathic concern for them. **Empathy** actually consists of three distinct components—emotional empathy, empathic accuracy, and empathic concern. All three components can serve as a basis for helping others. The **negative-state relief model** proposes that people help other people in order to relieve and make less negative their own emotional discomfort. The **empathic joy hypothesis** suggests that helping stems from the positive reactions recipients show when they receive help (e.g., gifts) and the positive feelings this, in turn, induces in helpers.

Recent evidence indicates that people around the world experience positive feelings (affect) when they engage in prosocial behavior. The competitive altruism theory suggests that we help others as a means of increasing our own status and reputation—and so benefit from helping in important ways. **Kin selection theory** suggests that we help others who are related to us because this increases the likelihood that our genes will be transmitted to future generations. Another motive for helping behavior is that of reducing the threat posed by outgroups to our own ingroup, known as **defensive helping**.

When an emergency arises and someone is in need of help, a bystander may or may not respond in a prosocial way—responses can range from apathy (and doing nothing) to heroism. In part because of **diffusion of responsibility**, the more bystanders present as witnesses to an emergency, the less likely each of them is to provide help and the greater the delay before help occurs (the *bystander effect*). This is true for helping between strangers, but is less likely to occur for helping among people who belong to same groups. The tendency for an individual surrounded by a group of strangers to refrain from acting is based on **pluralistic ignorance**: Because each of

the bystanders depends on the others to provide cues for appropriate action, no one does anything.

We are more likely to help others who are similar to ourselves than others who are dissimilar. This leads to lower tendencies to help people outside our own social groups. Helping is increased by exposure to prosocial models; it can also be increased by playing prosocial video games. Prosocial video games increase subsequent helping by priming prosocial thoughts, building cognitive frameworks related to helping.

Empathy is an important determinant of helping behavior. It is weaker across group boundaries than within social groups. Several factors reduce the tendency to help others. These include **social exclusion**, darkness, and putting an economic value on our time.

People who receive help from others do not always react positively, in part because it threatens their self-esteem. An important factor determining how recipients react to help is the motivation underlying such behavior. If it seems to stem from internal motives (e.g., a genuine desire to help), positive feelings and reactions may result. If, instead, it stems from external motives (i.e., the helper felt obligated to extend assistance), reactions tends to be far less favorable. Similar effects occur among helpers, too: They react more positively to helping others when the recipients express gratitude.

Crowdfunding, a new form of social behavior, allows individuals to make financial contributions to entrepreneurs, to help them start new companies. The contributors receive nothing in return for their help. Women and men do not differ in prosocial behavior overall, but women are more likely to engage in prosocial actions when these involve people with whom they personal relationships than with strangers, while men may be just as likely to help a stranger as a friend. Helping and prosocial behavior have many differences, but can share some underlying motives.

Chapter 10
Aggression
Its Nature, Causes, and Control

Chapter Overview

Learning Objectives

10.1 Describe contrasting views of why individuals aggress against others

10.2 Identify the social, cultural, personal, and situational conditions that influence aggressive behavior

10.3 Describe the types and causes of bullying

10.4 Identify techniques for reducing aggression

For as long as history has been recorded, intentional efforts to harm others—**aggression**—has been a part of human social behavior. Ancient accounts of human atrocities ranging from those committed by Genghis Khan and his army who, during the 13th century, conquered large parts of Asia—the Middle East, and even portions of Europe—to German Nazis killing of about 6 million Jewish people during World War II. These massive instances of intergroup violence, given the passage of time since their occurrence, may be ones we can consider from an emotional distance. But, coming to grips with aggressive events in our own lifetimes is a much harder process for most people. Consider the following examples of aggression and their potential impact, direct or indirect, on the way we live our lives today:

- Dharun Ravi, a student at Rutgers University in New Jersey, secretly set up a webcam in his dormitory room to capture video of his gay roommate, Tyler Clementi, in an intimate encounter with another man. Furthermore, Ravi invited his friends to watch. Soon after learning what had happened, Clementi committed suicide on September 22, 2010, by jumping off a bridge. Ravi was not charged with Clementi's death; he was though convicted of invasion of privacy and bias intimidation, and received a 30-day jail sentence.

- On December 14, 2012, Adam Lanza, who was 20 years old, went on a shooting rampage in Sandy Hook Elementary School, Newtown, Connecticut. He killed 20 children and 6 adults, before taking his own life.

- Nineteen-year-old Dzhokhar Tsarnaev and his 26-year-old brother Tamerlan planted two bombs near the finish line of the Boston Marathon, killing three people and wounding over 260 others on April 15, 2013. The older brother was killed in a shoot-out with police, but the younger brother received the death sentence in court.

- On June 17, 2015, 21-year-old Dylann Roof entered the Emanuel African Methodist Episcopal Church in Charleston, South Carolina. He was welcomed and took a seat. After about an hour, he rose to his feet and began shooting members of the Bible study group, killing nine people ranging in age from 26 to 87. Survivors included a girl who was told by her grandmother to pretend to be dead. Roof was arrested and indicted in both state and federal courts for the murders with a potential death sentence.

- On November 13, 2015, at least seven members of the organization ISIL (also called ISIS or the Islamic State) carried out a coordinated terrorism attack at six locations across the city of Paris. Over one hundred people were killed and more than 300 were injured by suicide bombers. Even before these attacks, other ISIL members carried out many incredible acts of violence in Lebanon, Tunisia, Iraq, Syria, and other parts of the Middle East and posted videos of executions they committed on social media.

Sadly, these events illustrate an unsettling fact: aggression—is an all-too-common part of social life. As illustrated in Figure 10.1, these examples remind us that acts of aggression are committed by individuals acting alone, as well as by individuals acting within the

Figure 10.1 Aggression: Individual and Group-Based

Intentional harm can be committed by one individual against another individual, or a single individual can commit grave harm against a mass of other people, or members of a group can engage in aggression toward another group. In all instances, the human costs can be tremendous.

framework of a group, large and small. Although harming others—often as many people as possible in instances of mass shootings, which in recent years in the United States have occurred virtually every day—may be a key goal of the aggressors in both types of situations, there are often other motivations. The goals underlying many forms of aggression are frequently ideological or political. For instance, Robert Lewis Dear, the person accused of the Planned Parenthood shooting in Colorado Springs, Colorado, on November 27, 2015, made remarks when arrested concerning his anti-abortion views. In other cases, political goals too seem to be paramount—prosecutors in the Dylann Roof case believed that he planned his actions in order to raise racial tension. Law enforcement officials indicated that Roof openly declared his hatred for black people, and the U.S. Justice Department classified Roof's actions as a hate crime. Similarly, members of ISIL do not merely seek to harm their victims, but they also aim to instill fear in other people. Indeed, the terrorist agenda is one of threatening those who they cannot directly reach to harm by creating a "climate of fear." Not only will people who live in areas controlled by ISIL be much less likely to resist ISIL's extreme religious views and practices because of fear, but the impact of induced terror can be felt among those considerably removed from the direct harm itself. In many other instances of mass shootings, the motivation appears to be retribution for perceived slights or actual conflicts with others, where those perceived as having done the aggressor harm are targets along with others who are simply in the vicinity.

Of course, most aggressive acts are not as extreme as those we described earlier. In fact, aggression can be as subtle as showing obvious boredom during a presentation by another person or deliberately ignoring them in a social setting—such as giving them the "cold shoulder" at a party. But, no matter what form it takes, as illustrated in Figure 10.2, aggression can damage or even tear the fabric of social life apart. Given the pervasiveness and human cost of aggression, it is not surprising that social psychologists have sought to obtain a greater understanding of why this dangerous aspect of social life occurs. The ultimate goal of such research is to develop improved techniques for reducing aggression in many different contexts (e.g., Bushman et al., 2016; Baumeister, 2005). In this chapter, we will summarize current knowledge about aggression gathered by social psychologists over several decades of careful research.

First, we will describe several *theoretical perspectives* on aggression, contrasting views about its nature and origins. Next, we will examine research illustrating important determinants of human aggression. These include *basic social factors*—the words or actions of other people, either "in the flesh" or as shown in the mass media

Figure 10.2 Aggression Can Be Devastating

Whether we consider the direct victims of mass aggression, their loved ones, or merely those who have witnessed the carnage caused, the suffering that results from such events can be intense and long-lasting.

(Fischer & Greitemeyer, 2006). Other possible determinants will also be considered, such as *personality traits* that predispose some people toward aggressive outbursts, and *situational factors*—aspects of the external world such as high temperatures, alcohol, and gun availability. Biological or genetic factors too will be examined, as well as how gender may influence the likelihood and forms of aggression. After delving into research concerning all of these factors, we will turn our attention to a very common but disturbing form of aggression to which children and teenagers are often exposed—*bullying*. Finally, we will examine various techniques for the prevention and control of aggression.

10.1: Perspectives on Aggression: In Search of the Roots of Violence

Objective   **Describe contrasting views of why individuals aggress against others**

Examples of unprovoked aggression, such as the ones described at the beginning of this chapter, raise a very basic question: Why do some human beings aggress against others in such frightening ways? Social psychologists have investigated these questions and offered many explanations. Here, we will examine several explanations that have been especially influential, ending with those that have emerged from recent social psychological research. It is important to note that though violent actions are rarely due to a single cause; rather they typically reflect the operation of multiple variables that often co-occur (Bushman et al., 2016).

10.1.1: The Role of Biological Factors: Are We Programmed for Violence?

The oldest and probably most famous explanation for human aggression attributed it to biological factors, our basic nature as a species. The most famous supporter of this theory was Sigmund Freud, who held that aggression stems mainly from a powerful *death wish* (thanatos) he believed all humans possess. According to Freud, this instinct is initially aimed at self-destruction, but is soon redirected outward, toward others. A related view was proposed by Konrad Lorenz, an ethologist (Lorenz, 1966, 1974), who suggested that aggression springs mainly from an inherited fighting instinct which assures that only the strongest males will obtain mates and pass their genes on to the next generation.

Until recently, most social psychologists rejected such ideas. Among the many reasons they did were: (1) Human beings aggress against others in many different ways—everything from excluding them from social groups to performing overt acts of violence against them. How can such a huge range of behaviors all be determined by genetic factors? (2) The frequency of aggressive actions varies tremendously across human societies, so that it is much more likely to occur in some than in others. Indeed, people in different cultures strongly differ in their support for aggressive or confrontational responses. Those in individualistic cultures such as the United States tend to support aggressive responding more than those in collectivistic cultures such as China, Turkey, or Ghana (Forbes, Collinsworth, Zhao, Kohlman, & LeClaire, 2011; Gunsoy, Cross, Uskul, Adams, & Gercek-Swing, 2015). Given such cultural variability in aggressive behavior and support for aggressive responses to the same conflict situations, social psychologists wonder, "How can aggressive behavior be determined by genetic factors?"

With the growth of the evolutionary perspective in psychology, however, the potential role of biology is being reconsidered. While most social psychologists continue to reject the view that human aggression stems largely from innate (i.e., genetic) factors, some now accept the possibility that genetic factors may play some role in human aggression. For instance, consider the following reasoning based on an evolutionary perspective (recall discussion of this theory in Chapter 1). In the evolutionary past (and even at present to some extent), males seeking desirable mates found it necessary to compete with other males. One way of eliminating such competition is through successful aggression, which drives such rivals away. Since males who were adept at such behavior may have been more successful in securing mates and in transmitting their genes to offspring, this may have led to the development of a genetically influenced tendency for males to aggress against other males. In contrast, males would not be expected to possess a similar tendency to aggress against females; in fact, development of such tendencies might be discouraged because females would tend to reject as mates males who are aggressive toward them or even ones who are aggressive in public, thus exposing themselves and their mates to unnecessary danger. As a result, males may have weaker tendencies to aggress against females than against other males. In contrast, while their frequency of aggression against others is considerably lower than that of males, females might aggress equally against males and females.

Some research findings are consistent with this reasoning. For instance, males tend to be more aggressive toward other males than toward females (although, of course, domestic violence is typically perpetrated by males against females). In contrast, similar differences in the targets of aggression do not exist (or are weaker) among females (e.g., Hilton, Harris, & Rice, 2000). In fact, as we will note later in this chapter, gender differences in aggression are not as large as many people have assumed, although the type of aggression expressed by each gender differs (Hawley, Card, & Little, 2007).

What role might testosterone (the male sex hormone) play in aggression? Flinn, Ponzi, and Muehlenbein (2012) measured testosterone in a group of soccer players. They found that following victories against strangers these levels increased, but they did not increase after losses or when playing against friends—people from their own community. This suggests that not only may males gain access to desirable mates through defeating others but, in addition, winning contests actually increases their testosterone which, in turn, raises their motivation to attain such mates. In addition, research indicates that when men's mating motivation is activated (by reading a story about meeting a very attractive woman)—they do indeed become more aggressive toward other men, which is consistent with their goal of driving off potential rivals (Griskevicius et al., 2009). Moreover, this is especially likely to occur when only other males can observe their behavior; if females are present, they do not become more aggressive, thus avoiding the possibility of turning off these potential mates. (women often find men who are aggressive in public to be frightening rather than attractive.)

Another reason why males may aggress against rivals is that if they succeed in driving off these rivals, not only does their level of testosterone increase, but they may gain in status—which then increases their attractiveness to at least some females. This may be why, at least to some degree, men who have "won" in life—whether

Figure 10.3 Defeating Opponents = Higher Status for Males

By defeating rivals, males gain in status, and this can increase their desirability—and so help them obtain attractive mates.

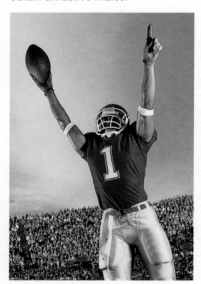

in sports, business, or any other context—are often eager to call attention to their success through external signs such as driving expensive cars, buying mansions, or private jets. Through these actions they are saying: "I have won—I have defeated rival males," which, they may believe, makes them highly attractive to females (see Figure 10.3). Of course, as we saw in Chapter 7, attraction is far more complex than this. But there does seem to be some evidence that it rests, at least in part, on status attainment.

More direct evidence for the role of genetic factors in aggression has been provided by research conducted by Hygen et al. (2015). They studied hundreds of children in Norway, and found that children who differed in terms of a gene related to chemicals produced in the brain also differed in aggression: Those with one gene were more aggressive as rated by their teachers than those who possessed the other gene. However, this was *only* true when the children were exposed to a high level of stress—for instance, abuse or serious illness. When such stress was absent, the children with the gene that facilitated aggression actually became *less* aggressive. The researchers explained these findings by suggesting that from the point of view of survival, having both groups in the population is adaptive: Those in the first group can cope better with changing environments, while those in the second group do better in relatively stable environments. The overall conclusion is that genetic factors may play some role in human aggression, but their effects are complex and fundamentally depend on environmental factors.

10.1.2: Drive Theories: The Motive to Harm Others

When social psychologists rejected the instinct views of aggression proposed by Freud and Lorenz, they countered with an alternative perspective: that aggression stems mainly from an externally elicited drive to harm others. This view is reflected in several different **drive theories of aggression** (e.g., Berkowitz, 1989; Feshbach, 1984). These theories propose that external conditions—especially those that create *frustration*—arouse a strong motive to harm others. As shown in Figure 10.4, when an aggressive drive is activated it can, in turn, lead to overt acts of aggression. Such an aggressive drive can be initiated by several factors discussed here (e.g., provocations from others), or even by the presence of a weapon in the room (Anderson, 1998).

By far the most famous of these theories is the **frustration-aggression hypothesis** (Dollard, Doob, Miller, Mowerer, & Sears, 1939), and we will discuss it in some detail in a later section. Here, we just want to note that this theory suggests that frustration—anything that prevents us from reaching goals we are seeking—leads to the arousal of a drive whose primary goal is that of harming some person or object—particularly the perceived cause of frustration (Berkowitz, 1989). Furthermore, the theory suggested that frustration is the strongest, or perhaps the *only*, cause of aggression. Social psychologists now realize that this theory is misleading, but it still enjoys widespread acceptance outside our field,

Figure 10.4 Drive Theories of Aggression: Motivation to Harm Others

Drive theories of aggression suggest that aggressive behavior is pushed from within by drives to harm or injure others. These drives are elicited by external events such as frustration. Such theories are no longer accepted as valid by most social psychologists, but one such view—the famous frustration-aggression hypothesis–continues to influence modern research, and many people's beliefs about the causes of aggression.

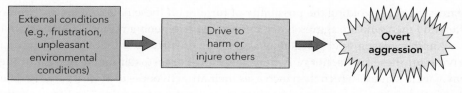

and you may sometimes hear people refer to it in such statements as: "He was so frustrated that he finally blew up," or "She was feeling frustrated, so she took it out on her roommate." We will explain here why such statements are often misleading.

10.1.3: Modern Theories of Aggression

Unlike earlier views, modern theories of aggression (Anderson & Bushman, 2002; Berkowitz, 1993; Zillmann, 1994) do not focus on a single factor (instincts, drives, and frustration) as the primary cause of aggression. Rather, they draw on advances in many areas of psychology in order to gain added insight into the factors that play a role in the occurrence of such behavior. One such theory, known as the *social learning perspective* (e.g., Bandura, 1997), begins with a very reasonable idea: Human beings are not born with a large array of aggressive responses at their disposal. Rather, they must acquire these in the much the same way that they acquire other complex forms of social behavior: through direct experience or by observing the behavior of others (i.e., social models—live persons or characters on television, in movies, or even in video games who behave aggressively; Anderson et al., 2010; Bushman & Anderson, 2002). Thus, depending on their past experience and the cultures in which they live, individuals learn (1) various ways of seeking to harm others, (2) which people or groups are appropriate targets for aggression, (3) what actions by others justify retaliation or vengeance on their part, and (4) what situations or contexts are ones in which aggression is permitted or even approved. In short, the social learning perspective suggests that whether a specific person will aggress in a given situation depends on many factors, including the person's past experience, the current rewards associated with past or present aggression, and attitudes and values that shape this person's thoughts concerning the appropriateness and potential effects of such behavior.

Building on the social learning perspective, a newer framework known as the **general aggression model (GAM)** (Anderson & Bushman, 2002) provides an even more complete account of the foundations of human aggression. According to this theory, a chain of events that may ultimately lead to overt aggression can be initiated by two major types of *input variables*: (1) factors relating to the current situation (situational factors) and (2) factors relating to the people involved (person factors). Variables falling into the first category include frustration, some kind of provocation from another person (e.g., an insult), exposure to other people behaving aggressively (*aggressive models*, real or in the media), and virtually anything that causes individuals to experience discomfort—everything from uncomfortably high temperatures to physical pain or even disrespectful treatment. Variables in the second category (*individual differences across people*) include traits that predispose some individuals toward aggression (e.g., high irritability), certain attitudes and beliefs about violence (e.g., believing that it is acceptable and appropriate), a tendency to perceive hostile intentions in others' behavior, and specific skills related to aggression (e.g., knowing how to fight or how to use various weapons).

According to the GAM, these situational and individual (personal) variables lead to overt aggression through their impact on three basic processes: *arousal*—they may increase physiological arousal or excitement; *affective states*—they can generate hostile feelings and outward signs of these (e.g., angry facial expressions); and *cognitions*—they can induce individuals to think hostile thoughts or can bring beliefs and attitudes about aggression to mind. Depending on individuals' interpretations (*appraisals*) of the current situation and restraining factors (e.g., the presence of police or the threatening nature of the intended target person), they then engage either in thoughtful action, which might involve restraining their anger, or impulsive action, which can lead to overt aggressive actions (see Figure 10.5 for an overview of this theory).

Bushman and Anderson (2002) have expanded this theory to explain why individuals who are exposed to high levels of aggression—either directly, in the actions

Figure 10.5 The GAM: A Modern Theory of Human Aggression

As shown here, the general aggression model (GAM) suggests that human aggression stems from many different factors. Input variables relating to the situation or person influence cognitions, affect, and arousal, and these internal states plus other factors such as appraisal and decision-making determine whether, and in what form, aggression occurs.

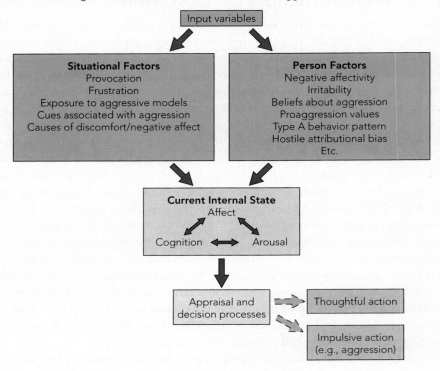

of others, or in films and video games—may tend to become increasingly aggressive themselves. Repeated exposure to such stimuli serves to strengthen *knowledge structures* related to aggression—beliefs, attitudes, schemas, and scripts relevant to aggression. As these knowledge structures related to aggression grow stronger, it is easier for these to be activated by situational or person variables. As a result, the people in question are truly "primed" for aggression.

The GAM is certainly more complex than earlier theories of aggression (e.g., the famous frustration-aggression hypothesis; Dollard et al., 1939). In addition, because it fully reflects recent progress in the field—growing understanding of the fact that what people *think* is crucial in determining in what they actually do—it seems much more likely to provide an accurate view of the nature of human aggression than these earlier theories—and that, of course, is what scientific progress is all about. Indeed, it has proven very valuable in terms of helping us understand the many causes of various forms of aggression (Bushman et al., 2016).

Key Points

- **Aggression** is the intentional infliction of harm on others. Research findings indicate that it derives from many different sources, including biological factors in interaction with environmental stressors and status-seeking.
- **Drive theories of aggression** suggest that aggression stems from externally elicited drives to harm or injure

others. The **frustration-aggression hypothesis** is the most famous example of such theories.
- Modern theories of aggression, such as the **general aggression model (GAM)**, recognize the importance of learning in aggression, various eliciting input variables, individual differences, affective states, and, especially, cognitive processes.

10.2: Causes of Human Aggression: Social, Cultural, Personal, and Situational

Objective Identify the social, cultural, personal, and situational conditions that influence aggressive behavior

Ray Rice, formerly a running back for the Baltimore Ravens, is well respected in his local community. In fact, he has engaged in many positive activities that benefitted Baltimore, such as running an anti-bullying campaign that was so effective, it lead the Maryland state government to pass a law that made repeated bullying a serious crime. Yet, in March 2014, he was videotaped dragging his unconscious fiancée from an elevator. From her injuries, and as shown in the tape, it seemed that he had knocked her unconscious. This frightening incident occurred after they had both been drinking, and after an argument escalated into physical assault. His fiancée, Janay Palmer, who married Rice after this incident, came to his defense, stating that this was the first time he had aggressed against her physically, and that their relationship was a very supportive one. Initially, Rice was suspended from playing in further games, but was ultimately reinstated after Rice agreed to undergo court-supervised counseling. Many observers noted, however, that it is well-known that domestic violence is rarely a one-time occurrence; rather it often continues for months or years, and is a frightening aspect of many intimate relationships.

But men are not the sole perpetrators of such violence. Hope Solo, a two-time Olympic gold medal winner was arrested in June 2014 for allegedly attacking her half sister and nephew. Although she initially injured both, the nephew who is 6'9" and weighs 280 pounds ultimately counterattacked, hitting Solo on the head with a broomstick, thus inflicting a serious concussion. When police arrived, Solo was said to be abusive and threatening, and had to be handcuffed to prevent her from attacking the officers. Despite that, Solo claims that in this incident she was the victim of domestic violence, and the courts have yet to decide in this seemingly complicated matter.

Why do such assaults occur—why do people attack those who they supposedly love the most? Research by social psychologists suggests that many factors combine to produce such unsettling incidents—provocation from the victim, who else is present on the scene, consumption of alcohol, and even environmental conditions such as high temperatures. The fact that domestic violence stems from many different factors is, of course, consistent with modern theories of aggression (Anderson & Bushman, 2002; DeWall, Twenge, Gitter, & Baumeister, 2009). Aggressive behavior is influenced by a wide range of social, cultural, personal, and situational conditions. Because these factors play a role not only in domestic violence, but also in many other forms of aggression, we will now examine the most important ones—conditions that increase the likelihood that people will engage in actions designed to hurt others.

10.2.1: Basic Sources of Aggression: Frustration and Provocation

Aggression, like other forms of social behavior, is often a response to something in the social world around us. In other words, it often occurs in response to something other people have said or done. Here are several ways in which this can—and often does—occur.

FRUSTRATION: WHY NOT GETTING WHAT YOU WANT CAN SOMETIMES LEAD TO AGGRESSION Suppose that you asked 20 people you know to name the single most important cause of aggression. The chances are good that most would reply "frustration." And if you asked them to define frustration, many would say: "The way I feel when something—or someone—prevents me from getting what I want or expect to get in some situation." This widespread belief in the importance of frustration as a cause of aggression stems from the **frustration-aggression hypothesis** mentioned in our discussion of drive theories of aggression (Dollard et al., 1939). In its original form, this hypothesis made two sweeping assertions: (1) Frustration *always* leads to some form of aggression, and (2) Aggression *always* stems from frustration. Bold statements like these are appealing, but it does not mean that they are necessarily accurate. In fact, existing evidence suggests that both portions of the frustration-aggression hypothesis assign far too much importance to frustration as a determinant of human aggression. In fact, individuals do *not* always respond with aggression when frustrated. On the contrary, they show many different reactions, ranging from sadness, despair, and depression on the one hand, to direct attempts to overcome the source of their frustration on the other. In short, aggression is definitely *not* an automatic response to frustration.

Furthermore, it is equally clear that not all aggression stems from frustration. As we have already noted, people aggress for many different reasons and in response to many different factors. Why, for instance, did Adam Lanza go on a shooting rampage at Sandy Hook Elementary School, after first killing his mother? Was he frustrated in any way? Were the children and teachers at Sandy Hook the cause of such feelings? Probably not. As this incident and others reveal, many factors other than frustration can influence aggression.

Accordingly, few social psychologists now accept the idea that frustration is the only, or even the most important, cause of aggression. It is simply one of many factors that can potentially lead to aggression. We should add that frustration *can* serve as a powerful determinant of aggression under certain conditions—especially when it is viewed as illegitimate or unjustified (Folger & Baron, 1996). For instance, if a student believes that she deserves a good grade on an exam but then receives a poor one, she might conclude that she has been treated very unfairly—that her legitimate needs have been thwarted. The result: She may have hostile thoughts, experience intense anger, and seek revenge against the perceived source of such frustration—in this case, her professor. If, though, she believes her poor grade is deserved because she failed to study, she may feel her goal or desire for good grades has been thwarted, but she will be unlikely to act aggressively toward the professor.

DIRECT PROVOCATION: WHEN AGGRESSION (OR EVEN TEASING) BREEDS AGGRESSION Major world religions often suggest that when provoked by another person, we should "turn the other cheek"—in other words, the most appropriate way to respond to being annoyed or hurt by another person is to do our best to not retaliate. In fact, however, research findings indicate that this is easier to say than to do, and that physical or verbal **provocation** from others is one of the strongest causes of human aggression. When we are on the receiving end of some form of provocation from others—criticism we consider unfair, sarcastic remarks, or physical assaults—we tend to reciprocate, returning as much aggression as we have received—or perhaps even more, especially if we are certain that the other person *meant* to harm us.

What kinds of provocation produce the strongest push toward aggression? Existing evidence suggests that *condescension*—expressions of arrogance or disdain on the part of others are very powerful (Harris, 1993). Harsh and unjustified criticism, especially criticism that attacks *us* rather than our behavior, is a powerful form of provocation, and when exposed to it, most people find it very difficult to avoid getting angry and retaliating in some manner, either immediately or later on (Baron & Richardson, 1994). Still another form of provocation to which many people respond with annoyance is **teasing**—provoking statements that call attention to an individual's flaws and imperfections, but can be, at the same time, somewhat playful in nature (e.g., Kowalski, 2001). Teasing can range from mild, humorous remarks (e.g., "Hey— you look you're having a bad hair day") through nicknames or comments that truly seem designed to hurt. Research findings indicate that the more individuals attribute teasing to hostile motives—a desire to embarrass or annoy them—the more likely they are to respond aggressively (Campos, Keltner, Beck, Gonzaga, & John, 2007).

One especially unfortunate effect of one person provoking another is that often, the recipient responds in kind, and a spiral in which aggression breeds aggression develops. The result is that verbal provocations can quickly escalate into physical aggression in which one or both parties are hurt.

Research findings indicate too that actions by others that threaten our status or public image are important triggers of aggression. For instance, in one revealing study (Griskevicius et al., 2009), participants (male and female college students) were asked to describe the primary reason why they had performed their most recent act of direct aggression against another person. A substantial proportion—48.3 percent of men and 45.3 percent of women—described concerns about their status or reputation—threats to their self-identity—as the main cause of their aggression. In sum, others' actions—especially when they are interpreted as stemming from hostile motives—from a desire to harm *us* are often a very powerful cause of aggression.

What about emotions—do they too play an important role in triggering aggression? Your first reaction is probably "Of course! People aggress when they are feeling angry—not when they are happy or relaxed." But in fact, the situation is more complex than this, as we explain in the special feature, **"What Research Tells Us About… the Role of Emotions in Aggression."**

What Research Tells Us About…

The Role of Emotions in Aggression

The view that strong emotions underlie many aggressive acts makes good sense, and seems intuitively obvious. For instance, when we are angry, one possible response is to express it overtly, by aggressing against another person, and especially the person who has aroused our anger. But all instances of aggression do not involve strong emotions or feelings. For instance, people who have a grudge against someone sometimes wait for long periods of time before attempting to harm their enemies—until conditions are "right" for doing the most damage with the least risk to themselves. An old Italian saying captures this idea: *Revenge is the only dish best served cold.* It suggests that when seeking revenge, it is sometimes best to do so *after* intense emotions have cooled because we can then develop a more effective strategy for "paying this person back." Here's another example: Paid assassins—professional killers who murder specific people—do so simply because they are paid for completing this task. Usually, as many movies have illustrated, they do not know the individuals, and feel no anger toward them; but it is their job, and the most effective ones do it coolly, with no emotional "baggage" to get in their way (see Figure 10.6).

And there's yet another complication in the simple idea that "aggression always involves strong emotion." Experts on emotion generally agree that there are two basic dimensions: a positive–negative dimension (happy to sad), and an activation dimension: low to high. This raises an intriguing question about the role of emotions in aggression: Can heightened arousal facilitate aggression even if it is unrelated to this behavior in any direct way? In other words, if we feel excited or energized by some events, can this arousal spill over into another situation and intensify our responses, including anger, in it? Suppose, for instance, that you are driving to the airport to catch a flight. You are late, so you

Figure 10.6 Sometimes Aggression Occurs Without Strong Emotions

Although emotions such as anger play an important role in many instances of aggression, sometimes they do not. For instance, hired assassins who are paid to kill other people often do so in a totally unemotional way. To them, this is simply their job, brutal as it is.

hurry as much as you can. On the way there, another driver cuts you off, and you almost have an accident. Your heart pounds wildly and your blood pressure shoots up; but fortunately, no accident occurs.

Now you arrive at the airport. You park and rush to the security line. There, the passenger in line ahead of you is very slow to open her carry-on case and also slow to remove her shoes. In addition, she hasn't placed her liquids in a separate plastic bag, so the agent sorts through them now, while you wait. Quickly, you become very irritated by this person, and say to yourself, "Why don't people like that stay home! I may miss my flight because of her . . ." You wish you could push the person out of the way and move forward to catch your plane.

Now for the key question: Do you think that your recent near miss in traffic played any role in your sudden surge of anger toward this other passenger? Could your emotional arousal from the recent traffic incident transfer to the present, unrelated situation and so intensify your feelings of annoyance? Research evidence suggests that it might (Zillmann, 1988, 1994). Under some conditions, heightened arousal—whatever its source—can enhance aggression in response to provocation, frustration, or other factors. In fact, in various experiments, arousal stemming from sources such as participation in competitive games (Christy, Gelfand, & Hartmann, 1971), exercise (Zillmann, 1979), and even some types of music (Rogers & Ketcher, 1979), have been found to increase subsequent aggression. Why is this the case? An explanation

for these effects is provided by **excitation transfer theory** (Zillmann, 1988, 1994).

This theory claims that because physiological arousal tends to dissipate slowly over time, a portion of such arousal may persist as a person moves from one situation to another. In the earlier example, some portion of the arousal you experienced because of the near miss in traffic may still be present as you approach the security gate in the airport. That arousal, which is unrelated to the current situation, intensifies your annoyance with the slow passenger. And this may occur *even if you are unaware of the residual arousal* (Zillmann, 1994).

Excitation transfer theory also suggests that such effects are especially likely to occur when the person recognizes the residual arousal but then wrongly attributes it to the events occurring right now (Taylor, Helgeson, Reed, & Skokan, 1991). In the airport incident, for instance, your anger would be intensified if you recognized the arousal but attributed it to the other passengers' actions rather than to the driver who nearly cut you off. Overall, it's clear that the relationship between emotion and aggression is more complex than common sense suggests.

10.2.2: Social Causes of Aggression

Social exclusion—being excluded or rejected by others—is an unpleasant experience, and one most of us would prefer to avoid. Exclusion not only means that we do not enjoy the benefits of social relations with others, but it also reflects negatively on our self-image. After all, if other people do not want us around, that seems to indicate that we have undesirable rather than desirable characteristics. Aggressive people are often excluded from groups or rejected by others *because* they are aggressive. But does rejection by others increase our likelihood of aggressing against them? Doing so would allow us to "even the score," and research findings do indicate that social rejection is often a powerful trigger for aggression (Leary, Twenge, & Quinlivan, 2006). Being rejected or excluded by others often leads to increase in aggression by the excluded individuals which, in turn, could lead to even more exclusion—a kind of self-perpetuating, negative cycle.

So, why, precisely, does this occur? Is it the emotional distress generated by being excluded that leads to "lashing out" against the sources of rejection? Although that seems like a reasonable explanation, studies designed to find out whether the emotional distress following rejection leads to aggression have *not* confirmed this idea. Negative emotions do not appear to mediate the effects of rejection on aggression. Another possibility is that rejection by others initiates a *hostile cognitive mindset*—it activates cognitive structures in our minds that lead us to perceive ambiguous or neutral actions by others as hostile in nature, and to perceive aggression as common in social interactions and as an appropriate kind of reaction (e.g., as suggested by the GAM; Anderson & Bushman, 2002; Tremblay & Belchevski, 2004). Evolutionary theory, too, suggests that a hostile cognitive mindset or bias might follow from exclusion. In the past, human beings needed others—and cooperation with them—to survive. So, being excluded from the group was a very serious and threatening matter. This suggests that exclusion by others would be interpreted as a very hostile action.

To test this reasoning, and find out if hostile cognitive bias does indeed underlie the effects of social exclusion on aggression, DeWall et al. (2009) conducted a series of studies. In one, some participants learned that their partner in an experiment had actively rejected them—refused to work with them, while others learned that their partner could not work with them because of factors beyond the partner's control—another appointment, for example. To find out if rejection triggered hostile cognitive bias, both groups were then asked to complete word fragments that could be completed to form aggressive or nonaggressive words (e.g., "r . . . pe" can be either *rape* or *ripe*). It was predicted that those who had been actively rejected would be more likely to complete the words in an aggressive way, and that indeed turned out to be the case.

In a follow-up study, participants completed a personality test and then were told either that their scores indicated that they would spend the future alone (i.e., they would be rejected by others) or that they would spend the future closely connected with other people in meaningful relationships. Next, they read a story in which another person acted in ambiguous ways. Afterward, they rated the extent to which the actions of the person in the story were accurately described by several adjectives related to hostility (e.g., angry, hostile, dislikable, unfriendly). It was predicted that learning that they would be socially excluded in the future would generate a hostile cognitive bias and lead participants in this group to rate a stranger's ambiguous actions as hostile. Again, this prediction was confirmed by the results. Finally, to determine if this hostile bias increased aggression, participants in both groups were given an opportunity to aggress against the stranger in the story; they were told that this person was seeking a position as a research assistant which they badly needed, and were asked to evaluate the stranger's suitability for the position. Negative evaluations, of course, would prevent this person from obtaining the needed position. It was predicted that participants who were told they would experience social exclusion in the future would rate this person lower than those told they would experience a rich, full social life. Once more, the findings confirmed these predictions. In an additional study, the authors found that these effects occurred even when the person they evaluated was not the one who caused their social exclusion.

Overall, the results of this research indicate that social exclusion does indeed operate through the generation of a hostile cognitive mindset or bias (see Figure 10.7). In short, rejection by others is indeed a strong antecedent of aggression, and it has such effects because it leads us to perceive others' actions as stemming from hostile motives and a desire on their part to harm *us*. Yes, rejection hurts and causes lots of emotional distress, but it appears to be the cognitive effects it produces rather than the emotional ones that are most strongly responsible for the fact that excluded people do often become highly aggressive—not simply toward the people who have excluded them, but toward others as well.

MEDIA VIOLENCE: THE POTENTIALLY HARMFUL EFFECTS OF FILMS, TELEVISION, AND VIDEO GAMES What was the last movie you saw? Did it contain aggression or violence? How often did the characters attack others or attempt to harm others? For instance, consider one giant hit of a few years back: *Avatar*. Certainly, it was exciting in many ways, but it certainly contained a tremendous amount of violence. In fact, a large proportion of the action on the screen fits into this category. And indeed, systematic surveys of the content of recent films, television shows, and other media indicate that violence is very frequent in the popular offerings of the mass media (Bushman & Anderson, 2002; Reiss & Roth, 1993; Waters, Block, Friday, & Gordon, 1993).

This fact raises an important question that social psychologists have studied for decades: Does exposure to media

Figure 10.7 Being Excluded or Rejected By Others Can Encourage Aggression

Research findings indicate that when individuals are excluded or are rejected by others, they often perceive even ambiguous actions by those people as hostile, and that, in turn, leads them to aggress against those people—and even against others who were not involved in their exclusion.

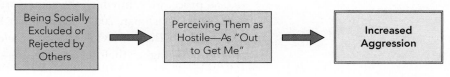

violence increase aggression among children and adults? Literally hundreds of studies have been performed to test this possibility, and the results are clear: Exposure to media violence is indeed one factor contributing to high levels of violence in countries where such materials are viewed by large numbers of people (e.g., Anderson et al., 2003; Bushman & Anderson, 2009; Paik & Comstock, 1994). In fact, in a summary of research findings in this area (Anderson, Bushman, Donnerstein, Hummer, & Warburton, 2015), leading experts on this topic who have provided testimony in U.S. Senate hearings on media and violence offered the following basic conclusions:

1. Research on exposure to violent television, movies, video games, and music indicates that such materials significantly increase the likelihood of aggressive behavior by people exposed to them.

2. Such exposure has both short-term and cumulative long-term effects on aggression.

3. The magnitude of these effects is large—at least as large as the various medical effects considered to be important by physicians (e.g., the effect of aspirin on heart attacks).

In other words, as a result of hundreds of studies using scientific methods investigating the effects of media violence in research involving hundreds of thousands of people have concluded that these effects are real, lasting, and substantial. These effects have important implications for society and for the safety and well-being of millions of people who are the victims of aggressive actions each year. Links between media violence and domestic partner assault, robbery, gang activity, and mass shootings have been obtained. As we will review here, many different types of research support these conclusions.

For example, in short-term laboratory experiments, children or adults exposed to violent films and television programs have been found to show more aggression than others exposed to nonviolent content (Bushman & Huesmann, 2001). The earliest research of this type was conducted by Albert Bandura and his colleagues in the early 1960s—a time when social psychology was still, in many respects, a new and rapidly growing science. To address this question, the research team (Bandura, Ross, & Ross, 1963a, b) devised an ingenious approach. Instead of using actual television programs, they constructed their own TV shows in which an adult model was shown aggressing against a large inflated toy clown (a Bobo doll) in unusual ways. For instance, the model sat on the doll, punched it repeatedly in the nose, struck it on the head with a toy mallet, and kicked it about the room. This "program," or a control one in which the model showed no aggressive actions toward the Bobo doll, was then shown to young school-age children.

Following exposure to one of these two programs, the children were placed in a room containing many toys, several of which had been used by the adult model in his or her attacks against the doll. They were allowed to play freely for 20 minutes and during this period their behavior was carefully observed to see if, perhaps, they would show actions similar to those of the model in the aggressive program. Results were clear: Young children exposed to the actions of an aggressive adult model showed strong tendencies to imitate these behaviors (see Figure 10.8). In contrast, those exposed to a nonaggressive adult model (the one who did not attack the inflated doll) did not show similar actions. Bandura and his associates reasoned that the children had learned new ways of aggressing from the "program" they watched and that the children also learned that aggression is an acceptable form of behavior.

Other research on the effects of media violence, in contrast, has employed *longitudinal* procedures, in which the same participants are studied for many years (e.g., Anderson & Bushman, 2002; Huesmann & Eron, 1984, 1986). Results of such research, too, are clear: The more violent films or television programs participants watched as children, the higher their levels of aggression as teenagers or adults—for instance, the higher the likelihood that they have been arrested for violent crimes. Such findings have been replicated in many different countries—Australia, Finland, Israel, Poland, and South Africa (Botha, 1990). Thus, they appear to hold across different cultural settings. Further, such effects are not restricted only to actual programs or films: They appear to be produced by violence in news programs, by violent lyrics in popular music (e.g., Anderson, Carnagey, & Eubanks, 2003), and by violent video games (Anderson, 2004; Bushman & Anderson, 2002).

This last media source—violent video games—has become the subject of intense study, because these games are very popular, and are played (often for hours each day) by millions of people all over the world. A large number of studies have sought

Figure 10.8 Bandura's "Bobo Doll" Studies: Early Evidence for the Effects of Televised Violence

In these famous studies, children saw a "television program" in which an adult model either attacked an inflated plastic doll (top row of photos) or sat quietly. When given a chance to play with the same toys, children imitated the actions of the aggressive model (bottom two rows of photos). These findings suggested that exposure to violence in the media may lead to similar actions by viewers.

to determine if playing such games produces effects similar to those produced by watching violent films or television shows, and the results are both consistent and alarming. For instance, a meta-analysis that examined the findings of all available well-conducted studies on the effects of aggressive video games (Anderson et al., 2010) found that playing such games consistently increases aggressive cognitions (thoughts related to harming others), aggressive affect (feelings of hostility, anger, and revenge), and subsequent aggressive behavior. In addition, playing aggressive video games reduces empathy for others and the tendency to engage in prosocial behavior. Such effects occur in Eastern (i.e., Asian) countries as well as Western ones (Europe, North America), and appear to generate long-term effects—relatively long-lasting increases in aggressive cognitions, affect, and overt behavior. Such effects are found in short-term laboratory studies as well as long-term longitudinal studies that follow the same participants for months or years. After reviewing this extensive evidence, Anderson et al. (2010, p. 171) offer the following somewhat unsettling conclusion: "Video games are neither inherently good nor inherently bad. But people learn. And content matters." When the content being learned is aggressive, it has substantial and large-scale undesirable social implications.

Figure 10.9 Why Do People Play Violent Video Games?

Research findings indicate that contrary to popular belief, people who play violent video games do not do so because of their violent content. Rather, they play these games because they enjoy the feeling of mastery and competence they provide.

One more question arises concerning the impact of violent video games: Why do so many people like to play them? An initial guess was that it is the violent content that makes them so popular; people find violence (especially in the safe context of a video game) exciting and enjoyable, so they purchase these games and play them. This suggestion is so compelling that it has generally been accepted as *the* explanation for the immense popularity of violent video games (see Figure 10.9). But is this really so? Research by Przybylski, Ryan and Rigby (2009) indicates that in fact, it is not. Drawing on *cognitive evaluation theory* (Ryan & Deci, 2000, 2007)—they suggest that it is *not* the violence in games such as "Grand Theft Auto" that make them so appealing, but rather it is the sense of autonomy and competence that the games provide. In other words, people enjoy playing such violent video games because they provide players with a sense of being in control—acting independently—and because they provide opportunities for experiencing competence by exercising their skills or abilities.

To test this reasoning, members of an Internet forum for discussion of video games completed measures of their feelings of competence and mastery while playing various games (e.g., "I experienced a lot of freedom in the game"; "The game provides me with interesting options and choices"). In addition, they rated their enjoyment of the games, their absorption in them, and their interest in a sequel (e.g., "I would buy a sequel to this game"). Finally, violent content in various games was coded by three raters; a rating of 1 was assigned to games with no violent content (e.g., *Tetris*), 2 was assigned to games with abstract violence (e.g., *Super Mario*), 3 to games with impersonal violence (e.g., *Civilization*), 4 to games with fantasy violence (e.g., *Starfox*), and 5 to games with realistic violence (e.g., *God of War 2*).

Results indicated that the extent to which the games satisfied needs for autonomy and competence were related to enjoyment of the games, absorption in them, and interest in purchasing a sequel, but were *not* related to violent content. So it appeared that the popularity of these games was not primarily due to their violent content, but rather to other factors. In several follow-up studies, the same authors examined the possibility that people who are high in aggressiveness would be more likely to prefer, enjoy, and become immersed in violent games relative to nonviolent ones. In these studies, participants played either a violent or nonviolent game, and then rated their preference for future play. Those high in trait aggressiveness did in fact prefer the violent games to the nonviolent ones, while people low in trait aggressiveness preferred the nonviolent games. However—and this is key—when the extent to which the games satisfied their needs for mastery and competence were held constant, this difference (between people high and low in aggressiveness) disappeared. This, too, suggests that it is *not* the violent content of these games that makes them appealing, even for highly aggressive people.

Overall, results of the research by Przybylski and colleagues (2009) indicate that although highly aggressive people are indeed attracted to violent video games, in general, it is *not* the violent content of these games, but rather the opportunity for autonomy and competence they provide that makes them so popular. This suggests that games that provide such experiences, but without violent content, might well be as popular as those with such content. So it may be possible for players of video games to enjoy important benefits without simultaneously experiencing the negative effects that stem from violent games. Now, if only the manufacturers of video games will give this possibility a try . . .!

THE EFFECTS OF MEDIA VIOLENCE: NEUROSCIENCE EVIDENCE FOR WHY THEY OCCUR One other factor that plays an important role in the effects of all types of media violence involves *desensitization*. In other words, as a result of exposure to large amounts of violent content in television programs, films, and video games, individuals become less sensitive to violence and its consequences (Anderson et al., 2015). Research findings suggest that such desensitization effects can contribute to increased aggression by people exposed to media violence (e.g., Funk, Bechtoldt-Baldacci, Pasold, & Baumgartner, 2004). Perhaps the most dramatic evidence for such desensitization, however, is provided by research using a social neuroscience perspective.

Research by Bartholow, Bushman, and Sestir (2006) provides a clear example of this approach. Individuals in that study reported on the extent to which they had played violent and nonviolent video games in the past and then participated in a competitive reaction time task in which they could determine the loudness of unpleasant sounds delivered to another person (who did not actually exist) when that person lost the competition. Before playing the competitive game, participants first viewed a series of neutral images (e.g., a man on a bicycle) and violent images (e.g., a person holding a gun to another person's head). Activity in their brains was recorded while they watched these images. In particular, the researchers carefully analyzed brain activity that had been found in previous research to indicate the extent to which incoming emotion-provoking stimuli are being processed. (This is known as P300 activity—one kind of *event-related brain potential*—changes in brain activity that occur as certain types of information are processed). If individuals have been desensitized to violent images by their past experience playing video games, P300 activity would be smaller when they view violent images. In fact, that is exactly what happened: Individuals who had previously played violent video games frequently showed smaller P300 reactions when viewing violent images than individuals who reported previously having played mainly nonviolent games. These findings suggest that exposure to media violence does indeed desensitize those who view it. Moreover, the degree of such desensitization, in turn, predicts the likelihood that those people will aggress against others.

Overall, it appears that exposure to violence in films, television, or video games does increase the tendency to aggress against others in several ways. First, as we just saw, it reduces individuals' emotional reactions to such events so that, in a sense, they perceive them as "nothing out of the ordinary." Second, it strengthens beliefs about the appropriateness of aggression, expectations about others' hostile intentions, and other cognitive processes related to aggression. As a result of repeated exposure to violent movies, television programs, or violent video games, individuals develop strong *knowledge structures* relating to aggression. When these knowledge structures are then activated by various events, people feel, think, and act aggressively because this is what, in a sense, they have learned to do.

More than 40 years of research on this issue has made clear that exposure to media violence can have very harmful effects on society. So why, then, is there so much of it on television, in movies, and in video games? The answer, sad to relate, is that violence *sells*. Moreover, because advertisers assume this is true, they "put their money where the action is" (Bushman, 1998). In short, this is a case where it would seem economic motives take precedence over everything else. We know what to do, as a society, with respect to media violence: We should reduce it, if decreasing violence is our goal. But as long as people are willing to pay to see aggressive shows and films or buy violent games, there seems little chance this will happen.

10.2.3: Why Some People Are More Aggressive Than Others

Several years ago, I worked in the same department as a person who had a strong reputation for behaving aggressively. While overt aggression is very rare in an academic setting, this individual—who was exceptionally talented and energetic—also literally exploded from time to time. He was in a position of authority, so often he could "get away with it." He would lose his temper and shout at people who, if they were not able to keep their own tempers in check, shouted back. Why was he so aggressive? Although several factors are likely to be involved, research on the role of personality factors in aggression offers some plausible answers. We will now briefly review some of the personal traits that seem to increase the likelihood that people having them will aggress against others.

HOSTILE ATTRIBUTIONAL BIAS   As we noted earlier, when individuals perceive hostility in others, they often respond aggressively. And research findings indicate that this is so because of aggressive cognition—for instance they think "If they are hostile toward me, I'll strike first." But large differences in the tendency to perceive others as aggressive exist. At one end of the dimension are people who seem to perceive everyone they meet as hostile, while at the other are people who rarely perceive others as hostile. Most of us fall in between: We recognize that other people vary greatly in terms of hostility; most are in the middle, and a few are very high or very low in their expectations of hostility in others. Research findings have confirmed the existence of such differences, and described them as involving the *hostile attributional bias* (Wu, Zhang, Chiu, Kwan, & He, 2014; Zhou, Yan, Che, & Meier, 2015). People high in this bias tend to attribute even innocent actions by others to the fact that they are hostile. In others words, to them, everyone they meet is "out to get them" in some way. So clearly, this form of bias is one important personal cause of aggression.

NARCISSISM: WHY INFLATED POSITIVE VIEWS OF ONESELF OFTEN LEAD TO AGGRESSION The ancient Greek myth of Narcissus tells of a handsome man who was literally in love with himself—he viewed himself as virtually perfect. The god Nemesis decided to punish him, and so directed him to a pool where he saw his own reflection. He found it so beautiful that he fell into the pool while trying to embrace it—and then drowned.

The spirit of Narcissus has been said to live in individuals who hold extremely positive—often unjustified—views of themselves, which is where we get the word *narcissism*. Interestingly, people's narcissism often leads them to be aggressive when others dare to question their overblown views of themselves. In such instances, they experience what has been termed **narcissistic rage**, in which they seek revenge against these "doubters," while simultaneously feeling threatened.

Research reveals that narcissism has two distinct parts: (1) What has been termed grandiosity—which refers to the tendency to show-off and exhibit arrogance and (2) Vulnerability—which reflects the tendency to be bitter, complaining, and defensive. Recent research suggests that only the second component is related to aggression (Krizan & Johar, 2015). Only people high in the vulnerability component experience rage when others call their inflated views of themselves into question. In a series of studies, Krizan and Johar (2015) obtained support for this prediction. In one study, they measured participants' grandiose and vulnerable narcissism, and also their tendencies to respond to conflict with others through either direct, or displaced aggression (that is, aggression toward another person aside from the one with whom they were in conflict). As predicted, only vulnerable narcissism predicted aggression.

In another experiment, supposedly, concerned with food preferences, participants were told that another person could choose whether they tasted a slightly bitter liquid (tea) or a very unpleasant and bitter liquid—bitter melon juice. They were then told that their partner had chosen for them to taste and rate the bitter melon juice. Next, they were given the choice of assigning a mild or extremely hot sauce to their partner for tasting. It was predicted that individuals high in vulnerable narcissism would choose the very hot sauce for their partners more often than those low in vulnerable narcissism, and findings offered support for the hypothesis. In other words, when they are provoked by others, people high in vulnerable narcissism feel a strong need to "punish" these people who, by provoking them, have not taken account of their supposed superiority (see Figure 10.10). So watch out for people who have inflated egos but who might harbor doubts—they can be dangerous when their egos are threatened in any way!

Figure 10.10 Narcissism and Aggression: Only for Those Who Feel Vulnerable

Research findings indicate that narcissism—inflated and often unjustified views of oneself—actually takes two forms: grandiosity and vulnerability. The latter is related to aggression when their inflated egos are threatened by others who, for instance, don't accept the narcissist's inflated self-image as accurate.

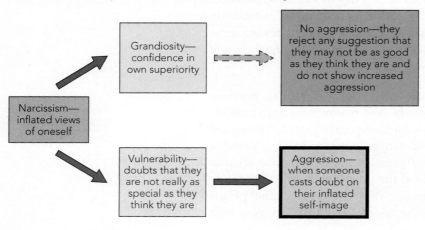

10.2.4: Gender and Aggression: Are Men More Aggressive Than Women?

It is generally assumed that men are more aggressive than women, and violent crime statistics provides ample support for this view. For instance, consider the Canadian victimization statistics shown in Table 10.1 (see Vaillancourt, 2010). As you can see, men are much more likely than women to be both the perpetrators and the victims of several kinds of violence. Research by social psychologists also tends to confirm these general patterns. For example, virtually all mass shootings are committed by males, and youth violence of all sorts is disproportionately committed by and affects males (see Bushman et al., 2016).

But, as revealed by a meta-analysis, when precisely gender differences in aggression emerge is more complex than these numbers suggest (Eagly & Steffen, 1986). For instance, men are indeed more likely to engage in aggression that produces pain or physical injury than women. Further, these differences exist across many different cultures (Archer, 2004). So, basically, around the world, men do engage in physical aggression more often, and with greater intensity, than women.

Another important point to consider is aggressive responses when direct provocation from others is present or absent. Research findings indicate that following strong provocation, males and females are equally likely respond with some form of aggression. However, in the absence of provocation, males are significantly more likely than females to respond with aggression (Bettencourt & Miller, 1996). This suggests that men are on a "shorter fuse" than women in this respect.

Another way in which individuals can aggress involves words rather than deeds—verbal aggression. Overall, there do not appear to be significant differences between men and women in this respect although men are more likely to use more extreme forms of verbal aggression than women—for instance, swearing. Perhaps the most intriguing differences between women and men with respect to aggression involves what is known as *indirect aggression*—actions designed to harm another person, but which are not performed directly against this person. For instance, such

---

Table 10.1   Men Are More Physically Aggressive Than Women

As shown here, recent data from Canada (which is a relatively nonviolent country) indicate that men are much more likely than women to engage in crimes involving aggression. Similar gender differences exist in many countries including the United States, which has been described as more violent than any other developed country.

Victims of Crimes in Canada by Gender, per 100,000 Residents			
Crime	Female Victims	Male Victims	Result
Aggravated assault	119	233	Males are 2 times more likely to be victims
Forcible confinement	22	7	Females are 3.1 times more likely
Homicide & attempted murder	2	7	Males are 3.5 times more likely
Robbery	62	114	Males are 1.8 times more likely
Sexual assault	68	6	Females are 11.3 times more likely
More severe crimes	273	367	Males are 1.3 times more likely
Simple assault	576	484	Females are 1.2 times more likely
Uttering threats	156	184	Males are 1.2 times more likely
Criminal harassment	135	51	Females are 2.6 times more likely
Less severe crimes	867	719	Females are 1.2 times more likely
Other assaults	16	62	Males are 3.9 times more likely
Other "person" crimes	1	2	Males are 2 times more likely

actions might involve spreading negative rumors about someone, "forgetting" to invite them to a social event, or even damaging or destroying their property. In all these cases, harm is done to the intended victim without him or her being present. Results of a review of existing evidence indicates that women are more likely than men to engage in this kind of indirect aggression, but this difference emerges only after puberty (Archer, 2004). One explanation for this might be that people who have lower status have more to fear from directly aggressing against another so they act more indirectly than those who have higher status. This would be consistent with women engaging in more indirect aggression than men. Because such indirect aggression involves planning, strategy, and perhaps subtlety than more impulsive forms of physical and verbal aggression, there is likely to be considerable learning involved so it is not surprising that it emerges later.

Overall, then, women and men do differ considerably with respect to physical aggression, but these differences are not uniform: Rather, the extent of the difference depends on the costs, type of aggression, and also age. Some evidence—far from final—also suggests that cultural factors play a role so that, for instance, differences between men and women are larger in cultures where men hold all the power. The overall conclusion that "common sense" beliefs about differences between the two genders where aggression is concerned is generally true when it comes to physical aggression, but ignores the fact that differences in some forms of aggression, when they occur, are influenced by external factors—that is, they differ by where, and when, and how aggression by the two genders actually occurs.

10.2.5: Situational Determinants of Aggression: The Effects of Heat, Alcohol, and Gun Availability

While aggression is often strongly influenced by social factors and is sometimes predicted by personal traits, it is also affected by the situation or context in which it occurs. Here, we will examine three of the many *situational factors* that can influence aggression: uncomfortably high temperatures, alcohol, and the availability of weapons.

Figure 10.11 The Long Hot Summer and Violence

It is widely believed that people are more aggressive when they are hot and uncomfortable, and research findings confirm that this is true; the "long, hot summer" effect does seem to be real.

IN THE HEAT OF ANGER: TEMPERATURE AND AGGRESSION *Boiling mad; Hot-tempered; In a white-hot rage . . .* Metaphors like these suggest a link between temperature (and perhaps anything else that makes people feel uncomfortable) and human aggression. There is, in fact, evidence that people report feeling especially irritable and short-tempered on hot and steamy days (see Figure 10.11). So, is there a systematic link between climate and human aggression? Social psychologists have studied this question for more than three decades, and during this period the methods they have used and the results they have obtained have become increasingly sophisticated.

The earliest studies on this topic were experiments conducted under controlled laboratory conditions, in which temperature was systematically varied as the independent variable. For instance, participants were exposed either to comfortably pleasant conditions (temperatures of 70–72° Fahrenheit) or to uncomfortably hot conditions (temperatures of 94–98° Fahrenheit), and were then given an opportunity to aggress against another person. (In fact, they only *believed* they could harm this person; ethical considerations made it necessary to assure that no harm could actually take place.) Results were surprising: High temperature *reduced* aggression for both provoked and unprovoked people. The initial explanation of these findings was that the high temperatures were so uncomfortable that participants focused on getting away from them—and this caused them to reduce their aggression (Baron & Richardson, 1994).

This seemed reasonable—when people are *very* hot, they do seem to become lethargic and concentrate on reducing their discomfort rather than on "evening the score" with others. However, these early studies suffered from important drawbacks which made it difficult to determine the validity of this interpretation. For instance, the exposure to the high temperatures lasted only a few minutes, while in the real world, this occurs over much longer periods. Other studies used very different methods (e.g., Anderson & Anderson, 1996; Bell, 1992) they examined long-term records of temperatures and police records of various aggressive crimes to determine whether the frequency of such crimes increased with rising temperatures.

Consider a careful study conducted by Anderson, Bushman, and Groom (1997). These researchers collected average annual temperatures for 50 cities in the United States over a 45-year period (1950–1995). In addition, they obtained information on the rate of both violent crimes (aggravated assault, homicide) and property crimes (burglary, car theft), as well as another crime that has often been viewed as primarily aggressive in nature: rape. They then performed analyses to determine if temperature was related to these crimes. In general, hotter years did indeed produce higher rates of violent crimes, but did not produce increases in property crimes or rape. This was true even though the effect of many other variables that might also influence aggressive crimes (e.g., poverty, age distribution of the population) were eliminated. These findings, and those of related studies (e.g., Anderson, Anderson, & Deuser, 1996), suggest that heat is indeed linked to at least some forms of aggression.

Excellent as this research was, however, it did not fully resolve one key question: Does this heat–aggression relationship have any limits? In other words, does aggression increase with heat indefinitely, or only up to some point, beyond which aggression actually declines as temperatures continue to rise? As you will recall, that is the pattern obtained in initial laboratory studies on this topic.

Additional studies by Rotton and Cohn (Cohn & Rotton, 1997; Rotton & Cohn, 2000) carefully addressed this issue. These researchers reasoned that if people do indeed try to reduce their discomfort when they are feeling very uncomfortable (e.g., when temperatures are very high), the relationship between heat and aggression should be stronger in the evening hours than at midday. That is because temperatures fall below their peak in the evening. In other words, a finer-grained analysis would reveal a curvilinear relationship between heat and aggression during the day, but a linear one at night. This is just what they found.

In sum, research on the effects of heat on aggression suggests that there is indeed a link between heat and aggression: When people get hot, they become irritable and may be more likely to lash out at others. However, there may be limits to this relationship, stemming from the fact that after prolonged exposure to high temperatures, people become so uncomfortable that they focus on reducing their discomfort—not on attacking others. Short of these extreme conditions, however, there is a big grain of truth in the metaphor "the heat of anger," and when temperatures rise, tempers may, too— with serious social consequences. That is, certainly something to consider in the context of global warming and the very real possibility that all of us will soon be exposed to uncomfortably hot outdoor temperatures more frequently than was true in the past.

ALCOHOL AND AGGRESSION: A DANGEROUS COMBINATION It is widely assumed that people become more aggressive when they consume alcohol. This idea is supported

Figure 10.12 Alcohol: Evidence That It Increases Aggression for Both Genders

Although women were less aggressive than men while playing a competitive reaction time task, aggression by both genders was increased by alcohol consumption.

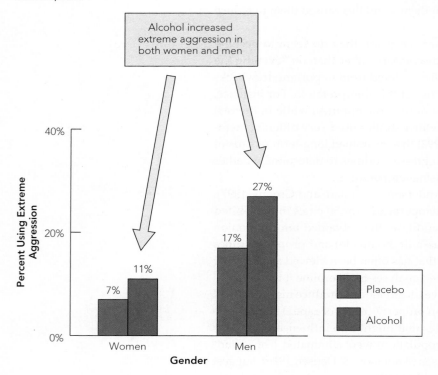

by the fact that bars and nightclubs are often the scene of violence. However, while alcohol is certainly consumed in these settings, other factors might be responsible for the fights—or worse—that often erupt: competition for desirable partners, crowding, and even cigarette smoke which irritates many people (Zillmann, Baron, & Tamborini, 1981). What does systematic research reveal about a possible link between alcohol and aggression? Interestingly, it tends to confirm the existence of such a link.

In several experiments, participants who consumed substantial doses of alcohol—enough to make them legally drunk—have been found to behave more aggressively, and to respond to provocations more strongly than those who did not consume alcohol (Bushman & Cooper, 1990; Gustafson, 1992). For example, Giancola, Levinson, Corman, and Godlaski (2009) had men and women participants consume either drinks containing alcohol (1 gram per kilogram of body weight for men, 0.90 grams per kilogram for women) or no alcohol (although a few drops were floated on the top to equate the smell of the two kinds of drinks). Then, the participants played a game in which they and an opponent competed in terms of reaction time—who could respond quicker. Participants were to set electric shocks for each other, and were supposed to receive these shocks if they lost on each trial. In fact, however, there was no opponent; the opponent's supposed responses were controlled by the experimenter. At first, the opponent set very weak shocks (which participants actually received after giving their permission to do so). But then, the opponent set extreme shocks at the highest level. The critical research question was how would the participants respond? As you can see from Figure 10.12, men were more than twice as likely to act aggressively compared to women in terms of the shocks they set for their opponent. But for both genders, extreme aggression (trials on which participants selected the strongest available shock for their opponent) was increased by alcohol. The effect was stronger for men than women, but alcohol increased such aggression for both.

Why does alcohol produce such effects? Does it simply eliminate inhibitions against acting in an impulsive, and possibly dangerous, way? Or does it make people especially sensitive to provocations, so that they are more likely to behave aggressively (Gantner & Taylor, 1992)? In other words, does alcohol lower their threshold for responding aggressively to provocations? All of these possibilities are reasonable and are supported by some evidence, but recent findings suggest that the effects of alcohol on aggression may stem, at least in part, from reduced cognitive functioning and what this does, in turn, to social perception. Specifically, the findings of several studies (e.g., Bartholow, Pearson, Gratton, & Fabiani, 2003) indicate that alcohol impairs higher-order cognitive functions such as evaluation of stimuli and memory. This may make it harder for individuals to evaluate others' intentions (hostile or non-hostile), and to evaluate the effects that various forms of behavior on their part, including aggression, may produce (e.g., Hoaken, Giancola, & Pihl, 1998). For instance, people who have consumed alcohol show reductions in their capacity to process positive information about someone they initially dislike. This means that if such a person provoked them, but then apologized, those who have consumed alcohol might be less able to process this information carefully, and so would remain likely to aggress, despite the apology. This does seem to fit other findings concerning the impact of alcohol on cognitive processes. For instance, alcohol has been shown to lower self-control and thereby limit people's abilities to inhibit aggressive responding following provocation (Denson, DeWall, & Finkel, 2012).

GUN AVAILABILITY: HOW WEAPONS ENABLE VIOLENCE   As we noted in the opening of this chapter, instances of mass killings in the United States almost always involve high powered weapons. Would Adam Lanza have killed so many people at Sandy Hook Elementary School in 2012, if he had not had access to his mother's high capacity weapons? Given the near-daily mass shooting event occurrence in the United States, which is a much higher rate than any other developed country—the question of what role the widespread availability of weapons (Americans are the best armed citizenry in the world) plays is hotly debated. On the assumption that weapon availability does not enable such violence, in December 2015, the U.S. Congress voted against a ban on assault weapons. Yet, careful epidemiologic research assessing firearm deaths following legislation to regulate firearms supports the opposite conclusion. Santaella-Tenorio, Cerda, Villaveces, and Galea (2016) examined 130 studies conducted in 10 countries following legislation changes restricting the purchase and access to firearms. They found that such legal changes were associated with lower intimate partner homicides and unintentional deaths in children.

How has social psychological research addressed these questions concerning gun availability? As Stroebe (2015) argues, there are two routes by which gun availability might affect homicide rates. First, such weapon availability could affect the intention to commit such acts, and second, it could affect the likelihood that an intention to kill is actually successful, or results in homicide. In terms of the first possibility—whether weapon availability can shape intentions—early experimental research on the *weapons effect* suggests that it can. Based on the idea that guns are perceived as a means of doing harm and serve to cue aggressive thoughts, Berkowitz and LePage (1967) exposed angered individuals in a research laboratory setting to either a gun or a tennis racket. They then gave the participants an opportunity to act aggressively toward the person who had angered them. The central finding, which has been replicated numerous times, was that participants acted more aggressively in the presence of a gun compared to a neutral object. Subsequent research in which men handled either a gun or a toy for 15 minutes revealed two important outcomes that are consistent with the earlier research (Klinesmith, Kasser, & McAndrew, 2006). In the gun-handling condition, the men's testosterone level increased as did the aggression they displayed toward another person compared to the toy-handling condition. Further, the increase in testosterone accounted for the gun-handling effect on the amount of subsequent aggression that was displayed. Although homicide is most certainly more aggressive than the sorts of behaviors measured in these studies, this research does suggest that weapons in the hands of people who are already angry may influence the likelihood that they will act more aggressively than otherwise.

In terms of the second question of whether the availability of guns, given an intention to kill—increases the likelihood of homicide—the answer is a resounding "yes." First, given an intention to kill, there is no doubt that guns are more effective than any other means (Zimring, 2004). This is true for both homicides and suicides; although other methods exist and are used by people (e.g., knives, drugs), guns are much more effective in causing death, including that of multiple people in mass shootings with assault weapons, very quickly. Indeed, many carefully conducted studies (e.g., Stroebe, 2015) have revealed that contrary to the widespread belief that gun ownership protects against homicide (e.g., is used effectively for self-defense), the evidence favors the opposite conclusion—that owning guns or living in a household with guns increases the risk of homicide (and suicide).

Key Points

- Contrary to the **frustration-aggression hypothesis**, not all aggression stems from frustration, and frustration does not always lead to aggression. Frustration is a strong elicitor of aggression only under certain limited conditions.
- In contrast, **provocation** from others is a powerful elicitor of aggression. The strongest form of provocation appears to be expressions of condescension, but even **teasing** can stimulate aggression.
- Heightened arousal can increase aggression if it persists beyond the situation in which it was induced and is unknowingly interpreted as anger generated in the new context. This process is referred to as **excitation transfer theory**.
- Exposure to media violence has been found to increase aggression among viewers. This is due to several factors, such as the priming of aggressive thoughts and a weakening of restraints against aggression, and also to desensitization to such materials.
- Playing violent video games increases aggressive cognitions, aggressive affect, and overt aggressive behavior.
- Individuals appear to enjoy playing these games not because of their aggressive content but because the games satisfy motives for competence and mastery.
- Existing evidence indicates that the widely accepted view that men are invariably more aggressive than women is not entirely correct. When gender differences emerge depends on the type of aggression and a variety of situational factors.
- **Narcissistic rage** can emerge when others question the individual's inflated self view.

- Men *are* more likely than women to engage in physical aggression, and to both perpetrate and be victims of several forms of violent crime. However the two genders do not differ significantly in terms of verbal aggression, although men tend to use stronger forms of such behavior.
- Following strong provocation, both men and women are similarly likely to respond with some form of aggression. However, men are more likely than women to behave aggressively in the absence of strong provocation.
- Women are slightly more likely than men to engage in *indirect* forms of aggression—actions intended to harm the victim in the absence of face-to-face confrontations.
- High temperatures tend to increase aggression but only up to a point. Beyond some level, aggression declines as temperatures rise.
- Consuming alcohol can increase aggression in both men and women, perhaps because alcohol reduces the individual's capacity to process some kinds of information and inhibits self-control following provocation.
- Research on the *weapons effect* indicates that weapon availability can affect the intention to commit aggressive acts. Handling a gun (versus a toy) increases aggressive behavior in males by increasing their testosterone levels.
- Research has also revealed that gun ownership does not provide a protective effect; rather living in a household with guns increases the risk of both homicide and suicide. In different countries following legislation restricting gun access, gun deaths have decreased.

10.3: Aggression in the Classroom and Workplace

Objective   **Describe the types and causes of bullying**

When you were in school, did you know any bullies—other students who frequently picked on various victims and made their lives truly miserable? Unfortunately, **bullying** is far from rare. Recent studies of this problem (Hymel & Swearer, 2015a) indicate that depending on age and location, anywhere from 10 percent to 33 percent of children report that they have been bullied, while 5 percent to 13 percent admit to having bullied one or more other children (see Figure 10.13). Given these findings, it is clear that bullying is a problem worthy of careful attention, so we will now review evidence concerning such issues as why it occurs, who becomes bullies or victims, its effects on both bullies and their victims, and how it can be reduced.

10.3.1: What Is Bullying?

In research on bullying, it is usually defined as a form of interpersonal aggression in which one individual—a bully—intentionally and repeatedly aggresses against another, and does so, in part, because the bully has more power or status than the person they seek to harm (Hymel & Swearer, 2015b).

Figure 10.13 Bullying: An All-too-Common Occurrence in Schools

A large proportion of children report that they have been bullied in school, and many others report that they have bullied their classmates. Some children indicate that they have been both the victim and bully.

Almost everyone has either experienced or observed bullying during their childhood or teen years, and it sometimes continues into adulthood, although in different forms. For instance, abusive bosses are, in a sense, bullying their subordinates. So why does bullying occur, and why is it focused on specific victims? These and related questions have been the focus of a growing amount of research and results indicate that the answers are complex. Bullying arises from many different factors including several personal characteristics that predispose individuals to become bullies. Among these personality factors are being callous toward the suffering of others (Muñoz, Qualter, & Padgett, 2011), endorsement of masculine traits (Navarro, Yubero, Larrañaga, & Martinez, 2011), and anxiety (Craig, 1998). Surprisingly, bullies also tend to be high in social intelligence—that is, they perceive others accurately, and are skilled at getting along with them. Yet, despite this, they seek to harm people who are unable to defend themselves.

Who are the victims? Again, research offers revealing findings (Hymel & Swearer, 2015b). Victims of bullying tend to be individuals who feel unhappy and unsafe, and their academic performance suffers as a result (Konishi, Hymel, Zumbo, & Li, 2010). They also tend to be lonely, withdrawn, and socially isolated—they have few friends and are awkward in interacting with their peers. Consequently, they are less well liked by their peers, and have no friends to rush to their aid when they are attacked by bullies.

But bullying does not only arise from the traits or skills (or lack of skills) of bullies and victims; it is also strongly influenced by contextual factors relating to their families, schools, and communities. For instance, with respect to families, poor parental supervision, conflict between parents, involvement of family members in gangs, and parental abuse are all related to bullying (Cook, Williams, Guerra, Kim, & Sadek, 2010). Turning to schools, such factors as poor teacher–student relationships, lack of teacher support, and a school climate that condones or even approves bullying may all play a role (Richard, 2012). Finally, communities, too, are important with such conditions as unsafe and dangerous environments and ones in which aggression and violence are shown by others and condoned all tend to encourage both bullying and victimization. A summary of the factors that, together, tend to increase bullying is shown in Figure 10.14.

Figure 10.14 Many Factors Encourage Bullying

Bullying is encouraged by factors relating to the bullies, the victims, and aspects of their school and community environments.

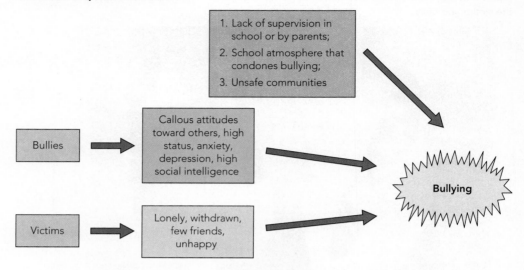

10.3.2: Cyberbullying: Electronic Means of Harm Doing

As is true of aggression generally, bullying can take many different forms, including direct physical harm, verbal taunts and threats, social exclusion, and rumor-spreading. Not surprisingly, verbal bullying and social exclusion are the most common: 51 percent of children in grades 4 to 12 have reported receiving such treatment, while a smaller number 31 percent indicated that they were the victims of physical assaults (Hymel & Swearer, 2015a).

In some ways, another form of bullying that has emerged in recent years—**cyberbullying**—is the most disturbing. Cyberbullying is often defined as the use of information and communication technologies such as e-mail, cell phones, instant messaging, and social media as means of engaging in deliberate, repeated, and hostile behavior that is intended to harm others. As indicated by a recent review of evidence relating to the causes and effects of cyberbullying, it resembles other forms of bullying in its intention to harm the victim, its origins in power differentials (the cyberbully being higher in status or power), and the fact that it occurs repeatedly. It differs from other forms of bullying in that the bullies often believe that they are anonymous, and their power often derives from the fact that they are more sophisticated with respect to technology and its uses (Kowalski, Giumetti, Schroeder, & Lattanner, 2014).

Despite these differences, cyberbullying seems to be at least as harmful to the victims as other forms of bullying, adversely influencing the physical, psychological, and social adjustment of victims. In addition, it leads to specific behavior problems such as reduced popularity, declines in school performance, and can even encourage use of dangerous drugs (Hymel & Swearer, 2015b). Since cyberbullying can occur through many outlets ranging from e-mail to social media, it is clearly a serious form of bullying—and one that reflects the conditions of modern society in which most people are interconnected with many others through electronic means.

10.3.3: Can Bullying Be Reduced?

Bullying is clearly an important problem; for instance, as we noted earlier, cyberbullying provides a new context and several new ways in which bullies can hurt their intended victims. This raises a key question: How can bullying of all types be reduced?

As you can probably guess there has been a large amount of research on this issue, and although the findings are complex, several tentative conclusions about the ways to proceed do exist (Bradshaw, 2015).

Some of the core elements of successful programs—ones that significantly reduce the frequency or magnitude of bullying—included the following features:

- Strong efforts to supervise children's behavior in playgrounds, classrooms, and other school settings.

- Training teachers to recognize, and, through consistent disciplinary practices either prevent or stop bullying when it occurs.

- Actively involving parents through meetings with them and providing them with information about the harmful effects of bullying.

- Involving bystanders who witness bullying, so that they know they should report it to teachers and certainly refrain from showing positive reactions toward the bully—approval that can encourage bullies to escalate their efforts to harm or humiliate their victims.

- Multicomponent models which include school-wide efforts to prevent bullying, which combine these steps, such as counseling individuals identified as either bullies or victims, increasing the involvement of parents, and also involving counselors who can help increase bullies' awareness of the inappropriateness of their behavior and the harm it produces.

- Tailoring programs to reflect children's initial reactions to prevention techniques so that children who do not change their behavior as a result of initial, mild interventions (e.g., efforts to enhance their social skills—ability to interact effectively with others; small changes in school climate), are exposed to stronger efforts (e.g., more intense training in social skills, actively involving their parents), and even stronger efforts for children who are most resistant to change their bullying behavior (e.g., enlisting the help of mental health professionals to help reduce the personal problems that lead to bullying).

- Providing potential or actual victims with the means for dealing with bullying—they must be told precisely what to do and how to seek help when bullying occurs.

One successful intervention that has been shown to substantially reduce school bullying involves changing the norms in schools by encouraging some "social referents," that many student pay attention to, to take a public stance against bullying and conflict. Because many students perceive bullying or conflict behavior in schools to be typical, expected, or desirable, intervening to change that perception of what is normative could serve to reduce bullying behavior. In an impressive experimental intervention in 56 schools, Paluck, Shepherd, and Aronow (2016) found that compared with control schools, those where a popular "social referent" was encouraged to be a public anti-conflict role model, incidence of school bullying dropped by 30 percent over a 1 year period. This research illustrates the power of social referents to change norms and thereby alter school climates to lessen bullying.

While bullying has often been viewed as a form of aggression that occurs primarily in schools, it is clear that it often exists in work settings, too. Abusive bosses who mistreat, shout at, and even threaten their subordinates are far from rare. Employees, too, often seek to harm others where they work, especially those who, in their view, have treated them badly or unfairly. These efforts to "right past wrongs" take many different forms, but in some cases, they have deadly consequences. In short, what is known as *workplace aggression* is another important form of aggression, and one with serious negative effects. What does research tell us about the causes, forms, and effects of workplace aggression? In the special feature, **"What Research Tells Us About... Workplace Aggression"** we will provide an overview of what is currently known about these questions.

What Research Tells Us About...

Workplace Aggression

Although aggression in workplaces can take many different forms—ranging from verbal insults, through more subtle actions such as blocking another person's promotion or pet project—it is instances of workplace violence that have most often captured public and media attention. Unfortunately, instances of extreme, physical violence in workplaces do occur. In what is, perhaps, the most disturbing occurrence, in 1987 David Burke, a ticket agent for USAir, was fired by his supervisor for theft. When his request for another chance was refused, he decided to take his revenge. He boarded a flight headed for San Francisco, and somehow, managed to smuggle a pistol with him. Shortly after the plane took off, he pulled out his gun and began shooting crew members; when he shot both the pilot and co-pilot, the plane crashed, killing 43 innocent people who had nothing to do with him losing his job. He left a note to his supervisor that survived the crash; it read: "I asked for some leniency for my family, remember? Well, I got none. And you'll get none."

Although such frightening instances of violence might lead us to think that workplaces are very dangerous locations decades of research (Barclay & Aquino, 2010) indicates that the overwhelming majority of instances in which individuals seek to harm others where they work take much less dramatic forms.

In fact, in most instances, workplace aggression involves quite subtle behavior, such as spreading negative rumors about their targets, reporting that they are getting ready to move to another company and taking important "secrets" with them or that they have engaged in unethical, if not illegal actions. Other forms of workplace aggression include removing equipment or resources the target people need to complete their work, expressing disapproval of projects these people favor, and even destroying their personal property. In fact, research findings (Barclay & Aquino, 2010) suggest that in aggressing against others at work, most people follow a "cost–benefit" rule: They attempt to do the most harm to the victim while at the same time, assuring that they cannot be identified as the source of this harm (see Figure 10.15).

Why do individuals aggress against others at work? Often, because they think they have been treated unfairly, that others have received benefits they have not, or have been humiliated by bosses or others. In such cases, workplace aggressors are often willing to wait a long time to gain their revenge. In sum, aggression does occur frequently at work, and sometimes it does indeed take the extreme form of violent actions. But in most instances, it occurs in more subtle and indirect ways—which can still be extremely harmful to their intended victims.

Figure 10.15 Workplace Aggression: A Cost–Benefit Calculation by the Aggressor

Most instances of workplace aggression do not involve overt physical attacks. Rather, they are rather subtle and designed to harm the victim without person being able to identify who caused the harm. This involves the kind of cost-benefit calculation shown here: Aggressors want to do the most harm at the least cost (or danger) to themselves.

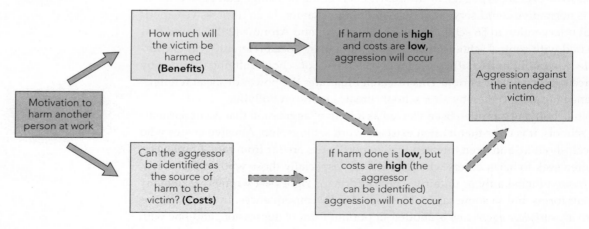

Key Points

- **Bullying** involves repeated aggression against individuals who, for various reasons, are unable to defend themselves against such treatment. Bullying occurs in many contexts, including schools and workplaces.
- Few children are solely bullies or victims; more play both roles. Bullies and bully-victims appear to have lower self-esteem than children who are not involved in bullying.
- There are a variety of techniques that are aimed at reducing bullying in schools. Among the most successful so far have been programs using popular students

as models against bullying, which serves to change the perceived norms in the schools.
- **Cyberbullying** involves using electronic means to harm others.
- Bullying occurs in work settings as well as schools. Abusive bosses bully their subordinates.
- Bullying in workplaces can sometimes lead the people who are bullied to engage in violent forms of aggression. Much of the time, though, *workplace aggression* is more subtle and aimed at harming the victim without that person being able to identify who caused the harm.

10.4: The Prevention and Control of Aggression: Some Useful Techniques

Objective   **Identify techniques for reducing aggression**

If there is one idea we hope you will take away with you from this chapter, it is this: Aggression is not an inevitable or unalterable form of behavior. On the contrary, since it stems from a complex interplay between cognitions, personal characteristics, and situational factors, it can be prevented or reduced. With that in mind, we will now examine several techniques that, when used appropriately, can be highly effective in reducing the frequency or intensity of human aggression.

10.4.1: Punishment: Revenge or Deterrence?

In most societies throughout the world, **punishment**—delivery of aversive consequences—is a major technique for reducing aggression. People who engage in prohibited aggressive behavior receive large fines, are put in prison, and in some countries are placed in solitary confinement or receive physical punishment for their actions (see Figure 10.16). In many cases, this involves spending time in prison, but in some locations, extreme cases of violence such as murder may result in *capital punishment*—legal execution of the convicted criminals. Why do so many societies punish aggressive acts? Basically, there are two major reasons (Darley, Carlsmith, & Robinson, 2000).

First, there is a widespread belief that individuals who engage in inappropriate acts of aggression *deserve* to be punished. They have inflicted harm on others—and on society in general—and should suffer in order to make amends for this harm. This perspective suggests that the amount of punishment people ought to receive should be matched to the magnitude of harm they have caused (e.g., breaking someone's arm should deserve less punishment than permanently harming or killing them). In addition, the magnitude of punishment should take account of extenuating

Figure 10.16 Punishment: An Effective Deterrent to Aggression?

Most societies use punishment for aggressive actions (e.g., fines, prison terms, or worse) to deter such behavior. Are these procedures effective? Existing evidence on this complex issue is mixed.

circumstances—for instance, was there some other motive for the aggressive action, such as self-defense or defense of one's family?

The second reason for punishing people who commit aggressive actions is to *deter* them (or others) from engaging in such behavior in the future. This basis for punishment implies that ease of detection of the crime should be given careful attention; if aggressive actions are hard to detect (e.g., they involve hidden or covert forms of harming others), they should be strongly punished because only strong punishment will deter people from engaging in actions they believe they can "get away with." Similarly, public punishment would be expected to be more effective in deterring future crimes than private punishment, especially in cultures where public shame is viewed as a truly negative outcome.

Which of these two perspectives is most important in determining the magnitude of punishment people feel is justified for specific aggressive acts or other offenses? Research by Carlsmith, Darley, and Robinson (2002) suggests that in general, the first perspective tends to dominate. So across many different contexts, people's beliefs about punishment involve morality or perceptions of the perpetrator's deservingness. Most people seem to believe that "the punishment should fit the crime."

There is still another rationale for using punishment to reduce aggressive behavior that we have not yet mentioned: Some kinds of punishment, at least, *remove dangerous people from society* (e.g., by placing them in prison), and in this way, prevent them from repeating their aggressive actions with new victims in the future. Is there any support for this view? In fact, statistics indicate that once people engage in violent crimes, they are likely to do so again. If that is true, then removing them from society might indeed help prevent additional acts of aggression against others (although not against other prisoners!). This is one rationale for giving people convicted of aggressive crimes long prison sentences, although it is rarely stated by judges or prosecuting attorneys. Surprisingly, this reason for imprisoning those convicted of crimes receives little attention in discussions of the pros and cons of punishment; yet, it does seem to offer the benefit of protecting potential future victims; and sadly, many criminals—when released—repeat the crimes for which they were found guilty.

Another important question relating to punishment concerns its effectiveness: Does it work? Can it reduce the tendency of specific people to engage in later harmful acts of aggression? Here, existing evidence is relatively clear. Punishment *can* reduce aggression, but only if it meets four basic requirements: (1) It must be *prompt*—it must follow aggressive actions as quickly as possible; (2) it must be *certain to occur*—the probability that it will follow aggression must be very high; (3) it must be *strong*—strong enough to be highly unpleasant to potential recipients; and (4) it must be perceived by recipients as *justified* or deserved.

Unfortunately, these conditions are typically not met in the criminal justice systems of many nations. In most societies, the delivery of punishment for aggressive actions is delayed for months or even years. Similarly, many perpetrators avoid arrest and conviction, so the certainty of punishment is low. The magnitude of punishment itself varies from one city, state, or even courtroom to another. Sentencing too is often harsher for minority group members than for whites. In fact, Eberhardt, Davies, Purdie-Vaughns, and Johnson (2006) found that when the victim of a crime was white, the degree to which the defendant looked "stereotypically black" predicted the likelihood the death sentence would be seen as deserved.

And often, punishment does not seem to fit the crime—it does not seem to be justified or deserved. In such cases, the people who are punished may view such treatment as aggression against *them*—as a kind of provocation. And as we saw earlier, provocation is a very powerful trigger *for* aggression. In view of these facts, it is hardly surprising that the threat of punishment—even severe punishment—does not seem to be effective in deterring violent crime. The conditions necessary for it to be effective simply do not exist, and probably, given the nature of most legal systems, cannot exist. For this reason, we must conclude that the belief that severe punishment for aggressive crimes will successfully deter such behavior is wildly optimistic and inaccurate. But, as we describe here, there are other techniques for reducing aggression, including several based on the principles of social cognition, which can be much more effective.

10.4.2: Self-Regulation: Internal Mechanisms for Restraining Aggression

From an evolutionary perspective, aggression can be viewed as adaptive behavior, at least in some situations. For instance, competition for desirable mates is often intense, and one way to "win" in such contests is through aggression against potential rivals. So, especially for males, strong tendencies to aggress against others can yield beneficial outcomes. On the other hand, living together in human society often requires restraining aggressive behavior. Lashing out at others in response to every provocation is definitely *not* adaptive, and can greatly disrupt social life. For this reason, it is clear that we possess effective internal mechanisms for restraining anger and overt aggression (Baumeister, 2005). Such mechanisms are described by the term *self-regulation* (or self-control), and refer to our capacity to regulate many aspects of own behavior, including aggression.

Unfortunately, such self-regulation often requires lots of cognitive effort, so one reason why this internal system of restraint sometimes fails is that we simply do not have the resources or skills required to do so. In other words, aggression often erupts because we have invested so much cognitive effort in other tasks that we have too little left to perform this important but demanding function. In fact, the results of many studies indicate that self-control can, like other resources, be depleted by tasks that require its exercise (Baumeister & Tierney, 2011; Baumeister, Vohs, & Tice, 2007). In such research, when participants had used up their self-control (e.g., by resisting the temptation to eat a delicious-looking donut), they displayed more aggression than those whose self-control had not been depleted.

Encouragingly, though, other research findings (Mauss, Evers, Wilhelm, & Gross, 2006) indicate that self-control of aggressive impulses does not necessarily involve the use of cognitive resources. In fact, when individuals have positive implicit attitudes toward regulating their own emotions, they may be able to restrain aggression almost effortlessly—simply because they have positive attitudes toward exerting such emotional control. Further, it appears that one way in which individuals self-regulate their behavior so as to avoid aggressing involves thinking *prosocial thoughts*—thinking about helping others, caring for them and so forth. The more readily people can bring such thoughts to mind when provoked or exposed to conditions that normally tend to trigger aggression, the less likely they are to behave in an aggressive manner (Meier, Robinson, & Wilkowski, 2006)

So where does this intriguing research leave us? With the suggestion that one effective means of reducing aggression—potentially a very effective one—is strengthening the *internal mechanisms* that usually operate to control such behavior. We all possess these mechanisms, so the major task is making them stronger and assuring that they are not overwhelmed by other demands on our cognitive resources. How can internal restraints against aggression be strengthened? There are several strategies for doing so. For instance, exposure to other people who show restraint even in the face of strong provocation (nonaggressive models; Baron & Richardson, 1994) can help, as would providing training designed to strengthen internal restraints. In addition, individuals can be taught to recognize when their cognitive resources are being "stretched," since those are the occasions on which inappropriate aggression is most likely to occur.

10.4.3: Catharsis: Does "Blowing Off Steam" Really Help?

When I was a child, my grandmother used to greet temper tantrums by saying: "That's OK darling, let it out . . . don't keep it bottled up inside—that's bad for you." In other words, she was a true believer in the **catharsis hypothesis**—the view that if individuals give vent to their anger and hostility in non-harmful ways, their tendencies to engage in more dangerous types of aggression will be reduced (Dollard et al., 1939).

Is this actually true? Most people seem to believe that it is; for instance, advice columnists often urge people to express their aggressive emotions and thoughts (e.g., by writing a nasty letter and not sending it) as a means of reducing them. This belief has given rise to a minor industry providing toys and games that, supposedly, allow people to "get rid" of their aggressive impulses. But systematic research by social psychologists on catharsis calls such advice into question; in fact, the widespread faith in the effectiveness of catharsis is not justified. On the contrary, it appears that so-called *venting* activities such as watching, reading about, or imagining aggressive actions, or even engaging in "play" aggression such as hammering a punching bag, are more likely to *increase* subsequent aggression than to reduce it (Bushman, 2001; Bushman, Baumeister, & Stack, 1999). A clear demonstration of this fact is provided by research conducted by Anderson, Carnagey, and Eubanks (2003).

These researchers reasoned that if catharsis really works, then exposure to songs with violent lyrics would allow people to "vent" aggressive thoughts or feelings; as a result, they would show lower levels of hostility and lower levels of aggressive thoughts. However, if catharsis does not work—and on the basis of previous findings the researchers did not expect that it would—exposure to songs with violent lyrics might actually increase hostility and aggressive cognitions. To test these competing predictions, they conducted a series of studies in which participants listened to violent or nonviolent songs and then completed measures of their current feelings (hostile or friendly) and their aggressive cognitions (e.g., how much similarity they perceived between aggressive and ambiguous words— ones that could have both an aggressive and nonaggressive meaning such as alley or police; the researchers measured how quickly participants pronounced aggressive and nonaggressive words that appeared on a computer screen). Results of all the studies were consistent: After hearing songs with violent lyrics, participants showed an increase in both hostile feelings and aggressive thoughts, and they responded more quickly to aggressive words than nonaggressive words. So catharsis definitely did *not* occur.

Why does "letting it out" fail to reduce aggression? There are several reasons. First, anger may actually be increased when individuals think about wrongs they have suffered at the hands of others and imagine ways of harming these people. Second, watching aggressive scenes, listening to songs with aggressive lyrics, or merely thinking about revenge and other aggressive actions may activate even more aggressive thoughts and feelings. These, in turn, may color interpretations of actual social interactions so that ambiguous actions by others are more likely to be perceived as hostile ones. As we saw earlier, research on the effects of playing violent video games confirms this. As a result of increased hostile thoughts, aggression is increased, not reduced, by activities that, according to the catharsis hypothesis should reduce it.

Is there even a small grain of truth in the catharsis hypothesis? Perhaps only this: Giving vent to angry feelings may make individuals feel better emotionally. Anyone who has punched their own pillow or a punching bag, thrown around objects that can't break or shouted angrily at other drivers who can't hear them, has experienced such effects (see Figure 10.17). But feeling better—less angry—may actually strengthen the link between anger and aggression—after all, "letting it all out" reduces emotional discomfort. So watch out: Catharsis is unlikely to reduce the tendency to engage in aggression when angry, it may even increase it. In short, systematic research by social psychologists suggests that "common sense" beliefs about the effectiveness of catharsis (as well as suggestions to this effect by Freud), are not really justified.

10.4.4: Reducing Aggression by Thinking Nonaggressive Thoughts

As we noted earlier, when one person angers another (e.g., through an insult, or behaving in a condescending manner), the recipient of such treatment often responds in kind, with the result that anger—and aggression—spiral upward. How can this potentially deadly outcome be prevented—or stopped? Research findings suggest that one way of doing so is by inducing thoughts and feelings that are incompatible with anger or aggression (Baron & Richardson, 1994). Several kinds of incompatible reactions have been found to be effective in reducing aggression—certain kinds of humor, feelings of empathy toward potential victims, and even mild sexual arousal. The feelings and thoughts involved are inconsistent or conflict with anger and intentions to harm another person. In other words, they get the potential aggressor "off the track," so that aggression itself becomes less likely.

Have you heard the expression "Count to 10 before losing your temper?" That describes a simple cognitive technique for changing the focus of your thoughts—and this momentary shift may sometimes be enough to reduce anger, just enough that it does not erupt into overt aggression. Are there others ways of reducing aggression through encouraging responses incompatible with it? A number of studies have been conducted to evaluate this idea—that inducing thoughts or feelings incompatible with aggression may actually reduce its occurrence—and they have generally reported findings that support it. In what is perhaps the most unusual research on this issue (Baron, 1976), a car driven by an assistant of the researcher pulled up at a red light and then failed to move when the light turned green. The number of seconds that passed until the driver in the car behind the assistant's honked her or his horn was measured—because it was reasoned that horn honking is a mild form of aggression. During the period when the light was still red, another assistant crossed between the two cars. In one condition, she wore a clown mask—to induce unexpected feelings of humor. In another, she wore a somewhat revealing outfit—to induce feelings of mild sexual arousal or interest among male drives. In a third condition, the assistant had a cast on her leg (to suggest that it was broken), and used crutches as she crossed the street—this was designed to induce empathy toward the assistant. As a control condition, she simply walked across the street in a normal manner.

It was predicted that all three conditions (empathy, sexual arousal, and humor) would induce incompatible responses among drivers and so increase the amount of time, relative to the control condition, until they honked when the driver in front of

Figure 10.17 Catharsis—Does It Really Work?

Does engaging in aggression at one time reduce the likelihood of subsequent aggression? Research findings indicate that it does not. Engaging in even nonharmful aggressive actions such as shouting angrily at other people who can't see or hear the person doing so can make the angry person feel better, at least temporarily. But this "reward" for expressing anger may actually strengthen the link between anger and aggression.

them did not move. Results offered strong support for this prediction. When coupled with findings from laboratory experiments, there is evidence that inducing incompatible feelings in others can reduce their tendency to aggress. If you have ever tried to shift a conversation that was becoming heated to another topic unrelated to the one being discussed, you have used this technique yourself. The basic idea of incompatible responses is expressed in the two quotations here which, in a few words, capture the idea that doing something that turns our thoughts or actions away from our anger or the temptation to aggress can often be effective in reducing it.

The best remedy for a short temper is a long walk. ~Jacqueline Schiff
Next time you're mad, try dancing out your anger. ~Terri Guillemets

So overall, is aggression inevitable, because it is part of our "human nature?" Absolutely not. Various techniques for reducing aggression exist, and if used appropriately, can significantly reduce the likelihood that overt acts of aggression will occur. In short, there is clear evidence that we are not the helpless pawns of our genes or situations that condemn us to engage in ever more dangerous acts of aggression.

Key Points

- **Punishment** can be effective in reducing aggression, but only when it is delivered under certain conditions that are rarely met.
- The **catharsis hypothesis** appears to be mainly false. The likelihood of subsequent aggression is not reduced by engaging in apparently "safe" forms of aggression.
- Aggression is often restrained by internal self-regulatory processes. If the cognitive resources needed by these processes are depleted, however, aggression is more likely to occur.
- Inducing feelings or responses incompatible with anger can sometimes reduce overt aggression.

Summary and Review

Aggression is the intentional infliction of harm on others. Research findings indicate that it derives from many different sources—even, as recent evidence suggests—from biological factors in interaction with situations we find ourselves in. **Drive theories of aggression** suggest that aggression stems from externally elicited drives to harm or injure others. The **frustration-aggression hypothesis** is the best-known of such theories. Modern theories of aggression, such as the **general aggression model (GAM)**, recognize the importance of learning, various eliciting input variables, individual differences, affective states, and, especially, cognitive processes in aggression.

Contrary to the frustration-aggression hypothesis, all aggression does not stem from frustration, and frustration does not always lead to aggression. Frustration is a strong elicitor of aggression only under certain limited conditions. In contrast, provocation from others is a powerful elicitor of aggression. The strongest form of provocation appears to be expressions of condescension, but even *teasing* can stimulate aggression. Social exclusion can lead the excluded people to engage in aggression as a means of "getting even" with the people who have rejected them.

Heightened arousal can increase aggression, especially if it persists beyond the situation in which it was induced and is unknowingly interpreted as anger generated in the new context.

Exposure to media violence has been found to increase aggression among viewers. This is due to several factors, such as the priming of aggressive thoughts and a weakening of restraints against aggression, and also to desensitization to such materials.

Playing violent video games increases aggressive cognition, aggressive affect, and overt aggressive behavior. It also reduces empathy toward others. Individuals like to play these games not because of the aggressive content but because the games satisfy motives for competence and mastery.

Existing evidence indicates that the widely accepted view that men are always more aggressive than women is not entirely accurate. Men do appear to be more likely than women to engage in physical aggression. However, the two genders do not differ significantly in terms of verbal aggression, although men tend to use stronger forms of such behavior. Following strong provocation, both men and women respond with some form of aggression, although men are more likely than women to behave aggressively in the absence of strong provocation. Women are slightly more likely than men to engage in indirect forms of aggression—actions intended to harm the victim in the absence of face-to-face confrontations. Overall then, differences between men and women with respect to aggression are consistent with the differing roles and status they occupy.

High temperatures tend to increase aggression, but only up to a point. Beyond some level, aggression declines as temperatures rise. Consuming alcohol can increase aggression in both men and women, perhaps because this drug reduces the individual's capacity to process some kinds of information and it reduces people's self-control. The availability of guns can encourage harmful forms of aggression (e.g., homicide and suicide). There is little evidence that gun ownership is a protective factor against aggression; in fact, it tends to be a risk factor for victimization. Findings are consistent—across countries—that legislative changes that reduce access to weapons reduces intentional and accidental gun deaths.

Bullying involves repeated aggression against individuals who, for various reasons, are unable to defend themselves against such treatment. Bullying occurs in many contexts, including schools and workplaces. Few children are solely bullies or victims; many play both roles. Bullies and bully-victims appear to have lower self-esteem than children who are not involved in bullying. Efforts to reduce or eliminate bullying use a combination of techniques such as increased supervision by teachers, and getting parents involved. Having popular peers in schools serve as antibullying advocates can effectively change school norms and reduce long-term bullying behavior. In recent years, **cyberbullying**—bullying that occurs through electronic means (e.g., in social media) has increased and has harmful effects on people who are the targets of this form of bullying.

Several techniques for reducing aggression exist and can be effective under various conditions. Punishment can be effective in reducing aggression, but *only* when it is delivered under certain conditions that are rarely met. The **catharsis hypothesis** appears to be mainly false. The likelihood of subsequent aggression is *not* reduced by engaging in apparently "safe" forms of aggression. Aggression can be restrained by internal self-regulatory processes. If the cognitive resources needed by these processes are depleted, however, aggression may be especially likely to occur. Inducing feelings or actions that are incompatible with anger can sometimes reduce aggression.

Chapter 11
Groups and Individuals
The Consequences of Belonging

Chapter Overview

Learning Objectives

11.1   Describe the types and features of groups

11.2   Identify how the presence of others impacts performance

11.3   Evaluate the factors that impact group cooperation and conflict

11.4   Recall that the way group fairness is judged impacts behavior

11.5   Evaluate the factors that impact the effectiveness of the group decision-making process

11.6   Analyze theories to understand leadership in group settings

We are all members of many different groups. Some of those groups are formally recognized—such as your citizenship in a nation, which has specific requirements for membership, as does the sorority or fraternity you may belong to. Other groups are more informal—such as a group of friends that you might play basketball with on weekends, a church youth group you may be part of, or the fellow students that you are assigned to work with by the professor on a joint class project.

In these groups, we may need to communicate effectively with other group members and act in a coordinated way to produce some desired outcome together. Successful teamwork can produce a strong sense of accomplishment and heightened camaraderie, while unsuccessful teams can be rife with conflict among the members, resulting in poorer outcomes. In this chapter, we will address factors that influence the extent to which teams facilitate creativity—are more than "the sum of their parts"— and when they do the opposite.

People also often need to communicate about their group's goals and products with the members of other groups. Much research suggests that communication across group lines—with members of different cultural groups or between different work groups in the same organization—can result in misunderstandings. We know that one key factor to effective communication and task performance in groups is the extent to which members feel they share a common identity (Greenaway, Wright, Willingham, Reynolds, & Haslam, 2015). When that is lacking, group performance and relations among members often suffers. As shown in Figure 11.1, groups can bring real joy to our lives, or they can be rather stressful and demoralizing.

Figure 11.1 Teamwork: When It Works and When It Doesn't

Sometimes being part of team brings a sense of togetherness and accomplishment, but when a shared identity is lacking and there is interpersonal competition among the members, conflict and poor outcomes are more likely.

Many people hold the belief that groups, compared to individuals, are more likely to make disaster-prone decisions or "go off the deep end." In this chapter, we will consider research addressing this question—do individuals or groups make more risky (or worse) decisions? Such a possibility is important because, if it is true that individuals are affected by processes that occur in groups, then understanding both the pitfalls and strengths of group decision making will be critical to managing our lives in the many group settings we find ourselves in.

Groups are central to most people's lives, and group life certainly cannot be eliminated. Even though being a member of a group can sometimes involve negative experiences—at other times it can entail considerable fulfillment. In this chapter, we seek to illuminate both the benefits and costs of belonging to groups.

Let's first consider a few of the potential hitches that come with joining a group. If it is a **cohesive group**—one where there are strong bonds among the members—it could be difficult to even get admitted, or it might result in some initiations we would wish to avoid. And, what if, after joining a group, we discover that there are group norms that we don't like? When a person is new to a group, one's status is likely to be low, which would make it rather difficult to change the group's norms. Moreover, as a newcomer, one's performance in the group may be judged by more established members, creating some evaluation anxiety.

Some conflict is likely within almost any group, and managing such difficult interactions can take a lot of effort. For this reason, people sometimes ask themselves whether they will have to put more effort into a group than the rewards they'd gain from being a member. Realistically, some groups do require major commitments of time, but it is also the case that some benefits can only be obtained by belonging to groups. For that reason, we will first turn to the question of why people join and stay in groups. Can we realistically just dispense with them, or might groups critically shape who we are?

Is being in groups a fundamental part of our evolutionary history? No one individual can know all the information necessary—particularly in our technologically complex world—to always make the best decisions alone on many issues. Perhaps we have to rely on other people for collective knowledge and information sharing, making being connected to groups essential to our survival. Brewer and Caporael (2006) argue that interdependence among group members is the *primary* strategy for survival among humans, with the group providing a critical buffer between the individual and the physical habitat. Such social coordination, and the skills necessary do so, could be therefore central to the species survival. There is certainly plenty of evidence that group memberships can enhance our health, serving as a resource that allows us to overcome adversity (Jetten, Haslam, Haslam, Dingle, & Jones, 2014).

What implications does an evolutionary perspective have for our attitudes toward groups in the here-and-now? Schachter (1959) concluded that the arousal of any strong emotion in humans tends to create the need to compare this reaction with that of other people. This suggests that the complex emotional lives of humans may, in fact, be one of the causes of the human need for group affiliation. Indeed, it is under the most threatening or uncertain conditions that we need our groups most. In these instances, for psychological security, we may increasingly identify with our social groups (Hogg, 2007). In fact, among the best predictors of psychological well-being across people is degree of connectedness to others (Diener & Oishi, 2005; Lyubomirsky, King, & Diener, 2005).

Are all groups equally important to us? While we are born into some of our groups, such as our family or ethnic group, others are self-selected—we choose to join groups such as fraternities and sororities, work organizations, and sports teams. Some groups are temporary, coming into existence to accomplish a specific purpose such as completing a team project, while others are longer lasting and less linked to specific goals, for example, being a member of your university student community. Some groups, such as those in the workplace, may be joined explicitly because of the benefits (i.e., the pay check) that they provide. In addition to this material benefit, people

Figure 11.2 Will You Identify Strongly with the Occupation You Join?

As illustrated here, people are often highly attached to their work group and savor its accomplishments. Research reveals that people who identify with the organization that employs them, exhibit greater commitment and show positive organizational citizenship behavior that goes beyond the "call of duty."

do form occupational identities that are of considerable personal importance to them, and many people also come to strongly identify with the organizations in which they are employed (Ashforth, Harrison, & Corley, 2008; Haslam, 2004). In fact, if you ask people "Who are you?" many will reply in terms of their occupations: "I'm a student majoring in history," "I'm a Kansas student," or "I'm a psychologist, accountant, or computer engineer." Will you, in the future, show equal pride in your occupational or organizational group and its accomplishments as the people shown in Figure 11.2 do?

For other groups, clear material benefits of membership might be hard to see, although such groups can still have considerable relevance for our identities, for example, a peer or friendship group. In fact, leaving behind our old friendship groups as we make life transitions, such as moving from high school to college, can be a stressful process (Iyer, Jetten, & Tsivrikos, 2008). Thus, we have emotional connectedness to groups—we like them, like being in them, and often develop strong bonds with the people in them. Perhaps that is the point: joining groups, and staying in them, feels perfectly natural—we really *want* to belong, and *freely choose* to join!

Now, let's turn to the issues of whether there are different types of groups, when we join them and why, and what determines when we choose to quit them. Then, we will examine the impact of what is, in some ways, the most basic group effect: the mere presence of others. As we will see, the presence of others, even if we are not in a formal group with them, can affect our performance on many tasks, as well as other important aspects of our behavior. Third, we will briefly examine the nature of cooperation and conflict in groups—why these contrasting patterns emerge and the effects they produce. After that, we will address the closely related question of perceived *fairness* in groups. Finally, we will turn to *decision making* in groups and the unexpected consequences of this process.

11.1: Groups: When We Join . . . and When We Leave

Objective **Describe the types and features of groups**

What is a group? Do we know one when we see it? Look at the photos in Figure 11.3. Which one would you say shows a group? You would probably identify the photo on the right as a group, but the one on the left as a mere collection of people waiting in

Figure 11.3 What Makes a Group a Group?

The photo on the left shows a collection of people who just happen to be in the same place; they are not part of a group. The photo on the right shows a real group, where the members interact with one another in a coordinated way and have shared goals and outcomes. Moreover, they will feel that they are, in fact, part of a group.

line. Perhaps that is because you have a definition of the term group that is close to the one adopted by many social psychologists—a **group** involves people who perceive themselves to be part of a coherent unit that they see as different from another group (Dasgupta, Banaji, & Abelson, 1999; Haslam, 2004).

The basis of this perceived coherence differs in different types of groups (Prentice, Miller, & Lightdale, 1994). In **common-bond groups**, which tend to involve face-to-face interaction among members, the individuals in the group are bonded *to each other*. Examples of these kinds of groups include the players on a sports team, friendship groups, a family, and work teams. In contrast, in **common-identity groups** the members are *linked via the category as a whole* rather than to each other with face-to-face interaction often being entirely absent. Our national, linguistic, university, and gender groups are ones where we might not know personally all, or even most, of the other group members. These are good examples of groups that we might identify with strongly, but not because of the bonds we have with specific other individual members. As you will see in this chapter, both of these types of group memberships can be of great importance to people.

Groups can also differ dramatically in terms of their **entitativity**—the extent to which they are perceived as a coherent whole (Campbell, 1958). Entitativity can range from, at the low end, a mere collection of individuals who happen to be in the same place at the same time and who have little or no connection with one another, to at the high end, where members of intimate groups, such as families share a name, history, and an identity. As shown in Table 11.1, when people are asked to freely name different types of groups, there is considerable agreement about which types of groups are perceived to be high and low in entitativity (Lickel et al., 2000). Those groups that are rated as high in entitativity also tend to be groups that people rate as relatively important to them. Groups high in entitativity are also perceived as persisting across time, although the specific members may change. In contrast, those low in entitativity are often not seen as possessing such continuity across time (Hamilton, Levine, & Thurston, 2008).

Groups clearly vary in their perceived entitativity—the extent to which they are seen as a distinct group. As shown here, while some groups are seen as being high in entitativity, others are not (1 = not a

Table 11.1 Is the Importance of a Group Dependent on Its Entitativity?

As you can see here, groups clearly vary in their perceived entitativity—the extent to which they are perceived to be a distinct group. While some groups are seen as being high in entitativity (1 = not a group; 9 = very much a group), others are not. The perceived importance of a group to its members was strongly correlated ($r = .75$) with how much of an entity it was perceived to be.

Type of Group	Entitativity	Importance to Self
Families	8.57	8.78
Friends/romantic partners	8.27	8.06
Religious groups	8.20	7.34
Music groups	7.33	5.48
Sports groups	7.12	6.33
Work groups	6.78	5.73
Ethnic groups	6.67	7.67
Common interest groups	6.53	5.65
National groups	5.83	5.33
Students in a class	5.76	4.69
Gender groups	4.25	3.00
Region of country	4.00	3.25
Physical attributes	3.50	2.50

group; 9 = very much a group). The perceived importance of a group to its members is strongly correlated ($r = .75$) with how much of an entity it is perceived to be.

What determines whether, and to what extent, we perceive a group as an entity? Groups high in entitativity tend to have the following characteristics: (1) members interact with one another often, although not necessarily in a face-to-face setting (e.g., it could be over the Internet), (2) the group is important in some way to its members, (3) members share common goals, and (4) members perceive themselves as similar to one another in important ways. The higher groups are on these dimensions, the more they will be seen by their members and nonmembers alike as forming coherent entities—real groups that can, and often do, exert powerful effects upon their members.

Highly entitative groups are more likely to be stereotyped than are groups low in entitativity (Yzerbyt et al., 2001). People even use different language to describe entitative groups compared to those low in entitativity (Spencer-Rodgers, Hamilton, & Sherman, 2007). Specifically, abstract language is used to imply that high entitativity groups are enduring and that they possess distinct characteristics that differentiate them from other groups, whereas groups low in entitativity are seen as less distinctive and their members are less likely to be characterized as sharing attributes. Perhaps, surprisingly, it is not the size of a group per se that matters for entitativity—some small and some large groups are perceived to be high in entitativity. It is behavioral features such as sharing of resources, reciprocating favors among group members, recognition of group authorities, and adherence to group norms that tend to result in greater entitativity rather than structural features of groups (Lickel, Rutchick, Hamilton, & Sherman, 2006).

11.1.1: Groups: Their Key Components

Before turning to the specific ways in which groups affect various aspects of our thought and behavior, it is useful to consider several basic features of groups—ones that are present in virtually every group. These features are *status, roles, norms*, and *cohesiveness*.

STATUS: HIERARCHIES IN GROUPS   When the President of the United States, or any other nation for that matter, enters the room, everyone stands, and no one sits down until the President has taken a seat. Why? Although the President is an American, like the rest of us, he (or she) occupies a special position within the group. Many groups have hierarchies like this, with members differing in **status**—their rank within the group. Sometimes it is an "official position" as in the case of the President, and sometimes it is not so explicit and instead is simply the "old-timers" in a group who are accorded higher status compared to "newcomers." People are often extremely sensitive to their status within a group because it is linked to a wide range of desirable outcomes—everything from respect and deference from other group members to material benefits such as salary received.

Evolutionary psychologists attach considerable importance to status attainment within a group, noting that in many different species, including our own, high status confers important advantages on those who possess it (Buss, 1999). But how, precisely, do people acquire high status? Physical attributes such as height may play some role— taller men and women have a consistent edge, especially in the workplace (Judge & Cable, 2004). Those who are taller are held in higher esteem compared to shorter people—they are literally "looked up to." Meta-analyses have revealed that taller people earn more in salary, are perceived as having more skills, and are more likely to be nominated as leader of groups relative to shorter people (Judge & Cable, 2004). Height even predicts who wins the American Presidency, within each election year's set of candidates. In fact, people judge those who have just won an election to be taller than they were before winning, while the losers of the election are seen as shorter (Higham & Carment, 1992). In fact, the average height of all Presidents is much higher than for the general population. This may change, of course, when women Presidents are elected, but even they, perhaps, will be taller than the average woman!

Factors relating to individuals' behavior also play a critical role in status acquisition. People who are seen as prototypical—by embodying the group's central attributes—are particularly likely to be accorded status and be selected as leader of a group (Haslam & Platow, 2001). Longevity or seniority in a group too can result in higher status—to the extent that it is seen as reflective of wisdom or knowledge of ingroup ways (Haslam, 2004).

Once status within a group is obtained, people with high status actually behave differently than those with lower status. Guinote, Judd, and Brauer (2002) observed that high-status group members are more "idiosyncratic and variable" in their behavior than are lower-status group members. Indeed, there appears to be an awareness of the need to conform to group norms more strongly among those who are junior in a group and therefore have lower status (Jetten, Hornsey, & Adarves-Yorno, 2006). Across a number of different samples from professional to student groups where status varied, people with high status report conforming less than people with lower status. As shown in Figure 11.4, when surveyed about "how susceptible to group influence" they were, social psychologists who were very senior in terms of number of years in a professional organization reported being less conforming than those who had few years in the organization or those who had just recently joined. By portraying themselves as open to group influence, low-status group members may be helping to ensure they become accepted in the organization. In fact, newcomers who lack status in a group are more likely to be subjected to punishments if they fail to yield to those with higher status (Levine, Moreland, & Hausmann, 2005). Thus, there can be little doubt that differences in status are an important fact of life in most groups.

ROLES: DIFFERENTIATION OF FUNCTIONS WITHIN GROUPS Think of a group to which you belong or have belonged—anything from a sports team to a sorority or

Figure 11.4 Status Matters for Conformity

As you can see, in every participant sample, those who were relatively high in status or more senior rated themselves personally as less conforming to the ingroup's norms than those who were lower in status or more junior members of their group. Status would appear to grant some degree of freedom to group members.

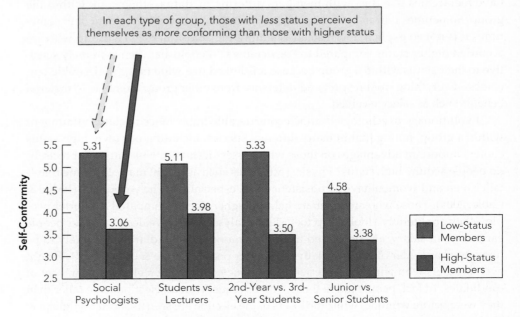

fraternity. Now consider this question: Did everyone in the group perform the same functions? Your answer is probably *no*. Different people performed different tasks and were expected to accomplish different things for the group. In short, they played different **roles**. Sometimes roles are assigned; for instance, a group may select different individuals to serve as its leader, treasurer, or secretary. In other cases, individuals gradually acquire certain roles without being formally assigned to them. Regardless of how roles are acquired, in many groups, someone often serves as the "good listener," taking care of members' emotional needs, while another person tends to specialize in "getting things done."

To the extent that people *internalize* their social roles—those roles are linked to key aspects of the self-concept—they can have important implications for psychological well-being. Indeed, enacting a role well can lead people to feel that their behavior reflects their *authentic* self. Consider students in one study whose key self-perceptions were first measured and then they were randomly assigned to fulfill a particular role in a class task (Bettencourt, Molix, Talley, & Sheldon, 2006). The behaviors called for when assigned to the "idea generating" role are rather different than the behaviors required when assigned to the "devil's advocate" role. The results showed that for those individuals whose traits were consistent with whichever role they were assigned; they perceived their behavior during the task as authentically reflecting themselves, exhibited more positive mood, and enjoyed the class task more than people for whom there was a discrepancy between their self-perceptions and the role they had enacted.

As we noted in Chapter 8, a recent simulated prison study obtained new answers concerning the question of when and why role assignments affect our behavior (Reicher & Haslam, 2006). The adult participants in that study were first randomly assigned to the role of either prisoner or guard. Over the course of the study, those assigned to be guards failed to identify with their role, in part because of their concerns with being liked by the prisoners and how others might perceive them when the study was over (and was televised). In contrast, the prisoners showed significant increases over the course of the study in the degree to which they identified with their role. Did this difference in identification with their assigned role make a difference for the behavior that was observed? The answer was a definite yes. Because the guards did not identify with their role, they failed to act cohesively, and they were eventually overcome by the other group whose members were highly identified with their more cohesive group. The guards also showed increased stress responses that the prisoners did not show—both self-reported burnout and greater cortisol reactivity, which is a physiological indicator of stress (Haslam & Reicher, 2006). Those assigned to the prisoner role, however, showed increasing identification with the other prisoners, developed a norm of rebellion, and showed reductions in depression over the course of the study.

So, while roles are not *automatic* determinants of behavior, when they are internalized they can affect how we see ourselves, who we identify with, and our actions. Once people identify with a role, the norms—or appropriate ways for "people like us" to act—guide our behavior and, as we will see below, even our emotions.

NORMS: THE RULES OF THE GAME   Groups powerfully affect the behavior of their members via **norms**—implicit rules that inform people about what is expected of them. Although we discussed the influence of norms on behavior in earlier chapters, here we consider how different norms can operate in different groups, and what happens when we deviate from what is normatively expected of us.

Have you ever considered the possibility that there might be "norms" that guide our emotions? Sometimes those are explicit **feeling rules**—expectations about the emotions that are appropriate to express (Hochschild, 1983). For example, as shown in Figure 11.5, many employers demand that service providers (cashiers, restaurant servers, and flight attendants) "always smile" at customers, no matter how annoying

Figure 11.5 Some Roles and Groups Have Emotion Norms: Happiness on Demand

Members of some social groups are told, or otherwise learn, what emotions they should express. These norms can be in the form of explicit rules: MacDonald's employees and flight attendants are told they must always smile at customers. Or, they can be more subtle, where learning to be a "good" group member means claiming to be "happier than you were before" you joined the group.

or rude they may be. In this case, norms for displaying positive feelings are specific to these types of employment settings. In contrast, if employed as a funeral director, there would be explicit instructions to interact with the bereaved family in a "sincere" way, and to display only a "serious face" while trying to communicate empathy. But perhaps socialization into groups involves more than being told how to "act" emotionally. Potentially, learning "how to be a good group member" may be guided by subtle emotional experience norms.

An interesting study of Evangelical Christians that was conducted by Wilkins (2008) reveals how feeling rules can reflect group membership acquisition. She found that initially, new converts did not perceive their participation in church lessons and meetings as pleasant. But over time, and through interactions with other community members, new members learned to model their emotions on others. A new emotional vocabulary was acquired; new members were encouraged to publicly talk about their old, pre-Christian self as unhappy and anxiety-ridden and to present their new Christian self as happy. Most participants in this study reported initially having to be pushed to devote the time to learning the new faith practices, but after doing so; they came to perceive themselves as having acquired an "authentic Christian self," in which negative emotions are disallowed. According to this research, to maintain this new identity and be fully accepted within this community, feeling happy appears to be necessary. For these participants, because happiness is equated with moral goodness, feeling happy with one's life is necessary to be perceived as a good group member.

An important norm that varies considerably across cultures, but can also apply differentially to groups within a culture is **collectivism** versus **individualism**. In collectivist groups, the norm is to maintain harmony among group members, even if doing so might entail some personal costs; in such groups, disagreement and conflict among members are to be avoided. In contrast, in individualistic groups, the norm is to value standing out from the group and be different from others; individual variability is to be expected and disagreeing with the group is often seen as courageous. Of course, people do differ in how much they value being a member of any particular group. Considerable research has illustrated that when being a member of a particular group is important to our self-concept (we highly identify with it); we are more likely to be guided by its norms, but ignore or even act contrary to its norms when we are not identified with that group (Jetten et al., 1997; Moreland & Levine, 2001). How then do people who are high or low in identification with an individualist or a collectivist group respond to someone who deviates from their group's norms?

This question was addressed in a series of studies by Hornsey, Jetten, McAuliffe, and Hogg (2006). First, participants were selected who were either high or low in identification with their university. Then, the norm of their "student group" was described as being "collectivist," with an emphasis on members achieving goals that will benefit the group as a whole rather than the students' personal goals, or as "individualist," where meeting personal goals is emphasized by members over achieving the goals of the student group as a whole. Responses to a student who was described as dissenting from the position of most students on an issue were then measured.

As can be seen in Figure 11.6, among those who highly identify with their student group, a dissenter was liked when the norm was individualist, but that same dissenter was disliked when the norm was collectivist. Among those low in identification with their student group, the norm did not affect evaluations of the dissenting student. This research illustrates the potential costs of violating a group's norms—at least in the eyes of those who highly value that group.

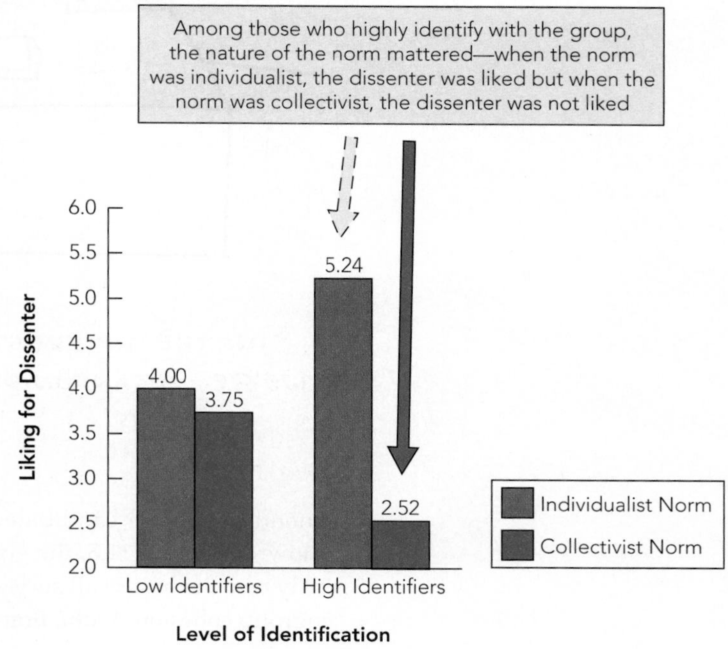

COHESIVENESS: THE FORCE THAT BINDS Consider two groups. In the first, members like one another very much, strongly concur with the goals their group is seeking, and feel that they could not possibly find another group that would better satisfy their needs. They have formed a group identity, and as a result are likely to perform their tasks well together. In the second, the opposite is true: Members don't like one another very much, don't share common goals, and are actively seeking other groups that might offer them a better deal. They lack a shared identity and are less likely to successfully perform tasks together. The reason for this difference in the experience and performance of these two groups is what social psychologists refer to as **cohesiveness**—all the forces that cause members to remain in the group (Ellemers, de Gilder, & Haslam, 2004).

Cohesive groups have a sense of *solidarity*: They see themselves as homogenous, support and cooperate with ingroup members, aim to achieve group goals, have high morale, and perform better than noncohesive groups (Hogg, 2007; Mullen & Cooper, 1994). In fact, the presence of an outgroup or other form of competitive threat increases cohesion in a variety of community groups (Putnam, 2000). As shown in Figure 11.7, outgroup members may find it difficult to gain acceptance in cohesive groups—they may not "fit" the norm all that well!

What might be less obvious is the effect that perceiving one's group to be potentially indistinguishable from another group has on emotions and actions aimed at protecting our own group's distinctiveness. Research has revealed that French Canadians who worry about not being able to maintain their culture as distinct from English Canadians favor the separation of Quebec from Canada (Wohl, Giguère, Branscombe, & McVicar, 2011). Likewise, English Canadians who are threatened with the possibility of a "North American Union" in which their distinctive Canadian identity might be lost by such a merger with their "superpower neighbor"—the United States—favor putting limits on the amount of American media shown in Canada and indicate they

Figure 11.6 Responses to a Dissenting Group Member: It Depends on the Group Norm

Dissent, or disagreeing with other group members, can result in negative evaluations by those who highly identify with the group when the group's norm is collectivist and conflict is to be avoided. In contrast, when the group's norm is individualist, those who highly identify with the group are tolerant of a group member who dissents. Among low identifiers, the norm of the group does not affect how a dissenting group member is evaluated.

Figure 11.7 Diversity in groups may not always be managed so well

As this "manager" notes, policies whereby we just look for others just 'like ourselves' will not produce a very diverse work environment.

"IN THE INTERESTS OF FOSTERING DIVERSITY, WE'RE ABANDONING OUR 'BIRDS OF A FEATHER' POLICY."

intend to vote for candidates who see Canada as too close to the United States. As shown in Figure 11.8, the general threat that your group's future might be in jeopardy can encourage all sorts of groups to advocate actions aimed at creating greater ingroup cohesion (Wohl, Branscombe, & Reysen, 2010).

11.1.2: The Benefits—and Costs—of Joining

If you consider how many different groups you belong to, you may be surprised at the length of the list—especially if you consider both common-bond (face-to-face) and common-identity (social categories) groups. While some people belong to more groups than others, most of us put forth effort to gain admittance and maintain membership in at least some groups. Why, then, if we work hard to get in and the benefits of group membership can be great, do we sometimes choose to leave groups? Withdrawing from a group to which we have belonged for months, years, or even decades can be a stressful experience. Here's what social psychologists have found out about why we join groups, and the processes involved in leaving them.

THE BENEFITS OF JOINING: WHAT GROUPS DO FOR US People sometimes go through a lot of difficulty to join a specific group: Membership in many groups is by "invitation only," and winning that invitation can be difficult. Perhaps more surprising is that once they gain admission, many people will stick with a group even when it experiences hard times. For instance, consider some sports fans and how they remain loyal to their team when it has a miserable season, even when it is the target of ridicule and gains a reputation as "the worst of the worst." What accounts for this strong desire to join—and remain a part of—social groups?

First, we often gain *self-knowledge* from belonging to various groups (Tajfel & Turner, 1986). Our membership can tell us what kind of person we are—or perhaps, would like to be—so group membership becomes central to our self-concept. As a result, it is fair to say, group memberships provide us with a sense of "existential security." Once we belong, we can find it hard to imagine not belonging because it makes our life meaningful by defining, to some extent, who we are.

Figure 11.8 Perceived Future Jeopardy Elicits Actions That Will Make the Ingroup More Cohesive

Imagining how the future of your group might be in jeopardy—either by a union with another nation, your university is destroyed by a tornado, or thinking about a historical attempt to eliminate your group—can result in actions aimed at keeping the ingroup cohesive. These cohesion-maintaining actions can include marrying other ingroup members, educating children in schools for ingroup members only, and voting for politicians who say they will protect the ingroup.

Being part of a group can also increase our perceived ability to cope with stress, in part by making us feel a greater sense of control. Greenaway, Haslam, Cruwys, Branscombe, Ysseldyk, & Heldreth (2015) illustrated this in a variety of studies. First, in an analysis of people in 47 countries, it was found that people who felt a part of and identified with their community, nation, and all of humanity reported feeling greater personal control over their lives. In addition, following the U.S. Presidential election of 2012, those who identified with *either* major political group—Republicans or Democrats—reported more perceived personal control than those who did not identify. This was the case even though one of those political groups had just experienced a stressor—an election defeat. The same effect was observed among students experiencing a stressor—completion of their undergraduate honors thesis. Regardless of the grade they received on this important work project, the students felt more in control of their lives when they identified closely with their student group.

Another obvious benefit of belonging to groups is that they can help us reach our goals. One important goal may be attaining prestige. When an individual is accepted into a certain type of group—a highly selective school, an exclusive social club, and a varsity sports team—self-esteem can increase. Just how important is this boost from joining and identifying with particular groups? As you can probably guess, the more an individual is seeking **self-enhancement**—boosting one's own public image—the more important will a group's status be to that person and the more strongly he or she will identify with it (Roccas, 2003).

People are also attracted to groups when they fit their goals—even if those goals are relatively transient. Suppose you feel willing to take risks and try something new or, conversely, want to feel secure and are a little cautious. How might these different orientations affect the kind of group you would join and value being in it? Would you prefer a relatively high power group (that is able to exert influence and get things done) or a relatively low power group with less of those capabilities? Research findings indicate that people like being in a group best when it matches their current goal orientation (Sassenberg, Jonas, Shah, & Brazy, 2007).

Another important benefit of joining groups is that doing so often helps us to accomplish goals we could not achieve alone—for example, social change. How can members of groups that have been the target of oppression attain equal rights? One way devalued groups cope with the discrimination they experience is to gain strength from and identify with their disadvantaged group (Branscombe, Schmitt, & Harvey, 1999). As a result of recognizing shared grievances, people can develop a **politicized**

Figure 11.9 Producing Social Change: One Reason Why People Join Groups

Individuals can benefit from joining groups to achieve social change. For instance, by joining together, members of gay rights groups have collectively lobbied to change the law to allow same-sex marriage. In 2015, the U.S. Supreme Court agreed, and made same-sex marriage legal throughout the nation.

collective identity, which prepares them to engage in a power struggle on behalf of their group. As shown in Figure 11.9, by joining together, people who have been the victims of prejudice gain "social clout" and can succeed in winning better treatment for their group (Simon & Klandermans, 2001). Clearly, then, we derive many benefits—some personal and some collective—from belonging to and identifying with various groups.

Considerable research has revealed that to be rejected by a group—even one we have recently joined—can be among the most painful of experiences. For example, being ostracized from a mere online computer group can lower feelings of control and self-esteem both immediately after it occurs as well as after a 45-minute delay (Williams, 2001). Indeed, neuroimaging research makes clear that the brain circuitry involved in processing physical pain and social pain—from losing important social bonds—overlap considerably (Eisenberger & Lieberman, 2004; Williams & Nida, 2011). For example, when rejected by a group playing a computer ball-tossing game, neural activation in the anterior cingulated cortex was highly correlated with participants' feelings of distress. Neuroimaging studies have likewise revealed that his same brain area is activated when participants experience painful stimulation in their abdomen. So, not only are there plenty of benefits of being in and feeling a part of groups, but there are clear psychological costs of being excluded from them.

THE COSTS OF GETTING ACCEPTED INTO A GROUP   Perhaps because of the importance of groups and the benefits derived by those who are part of them, many groups erect barriers to entry: They want only *some* people to join, and they insist that those who do be highly motivated to enter. Steep initiation fees, substantial efforts to prove one's credentials as suitable, and long trial or probationary periods are common methods of restricting group membership.

Social psychologists have addressed the question: What are the consequences of undergoing severe admission processes in terms of their impact on commitment to the group? Does paying a very high price to secure membership in such selective groups require us to cognitively justify our time and effort in doing so, and might that make it difficult to later admit that joining might have been a mistake?

To increase our commitment to a group because we have paid a heavy material or psychological price to join it might at first appear to be a rather strange idea. In a classic experiment, Aronson and Mills (1959) illustrated why this sometimes happens. In order to imitate a mild initiation rite, students in their study either were asked to read very embarrassing material in front of a group or mildly embarrassing material or did not read any material. As we saw in Chapter 5, according to cognitive dissonance theory, people feel discomfort when their attitudes and behavior are discrepant. When we have put forth considerable effort to achieve membership in a group, we may need to change our attitudes toward that group in a positive direction in order to justify our effort. As a result, after going through an initiation in order to be admitted to a group and then learning that the group is unattractive after all, our commitment toward that group should actually *increase*. As these researchers predicted, liking for the group was greater as the severity of the initiation increased; the more embarrassing the material the students had to read, the more attractive they subsequently found this boring group. This may account for the increased commitment with new members of sororities and fraternities feel, after engaging in various types of initiation experiences.

THE COSTS OF MEMBERSHIP: WHY GROUPS SOMETIMES SPLINTER While groups can help us to reach our goals, help to boost our status along the way, and form an important part of who we are, they also impose certain costs. First, group membership often restricts personal freedom. Members of various groups are expected to behave in certain ways—and if they don't, the group may impose sanctions or even expel such violators from membership.

Similarly, groups often make demands on members' time, energy, and resources, and members must meet these demands or surrender their membership. Some churches, for instance, require that their members donate 10 percent of their income to the church. Persons wishing to remain in these groups must comply—or face expulsion. Finally, groups can adopt positions or policies of which some members disapprove.

Withdrawing from groups can be a major step with lasting repercussions. Why might individuals take this ultimate action—exiting a group they perhaps once highly valued? One intriguing answer is provided by a series of studies involving political parties and church groups (Sani, 2005, 2009). When individuals identify with these sorts of groups, other members of the group are categorized together with the self to, in effect, become "we." To the extent that people identify themselves and others as part of the same category, then they may choose to withdraw from groups that they no longer see as meeting the definition of the "we-ness" they initially adopted. Thus, individuals may decide to leave a group when they conclude that the group has changed sufficiently that it can no longer be seen as representing "us." This is particularly likely when differences in **ideology**—the philosophical and political values of a group—among different factions become so disparate that some members cannot see themselves as sharing a social identity with other members of the group.

Evidence for this ideological splintering process among members of the Church of England was obtained by Sani (2005). In 1994, the first women were ordained as priests, and as a result, hundreds of clergy who objected to this ideological change—from the 500-year tradition of permitting only males to enter the priesthood—decided to leave the church (see Figure 11.10). Why did they feel this drastic action was necessary? After all, they had been officials of this church for much of their lives, and their identities were strongly bound up with it.

To investigate what led to this upheaval, over 1,000 priests and deacons in the Church of England were asked to express their views about the new policy of ordaining women as priests, the extent to which they felt this had changed the church greatly, how much they identified with the Church of England, the degree to which they felt emotionally distressed by the change, and whether they believed their views (if they were opposed to the policy change) would be heard. Results indicated that clergy who left the church did so because they felt this policy change altered fundamental doctrines so much that it was no longer the same organization as the one they originally joined, and that it no longer represented their views. Furthermore, they felt strongly that no one would pay attention to their dissenting opinions. As shown in Figure 11.11, perceiving their group identity as being subverted by

Figure 11.10 Groups Change: Women Become Priests in the Church of England

In 1994, the first women were ordained as priests in the Church of England. Some existing clergy found this change ideologically intolerable and left the church, while others saw the admission of women to the priesthood as enhancing their group identity.

Figure 11.11 Why Groups Sometimes Splinter

Research indicates that groups splinter when members perceive that the group has changed so much (subversion) that it is no longer the same entity (group); they originally joined, and when they conclude that no one will listen to their protests over this change (there is no chance of reversing it), the group splinters apart.

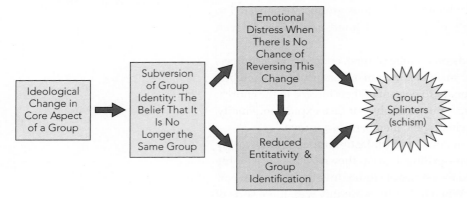

this change resulted in emotional distress, reduced the perception that the church was an entitative group, and lowered identification with the church. These processes lead to a **schism**—splintering of the group into distinct factions that could not stay united by a single identity. For those members who felt compelled to leave, the emotional distress experienced reflected the loss of this important identity and was akin to bereavement.

The potential for splintering as groups undergo change is not restricted to religious groups. Similar schisms have occurred in other types of groups—political parties, social movements, and in any group that is built on shared beliefs and values (Sani, 2009). Groups change, and when they do so to the extent that members feel that they can no longer identify with the group, they are likely to withdraw because, they believe, the group is no longer the same as the one they originally joined. But does that mean that groups will never tolerate criticism from their members? For more information about how groups manage dissent from within, see our special feature, **"What Research Tells Us About…Dissent and Criticism of Our Groups—'Because We Care.'"**

What Research Tells Us About…

Dissent and Criticism of Our Groups—"Because We Care"

When we identify with a group, we want to see it in a positive light. But what if we believe our group is acting in ways that are harmful? Suppose you work for an organization that decides to engage in unsafe practices and hide them from the public. It might even be General Motors (GM), which in 2015 settled a case where it was accused of withholding information about defective ignition switches that ultimately were blamed for the death of 100 people. In such cases, would your only choice be to stay silent and let the organization you really value make such a mistake—so, in effect, go along with it—or withdraw because you disagreed with its decisions and leave the organization?

Mary Barra, who took over as CEO of General Motors just days after a scandal of this sort broke (see Figure 11.12), chose to apologize for the decisions of the organization she loves and argued in a surprising speech to GM employees that the culture of the organization needs to change so that problems are openly tackled rather than continuing GM's long-standing tactics of minimizing and hiding them. Not only was it moral to do so, but she proposed it was necessary for the long-term interests of the organization.

Is dissent and criticism of one's own group so unusual? Are people who do so typically seen as "troublemakers," or are they sometimes admired and, consequently, able to bring about improvements in the norms and practices of their group? To answer these questions, we first need to acknowledge that there are different types of ingroup critics, or dissenters (Jetten & Hornsey, 2014).

There are "individualists" who lack understanding of the group's norms and may violate them for that reason or, alternatively, because they don't care about the group enough to protect it. They may criticize their group in public—to an outgroup audience, what has been referred to as "airing dirty laundry" (Packer, 2014)—and they are likely to be perceived as disloyal to the group either because they lack concern for the consequences or because they are seen as deriving some personal benefit from doing so (Branscombe, Wann, Noel, & Coleman, 1993; Packer & Chasteen, 2010).

The second form of ingroup criticism has been labeled "constructive dissent" because it is seen as reflecting genuine concern for the group—with an aim of provoking change to improve the group or prevent harm to its interests. This latter type we suggest is expressed by Mary Barra who seeks to change GM's "faulty" procedures, but also can be shown by loyal patriots who protest a war or other action on the part of their nation out of concern that its decisions may harm the group well into the future.

Figure 11.12 When Criticism of One's Group Can Lead to Improvement

Mary Barra, who became CEO of General Motors just after a scandal broke revealing the company had knowingly withheld information about a defect in its product, chose to criticize her own organization's culture of silence and cover-up. By doing so, she hoped to change behavior and practices that had damaged the group that she is highly identified with.

Ingroup critics are generally responded to more positively than outgroup members who utter the same criticism (Hornsey, Oppes, & Svensson, 2002), what has been termed the **intergroup sensitivity effect**. This is primarily due to ingroup members who criticize the group being seen as motivated to create constructive change, which is not the case for outgroup members. Yet, ingroup critics who appear to be motivated by individualistic gains and show a lack of regard for the ingroup's reputation, or who undermine the ingroup with a competitor, tend to be responded to rather negatively.

Does ingroup criticism have the potential for improving the procedures used by the group and its ultimate outcomes? There is indeed evidence that dissent within groups can improve the quality of decision making, lead to more creative ideas, and innovation (De Dreu & West, 2001). In fact, dissent in educational settings, by eliciting divergent thinking, can promote higher quality learning (Butera, Darnon, & Mugny, 2011). This means that ingroup critics, when assumed to have the group's interests at heart, can be accepted and effective at bringing about improved outcomes.

Key Points

- Groups are an indispensible part of our lives; evolutionary theorists suggest that groups are necessary for human survival.
- There are different kinds of groups: **common-bond** where the individual members have bonds with each other and **common-identity** where the members are linked via the category as a whole.
- **Groups** are composed of people who perceive themselves and are perceived by others as forming a coherent unit. The extent to which the group is perceived to form a coherent entity is known as **entitativity**.

- Basic features of groups include: **status**, **roles**, **norms**, and **cohesiveness**.
- People gain status in a group for many reasons, ranging from physical characteristics (e.g., height), to various aspects of their behavior (e.g., conforming to group norms). Status tends to be higher for those who are prototypical of the group, or those who have seniority within the group.
- The effects of roles on our behavior are often powerful, especially when we internalize the role as part of our identity. In some roles there are explicit **feeling rules** about the emotions we should express.

- Deviating from group norms can affect how other group members, especially those who highly identify with the group, evaluate us. Norms can be **collectivist**, where harmony is valued, or **individualist**, where being different from the rest of the group is valued.
- Groups differ in their level of **cohesiveness**—the sum of all the factors that cause people to want to remain members. Perceiving a threat to one's group can encourage actions aimed at increasing group cohesiveness and solidarity.
- Joining groups confers important benefits on members, including increased self-knowledge, progress toward important goals, **self-enhancement**, and when a **politicized collective identity** is formed, a means of attaining social change.
- However, group membership also exacts important costs, such as loss of personal freedom and demands on time, energy, and resources.

- The desire to join exclusive and prestigious groups may be so strong that individuals are willing to undergo painful and dangerous initiations in order to become members. Having undergone such initiations can result in increased commitment to the group.
- Individuals withdraw from groups when they feel that the group's **ideology** has changed so much that it no longer reflects their basic values. When a **schism** or splintering of a group into distinct factions occurs, some members experience emotional distress and feel they can no longer identify with or see the group as the one they originally joined.
- Ingroup critics are generally responded to more positively than outgroup critics—the **intergroup sensitivity effect**. This is because ingroup critics are believed to be motivated to create constructive change, which is not the case for outgroup critics.
- Ingroup criticism can help bring about improved group outcomes.

11.2: Effects of the Presence of Others: From Task Performance to Behavior in Crowds

Objective   **Identify how the presence of others impacts performance**

The fact that our behavior is often strongly affected by the groups to which we belong is far from surprising; after all, in these groups there are usually well-established norms that tell us how we are expected to behave. Perhaps much more surprising is the fact that often, we are strongly affected by the *mere presence of others*, even if we are not part of a formal group. You are probably already familiar with such effects from your own experience. For instance, suppose you are sitting alone in a room studying. You may sit any old way you find comfortable, including putting your feet up on the furniture. But, if a stranger enters the room, all this may change. You will probably refrain from doing some things you might have done when alone, and you may change many other aspects of your behavior—even though you don't know this person and are not directly interacting with him or her (see Figure 11.13). So, clearly, we are often affected by the mere physical presence of others. While such effects take many different forms, we will focus here on two that are especially important: the effects of the presence of others on our performance of various tasks and the effects of being in a large crowd.

11.2.1: Social Facilitation: Performing in the Presence of Others

Sometimes, when we perform a task, we work totally alone; for instance, you might study alone in your room. In many other cases, even if we are working on a task by ourselves, other people are present—for instance, you might study at a café, or in your room while your roommate also studies. How does the presence of others affect our performance, and why does having an audience matter?

Imagine that you have to give a speech in a class—and that you are preparing for this important performance (most of your grade depends on how you do). You repeatedly practice your speech alone. Finally, the big day arrives and you walk out

Figure 11.13 Effects of the Mere Presence of Others

Often, the mere presence of other people, even if they are total strangers, can influence our behavior. We change from casual slouching and having our feet on the furniture to a more "socially acceptable" posture.

onto the stage to find a large audience seated there waiting to hear you. How will you do? Most of us can recall times when we have been nervous about performing in front of others (I can still remember the first time I ever lectured in a big undergraduate class). Some of us have even "choked" when the time came, whereas others have felt that their abilities really shone with an audience. Evidence from several different studies confirms that the presence of others can affect our performance—sometimes positively and sometimes negatively.

Almost 50 years ago, Zajonc, Heingartner, and Herman (1969) conducted a seemingly zany experiment. They arranged to have cockroaches run a maze. That would have been strange enough for social psychologists, but these researchers added a curious twist to the roach maze—they constructed clear plastic boxes close enough to the maze so that a roach "audience" could observe the maze-running "participants." With this setup the roaches in the maze would also "know" they were being watched—they would be aware of the presence of the onlooking audience.

As it turned out, those cockroaches who were watched by other roaches ran the maze faster than cockroaches without an audience. Zajonc and his colleagues (1969) were intent on making a point about a group phenomenon called **social facilitation**, that is, the effects of the presence of others on performance. Although, as social psychologists, we typically study human, as opposed to cockroach, behavior, why did Zajonc et al. choose to conduct an animal experiment of this type?

Zajonc (1965) argued that the mere presence of others would *only* facilitate a well-learned response, but that it could inhibit a less-practiced or "new" response. He noted that the presence of others increases physiological arousal (our bodies become more energized), and, as a result, any *dominant response* will be facilitated. This means that we can focus better on something we *know* or have *practiced* when we are aroused, but that same physiological arousal will create problems when we are dealing with something new or complex. This reasoning—depicted in Figure 11.14—became known as the **drive theory of social facilitation** because it focuses on arousal or drive-based effects on performance. The presence of others will improve individuals' perfor-

Figure 11.14 The Drive Theory of Social Facilitation

According to this theory, the presence of others, either as an audience or co-actors, increases arousal and this, in turn, strengthens the tendency to perform dominant responses. If these responses are correct, performance is improved; if they are incorrect, performance is harmed.

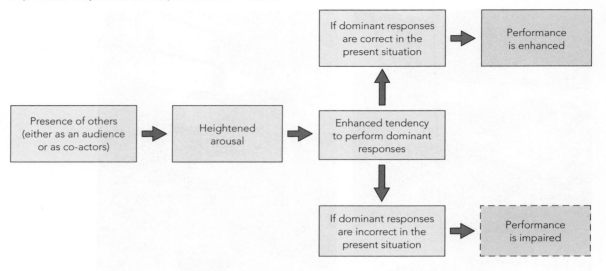

mance when they are highly skilled at the task in question (in this case their dominant responses would tend to be correct), but will interfere with performance when they are not highly skilled—for instance, when they are learning to perform it (for their dominant responses would not be correct in that case).

However, other researchers thought that performance might sometimes be disrupted by the presence of an audience because of apprehension about having their performance evaluated (remember the professor who will be grading your speech!). This **evaluation apprehension** idea was studied by Cottrell, Wack, Sekerak, and Rittle (1968). In fact, several of their experiments found that social facilitation did *not* occur when an audience was blindfolded, or displayed no interest in watching the person performing the task, which lent support to this interpretation that concerns about evaluation might play a role. But Zajonc did not believe the fear of potential evaluation was *necessary* for social facilitation to occur, so that was why he performed the cockroach experiment. Given that we can assume that cockroaches do not worry about their maze-running abilities being evaluated, it is safe to say that social facilitation does not *require* evaluation apprehension to work, at least for some species.

CAN HAVING AN AUDIENCE DISTRACT US?   Some have suggested that the presence of others, either as an audience or as co-actors, can be distracting and, for this reason, it can produce cognitive overload (e.g., R.S. Baron, 1986). Because performers must divide their attention between the task and the audience, such increased cognitive load can result in a tendency to restrict one's attention so as to focus only on essential cues or stimuli while "screening out" nonessential ones. Several findings offer support for this view, known as **distraction conflict theory**. So, which is more important—increased arousal with an audience (Zajonc, 1965) or this tendency toward a narrowed attentional focus?

Hetherington, Anderson, Norton, and Newson (2006) applied these ideas to understand the effects of others on eating as a function of distraction. Caloric intake was measured in male participants under differing distraction conditions. Both eating with friends and while watching TV increased eating. Because both friends and TV can be distracting, it can result in a greater focus on the food and thus lead to improved eating performance (i.e., greater caloric intake). In contrast, eating in the presence of strangers was less distracting, and, therefore, caused no increased focus on food and no increased caloric intake. One advantage of this cognitive perspective is that it helps explain when and why animals, as well as people, are affected by the presence of an audience that differs in how distracting it is to the performer. After all, animals, too (even cockroaches) can experience conflicting tendencies to work on a task *and* pay attention to an audience.

11.2.2: Social Loafing: Letting Others Do the Work

You have probably had the experience of seeing a construction crew in which some appear to be working hard while others seem to be standing around not doing much at all. When it comes to a task like the physically demanding one shown in Figure 11.15, do you think everyone will fully "pitch in" and exert equal effort? Probably not. Some will contribute by taking on as much of the load as they can, while some may simply pretend to be trying hard when, in fact, they are not.

This pattern is quite common in situations where groups perform what are known as **additive tasks**—ones in which the contributions of each member are combined into a single group output. On such tasks, some people will work hard, while others goof off and do less than they would if working alone. Social psychologists refer to such effects as **social loafing**—reductions in effort when individuals work collectively compared to when they work individually (Karau & Williams, 1993).

Social loafing has been demonstrated for many different types of tasks. In one of the first studies on this topic, Latane, Williams, and Harkins (1979) asked groups of male students to clap or cheer as loudly as possible at specific times, supposedly so that the experimenter could determine how much noise people make in social settings. To make sure participants were not affected by the actual noise of other participants, they wore headphones, through which noise-making was played at a constant volume. Furthermore, they could not see the other participants, but were only told how many others they were shouting with. They performed these tasks in groups of two, four, or six people. Although the total amount of noise rose as group size increased, the amount produced by each participant dropped. In other words, each person put out less effort as the size of the group increased.

Figure 11.15 Does Everyone Do Their Share of the Work?

When several people work together to accomplish a task like this, it is probable that they will not all exert the same amount of effort. Some will work very hard, others will exert themselves less, and perhaps a few will do nothing at all, while pretending to work hard!

Such effects occur with both cognitive tasks and those involving physical effort (Weldon & Mustari, 1988; Williams & Karau, 1991). As anyone who has worked as a server in a restaurant knows, tips tend to be proportionally less as the size of the group increases, which may be one reason that a standard tip is often added by the restaurant when there are six or more in a party.

To ask whether social loafing occurs in school settings might elicit a "duh" response from students. Englehart (2006) suggests that social loafing can explain patterns of student participation, as a function of the size of the class; students participate less in larger classes. Likewise, social loafing occurs among students working on team projects. Price, Harrison, and Gavin (2006) identified several psychological factors that affect students' social loafing on team projects. First, those who felt "dispensable" to the group were more likely to loaf. Second, the more fairness that was perceived in the group generally, the less likely students were to loaf. What determined these two perceptions—dispensability and fairness? When participants had substantial knowledge and skills relating to the task, they felt less dispensable. So, in effect, being able to offer task-relevant help to the group served to counteract loafing. In addition, dissimilarity from the other group members led participants to feel more dispensable, and thus more likely to loaf. So, what can be done to reduce social loafing?

REDUCING SOCIAL LOAFING: SOME USEFUL TECHNIQUES   The most obvious way to reduce social loafing involves making the output or effort of each participant readily identifiable (Williams, Harkins, & Latané, 1981). Under these conditions, people can't sit back and let others do their work, so social loafing is reduced. Research in organizations has found that when individual contributions to a team effort are publicly posted, performance in a group can be even better than working alone (Lount & Wilk, 2014). As a result of the public recognition of their individual contributions to the team—and the desire to be seen as doing the "most" for the group—performance increased.

When people believe their contribution matters, and a strong performance on the part of the group will lead to a desired outcome, individuals also tend to try harder (Shepperd & Taylor, 1999). So pooling contributions to a task—such as performance on a basketball sports team—will be effective to the extent that each player feels their contribution is clear and each player feels identified with a cohesive team (Backer, Boen, De Cuyper, Hoigaard, & Vande Broek, 2015).

Second, groups can reduce social loafing by increasing group members' commitment to successful task performance (Brickner, Harkins, & Ostrom, 1986). Pressures toward working hard will then serve to offset temptations to engage in social loafing. Third, social loafing can be reduced by increasing the apparent importance or value of a task (Karau & Williams, 1993). Fourth, people are less likely to loaf if they are given some kind of standard of performance—either in terms of how much others are doing or their own past performance (Williams et al., 1981). An interesting study with students in a marketing class showed that group members themselves can provide such feedback to each other over the course of a joint project and that doing so reduces social loafing (Aggarwal & O'Brien, 2008). Together, use of these tactics can sharply reduce social loafing.

11.2.3: Effects of Being in a Crowd

Have you ever attended a football or basketball game at which members of the crowd screamed insults, threw things at the referees, or engaged in other violent behavior they would probably never show in other settings? Most of us have not, since such extreme events are relatively rare, although, interestingly enough, this is part of the "stereotype" of how people behave in crowds, particularly those at sporting events. English soccer fans have become especially famous for **hooliganism**—incidents throughout Europe of serious disorder at matches involving England's team (Stott, Hutchison, & Drury, 2001). Such effects in crowds—where there is a drift toward wild, unrestrained behavior— were initially termed **deindividuation** because they seemed to stem, at least in part, from the possibility that when people are in a large crowd they tend to "to lose their individuality" and instead act as others do. More formally, the term *deindividuation* was used to indicate a psychological state characterized by reduced self-awareness, brought on by external conditions such as being an anonymous member of a large crowd.

Initial research on deindividuation (Zimbardo, 1970) seemed to suggest that being in a crowd makes people anonymous and therefore less responsible for their own actions, which encourages unrestrained, antisocial actions. More recent evidence, though, indicates that deindividuation leads to *greater* normative behavior, not less. When we are part of a large crowd we are more likely to obey the norms of this group—whatever those may be (Postmes & Spears, 1998). For instance, at a sporting event, when norms in that situation suggest that it is appropriate to boo the opposing team, that is what many people—especially highly identified fans—will do. Certainly that seems to have been the norm that was active for "English hooligans" at soccer games in the past. However, recent evidence indicates that, as a result of social psychological intervention with police agencies, those norms can be changed (Stott, Adang, Livingstone, & Schreiber, 2007). As a result of a shift in norms, at more recent soccer matches, England's fans no longer defined "hooliganism" as characteristic of their fan group; they self-policed by marginalizing those few English fans who attempted to create conflict, and no violent incidents have taken place.

Overall, then, being part of a large crowd and experiencing deindividuation does not necessarily lead to negative or harmful behaviors: It simply increases the likelihood that crowd members will follow the norms of the group. Those norms might be of "showing respect" by silently crying—behaviors demonstrated at the immense gatherings following Diana, Princess of Wales' death, or at the vigils that took place on the campus of Virginia Tech in Blacksburg following the shooting deaths that took place there in 2007. Or, the critical norms might involve working together for a purpose—coordinating efforts to save people from crumbled buildings after the earthquake in Haiti in 2010, or praying and singing joyously together at huge Christian revival meetings. When people are in large crowds, as shown in Figure 11.16, what behavior they will exhibit—for good or ill—will depend on what norms are operating.

Figure 11.16 The Crowd: Conforming to Norms for Good or Ill

Crowds sometimes engage in actions that individual members would never dream of performing alone. Those actions can be dramatically destructive as shown in Panel A, or peaceful as shown in Panel B. By identifying with others in a crowd, it can affect our behavior by encouraging conformity to the salient norms governing that particular crowd.

Key Points

- The mere presence of other people either as an audience or as co-actors can influence our performance on many tasks. Such effects are known as **social facilitation**.
- The **drive theory of social facilitation** suggests that the presence of others is arousing and can either increase or reduce performance, depending on whether dominant responses in a given situation are correct or incorrect.
- The **evaluation apprehension** view suggests that an audience disrupts performance because of the actor's concerns about being evaluated.
- The **distraction conflict** perspective suggests that the presence of others induces conflicting tendencies to focus on the task being performed and on the audience or co-actors. This can result both in increased arousal and narrowed attentional focus.
- Recent findings offer support for the view that several kinds of audiences produce narrowed attentional focus when performing a task. Both the arousal and cognitive views of social facilitation can help explain why social facilitation occurs among animals as well as people.

- When individuals work together on an **additive task**, where their contributions are combined, **social loafing**—reduced output by each group member—frequently occurs. Such loafing has been found on physical and cognitive tasks.
- Social loafing can be reduced in several ways: by making outputs individually identifiable or unique, ensuring individuals do not feel dispensable, providing feedback on each person's performance, and increasing commitment to the success of the task. When people feel their contribution is identifiable and they are identified with the team, performance can be even better than working alone.
- When we are part of a large crowd, **deindividuation**—where we are thought to be less aware of our personal self—can occur. Initially it was believed that **hooliganism**—wild and destructive behavior—was inevitable in crowds.
- However, people act on the basis of whatever norms are operative in crowds, which differ depending on what group identity is salient. Those norms can sanction either antisocial or prosocial actions.

11.3: Coordination in Groups: Cooperation or Conflict?

Objective **Evaluate the factors that impact group cooperation and conflict**

Cooperation—helping that is mutual, where both sides benefit—is common in groups working together to attain shared goals. As we discussed in the beginning of this chapter, by cooperating, people can attain goals they could never hope to reach by themselves. Surprisingly, though, cooperation does not always develop in groups. Sometimes, group members may perceive their personal interests as incompatible, and instead of coordinating their efforts, may work *against* each other, often producing negative results for all. This is known as **conflict**, and can be defined as a process in which individuals or groups perceive that others have taken, or will soon take, actions incompatible with their own interests (DeDreu, 2010). Conflict is indeed a process, for, as you probably know from your own experience; it has a nasty way of escalating—from simple mistrust, through a spiral of anger, to actions designed to harm the other side.

Part of what makes for good cooperation is **social embeddedness**, which is a sense of knowing the reputation of the other parties involved, often by knowing someone else who knows them (Riegelsberger, Sasse, & McCarthy, 2007). In the world of work, with increasing numbers of people *telecommuting*, communicating over the Internet with people you don't know well, or at all, is becoming increasingly common (Brandon & Hollingshead, 2007). Attempting to work on group projects with people you don't know always raises questions about how they will turn out. This is especially true when you consider that such projects often require considerable trust and cooperation. Interpersonal cues that can convey co-worker trustworthiness are absent in such distant situations. Because this could lead to conflict—the very opposite of cooperation—many organizations and individuals working together from a distance have turned to video computer-mediated programs to provide the interpersonal cues that would be otherwise missing (see Figure 11.7).

Figure 11.17 To Skype or Not to Skype: That Is the Question

Increasingly, people are working via long distances and communicating via the internet. Work activities that used to take place face-to-face can now be done using Skype or other video conferencing programs, which allows for all the normal interpersonal cues to be present during long distance communication.

Can cooperation be promoted in groups that work at a distance by allowing people to share how others have behaved—whether cooperatively or not—for example, provide reputational information? Might doing so help increase trust and cooperative performance ultimately? Recent research suggests that this is so (Feinberg, Willer, & Schultz, 2015). Participants in this study played a series of games with others over a computer. Everyone first received 10 points at the start of each round, with each player deciding how much of that to donate to the group—with the total donated to the group by all the players being doubled and given equally to all the group members. This means there is a clear incentive for behaving cooperatively and donating to the group—the more everyone does so, the more everyone gains. In some versions of the game, participants simply learned how much each of the other three people in their group had contributed. In another version, they were able to tell another person they would be playing the next round of the game with how much (or how little) one person had contributed to the group. In the last version, participants could not only tell on one of the players, but they could exclude someone from the next round and thereby cost that person potential earnings.

What were the consequences? First, people did use the "reputational" information to select partners for the next round of the game—favoring those who had cooperated previously. Those who gained a negative reputation and were excluded subsequently "saw the light," and in later rounds started behaving considerably more cooperatively. So, even when working separately or at a distance from each other, cooperation in groups can be encouraged when people know others' reputations and can act on that basis.

11.3.1: Cooperation: Working with Others to Achieve Shared Goals

Cooperation is often highly beneficial to the people involved. So, why would group members not consistently cooperate? One answer is straightforward: because some outcomes that people seek simply can't be shared. Several people seeking the same job or romantic partner can't combine forces to attain these goals: The rewards can go to only one. Social psychologists refer to this situation as one of **negative interdependence**—where if one person obtains a desired outcome, others cannot (DeDreu, 2010).

In many other situations, however, cooperation *could* develop but often does not. Social psychologists study these kinds of situations with the aim of identifying the factors that tip the balance either toward or away from cooperation. Often the people involved in such conflicts do not realize that a compromise *is* possible. Consider the following example. Suppose we wanted to go on vacation together. You say you want to go to Switzerland, and I say I want to go to Hawaii. Does this conflict seem solvable, without one person losing? Perhaps, but one thing conflict mediators do know is that to solve this kind of conflict of seemingly incompatible goals—without one person simply capitulating to the other—we have to get to the essence of what lies behind each person's demands. Now suppose your "real" goal is to see some mountains (which Switzerland certainly has, but so do many other places), and my "real" goal is to be by the sea and swim in warm water. Once the underlying goal of each party is known, it can often be settled, with the help of a little imagination. In this case, we could go to Greece—visit some mountains *and* the beach on some lovely Greek island! Of course, not all social conflicts are solvable by this method, but many are. Let's examine now classic research on dilemmas where a lack of cooperation frequently results in poor outcomes for all parties involved.

SOCIAL DILEMMAS: WHERE COOPERATION COULD OCCUR, BUT OFTEN DOESN'T **Social dilemmas** are situations in which each person can increase his or her individual gains by acting in a purely selfish manner, but if all (or most) people do the same thing, the outcomes experienced by all are reduced (Komorita & Parks, 1994; Van Lange & Joireman, 2010). A classic illustration of this kind of situation is known as the *prisoner's dilemma*—a situation faced by two suspects who have been caught by the police. They are being held in separate rooms, so each does not know what the other will do. Here, either or both people can choose to cooperate (e.g., stay silent and not confess) or compete (e.g., "rat the other person out"). If both remain silent, then they each serve a one-year prison sentence. If both compete, each will serve a two-year prison sentence. What happens if one chooses to compete while the other chooses to cooperate? In this case, the one who competes goes free, while the one who stays silent serves a three-year prison sentence. So in order to achieve a maximally beneficial outcome for *both* of them, they must individually cooperate without the assurance of that outcome. If they decide to compete, however, in an effort to maximize their own *individual* outcome, they risk *both* losing the benefits of cooperation. Social psychologists have used this type of situation to examine the factors that tip the balance toward trust and cooperation or mistrust and competition (Balliet & Van Lange, 2013).

It might be reasonable to suppose that decreasing the attractiveness of competition should increase cooperation. One way to do this would be to increase the sanctions given in a social dilemma for noncooperative choices. But doing so might change how people perceive such situations—from one involving trust in others to one based on economic self-interest. When seen as based in trust, cooperation should be higher than when the dilemma is seen as a situation in which people act on their own self-interest. To what degree, then, does the presence of sanctions for noncooperation undermine people's subsequent cooperative behavior—the exact opposite of its intended effect?

Mulder, van Dijk, De Cremer, and Wilke (2006) addressed this question by first telling their participants about a "game" that "other participants in a prior study" were said to have engaged in. All participants were told about a situation in which four group members had to decide whether to keep chips for themselves or donate them to the group. The total number of chips that were donated by the members to the group would be doubled in value by the experimenter and then equally divided among the members. This information phase of the study was included so that the presence of sanctioning for noncooperative group members could be varied. The crucial manipulation was whether a sanctioning system—applied to the two lowest chip-donating people—was said to have been operating or not. Later, when the participants took part in a different social dilemma where no sanctioning was mentioned, the influence of exposure to the prior sanctioning system for noncooperation could be assessed.

As you can see in Figure 11.18, prior exposure to the sanctioning for noncooperation subsequently lowered cooperation when the participants made their behavioral choices in a social dilemma. The reduction in cooperation among those exposed to a sanctioning system stemmed from changes in participants' perceptions of the extent to which they could trust that others will behave cooperatively. So, having sanctions be present, over time, has the opposite effect on cooperation than might be intended. In fact, research has revealed that merely thinking about the law as a sanctioning system fosters people's beliefs that others are competitive, that they cannot be trusted, and leads people to make more competitive choices during a prisoner's dilemma game (Callan, Kay, Olson, Brar, & Whitefield, 2010).

11.3.2: Responding to and Resolving Conflicts

Most definitions of conflict emphasize the existence of incompatible interests. But conflict can sometimes occur when the two sides don't really have opposing interests—they simply *believe* that these exist (DeDreu & Van Lange, 1995). Indeed, errors concerning the causes of others' behavior—*faulty attribution*—can play a critical role in conflict.

Consider how you feel when someone misunderstands your actions. Do you attempt to make them "see the light" or do you "simply withdraw," assuming there is nothing you can do to change their mind? "Feeling misunderstood" by others leads to different responses in members of various ethnic groups. In a series of studies by Lun, Oishi, Coan, Akimoto, and Miao (2010), EEG (left prefrontal) brain activity was measured when group members were led to believe they had been "misunderstood or understood by others." Because European Americans were expected to feel challenged and be prepared to confront others when they felt misunderstood, whereas Asian Americans were expected to be motivated to withdraw from such situations, brain activity in the area reflecting approach motivation should be differentially observable in these circumstances. As shown in Figure 11.19, that is exactly what occurred. European Americans showed elevated activity reflective of approach motivation when they were misunderstood, but Asian Americans showed reductions in such activity in this case. Conversely, Asian Americans' brain activation was especially high when they felt understood, whereas European Americans appeared not to be motivated to approach when they felt understood.

Figure 11.18 Awareness of Sanctions for Noncooperation Can Undermine Trust and Cooperation

At first, as shown on the left side of the graph, awareness that there are sanctions for noncooperation might serve to ensure people cooperate with others. However, as shown on the right side of the graph, later responses to a new social dilemma may be less cooperative following exposure to sanctions for noncooperation because it serves to undermine trust in others.

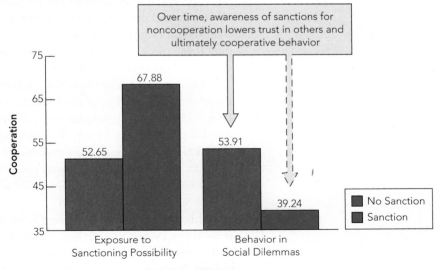

Figure 11.19 Brain Activity While Being Misunderstood

Shown here is EEG left frontal brain activity in Asian Americans and European Americans when they felt either understood or misunderstood by others. When European Americans felt misunderstood they prepared to confront, whereas Asian Americans showed evidence of withdrawal when they felt misunderstood.

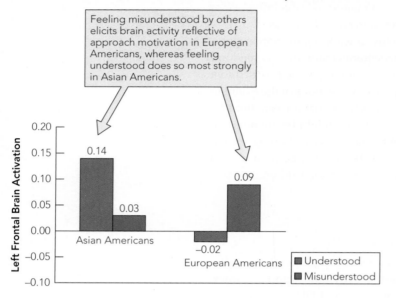

Feeling misunderstood by others elicits brain activity reflective of approach motivation in European Americans, whereas feeling understood does so most strongly in Asian Americans.

Conflicts within groups are often likely to develop under conditions of scarce resources where group members must compete with each other to obtain them. What begins as a task conflict can rapidly turn into relationship conflict (DeDreu, 2010). Imagine that you and your sibling are told you have to clean out the garage, and you are told that whoever completes their half of the task first gets to use your parent's car for the weekend. Both of you can't have the car—a desirable resource—so conflict is likely to happen. And, you can easily imagine how conflict over who gets to use the vacuum cleaner first and so on could rapidly deteriorate into name calling and other actions that would ultimately harm your relationship. So, a variety of social factors can play a strong role in initiating and intensifying conflicts. Because conflicts are often very costly, knowing effective steps to resolve them as quickly as possible is useful. Two frequently used strategies are **bargaining** and employment of **superordinate goals**.

BARGAINING: THE UNIVERSAL PROCESS By far the most common strategy for resolving conflicts is bargaining, or *negotiation* (Pruitt & Carnevale, 1993). In this process, opposing sides exchange offers, counteroffers, and concessions, either directly or through representatives. If the process is successful, a solution acceptable to both sides is attained, and the conflict is resolved. If, instead, bargaining is unsuccessful, costly deadlock may result and the conflict is likely to intensify. What factors determine which of these outcomes occurs?

First, and perhaps most obviously, the outcome of bargaining is determined, in part, by the specific tactics adopted by the bargainers (Thompson, 1998). Many of these are designed to accomplish a key goal: Reduce the opponent's *aspirations* (i.e., hopes or goals), so that this person or group becomes convinced that it cannot get what it wants and should, instead, settle for something less favorable to their side. Tactics for accomplishing this goal include: (1) beginning with an extreme initial offer—one that is very favorable to the side proposing it, (2) attempting to convince the other side that one's break-even point is much higher than it is so that they offer more than would otherwise be the case; for example, claiming you will lose money on the deal if the price is lowered, and (3) convincing the other side that you can go elsewhere and get even better terms.

A second, and very important, determinant of the outcome of bargaining involves the overall orientation of the bargainers to the process (Pruitt & Carnevale, 1993). People taking part in negotiations can approach such discussions from either of two distinct perspectives. In one, they can view the negotiations as "win–lose" situations in which gains by one side are necessarily linked with losses for the other. In the other, they can approach negotiations as potential "win–win" situations, in which the interests of the two sides are not necessarily incompatible and in which the potential gains of both sides can be maximized.

This approach produces more favorable results in the long run—and is typically what is used when negotiating national conflicts such as the one between the Israelis and Palestinians, or the conflict between Protestants and Catholics in Northern Ireland. Such peace agreements, when achieved, are known as *integrative agreements*—ones that offer greater joint benefits than would be attained by simply splitting all

Table 11.2 Tactics for Reaching Integrative Agreements

Many strategies can be useful in attaining integrative agreements—ones that offer better outcomes than simple compromise. Several of these are summarized here.

Tactic	Description
Broadening the pie	Available resources are increased so that both sides can obtain their major goals.
Nonspecific compensation	One side gets what it wants; the other is compensated on an unrelated issue.
Logrolling	Each party makes concessions on low-priority issues in exchange for concessions on issues it values more highly.
Bridging	Neither party gets its initial demands, but a new option that satisfies the major interests of both sides is developed.
Cost cutting	One party gets what it desires, and the costs to the other party are reduced in some manner.

differences down the middle, or one side simply giving in to the demands of the other side. This is very much like the situation we described earlier in which there was a conflict between two individuals about picking a vacation destination. When the two parties communicate clearly about their underlying needs, a new option that satisfies both parties' needs can often be found. This technique—called *bridging*—is one of many techniques for attaining such integrative solutions to conflicts. Several strategies that can be useful in attaining integrative agreements, which offer better outcomes than simple compromise, are shown in Table 11.2.

Often negotiators believe that displaying anger at the other party will further their interests, that is, lead the other party to make larger concessions. However, there are cultural differences in the norms concerning the appropriateness of expressing anger in negotiations so this strategy must be used with care. Adam, Shirako, and Maddux (2010) found that expressing anger in a negotiation resulted in greater concessions from European Americans, but smaller concessions from Asian Americans. These researchers showed that the effectiveness of different bargaining strategies involving displays of emotion depend on cultural norms.

SUPERORDINATE GOALS: WE'RE ALL IN THIS TOGETHER As we saw in Chapter 6, members of groups in conflict often divide the world into two opposing camps—"us" and "them." They perceive members of their own group (us) as quite different from, and usually better than, people belonging to other groups (them). This tendency to magnify differences between one's own group and other groups and to disparage the other is very powerful and often plays a critical role in the occurrence and persistence of conflicts. Fortunately, it can be countered through the induction of **superordinate goals**—goals that both sides seek, and that tie their interests together rather than driving them apart (Gaertner et al., 1994; Sherif et al., 1961). When opposing sides can be made to see that they share overarching goals, conflict is often sharply reduced and may, in fact, be replaced by overt cooperation.

Key Points

- **Cooperation**—working together with others to obtain shared goals—is a common aspect of social life. However, cooperation does not develop in many situations where it is possible, partly because such situations involve **social dilemmas** in which individuals can increase their own gains by not cooperating or because there is perceived to be a **conflict** of interests between the individuals involved.

- Cooperation in teams such as might occur when people work on computers at a distance can be difficult to achieve because of the absence of interpersonal cues that are present during face-to-face interactions. However, **social embeddedness**, which is a sense of knowing the reputation of the other parties involved, can improve cooperation by making those who do not cooperate accountable.

- **Negative interdependence**—where if one person obtains a desired outcome, others cannot—lowers the likelihood of cooperation. Social dilemmas such as the *prisoner's dilemma* are cases where cooperation could occur and both parties would benefit, but where it often does not because the parties do not trust each other.
- Having sanctions for noncooperation can change the extent to which people trust others, and thereby lower the extent to which they engage in cooperation on other tasks.
- Conflict often begins when individuals or groups perceive that others' interests are incompatible with their own

interests. Social factors such as *faulty attributions* can play a role in conflict.
- Members of different ethnic groups often respond differently when they feel misunderstood by others. European Americans appear to prepare for confrontation and Asian Americans seem to withdraw under these conditions.
- Conflict can be reduced in many ways, but **bargaining** and the induction of **superordinate goals** can be particularly effective.

11.4: Perceived Fairness in Groups: Its Nature and Effects

Objective   **Recall that the way group fairness is judged impacts behavior**

Have you ever been in a situation where you felt that you were getting less than you deserved from some group to which you belong? If so, you probably experienced anger and resentment in response to such *perceived unfairness or injustice* (Cropanzano, 1993). Were you ready to act to rectify it and attempt to get whatever it was you felt you deserved, or were you afraid of potential retaliation (Miller, Cronin, Garcia, & Branscombe, 2009)? Social psychologists have conducted many studies to understand (1) what leads people to infer they have been treated fairly or unfairly and (2) what they do about it—their efforts to deal with perceived unfairness (Adams, 1965; Walker & Smith, 2002). We will now consider both of these questions.

11.4.1: Rules for Judging Fairness: Distributive, Procedural, and Transactional Justice

Deciding whether we have been treated fairly in our relations with others can be quite tricky. First, we rarely have all the information needed to make such a judgment accurately (Van den Bos & Lind, 2002). Second, even if we did, fairness is very much "in the eye of the beholder," so is subject to many forms of bias. Despite such complexities, research on perceived fairness in group settings indicates that, in general, we make these judgments by focusing on three distinct aspects or rules.

The first, known as **distributive justice**, or *fairness*, involves the *outcomes* we and others receive. According to the *equity rule*, available rewards should be divided among group members in accordance with their contributions: The more they provide in terms of effort, experience, skills, and other contributions to the group, the more they should receive. For example, people may expect that those who have made major contributions toward reaching the group's goals should receive greater rewards than people who have contributed very little. In short, we often judge fairness in terms of the ratio between the contributions group members have provided and the rewards they receive (Adams, 1965).

But equity, which is essentially merit-based distributive justice, is not the only justice rule people can and do use. New research assessing the distribution rules favored by people in different cultural contexts has found considerable variability (Schafer, Haun, & Tomasello, 2015). While in Western countries fairness in the workplace in particular is often determined by perceived merit, in other societies outcomes can be distributed based on desire for maintaining harmony among group members so awarded equally. Other distributive rules may be favored too in some contexts—such as seniority rules where older people get more resources, or in terms of differential member needs (a frequent distribution rule in families).

To assess the extent to which children use merit as the basis for distributing rewards differentially depending on the norms of their culture, Schafer et al. (2015) had children from three different types of cultures participate in a task that was rigged so that some children were able to retrieve more balls from a tank than others (thereby creating differential merit), or they were simply given more balls by the experimenter. The German children in this research distributed rewards to the others according to *merit*—based on how many balls a given child had retrieved. However, children from the two small African societies, where people's interactions tend to be face-to-face much of the time, were considerably less sensitive to merit and their reward allocations were not based on an abstract rule as it was by the German children. This suggests that how we favor distributing resources is a learned cultural norm.

While people are often concerned with the outcomes they receive, this is far from the entire story where judgments of fairness are concerned. In addition, people are also interested in the fairness of the *procedures* through which rewards have been distributed, what is known as **procedural justice** (Tyler & Blader, 2003). We base our judgments about it on factors such as: (1) the extent to which the procedures are applied in the same manner to all people, (2) there are opportunities for correcting any errors in distribution, and (3) decision makers avoid being influenced by their own self-interest.

Evidence that such factors really do influence our judgments concerning procedural justice has been obtained in many studies (Tyler & Blader, 2003). For instance, in one investigation, when people perceived authorities as holding attitudes that are biased against them, and when they believed they lack "voice" (e.g., cannot complain or won't be listened to), the more they report feeling treated unjustly (Van Prooijen, Van den Bos, Lind, & Wilke, 2006). In a large study of people who had been laid off from their jobs, those who felt the procedures used to decide who would be let go were unfair expressed greater hostility and intentions to retaliate against organizational authorities (Barclay, Skarlicki, & Pugh, 2005).

We also judge fairness in terms of the way information about outcomes and procedures is given to us. This is known as **transactional justice**: The extent to which we are given clear and rational reasons for why rewards were divided as they were (Bies, Shapiro, & Cummings, 1988), and the courtesy or respect with which we are informed about these divisions (Greenberg, 1993; Tyler, Boeckmann, Smith, & Huo, 1997). For more information about how group members respond when feel they are treated with respect or with disrespect, see the special feature, **"What Research Tells Us About… The Importance of Being Treated with Respect."**

What Research Tells Us About…

The Importance of Being Treated with Respect

It is difficult to underestimate the importance of feeling respected—both as an individual person and on the basis of one's group membership. Receiving respect strongly affects relations between groups, and is an important influence on psychological well-being. When a group perceives itself to be unjustly devalued by another group, people who believe they are highly valued by their disadvantaged group will be inclined to exhibit hostility toward the devaluing outgroup (Branscombe, Spears, Ellemers, & Doosje, 2002). Conversely, when members of disadvantaged groups (Latinos and African Americans) feel respected and treated fairly by peers who are members of a more powerful group in society (white Americans), they display more positive social engagement with the school of which they are both part (Huo, Binning, & Molina, 2010).

How does a disadvantaged group's perceived respect and recognition from the broader society in which it is located affect responses to another minority? In other words, does feeling respected create a willingness to respect others? To examine this idea, Simon and Grabow (2014) asked a large sample of members of the gay and lesbian community in Germany to what extent they felt the general population of Germany recognized and respected gays and lesbians as equal citizens. They found that the more gays and lesbians felt respected in their society, the more they were willing to accord respect to another minority—Muslim immigrants in Germany. This suggests that being respected as an equal translates into respecting others.

Might the opposite be true as well—will minority group members who feel disrespected exhibit lower trust and greater resentment of societal authorities? As an initial test of this idea, Belmi, Cortes Barragan, Neale, and Cohen (2015) first sampled black and white American college students and asked them how much they feel disrespected at school because of their ethnicity, and whether they expected that treatment to continue in the future. The researchers also asked them a wide variety of questions concerning their school-related delinquency in the past year—for example, whether they had cheated on tests and

picked a fight. They found that the more students worried about being disrespected based on their ethnicity at school, the more they were likely to engage in deviance, and this relationship was stronger for the minority students than majority students. In samples of employees, similar relationships were observed: Those who felt more disrespected by their employer, especially minority respondents, the more they reported counterproductive work attitudes (e.g., damaging equipment on purpose, taking office supplies, bad-mouth the company to others). In a final study, the investigators led some white Americans to expect disrespectful treatment on the job because of their identity and then had them complete a series of anagrams, for which they had to report on how many they had solved. Just like minority participants in the prior studies, these respondents who expected disrespectful treatment based on their social identity on the job were more likely to dishonestly report their performance on the anagram task. This work revealed that not only are people profoundly sensitive to the evaluations of others in the form of group-based disrespect, but perceived disrespect has negative consequences for social deviance as well as the treatment of other minorities. These processes and consequences are shown in Figure 11.20.

In sum, we judge fairness in several different ways—in terms of the rewards we have received (distributive justice), the procedures used to reach these divisions (procedural justice), and the style in which we are informed about these divisions (transactional justice). All three forms of justice can have strong effects on our behavior.

In many situations in which we ask the question "Am I being treated fairly?" we do not have sufficient information about the outcomes or procedures used to clearly apply rules of distributive and procedural justice. We don't know exactly what rewards others have received (e.g., their salaries), and we may not know all the procedures or whether they were consistently followed when distributing rewards to group members. What do we do in such situations? A meta-analysis of these studies has revealed that we treat our feelings as a source of information (Barsky & Kaplan, 2007) and base our judgments on them, reasoning "If I feel good, this must be fair," or "If I feel bad, this must be unfair."

HOW EMOTIONS AFFECT INTERGROUP INTERACTIONS Members of one group often have to interact with and get along with members of another group. Corporations may merge—some successfully (Disney and Pixar) and others not so successfully (AOL and Time Warner)—requiring employees of each organization (often former competitors) to get along. Such group mergers can trigger threat in members of each group. Among those who were members of the lower-status group, particularly those who were highly identified with the original organization, negative social comparisons with the higher-status merger group can be stressful (Amiot, Terry, & Callan, 2007). For members of the former high status group, if the merger is seen as diminishing their distinctiveness or their group may be dragged down by the lower-status group that they are merging with, it can create a sense of injustice and have undesirable interaction consequences (Boen, Vanbeselaere, & Wostyn, 2010). Members of each of the merged groups may fail to identify with the new corporate entity, and instead show hostility toward members of the other group and favoritism toward members of their old group (Gleibs, Noack, & Mummendey, 2010).

Figure 11.20 Responses to Respectful and Disrespectful Group-Based Treatment

When people feel they are accorded respect based on their minority identity they show respect to others. In contrast, when people feel disrespected based on their minority identity they are less willing to abide by social norms and instead are more likely to engage in social deviance.

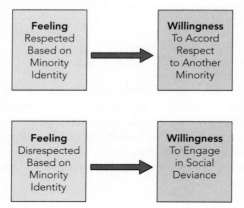

Such potential for negative emotion is not only the case for corporate groups experiencing a merger. Because people are profoundly sensitive to the evaluations of others, whenever group members perceive another group as potentially rejecting their group, negative emotions can be elicited, creating awkward social interactions, and intensifying conflict between groups (Vorauer, 2006). Studies investigating this type of threat-based conflict between majority and minority groups have revealed that interethnic behavior is affected by such beliefs about the other group. For example, white Americans who were concerned that their group would be perceived as bigoted, sat further away from an African American with whom they expected to discuss racial profiling compared to when they expected to discuss interpersonal relationships (Goff, Steele, & Davies, 2008). So, emotions in group settings can affect how interactions proceed.

Key Points

- Individuals wish to be treated fairly by the groups to which they belong. Fairness can be judged in terms of outcomes (**distributive justice**), in terms of procedures (**procedural justice**), or in terms of how the treatment is delivered (**transactional justice**).
- People may not have the necessary information to determine whether their outcomes or the procedures used are fair or not. When such information is unknown, people may use their feelings of *respect* as a guide.

- Feeling respected based on social identity can encourage people to accord respect to other minorities. Conversely, feeling disrespected based on minority identity can result in lowered willingness to abide by social norms and increased deviance.
- When formerly distinct groups are involuntarily merged, members of both groups can feel threatened and consequently show favoritism toward members of their old group.

11.5: Decision Making by Groups: How It Occurs and the Pitfalls It Faces

Objective   **Evaluate the factors that impact the effectiveness of the group decision-making process**

One of the most important activities that groups perform is **decision making**—deciding on one out of several possible courses of action. Governments, corporations, and many other organizations entrust key decisions to groups. Yet, as we noted in our opening, people often believe that groups reach worse decisions than individuals. Despite groups being able to pool the expertise of their members and potentially avoid the biases that might operate when individuals act alone, many in our culture believe groups make worse decisions than individuals. But, are such beliefs about group decision making accurate?

In their efforts to address this issue, social psychologists have focused on three major questions: (1) How do groups *actually* make their decisions and reach a consensus? (2) Do decisions reached by groups differ from those made by individuals? (3) What accounts for the fact that groups sometimes do make disastrous decisions?

11.5.1: The Decision-Making Process: How Groups Attain Consensus

When groups first begin to discuss any issue, their members rarely start out in complete agreement. Rather, they come to the decision-making task with a range of views (Brodbeck, Kerschreiter, Mojzisch, Frey, & Schulz-Hardt, 2002; Postmes, Spears, Lee, & Novak, 2005). After some period of discussion, however, groups usually do reach a decision. How is this accomplished, and can the final outcome be predicted from the views initially held by the members of the group?

THE DECISION QUALITY OF GROUPS: LESS OR MORE EXTREME? Some have suggested that groups are far less likely than individuals to make extreme decisions. Is that view correct? A large body of evidence indicates that groups are actually *more* likely to adopt extreme positions than if its members made those same decisions alone. Across many different kinds of decisions and many different contexts, groups show a pronounced tendency to shift toward views that are more extreme than the ones with which they initially began (Burnstein, 1983; Rodrigo & Ato, 2002). This is known as **group polarization**, and its major effects can be summarized as follows: Whatever the initial leaning or preference of a group prior to its discussions, this preference is strengthened during the group's deliberations. As a result, groups make more extreme decisions than individuals. Initial research on this topic (Kogan & Wallach, 1964) suggested that groups move toward riskier alternatives as they discuss important issues—a change described as the *risky shift*. But additional research showed that the shift was not always toward risk—the shift toward risk *only* happened in situations where the initial preference of the group leaned in that direction. The shift could be in the opposite direction—toward increased caution—if *caution* was the group's initial preference.

Why do groups tend to move, as shown in Figure 11.21, over the course of their discussions, toward increasingly extreme views and decisions? Two major factors are involved. First, *social comparison* plays a role. If we all want to be "above average," where opinions are concerned, this implies holding views that are "better" than other group members. Being "better" would mean holding views that are more prototypical of the group's overall preference, but even more so (Turner, 1991). So, for example, in a group of liberals, "better" would mean "more liberal." Among a group of conservatives, "better" would mean "more conservative."

A second factor involves the fact that during group discussion, most arguments favor the group's initial preference. As a result of hearing such arguments members shift, increasingly, toward the majority's view. Consequently, the proportion of discussion favoring the group's initial preference increases, so that ultimately, members convince themselves that this must be the "right" view (Postmes, Spears, & Cihangir, 2001). In support of this idea, recent research has revealed that if other group members' opinions are not known before discussion, group decisions improve because more diverse arguments are considered (Mojzisch & Schulz-Hardt, 2010).

11.5.2: The Downside of Group Decision Making

The drift of many decision-making groups toward polarization is a serious problem—one that can interfere with their ability to make sound decisions, but this is not the only process that can exert such negative effects (Hinsz, 1995). Among the most important of these other processes are (1) *groupthink* and (2) groups' seeming inability to share and use information held by only some of their members.

Figure 11.21 Group Polarization: How It Works

Group polarization involves the tendency for decision-making groups to shift toward views that are more extreme than the ones with which the groups initially began, but in the same general direction. Thus, if groups start out slightly in favor of one view or position, they often end up holding this view more strongly or extremely after discussion.

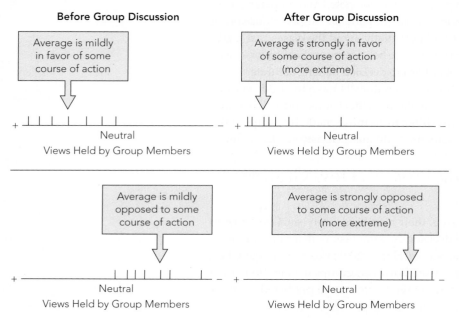

GROUPTHINK: WHEN COHESIVENESS IS DANGEROUS Earlier we described how high levels of cohesiveness in groups has benefits: it can increase members' commitment to the group and make those groups more satisfying. But, like anything else, there can be too much of a good thing. When cohesiveness reaches very high levels, **groupthink** may develop. This is a strong tendency for decision-making groups to "close ranks" around a decision, to assume that the group *can't* be wrong, with pressure for all members to support the decision strongly, and to reject any information contrary to the decision. Research indicates that once groupthink develops, groups become unwilling to change their decisions, even when initial outcomes suggest that those decisions were very poor ones (Haslam et al., 2006).

Consider the decisions of three United States Presidents (Kennedy, Johnson, and Nixon) to escalate the war in Vietnam. Each escalation brought increased American casualties and no progress toward the goal of ensuring the survival of South Vietnam as an independent country. Likewise, President George W. Bush and his cabinet chose to invade Iraq, without critically considering the assumption that is now known to be incorrect—that Saddam Hussein possessed weapons of mass destruction. According to Janis (1982), the social psychologist who originated the concept of groupthink, this process—and the fact that it encourages an unwillingness among members of cohesive groups to consider alternative courses of action—may well have contributed to these events.

Why does groupthink occur? Research findings (Tetlock et al., 1992; Kameda & Sugimori, 1993) suggest that two factors are crucial. One of these is a very high level of cohesiveness among group members and the fact that supportive group members in the leader's "inner circle" exert a disproportional impact on the ultimate decision making (Benabou, 2013; Burris, Rodgers, Mannix, Hendron, & Oldroyd, 2009). The second is *emergent group norms*—norms suggesting that the group is infallible, morally superior, and because of these factors, there should be no further discussion of the issues at hand: the decision has been made, and the only valid response is to support it as strongly as possible. Closely related to these effects is a tendency to reject any criticism by outside sources. Criticism from outsiders is viewed with suspicion and attributed negative motives. Consequently it is largely ignored, and may even tend to strengthen the group's cohesiveness, as members rally to defend the group against perceived assaults by outsiders.

Such rejection of criticism on the part of outsiders has been reported by Hornsey and Imani (2004). They asked Australian college students to read comments supposedly made during an interview that were either positive ("When I think of Australians I think of them as being fairly friendly and warm people . . .") or negative ("When I think of Australians I think of them as being fairly racist . . ."). The comments were attributed either to another Australian (an ingroup member), a person from another country who had never lived in Australia (inexperienced outgroup member), or to a person from another country who had once lived in Australia and therefore had experience with Australians (experienced outgroup member). Participants then evaluated the source of the comments and rated the extent to which this person's comments were designed to be constructive.

Hornsey and Imani (2004) reasoned that when the comments were negative, both the speaker and the comments would receive lower ratings when this person was an outgroup member than an ingroup member. Furthermore, an outgroup member's experience with the ingroup (having lived in Australia) would not make any difference because this person was still not a member of the ingroup. When the comments were positive, such effects were not expected to occur; after all, praise is acceptable no matter what its source!

This is precisely what happened. When the stranger's comments were positive, whether this person was an Australian or not made no difference. But when this person made negative comments, both the speaker and the comments were viewed more negatively when this person was from an outgroup—regardless of degree of experience with

Australia—than when this person was a member of the ingroup. In fact, when criticism of the ingroup is aired in front of an outgroup audience, evaluations of the critic are even worse than if the criticism were voiced to the ingroup only (Hornsey et al., 2005).

THE FAILURE TO SHARE INFORMATION UNIQUE TO EACH MEMBER A second potential source of bias in decision-making groups involves the fact that such groups do not always pool their resources—share information and ideas unique to each member. In fact, research (Gigone & Hastie, 1997; Stasser, 1992) indicates such pooling of resources or information may be the exception rather than the rule. The result: The decisions made by groups tend to reflect the shared information rather than the total information available—such as that which only some group members possess. This is not a problem if the shared information points to the best decision. But consider what happens when information pointing to the best decision is *not* shared by most members. In such cases, the tendency of group members to discuss mainly the information they all already possess may prevent them from reaching the best decision. Consequently, the presence of dissent in groups can be critical; it can lead members to consider nonshared information and this improves decision quality (Schulz-Hardt, Brodbeck, Mojzisch, Kerschreiter, & Frey, 2006; Lu, Yuan, & McLeod, 2012).

BRAINSTORMING: IDEA GENERATION IN GROUPS When groups work on creative tasks together they tend to produce different kinds of solutions than when working alone (Adarves-Yorno, Postmes, & Haslam, 2007). But are they better solutions? In **brainstorming**—a process whereby people meet as a group to generate new ideas—it has generally been assumed that more creative output will emerge than when the same people work as individuals (Stroebe, Diehl, & Abakoumkin, 1992). But in contrast to this expectation, brainstorming does *not* on the whole result in more creative ideas being generated than if the same people worked alone. So why doesn't such a great idea in theory work in practice?

Dugosh and Paulus (2005) investigated both cognitive and social aspects of brainstorming, particularly the effects of idea exposure. This is especially important because the benefits of brainstorming were assumed to result from group members' exposure to others' creativity. These researchers considered whether exposure to common or unique ideas by other group members would result in similar quality ideas being generated by the other participants, as well as whether people engage in social comparison during brainstorming. Some research has suggested that "performance matching" could lead to lowered motivations for idea output, that is, everyone sort of "dumbing down" to conform to a low-output norm. Munkes and Diehl (2003) have suggested, however, that such social comparison ought to result in *competition* and raise the quality of the ideas generated.

Dugosh and Paulus' study tested this idea by having some participants believe that the ideas they were exposed to were selected by a computer from an "idea database," whereas other participants were told that the ideas came from people similar to themselves. First, exposure to a larger quantity of ideas did in fact result in more ideas being generated by participants. Moreover, participants who were led to believe they were being exposed to people-generated ideas, as opposed to computer-selected ideas, produced more high quality ideas—presumably because participants felt the need to be as creative as those "other people."

Nemeth, Personnaz, Personnaz, and Goncalo (2004), point out that dissent or debating competing views are widely valued as stimuli for creative ideas. These researchers gave two different instructions to brainstorming groups: Either traditional brainstorming instructions to just listen without evaluating or instructions encouraging people to debate the merits of ideas. In general, debate instructions produced results superior to traditional instructions. Thus a central tenet of brainstorming, the lack of criticism of new ideas, seems, on balance, to add less in the way of stimulation of idea production, than does the cognitive stimulation provided by dissent and debate.

Key Points

- It is often supposed that groups make worse decisions than individuals. Research findings indicate that groups are subject to **group polarization**, which leads them to make more extreme decisions than individuals; that is, their **decision making** is flawed. This occurs for two reasons: members want to hold views that are more prototypical than others, which means more extreme than average, and because during group discussions members are persuaded by the arguments that other members make and, therefore, they subsequently move their own views in that direction.
- In addition, groups often suffer from **groupthink**—a tendency for highly cohesive groups to assume that they can do no wrong and that information contrary to the group's view should be rejected.
- Groups do tend to reject criticism from outgroup members relative to the identical criticism from ingroup members.

It is also more distressing to hear one's ingroup criticized in front of an outgroup compared to when the audience consists of other ingroup members only.

- Group members often fail to share information during discussion that only some members possess. Instead, discussions tend to focus on the information that all members already know, so the decisions they make tend to reflect this shared information. One way to prevent this is to ensure group members do not know other members' views and what information they have before discussion begins.
- **Brainstorming**—generating ideas in a group without critically evaluating them—does not result in more creativity than individuals producing the ideas on their own. *Debate* about ideas though does tend to stimulate more creative idea production.

11.6: The Role of Leadership in Group Settings

Objective   **Analyze theories to understand leadership in group settings**

Leadership—the very word conjures up images of heroic figures leading their followers toward something better: victory, prosperity, or social justice. But what precisely is **leadership**? Researchers in several different fields have considered this question for decades, and the result is that at present, there is general agreement that leadership involves *influence*—influencing others in a group by establishing a direction for collective effort and then encouraging the activities needed to move in that direction to attain the group's common goals (Yukl, 2006; Turner, 2005; Zaccaro, 2007).

Research on leadership has been part of social psychology for many years (Haslam, Reicher, & Platow, 2010). Here, we will consider three key aspects of the findings on leadership in terms of (1) why some individuals, but not others, become leaders; (2) when nontraditional leaders are most likely to emerge; and (3) how leaders influence group members' satisfaction with their performance.

Why do some people become leaders, but not others? Are some people simply born to lead? Indeed, some famous leaders were born to the job (e.g., Queen Elizabeth I). Others clearly were not: Abraham Lincoln, Nelson Mandela, Adolf Hitler, Bill Gates, Barack Obama, to name a few, all of whom, frankly, came from rather ordinary circumstances. Although leaders tend to reflect dominant majorities in their societies (Chin, 2010), and in the case of the United States that means they have been, historically, white, heterosexual, Protestant males, to explain *which* individual from within those categories becomes a leader, early researchers formulated the *great person* theory of leadership—the view that great leaders possess certain traits that set them apart from other human beings—traits that differentiate them from those who are merely followers.

Early research designed to test this notion was not encouraging. Try as they might, researchers could not come up with a short list of key traits shared by all great leaders (Yukl, 1998). Although the relationships obtained have been consistently weak—generally accounting for less than 5 percent of the variability across people— some attributes do appear to differentiate between leaders and nonleaders. Leaders tend to be slightly more intelligent, socially skilled, open to new experiences, and extroverted than nonleaders (Haslam, 2004; Hogg, 2001). Of course, we cannot know from such studies whether these attributes resulted in those individuals becoming leaders as is assumed, or if experience as a leader resulted in the development of those attributes.

So if leaders and followers cannot be differentiated from one another so easily in terms of the traits they possess, perhaps effective and ineffective leaders can be? Not really. Research seeking to predict U.S. Presidential leader effectiveness has found that Presidents rated effective by historians are more intelligent and they were not involved in scandals compared to those rated ineffective leaders (Simonton, 2009), but otherwise aspects of the context appear to be more important in predicting effectiveness (they were President during war—ensuring there was high national cohesiveness and certainty of the priorities to achieve).

In a sense, there can be no leadership without followers. The importance of followers is given consideration in modern theories of leadership. For instance, experts on leadership (Hackman & Wageman, 2007; Turner, 2005) suggest that leaders and followers are both essential parts of the leadership relationship, and that all theories of leadership should note that *both* play a crucial role and that both exert influence as well as receive it. For this reason, recent research has considered whether some people are more likely to become leader in some contexts (or times), while others emerge as leaders in other contexts. Indeed, a meta-analysis of research assessing the effectiveness of "shared" leadership in teams has found that overall it produces positive effects on attitudes and outcomes (Wang, Waldman, & Zhang, 2014).

In 2012, Barack Obama was elected President of the United States for the second time (see Figure 11.22). What is notable here is that not only was he from an "underrepresented leadership group" but he came to the fore during a period of national crisis. This is precisely the kind of context in which Ryan and Haslam (2005) predict the selection of nontraditional leaders will occur. In a study of appointments of women to CEO positions, Haslam, Ryan, Kulich, Trojanowski, and Atkins (2010) found that women were appointed to these positions when the organization was in crisis and there was a high risk of failure, whereas men were more likely to be appointed when the organization was doing well and the likelihood of failure was low.

In an archival study of appointments to the board of directors in major corporations listed on the London Stock Exchange, Ryan and Haslam (2005) found that when men were appointed, the share price of the company had been relatively stable before the appointment. However, women were appointed to boards of directors only after consistently poor share performance in the months preceding their appointments. These findings were characterized in terms of nontraditional group members being appointed to leadership positions only when a **glass cliff** exists—that is, when the leadership position can be considered precarious or relatively risky because the organization is in crisis. What this research suggests is that being seen as "leader material" may depend more on the "times" than on the "person."

What role do leaders play in enhancing group members' satisfaction with the group and its performance? Research has documented that, for a variety of kinds of groups, having a leader that is seen as prototypical of the group (rather than different from group members) predicts both member satisfaction (Cicero, Pierro, & van Knippenberg, 2007) and perceived leader effectiveness (Fielding & Hogg, 1997). Why does the leader being seen as prototypical of the group have such important consequences? Giessner and van Knippenberg (2008) propose that it is due to its impact on group members' trust in the leader. Sometimes leaders have to make choices that

Figure 11.22 Leaders from Underrepresented Groups Are More Likely to Be Selected in Risky Situations

Barack Obama's successful re-election as U.S. President may be an instance of "underrepresented groups" being selected during precarious or especially risky times. After all, the United States was involved in two wars at the time and was suffering the effects of the immense 2008 financial recession.

all group members do not experience as positive, or as consistent with their own interests. Furthermore, sometimes leader decisions can lead to failure to achieve group goals. But leaders who are seen as prototypical of the group are seen as more likely to take actions that serve the group's interests, and trust in the leader's intentions enables group members to weather such poor outcomes. Giessner and van Knippenberg (2008) found that even when participants knew their leader's decision had resulted in failure to reach an important goal, because the leader who was prototypical of the group was seen as trustworthy, the leader was more likely to be forgiven than when the leader was nonprototypical of the group.

Key Points

- **Leadership** researchers long sought personality characteristics that differentiate leaders from followers. There is evidence that leaders may be somewhat more intelligent and sociable than nonleaders. However, despite its intuitive appeal, traits explain little of the variability and do a poor job differentiating leaders from nonleaders or even effective leaders from ineffective leaders.
- Nontraditional leaders tend to emerge in periods of crisis—which means they can find themselves on **glass cliffs**

where failure is more likely because the situation they are attempting to lead in contains greater risk.
- Leaders that are seen as prototypical of the group (rather than different from other group members) instill greater member satisfaction and perceived leader effectiveness. The greater trust felt in leaders who are prototypical of the group allows group members to weather poor outcomes and forgive the leader for failures relative to leaders who are seen as not prototypical of the group.

Summary and Review

Groups are collections of people who perceive themselves as forming a **cohesive** unit to some degree. Groups have played a critical role in human evolutionary history and often are of great psychological importance to us. In **common-bond groups**, the members tend to be bonded with each other, whereas in **common-identity groups**, members tend to be linked via the category as a whole. The extent to which the group is perceived to form a coherent entity is known as **entitativity**.

Basic aspects of groups involve **status**, **roles**, and **norms**. People achieve high status—position or rank within a group—for many reasons, ranging from physical characteristics (e.g., height), how long they have been members of the group, how prototypical of the group they are, and various aspects of their behavior. To the extent that people internalize their social roles, where those roles are linked to aspects of their self-concept, they can have important implications for behavior and well-being. Being assigned to act as "prisoner" or "guard" in a prison simulation (e.g., the BBC Prison Experiment) resulted in behavioral changes to the extent that people identified with those roles and were guided by the norms associated with them. Group norms—implicit rules about what is appropriate—can affect our emotional expressions and experience through adherence to **feeling rules**. Norms of **individualism** and **collectivism** can affect our willingness to tolerate dissent within groups. **Cohesiveness**—factors that cause people to want to remain members—produces a sense of solidarity among group members. Anxiety about our group's future can encourage actions aimed at strengthening ingroup cohesion.

Joining groups confers important benefits on members, including increased self-knowledge, progress toward important goals, higher status, enhanced sense of control, and the possibility of attaining social change especially if a **politicized collective identity** develops. However, group memberships can also exact important costs, such as loss of personal freedom and heavy demands on time, energy, and resources. The desire to join exclusive and prestigious groups may be so strong that individuals are willing to undergo painful and dangerous initiations in order to become members. Undergoing severe initiation processes to obtain admission in a group frequently increases commitment to that group.

Individuals often withdraw from groups when they feel that the group has changed so much that it no longer reflects their basic values or beliefs. When a group undergoes a **schism**—splintering into distinct factions based on **ideology**—it can produce emotional distress in those who feel compelled to leave. There are different types of dissenters or ingroup critics in groups—individualists and constructive dissenters. Ingroup critics are tolerated more than outgroup critics—the **intergroup sensitivity effect**—because they are seen as having the ingroup's interests at heart.

The mere presence of other people either as an audience or as co-actors can influence our performance on many tasks. Such effects are known as **social facilitation**. The **drive theory of social facilitation** suggests that the presence of others is arousing and can either increase or reduce performance, depending on whether dominant responses in a given situation are correct or incorrect. The **distraction conflict theory** suggests that the presence of others induces conflicting tendencies to focus on the task being performed and on an audience or co-actors. This can result both in increased arousal and narrowed attentional focus, explaining why social facilitation occurs in many species. The **evaluation apprehension** view suggests that an audience disrupts our performance because we are concerned about their evaluation of us.

When individuals work together on a task, **social loafing**—reduced output by each group member—sometimes occurs, especially on **additive tasks** where member contributions are combined. Social loafing can be reduced in several ways: by making outputs individually identifiable, increasing commitment to the task and task importance, and ensuring that each member's contributions to the task are unique.

Being part of a large crowd has been stereotyped as inducing **hooliganism**—violent and antisocial incidents—due to the presumed reduction in self-awareness that occurs with **deindividuation**. Contrary to this idea, anonymity in a crowd actually induces more normative or conforming behavior. The norms operating in some crowds may be changed, and the likelihood of violence reduced. Deindividuation can intensify *either* aggressive or prosocial behavior, depending on what norms are operating in a particular crowd context.

Cooperation—working together with others to obtain shared goals—is a common aspect of social life. However, cooperation does not develop in many situations where it is possible especially under conditions of **negative interdependence**. When there is a lack of **social embeddedness** where the reputation of others is unknown, being able to communicate about past performance can increase cooperation. Situations involving **social dilemmas**, where individuals can increase their own gains at the expense of the other, are used to study the development of trust and distrust. Sanctioning for noncooperation can decrease people's trust in the other and thereby undermine their subsequent willingness to cooperate.

Conflict is a process that begins when individuals or groups perceive that others have interests that are incompatible with their own, and *faulty attributions* are made. Members of different cultural groups respond differently to feeling misunderstood by others. Conflict can be reduced in many ways, but **bargaining** and the induction of **superordinate goals** seem to be most effective.

Individuals wish to be treated fairly by the groups to which they belong. Fairness can be judged in terms of outcomes (**distributive justice**), in terms of procedures (**procedural justice**), or in terms of courteous treatment (**transactional justice**). When individuals feel that they have been treated disrespectfully, they may be willing to engage in socially deviant actions.

Research findings indicate that groups are often subject to **group polarization** which leads them to make more extreme decisions than individuals. This occurs for two reasons: group members want to be "good" group members, which, in practice, means holding views that are prototypical of the group, and members are influenced by the group's discussion which tends to focus on arguments that favor the group's initial preference. In addition, groups often suffer from **groupthink**—a tendency

to assume that they can't be wrong and that information contrary to the group's view should be rejected. Groups do tend to reject criticism from outgroup members relative to identical criticism from ingroup members. Groups often fail to share information that only some members possess and this can lead to biased decisions.

People tend to believe that **brainstorming**—where people attempt to generate new ideas in a group—will be more effective than individuals working alone. Research illustrates that this is generally not true. In fact, dissent and debate in group discussions tends to produce more creative ideas.

The great person theory of leadership suggested that leaders and nonleaders have different traits. This largely turns out not to be the case. Nontraditional leaders often emerge during times of crisis—**the glass cliff**—conditions that carry a greater risk of failure. Leaders who are seen as prototypical of their group are perceived as more effective, and even when they fail they are more likely to be forgiven because they are seen as more trustworthy than leaders who are nonprototypical of the group.

Chapter 12
Dealing with Adversity and Achieving a Happy Life

Chapter Overview

Learning Objectives

12.1 Examine how social causes lead to physical and psychological ailments

12.2 Identify social and individual strategies that help alleviate the harmful effects of stress

12.3 Describe the sources of errors and biases that have to be overcome in order to make the legal system fair

12.4 Describe the influences on our happiness and explain how happiness can be increased

"What does not kill me makes me stronger."

Friedrich Nietzsche (1889)

Life is not always easy. Most of us experience various forms of adversity—rejections, disappointments, obstacles, and defeats. These difficulties may take the form of a low grade on an important exam, the painful break-up of a relationship, bad news about the health of a relative, failure to receive an important promotion, rejection from a sports team you badly wanted to join, or feeling unwelcome in a new environment. The list of potential forms of adversity we might face is seemingly endless.

Yet it is also the case that life offers us a wealth of positive events and experiences—times when we enjoy great happiness as a result of feeling loved and included by others. There is also the sense of excitement or satisfaction that comes from many experiences, such as winning a scholarship, receiving unexpected good news, knowing someone believes in us, or achieving an athletic feat that few others do. So, it is fair to say that life has highs and lows, and plenty in between. Although it is certainly the case that most of us seek and expect to be happy, how to achieve it is not always so obvious.

In this chapter, we describe what the science of "happiness" tells us about how people overcome adversities and go on to enjoy lives that are not only happy but meaningful, too. Let's first consider the example of someone famous who overcame considerable adversity in her early life to ultimately become the first Latina Justice on the U.S. Supreme Court— Sonia Sotomayor (see Figure 12.1).

In her recent memoir, Justice Sotomayor candidly describes her journey from a crime-infested New York housing project to the highest court in the land (Sotomayor, 2014). Her journey involved overcoming numerous difficulties: Parents whose troubled marriage produced lots of conflict at home; an alcoholic father who died young, leaving the family in poverty; her development of childhood diabetes; plenty of ethnic and gender discrimination; and her own painful divorce.

Many aspects of the journey she describes are noteworthy. So, too, are the strategies she employed to make her life a happy one. Such ingredients for a happy life include counting her blessings, even for the negative experiences that helped shape who she is today. She describes the valuable support and direction she received from both her mother and her grandmother, particularly in terms of their emphasis on education and preparation for lifelong employment. She also describes numerous professional mentors who helped with problems and obstacles in achieving her legal and judicial career.

Figure 12.1 Success in Spite of Adversity

Sonia Sotomayor, the daughter of Puerto Rican immigrants, grew up in a New York housing project. In spite of social, family, and health challenges, she became the first Latina Supreme Court Justice in U.S. history.

Ultimately, her optimism was stronger than the adversity she faced. As Judge Sotomayor writes in her book's preface, "People who live in difficult circumstances need to know that happy endings are possible." She goes on to write, "You cannot value dreams according to the odds of their coming true. Their real value is in stirring within us the will to aspire."

Social psychological research has played an important role in identifying strategies for handling the setbacks people experience, revealing what it takes to become flourishing and happy people. If carefully applied, the messages of this research can help us turn adversity into strength and achievement. In this chapter, we will provide an overview of some of the important ways in which social psychology—with its scientific approach to the social side of life—can help us attain better health by reducing the harmful effects of stress. We will closely examine research from "a social cure" perspective—with its concrete steps that individuals can take to cope with loneliness and build enduring and satisfying relationships (Jetten, Haslam, Haslam, & Branscombe, 2009).

After that, we will consider the contributions of social psychology to an important goal: making our legal system more open, fair, and effective—a major goal that inspired Justice Sotomayor. As it exists now, the legal system in the United States, as well as those in many other countries, has flaws and tendencies that sometimes prevent fair and impartial justice. The goal of research by social psychologists working on such issues is straightforward: Ensuring the legal system is one that protects human rights and enables all people to have equal opportunity for attaining "life, liberty, and the pursuit of happiness."

We will then address the major ingredients that play a role in increasing happiness and explore how happiness confers advantages on the people who attain it. Some of the questions we will consider are: Can people be too happy? What roles do culture and age play in defining the meaning of happiness? What do we know about how the happiness of people in different nations can be improved? And, what can we do to make ourselves happier individuals, and satisfied with what we have and the choices we have made? In short, this chapter describes social psychological knowledge that can help you in your quest to build the happy and fulfilling life we all seek.

12.1: Social Sources of Stress and Their Effects on Personal Well-Being

Objective **Examine how social causes lead to physical and psychological ailments**

Have you ever felt that you were at the edge of being overwhelmed by negative events or by pressures in your life? If so, you are already quite familiar with **stress**: our response to events that disrupt, or threaten to disrupt, our physical or psychological functioning (Lazarus & Folkman, 1984; Taylor, 2002). Unfortunately, stress is a common part of modern life—few of us can avoid it altogether. For this reason, and because it seems to exert negative effects on both physical health and psychological well-being, we describe some of the major contributions made by social psychologists to our understanding of stress and how we cope with it.

12.1.1: The Impact of Social Relationships on Health

What are the major sources of stress in our lives? Unfortunately, the list is a very long one: Many conditions and events can add to our total "stress quotient." Among the most important of these, though, are life events related to our relationships with other people (e.g., the death of a loved one, a painful divorce, being excluded from important life arenas as a result of discrimination, childhood neglect, exposure to and experience of violence). It is clear that the effects of such social stressors can be devastating and long-lasting (McInnis, McQuaid, Matheson, & Anisman, 2015). In fact, existing evidence indicates that people who experience high levels of stress are more likely to become seriously ill than those who do not. Overall, stress is a key contributing factor to a very wide range of psychological and physical health problems (Blackburn & Epel, 2012; Cohen et al., 1998; Cohen & Janicki-Deverts, 2009).

Although major life events can be traumatic and deeply disturbing, they are not the only social causes of stress in our lives. In fact, the minor annoyances of daily life—often termed **hassles**—are also important, making up for their relatively low intensity by their much higher frequency. The findings of several studies by Lazarus and his colleagues (e.g., DeLongis, Folkman, & Lazarus, 1988; Lazarus, Opton, Nomikos, & Rankin, 1985) suggest that daily hassles are an important cause of stress. These researchers developed a *Hassles Scale* on which individuals indicate the extent to which they have felt "hassled" by common events during the past month. The items included in this scale deal with a wide range of everyday events, such as having too many things to do at once, misplacing or losing things, troublesome neighbors or roommates, and concerns over money. While such events may seem relatively minor, they can be cumulatively quite important. When scores on the Hassles Scale are related to reports of psychological symptoms, strong correlations are obtained (Lazarus et al., 1985). In short, the more stress people report as a result of daily hassles, the poorer their psychological well-being.

HOW DOES STRESS AFFECT HEALTH?   The evidence that stress exerts harmful effects on both psychological and physical health is overwhelming. But *how* does stress produce these effects? While the precise mechanisms involved are the subject of ongoing research, growing evidence suggests that the process goes something like this: by draining our resources and inducing negative affect, stress upsets our complex internal chemistry. Chronic stress stemming from physical abuse, unemployment, or death of a family member can be measured at the cellular level in terms of decreased *telomere* size, which is the protective cap at the end of our chromosomes found in every cell. Reduction in telomere size is a strong predictor of several immune-related aging diseases and mortality (Epel et al., 2004; Kiecolt-Glaser et al., 2011).

We know that stress interferes with efficient operation of our *immune system*—the mechanism through which our bodies recognize and destroy potentially harmful substances and intruders such as bacteria, viruses, and cancerous cells. When functioning normally, the immune system is nothing short of amazing. Each day it removes many potential threats to our health. Yet, prolonged exposure to stress disrupts this system. Chronic exposure to stress can reduce circulating levels of *lymphocytes* (white blood cells that fight infection and disease) and increase levels of the hormone *cortisol*, a substance that suppresses immune system functioning (Kemeny, 2003). These findings indicate that stress does indeed weaken our immune systems, leaving us more vulnerable to a wide range of illnesses.

Overall, research findings support a stress model that involves both direct and indirect harmful effects. Direct effects, as described earlier, weaken our immune system and also harm other bodily functions. Indirect effects of stress influence the lifestyles we adopt. Stress can encourage behaviors that can provide immediate pleasure but have long-term health risks (e.g., smoking, alcohol use). In a representative sample of Americans, evidence for a link between stress and unhealthy behavior was found, especially among low-income individuals (Krueger & Chang, 2008).

Likewise, stress has been associated with reductions in factors that are protective of health (e.g., less sleep and fitness-related exercise behavior). In the case of American teenagers, such findings are especially alarming since these young people do not typically perceive stress as having any impact on their physical health (American Psychological Association Survey, 2014). While the model shown in Figure 12.2 may not include all the potential ways that stress can affect our health, it offers a useful overview of several routes by which stress effects can arise.

Figure 12.2 How Stress Harms Our Health

Stress harms health in many ways. It weakens our immune system and harms other key systems within our bodies. In addition, stress can lead us to adopt potentially harmful lifestyles—for instance, overeating, smoking, or alcohol use. At the same time, stress can reduce our tendency to adopt positive long-term strategies, such as participating in exercise programs and obtaining social support.

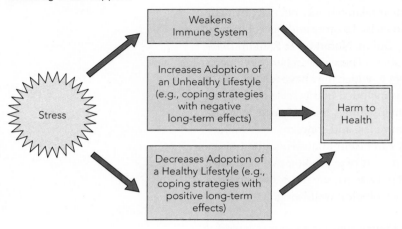

WHY RELATIONSHIPS MATTER: THE BENEFITS OF SOCIAL SUPPORT Since stress is an inescapable part of life, the key task we face is not trying to eliminate it, but rather to *cope* with it effectively—in ways that reduce its adverse effects. Direct coping with stress can entail seeking **social support**—drawing on the emotional resources provided by friends, family members, and people with whom we work. More specifically, social support refers to the perception or experience that one is cared for by others, is valued and esteemed, and is part of a social network of mutual assistance (Taylor et al., 2010).

Research findings indicate that social support can be a highly effective means of protecting our health from the ravages of stress (House, Landis, & Umberson, 1988). In fact, the availability of social support has been found to reduce psychological distress, including depression and anxiety, and to promote better adjustment to high levels of stress that are chronic—ones that continue over time (Taylor, 2007). In one revealing study, Brown and her colleagues (2003) examined the effects that giving social support had on mortality rates. In a sample of 846 elderly people, participants who reported providing high levels of support to others (friends, relatives, neighbors) were significantly less likely to die over a 5-year period than participants who provided little or no support to others.

But you don't have to have contact with another person to experience health benefits. As shown in Figure 12.3, *therapy* or *companion animals* (commonly dogs) are utilized in many different settings, including hospitals, retirement centers, schools,

Figure 12.3 Animals Can Help Reduce Stress

Dogs and other animals are brought to hospitals, retirement homes, and other locations to help reduce people's stress and feelings of isolation—a strategy that has been shown to be very effective in improving health and well-being.

prisons, and homes. Results have been very positive: Playing with, caring for, or simply holding these "therapist animals" has been found to significantly reduce stress (Griffin, McCune, Maholmes, & Hurley, 2011).

Such beneficial effects of pets were illustrated in a study by Allen, Shykoff, and Izzo (2001). The participants were stockbrokers who lived alone and described their work as very stressful; all of them had high blood pressure. Participants were randomly selected to receive a pet cat or dog from an animal shelter, or to not receive a pet. Results indicated that the pets were an excellent source of social support, significantly reducing stress among those who received them. In fact, when exposed to high levels of stress, participants who acquired pets cut their blood pressure elevation by half compared to those who did not receive pets. Why are animals so effective in this regard? One possibility is that pets provide nonjudgmental social support. Another possibility is that the responsibility of caring for a pet is a form of prosocial giving, which is predictive of improvements in well-being (Dunn, Aknin, & Norton, 2014).

CONSEQUENCES OF BEING LONELY Most of us experience feelings of loneliness at some time in our lives. It can happen when we go somewhere new such as attending university far from home, or even visiting a foreign country where we may have trouble communicating with others in a different language. Social psychologists define **loneliness** as a state that involves emotional and cognitive reactions to having fewer and less satisfying relationships than an individual desires (Archibald, Bartholomew, & Marx, 1995).

Fortunately, for most of us, loneliness is a temporary state. As we will soon see, the groups we belong to not only help prevent us from feeling isolated but also have beneficial effects on our physical and psychological well-being (Jetten et al., 2015). For some people, of course, social isolation is a choice. They prefer to live their lives without any close ties to others (Burger, 1995), and as a result, they don't feel deprived of social contact. But many others lead lives of isolation and experience loneliness not by choice, but because they have not been successful in forming bonds with others, or because their social ties have been severed (divorce, relocation, death of loved ones). In other words, they experience involuntary loneliness. In short, loneliness is an all-too-common source of social stress, occurring in many cultures all around the world (Goodwin, Cook, & Young, 2001; Rokach & Neto, 2000; Shams, 2001).

As shown in Figure 12.4, loneliness is unpleasant. The negative feelings it involves include depression, anxiety, pessimism about the future, self-blame, and shyness (Anderson, Miller, Riger, Dill, & Sedikides, 1994; Jackson, Soderlind, & Weiss, 2000; Jones, Carpenter, & Quintana, 1985). Not surprisingly, people who feel lonely tend to spend their leisure time in solitary activities, have very few connections that are important to them, and have only casual friends or acquaintances (Berg & McQuinn, 1989). Lonely individuals often feel left out and believe they have very little in common with those they meet (Bell, 1993). However, even if a child has only *one* close friend, that is enough to reduce feelings of loneliness (Asher & Paquette, 2003).

Loneliness is associated with poor health (Cacioppo, Hughes, Waite, Hawkley, & Thisted, 2006; Hawkley, Burleson, Berntson, & Cacioppo, 2003). In one study, Jetten and colleagues (2010) studied first-year students at a university for several months, both before they came to the university and afterward. Students completed several measures of well-being and also reported on the number of groups to which they belonged before coming to campus. Results indicated that the more groups they belonged to, the less likely they were to become depressed when they moved to this new environment. In short, membership in many groups buffered them against the high levels of stress freshmen generally encounter. Additional studies with elderly people (Haslam, Cruwys, & Haslam, 2014) indicate that the more groups to which they belong—or even, the more groups to which they *believe* they belong—the healthier they feel. Overall, then, it seems clear that *not* belonging to groups (*not* being socially connected) is a key component of loneliness with negative effects on health.

Figure 12.4 Loneliness: Alone, But Not by Choice

Although some people may choose to be alone, a much greater number are alone not by choice, but because they lack close relationships with others. This typically leads to unpleasant, and sometimes intense, feelings of loneliness.

12.1.2: How Self-Views Affect Outcomes

The way you view yourself, including what you think about your abilities and your role in society, can influence the way that stressful circumstances or events affect your life over the long term. In other words, all of us experience the negative effects of stress, but how we choose to respond to adversity can make a big difference in life outcomes. We will next explore how self-views and attitudes toward change factor into our choices and well-being.

THE IMPORTANCE OF BELIEVING WE CAN CHANGE If we experience repeated rejection that results in chronic loneliness, our conceptions of ourselves can be negatively affected. That is, when we experience rejection as stemming from something that we see as reflecting "who we really are," then psychological recovery from that rejection may be more difficult.

People differ in the extent to which they believe they can change or the extent to which their attributes—both abilities and personality—are malleable or fixed (Dweck & Legget, 1988). Individuals who see themselves as "entities" with fixed traits are inclined to cut themselves off from others if they experience a rejection and see it as predicting future negative experiences with others. They also see themselves as unable to change and grow or learn from such unfortunate experiences with others.

In contrast, people who see themselves as "a work in progress," or have an incremental theory of the self as capable of growing and changing as a result of experience, are less likely to direct negative emotion toward themselves following rejection. They tend to experience less fear of recurring rejection in the future. They are also more likely to feel less need to hide their rejection experiences because they see them as an opportunity for self-growth.

To test these ideas concerning how the self is defined during recovery from rejection, Howe and Dweck (2016) conducted several studies. In some studies, they first measured individuals' theories about whether people can change (assessing the extent to which they held an incremental theory), or whether there are basic things about themselves that can't be changed much (assessing the extent to which they subscribed to an entity theory).

Next, these researchers asked participants to recall a time when they were rejected by another person. Participants were asked to indicate the extent to which they perceived the rejection as relevant to their self-definition (e.g., "I worry that there is something 'wrong' with me because I got rejected"), and whether they feared this kind of rejection in the future. Lastly, they assessed participants' emotions when they thought about the rejection (e.g., ashamed, dissatisfied with myself). Howe and Dweck found that people who perceived themselves as a relatively fixed entity reported that the rejection made them redefine themselves as having something wrong with them. In turn, this made them fear a recurrence of rejection and more feelings of shame.

Additional studies by Howe and Dweck (2016) further assessed the effect of rejection among participants with entity self-definitions versus incremental self-definitions. Effects were measured more extensively in terms of the degree in which participants saw rejection as "revealing who I truly am" and "worrying that I am unlikable." Results revealed that such experienced rejection was associated with "putting up walls" to protect the self. Figure 12.5 illustrates the processes and implications for future behavior when rejection is experienced by people who see themselves as an unchanging entity, as opposed to being malleable.

Other studies by Howe and Dweck (2016) experimentally influenced some people to think of themselves as having "set qualities" (e.g., an entity theory) and others to see those same qualities as changeable at any point in a person's life (e.g., an incremental theory). Results showed that this experimental intervention had an effect on participants' responses to rejection. Participants who thought of themselves as a fixed entity attributed rejection to their unlikable self. In contrast, those who thought of themselves as able to change did not anticipate rejection as likely in their future. This work is important in showing how changes in people's beliefs about personality—as not being "set," but capable of change—can help people to avoid closing themselves off following rejection and instead see it as an opportunity for future growth.

SELF-CHANGE BELIEFS CAN HELP US WEATHER ADVERSITY People who are making transitions in life—changing schools or jobs, moving from high school to university, immigrating to a new country—are most susceptible to loneliness. Interventions that encourage people to believe they have the potential to change, and weather adversities may help prevent depression at transitional life points. Research has shown that believing intelligence is malleable—that "smartness" is not a fixed

---

Figure 12.5 When the Self Can't Change, Rejection Has Lasting Consequences

People who see themselves as "fixed" experience rejection as reflecting something fundamental about themselves. As a result, they fear future rejection, put up "walls" to prevent others from getting close, and feel ashamed. In contrast, when the self is seen as changeable, rejection has less implications for the future and is often seen as an opportunity for growth.

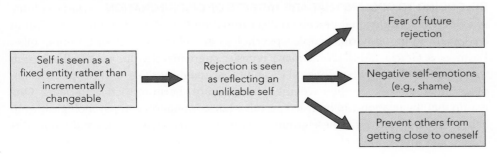

trait—increases student persistence in school and improves academic achievement (Yeager & Dweck, 2012). In light of this evidence, interventions related to self-change might also improve students' well-being during the transition to high school—a time of great social uncertainty and unstable peer relationships.

To test this idea, students in California who were in their first few weeks of high school indicated on a survey whether they had experienced adversities in their interactions with peers, including verbal or physical aggression. They also completed a measure of depressive symptoms (Miu & Yeager, 2015). One week later, students were randomly assigned into intervention and control groups. In the *people are malleable* group, the students were given scientific evidence that "if you are excluded or victimized, it is not due to a fixed, personal deficiency on your part; and people who exclude or victimize you are not fixed, bad people but, instead, have complicated motivations that are subject to change" (p. 731). In the control group, students were given information about the malleability of athletic ability, but no mention of exclusion or victimization was made.

Evidence showed that students had correctly learned the information taught in the intervention, as indicated by coding the students' written summary of the lesson given to them. In fact, this single intervention concerning the changeability of aggressors and victims was shown to be effective in preventing depression among these vulnerable students. Nine months after the "people can change" intervention had occurred, the 600 adolescents in this study had 40 percent lower incidence of clinical depression symptoms. Effects on self-esteem and negative moods were similarly positive in the intervention group compared to the control group. This work powerfully demonstrates that believing that negative events can improve is a simple and effective means of creating resilience in the face of stress.

12.1.3: The Struggle to "Belong"

If, as existing evidence strongly suggests, loneliness is harmful to our physical and psychological well-being (Hawkley, Thisted, Masi, & Cacioppo, 2010), then it is even more important that people realize the importance of forming and maintaining social relationships with others. Many kinds of relationships can fulfill our need for being connected to others—friends, romantic partners, family, neighbors, work colleagues, to mention just a few. These relationships also help us establish a clear social identity so we know where we fit in.

Consider, for example, individuals who join religious organizations that require them to isolate themselves from society or may specifically forbid them from marrying (e.g., priests and nuns in the Catholic Church). These individuals can fill their need to "belong" through their relationship with their church and the roles they fill within it, even though they don't join many other groups and don't form romantic relationships. Other people identify closely with organizations for which they work or professions to which they belong and fulfill their need to feel socially connected in this way. What's basic to not feeling lonely is having social connections, which may involve joining social groups. Such connections do *not* have to take the form of romantic relationships.

BELONGING TO GROUPS THAT ARE TARGETS OF DISCRIMINATION A large volume of evidence indicates that perceived discrimination that stems from membership in a stigmatized group harms people's psychological well-being (Schmitt, Branscombe, Postmes, & Garcia, 2014). Of the many types of stigmatized groups studied, research indicates that those with a physical disability, sexual minorities, and people who are discriminated based on their weight suffer the most harm to their well-being. One reason that the relationship between perceived discrimination and psychological well-being is most negative for these groups (compared to racial minorities and women) is that the discrimination and exclusion they experience often comes from people who might otherwise provide social support.

For example, among sexual minorities, perceived discrimination is associated with strained relationships between family members and friends, and predicts increased loneliness (Doyle & Molix, 2015). For people with disabilities, the exclusion they experience may be especially pervasive across situations and isolation due to their geographical dispersion is likely. For instance, disabled people are often the only person in their family, school, or community with a disability. As such, they may find it difficult to connect with others who share their condition. Without these social connections, it is hard to develop a sense of belonging in order to combat the discrimination experienced (Branscombe, Fernández, Gómez, & Cronin, 2011; Nario-Redmond, Noel, & Fern, 2013).

CONSEQUENCES OF WEIGHT DISCRIMINATION Around the globe, the percentage of people who substantially exceed their ideal weight is increasing (King, 2013). In fact, it is estimated that in the United States 66 percent of people exceed their ideal weight. Since obesity is increasing—but the acceptance of it is not—the implications for psychological and physical health are potentially substantial. First, consider social norms concerning weight: "Thin" is definitely "in," and most people report that they want to weigh less than they do. This means that discrimination against people based on their weight may be widely perceived as legitimate. As a result, discrimination may be perpetrated by both strangers and loved ones who would otherwise be sources of social support (Crandall, 1995).

Although being overweight is a risk factor for a variety of diseases (e.g., diabetes, hypertension), recent research addressed the question of whether "the stigma associated with being overweight is more harmful than actually being overweight" (Sutin, Stephan, & Terracciano, 2015, p. 1807). The researchers analyzed a large, nationally representative longitudinal survey of Americans, started in 2004 and completed in 2012. As a measure of discrimination, respondents were asked whether they were "treated with less courtesy or respect than other people" based on their weight. In addition, actual body mass index information (i.e., weight) was assessed, and numerous demographic (gender, race, age) and relevant health variables (e.g., smoking, exercise, depression) were obtained. Then, the crucial variable of mortality (death rates) was determined.

The results indicated that even after accounting for other risk factors, people who reported experiencing discrimination based on their weight had a shorter life expectancy (higher mortality) than those who were not routinely disrespected because of their weight. These potentially serious consequences of experiencing weight discrimination indicate that counteracting the "antifat" stigma is critical. The National Association to Advance Fat Acceptance (NAAFA) is a nonprofit organization doing its part to counteract size discrimination and improve the well-being of overweight people. NAAFA uses public education to promote equality and provides support to those who are experiencing discrimination (see Figure 12.6).

Figure 12.6 Providing a Safe Haven in an Antifat World

The National Association to Advance Fat Acceptance is a civil rights organization that aims to counter the stigma and discrimination that is directed toward people based on their weight. Given the severe psychological and physical health consequences of experiencing discrimination and exclusion based on weight, this organization attempts to be a safe haven in society where the "thin is beautiful" norm is pervasive.

Key Points

- **Stress** is a contributing factor to psychological and physical health problems. It often stems from and affects our relationships with other people. Stress interferes with the operation of the body's *immune system* by reducing *lymphocytes* and increasing *cortisol*. Chronic stress can also be measured at the cellular level—reduced *telomere* size is a strong predictor of disease and mortality.

- Daily **hassles**, which tend to be lower intensity but higher in frequency, are another form of stress. The higher a person scores on the *Hassles Scale*, the more he or she is at risk for developing stress-related illnesses.

- Stress can be directly coped with by seeking **social support**—emotional resources provided by people who care about us—which helps to reduce psychological distress. Spending time with *therapy* or *companion animals*, or our own pets, is another aid in reducing stress.

- **Loneliness** occurs when a person has fewer and less satisfying relationships than desired. A lack of social connections has negative effects on health. Negative consequences associated with loneliness include depression, anxiety, self-blame, and a lower life expectancy.

- When people believe their personality is "fixed" and cannot change, they are likely to react to rejection by cutting themselves off from others to avoid future negative experiences. But for people who see themselves as capable of change, rejection experiences are more likely to be construed as an opportunity for growth.

- Interventions related to self-change can help improve people's resilience in the face of stress. Vulnerable students entering high school who were given a "people are malleable" intervention showed a substantial reduction in depression 9 months later, compared to students in the control group.

- When people experience discrimination based on disability, sexual minorities, and weight, the discrimination is associated with harm to well-being. One reason is that the discrimination often comes from those who would normally be expected to provide social support. Weight discrimination, even controlling for other risk factors, predicts mortality.

12.2: Social Tactics for Decreasing the Harmful Effects of Stress

Objective **Identify social and individual strategies that help alleviate the harmful effects of stress**

While there are many ways to lower stress and improve well-being, two areas of particular interest to social psychologists are related to social groups and self-acceptance. In this section, we will first examine the use of social groups to manage stress through exercise, social identification, and other coping mechanisms. Later, we will take a look at the important issue of learning to accept ourselves—a condition needed to thrive.

12.2.1: Using Social Groups to Improve Health

One important means of managing stress and improving both mental and physical health in adults is regular physical exercise (Biddle & Mutrie, 2008; Colcombe & Kramer, 2003; Singh, Clements, & Singh, 2001). Yet maintaining the motivation to participate in regular exercise is a major obstacle to attaining those benefits. The role of social support, in terms of accessing and connecting with others in our social networks, may be crucial to achieving adherence to an exercise regime. Two major meta-analytic reviews of the effects of exercise interventions on health have found that exercise in groups—especially groups that induce a sense of shared identity among participants—produces more positive outcomes than exercise interventions delivered individually (Burke, Carron, Eys, Ntoumanis, & Estabrooks, 2006; Dishman & Buckworth, 1996).

To benefit from exercising with others, we don't need to be face-to-face. Technology such as Fitbit and other activity trackers may serve the same social purposes to keep people motivated and improving to the extent they increase or continue exercising (see Figure 12.7). One study (Duus & Cooray, 2015) found that a substantial number of Fitbit users came to see the device as "part of themselves"—they stopped

Figure 12.7 Exercising with Others, Face-to-Face or Virtually

Use of Fitbit and other activity tracking devices can encourage people to increase their exercise to meet their own goals. By linking individuals with others through technology, these devices may encourage motivation to continue exercising and thereby improve happiness.

perceiving it as just external technology. Fitbit users compared their activity rates with others using the device. Most people reported using it to increase their daily steps and overall amount of weekly exercise. The social element of being able to cheer on other Fitbit users after seeing their step counts was perceived as encouraging their own activity levels. Furthermore, by reaching daily targets, virtually all users in this study reported that their happiness and motivation increased. Nonetheless, some people felt that wearing the device made them feel controlled by it. They also reported perceiving the Fitbit as an "enemy" because it made them feel guilty for not achieving their goals.

12.2.2: Social Identification as a Means for Managing Stress

Some people in highly stressful occupations (e.g., firefighters, pilots, military personnel) find the social groups they belong to can influence how much stress they are likely to experience and how they respond to stressful situations. How might identifying with others who share one's stressful occupation help people to deal with the strain they experience on the job? Research by Haslam, O'Brien, Jetten, Vormedal, and Penna (2011) investigated this question with a sample of British air force bomb disposal experts. In this case, identifying with their work group was associated with lower levels of stress (burnout) and higher levels of job satisfaction. As a result of perceiving their fellow workers as lending them social support, it served as a buffer against the very real and adverse forms of stress experienced in this job.

Social identification, which is the psychological vehicle through which "I" is translated into "us," can allow people to feel they have control in stressful situations that might otherwise be absent. Indeed, being part of a group allows us to achieve goals that we could not possibly accomplish alone. Perceiving we have control over and are able to influence events that happen to us is strongly predictive of well-being (Langer & Rodin, 1976) and reduces biological stress reactions (Dickerson & Kemeny, 2004). Identifying with one's community might provide people with a sense of control over their way of life and through this achieve greater life satisfaction. To test this idea, Greenaway et al. (2015) analyzed community identification, perceived personal control, and life satisfaction among 62,000 participants in 47 countries, while controlling for a variety of demographic variables. As expected, these researchers found that greater community identification was associated with higher life satisfaction through increased perceived personal control.

Does identifying with a social group help people maintain a sense of perceived control and enhance their well-being even when the group experiences a stressful event? Greenaway et al. (2015) analyzed responses among Democrats and Republicans in the United States following the 2012 Presidential election. The researchers wanted to know if identification with a political group would serve as a psychological resource and protect well-being only when the group was successful (i.e., among Democrats following an election win), or if the group could do so even when it suffered a setback (i.e., among Republicans after an election loss). The findings revealed that regardless of political party membership (i.e., results were the same for both Republicans and Democrats), people who identified more with their political party reported higher life satisfaction. This resulted from the greater sense of perceived personal control they felt over their lives.

So, can joining groups, as a means of fostering social connectedness, help to prevent depression? Using a large nationally representative sample in Britain, Cruwys et al. (2013) found that people who belonged to more groups were less likely to develop depression. With each new group membership added by an individual over a 4-year period, the individual's risk of depression declined by 24 percent.

To determine what it is about social identities that prevents depressive symptoms, Cruwys, South, Greenaway, and Haslam (2015) first randomly assigned students to one of the following: (a) Write about one group you are a member of, and why it is an important part of who you are; (b) list three groups you are a member of and write why each of those groups are an important part of who you are; or (c) a control condition with no writing reflection task. Then, all participants in the study were asked to engage in an unsolvable problem task. Afterward they all received a score of zero indicating they had failed. Negative emotion symptoms were then assessed, as was the participants' tendency to make depression-related attributions for failure (e.g., "when bad things happen I think it is my fault").

Depressive attributions (such as "failure reflects something stable and negative about me") and negative emotions were significantly lower in the social identity salient conditions compared to the control condition. Merely thinking about groups (either one or three) that they belonged to, and that were important to them, undermined depressive attributions. This, in turn, protected participants from experiencing depressive emotional symptoms following a failure experience. This research is important because it demonstrates how groups and the identities we derive from membership in them can affect how we think about stressful events that happen to us. In this way, they serve to protect our psychological well-being.

Many veterans who served in the military have returned home suffering from what is known as **post-traumatic stress disorder (PTSD)**, a psychological condition caused by experiencing or witnessing extremely frightening, often life-threatening, events. Social support is a key factor in helping these veterans cope with PTSD. See the **"What Research Tells Us...About Reducing Post-Traumatic Stress Among Veterans"** feature for more information about this condition and the social tactics used to deal with it.

12.2.3: Accepting Ourselves

To perform well and manage the stress of new challenges, students entering college need to realize that they may feel uncertain about whether they belong in this new environment. They may also worry about whether they can "measure up," particularly students from under-represented groups (e.g., first-generation college students, members of ethnic minorities). Students from such under-represented groups may be tempted to wonder if universities "value people like them."

To the extent that students' concerns can be alleviated, stress can be lowered and mental health improved (Walton & Cohen, 2011). For example, simply learning that

What Research Tells Us About…

Reducing Post-Traumatic Stress Among Veterans

When veterans return from active duty—usually from wars being waged far from home—they are typically happy to be back and seek to resume their normal lives (see Figure 12.8). Unfortunately, this is often not as easy as it sounds. As a result of the terrible and often life-threatening experiences they had, veterans often experience a serious psychological disturbance known as **post-traumatic stress disorder (PTSD).** Symptoms of PTSD include flashbacks—repeatedly imagining the traumatic situations they experienced and hyperarousal—being easily startled and the inability to concentrate on tasks because of intense emotional feelings.

Clearly, such feelings and memories can make it difficult for sufferers of PTSD to successfully adjust to their return. Recent research with American veterans returning from Iraq with mild traumatic brain injuries has found that the extent of their PTSD symptoms is a strong predictor of their satisfaction with life (Travis Seidl et al., 2015). What can be done to help these veterans recover their health and well-being? Research by social psychologists offers some answers (Romero, Riggs, & Ruggero, 2015).

The coping style that veterans adopt—how they seek to reduce or control their stress—plays a key role. Avoidant coping, in which they attempt to deny or minimize their feelings, is counterproductive. The more they engage in avoidant behavior, the worse the PTSD effects become on their health. Another coping style, problem-focused, has been found to reduce stress in many situations, but by itself does not do so in PTSD cases. Rather, support from family members, when combined with a problem-focused approach, is central to stress reduction (Romero et al., 2015). In others words, when family members help veterans cope with the stress of their symptoms—vivid memories/nightmares of past traumatic events, "jumpiness" and easy excitability—improvement can be made.

Research findings indicate that a particular approach to managing traumatic memories can help reduce the physiological arousal often reported among veterans with PTSD. In one study, veterans with PTSD were randomly assigned to recall their worst traumatic experience either "as if it were happening to you all over again" (the immersed condition) or "to move away from the situation and watch it unfold from a distance and see yourself in the event" (the distanced condition). Physiological reactivity—measured in terms of heart rate and skin conductance—was significantly reduced in the distanced condition compared to the immersed condition (Wisco et al., 2015). However, the negative emotions experienced following the trauma recall remained high in both conditions. This suggests that some treatments are successful in dealing with traumatic memories, while other treatments are needed for improving overall well-being.

Further evidence for the critical role of social support from family members during psychological adjustment emerged from

Figure 12.8 Social Support Is Important for Recovery of Veterans Returning Home

Veterans who receive social support from their families and military support groups recover better than those who do not. This is especially the case for veterans suffering from PTSD.

a large study of American veterans who were prisoners of war in Vietnam and who suffered considerable physical harm while in captivity (King et al., 2015). Interestingly enough, men who were older and better educated at the time they experienced the trauma were better able to make use of the social support they received upon their return, to attain improved emotional functioning. This group of veterans mostly retained their military membership after their release. So, they were able to access the identity and material resources of the institution. These resources may have also contributed to the veterans' positive adjustment back into regular society, despite having experienced great pain from physical torture.

older students also had concerns about belonging when they first arrived on campus increased new students' feelings of "belonging," and resulted in higher grades. Indeed, interventions aimed at helping students feel like they "fit in" have been shown to reduce the racial achievement gap by half. This illustrates the importance of feeling accepted, especially for minority students (Walton & Cohen, 2007). Two tactics that people can employ to create greater self-acceptance and improve their own well-being are described in the next sections.

PRACTICING SELF-FORGIVENESS All of us experience failures, make mistakes, commit transgressions against others, and sometimes hurt other people—whether we intended to or not. On occasion, we may even find we have violated moral principles that we actually hold dear. Learning to forgive ourselves, and avoiding numerous forms of self-condemnation and maladaptive behaviors, appears to be critical for our well-being.

After offending someone, people often feel guilty, which can motivate them to apologize or otherwise make reparations for their actions. Such behavioral indications of remorse can allow people who have offended another or violated their values to feel worthy again (Shnabel & Nadler, 2008; Zechmeister & Romero, 2002). In contrast, an inability to forgive oneself is associated with higher guilt and anxiety (Hall & Fincham, 2005) and reduced perceived global physical health in college students (Wilson, Milosevic, Carrol, Hart, & Hibbard, 2008).

Is self-forgiveness for regrettable actions that harm *ourselves* rather than others, also important for well-being? And, does forgiving ourselves for a lapse on one occasion help to prevent us from engaging in similar behavior in the future? To address these questions, Wohl, Pychyl, and Bennett (2010) focused on a common behavior among first-year university students—procrastinating or failing to study for important exams. Not only is this a behavior that people often engage in, it is also one that is self-defeating with potential negative consequences for students: lower grades and increased risk for depression. By forgiving ourselves for one such instance of procrastination, negative feelings about the self are reduced, thereby discouraging repetition of the same behavior.

To test these ideas, Wohl, et al. (2010) first measured the extent to which first-year psychology students reported having engaged in procrastination before their first exam (e.g., delayed preparing for the exam later than intended). They also measured how much the students forgave themselves for doing so. Several weeks later, before their midterm exam, the students were asked to indicate how they felt about their performance on the first exam. Then, just before their second midterm exam, students indicated the extent to which they had engaged in procrastination.

Results revealed that students who procrastinated more before their first exam, reported worse performance on that exam than those who had not procrastinated. However, the more the students forgave themselves for having procrastinated before their first exam, the less negative emotion they felt about their performance. Even more importantly, those who forgave themselves for initially procrastinating were less likely to report having procrastinated before their midterm exam. Conversely, students who did *not* forgive themselves, continued to display the same problematic behavior and engaged in procrastination before their midterm exam. So, self-forgiveness appears to have two important effects. It helps reduce negative feelings about our prior poor performance and seems to encourage us to not make the same mistake the next time.

ADJUSTING HOW WE SEE OURSELVES Given that our past selves and behavior have some imperfections, are there other means besides self-forgiveness that can help us to change and improve our behavior? People often try to set dates when they will change (e.g., make New Year's resolutions, the start of a new semester). For example, they set "quit smoking dates," or they pick a date when they will start a new exercise program or diet. This type of date-setting often coincides with other changes: moving to a new city, getting married, or getting divorced. Dai, Milkman, and Riis (2015) suggested that "temporal landmarks" that signal a new time period can motivate people to change in ways that facilitates their goal achievement. Let's consider the different ways the researchers examined this idea.

In one study, participants were asked to describe a new goal that they would like to begin pursuing the next month. All participants were told that they could receive an email reminder, if they wished. The dates given for this reminder were described in one of two ways: as either a new beginning or without that implication. So, for example, they could be offered the date with or without a "new beginning" suggestion: March 20, 2014 (Thursday, the first day of Spring), or March 20, 2014 (Thursday, the third Thursday in March). As the researchers predicted, participants who were offered a date that sounded like a new beginning were more likely (25.6 percent) to ask for the change reminder than those for whom the date specified sounded like an ordinary day (7.2 percent).

Dai et al. (2015) theorized that temporal landmarks that signal new beginnings are preferred as dates for initiating change because they allow people to separate themselves psychologically from their prior imperfect selves. In another study these researchers conducted, participants were first asked to think about a goal they had not achieved and would like to pursue in the future. Then, they were asked to imagine that they had just moved to a new apartment. For half the participants, this move was said to be their first one since coming to that city 9 years ago (the new beginning case). The other half of participants were told they had moved once every year of those prior 9 years (the control case). All participants were then asked to indicate how motivated they would be to pursue the goal they had previously described, after moving to a new apartment.

The process revealed by the results is displayed in Figure 12.9. People for whom the move was framed as a new beginning were significantly more motivated to pursue a new personal goal than those for whom the move was framed as an ordinary one. The new beginning framing led people to feel more disconnected from their imperfect past self, which motivated pursuit of new goals. By "marking" the past self, in terms of a dividing line between it and our potential new and improved self, we can motivate ourselves to engage in actions that may actually bring about that new and improved self.

It is also the case that sometimes we need to see our past as a source of strength, even inspiration. If we see ourselves as having overcome disadvantage, reminders of successfully overcoming that history may help us to deal with stress in the present. This idea is similar to Nietzsche's famous quote, with which we began this chapter, "What does not kill me makes me stronger."

First-generation college students (whose parents do not have college degrees) received information about how their background might present certain obstacles in college, but also how it could serve as a strength. Other first-generation college students learned similar information about obstacles in college, but overcoming those difficulties was not linked to their social-class backgrounds. Stephens, Hamedani, and Destin (2014) found that encouraging these first-generation students to see their class difference as a source of strength resulted in greater academic identification and performance, better psychological well-being, and coping strategies that were adaptive in the face of stressful college situations.

Figure 12.9 Signals of New Beginnings Help Dissociate Us from the Past

Research has revealed that framing points in time as "new beginnings" help us to separate our imperfect past self from the desired new self. In turn, this increases our motivation to pursue new goals.

Key Points

- Exercise is an important method of dealing with stress, but adherence is difficult without social support. Technology such as Fitbit can help people stay motivated by creating a shared identity with others using the device.
- Identifying with groups can help people feel less strain and burnout in stressful occupations by providing a sense of personal control.
- Joining groups can foster social connectedness and help prevent depression. Following a failure experience, thinking about groups we belong to protects us by undermining depression attributions.
- Military veterans with **post-traumatic stress disorder (PTSD)** tend to be dissatisfied with their lives, but they show improvement when family members provide social support.
- Interventions that encourage students to feel they "belong" in college can improve academic performance and overall well-being.

- Practicing self-forgiveness for our failures and harmful acts against others is an important step toward greater well-being. Forgiving ourselves for failing ourselves (as in the behavior of procrastination) can improve performance, lower the risk for depression, and encourage us not to make the same mistake next time.
- People are better able to change when a new behavior is framed as a new beginning. This approach helps to disconnect them from their past imperfect self and sets the stage for pursuing new goals.
- When we have a disadvantaged past, reminders of having overcome obstacles and seeing those circumstances as a source of strength enables first-generation college students to adaptively cope with the stress they experience because of their backgrounds.

12.3: Making the Legal System More Fair and Effective

Objective **Describe the sources of errors and biases that have to be overcome in order to make the legal system fair**

Outside many court buildings throughout the world is a statue of "Lady Justice." As shown in Figure 12.10, she is depicted as blindfolded, which represents the idea that all people should be equal under the law and treated in the same, impartial manner. While this is an admirable ideal, it can be very hard to achieve in real life. As you learned in Chapters 2 and 6, it is very difficult for us to ignore the words, behaviors, or personal attributes of other people and to dismiss our preconceived ideas, beliefs, and stereotypes when thinking about and making decisions about people. Therefore, to achieve a fair and impartial legal system, many social psychologists believe that we must first understand the potential sources of error and bias that exist within the current legal system. By better understanding how people actually think about others and recognizing the possible risks for biased judgments in a legal context, we may then be able to take effective steps toward correcting problems. Let's look at what research has revealed about potential pitfalls and how we can seek to reduce them.

12.3.1: Social Influence in the Legal Process

In a sense, most legal processes involve an element of social influence. For example, during crime investigations, although police detectives attempt to discover the truth from the people they interview, they may inadvertently affect people's responses. Likewise, during trials attorneys attempt to persuade jurors, and perhaps the presiding judge, of the guilt or innocence of the person(s) on trial. While social influence is a potential factor affecting many legal system activities, we will focus here on two particular areas where social psychology has identified issues that can affect the fairness of outcomes: how police lineups are conducted and the use of prior legal judgment information.

Figure 12.10 Is Justice Really Blind?

Ideally, justice is "blind"—relying on facts and evidence rather than subjective factors. Unfortunately, research findings indicate that in practice this is not always true. Decisions by juries, judges, attorneys, witnesses, and law enforcement are often influenced by personal or social biases.

LINEUPS: HOW SOCIAL PRESSURE CAN LEAD TO ERRORS One technique commonly used by police to help identify suspects is the **lineup** (see Figure 12.11). In this procedure, witnesses to a crime are shown several people, one of whom is typically a suspect in the case. The witnesses are then individually asked if they recognize anyone in the lineup as the person(s) who committed the crime. To protect anonymity, witnesses may view people through a one-way glass window or be shown photographs of them, which is likely to occur weeks or even months after the crime initially occurred. Although lineups are intended to reveal the truth, they can be subject to several forms of serious bias. In fact, despite the widespread belief in the truth-value of eyewitnesses, they are notoriously error-prone (Wells, Steblay, & Dysart, 2015). We will examine several reasons why that is the case.

Consider the way in which suspects are presented in a lineup. In *sequential lineups,* suspects are presented one at a time, and witnesses indicate whether they recognize each one or not. However, in *simultaneous lineups,* all the suspects are shown at once, and witnesses are asked to indicate which one (if any) they recognize. Results of many studies indicate that sequential lineups are better in the sense that they reduce the likelihood that witnesses will make a serious mistake—identify someone who did not commit the crime.

Steblay, Dysart, and Wells (2011) performed a meta-analysis of the many studies that compared rates of false identification using these two lineup presentation strategies, when

Figure 12.11 Are Lineups Always Accurate?

Research findings indicate that eyewitnesses often make errors when attempting to identify a suspect. Sometimes, this is due to the specific procedures used.

the actual perpetrator was in the array presented to the witnesses. The meta-analysis confirmed that sequential lineups produce greater accuracy than simultaneous lineups. This is because in sequential lineups witnesses are forced to make absolute judgments, by comparing each individual to their memory of the person. In contrast, simultaneous lineups result in witnesses making comparative judgments between the suspects in the array they are presented with, which results in witnesses selecting the person who looks *most* similar to their memory of the person. When eyewitnesses of actual crimes are randomly assigned to view the same array of photo lineups in either a simultaneous or sequential procedure (Wells et al., 2015), no differences in correct identification occurs (25 percent overall). But, importantly, a reduction in false identifications occurs with the sequential procedure (11 percent) compared to the simultaneous procedure (18 percent).

Another important, but subtle, form of social influence on lineups is the type of instructions given to witnesses. Totally neutral instructions simply ask witnesses to identify the person who committed the crime; no statements are made about whether this person is or is not present in the lineup. In contrast, biased instructions suggest that the suspect is present and the witnesses' task is to pick this person out from the others (Pozzulo & Lindsay, 1999). Such instructions can cause witnesses to feel pressured to identify someone as the suspect, even if they do not recognize anyone present.

Research by Pozzulo and Dempsey (2006) very clearly illustrates the danger of biased instructions. They had both children and adults watch a videotape of a staged crime—one in which a woman's purse was stolen. Both groups were then shown a lineup consisting of photos of people who resembled the person who committed the crime. Simultaneous presentation of the photos was used. A key aspect of the study involved instructions to the participants. In one condition (neutral instructions), they were told that the criminal might or might not be present in the lineup. In the biased instructions condition, participants were led to believe that the suspect was indeed present in the lineup. In fact, though, this person was *not* included in the lineup. The key question was: "Would the biased instructions lead participants to falsely identify someone—an innocent person—as the culprit?" That's exactly what happened. Both adults and children were more likely to falsely identify an innocent person after hearing the biased instructions (ones leading them to conclude that the suspect was present) than after hearing the neutral instructions.

Further, when lineup administrators suggest to witnesses that their identifications are correct, rather than giving no feedback, this strongly increases the witnesses' confidence in their identifications (Smalarz & Wells, 2015). As these researchers noted, mistaken but confident eyewitnesses have been involved in 72 percent of the instances where innocent people have been convicted and later revealed to be innocent as a result of DNA testing.

These findings indicate that social influence is at work in police lineups, and stringent procedures should be adopted to avoid such effects. Instructions to witnesses should be neutral and not imply that the potentially guilty party is actually present, or that the witness after identifying someone has indeed picked the person suspected by police. Sequential rather than simultaneous lineups should be used whenever possible. Social influence is a powerful and often very subtle process, so guarding against it is a difficult task. But doing so will help to increase the likelihood that lineups, which are commonly used around the world, provide more accurate results.

EFFECTS OF PRIOR CONVICTIONS AND PRIOR ACQUITTALS As shown in Figure 12.12, you've likely seen a trial in a movie or TV show in which the judge tells the jury: "Ignore that information." However, once we have been exposed to information, people do not function like a computer and just delete it from their memory. In fact, there is a large body of evidence indicating that jurors cannot "strike inadmissible evidence from the record"—and behave as if they never heard or saw it (Lieberman & Arndt, 2000). This is not due only to the ways in which memory works, but also to several social psychological effects we described in earlier chapters. For instance, belief perseverance is the tendency to adhere to our beliefs or attitudes, even when new evidence indicates inaccuracies. Another example is the hindsight bias—the tendency to believe that "I knew it all along," when an event occurs or new information is received that is consistent with the conclusion reached. So, when evidence is presented that jurors are not supposed to remember and use, they may later assume they knew the information before it was presented in court and be actually influenced by it.

Effects like these can occur with respect to a defendant's past convictions. If this information is revealed to members of a jury, they are more likely to convict the defendant of the present charges. After all, jurors may reason, this person already has a criminal record, so the chances are good that he or she also committed the present crime (e.g., Greene & Dodge, 1995). Might information concerning prior acquittals also increase the likelihood of juries reaching a guilty verdict since the defendant already is believed to have a criminal record? On the other hand, it is possible that information on past acquittals could actually help the defendant and reduce the likelihood of a guilty verdict. From this perspective, because the defendant was declared innocent in the past, she or he may well be seen as innocent now. Which of these effects is most

Figure 12.12 Can Jurors Truly Ignore Information They Have Received?

Although a judge may instruct a jury to disregard a particular piece of information, research shows that jurors are unable to completely do so because of memory processes and social psychological effects.

likely to occur? And, does a judge's instruction to a jury to ignore such information about a defendant's past help them to do so?

A study conducted by Greene and Dodge (1995) tested these possibilities. The researchers arranged for mock juries to read a description of a bank robber trial. Some of these juries were presented with information about the defendant's past while others received no information of this type. In addition, some of the juries were instructed by the judge to ignore the information provided, while others were not. Then, all juries rated the defendant's guilt, and how confident they were of their decisions. Results indicated that juries that received information on both past convictions and acquittals were more likely to decide that the defendant was guilty now, than those who received no information on the defendant's past record. Moreover, instructions to ignore such information had virtually no effect: Information about the defendant's past, still influenced juror decisions. In short, once evidence was introduced, warnings to ignore it had little or no effect. Understanding how information that people have when impressions of others are being formed—even if such information is false—clearly has important implications for the legal system.

12.3.2: The Influence of Prejudice and Stereotypes in the Legal System

If justice were truly blind, then, it would be completely unaffected by race, gender, ethnic background, and other factors. In other words, decisions by judges and juries would be based entirely on evidence, and the characteristics of defendants would have no effect. However, as human beings, each of us enters any social situation, including legal proceedings, with complex sets of attitudes, beliefs, values, and stereotypes concerning various groups. It is unquestionably the case that these factors can influence the decisions people reach as jurors, even if they intend for them not to do so.

THE IMPORTANCE OF RACIALLY DIVERSE JURIES Before members of juries are selected, they are questioned by the opposing attorneys (defense, prosecution). Individuals whose answers indicate strong biases that could interfere with their fair evaluation of the evidence are not chosen to be jurors. This examination process is known as *voir dire*, an Anglo-French phrase that means "to speak the truth." In instances where the case may be race relevance, pretrial questioning can ask potential jurors if they have any biases or prejudices that would prevent them from judging an African American defendant fairly. Jurors selected as a result of such questioning tend to be less likely to vote guilty when the defendant is black compared to those jurors not subjected to questions about their potential racial biases.

One factor that might influence jurors' actual decision making is the racial composition of the jury. Sommers (2006) investigated the effects of jurors' racial diversity on their deliberations and decisions. Prior to this research, the role of juror diversity was not known. One possibility is that, in racially diverse juries, white members might be more reluctant to discuss negative evidence for a black defendant than a white one. And, perhaps information about racial injustice would be more likely discussed in racially mixed juries than in all white or all black juries. This research sought to determine whether there might be important beneficial effects of juries with racial diversity among the jurors.

To test these possibilities, Sommers (2006) assembled two different types of mock juries: Half were all white and the other half were racially diverse. The juries were then shown a tape of an actual trial in which a black defendant was charged with sexual assault. The evidence was mixed, so there was much for the juries to discuss. Measures of the quality of their discussions were then obtained, for instance, the length of deliberations, the number of facts discussed, the number of relevant facts ignored, and the number of inaccurate statements made about the evidence.

As you can see in Table 12.1, the diverse juries were superior to the homogeneous (all white) juries in several respects. The diverse juries spent more time deliberating, discussed more facts, were less likely to make errors in discussing the evidence, and were less likely to ignore relevant information. In short, racially diverse juries functioned more effectively—and fairly—than those that were not diverse. The overall message, then, is clear: Attorneys conducting voir dire to choose jurors should do their best to construct racially diverse juries.

HOW CHARACTERISTICS OF DEFENDANTS AND JURORS CAN INFLUENCE LEGAL PROCEEDINGS Characteristics of defendants on trial have been found to influence jury decisions and other legal outcomes. In the United States, African American defendants have generally been found to be at a disadvantage. For example, they are more likely than whites to be convicted of murder and to receive the death penalty and are disproportionally over-represented on death row (Price, 2015). In addition to race, physical appearance (attractiveness), gender, and socioeconomic status can be influential factors in legal proceedings. For example, people accused of most major crimes are less likely to be found guilty if they are physically attractive, female, and of high socioeconomic status rather than low (Mazzella & Feingold, 1994). Attractiveness has

Table 12.1 Advantages of Racially Diverse Juries

As shown in this table, racially diverse juries were more effective during case deliberations—made fewer errors and discussed more of the evidence presented—than racially homogeneous (all white) juries.

	Racially Diverse	Racially Homogenous
Length of Jury Deliberations (Minutes)	50.67	39.49
Number of Facts Discussed	30.48	25.93
Number of Errors About Facts in the Case	4.14	7.28

been studied the most. In real as well as mock trials, attractive defendants have a major advantage over unattractive ones with respect to being acquitted, receiving a light sentence, and gaining the sympathy of the jurors (Downs & Lyons, 1991; Quigley, Johnson, & Byrne, 1995; Wuensch, Castellow, & Moore, 1991).

In addition to race and attractiveness, another visible characteristic—gender—plays an important role in legal proceedings. In general, female defendants tend to be treated more leniently by juries and courts than male defendants, but this depends on the specific crime. For instance, in cases involving assault, female defendants are more likely to be found guilty than male defendants, perhaps because assault is considered an even more unacceptable and unusual behavior for women than men (Cruse & Leigh, 1987).

The gender of jurors, too, can be important. One of the consistent differences between male and female jurors is in their reactions to cases involving sexual assault. In judging what occurred in cases of rape, men are more likely than women to conclude that the sexual interaction was consensual (Harris & Weiss, 1995). An analysis of the results of 36 studies of simulated cases of rape and child abuse revealed that in responding to defendants accused of either crime, women were more likely than men to vote for conviction (Schutte & Hosch, 1997).

HOW PREJUDICE AFFECTS JURY DELIBERATIONS   Growing evidence suggests that although the factors we have discussed do indeed influence legal outcomes, these effects may not be as large as previously suspected and may be overcome—at least to some degree—by some aspects of legal processes. Perhaps the most encouraging evidence in this respect is provided by Bothwell, Piggott, Foley, and McFatter (2006). Taking account of past research on prejudice and stereotypes, these researchers reasoned that often these operate at an automatic or unconscious level. In other words, they influence behavior, but they do so in subtle rather than overt ways. This suggests that prejudiced views would be more likely to influence people's private judgments more so than their public decisions as jurors (Hebl & Kleck, 2006). Jury deliberations, which are often lengthy and detailed, might serve to reduce the impact of subtle and nonconscious forms of prejudice.

To test this reasoning, Bothwell et al. (2006) conducted research in which both students and prospective jurors in actual legal cases read about a sexual harassment suit in which a supervisor demanded sexual favors from a subordinate. In the case description, the race of the supervisor and the subordinate (who had made the complaint) was varied so that each could be either African American or white. Gender was also a factor in the study, so that information too was varied: The supervisor and the subordinate could each be either a man or a woman. Participants read a case that presented one of these various combinations (e.g., an African American male supervisor and a white female subordinate; white female supervisor and an African American male subordinate). Participants then rated the responsibility of the person making the complaint and how much monetary compensation the victim should receive from the company.

Results for these measures indicated that racial and gender prejudice exerted significant effects. For instance, the person making the complaint was held more responsible for what happened to him or her when the supervisor was African American than when this person was White. Similarly, participants awarded less compensation when the supervisor was African American than when he or she was White. Participants reasoned—at the private level—that when the supervisor was African American, the subordinates "should have known better" than to go to this person's hotel room, where the sexual harassment occurred.

After making their private decisions and judgments, a mock trial was held in which jurors met and then recommended compensation for the victim. At the end of the mock trials, the effects of race and gender largely disappeared. In other words, although the impact of these variables was present prior to actual jury deliberations, it was essentially eliminated by jury deliberations. Figure 12.13 illustrates the study participants' private judgments versus their jury judgments.

These findings and those in related studies (e.g., Greene & Bornstein, 2003) suggest that while justice is certainly not entirely blind, the procedures used for reaching legal decisions can, at least sometimes, help to counter the impact of various characteristics of defendants and perhaps of jurors, too. In addition, a review by Devine and Caughlin (2014) suggests that the effects of some defendant characteristics on jury decisions may be weaker than was previously believed. Their meta-analysis revealed that across studies defendant gender and juror education did not matter. Yet among the characteristics that had the strongest effects were defendant race, prior criminal record, defendant socioeconomic status, juror authoritarianism, and juror trust in the legal system. Although this means there is reason for some optimism that some biases may be overcome, the legal system must continue to be aware of their potential role. The knowledge provided by social psychological research can help legal, judicial, and law-enforcement professionals make progress toward a more fair, impartial, and accurate legal system.

Figure 12.13 Do Juries Overcome Bias in Legal Proceedings?

When participants made individual (private) recommendations for compensation to a victim of sexual harassment, they recommended larger awards when the defendant was white than when he or she was black. After jury deliberation, however, this difference—and others reflecting racial and gender bias—tended to disappear. These findings suggest that jury deliberations may help to reduce the impact of prejudices held by individual jurors related to the race, gender, and attractiveness of defendants.

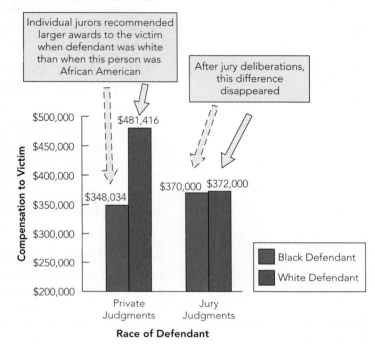

Key Points

- Social influence is a possible risk factor in many legal-related activities. To make the legal system more fair, impartial, and protective of basic human rights, it is necessary to understand potential sources of error and bias within the current system.
- **Lineups** used to identify criminal suspects are subject to bias, depending on how they are conducted. *Sequential lineups* requiring absolute judgments produce greater accuracy than *simultaneous lineups* that result in comparative judgments. Some types of instructions and feedback provided to witnesses during lineups can also lead to identification errors.
- Although judges often instruct jurors to ignore certain information, such as the defendant's prior convictions,

or even acquittals, research indicates that jurors cannot actually do so.
- The pretrial examination process of *voir dire* helps to reduce the risk of biased jurors. Research also shows that racially diverse juries function more fairly and effectively than homogeneous juries.
- In legal proceedings, defendants' race, gender, physical attractiveness, and socioeconomic status can influence jurors' perceptions and judgments. However, a recent review of existing evidence indicates that prejudicial effects may be weaker than previously believed.
- Careful deliberations by juries as they review available evidence, tend to reduce prejudicial effects, although not, of course, in all instances.

12.4: Fostering Happiness in Our Lives

Objective   **Describe the influences on our happiness and explain how happiness can be increased**

We all want to be happy and satisfied with our lives, but what does that mean, specifically? After decades of research on the nature, causes, and effects of **happiness**, most social psychologists agree that our *subjective well-being* involves four basic components (Diener, 2000):

- *Global life satisfaction*—feeling generally satisfied or happy with our lives
- *Satisfaction with important life domains*—being satisfied with our work, relationships, and family
- *Positive feelings*—experiencing positive emotions and moods often
- *Negative feelings*—experiencing negative emotions less often than positive ones, or preferably, rarely

In short, happiness with our lives seems to consist of multiple, interrelated factors. To the degree these factors are present in our lives, they strongly influence how happy we are and the extent to which we see our lives as meaningful and fulfilling (Krause, 2007). We will now present an overview of some key research findings on happiness. Get ready for some surprises because research has indicated that the ingredients in happiness are different, in important ways, from what many people might guess.

12.4.1: How Happy Are People, in General?

Let's begin with a very basic question: How happy are people, in general, with their lives? Efforts to investigate happiness sometimes focus on differing aspects of life, but because they are highly correlated, researchers frequently use short and straightforward measures of happiness—ones in which individuals respond to questions such as "How satisfied or dissatisfied are you with your life overall?" (Weiss, Bates, & Luciano, 2008). As perhaps you might expect, there are *huge* differences in people's responses to questions like these, depending on the country in which they live. As shown in Table 12.2, on a scale ranging from 0 (worst possible life) to 10 (best possible life), nations can be rank-ordered in terms of people's happiness. For the years 2012–2014, Switzerland and most Nordic countries consistently appeared at the top of the 158-nation list, while sub-Saharan African countries were at the bottom (Helliwell, Layard, & Sachs, 2015).

What accounts for these national differences in happiness? According to research presented in the *World Happiness Report 2015* by Helliwell et al. (2015) there are seven variables that consistently account for more than half of the variability in these nations' average happiness levels, or people's own assessments of the quality of their lives. These seven variables concern social aspects of people's lives and the kind of institutions that structure how people live. In order of importance in accounting for differences in national levels of happiness, these variables are degree of social support, per capita income, healthy life expectancy, freedom to make life choices, generosity toward or trust in others, amount of violence, and degree of corruption.

However, if we look only at the subset of rich, industrialized countries—those in which people report fairly high levels of happiness—we see that despite the small differences between those countries, about 80 percent of those nations' respondents indicate that they are quite

Table 12.2 Happiness Varies According to Where You Live

Research provided in the *World Happiness Report 2015* shows that people's happiness levels vary greatly according to the country where they live. The average happiness was reported on a 0 to 10 scale by people across 158 nations. Shown here is a sample of happiness rankings by country for the years 2012–2014.

Country	Ranking	Average Happiness
Switzerland	1	7.59
Denmark	3	7.53
Canada	5	7.43
Netherlands	7	7.38
New Zealand	9	7.29
Israel	11	7.28
Austria	13	7.20
United States	15	7.12
Argentina	30	6.57
Poland	60	5.79
Philippines	90	5.07
Congo	120	4.52
Guinea	150	3.66
Rwanda	154	3.47
Syria	156	3.01
Togo	158	2.84

happy and satisfied with their lives (Diener, Lucas, & Scollon, 2006). One question researchers have pursued is: How can people within these rich countries all be fairly happy, given that people lead very different lives within these nations? The answer seems to involve the fact that there are many sources of happiness, and human beings are adept at securing many of these. Thus, happiness levels within specific nations can be high for different reasons (Diener, Ng, Harter, & Arora, 2010). Let's consider some of the factors that appear to contribute to happiness in these rich nations.

12.4.2: Factors That Influence Happiness

What makes people happy with their lives? First, happy people report a higher frequency of positive emotions and a lower frequency of negative emotions than people who are less happy (Lyubomirsky, King, & Diener, 2005). A higher frequency of positive emotions leads people to think and act in ways that help to broaden and build their emotional, physical, and social resources (Fredrickson, 2001; Fredrickson & Joiner, 2002).

Second, good social relations with other people—friends, family, romantic partners—is an important ingredient for being happy. Such close relationships are available to all people, regardless of personal wealth (see Figure 12.14). In fact, close family relationships may be more prevalent in less wealthy societies than in generally wealthy ones. For example, in more wealthy (and individualistic) societies, people tend to move more frequently. This means they may live hundreds or even thousands of miles from their family and close friends, whom they left behind when they went to college or took a new job.

Additional research findings (Diener, Suh, Lucas, & Smith, 1999) suggest that happiness may also be influenced by other factors, such as having goals and the means necessary to reach them—personal, economic, and other resources. Many studies indicate that people who have concrete goals, especially realistic ones, and who feel they are making progress toward those goals, are happier than people who lack goals (Cantor & Sanderson, 1999).

12.4.3: Does Monetary Wealth Create Happiness?

Does more money equal more happiness? Many people seem to believe that it does. In fact, economists have long assumed that the wealth of a nation—termed gross domestic product (GDP)—should be the primary measure of the well-being of

---

Figure 12.14 Close Family Relationships: An Important Factor in Happiness

Research findings indicate that close relationships with family and friends are an important source of happiness. Such relationships are possible for people everywhere, regardless of their personal or societal monetary wealth.

a nation. In other words, people assume that wealth will buy the things and conditions that produce happiness. Yet, research on the link between monetary wealth and happiness both within and between nations indicates that this matter is rather complex.

Overall, there is *some* connection between income and happiness. As we saw earlier from the *World Happiness Report 2015*, GDP (per capita income) does predict differences across countries in the level of happiness and how satisfied people are with their lives. But studies that have examined the relationship between income and happiness within fairly wealthy nations reveal that it is not as strong as you might think (Diener et al., 2010; Kahneman, Diener, & Schwarz, 2003). At low-income levels, a lack of money is likely to make people feel unhappy because without it, they can't meet their basic needs—such as food, clothing, and shelter. At higher income levels, however, income is not strongly related to how happy people feel. In cases, where people have enough money to meet all their basic needs, plus some of the "luxuries," increasing wealth further does not result in improved happiness or life satisfaction.

Kahneman and Deaton (2010), who examined a nationally representative sample of Americans, showed that increased income above $75,000 per year had little connection with the positive feelings people experience on a daily basis. Since positive feelings are crucial for happiness, this finding indicates that monetary wealth beyond a certain point does not necessarily increase happiness.

Furthermore, monetary wealth is not clearly linked to happiness and the social side of life (Diener et al., 2010). One reason for this is that close relationships with friends and family are independent of income. As shown in Table 12.3, many countries high in societal wealth (GDP) are relatively *low* in terms of social prosperity and positive feelings, which are typically derived from having strong community ties (see Putnam, 2000). As Diener et al. (2010, p. 60) put it: "Some nations that do well in economic terms do only modestly well in social psychological prosperity, and some nations that rank in the middle in economic development are stars . . . in social psychological prosperity."

One factor that is critical for positive feelings is the extent to which people are satisfied with their everyday experiences with public and common goods—quality education and health care systems, safe roads and accessible public transportation, good air and water quality, and good affordable housing. Oishi, Schimmack, and Diener (2012) analyzed responses from 54 nations in regard to public goods. Even after controlling for income, the researchers found that people living in nations with more progressive taxation—defined in terms of a greater difference between the highest and lowest tax rates—had more positive daily experiences and greater life satisfaction as a result of their contentment with the public goods provided by their government.

Why doesn't personal wealth necessarily result in happiness? Consider research by Boyce, Brown, and Moore (2010) who found that wealth itself is not as important as *relative* judgments about one's wealth. People seem to care more about how their income (wealth) compares with that of others than they do about its absolute level. When individuals were asked to report on the number of people in their society who had income lower than or higher than theirs, these relative judgments were strongly tied to life satisfaction. On the other hand, absolute income was not.

Consistent with this research, Luttmer (2005) found that individuals who earned the same amount

Table 12.3 Does Wealth Equal Happiness?

As shown here, countries ranked high in income (e.g., the United States) are *not* necessarily high in social prosperity (e.g., people feel respected by others, good relationships with friends and family) or in experiencing positive feelings. In fact, countries such as Denmark, Costa Rica, and New Zealand score very high in positive feelings and social prosperity, although they are lower in per capita wealth than the United States. Wealth does not automatically translate into the highest national happiness ratings.

Country	Income per Capita	Social Prosperity Ranking	Positive Feelings Ranking
United States	1	19	26
Denmark	5	13	7
Italy	18	33	67
New Zealand	22	12	1
South Korea	24	83	58
Costa Rica	41	6	4
India	61	85	63
Tanzania	89	58	52

but lived in richer neighborhoods were less happy than those who lived in poorer neighborhoods. In fact, this effect was stronger for people who interacted more with their neighbors, suggesting that a stronger opportunity existed to negatively compare themselves with richer neighbors than poorer neighbors.

This tendency to care more about doing better than others—as opposed to just being wealthy ourselves—illustrates the important role that social comparison plays in our subjective well-being. Even when countries experience rising standards of living, the people living in those countries do not necessarily report that they are happier because others with whom they compare also are experiencing a rise in income.

In the United States, for instance, per capita income (adjusted for inflation) rose more than 50 percent in recent decades, but people do *not* report being happier. In fact, they report being *less* happy than in the "good old days" when their incomes were actually lower. This is due, in part, to the fact that Americans are working longer hours and spend more time commuting, both of which decrease happiness. And, compared to previous decades, they spend less time in leisure activities and interacting with others, both of which increase happiness (Kahneman, Krueger, Schkade, Schwarz, & Stone, 2006).

12.4.4: Is Happiness Getting What You Want or Enjoying What You Have?

How might striving for more and more material wealth affect our capacity to enjoy life? Research by Quoidbach, Dunn, Petrides, and Miklajczak (2010) suggests that obtaining material possessions does not really add to our happiness, since doing so may reduce our capacity to enjoy those items once we have them. To test this idea, students at a Canadian university were each given a piece of chocolate and then were observed as they ate it. Before receiving the chocolate, some participants were primed to think about their desire for wealth by being exposed to photos of Canadian money. Others saw neutral photos unrelated to money. On a scale from 1 (not at all) to 7 (a great deal), observers rated the amount of enjoyment shown by the participants as they ate the chocolate. Observers also tracked how long the participants spent eating the chocolate. Participants who had looked at photos of money before eating the chocolate appeared to enjoy the chocolate less, and spent less time savoring it, than those who saw neutral photos. These findings suggest that even though money may provide many of the things we want, money may also reduce our ability to enjoy the pleasures in life it can bring.

The findings of other research (Larsen & McKibban, 2008) indicate that happiness comes from *both* having what we want and being grateful for what we have. The fundamental message here is that having things is not the sole ingredient of happiness. Rather, happiness comes from valuing the things we have—being grateful for them and enjoying them, rather than striving for yet more and better possessions. Sadly, many people seem to lose the capacity to enjoy their wealth after they obtain it. They often continue to believe that if they could get just one more thing—that new car, a newer and larger home, one more designer item for their wardrobe, one more tool for their shop, one more piece of art—they will finally attain the happiness they seek (see Figure 12.15). But, in fact, this attitude is likely to lead to a frustrating cycle of striving and discontent.

12.4.5: Differences Between Happy and Unhappy People

As we have illustrated, many factors influence happiness. In addition to having strong social ties to others whom we value (Jetten et al., 2015) and being grateful for what we have, are there other important cognitive and motivational differences in how happy

Figure 12.15 Having What We Want or Wanting What We Have? Which Brings Happiness?

Research indicates that having what we want does not in and of itself bring happiness. Rather, it is both having what we want and appreciating what we have that together generates high levels of happiness. This is one reason why many people who have lots of possessions and high levels of wealth are not happy: They constantly expand their list of "wants" and take little pleasure in these items when they actually obtain them.

people approach life, compared to those who are unhappy? We know that happy people are more community-oriented and express greater concern for others than unhappy people. For example, happy people are more likely to donate blood (Priller & Schupp, 2011) than are unhappy people. Aknin, Sandstrom, Dunn, and Norton (2011) also found (across 122 countries) that prosocial behavior in terms of donating money to charity was more likely among people who were happy with their lives than those who were unhappy.

Lyubomirsky (2001) found evidence that happy and unhappy people respond differently to the same social information. For instance, when comparing themselves to others, happy people (as compared to unhappy people) are less distressed by information that suggests others have outperformed them in various ways. People who are happy are generally not upset by such negative social comparisons; they may even experience positive reactions to others' success. In contrast, unhappy people are more likely to be emotionally crushed when they "come up short" in comparisons with others.

Similarly, when choosing between several options (e.g., a dessert, a college), happy people are generally pleased with the choices they have made and feel little pressure to down-rate the options they rejected. In other words, they are less likely to suffer from cognitive dissonance and are less likely to experience regret over choices made, a process described in Chapter 5. In contrast, unhappy people tend to worry about the choices they have made, and feel strong pressure to down-rate the options they did not choose, suggesting ongoing rumination about the past.

Another difference is that happy people tend to interpret events in a positive way, while unhappy ones interpret the same events more negatively. It is the difference between "seeing the glass as half full or seeing it as half empty." So, when they think about events in the past, happy people tend to remember those events in a generally positive light, while unhappy people perceive past events in a more negative light. For instance, consider two individuals who are interviewing for the same job—one with a strong tendency to be happy, and the other with a strong tendency to be unhappy. Both interview for the same job. After the interview, the happy person tends to perceive the experience as positive—even if he or she doesn't get the job. The happy person also likely feels that lessons have been learned from the experience, which can be used to do even better in the next interview. In contrast, the unhappy person tends to perceive the interview as a negative experience. This person probably worries incessantly about her or his performance, and whether he or she will ever get a good job.

Another process that differs for people who are happy or unhappy is *self-reflection*—thinking about ourselves. Happy people tend to focus on their strong or positive qualities and feelings. Unhappy people are more likely to focus on their weaknesses or negative characteristics—often to the point where they feel depressed, lacking the energy or will to pursue their goals. It is also the case that unhappy people tend to have more friends who are unhappy, whereas happy people have a larger number of friends who are also happy (Fowler & Christakis, 2008). So, who we associate with can have an impact on our own emotions. The following special feature, **"What Research Tells Us About…The Relationship Between Emotions and Life Satisfaction Within Different Cultures,"** further explores how positive and negative emotions influence levels of well-being.

What Research Tells Us About…

The Relationship Between Emotions and Life Satisfaction Within Different Cultures

Emotional experiences can have an impact on levels of happiness. Kuppens, Realo, and Diener (2008) wanted to know what role the frequency of positive and negative emotions played in people's satisfaction with life. They investigated this question with a sample of more than 8,500 participants from 46 different countries. Overall, the findings indicated that positive emotions are strongly related to happiness, while negative emotions are related to unhappiness. Perhaps more surprising is that the strength of these relationships varies between cultures.

Cultures vary along many dimensions, but a central one is the extent to which they lean toward either individualistic or collectivist values. Individualistic cultures, such as the United States, emphasize each person's individual achievements and her or his particular attributes. On the other hand, collectivist cultures, such as Japan and China, tend to emphasize harmony within the groups to which people belong—ethnic, educational, professional, or religious groups. How well people fit the norms of their groups predicts life satisfaction in such cultures (Diener, Tay, & Myers, 2011).

Kuppens et al. (2008) found that positive and negative emotions were more strongly related to happiness and unhappiness in individualistic cultures than in collectivistic cultures. For instance, in individualistic cultures such as Australia, Belgium, Germany, and the United States, the relationship between these emotions and happiness was stronger than in collectivist cultures such as Thailand, Indonesia, and Venezuela. Thus, individual emotional experiences appear to be more important to the happiness of people in individualistic cultures than in cultures that are collectivistic in orientation (see Figure 12.16).

Research also shows that some types of interventions aimed at increasing happiness are more effective in some cultures than others. Interventions that are consistent with individualistic values and emphasize personal self-improvement and personal agency improve the happiness of Anglo Americans relative to a control condition. However, those same interventions do not improve the happiness of foreign-born Asian Americans whose cultural values are more collectivist and emphasize the basis of happiness as attaining social harmony (Boehm, Lyubomirsky, & Sheldon, 2011).

Figure 12.16 Are Positive Feelings Related to Happiness the Same Everywhere?

In general, positive feelings are related to happiness. However, this relationship is stronger in cultures that focus on individuals and their behavior or performance (left), than in cultures that focus more on group success and harmony (right).

The relationship between emotions and happiness also depends on people's age. For example, younger people in the United States consistently report experiencing more anger and are more reactive to stress than are older people (Isaacowitz & Livingstone, 2015). It is not surprising, then, that older Americans generally report being happier than younger people, and especially compared to the middle-aged who experience considerably more workplace stress and familial strains.

People also tend to shift the basis of their happiness as they age. In a study comparing American 20-year-olds with adults 50 years and older, Mogilner, Kamvar, and Aaker (2011) found that younger people associated the experience of happiness with excitement or high arousal considerably more than older people. In contrast, older people were eight times more likely to associate happiness with peacefulness and serenity, which are states with low arousal.

This age difference appears to be due to the shift in temporal focus that often occurs as people age. For young people, the future appears to be expanding before them, whereas for older people the future is less expansive. Focusing on the present, as older people are more inclined to do, results in happiness that is experienced as feeling calm or serene. This difference in temporal focus also helps explain cultural differences in emotion ideals. Tsai (2007) indicates that Chinese people ideally want to feel calm and serene, whereas Americans are more likely to value feeling excitement. These ideals reflect the respective cultural differences in focus on the present versus the future.

12.4.6: Benefits of Happiness

Being happy certainly feels good—it is the state we would prefer to be in most, if not all, of the time. Besides feeling good, happy people generally experience many tangible benefits related to their high levels of satisfaction with their lives (Lyubomirsky et al., 2005). With regard to work, individuals high in subjective well-being are more likely to experience better work outcomes, including increased productivity, higher quality of work, higher income, more rapid promotions, and greater job satisfaction (Borman, Penner, Allen, & Motowidlo, 2001; Wright & Cropanzano, 2000). They also tend to have more, and higher quality, social relationships—more friends, more satisfying romantic relationships, and stronger social support networks than less happy people (Lyubomirsky, Sheldon, & Schkade, 2005; Pinquart & Sorensen, 2000).

Happy people also tend to report better health and fewer unpleasant physical symptoms, and they deal with illness more effectively when it does occur (Lyubomirsky et al., 2005). Specific health-related benefits associated with higher levels of well-being include increased resistance to cold and flu viruses (Cohen, Doyle, Turner, Alper, & Skoner, 2003), a greater ability to deal with pain (Muller et al., 2016), lower incidence of depression (Maruta, Colligan, Malinchoc, & Offord, 2000), and improved recovery from surgery (Lamers, Bolier, Westerhof, Smit, and Bohlmeijer, 2012).

Perhaps most intriguing of all is the fact that happy people appear to live longer than unhappy people. For instance, Xu and Roberts (2010) related subjective well-being to longevity in a large sample of people living in California. They examined death from natural causes over a 28-year period and correlated it with measures of global life satisfaction, positive feelings, negative feelings, and satisfaction with important life domains. All of these measures were available because the people in this research were participating in a county-wide longitudinal public health study. Results were compelling: All the components of happiness (life satisfaction, satisfaction with important life domains, high positive affect, low negative affect) were related to longevity. In other words, the better people scored on these components of happiness, the less likely they were to die during the study. Interestingly, these findings were found among both younger and older adults. Being happy, it appears, not only makes our lives more enjoyable; it prolongs them, too.

12.4.7: Is It Possible to Be Too Happy?

Happiness is certainly one of the goals most people seek in life, but is it possible to be too happy? Initially, you might be tempted to answer "No, the more the better!" But sometimes in life, there can be too much of a good thing. Even characteristics or conditions that are generally beneficial can be overdone, resulting in negative rather than positive outcomes. Surprisingly, there are some grounds for suggesting that this principle also applies to happiness.

First, consider a theory proposed by Oishi, Diener, and Lucas (2007)—**optimum level of well-being theory**—which concerns the effects of well-being on task performance. This theory proposes that for any specific task, there is an optimum (i.e., best) level of subjective well-being. Thus, for any task, there may be an optimum level of positive affect that is associated with maximum performance. Up to that point, performance on many different tasks improves as well-being increases, but beyond it, performance declines. This is similar to Zajonc's (1965) drive theory of social facilitation, discussed in Chapter 11. In this theory, an audience is a source of arousal that improves performance on tasks up to a point, beyond which performance declines.

Research findings, involving thousands of participants in many nations, provide support for applying Zajonc's theory to happiness. At very high levels of happiness, people's performance suffers, compared to those who are just a little less happy. With a variety of different tasks relating to career success, income, and educational attainment, performance has been found to increase with subjective well-being, but only up to a specific point. This is not the case, however, for the relationship between happiness and satisfaction with social relationships. People who are happier are more likely to be have longer lasting and more satisfying social relationships.

So why does income, educational attainment, and career success show a downturn at the very highest levels of happiness? See Figure 12.17 for an amusing take on this question. Oishi et al. (2007) explain the reduction in task performance among extremely happy people as follows. For tasks related to achievement (e.g., career success, educational attainment), very high levels of positive affect may foster complacency or satisfaction with less than perfect outcomes. As a result, motivation and effort are reduced. So, when people are feeling very happy, they may "take it easy," rather than exerting maximal effort on difficult tasks since they are already quite satisfied with their lives. Thus, performance declines at very high levels of positive affect.

Very high levels of subjective well-being may also be related to cognitive errors, such as those examined in Chapter 2: overoptimism, overconfidence, and the planning fallacy (the false belief that more can be accomplished in a given period of time than is actually true). It is also the case that some amount of negative emotion is necessary to

Figure 12.17 Very High Levels of Happiness May Lead to Complacency

For those who are already extremely happy, it may be hard to entice them to work toward achieving more trappings of success.

confront others to bring about improvements in performance, and people who are extremely happy may find doing so more difficult than people who are a little lower in positive affect (Gruber, Mauss, & Tamir, 2011).

Finally, with respect to personal health, very high levels of subjective well-being may lead people to believe that they can "get away" with doing things that are dangerous or harmful to their health. They may eat or drink too much, engage in risky actions, and so on. This kind of illusion can, of course, be very harmful and undermine the benefits to personal health conferred by subjective well-being. For these and other reasons, very high levels of subjective well-being can have both harmful and beneficial effects. So, surprising as it may be, it is possible to be too happy under certain circumstances.

12.4.8: Increasing Happiness Levels

Initial research on subjective well-being suggested that happiness is relatively fixed: People are born with strong tendencies to be happy or unhappy and these are difficult to change. In other words, some people tend to be happy even under very difficult life circumstances, while others tend to be unhappy, even if they are blessed with fortunate circumstances. Support for this view was provided by studies suggesting that subjective well-being is fairly stable over time (Eid & Diener, 2004).

A related perspective emerged from the idea that emotions can vary, including happiness, but they do so around a *set point* that is fairly stable throughout life. Thus, after experiencing intense emotion-generating events (e.g., winning the lottery, becoming disabled as a result of an auto accident), people tend to adapt and ultimately return to their basic, personal set points (e.g., Brickman & Campbell, 1971; Frederick & Loewenstein, 1999). There is, however, growing evidence that counters this *hedonic treadmill* view that events and circumstances only temporarily change people.

First, recall the substantial national differences in average happiness levels of people around the world, illustrated earlier in Table 12.2. There is little reason to suppose that people living in Denmark, with an average happiness level of 7.53 on a 10-point scale, simply have different and unchangeable "personal set points" from people living in war-torn Syria, whose average happiness level is 3.01. Recall, too, that the types of factors that account for a large proportion of these national differences in happiness levels are social and institutional in nature. In other words, the factors that account for these large cross-national differences in happiness are fundamentally changeable—to the extent that people feel they are socially supported—are able to control their own lives, can trust in and act generously toward other people, have governments and other institutions that are relatively free of corruption, live their lives with low exposure to violence, and have reasonably healthy life expectancies.

We also know there are changeable factors that systematically predict increasing *un*happiness across nations, as well as across the United States, over time. As Wilkinson and Pickett (2010) showed, as income inequality increases (as measured by the Gini coefficient, 0 = perfect income equality and 1 = all income goes to one person), happiness and numerous other indicators of well-being decline. Furthermore, as the distribution of income becomes more unequal within highly developed countries, the various factors that are critical to people's happiness levels decline. That is, as income inequality grows, trust in other people declines, the frequency of experiencing negative emotions increases, life expectancies decline, homicides and other violent crimes increase, and social cohesion declines.

Nations that used the above knowledge and made changes in 2005—such as improved government quality and delivery of public services—have produced sustained increases in the life satisfaction of their populations, as measured in 2012 (Helliwell, Huang, & Wang, 2014). These and many other national interventions aimed at improving population well-being, argue against the set-point idea and instead lend support to the optimistic conclusion that population happiness levels can be changed.

Happiness too varies considerably between individuals and is responsive to changes in circumstances (Diener et al., 2006). What types of interventions aimed at individuals can improve their happiness levels? There are several that research has found will do so, including ones that strengthen social connections, change how we engage with the world, and involve intentional activities (Lyubomirsky et al., 2005).

Interventions targeting intentional activity—a term used to describe things that people voluntarily think or regularly do in their daily lives—have been shown to produce relatively lasting effects on happiness. For example, careful research has confirmed that relatively simple behavioral interventions, such as engaging in regular exercise, can improve well-being. Other simple interventions where participants are randomly assigned to be kind to others for a day spend a small amount of money on others rather than themselves, or pause to count and consider their blessings, can exert lasting effects on measures of happiness (Aknin et al., 2013; Lyubomirsky et al., 2005; Seligman, Steen, Park, & Peterson, 2005). Here are some other steps you can take to increase your happiness:

- **Start an upward spiral**. Experiencing positive emotions appears to be one way of "getting the ball rolling," so to speak. Positive emotions help us adopt effective ways of coping with life's unavoidable problems, and this in turn can generate even more positive emotions. So the hardest step, as in many tasks, may be the first step. Once you begin experiencing positive feelings, it may become easier to experience more of them.

- **Build close personal relationships or join groups that you value.** Developing and maintaining good relationships requires a lot of time and may involve joining one or more groups, but the rewards appear to make this effort well worthwhile (Jetten et al., 2015). In fact, this may be the single most important thing you can do to increase your happiness. Try thinking more about the people who are important to you, and how you can help make them happier (Aknin et al., 2013). The result may be a major boost to your own well-being.

- **Invest in experiences over material goods.** Many people believe that getting that new car, jewelry, sweater, or some other kind of material object will contribute to their happiness. But, considerable research has revealed that if you have to pick between buying a material object and buying an experience, you will gain greater and more lasting happiness from the experience over the object (Van Boven, 2005). This is because experiences are less comparative than objects, so they are much less likely to produce regret (Carter & Gilovich, 2010). Experiences are also more likely to build social relationships, which in turn contribute to happiness. Consider, for example, whether taking a friend out to a concert or dinner as a birthday gift will produce more happiness than spending equivalent funds on a material object. The experience is far more likely to make both you and the friend happy because it will result in longer lasting positive memories than the object would.

- **Build personal skills that contribute to being happy.** Happy people possess a number of personal characteristics that contribute to their happiness. These include being friendly and outgoing (extroverted), agreeable (i.e., approaching others with the belief that you will like and trust them), and emotionally stable. So, consider where you stand on these dimensions, and build from there—preferably with the help of close friends.

- **Stop doing counterproductive things**. In spite of wanting to be happy, you may nevertheless find yourself engaging in thoughts and actions that generate negative emotions rather than positive emotions. With the help of others, many negative behavioral and thought patterns can be changed, such as worrying excessively, trying to be perfect, or setting unreasonable goals for yourself. Likewise, by changing your focus, you can choose to live more in the present than in the future. For example, instead of telling yourself that you will be happy when X occurs, focus instead on the small pleasures and enjoyable experiences in your day-to-day life. Set your intentions to reduce negative factors in your life that contribute to unhappiness and increase the positive factors that improve happiness.

12.4.9: Entrepreneurship as a Means of Seeking Happiness

Many of the characteristics needed to be a successful **entrepreneur** are also ones that contribute to happiness levels. The origin of "entrepreneur" is a French word that means "to undertake." However, in today's language, this term can have several variations of meaning depending on the context in which it is used. For instance, in a very broad context, an entrepreneur is a person who initiates change. In a business context, an entrepreneur can be someone who starts a new company, creates a new product, or designs a new way of doing something. In some cases, this term may simply refer to people who work for themselves, as opposed to being employees—working for others. Now that you have a basic sense of entrepreneurship, let's examine the motivations and skills exhibited by entrepreneurs that relate to happiness.

Entrepreneurship can be said to be risky behavior. Anytime someone starts a new company or ventures out to become his or her "own boss," there is usually more risk involved than there typically is with being an employee. So, then, how can entrepreneurship be considered a means of generating happiness? In other words, what motivates people to become entrepreneurs? A positive outlook may be one reason; entrepreneurs tend to be optimists. They believe they will experience positive outcomes in life, even if this belief is not fully justified (Hmieleski & Baron, 2009).

In the past, it was widely assumed, that peoples' motives for becoming entrepreneurs were the desires for monetary wealth and fame. But more recent research—much of it inspired by social psychological theories—indicates that financial motives are only a small part of the total picture. Of course, most entrepreneurs would not object if they made a lot of money, but that outcome is usually not their key or central motive. In many cases, they seek to escape from jobs and lives that they find dull or unfulfilling. In other words, they become entrepreneurs to find more meaning in their lives—which, as you may recall, is a key aspect of happiness. Others become entrepreneurs because they want to have greater personal freedom—they want to be able to take greater charge of their lives and make the decisions that affect their quality of life. They are tired of working with bosses whom, they often believe, are unreasonable and perhaps less talented or hard-working than they are.

An important theory of motivation and well-being developed by social psychologists—**self-determination theory (SDT)** (Deci & Ryan, 2000; 2008)—is directly relevant to understanding entrepreneurs' motives. This theory focuses, in part, on the distinction between two kinds of motivation: intrinsic and extrinsic. *Intrinsic* motivation refers to activities that individuals pursue for their own sake—that is, for pure enjoyment. For instance, an individual who collects stamps or baseball cards is usually intrinsically motivated. Such a collector typically does not expect to obtain great financial gains from these activities; they pursue their hobbies because they enjoy them.

In contrast, *extrinsic* motivation refers to situations in which individuals *do* seek external rewards. They may perform tasks they don't enjoy—or may actually dislike—in order to obtain rewards such as money, high status, or a better job. As you might guess, intrinsic motives tend to promote higher levels of happiness and well-being than extrinsic ones. Applying self-determination theory to entrepreneurs helps to explain why many of them are not primarily seeking monetary wealth. Rather, they want to enjoy their work and be happy.

In addition to understanding the motivations behind entrepreneurship, what other attributes do successful entrepreneurs have that also play important roles in happiness? First, entrepreneurs, as a group, tend to have a high degree of confidence in themselves (Zhao, Seibert, & Hills, 2005). They generally believe they can accomplish the tasks they set out to perform. This is known as *self-efficacy* and is closely related to self-esteem and other aspects of the self that were discussed in Chapter 4. The degree to which we perceive ourselves positively or negatively—our overall attitude toward ourselves—directly impacts our level of happiness.

Another characteristic that entrepreneurs tend to display is a high level of social skills, which is important for convincing potential investors to contribute to their companies (see Figure 12.18). Social skills include the ability to "read" other people accurately, the ability to influence people, skill in generating enthusiasm among others, and the capacity to change or adapt behavior from one social situation to another. From a happiness point of view, people who are high in social skills are more likely to be promoted and receive positive feedback, and they tend to attract more friends than people who are low in such skills.

Another closely related variable involves an entrepreneur's ability to develop a strong social network (Baron, 2012). Social networks can help entrepreneurs in various ways. For instance, suppose an entrepreneur needs the expertise of a particular kind of engineer. If she or he has a large social network, someone in it might be able to help by recommending a person who can fill the need. How do entrepreneurs develop social networks? Recent research (Fang, Chi, Chen, & Baron, 2015) indicates they start

Figure 12.18 Social Skills Affect Both Entrepreneurial Success and Happiness

Good social skills are important for those who want to be successful entrepreneurs. People who are high in social skills are also typically happier than those low in social skills.

by developing positive relations with others they trust, and then expand their social networks to include others who may help them improve their business. As you may recall, having good social relationships and a diverse network of support to rely on is a central component of happiness.

In summary, research concerning people who seek to develop something new—entrepreneurs—reveals that they are intrinsically motivated by their work, which tends to promote happiness. The work that entrepreneurs undertake requires self-confidence. Entrepreneurial success is more likely for those with strong social skills, which allow them to build positive relationships with others. By extending their social networks, entrepreneurs rely on these more distant connections to help them improve their businesses. The same social ingredients that are associated with happiness among entrepreneurs have also proven important in predicting well-being among nonentrepreneurs.

Key Points

- Everyone seeks **happiness**, often referred to by social psychologists as *subjective well-being*. Systematic research on this topic suggests that it involves four basic components: global life satisfaction, satisfaction with specific life domains, a high level of positive feelings, and a minimum of negative feelings.

- People respond differently to questions about their levels of happiness and life satisfaction depending on the country in which they live. A number of central factors consistently account for more than half of the variability in nations' average happiness levels: degree of social support, per capita income, healthy life expectancy, freedom to make life choices, generosity toward others, amount of violence, and degree of corruption.

- One important source of happiness is close ties with friends and family—being part of an extended social network. Other factors involve having concrete goals and the resources to attain them. In addition, happy people report experiencing a higher frequency of positive emotions and a lower frequency of negative emotions than unhappy people do.

- According to research, increased income above a certain level has little connection with the positive feelings that people experience on a daily basis. This suggests that monetary wealth beyond a certain point does not necessarily increase happiness.

- Social comparison often plays a role in subjective well-being. Monetary wealth itself is not as important to people's happiness as *relative* wealth—knowing that they are wealthier than others in their neighborhoods or social circles.

- The possessions we own do not necessarily produce happiness. Happiness also appears to come from valuing the things we have—being grateful for them and enjoying them. A continual focus on obtaining more and better possessions can reduce our capacity to savor current pleasant experiences.

- Many differences exist between happy and unhappy people. Happy people are more community-oriented than unhappy people. Happy people also tend to focus on the positive: They are less affected by negative social comparisons, generally pleased with their choices, tend to interpret events in a positive way, and place more emphasis on their strengths than weaknesses when *self-reflecting*. In contrast, unhappy people tend to perceive past choices, events, and themselves in a more negative light.

- Individual, emotional experiences appear to play a greater role in the happiness levels within individualistic cultures (those that place emphasis on a person's particular achievements) than in collectivistic cultures (those that emphasize group harmony).

- In addition to feeling good, happiness has many tangible benefits. People who are high in subjective well-being are more likely to experience better work outcomes (raises, productivity, promotions, job satisfaction); have more, high-quality social relationships; report better health; and live longer than unhappy people.

- The **optimum level of well-being theory** helps explain why under some circumstances people can be *too* happy. Very high levels of happiness can foster complacency or lead to unjustified overoptimism. As a result, extreme happiness may interfere with task performance or cause cognitive errors. It may also encourage people to take more risks.

- Growing evidence supports the idea that happiness levels are fundamentally changeable. This evidence counters the *hedonic treadmill*—a view that suggests people ultimately return to their personal *set points* after experiencing intense emotion-generating events. Interventions that target intentional activity can exert lasting effects on measures of happiness.

- Steps you can take to increase happiness include building close personal relationship or joining groups you value, investing in experiences over material goods, building personal skills that contribute to being happy, and ceasing to engage in counterproductive thoughts and actions.

- Many of the characteristics needed to be a successful **entrepreneur** are also ones that contribute to happiness levels. Despite risks, entrepreneurs are motivated to start new businesses or work for themselves in order to find more meaning in their lives and gain greater personal freedom—two key aspects of happiness. Entrepreneurs are also high in *self-efficacy*, social skills, and use their social networks to help themselves succeed. These elements are also components related to happiness levels among nonentrepreneurs.

- **Self-determination theory (SDT)** helps to explain entrepreneurs' motives. Entrepreneurs tend to exhibit *intrinsic* motivation (engaging in activities for enjoyment) as opposed to *extrinsic* motivation (performing tasks in order to obtain external rewards). Intrinsic motives promote higher levels of happiness and well-being than extrinsic ones.

Summary and Review

Stress is a contributing factor to psychological and physical health problems. Stress can stem from traumatic events, or daily **hassles,** which tend to be lower intensity but higher in frequency. Stress interferes with the operation of the body's *immune system,* and can even be measured at the cellular level. **Social support**—emotional resources provided by people who care about us—helps to reduce the psychological distress induced by stressful experiences.

Loneliness occurs when a person has fewer and less satisfying relationships than desired. The lack of social connections that produces loneliness can be temporary, following a life change, or more chronic. Lonely people often feel left out. To the extent that people see their personality as "fixed" and unable to change, they are likely to react to rejection by cutting themselves off from others to avoid future negative experiences. In contrast, perceiving the self as capable of change, allows people to experience rejection as an opportunity for future improvement or growth. Interventions related to self-change—from seeing ourselves as fixed entities, to instead believing we are malleable and capable of incremental change—help to improve people's resilience in the face of stress and reduce the likelihood of depression.

Experiencing discrimination based on disability, sexual minorities, and weight, is associated with harm to well-being. One reason is because discrimination experienced by these groups often comes from those who would normally be expected to provide social support. Weight discrimination, even controlling for other risk factors, predicts mortality.

One method of dealing with stress and improving mental and physical health is regular exercise. Yet, adherence is difficult without social support. Technology such as Fitbit can link people with others monitoring their exercise, and help people stay motivated by creating a shared identity with others using the device. Identifying with groups can help people feel less strain and burnout in stressful occupations by providing a sense of personal control. Joining groups can foster social connectedness and help prevent depression. Following a failure experience, thinking about groups we belong to protects us by undermining depression attributions. Military veterans with **post-traumatic stress disorder (PTSD)** tend to show improvement when they receive social support from family members. Interventions that encourage students to feel they "belong" in college can improve academic performance and overall well-being.

An important means of coping with the stress of new challenges, especially when we find ourselves in new uncertain environments or feel we have made mistakes in the past, is to practice self-forgiveness. Forgiving ourselves for failing ourselves (as in the behavior of procrastination) can improve performance, lower the risk for depression, and encourage us not to make the same mistake next time. People are better able to enact self-change when it is framed as a new beginning. This approach helps to disconnect them from their past imperfect self and sets the stage for pursuing new goals. Reminders of having overcome obstacles and seeing those circumstances as a source of strength can allow first-generation college students to adaptively cope with the stress they experience because of their backgrounds.

To make the legal system more fair, impartial, and protective of basic human rights, it is necessary to understand potential sources of error and bias within the current system. **Lineups** used to identify criminal suspects are subject to bias, depending on how they are conducted. *Sequential lineups* requiring absolute judgments produce greater accuracy than *simultaneous lineups* that result in comparative judgments. Some types of instructions and feedback provided to witnesses during lineups can also lead to identification errors. Although judges often instruct jurors to ignore certain information, such as the defendant's prior convictions, or even acquittals, research indicates that jurors cannot actually do so.

In legal proceedings, defendants' race, gender, physical attractiveness, and socioeconomic status can influence jurors' perceptions and judgments. Racially diverse juries function more fairly and effectively than homogeneous juries.

Everyone seeks **happiness**, often referred to as *subjective well-being* with four basic components: global life satisfaction, satisfaction with specific life domains, a high level of positive feelings, and a minimum of negative feelings. People respond differently to questions about their levels of happiness and life satisfaction depending on the country in which they live. Several factors consistently account for more than half of the variability in nations' average happiness levels: degree of social support, per capita income, healthy life expectancy, freedom to make life choices, generosity toward others, amount of violence, and degree of corruption.

Happy people report experiencing a higher frequency of positive emotions and a lower frequency of negative emotions than unhappy people do. One important source of happiness is close ties with friends and family—being part of an extended social network. Happy people are more community-oriented than unhappy people. Happiness can be increased by building close personal relationships or joining groups you value, investing in experiences over material goods, building personal skills that contribute to being happy, and avoiding counterproductive thoughts and actions.

Monetary wealth beyond a certain point does not necessarily increase happiness. In fact, absolute amount of monetary wealth is not as important to people's happiness as *relative* wealth. Happiness also appears to come from valuing the things we have—being grateful for them and enjoying them—rather than focusing on obtaining more things, which can reduce our capacity to savor current pleasant experiences. People who are high in subjective well-being are more likely to experience better work outcomes (raises, productivity, promotions, job satisfaction), have more high-quality social relationships, report better health, and live longer than unhappy people.

The **optimum level of well-being theory** helps explain why, under some circumstances, people can be *too* happy. Very high levels of happiness can foster complacency or lead to unjustified overoptimism. Growing evidence supports the idea that happiness levels are fundamentally changeable. This evidence counters the *hedonic treadmill*—a view that suggests that people ultimately return to their personal *set points* after experiencing intense emotion-generating events.

Many of the characteristics needed to be a successful **entrepreneur** are the same ones that contribute to happiness levels. By starting new businesses or working for themselves, they gain meaning in their lives and feel greater personal freedom. Entrepreneurs are also high in *self-efficacy*, social skills, and use their social networks to help themselves succeed. **Self-determination theory (SDT)** helps to explain why entrepreneurs typically have strong *intrinsic* motivation; they want to perform work or activities that they enjoy. Whereas *extrinsic* motivation to obtain rewards does not bring the same level of happiness.

Glossary

above average effect The tendency for people to rate themselves as above the average on most positive social attributes.

action identification The level of interpretation we place on an action; low-level interpretations focus on the action itself, whereas higher-level interpretations focus on its ultimate goals.

actor-observer effect The tendency to attribute our own behavior mainly to situational causes but the behavior of others mainly to internal (dispositional) causes.

additive tasks Tasks for which the group product is the sum or combination of the efforts of individual members.

affect Our current feelings and moods.

affective forecasts Predictions about how we would feel about events we have not actually experienced.

aggression Behavior directed toward the goal of harming another living being who is motivated to avoid such treatment.

anchoring and adjustment heuristic A heuristic that involves the tendency to use a number of values as a starting point to which we then make adjustments.

attachment style The degree of security experienced in interpersonal relationships. Differential styles initially develop in the interactions between infant and caregiver when the infant acquires basic attitudes about self-worth and interpersonal trust.

attitude Evaluation of various aspects of the social world.

attitude clarity When there is no ambivalence in attitude; the person feels clear about what attitude to hold.

attitude correctness Believing one's attitude is the valid or proper one to hold.

attitude similarity The extent to which two individuals share the same attitude.

attitude-to-behavior process model A model of how attitudes guide behavior that emphasizes the influence of attitudes and stored knowledge of what is appropriate in a given situation on an individual's definition of the present situation. This definition, in turn, influences overt behavior.

attribution The process through which we seek to identify the causes of others' behavior and so gain knowledge of their stable traits and dispositions.

autobiographical memory Concerns memory of ourselves in the past, sometimes over the life course as a whole.

autokinetic phenomenon The apparent movement of a single, stationary source of light in a dark room. Used to study the emergence of social norms and social influence.

automatic processing This occurs when, after extensive experience with a task or type of information, we reach the stage where we can perform the task or process the information in a seemingly effortless, automatic, and nonconscious manner.

availability heuristic A strategy for making judgments on the basis of how easily specific kinds of information can be brought to mind.

balance theory Heider's perspective specifies the relationships among (1) an individual's liking for another person, (2) his or her attitude about a given topic, and (3) the other person's attitude about the same topic. Balance (liking plus agreement) results in a positive emotional state. Imbalance (liking plus disagreement) results in a negative state. Nonbalance (disliking plus either agreement or disagreement) leads to indifference.

bargaining (negotiation) A process in which opposing sides exchange offers, counteroffers, and concessions, either directly or through representatives.

body language Cues provided by the position, posture, and movement of others' bodies or body parts.

bona fide pipeline A technique that uses priming to measure implicit racial attitudes.

brainstorming A process in which people meet as a group to generate new ideas freely.

bullying A pattern of behavior in which one individual is chosen as the target of repeated aggression by one or more others; the target person (the victim) generally has less power than those who engage in aggression (the bullies).

catharsis hypothesis The view that providing angry people with an opportunity to express their aggressive impulses in relatively safe ways will reduce their tendencies to engage in more harmful forms of aggression.

central route to persuasion Attitude change resulting from systematic processing of information presented in persuasive messages.

classical conditioning A basic form of learning in which one stimulus, initially neutral, acquires the capacity to evoke reactions through repeated pairing with another stimulus. In a sense, one stimulus becomes a signal for the presentation or occurrence of the other.

close friendships Relationships in which two people spend a great deal of time together, interact in a variety of situations, and provide mutual emotional support.

cognitive dissonance An internal state that results when individuals notice inconsistency between two or more attitudes or between their attitudes and their behavior.

cohesive group One where there are strong bonds among the members creating a sense of solidarity.

cohesiveness The extent to which we are attracted to a social group and want to belong to it. All forces (factors) that cause group members to remain in the group.

collective guilt The emotion that can be experienced when we are confronted with the harmful actions done by our ingroup against an outgroup. It is most likely to be experienced when the harmful actions are seen as illegitimate.

collectivism Groups in which the norm is to maintain harmony among group members, even if doing so might entail some personal costs.

common ingroup identity model A theory suggesting that to the extent individuals in different groups view themselves as members of a single social entity, intergroup bias will be reduced.

common-bond groups Groups that tend to involve face-to-face interaction and in which the individual members are bonded to each other.

common-identity groups Face-to-face interaction is often absent, and the members are linked together via the category as a whole rather than each other.

companionate love Love that is based on friendship, mutual attraction, shared interests, respect, and concern for one another's welfare.

competitive altruism Refers to situations in which individuals behave in a prosocial way in order to boost their own status—to show that they are even more helpful than others.

compliance   A form of social influence involving direct requests from one person to another.

conditioned stimulus   The stimulus that comes to stand for or signal a prior unconditioned stimulus.

conditions of uncertainty   Where the "correct" answer is difficult to know or would take a great deal of effort to determine.

conflict   A process in which individuals or groups perceive that others have taken or will soon take actions incompatible with their own interests.

conformity   A type of social influence in which individuals change their attitudes or behavior to adhere to existing social norms.

consensus   The extent to which other people react to some stimulus, or even in the same manner as the person we are considering.

consistency   The extent to which an individual responds to a given stimulus, or situation in the same way on different occasions (i.e., across time).

consummate love   In Sternberg's triangular model of love, a complete and ideal love that combines intimacy, passion, and decision (commitment).

contact hypothesis   The view that increased contact between members of various social groups can be effective in reducing prejudice between them.

controlled processing   A mode of social thought that is logical, systematic, and effortful.

cooperation   Behavior in which group members work together to attain shared goals.

correlational method   A method of research in which a scientist systematically observes two or more variables to determine whether changes in one are accompanied by changes in the other.

correspondence bias (fundamental attribution error)   The tendency to explain others' actions as stemming from dispositions even in the presence of clear situational causes.

correspondent inference   A theory describing how we use others' behavior as a basis for inferring their stable dispositions.

counterfactual thinking   The tendency to imagine other outcomes in a situation than the ones that actually occurred ("What might have been").

crowdfunding   A new form of prosocial behavior in which entrepreneurs describe the products or services their new company will provide and ask people to contribute.

cyberbullying   Involves the use of communication technologies, such as e-mail, cell phones, instant messaging, and offensive personal websites, to engage in deliberate, repeated, and hostile behavior that is intended to harm others.

deadline technique   A technique for increasing compliance in which targeted people are told that they have only limited time to take advantage of some offer or to obtain some item.

debriefing   Procedures at the conclusion of a research session in which participants are given full information about the nature of the research and the hypothesis or hypotheses under investigation.

deception   A technique whereby researchers withhold information about the purposes or procedures of a study from people participating in it.

decision/commitment   In Sternberg's triangular model of love, these are the cognitive processes involved in deciding that you love another person and are committed to maintain the relationship.

deindividuation   A psychological state characterized by reduced self-awareness brought on by external conditions, such as being an anonymous member of a large crowd.

dependent variable   The variable that is measured in an experiment.

descriptive norms   Norms simply indicating what most people do in a given situation.

diffusion of responsibility   A principle suggesting that the greater the number of witnesses to an emergency the less likely victims are to receive help. This is because each bystander assumes that someone else will assume responsibility for helping.

discrimination   Differential (usually negative) behaviors directed toward members of different social groups.

dismissing attachment style   A style characterized by high self-esteem and low interpersonal trust. This is a conflicted and somewhat insecure style in which the individual feels that he or she deserves a close relationship, but is frustrated because of mistrust of potential partners. The result is the tendency to reject the other person at some point in the relationship to avoid being the one who is rejected.

distinctiveness   The extent to which an individual responds in the same manner to different stimuli or events.

distraction conflict theory   A theory suggesting that social facilitation stems from the conflict produced when individuals attempt, simultaneously, to pay attention to the other people present and to the task being performed.

distributive justice (fairness)   Refers to individuals' judgments about whether they are receiving a fair share of available rewards—a share proportionate to their contributions to the group or any social relationship.

door-in-the-face technique   A procedure for gaining compliance in which requesters begin with a large request and then, when this is refused, retreat to a smaller one (the one they actually desired all along).

downward social comparison   A comparison of the self to another who does less well than or is inferior to us.

drive theories (of aggression)   Theories suggesting that aggression stems from external conditions that arouse the motive to harm or injure others. The most famous of these is the frustration-aggression hypothesis.

drive theory of social facilitation   Claims that physiological arousal due to the presence of others facilitate performance on well-practiced tasks.

ego-depletion   The lowered capacity to exert subsequent self-control following earlier efforts to exert self-control. Performance decrements occur when people's ego strength has been depleted by prior efforts at self-control.

elaboration-likelihood model (ELM)   A theory suggesting that persuasion can occur in either of two distinct ways, differing in the amount of cognitive effort or elaboration the message receives.

emotional contagion   The spread of emotion from one person to another person who observes this emotion.

empathic joy hypothesis   The view that helpers respond to the needs of a victim because they want to accomplish something, and doing so is rewarding in and of itself.

empathy   Emotional reactions that are focused on or oriented toward other people and include feelings of compassion, sympathy, and concern.

empathy-altruism hypothesis   The suggestion that some prosocial acts are motivated solely by the desire to help someone in need.

entrepreneur   An individual who has an idea for something new—for instance, a new product or service—and takes active steps to develop this idea and turn it into reality.

entitativity   The extent to which a group is perceived as being a coherent entity.

essence   Typically some biologically based feature that is used to distinguish one group and another; frequently can serve as justification for the differential treatment of those groups.

evaluation apprehension   Concern over being evaluated by others. Such concern can increase arousal and so contribute to social facilitation effects.

evolutionary psychology   A new branch of psychology that seeks to investigate the potential role of genetic factors in various aspects of human behavior.

excitation transfer theory   A theory suggesting that arousal produced in one situation can persist and intensify emotional reactions occurring in later situations.

existential threat   The anxiety that results from awareness of our own mortality.

experimentation (experimental method)   A method of research in which one or more factors (the independent variables) are systematically changed to determine whether such variations affect one or more other factors (dependent variables).

explicit attitudes   Consciously accessible attitudes that are controllable and easy to report.

fear appeals   Attempting to change people's behaviors by use of a message that induces fear.

fearful-avoidant attachment style   A style characterized by low self-esteem and low interpersonal trust. This is the most insecure and least adaptive attachment style.

feeling rules   Expectations about the appropriate emotions to display or express.

foot-in-the-door technique   A procedure for gaining compliance in which requesters begin with a small request and then, when this is granted, escalate to a larger one (the one they actually desired all along).

forewarning   Advance knowledge that one is about to become the target of an attempt at persuasion; Forewarning often increases resistance to the persuasion that follows.

frustration-aggression hypothesis   The suggestion that frustration is a very powerful determinant of aggression.

fundamental attribution error (correspondence bias)   The tendency to overestimate the impact of dispositional cues on others' behavior.

gender stereotypes   Stereotypes concerning the traits possessed by females and males and that distinguish the two genders from each other.

general aggression model (GAM)   A modern theory of aggression suggesting that aggression is triggered by a wide range of input variables that influence arousal, affective stages, and cognitions.

glass ceiling   Barriers based on attitudinal or organizational bias that prevent qualified females from advancing to top-level positions.

glass cliff   When women and minorities are seen as better leaders because of their ability to manage crises, they are more likely to be selected as leader when the situation contains more risk.

glass cliff effect   Choosing women for leadership positions that are risky, precarious, or when the outcome is more likely to result in failure.

group   A collection of people who are perceived to be bonded together in a coherent unit to some degree.

group polarization   The tendency of group members to shift toward a more extreme position than initially held by those individuals as a result of group discussion.

groupthink   The tendency of the members of highly cohesive groups to assume that their decisions can't be wrong, that all members must support the group's decisions strongly, and that contrary information should be ignored.

habit   Repeatedly performing a specific behavior, so responses become relatively automatic whenever that situation is encountered.

happiness   Refers to subjective well-being, which involves global life satisfaction, satisfaction with specific life domains, frequent positive feelings, and relatively few negative feelings.

hassles   Minor annoyances experienced in daily life that may be low in intensity, but contribute to stress in our lives.

heuristic processing   Processing of information in a persuasive message that involves the use of simple rules of thumb or mental shortcuts.

heuristic-systematic model   Two distinct routes to persuasion: one where heuristic low-effort strategies are employed, and the other where effortful and systematic information processing is used.

heuristics   Simple rules for making complex decisions or drawing inferences in a rapid manner and seemingly effortless manner.

hooliganism   Negative stereotype about how people behave in crowds at sporting events, especially applied to incidents involving England's soccer fans.

hubris   The tendency to hold exaggerated self-confidence and overly positive views about oneself.

hypocrisy   Publicly advocating some attitudes or behavior and then acting in a way that is inconsistent with these attitudes or behavior.

hypothesis   An as yet unverified prediction concerning some aspect of social behavior or social thought.

identity fusion   The extent to which you see yourself and your group as overlapping.

ideology   The philosophical and political values that govern a group.

illusion of truth effect   The mere repetition of information creates a sense of familiarity and more positive attitudes.

implementation plan   A plan for how to implement our intentions to carry out some action.

implicit associations   Links between group membership and trait associations or evaluations that the perceiver may be unaware of. They can be activated automatically based on the group membership of a target.

implicit attitudes   Unconscious associations between objects and evaluative responses.

implicit self-esteem   Feelings about the self of which we are not consciously aware.

impression formation   The process through which we form impressions of others.

impression management (self-presentation)   Efforts by individuals to produce favorable first impressions on others.

incidental feelings   Those feelings induced separately or before a target is encountered; as a result, those feelings are irrelevant to the group being judged but can still affect judgments of the target.

independent variable   The variable that is systematically changed (i.e., varied) in an experiment.

individualism   Groups where the norm is to stand out and be different from others; individual variability is expected and disagreement among members is tolerated.

information overload   Instances in which our ability to process information is exceeded.

informational social influence   Social influence based on the desire to be correct (i.e., to possess accurate perceptions of the social world).

informed consent   A procedure in which research participants are provided with as much information as possible about a research project before deciding whether to participate in it.

ingratiation   When we try to make others like us by conveying that we like them; praising others to flatter them.

injunctive norms   Norms specifying what ought to be done; what is approved or disapproved behavior in a given situation.

instrumental conditioning   A basic form of learning in which responses that lead to positive outcomes, or which permit avoidance of negative outcomes, are strengthened.

intergroup comparisons   Judgments that result from comparisons between our group and another group.

intergroup sensitivity effect   When criticism of a group by an in-group member is responded to more favorably than when made by an outgroup member.

interpersonal trust   An attitudinal dimension underlying attachment styles that involves the belief that other people are generally trust-worthy, dependable, and reliable as opposed to the belief that others are generally untrustworthy, undependable, and unreliable. This is the most successful and most desirable attachment style.

intimacy   In Sternberg's triangular model of love, the closeness felt by two people—the extent to which they are bonded.

intragroup comparisons   Judgments that result from comparisons between individuals who are members of the same group.

introspection   To privately contemplate "who we are." It is a method for attempting to gain self-knowledge.

introspection illusion   Our belief that social influence plays a smaller role in shaping our own actions than it does in shaping the actions of others.

kin selection theory   A theory suggesting that a key goal for all organisms—including human beings—is getting our genes into the next generation; one way in which individuals can reach this goal is by helping others who share their genes.

leadership   Involves setting the group's agenda and influencing oth-ers to act in ways that will achieve those goals.

less-leads-to-more effect   The fact that offering individuals small rewards for engaging in counterattitudinal behavior often produces more dissonance, and so more attitude change, than offering them larger rewards.

lineup   A procedure in which witnesses to a crime are shown several people, one or more of whom may be suspects in a case, and asked to identify those that they recognize as the person who committed the crime.

linguistic style   Aspects of speech apart from the meaning of the words employed.

loneliness   The unpleasant emotional and cognitive state based on desiring close relationships but being unable to attain them.

love   A combination of emotions, cognitions, and behaviors that often play a crucial role in intimate relationships.

low-ball procedure   A technique for gaining compliance in which an offer or deal is changed to make it less attractive to the target person after this person has accepted it.

the Lure effect   A technique for gaining compliance in which individuals are first asked to do something they find appealing and then, once they agree, are asked to do something they dislike.

magical thinking   Thinking involving assumptions that don't hold up to rational scrutiny—for example, the belief that things that resemble one another share fundamental properties.

matching hypothesis   The tendency for individuals in a roman-tic relationship to be similar to each other in terms of physical attractiveness.

mediating variable   A variable that is affected by an independent variable and then influences a dependent variable. Mediating vari-ables help explain why or how specific variables influence social behavior or thought.

mere exposure   By having seen before, but not necessarily remem-bering having done so, attitudes toward an object can be formed.

meta-analysis   An average effect size observed across many studies is computed permitting assessment of the strength of an effect. This allows for strong conclusions, in part because of the increased sam-ple size and reduced error when many studies are combined.

metaphor   A linguistic device that relates or draws a comparison between one abstract concept and another dissimilar concept.

microexpressions   Fleeting facial expressions lasting only a few tenths of a second.

minimal groups   When we are categorized into different groups based on some "minimal" criteria we tend to favor others who are categorized in the same group as ourselves compared to those categorized as members of a different group.

mirror neurons   Refers to systems in the brain that appear to provide a neural foundation for our capacity to experience empathy.

moderators   Factors that are treated as independent variables and can change the size or even direction of a relationship between two variables. By comparing an effect or strength of a relationship under different conditions, knowledge of when and how effects emerge is gained, ensuring science is a cumulative enterprise.

modern racism   More subtle beliefs than blatant feelings of supe-riority. It consists primarily of thinking minorities are seeking and receiving more benefits than they deserve and a denial that discrimi-nation affects their outcomes.

mood congruence effects   The fact that we are more likely to store or remember positive information when in a positive mood and nega-tive information when in a negative mood.

mood dependent memory   The fact that what we remember while in a given mood may be determined, in part, by what we learned when previously in that mood.

moral disengagement   No longer seeing sanctioning as necessary for perpetrating harm that has been legitimized.

multicultural perspective   A focus on understanding the cultural and ethnic factors that influences social behavior.

narcissism   An aspect of personality; persons high in narcissism have unjustified overinflated self-esteem, which leads them to focus on themselves while largely ignoring the needs and feelings of others.

narcissistic rage   Intense anger experienced by narcissistic persons who have doubts about the accuracy of their exaggerated self-image when someone calls these views into question.

need for affiliation   The basic motive to seek and maintain interper-sonal relationships.

negative interdependence   A situation where if one person obtains a desired outcome, others cannot obtain it.

negative-state relief model   The proposal that prosocial behavior is motivated by the bystander's desire to reduce his or her own uncomfortable negative emotions or feelings.

noncommon effects   Effects produced by a particular cause that could not be produced by any other apparent cause.

nonverbal communication   Communication between individu-als that does not involve the content of spoken language. It relies instead on an unspoken language of facial expressions, eye contact, and body language.

normative focus theory   A theory suggesting that norms will influ-ence behavior only to the extent that they are focal for the people involved at the time the behavior occurs.

normative social influence   Social influence based on the desire to be liked or accepted by other people.

norms   Rules or expectations within a group concerning how its members should (or should not) behave.

obedience   A form of social influence in which one person simply orders one or more others to perform some action(s).

objective scales Those with measurement units that are tied to external reality so that they mean the same thing regardless of category membership (e.g., dollars earned, feet and inches, chosen or rejected).

observational learning A basic form of learning in which individuals acquire new forms of behavior as a result of observing others.

optimistic bias Our predisposition to expect things to turn out well overall.

optimum level of well-being theory A theory suggesting that for any specific task there is an optimum level of subjective well-being. Up to this point, performance increases, but beyond it, performance on the task declines

overconfidence bias The tendency to have more confidence in the accuracy of our own judgments than is reasonable.

passion In Sternberg's triangular model of love, the sexual motives and sexual excitement associated with a couple's relationship.

passionate love An intense and often unrealistic emotional response to another person. When this emotion is experienced, it is usually perceived as an indication of true love, but to outside observers it appears to be infatuation.

peripheral route to persuasion Attitude change that occurs in response to peripheral persuasion cues, which is often based on information concerning the expertise or status of would-be persuaders.

perseverance effect The tendency for beliefs and schemas to remain unchanged even in the face of contradictory information.

personal-versus-social identity continuum At the personal level, the self is thought of as a unique individual, whereas at the social identity level, the self is seen as a member of a group.

persuasion Efforts to change others' attitudes through the use of various kinds of messages.

physical attractiveness The combination of characteristics that are evaluated as beautiful or handsome at the positive extreme and as unattractive at the negative extreme.

planning fallacy The tendency to make optimistic predictions concerning how long a given task will take for completion.

playing hard to get A technique that can be used for increasing compliance by suggesting that a person or object is scarce and hard to obtain.

pluralistic ignorance When we collectively misunderstand what attitudes others hold and believe erroneously that others have different attitudes than us.

politicized collective identity Recognizing shared grievances and engaging in a power struggle on behalf of one's devalued group.

portion size effect The tendency to eat more when a larger portion of food is received than if a smaller portion is received. Portion size acts as a starting point (anchor) for how much food is perceived to be appropriate to eat. Since portion sizes have steadily increased over time, this effect is believed to play an important role in overeating in western societies.

possible selves Image of how we might be in the future—either a "dreaded" potential to be avoided or "desired" potential that can be strived for.

post-traumatic stress disorder (PTSD) A psychological condition caused by experiencing or witnessing an extremely frightening, often life-threatening, ordeal or event.

prejudice Negative emotional responses based on group membership.

preoccupied attachment style A style characterized by low self-esteem and high interpersonal trust. This is a conflicted and somewhat insecure style in which the individual strongly desires a close relationship but feels that he or she is unworthy of the partner and is thus vulnerable to being rejected.

priming A situation that occurs when stimuli or events increase the availability in memory or consciousness of specific types of information held in memory.

procedural justice Judgments concerning the fairness of the procedures used to distribute available rewards among group members.

proportion of similarity The number of topics on which two people express similar views is divided by the total number of topics on which those two people have communicated, resulting in a proportion that can be used to predict attraction.

prosocial behavior Actions by individuals that help others with no immediate benefit to the helper.

prototype Summary of the common attributes possessed by members of a category.

provocation Actions by others that tend to trigger aggression in the recipient, often because they are perceived as stemming from malicious intent.

proximity In attraction research, the physical closeness between two individuals with respect to where they live, where they sit in a classroom, where they work, and so on. The smaller the physical distance, the greater the probability that the two people will come into repeated contact experiencing repeated exposure to one another, positive affect, and the development of mutual attraction.

punishment Procedures in which aversive consequences are delivered to individuals when they engage in specific actions.

random assignment of participants to experimental conditions A basic requirement for conducting valid experiments. According to this principle, research participants must have an equal chance of being exposed to each level of the independent variable

reactance Negative reactions to threats to one's personal freedom. Reactance often increases resistance to persuasion and can even produce negative attitude change or opposite to what was intended.

realistic conflict theory The view that prejudice stems from direct competition between various social groups over scarce and valued resources.

recategorization Shifts in the boundaries between our ingroup ("us") and some outgroup ("them"). As a result of such recategorization, people formerly viewed as outgroup members may now be viewed a belonging to the ingroup and consequently are viewed more positively.

reference groups Groups of people with whom we identify and whose opinions we value.

relationships Our social ties with other individuals, ranging from casual acquaintance or passing friendships, to intense, long-term relationships such as marriage or lifetime friendships.

repeated exposure effect Zajonc's finding that frequent contact with any mildly negative, neutral, or positive stimulus results in an increasingly positive evaluation of that stimulus.

representativeness heuristic A strategy for making judgments based on the extent to which current stimuli or events resemble other stimuli or categories.

risk averse We weigh possible losses more heavily than equivalent potential gains. As a result, we respond more negatively to changes that are framed as potential losses than positively to changes that are framed as potential gains.

roles The set of behaviors that individuals occupying specific positions within a group are expected to perform.

salience When someone or some object stands out from its background or is the focus of attention.

schemas Mental frameworks centering on a specific theme that help us to organize social information.

schism Splintering of a group into distinct factions following an ideological rift among members.

secure attachment style A style characterized by high self-esteem and high interpersonal trust. This is the most successful and most desirable attachment style.

selective avoidance A tendency to direct attention away from information that challenges existing attitudes. Such avoidance increases resistance to persuasion.

self-affirmation Refers to the tendency to respond to a threat to one's self-concept by affirming one's competence in another area (different from the threat).

self-construal How we characterize ourselves, which can vary depending on what identity is salient at any given moment.

self-control Achieved by refraining from actions, we like and instead performing actions we prefer not to do as a means of achieving a long-term goal.

self-depreciating Putting ourselves down or implying that we are not as good as someone else.

self-determination theory (SDT) A framework used to study motivation that involves two forms of human initiative: intrinsic and extrinsic. People persist longer at tasks they are intrinsically motivated to complete and gain enjoyment from, whereas extrinsic motivation to achieve awards or financial gains is less likely to promote happiness.

self-enhancement The goal of increasing the positivity of one's self-image.

self-esteem The degree to which we perceive ourselves positively or negatively; our overall attitude toward ourselves. It can be measured explicitly or implicitly.

self-evaluation maintenance model This perspective suggests that to maintain a positive view of ourselves, we distance ourselves from others who perform better than we do on valued dimensions and move closer to others who perform worse than us. This view suggests that doing so will protect our self-esteem.

self-promotion Attempting to present ourselves to others as having positive attributes.

self-regulation Limited capacity to engage our willpower and control our own thinking and emotions.

self-serving bias The tendency to attribute positive outcomes to internal causes (e.g., one's own traits or characteristics) but negative outcomes or events to external causes (e.g., chance, task difficulty).

self-verification perspective Theory that addresses the processes by which we lead others to agree with our views of ourselves; wanting others to agree with how we see ourselves.

shining standards When we use one group as the standard but shift to use another group as the comparison standard when judging members of a different group.

similarity-dissimilarity effect The consistent finding that people respond positively to indications that another person is similar to themselves and negatively to indications that another person is dissimilar from themselves.

singlism Negative stereotyping and discrimination directed toward people who are single.

social cognition The manner in which we interpret, analyze, remember, and use information about the social world.

social comparison The process through which we compare ourselves to others to determine whether our view of social reality is, or is not, correct.

social comparison theory Festinger (1954) suggested that people compare themselves to others because for many domains and attributes there is no objective yardstick to evaluate ourselves against, and other people are therefore highly informative.

social contagion Refers to the process by which emotions experienced by one person spread to others.

social dilemmas Situations in which each person can increase their individual gains by acting in one way, but if all (or most) people do the same thing, the outcomes experienced by all are reduced.

social embeddedness Having a sense of that you know other persons because you know their reputations, often by knowing other people they know too.

social facilitation When the presence of an audience improves task performance.

social identity theory Addresses the consequences of perceiving ourselves as a member of a social group and identifying with it; predicts how we respond when our group identity is salient. Suggests that we will move closer to positive others with whom we share an identity but distance from other ingroup members who perform poorly or otherwise make our social identity negative.

social influence Efforts by one or more persons to change the behavior, attitudes, or feelings of one or more others.

social learning The process through which we acquire new information, forms of behavior, or attitudes from other people.

social learning view (of prejudice) The view prejudice is acquired through direct and vicarious experiences in much the same manner as other attitudes.

social loafing Reductions in motivation and effort when individuals work in a group compared to when they work individually.

social networks Composed of individuals with whom we have interpersonal relationships and interact with on a regular basis.

social norms Rules indicating how individuals are expected to behave in specific situations.

social perception The process through which we seek to know and understand other people.

social skills A combination of aptitudes that help individuals who possess them to interact effectively with others, thereby increasing their attractiveness.

social support Drawing on the emotional and task resources provided by others as a means of coping with stress.

staring A form of eye contact in which one person continues to gaze steadily at another regardless of what the recipient does.

status The individual's position or rank within the group.

stereotype threat Can occur when people believe that they might be judged in light of a negative stereotype about their group or that, because of their performance, they may in some way confirm a negative stereotype of their group.

stereotypes Beliefs about social groups in terms of the traits or characteristics that they are believed to share. Stereotypes are cognitive frameworks that influence the processing of social information.

stress Our response to events that disrupt, or threaten to disrupt, our physical or psychological functioning.

subjective scales Response scales that are open to interpretation and lack an externally grounded referent, including scales labeled from good to bad or weak to strong. They are said to be subjective because they can take on different meanings depending on the group membership of the person being evaluated.

subliminal conditioning Classical conditioning of attitudes by exposure to stimuli that are below individuals' threshold of conscious awareness.

subtype A subset of a group that is not consistent with the stereotype of the group as a whole.

superordinate goals Goals that tie the interests of both sides in a conflict together rather than driving them apart. These are goals that can only be achieved by cooperation between groups.

survey method A method of research in which a large number of people answer questions about their attitudes or behavior.

symbolic social influence Social influence resulting from the mental representation of others or our relationships with them.

synchronous behavior Behavior in which individuals closely match their actions to those of others.

systematic observation A method of research in which behavior is systematically observed and recorded.

systematic processing Processing of information in a persuasive message that involves careful consideration of message content and ideas.

teasing Provoking statements that call attention to the target's flaws and imperfections.

terror management theory A view that human awareness of death evokes existential terror that can be reduced by adhering to cultural worldviews that give meaning to one's life.

that's-not-all technique A technique for gaining compliance in which requesters offer additional benefits to target people before they have decided whether to comply with or reject specific requests.

theory of planned behavior An extension of the theory of reasoned action, suggesting that in addition to attitudes toward a given behavior and subjective norms about it, individuals also consider their ability to perform the behavior.

theory of reasoned action A theory suggesting that the decision to engage in a particular behavior is the result of a rational process in which behavioral options are considered, consequences or outcomes of each are evaluated, and a decision is reached to act or not to act. That decision is then reflected in behavioral intentions, which strongly influence overt behavior.

thin slices Refers to small amounts of information about others we use to form first impressions of them.

tightness versus looseness In some cultures people are expected to adhere to many strong social norms (tight cultures), whereas in other cultures norms are weaker and less strongly enforced (loose cultures).

threat It primarily concerns fear that our group interests will be undermined or our self-esteem is in jeopardy.

tokenism Tokenism can refer to hiring based on group membership. It can concern a numerically infrequent presence of members of a particular category, or it can refer to instances where individuals perform trivial positive actions for members of outgroups that are later used as an excuse for refusing more meaningful beneficial actions for members of these groups.

transactional justice Refers to the extent to which people who distribute rewards explain or justify their decisions and show respect and courtesy to those who receive the rewards.

triangular model of love Sternberg's conceptualization of love relationships.

unconditioned stimulus A stimulus that evokes a positive or negative response without substantial learning.

unintentional social influence Instances in which other persons change our behavior without intending to do so.

unpriming Refers to the fact that the effects of the schemas tend to persist until they are somehow expressed in thought or behavior and only then do their effects decrease.

unrequited love Love felt by one person for another who does not feel love in return.

upward social comparison A comparison of the self to another who does better than or is superior to us.

zero-sum outcomes Those that only one person or group can have. So, if one group gets them, the other group can't.

References

Adam, H., Shirako, A., & Maddux, W. W. (2010). Cultural variance in the interpersonal effects of anger in negotiations. *Psychological Science, 21,* 882–889.

Adams, G., Biernat, M., Branscombe, N. R., Crandall, C. S., & Wrightsman, L. S. (2008). Beyond prejudice: Toward a sociocultural psychology of racism and oppression. In G. Adams, M. Biernat, N. R. Branscombe, C. S. Crandall, & L. S. Wrightsman (Eds.), *Commemorating Brown: The social psychology of racism and discrimination* (pp. 215–246). Washington, DC: American Psychological Association.

Adams, J. S. (1965). Inequity in social exchange. In L. Berkowitz (Ed.), *Advances in experimental social psychology* (Vol. 2, pp. 267–299). New York: Academic Press.

Adarves-Yorno, I., Postmes, T., & Haslam, S. A. (2007). Creative innovation or crazy irrelevance? The contribution of group norms and social identity to creative behavior. *Journal of Experimental Social Psychology, 43,* 410–416.

Aggarwal, P., & O'Brien, C. L. (2008). Social loafing on group projects: Structural antecedents and effect on student satisfaction. *Journal of Marketing Education, 30,* 255–264.

Ajzen, I. (1987). Attitudes, traits, and actions: Dispositional prediction of behavior in personality and social psychology. In L. Berkowitz (Ed.), *Advances in experimental social psychology* (Vol. 20, pp. 1–63). San Diego, CA: Academic Press.

Ajzen, I. (1991). The theory of planned behavior: Special issue: Theories of cognitive self-regulation. *Organizational Behavior and Human Decision Processes, 50,* 179–211.

Ajzen, I., & Fishbein, M. (1980). *Understanding attitudes and predicting social behavior.* Englewood Cliffs, NJ: Prentice-Hall.

Ajzen, I., & Fishbein, M. (2005). The influence of attitudes on behavior. In D. Albarracin, B. T. Johnson, & M. P. Zanna (Eds.), *The handbook of attitudes* (pp. 173–221). Mahwah, NJ: Erlbaum.

Akerlof, G. A., & Shiller, R. J. (2009). *Animal spirits: How human psychology drives the economy, and why it matters for global capitalism.* Princeton, NJ: Princeton University Press.

Aknin, L. B., Barrington-Leigh, C. P., Dunn, E. W., Helliwell, J. F., Burns, J., Biswas-Diener, R., et al. (2013). Prosocial spending and well-being: Cross-cultural evidence for a psychological universal. *Journal of Personality and Social Psychology, 104,* 635–652.

Aknin, L., Sandstrom, G. M., Dunn, E. W., & Norton, M. I. (2011). Investing in others: Prosocial spending for (pro) social change. In R. Biswas-Diener (Ed.), *Positive psychology in social change* (pp. 219–234). Dordrecht, Netherlands: Springer.

Alagna, F. J., Whitcher, S. J., & Fisher, J. D. (1979). Evaluative reactions to interpersonal touch in a counseling interview. *Journal of Counseling Psychology, 26,* 465–472.

Albarracin, D., Johnson, B. T., Fishbein, M., & Muellerleile, P. A. (2001). Theories of reasoned action and planned behavior as models of condom use: A meta-analysis. *Psychological Bulletin, 127,* 142–161.

Albarracin, D., Johnson, B. T., & Zanna, M. P. (2005). *The Handbook of attitudes.* Hillsdale, NJ: Erlbaum.

Alicke, M. D., Vredenburg, D. S., Hiatt, M., & Govorun, O. (2001). The better than myself effect. *Motivation and Emotion, 25,* 7–22.

Allen, J. P., Uchino, B. N., & Hafen, C. A. (2015). Running with the pack: Teen peer-relationship qualities as predictors of adult physical health. *Psychological Science.* doi:10.1177/0956797615594118

Allen, K., Shykoff, B. E., & Izzo, J. L. (2001). Pet ownership, but not ACE inhibitor therapy, blunts home blood pressure responses to mental stress. *Hypertension, 38,* 815–820.

Alquist, J. L., Ainsworth, S. E., Baumeister, R. F., Daly, M., & Stillman, T. F. (2015). The making of might-have-beens: Effects of free will belief on counterfactual thinking. *Personality and Social Psychology Bulletin, 41,* 268–283.

Amato, P. R. (1986). Marital conflict, the parent-child relationship and child self-esteem. *Family Relations, 35,* 403–410.

Ambady, N., Bernieri, F. J., & Richeson, J. A. (2000). Towards histology of social behavior: Judgmental accuracy from thin slices of the behavioural stream. *Advances in Experimental Social Psychology, 32,* 201–271.

American Psychological Association Survey. (2014). *Stress in America.* Retrieved from http://www.apa.org/news/press/releases/2014/02/teen-stress.aspx

Ames, D. R., Kammrath, L. K., Suppes, A., & Bolger, N. (2010). Not so fast: The (not-quite-complete) dissociation between accuracy and confidence in thin-slice impressions. *Personality and Social Psychology Bulletin, 36,* 264–277.

Amiot, C. E., Terry, D. J., & Callan, V. J. (2007). Status, fairness, and social identification during an intergroup merger: A longitudinal study. *British Journal of Social Psychology, 46,* 557–577.

Amirkhan, J. H. (1998). Attributions as predictors of coping and distress. *Personality and Social Psychology Bulletin, 24,* 1006–1018.

Andersen, R., & Fetner, T. (2008). Economic inequality and intolerance: Attitudes toward homosexuality in 35 democracies. *American Journal of Political Science, 52,* 942–958.

Anderson, C. A. (1989). Temperature and aggression: Effects on quarterly, yearly, and city rates of violent and nonviolent crime. *Journal of Personality and Social Psychology, 52,* 1161–1173.

Anderson, C. A. (1998). Does the gun pull the trigger?: Automatic priming effects of weapon pictures and weapon names. *Psychological Science, 9,* 308–314.

Anderson, C. A. (2004). *The influence of media violence on youth.* Paper presented at the annual convention of the Association for Psychological Science, Los Angeles, CA.

Anderson, C. A., & Anderson, K. B. (1996). Violent crime rate studies in philosophical context: A destructive testing approach to heat and Southern culture of violence effects. *Journal of Personality and Social Psychology, 70,* 740–756.

Anderson, C. A., Anderson, K. B., & Deuser, W. E. (1996). Examining an affective aggression framework: Weapon and temperature effects on aggressive thoughts, affect, and attitudes. *Personality and Social Psychology Bulletin, 22,* 366–376.

Anderson, C. A., Berkowitz, L., Donnerstein, E., Huesmann, L. R., Johnson, J., Linz, D., et al. (2003). The influence of media violence on youth. *Psychological Science in the Public Interest, 4,* 81–110.

Anderson, C. A., & Bushman, B. J. (2001). Effects of violent video games on aggressive behavior, aggressive cognition, aggressive affect, physiological arousal, and prosocial behavior: A meta-analytic review of the scientific literature. *Psychological Science, 12,* 353–359.

Anderson, C. A., & Bushman, B. J. (2002). Human aggression. *Annual Review of Psychology, 53,* 27–51.

Anderson, C. A., Bushman, B. J., Donnerstein, E., Hummer, T. A., & Warburton, W. (2015). SPSSI research summary on media violence. *Analyses of Social Issues and Public Policy.* doi: 10.1111/asap.12093

Anderson, C. A., Bushman, B. J., & Groom, R. W. (1997). Hot years and serious and deadly assault: Empirical tests of the heat hypothesis. *Journal of Personality and Social Psychology, 73*, 1213–1223.

Anderson, C. A., Carnagey, N. L., & Eubanks, J. (2003). Exposure to violent media: The effects of songs with violent lyrics on aggressive thoughts and feelings. *Journal of Personality and Social Psychology, 84*, 960–971.

Anderson, C. A., Miller, R. S., Riger, A. L., Dill, J. C., & Sedikides, C. (1994). Behavioral and characterological attributional styles as predictors of depression and loneliness: Review, refinement, and test. *Journal of Personality and Social Psychology, 66*, 549–558.

Anderson, C. A., Shibuya, A., Ihori, N., Swing, E. L., Bushman, B. J., Sakamoto, A., et al. (2010). Violent video game effects on aggression: Empathy and prosocial behavior in Eastern and Western countries: A meta-analytic review. *Psychological Bulletin, 136*, 151–172.

Anderson, S. L., Adams, G., & Plaut, V. C. (2008). The cultural grounding of personal relationship: The importance of attractiveness in everyday life. *Journal of Personality and Social Psychology, 95*, 352–368.

Apanovitch, A. M., McCarthy, D., & Salovey, P. (2003). Using message framing to motivate HIV testing among low-income, ethnic minority women. *Health Psychology, 22*, 60–67.

Aquino, K., Reed, A., Thau, S., & Freeman, D. (2006). A grotesque and dark beauty: How moral identity and mechanisms of moral disengagement influence cognitive and emotional reactions to war. *Journal of Experimental Social Psychology, 43*, 385–392.

Archer, J. (2004). Sex differences in aggression in real-world settings: A meta-analytic review. *Journal of General Psychology, 8*, 291–322.

Archibald, F. S., Bartholomew, K., & Marx, R. (1995). Loneliness in early adolescence: A test of the cognitive discrepancy model of loneliness. *Personality and Social Psychology Bulletin, 21*, 296–301.

Arkes, H. R., & Tetlock, P. E. (2004). Attributions of implicit prejudice, or "Would Jesse Jackson 'Fail' the Implicit Association Test?" *Psychological Inquiry, 15*, 257–278.

Armor, D. A., & Taylor, S. E. (2002). When predictions fail: The dilemma of unrealistic optimism. In T. Gilovich, D. Griffin, & D. Kahneman (Eds.), *Heuristics and biases: The psychology of intuitive judgment* (pp. 334–347). New York: Cambridge University Press.

Aron, A., Aron, E. N., & Allen, J. (1998). Motivations for unreciprocated love. *Personality and Social Psychology Bulletin, 24*, 787–796.

Aron, A., & Westbay, L. (1996). Dimensions of the prototype of love. *Journal of Personality and Social Psychology, 70*, 535–551.

Aronson, E., & Mills, J. S. (1959). The effect of severity of initiation on liking for a group. *Journal of Abnormal and Social Psychology, 59*, 177–181.

Aronson, J., Lustina, M. J., Good, C., Keough, K., Steele, C. M., & Brown, J. (1999). When white men can't do math: Necessary and sufficient factors in stereotype threat. *Journal of Experimental Social Psychology, 35*, 29–46.

Arriaga, X. B., Reed, J. T., Goodfriend, W., & Agnew, C. R. (2006). Relationship perceptions and persistence: Do fluctuations in perceived partner commitment undermine dating relationships? *Journal of Personality and Social Psychology, 91*, 1045–1065.

Asch, S. E. (1946). Forming impressions of personality. *Journal of Abnormal and Social Psychology, 41*, 258–290.

Asch, S. E. (1951). Effects of group pressure upon the modification and distortion of judgment. In H. Guetzkow (Ed.), *Groups, leadership, and men* (pp. 222–236). Pittsburgh, PA: Carnegie.

Asch, S. E. (1955). Opinions and social pressure. *Scientific American, 193*(5), 31–35.

Asch, S. E. (1956). Studies of independence and conformity: A minority of one against unanimous majority. *Psychological Monographs, 70* (Whole No. 416).

Asch, S. E. (1959). A perspective on social psychology. In S. Koch (Ed.), *Psychology: A study of a science* (Vol. 3, pp. 363–383). New York: McGraw-Hill.

Asher, S. R., & Paquette, J. A. (2003). Loneliness and peer relations in childhood. *Current Directions in Psychological Science, 12*, 75–78.

Ashforth, B. E., Harrison, S. H., & Corley, K. G. (2008). Identification in organizations: An examination of four fundamental questions. *Journal of Management, 34*, 325–374.

Ashmore, R. D., Solomon, M. R., & Longo, L. C. (1996). Thinking about fashion models' looks: A multidimensional approach to the structure of perceived physical attractiveness. *Personality and Social Psychology Bulletin, 22*, 1083–1104.

Atchley, P., Hadlock, C., & Lane, S. (2012). Stuck in the 70s: The role of social norms in distracted driving. *Accident Analysis and Prevention, 48*, 279–284.

Avenanti, A., Sirigu, A., & Aglioti, S. M. (2010). Racial bias reduces empathic sensorimotor resonance with other-race pain. *Current Biology, 20*, 1018–1022.

Averill, J. R., & Boothroyd, P. (1977). On falling in love: Conformance with romantic ideal. *Motivation and Emotion, 1*, 235–247.

Azar, O. H. (2007). The social norm of tipping: A review. *Journal of Applied Social Psychology, 137*, 380–402.

Baas, M., De Dreu, C. K. W., & Nijstad, B. A. (2008). A meta-analysis of 25 years of mood-creativity research: Hedonic tone, activation, or regulatory focus? *Psychological Bulletin, 134*, 779–806.

Back, M. D., Schmukle, S. C., & Egloff, B. (2011). A closer look at first sight: Social relations lens model analysis of personality and interpersonal attraction at zero acquaintance. *European Journal of Personality, 25*, 225–238.

Back, M. J., Hopfer, J. M., Vazire, S., Gaddis, S., Schmukle, S. C., Egloff, B., et al. (2010). Facebook profiles reflect actual personality, not self-idealization. *Psychological Science, 21*, 372–374.

Baddeley, A. D. (1990). *Human memory.* Boston: Allyn & Bacon.

Baird, A. D., Scheffer, I. D., & Wilson, S. J. (2011). Mirror neuron system involvement in empathy: A critical look at the evidence. *Social Neuroscience, 66*, 327–335.

Baldwin, M. W., Carrell, S. E., & Lopez, D. F. (1990). Priming relationship schemas: My advisor and the Pope are watching me from the back of my mind. *Journal of Experimental Social Psychology, 26*, 435–454.

Ball, H., & Goodboy, A. K. (2014). An experimental investigation of the antecedents and consequences of psychological reactance in the college classroom. *Communication Education, 63*, 192–209.

Balliet, D., & Van Lange, P. A. M. (2013). Trust, conflict, and cooperation: A meta-analysis. *Psychological Bulletin, 139*, 1090–1112.

Banaji, M., & Hardin, C. (1996). Automatic stereotyping. *Psychological Science, 7*, 136–141.

Bandura, A. (1990). Selective activation and disengagement of moral control. *Journal of Social Issues, 46*, 27–46.

Bandura, A. (1997). *Self-efficacy: The exercise of control.* New York: W. H. Freeman.

Bandura, A. (1999). Moral disengagement in the perpetration of inhumanities. *Personality and Social Psychology Review, 3*, 193–209.

Bandura, A., Ross, D., & Ross, S. (1963a). Imitation of film-mediated aggressive models. *Journal of Abnormal and Social Psychology, 66*, 3–11.

Bandura, A., Ross, D., & Ross, S. (1963b). Vicarious reinforcement and imitative learning. *Journal of Abnormal and Social Psychology, 67*, 601–607.

Bar, M., Neta, M., & Linz, H. (2006). Very first impressions. *Emotion, 6*, 269–278.

Bar-Tal, D. (2003). Collective memory of physical violence: Its contribution to the culture of violence. In E. Cairns & M. D. Roe (Eds.), *The role of memory in ethnic conflict* (pp. 77–93). New York: Palgrave Macmillan.

Barclay, L. J., & Aquino, K. (2010). Workplace aggression and violence. In S. Zedeck (Ed.), *APA handbook of industrial and organizational psychology* (Vol. 3, pp. 615–640). Washington, DC: American Psychological Association.

Barclay, L. J., Skarlicki, D. P., & Pugh, S. D. (2005). Exploring the role of emotions in injustice perceptions and retaliation. *Journal of Applied Psychology, 90,* 629–643.

Bargh, J. A., & Chartrand, T. L. (2000). Studying the mind in the middle: A practical guide to priming and automaticity research. In H. Reis & C. Judd (Eds.), *Handbook of research methods in social psychology* (pp. 253–285). New York: Cambridge University Press.

Bargh, J. A., Chen, M., & Burrows, L. (1996). Automaticity of social behavior: Direct effects of trait construct and stereotype activation on action. *Journal of Personality and Social Psychology, 71,* 230–234.

Baron, R. A. (1976). The reduction of human aggression: A field study of the influence of incompatible responses. *Journal of Applied Social Psychology, 6,* 260–674.

Baron, R. A. (1990). Attributions and organizational conflict. In S. Graha & V. Folkes (Eds.), *Attribution theory: Applications to achievement, mental health, and interpersonal conflict* (pp. 185–204). Hillsdale, NJ: Erlbaum.

Baron, R. A. (1997). The sweet smell of helping: Effects of pleasant ambient fragrance on prosocial behavior in shopping malls. *Personality and Social Psychology Bulletin, 23,* 498–503.

Baron, R. A. (2008). The role of affect in the entrepreneurial process. *Academy of Management Review, 33,* 328–340.

Baron, R. A. (2012). *Entrepreneurship: An evidence-based guide.* Cheltenham, UK: Edward Elgar.

Baron, R. A., & Richardson, D. R. (1994). *Human aggression* (2nd ed.). New York: Plenum.

Baron, R. A., & Shane, S. A. (2007). *Entrepreneurship: A process perspective.* Mason, OH: Thomson.

Baron, R. A., & Thomley, J. (1994). A whiff of reality positive affect as a potential mediator of the effects of pleasant fragrances on task performance and helping. *Environment and Behavior, 26,* 766–784.

Baron, R. S. (1986). Distraction/conflict theory: Progress and problems. In L. Berkwoitz (Ed.), *Advances in experimental social psychology* (Vol. 19, pp. 1–40). Orlando, FL: Academic Press.

Baron, R. S., Vandello, U. A., & Brunsman, B. (1996). The forgotten variable in conformity research: Impact of task importance on social influence. *Journal of Personality and Social Psychology, 71,* 915–927.

Barreto, M., & Ellemers, N. (2015). Detecting and experiencing prejudice: New answers to old questions. *Advances in Experimental Social Psychology, 52,* 139–219.

Barrick, M. R., & Mount, M. K. (1991). The big five personality dimensions and job performance: A meta-analysis. *Personnel Psychology, 44,* 109–141.

Barrick, M. R., Swider, B. W., & Stewart, G. J. (2010). Initial evaluations in the interview: Relationships with subsequent interviewer evaluations and employment offers. *Journal of Applied Psychology, 95,* 1161–1172.

Barsky, A., & Kaplan, S. A. (2007). If you feel bad, it's unfair: A quantitative synthesis of affect and organizational justice perceptions. *Journal of Applied Psychology, 92,* 286–295.

Bartholow, B. D., Bushman, B. J., & Sestir, M. A. (2006). Chronic violent video game exposure and desensitization to violence: Behavioral and event-related brain potential data. *Journal of Experimental Social Psychology, 42,* 532–539.

Bartholow, B. D., Dickter, C. L., & Sestir, M. A. (2006). Stereotype activation and control of race bias: Cognitive control of inhibition and its impairment by alcohol. *Journal of Personality and Social Psychology, 90,* 272–287.

Bartholow, B. D., Pearson, M. A., Gratton, G., & Fabiani, M. (2003). Effects of alcohol on person perception: A social cognitive neuroscience approach. *Journal of Personality and Social Psychology, 85,* 627–638.

Barz, M., Parschau, L., Warner, L. M., Lange, D., Fleig, L., Knoll, N., et al. (2014). Planning and preparatory actions facilitate physical activity maintenance. *Psychology of Sport and Exercise, 15,* 516–520.

Bassili, J. N. (2003). The minority slowness effect: Subtle inhibitions in the expression of views not shared by others. *Journal of Personality and Social Psychology, 84,* 261–276.

Bastian, B., Kuppens, P., De Roover, K., & Diener, E. (2014). Is valuing positive emotion associated with life satisfaction? *Emotion, 14,* 630–645.

Batson, C. D., Kobrynowicz, D., Dinnerstein, J. L., Kampf, H. C., & Wilson, A. D. (1997). In a very different voice: Unmasking moral hypocrisy. *Journal of Personality and Social Psychology, 72,* 1335–1348.

Baumeister, R. F. (1991). *Escaping the self.* New York: Basic Books.

Baumeister, R. F. (1998). The self. In D. T. Gilbert, S. T. Fiske, & G. Lindzey (Eds.), *Handbook of social psychology* (4th ed., Vol. 1, pp. 680–740). New York: McGraw-Hill.

Baumeister, R. F. (2005). *The cultural animal: Human nature, meaning, and social life.* New York: Oxford University Press.

Baumeister, R. F., & Leary, M. R. (1995). The need to belong: Desire for interpersonal attachments as a fundamental human motivation. *Psychological Bulletin, 117,* 497.

Baumeister, R. F., & Tierney, J. (2011). *Willpower: Rediscovering the greatest human strength.* New York: Penguin Press.

Baumeister, R. F., & Twenge, J. M. (2003). The social self. In T. Millon & M. J. Lerner (Eds.), *Handbook of psychology* (pp. 327–325). Hoboken, NJ: Wiley.

Baumeister, R. F., Twenge, J. M., & Nuss, C. K. (2002). Effects of social exclusion on cognitive processes: Anticipated aloneness reduces intelligent thought. *Journal of Personality and Social Psychology, 83,* 817.

Baumeister, R. F., Vohs, K. D., & Tice, D. M. (2007). The strength model of self-control. *Current Directions in Psychological Science, 16,* 351–355.

Beall, A. E., & Sternberg, R. J. (1995). The social construction of love. *Journal of Social and Personal Relationships, 12,* 417–438.

Beaman, A. L., Cole, C. M., Preston, M., Klentz, B., & Steblay, N. M. (1983). Fifteen years of foot-in-the-foot research: A meta-analysis. *Personality and Social Psychology Bulletin, 9,* 181–196.

Bebchuk, L. A., & Fried, J. M. (2005). Pay without performance: Overview of the issues. *Journal of Applied Corporate Finance, 17,* 8–23.

Bell, B. (1993). Emotional loneliness and the perceived similarity of one's ideas and interests. *Journal of Social Behavior and Personality, 8,* 273–280.

Bell, P. A. (1992). In defense of the negative affect escape model of heat and aggression. *Psychological Bulletin, 111,* 342–346.

Bell, P. A., Greene, T. C., Fisher, J. D., & Baum, A. (2001). *Environmental psychology* (5th ed.). Belmont, CA: Wadsworth/Thomson Learning.

Bellezza, S., Gino, F., & Keinan, A. (2014). The red sneakers effect: Inferring status and competence from signals of nonconformity. *Journal of Consumer Research, 41,* 35–54.

Belmi, P., Cortes Barragan, R., Neale, M. A., & Cohen, G. L. (2015). Threats to social identity can trigger social deviance. *Personality and Social Psychology Bulletin, 41,* 467–484.

Ben-Porath, D. D. (2002). Stigmatization of individuals who receive psychotherapy: An interaction between help-seeking behavior and the presence of depression. *Journal of Social and Clinical Psychology, 21,* 400–413.

Benabou, R. (2013). Groupthink: Collective delusions in organizations and markets. *Review of Economic Studies, 80,* 429–462.

Benish-Weisman, M., Daniel, E., Schiefer, D., Mollering, A., & Knafo-Noam, A. (2015). Multiple social identifications and adolescents' self-esteem. *Journal of Adolescence, 44,* 21–31.

Benjamin, E. (1998, January 14). Storm brings out good, bad and greedy. Albany *Times Union,* pp. A1–A6.

Benoit, W. L. (1998). Forewarning and persuasion. In M. Allen & R. riess (Eds.), *Persuasion: Advances through meta-analysis* (pp. 159–184). Cresskill, NJ: Hampton Press.

Berg, J. H., & McQuinn, R. D. (1989). Loneliness and aspects of social support networks. *Journal of Social and Personal Relationships, 6,* 359–372.

Berkowitz, L. (1989). Frustration-aggression hypothesis: Examination and reformulation. *Psychological Bulletin, 106,* 59–73.

Berkowitz, L. (1993). *Aggression: Its causes, consequences, and control.* New York: McGraw-Hill.

Berkowitz, L., & LePage, A. (1967). Weapons as aggression-eliciting stimuli. *Journal of Personality and Social Psychology, 7,* 202–207.

Berns, G. S., Chappelow, J., Zink, C. F., Pagnoni, G., Martin-Skurski, M. E., & Richards, J. (2005). Neurobiological correlates of social conformity and independence during mental rotation. *Biological Psychiatry, 58,* 245–253.

Berry, D. S., & Hansen, J. S. (1996). Positive affect, negative affect, and social interaction. *Journal of Personality and Social Psychology, 71,* 796–809.

Berscheid, E., Dion, K., Walster, E., & Walster, G. W. (1971). Physical attractiveness and dating choice: A test of the matching hypothesis. *Journal of Experimental Social Psychology, 7,* 173–189.

Berscheid, E., & Hatfield, E. (1974). A little bit about love. In T. L. Huston (Ed.), *Foundations of interpersonal attraction* (pp. 355–381). New York: Academic Press.

Bettencourt, B. A., & Miller, N. (1996). Gender differences in aggression as a function of provocation: A meta-analysis. *Psychological Bulletin, 119,* 422–447.

Bettencourt, B. A., Molix, L., Talley, A. E., & Sheldon, K. M. (2006). Psychological need satisfaction through social roles. In T. Postmes & J. Jetten (Eds.), *Individuality and the group: Advances in social identity* (pp. 196–214). London: Sage.

Biddle, S. J. H., & Mutrie, N. (2008). *Psychology of physical activity and psychological well-being.* New York: Routledge.

Biernat, M. (2012). Stereotypes and shifting standards: Forming, communicating, and translating person impressions. *Advances in Experimental Social Psychology, 45,* 1–60.

Biernat, M., Collins, E. C., Katzarska-Miller, I., & Thompson, E. R. (2009). Race-based shifting standards and racial discrimination. *Personality and Social Psychology Bulletin, 35,* 16–28.

Biernat, M., Eidelman, S., & Fuegan, K. (2002). Judgment standards and the social self: A shifting standards perspective. In J. P. Forgas & K. D. Williams (Eds.), *The social self: Cognitive, interpersonal, and intergroup perspectives* (pp. 51–72). Philadelphia: Psychology Press.

Bies, R. J., Shapiro, D. L., & Cummings, L. L. (1988). Causal accounts and managing organizational conflict: Is it enough to say it's not my fault? *Communication Research, 15,* 381–399.

Bizer, G. Y., Tormala, Z. L., Rucker, D. D., & Petty, R. E. (2006). Memory-based versus on-line processing: Implications for attitude strength. *Journal of Experimental Social Psychology, 42,* 646–653.

Bjorklund, D. F., & Kipp, K. (1996). Parental investment theory and gender differences in the evolution of inhibition mechanisms. *Psychological Bulletin, 120,* 163–188.

Blackburn, E., & Epel, E. (2012). Psychological stress and telomeres. *Nature, 490,* 169–171.

Blanchette, I., & Richards, A. (2010). The influence of affect on higher level cognition: A review of research on interpretation, judgement, decision making and reasoning. *Cognition and Emotion, 24,* 561–595.

Blankenship, K. L., & Wegener, D. T. (2008). Opening the mind to close it: Considering a message in light of important values increases message processing and later resistance to change. *Journal of Personality and Social Psychology, 94,* 196–213.

Blazer, D. G., Kessler, R. C., McGonagle, K. A., & Swartz, M. S. (1994). The prevalence and distribution of major depression in a national community sample: The National Comorbidity Survey. *American Journal of Psychiatry, 151,* 979–986.

Blease, C. R. (2015). Too many 'friends,' too few 'likes'? Evolutionary psychology and 'facebook depression.' *Review of General Psychology, 19*(1), 1–13.

Bobo, L. (1983). Whites' opposition to busing: Symbolic racism or realistic group conflict? *Journal of Personality and Social Psychology, 45,* 1196–1210.

Bodenhausen, G. F. (1993). Emotion, arousal, and stereotypic judgment: A heuristic model of affect and stereotyping. In D. Mackie & D. Hamilton (Eds.), *Affect, cognition, and stereotyping: Intergroup processes in intergroup perception* (pp. 13–37). San Diego, CA: Academic Press.

Bodenhausen, G. V., & Hugenberg, K. (2009). Attention, perception, and social cognition. In F. Strack & J. Förster (Eds.), *Social cognition: The basis of human interaction* (pp. 1–22). Philadelphia: Psychology Press.

Boehm, J. K., Lyubomirsky, S., & Sheldon, K. M. (2011). A longitudinal experimental study comparing the effectiveness of happiness-enhancing strategies in Anglo Americans and Asian Americans. *Cognition and Emotion, 25,* 1263–1272.

Boen, F., Vanbeselaere, N., & Wostyn, P. (2010). When the best become the rest: The interactive effect of premerger status and relative representation on postmerger identification and ingroup bias. *Group Processes and Intergroup Relations, 13,* 461–475.

Boer, F., Westenberg, M., McHale, S. M., Updegraff, K. A., & Stocker, C. M. (1997). The factorial structure of the Sibling Relationship Inventory (SRI) in American and Dutch samples. *Journal of Social and Personal Relationships, 14,* 851–859.

Bolino, M. C., & Turnley, W. H. (1999). Measuring impression management in organizations: A scale development based on the Jones and Pittman taxonomy. *Organizational Research Methods, 2,* 187–206.

Bollich, K. L., Rogers, K. H., & Vazire, S. (2015). Knowing more than we can tell: People are aware of their biased self-perceptions. *Personality and Social Psychology Bulletin, 41,* 918–929.

Bond, C. F. Jr., & DePaulo, B. M. (2006). Accuracy of deception judgments. *Personality and Social Psychology Review, 10,* 214–234.

Bond, C. F. Jr., Omar, A., Pitre, U., Lashley, L. M., Skaggs, L. M., & Kirk, C. T. (1992). Fishy-looking liars: Deception judgment from expectancy violation. *Journal of Personality and Social Psychology, 63,* 669–677.

Bond, R., & Smith, P. B. (1996). Culture and conformity: A meta-analysis of studies using Asch's (1952b, 1956) line judgment task. *Psychological Bulletin, 119,* 111–137.

Borkenau, P., Mauer, N., Riemann, R., Spinath, F. M., & Angleitner, A. (2004). Thin slices of behavior as cues of personality and intelligence. *Journal of Personality and Social Psychology, 86,* 599–614.

Borman, W. C., Penner, L. A., Allen, T. D., & Motowidlo, S. J. (2001). Personality predictors of citizenship performance. *International Journal of Selection and Assessment, 9,* 52–69.

Bornstein, R. F., & D'Agostino, P. R. (1992). Stimulus recognition and the mere exposure effect. *Journal of Personality and Social Psychology, 63,* 545–552.

Bossard, J. H. S. (1932). Residential propinquity as a factor in marriage selection. *American Journal of Sociology, 38,* 219–224.

Bosson, J. K., Haymovitz, E. L., & Pinel, E. C. (2004). When saying and doing diverge: The effects of stereotype threat on self-reported versus non-verbal anxiety. *Journal of Experimental Social Psychology, 40,* 247–255.

Botha, M. (1990). Television exposure and aggression among adolescents: A follow-up study over 5 years. *Aggressive Behavior, 16,* 361–380.

Bothwell, R. K., Pigott, M. A., Foley, L. A., & McFatter, R. M. (2006). Racial bias in juridic judgment at private and public levels. *Journal of Applied Social Psychology, 36,* 2134–2149.

Bowlby, J. (1969). *Attachment and loss: Vol. 1. Attachment.* New York: Basic Books.

Bowlby, J. (1973). *Attachment and loss: Vol. 2. Separation.* New York: Basic Books.

Bowles, H. R. (2013). Psychological perspectives on gender in negotiation. In M. K. Ryan & N. R. Branscombe (Eds.), *The Sage handbook of gender and psychology* (pp. 465–483). London: Sage.

Boyce, C. R., Brown, G. D. A., & Moore, S. C. (2010). Money and happiness: Rank of income, not income, affects life satisfaction. *Psychological Science, 21,* 471–475.

Bradshaw, C. P. (2015). Translating research to practice in bullying prevention. *American Psychologist, 70,* 322–332.

Brandon, D. P., & Hollingshead, A. B. (2007). Characterizing online groups. In A. N. Joinson, K. Y. A. McKenna, T. Postmes, & U.-D. Reips (Eds.), *The Oxford handbook of internet psychology* (pp. 105–119). New York: Oxford University Press.

Branscombe, N. R. (2004). A social psychological process perspective on collective guilt. In N. R. Branscombe & B. Doosje (Eds.), *Collective guilt: International perspectives* (pp. 320–334). New York: Cambridge University Press.

Branscombe, N. R., Fernández, S., Gómez, A., & Cronin, T. (2011). Moving toward or away from a group identity: Different strategies for coping with pervasive discrimination. In J. Jetten, C. Haslam, & S. A. Haslam (Eds.), *The social cure: Identity, health and well-being* (pp. 115–131). New York: Psychology Press.

Branscombe, N. R., & Miron, A. M. (2004). Interpreting the ingroup's negative actions toward another group: Emotional reactions to appraised harm. In L. Z. Tiedens & C. W. Leach (Eds.), *The social life of emotions* (pp. 314–335). New York: Cambridge University Press.

Branscombe, N. R., Owen, S., Garstka, T., & Coleman, J. (1996). Rape and accident counterfactuals: Who might have done otherwise and would it have changed the outcome? *Journal of Applied Social Psychology, 26,* 1042–1067.

Branscombe, N. R., Schmitt, M. T., & Harvey, R. D. (1999). Perceiving pervasive discrimination among African Americans: Implications for group identification and well-being. *Journal of Personality and Social Psychology, 77,* 135–149.

Branscombe, N. R., Schmitt, M. T., & Schiffhauer, K. (2007). Racial attitudes in response to thoughts of White privilege. *European Journal of Social Psychology, 37,* 203–215.

Branscombe, N. R., Spears, R., Ellemers, N., & Doosje, B. (2002). Intragroup and intergroup evaluation effects on group behavior. *Personality and Social Psychology Bulletin, 28,* 744–753.

Branscombe, N. R., & Wann, D. L. (1994). Collective self-esteem consequences of outgroup derogation when a valued social identity is on trial. *European Journal of Social Psychology, 24,* 641–657.

Branscombe, N. R., Wann, D. L., Noel, J. G., & Coleman, J. (1993). In-group or out-group extremity: Importance of the threatened identity. *Personality and Social Psychology Bulletin, 19,* 381–388.

Brehm, J. W. (1966). *A theory of psychological reactance.* New York: Academic Press.

Brewer, M. B., & Brown, R. (1998). Intergroup relations. In D. T. Gilbert, S. T. Fiske, & G. Lindzey (Eds.), *The handbook of social psychology* (4th ed., Vol. 2, pp. 554–594). New York: McGraw-Hill.

Brewer, M. B., & Caporael, L. R. (2006). An evolutionary perspective on social identity: Revisiting groups. In M. Schaller, J. A. Simpson, & D. T. Kenrick (Eds.), *Evolution and social psychology* (pp. 143–161). New York: Psychology Press.

Brickman, P., & Campbell, D. T. (1971). Hedonic relativism and planning the good society. In M. H. Appley (Ed.), *Adaptation level theory: A symposium* (pp. 287–302). New York: Academic Press.

Brickner, M., Harkins, S., & Ostrom, T. (1986). Personal involvement: Thought provoking implications for social loafing. *Journal of Personality and Social Psychology, 51,* 763–769.

Bringle, R. G., & Winnick, T. A. (1992, October). *The nature of unrequited love.* Paper presented at the first Asian Conference in Psychology, Singapore.

Brinol, P., Rucker, D. D., Tormala, Z. L., & Petty, R. E. (2004). Individual differences in resistance to persuasion: The role of beliefs and meta-beliefs. In E. S. Knowles & J. A. Linn (Eds.), *Resistance to persuasion* (pp. 83–104). Mahwah, NJ: Erlbaum.

Brodbeck, F. C., Kerschreiter, R., Mojzisch, A., Frey, D., & Schulz-Hardt, S. (2002). The dissemination of critical, unshared information in decision-making groups: The effects of pre-discussion dissent. *European Journal of Social Psychology, 32,* 35–56.

Broemer, P. (2004). Ease of imagination moderates reactions to differently framed health messages. *European Journal of Social Psychology, 34,* 103–119.

Brooks, J., Oxley, D., Vedlitz, A., Zahran, S., & Lindsey, C. (2014). Abnormal daily temperature and concern about climate change across the United States. *Review of Policy Research, 31,* 199–217.

Brooks-Gunn, J., & Lewis, M. (1981). Infant social perception: Responses to pictures of parents and strangers. *Developmental Psychology, 17,* 647–649.

Brown, J. D. (1991). Staying fit and staying well: Physical fitness as a moderator of life stress. *Journal of Personality and Social Psychology, 60,* 555–561.

Brown, J. D., & Rogers, R. J. (1991). Self-serving attributions: The role of physiological arousal. *Personality and Social Psychology Bulletin, 17,* 501–506.

Brown, L. M. (1998). Ethnic stigma as a contextual experience: Possible selves perspective. *Personality and Social Psychology Bulletin, 24,* 165–172.

Brown, R. P., Charnsangavej, T., Keough, K. A., Newman, M. L., & Rentfrow, P. J. (2000). Putting the "affirm" into affirmative action: Preferential selection and academic performance. *Journal of Personality and Social Psychology, 79,* 736–747.

Brown, S. L., Nesse, R. M., Vinokur, A. D., & Smith, D. M. (2003). Providing social support may be more beneficial than receiving it. *Psychological Science, 14,* 320–327.

Bruckmuller, S., & Branscombe, N. R. (2010). The glass cliff: When and why women are selected as leaders in crisis contexts. *British Journal of Social Psychology, 49,* 433–451.

Bruckmüller, S., Ryan, M. K., Rink, F., & Haslam, S. A. (2014). Beyond the glass ceiling: The glass cliff and its lessons for organizational policy. *Social Issues Policy Review, 8,* 202–232.

Bryan, J. H., & Test, M. A. (1967). Models and helping: Naturalistic studies in aiding behavior. *Journal of Personality and Social Psychology, 6,* 400–407.

Buckley, K. E., Winkel, R. E., & Leary, M. R. (2004). Reactions to acceptance and rejection: Effects of level and sequence of relational evaluation. *Journal of Experimental Social Psychology, 40,* 14–28.

Budson, A. E., & Price, B. H. (2005). Memory dysfunction. *New England Journal of Medicine, 352,* 692–699.

Buehler, R., & Griffin, D. (1994). Change-of-meaning effects in conformity and dissent: Observing construal processes over time. *Journal of Personality and Social Psychology, 67,* 984–996.

Buehler, R., Griffin, D., & Ross, M. (1994). Exploring the "planning fallacy": Why people underestimate their task completion times. *Journal of Personality and Social Psychology, 67,* 366–381.

Burger, J. M. (1986). Increasing compliance by improving the deal: The that's-not-all technique. *Journal of Personality and Social Psychology, 51,* 277–283.

Burger, J. M. (1995). Individual differences in preference for solitude. *Journal of Research in Personality, 29,* 85–108.

Burger, J. M. (2009). Replicating Milgram: Would people still obey today? *American Psychologist, 64,* 1–11.

Burger, J. M. (2014). Situational features in Milgram's experiments that kept his participants shocking. *Journal of Social Issues, 70,* 489–500.

Burger, J. M., & Cornelius, T. (2003). Raising the price of agreement: Public commitment and the lowball compliance procedure. *Journal of Applied Social Psychology, 33,* 923–934.

Burger, J. M., Messian, N., Patel, S., del Pardo, A., & Anderson, C. (2004). What a coincidence! The effects of incidental similarity on compliance. *Personality and Social Psychology Bulletin, 30,* 35–43.

Burke, S. M., Carron, A. V., Eys, M. A., Ntoumanis, N., & Estabrooks, P. A. (2006). Group versus individual approach? A meta-analysis of the effectiveness of interventions to promote physical activity. *Sport and Exercise Psychology Review, 2,* 19–35.

Burkley, E. (2008). The role of self-control in resistance to persuasion. *Personality and Social Psychology Bulletin, 34,* 419–431.

Burleson, M. H., Poehlmann, K. M., Hawkley, L. C., Ernst, J. M., Berntson, G. G., Malarkey, W. B., et al. (2002). Stress-related immune changes in middle-aged and older women: 1-year consistency of individual differences. *Health Psychology, 21,* 321–331.

Burnstein, E. (1983). Persuasion as argument processing. In M. Brandstatter, J. H. Davis, & G. Stocker-Kriechgauer (Eds.), *Group decision processes* (pp. 103–124). London: Academic Press.

Burnstein, E., Crandall, C., & Kitayama, S. (1994). Some neo-Darwinian rules for altruism: Weighing cues for inclusive fitness as a function of the biological importance of the decision. *Journal of Personality and Social Psychology, 67,* 773–789.

Burris, E. R., Rodgers, M. S., Mannix, E. A., Hendron, M. G., & Oldroyd, J. B. (2009). Playing favorites: The influence of leaders' inner circle on group processes and performance. *Personality and Social Psychology Bulletin, 35,* 1244–1257.

Burrus, J., & Roese, N. J. (2006). Long ago it was meant to be: The interplay between time, construal, and fate beliefs. *Personality and Social Psychology Bulletin, 32,* 1050–1058.

Bushman, B. J. (1988). The effects of apparel on compliance: A field experiment with a female authority figure. *Personality and Social Psychology Bulletin, 14,* 459–467.

Bushman, B. J. (1998). Effects of television violence on memory for commercial messages. *Journal of Experimental Psychology: Applied, 4,* 1–17.

Bushman, B. J. (2001). Does venting anger feed or extinguish the flame? Catharsis, rumination, distraction, anger, and aggressive responding. Manuscript under review.

Bushman, B. J., & Anderson, C. A. (2002). Violent video games and hostile expectations: A test of the general aggression model. *Personality and Social Psychology Bulletin, 28,* 1679–1686.

Bushman, B. J., & Anderson, C. A. (2009). Comfortably numb: Desensitizing effects of violent media on helping others. *Psychological Science, 20,* 273–277.

Bushman, B. J., Baumeister, R. F., & Stack, A. D. (1999). Catharsis messages and anger-reducing activities. *Journal of Personality and Social Psychology, 76,* 367–376.

Bushman, B. J., & Cooper, H. M. (1990). Effects of alcohol on human aggression: An integrative research review. *Psychological Bulletin, 107,* 341–354.

Bushman, B. J., & Huesmann, L. R. (2001). Effects of televised violence on aggression. In D. Singer & J. Singer (Eds.), *Handbook of children and the media* (pp. 223–254). Thousand Oaks, CA: Sage.

Bushman, B. J., Newman, K., Calvert, S. L., Downey, G., Dredze, M., Gottfredson, M., et al. (2016). Youth violence: What we know and what we need to know. *American Psychologist, 71,* 17–39.

Buss, D. M. (1994). The strategies of human mating. *American Scientist, 82,* 238–249.

Buss, D. M. (1999). *Evolutionary psychology: The new science of the mind.* Needham Heights, MA: Allyn & Bacon.

Buss, D. M. (2004). *Evolutionary psychology: The new science of the mind* (2nd ed.). Boston: Allyn & Bacon.

Buss, D. M. (2008). *Evolutionary psychology: The new science of the mind* (3rd ed.). Boston: Allyn & Bacon.

Buss, D. M., Larsen, R. J., Westen, D., & Semmelroth, J. (1992). Sex differences in jealousy: Evolution, physiology, and psychology. *Psychological Science, 3,* 251–255.

Buss, D. M., & Shackelford, T. K. (1997). From vigilance to violence: Mate retention tactics in married couples. *Journal of Personality and Social Psychology, 72,* 346–361.

Butera, F., Darnon, C., & Mugny, G. (2011). Learning from conflict. In J. Jetten & M. J. Hornsey (Eds.), *Rebels in groups: Dissent, deviance, difference and defiance* (pp. 36–54). Chichester, UK: Wiley.

Byrne, D. (1961a). The influence of propinquity and opportunities for interaction on classroom relationships. *Human Relations, 14,* 63–69.

Byrne, D. (1961b). Interpersonal attraction and attitude similarity. *Journal of Abnormal and Social Psychology, 62,* 713–715.

Byrne, D. (1971). *The attraction paradigm.* New York: Academic Press.

Byrne, D. (1991). Perspectives on research classics: This ugly duckling has yet to become a swan. *Contemporary Social Psychology, 15,* 84–85.

Byrne, D. (1997). An overview (and underview) of research and theory within the attraction paradigm. *Journal of Social and Personal Relationships, 14,* 417–431.

Byrne, D., & Nelson, D. (1965). Attraction as a linear function of proportion of positive reinforcements. *Journal of Personality and Social Psychology, 1,* 659–663.

Byrne, R. L. (2001, June 1). *Good safety advice.* Internet.

Cacioppo, J. T., Berntson, G. G., Long, T. S., Norris, C. J., Rickhett, E., & Nusbaum, H. (2003). Just because you're imaging the brain doesn't mean you can stop using your head: A primer and set of first principles. *Journal of Personality and Social Psychology, 85,* 650–661.

Cacioppo, J. T., Hughes, M. E., Waite, L. J., Hawkley, L. C., & Thisted, R. A. (2006). Loneliness as a specific risk factor for depressive symptoms: Cross-sectional and longitudinal analyses. *Psychology and Aging, 21,* 140–151.

Callan, M. J., Kay, A. C., Olson, J. M., Brar, N., & Whitefield, N. (2010). The effects of priming legal concepts on perceived trust and competitiveness, self-interested attitudes, and competitive behavior. *Journal of Experimental Social Psychology, 46,* 325–335.

Campbell, D. T. (1958). Common fate, similarity, and other indices of the status of aggregates of persons as social entities. *Behavioral Science, 4,* 14–25.

Campbell, W. K., Bonacci, A. M., Shelton, J., Exline, J. J., & Bushman, B. J. (2004). Psychological entitlement: Interpersonal consequences and validation of a self-report measure. *Journal of Personality Assessment, 83,* 29–45.

Campos, B., Keltner, D., Beck, J. M., Gonzaga, G. C., & John, O. P. (2007). Culture and teasing: The relational benefits of reduced desire for positive self-differentiation. *Personality and Social Psychology Bulletin, 33,* 3–16.

Canadian Gaming Association. (2011). 2010 economic impact of the Canadian gaming industry: Key findings report. Retrieved from http://www.canadiangaming.ca/images/stories/media_releases/CGA_Economic_Impact_Report_Final.pdf

Canetti, D., & Lindner, M. (2015). Exposure to political violence and political behavior: Psychological mechanisms of transformation. In K. J. Reynolds & N. R. Branscombe (Eds.), *Psychology of change: Life contexts, experiences, and identities* (pp. 77–94). New York: Psychology Press.

Cann, A., Calhoun, L. G., & Banks, J. S. (1997). On the role of humor appreciation in interpersonal attraction: It's no joking matter. *Humor: International Journal of Humor Research, 10,* 77–90.

Cantor, N., & Sanderson, C. A. (1999). Life task participation and well-being: The importance of taking part in daily life. In D. Kahneman, E. Diener, & N. Schwarz (Eds.), *Well-being: Foundations of hedonic psychology* (pp. 230–243). New York: Russell Sage Foundation.

Caputo, D., & Dunning, D. (2005). What you don't know: The role played by errors of omission in imperfect self-assessments. *Journal of Experimental Social Psychology, 41,* 488–505.

Carey, M. P., Morrison-Beedy, D., & Johnson, B. T. (1997). The HIV-Knowledge Questionnaire: Development and evaluation of a reliable, valid, and practical self-administered questionnaire. *AIDS and Behavior, 1,* 61–74.

Carlsmith, K. M., Darley, J. M., & Robinson, P. H. (2002). Why do we punish? Deterrence and just deserts as motives for punishment. *Journal of Personality and Social Psychology, 83,* 284–299.

Carney, D. R., Colvin, D. W., & Hall, J. A. (2007). A thin slice perspective on the accuracy of first impressions. *Journal of Research in Personality, 41,* 1054–1072.

Carney, D. R., Cuddy, A. J. C., & Yap, A. J. (2010). Power posing: Brief nonverbal displays affect neuroendrocrine levels and risk tolerance. *Psychological Science, 21,* 1363–1368.

Carney, D. R., & Harrigan, J. A. (2003). It takes one to know one: Interpersonal sensitivity is related to accurate assessment of others' interpersonal sensitivity. *Emotion, 3,* 194–204.

Carroll, J. M., & Russell, J. A. (1996). Do facial expressions signal specific emotions? Judging emotion from the face in context. *Journal of Personality and Social Psychology, 70,* 205–218.

Carter, T. J., & Gilovich, T. (2010). The relative relativity of material and experiential purchases. *Journal of Personality and Social Psychology, 98,* 146–159.

Caruso, E. M. (2008). Use of experienced retrieval ease in self and social judgments. *Journal of Experimental Social Psychology, 44,* 148–155.

Carvallo, M., & Gabriel, S. (2006). No man is an island: The need to belong and dismissing avoidant attachment style. *Personality and Social Psychology Bulletin, 32,* 697–709.

Caspi, A., & Herbener, E. S. (1990). Continuity and change: Assortative marriage and the consistency of personality in adulthood. *Journal of Personality and Social Psychology, 58,* 250–258.

Castilla, E. J., & Benard, S. (2010). The paradox of meritocracy in organizations. *Administrative Science Quarterly, 55,* 543–576.

Catalyst (June 7, 2009). *2008 Catalyst Census of Women Corporate Officers and Top Earners of the FP500.* Retrieved from http://www.catalyst.org/publication/295/2008-catalyst-censusof-women-corporate-officers-and-top-earners-of-the-fp500

Center for American Women and Politics. (2010). *Can more women run? Reevaluating women's election to the state legislatures.* Retrieved from http://www.cawp.rutgers.edu/research

Cervone, D., & Shoda, Y. (Eds.). (1999). The coherence of personality: Social-cognitive bases of consistency, variability, and organization. New York: Guilford Press.

Cesario, J., Plaks, J. E., & Higgins, E. (2006). Automatic social behavior as motivated preparation to interact. *Journal of Personality and Social Psychology, 90,* 893–910.

Chaiken, S., Liberman, A., & Eagly, A. H. (1989). Heuristic and systematic processing within and beyond persuasion context. In J. S. Uleman & J. A. Bargh (Eds.), *Unintended thought* (pp. 212–252). New York: Guilford Press.

Chaiken, S., & Trope, Y. (1999). *Dual-process theories in social psychology.* New York: Guilford Press.

Chajut, E., & Algom, D. (2003). Selective attention improves under stress: Implications for theories of social cognition. *Journal of Personality and Social Psychology, 85,* 231–248.

Chambers, J. R., Epley, N., Savitsky, K., & Windschitl, P. D. (2008). Knowing too much: Using private knowledge to predict how one is viewed by others. *Psychological Science, 19,* 542–548.

Chan, K. Q., Tong, E. M. W., Tan, D. H., & Koh, A. H. (2013). What do love and jealousy taste like? *Emotion, 13,* 1142–1149.

Chan, M. E., & Arvey, R. D. (2012). Meta-analysis and the development of knowledge. *Perspectives in Psychological Science, 7,* 79–92.

Chaplin, W. F., Phillips, J. B., Brown, J. D., Clanton, N. R., & Stein, J. L. (2000). Handshaking, gender, personality, and first impressions. *Journal of Personality and Social Psychology, 19,* 110–117.

Chasteen, A. L., Burdzy, D. C., & Pratt, J. (2010). Thinking of God moves attention. *Neuropsychologia, 48,* 627–630.

Chen, S., Chen, K., & Shaw, L. (2004). Self-verification motives at the collective level of self-definition. *Journal of Personality and Social Psychology, 86,* 77–94.

Cheung, M. Y., Luo, C., Sia, C. L., & Chen, H. (2009). Credibility of electronic word-of-mouth: Informational and normative determinants of on-line consumer recommendations. *International Journal of Electronic Commerce, 13,* 9–38.

Chin, J. L. (2010). Introduction to the special issue on diversity and leadership. *American Psychologist, 65,* 150–156.

Choi, I., Dalal, R., Kim-Prieto, C., & Park, H. (2003). Culture and judgment of causal relevance. *Journal of Personality and Social Psychology, 84,* 46–59.

Christy, P. R., Gelfand, D. M., & Hartmann, D. P. (1971). Effects of competition-induced frustration on two classes of modeled behavior. *Developmental Psychology, 5,* 104–111.

Chung, J. M., Robins, R. W., Trzesniewski, K. H., Noftle, E. E., Roberts, B. W., & Widaman, K. F. (2014). Continuity and change in self-esteem during emerging adulthood. *Journal of Personality and Social Psychology, 106,* 469–483.

Cialdini, R. B. (1994). *Influence: Science and practice* (3rd ed.). New York: HarperCollins.

Cialdini, R. B. (2000). *Influence: Science and practice* (4th ed.). Boston: Allyn & Bacon.

Cialdini, R. B. (2006). *Influence: The psychology of persuasion.* New York: Collins.

Cialdini, R. B. (2008). *Influence: Science and practice* (5th ed). Boston: Allyn & Bacon.

Cialdini, R. B., Baumann, D. J., & Kenrick, D. T. (1981). Insights from sadness: A three-step model of the development of altruism as hedonism. *Developmental Review, 1*, 207–223.

Cialdini, R., Brown, S., Lewis, B., Luce, C., & Neuberg, S. (1997). Reinterpreting the empathy-altruism relationships: When one into one equals oneness. *Journal of Personality and Social Psychology, 61*, 773–789.

Cialdini, R. B., Cacioppo, J. T., Bassett, R., & Miller J. A. (1978). A low-ball procedure for producing compliance: Commitment then cost. *Journal of Personality and Social Psychology, 36*, 463–476.

Cialdini, R. B., Kallgren, C. A., & Reno, R. R. (1991). A focus theory of normative conduct. *Advances in Experimental Social Psychology, 24*, 201–234.

Cialdini, R. B., Kenrick, D. T., & Baumann, D. J. (1982). Effects of mood on prosocial behavior in children and adults. In N. Eisenberg-Berg (Ed.), *Development of prosocial behavior* (pp. 339–359). New York: Academic Press.

Cialdini, R. B., & Petty, R. E. (1981). Anticipatory opinion effects. In R. Petty, T. Ostrom, & T. Brock (Eds.), *Cognitive responses in persuasion* (pp. 217–235). Hillsdale, NJ: Erlbaum.

Cialdini, R. B., Reno, R. R., & Kallgren, C. A. (1990). A focus theory of normative conduct : Recycling the concept of norms to reduce littering in public places. *Journal of Personality and Social Psychology, 91*, 105–1026.

Cialdini, R. B., Schaller, M., Houlainham, D., Arps, K., Fultz, J., & Beaman, A. L. (1987). Empathy-based helping: Is it selflessly or selfishly motivated? *Journal of Personality and Social Psychology, 52*, 749–758.

Cialdini, R. B., Vincent, J. E., Lewis, S. K., Catalan, J., Wheeler, D., & Darby, B. L. (1975). Reciprocal concessions procedure for inducing compliance: The door-in-the-face technique. *Journal of Personality and Social Psychology, 31*, 206–215.

Cicero, L., Pierro, A., & van Knippenberg, D. (2007). Leader group prototypicality and job satisfaction: The moderating role of job stress and team identification. *Group Dynamics: Theory, Research, and Practice, 11*, 165–175.

Cikara, M., & Fiske, S. T. (2009). Warmth, competence, and ambivalent sexism: Vertical assault and collateral damage. In M. Barreto, M. K. Ryan, & M. T. Schmitt (Eds.), *The glass ceiling in the 21st century* (pp. 73–96). Washington, DC: American Psychological Association.

Clark, L. A., Kochanska, G., & Ready, R. (2000). Mothers' personality and its interaction with child temperament as predictors of parenting behavior. *Journal of Personality and Social Psychology, 19*, 274–285.

Clarkson, J. J., Tormala, Z. L., Rucker, D. D., & Dugan, R. G. (2013). The malleable influence of social consensus on attitude certainty. *Journal of Experimental Social Psychology, 49*, 1019–1022.

Clore, G. L., Schwarz, N., & Conway, M. (1993). Affective causes and consequences of social information processing. In R. S. Wyer & T. K. Srull (Eds.), *Handbook of social cognition* (2nd ed., pp. 323–417). Hillsdale, NJ: Erlbaum.

Cohen, J. D. (2005). The vulcanization of the human brain: A neural perspective on interactions between cognition and emotion. *Journal of Economic Perspectives, 19*, 3–24.

Cohen, S., Doyle, W. J., Turner, R. B., Alper, C. M., & Skoner, D. P. (2003). Emotional style and susceptibility to the common cold. *Psychosomatic Medicine, 65*, 652–657.

Cohen, S., Frank, E., Doyle, W. J., Skoner, D. P., Rabin, B. S., & Gwaltuey, J. M., Jr. (1998). Types of stressors that increase susceptibility to the common cold in healthy adults. *Health Psychology, 17*, 214–223.

Cohen, S., & Janicki-Deverts, D. (2009). Can we improve our physical health by altering our social networks? *Perspectives on Psychological Science, 4*, 375–378.

Cohen, T. R., Montoya, R. M., & Insko, C. A. (2006). Group morality and intergroup relations: Cross-cultural and experimental evidence. *Personality and Social Psychology Bulletin, 32*, 1559–1572.

Cohn, E. G., & Rotton, J. (1997). Assault as a function of time and temperature: A moderator-variable time-series analysis. *Journal of Personality and Social Psychology, 72*, 1322–1334.

Colcombe, S., & Kramer, A. F. (2003). Fitness effects on the cognitive function of older adults: A meta-analytic study. *Psychological Science, 14*, 125–130.

Cole, S. W., Kemeny, M. E., Taylor, S. E., & Visscher, B. R. (1996). Elevated physical health risk among gay men who conceal their homosexual identity. *Health Psychology, 15*, 243–251.

Collins, M. A., & Zebrowitz, L. A. (1995). The contributions of appearance to occupational outcomes in civilian and military settings. *Journal of Applied Social Psychology, 25*, 129–163.

Collins, N. L., & Feeney, B. C. (2000). A safe haven: An attachment theory perspective on support seeking and caregiving in intimate relationships. *Journal of Personality and Social Psychology, 78*, 1053–1073.

Condon, J. W., & Crano, W. D. (1988). Inferred evaluation and the relation between attitude similarity and interpersonal attraction. *Journal of Personality and Social Psychology, 54*, 789–797.

Cone, T. C., & Ferguson, M. J. (2015). Can we undo our first impressions? The role of reinterpretation in reversing implicit evaluations. *Journal of Personality and Social Psychology, 108*, 823–849.

Cook, C. L., Cohen, F., & Solomon, S. (2015). What if they're right about the afterlife? Evidence of the role of existential threat on anti-atheist prejudice. *Social Psychological and Personality Science, 6*, 840–846.

Cook, C. R., Williams, K. R., Guerra, N. G., Kim, T. E., & Sadek, S. (2010). Predictors of bullying and victimization in childhood and adolescence: A meta-analytic investigation. *School Psychology Quarterly, 25*, 65–83.

Corneo, G., & Neher, F. (2014). Income inequality and self-reported values. *Journal of Economic Inequality, 12*, 49–71.

Correll, J., Urland, G. R., & Ito, T. A. (2006). Event-related potentials and the decision to shoot: The role of threat perception and cognitive control. *Journal of Experimental Social Psychology, 42*, 120–128.

Cottrell, C. A., & Neuberg, S. L. (2005). Different emotional reactions to different groups: A sociofunctional threat-based approach to "prejudice." *Journal of Personality and Social Psychology, 88*, 770–789.

Cottrell, C. A., Neuberg, S. L., & Li, N. P. (2007). What do people desire in others? A sociofunctional perspective on the importance of different valued characteristics. *Journal of Personality and Social Psychology, 92*, 208–231.

Cottrell, N. B., Wack, K. L., Sekerak, G. J., & Rittle, R. (1968). Social facilitation of dominant responses by the presence of an audience and the mere presence of others. *Journal of Personality and Social Psychology, 9*, 245–250.

Craig, W. M. (1998). The relationship among bullying, victimization, depression, anxiety, and aggression in elementary school children. *Personality and Individual Differences, 24*, 123–130.

Cramer, R. E., McMaster, M. R., Bartell, P. A., & Dragma, M. (1988). Subject competence and minimization of the bystander effect. *Journal of Applied Social Psychology, 18*, 1133–1148.

Crandall, C. C., & Martinez, R. (1996). Culture, ideology, and antifat attitudes. *Personality and Social Psychology Bulletin, 22*, 1165–1176.

Crandall, C. S. (1988). Social contagion of binge eating. *Journal of Personality and Social Psychology, 55*, 588–598.

Crandall, C. S. (1995). Do parents discriminate against their heavyweight daughters? *Personality and Social Psychology Bulletin, 21,* 724–735.

Crandall, C. S., Eidelman, S., Skitka, L. J., & Morgan, G. S. (2009). Status quo framing increases support for torture. *Social Influence, 4,* 1–10.

Crandall, C. S., Eshleman, A., & O'Brien, L. T. (2002). Social norms and the expression and suppression of prejudice: The struggle for internalization. *Journal of Personality and Social Psychology, 82,* 359–378.

Crano, W. D. (1995). Attitude strength and vested interest. In R. E. Petty & J. A. Krosnick (Eds.), *Attitude strength: Antecedents and consequences* (Vol. 4, pp. 131–157). Hillsdale, NJ: Erlbaum.

Crawford, L. E., Margolies, S. M., Drake, J. T., & Murphy, M. E. (2006). Affect biases memory of location: Evidence for the spatial representation of affect. *Cognition and Emotion, 20,* 1153–1169.

Crites, S. L., & Cacioppo, J. T. (1996). Electrocortical differentiation of evaluative and nonevaluative categorizations. *Psychological Science, 7,* 318–321.

Crocker, J., & Major, B. (1989). Social stigma and self-esteem: The self-protective properties of stigma. *Psychological Review, 96,* 608–630.

Cropanzano, R. (Ed.). (1993). *Justice in the workplace* (pp. 79–103). Hillsdale, NJ: Erlbaum.

Crosby, F. J. (2004). *Affirmative action is dead: Long live affirmative action.* New Haven, CT: Yale University Press.

Cruse, D. F., & Leigh, B. C. (1987). "Adam's Rib" revisited: Legal and non-legal influences on the processing of trial testimony. *Social Behavior, 2,* 221–230.

Crutchfield, R. A. (1955). Conformity and character. *American Psychologist, 10,* 191–198.

Cruwys, T., Bevelander, K. E., & Hermans, R. C. J. (2015). Social modeling of eating: A review of when and why social influence affects food intake and choice. *Appetite, 86,* 3–18.

Cruwys, T., Dingle, G. A., Haslam, C., Haslam, S. A., Jetten, J., & Morton, T. A. (2013). Social group memberships protect against future depression, alleviate depression symptoms and prevent depression relapse. *Social Science & Medicine, 98,* 179–186.

Cruwys, T., South, E. I., Greenaway, K. H., & Haslam, S. A. (2015). Social identity reduces depression by foster positive attributions. *Social Psychological and Personality Science, 6,* 65–74.

Cunningham, M. R. (1979). Weather, mood, and helping behavior: Quasi-experiments with the sunshine Samaritan. *Journal of Personality and Social Psychology, 37,* 1947–1956.

Cunningham, M. R. (1986). Measuring the physical in physical attractiveness: Quasi-experiments on the sociobiology of female facial beauty. *Journal of Personality and Social Psychology, 50,* 925–935.

Cunningham, M. R., Roberts, A. R., Wu, C.-H., Barbee, A. P., & Druen, P. B. (1995). "Their ideas of beauty are, on the whole, the same as ours": Consistency and variability in the cross-cultural perception of female physical attractiveness. *Journal of Personality and Social Psychology, 68,* 261–279.

Cunningham, M. R., Shaffer, D. R., Barbee, A. P., Wolff, P. L., & Kelley, D. J. (1990). Separate processes in the relation of elation and depression to helping: Social versus personal concerns. *Journal of Experimental Social Psychology, 26,* 13–33.

Cunningham, W. A., Johnson, M. K., Gatenby, J. C., Gore, J. C., & Banaji, M. R. (2003). Neural components of social evaluation. *Journal of Personality and Social Psychology, 85,* 639–649.

Dai, H., Milkman, K. L., & Riis, J. (2015). Put your imperfections behind you: Temporal landmarks spur goal initiation when they signal new beginnings. *Psychological Science, 26,* 1927–1936.

Danaher, K., & Branscombe, N. R. (2010). Maintaining the system with tokenism: Bolstering individual mobility beliefs and identification with a discriminatory organization. *British Journal of Social Psychology, 49,* 343–362.

Dancygier, R. M., & Green, D. P. (2010). Hate crime. In J. F. Dovidio, M. Hewstone, P. Glick, & V. M. Esses (Eds.), *Sage handbook of prejudice, stereotyping and discrimination* (pp. 294–311). London: Sage.

Darley, J. M. (1995). Constructive and destructive obedience: A taxonomy of principal-agent relationships. *Journal of Social Issues, 125,* 125–154.

Darley, J. M., Carlsmith, K. M., & Robinson, P. H. (2000). Incapacitation and just desserts as motives for punishment. *Law and Human Behavior, 24,* 659–684.

Darley, J. M., & Latane, B. (1968). Bystander intervention in emergencies: Diffusion of responsibility. *Journal of Personality and Social Psychology, 8,* 377–383.

Dasgupta, N., & Asgari, S. (2004). Seeing is believing: Exposure to counterstereotypic women leaders and its effect on the malleability of automatic gender stereotyping. *Journal of Experimental Social Psychology, 40,* 642–658.

Dasgupta, N., Banaji, M. R., & Abelson, R. P. (1999). Group entiativity and group perception: Association between physical features and psychological judgment. *Journal of Personality and Social Psychology, 75,* 991–1005.

Davis, C. G., Lehman, D. R., Wortman, C. B., Silver, R. C., & Thompson, S. C. (1995). The undoing of tragic life events. *Personality and Social Psychology Bulletin, 21,* 109–124.

Davis, J. I., Senghas, A., Brandt, F., & Ochsner, K. N. (2010). The effects of BOTOX injections on emotional experience. *Emotion, 10,* 433–40.

Dawtry, R. J., Sutton, R. M., & Sibley, C. G. (2015). Why wealthier people think people are wealthier, and why it matters: From social sampling to attitudes to redistribution. *Psychological Science, 26,* 1389–1400.

De Backer, M., Boen, F., De Cuyper, B., Hoigaard, R., & Vande Broek, G. (2015). A team fares well with a fair coach: Predictors of social loafing in interactive female sport teams. *Scandinavian Journal of Medicine and Science in Sports, 25,* 897–908.

De Dreu, C. K. W., & West, M. A. (2001). Minority dissent and team innovation: The importance of participation in decision making. *Journal of Applied Psychology, 86,* 1191–1201.

De Hoog, N., Stroebe, W., & de Wit, J. B. F. (2007). The impact of vulnerability to and severity of a health risk on processing and acceptance of fear-arousing communications: A meta-analysis. *Review of General Psychology, 11,* 258–285.

Deaux, K., & LaFrance, M. (1998). Gender. In D. T. Gilbert, S. T. Fiske, & G. Lindzey (Eds.), *The handbook of social psychology* (4th ed., Vol. 1, pp. 788–827). New York: McGraw-Hill.

Deci, E. L., & Ryan, R. M. (2000). The 'what' and 'why' of goal pursuits: Human needs and the self-determination of behavior. *Psychological Inquiry, 11,* 227–268.

Deci, E. L., & Ryan, R. M. (2008). Self-determination theory: A macrotheory of human motivation, development, and health. *Canadian Psychology, 49,* 182–185.

DeDreu, C. K. W. (2010). Conflict at work: Basic principles and applied issues. In S. Zedeck (Ed.), *Handbook of industrial and organizational psychology* (pp. 461–493). Washington, DC: American Psychological Association.

DeDreu, C. K. W., & Van Lange, P. A. M. (1995). Impact of social value orientation on negotiator cognition and behavior. *Personality and Social Psychology Bulletin, 21,* 1178–1188.

DeHart, T., & Pelham, B. W. (2007). Fluctuations in state implicit self-esteem in response to daily negative events. *Journal of Experimental Social Psychology, 43,* 157–165.

DeHart, T., Pelham, B. W., & Tennen, H. (2006). What lies beneath: Parenting style and implicit self-esteem. *Journal of Experimental Social Psychology, 42,* 1–17.

DeLongis, A., Folkman, S., & Lazarus, R. S. (1988). The impact of daily stress on health and mood: Psychological and social resources as mediators. *Journal of Personality and Social Psychology, 54*, 486–595.

Denson, T. F., DeWall, C., & Finkel, E. J. (2012). Self-control and aggression. *Current Directions in Psychological Science, 21*, 20–25.

DePaulo, B. M. (2006). *Singled out: How singles are stereotyped, stigmatized, and ignored, and still live happily ever after*. New York: St. Martin's Press.

DePaulo, B. M. (2008). *Singled out: How singles are stereotyped, stigmatized, and ignored, and still live happily ever after*. New York: St. Martin's Press.

DePaulo, B. M., & Kashy, D. A. (1998). Everyday lies in close and casual relationships. *Journal of Personality and Social Psychology, 74*, 63–79.

DePaulo, B. M., Brown, P. L., Ishii, S., & Fisher, J. D. (1981). Help that works: The effects of aid on subsequent task performance. *Journal of Personality and Social Psychology, 41*, 478–487.

DePaulo, B. M., Lindsay, J. J., Malone, B. E., Muhlenbruck, L., Chandler, K., & Cooper, H. (2003). Cues to deception. *Psychological Bulletin, 129*, 74–118.

DePaulo, B. M., & Morris, W. L. (2006). The unrecognized stereotyping and discrimination against singles. *Current Directions in Psychological Science, 15*, 251–254.

DeSteno, D. (2004). *New perspectives on jealousy: An integrative view of the most social of social emotions*. Paper presented at the meeting of the American Psychological Society, Chicago, IL.

DeSteno, D., Dasgupta, N., Bartlett, M. Y., & Cajdric, A. (2004). Prejudice from thin air: The effect of emotion on automatic intergroup attitudes. *Psychological Science, 15*, 319–324.

Deutsch, M., & Gerard, H. B. (1955). A study of normative and informational social influences upon individual judgment. *Journal of Abnormal and Social Psychology, 51*, 629–636.

Devine, D. J., & Caughlin, D. E. (2014). Do they matter? A meta-analytic investigation of individual characteristics and guilt judgement. *Psychology, 21*, 109–134.

Devine, P. G., Plant, E. A., & Blair, I. V. (2001). Classic and contemporary analyses of racial prejudice. In R. Brown & S. Gaertner (Eds.), *Blackwell handbook of social psychology: Intergroup processes* (pp. 198–217). Oxford, UK: Blackwell.

DeVoe, S. E., & Pfeffer, J. (2010). The stingy hour: How accounting for time affects volunteering. *Personality and Social Psychology Bulletin, 36*, 470–483.

DeWall, C. N., MacDonald, G., Webster, G. D., Masten, C. L., Baumeister, R. F., Powell, C., et al. (2010). Acetaminophen reduces social pain: Behavioral and neural evidence. *Psychological Science, 21*, 931–937.

DeWall, C. N., Twenge, J. M., Gitter, S. A., & Baumeister, R. F. (2009). It's the thought that counts: The role of hostile cognition in shaping aggressive responses to social exclusion. *Journal of Personality and Social Psychology, 96*, 45–59.

Dickerson, S. S., & Kemeny, M. E. (2004). Acute stressors and cortisol responses: A theoretical integration and synthesis of laboratory research. *Psychological Bulletin, 130*, 355–391.

Diener, D., Ng., W., Harter, J., & Raksha, A. (2010). Wealth and happiness across the world: Material prosperity predicts life evaluation, whereas psychosocial prosperity predicts positive feelings. *Journal of Personality and Social Psychology, 99*, 52–61.

Diener, E. (2000). Subjective well-being: The science of happiness, and a proposal for a national index. *American Psychologist, 55*, 34–43.

Diener, E., Lucas, R., & Scollon, C. N. (2006). Beyond the hedonic treadmill: Revising the adaptation theory of well-being. *American Psychologist, 61*, 305–314.

Diener, E., Ng, W., Harter, J., & Arora, R. (2010). Wealth and happiness across the world: Material prosperity predicts life evaluation, whereas psychosocial prosperity predicts positive feelings. *Journal of Personality and Social Psychology, 99*, 52–61.

Diener, E., & Oishi, S. (2005). The nonobvious social psychology of happiness. *Psychological Inquiry, 16*, 162–167.

Diener, E., Suh, E. M., Lucas, R. E., & Smith, H. L. (1999). Subjective well-being: Three decades of progress. *Psychological Bulletin, 125*, 276–302.

Diener, E., Tay, L., & Myers, D. (2011). The religion paradox: If religion makes people happy, why are so many dropping out? *Journal of Personality and Social Psychology, 101*, 1278–1290.

Diener, E., Wolsic, B., & Fujita, F. (1995). Physical attractiveness and subjective well-being. *Journal of Personality and Social Psychology, 69*, 120–129.

Dietrich, D. M., & Berkowitz, L. (1997). Alleviation of dissonance by engaging in prosocial behavior or receiving ego-enhancing feedback. *Journal of Social Behavior and Personality, 12*, 557.

Dijksterhuis, A. (2004). I like myself but I don't know why: Enhancing implicit self-esteem by subliminal evaluative conditioning. *Journal of Personality and Social Psychology, 86*, 345–355.

Dijksterhuis, A., & Nordgren, L. F. (2006). A theory of unconscious thought. *Perspectives on Psychological Science, 1*, 95–109.

Dijksterhuis, A., & van Olden, Z. (2006). On the benefits of thinking unconsciously: Unconscious thought can increase post-choice satisfaction. *Journal of Experimental Social Psychology, 42*, 627–631.

Dimatteo, R. M., & Taranta, A. (1979). Nonverbal communication and physician-patient rapport: An empirical study. *Professional Psychology, 10*, 540–547.

Dion, K. K., Berscheid, E., & Hatfield (Walster), E. (1972). What is beautiful is good. *Journal of Personality and Social Psychology, 24*, 285–290.

Dishman, R. K., & Buckworth, J. (1996). Increasing physical activity: A quantitative synthesis. *Medicine and Science in Sports and Exercise, 28*, 706–719.

Dissanayake, E. (2000). *Art and intimacy*. Seattle: University of Washington Press.

Dollard, J., Doob, L., Miller, N., Mowerer, O. H., & Sears, R. R. (1939). *Frustration and aggression*. New Haven, CT: Yale University Press.

Dong, P, Dai, X., & Wyer, R. S. Jr. (2014). Actors conform, observers react: The effects of behavioral synchrony on conformity. *Journal of Personality and Social Psychology, 108*, 60–75.

Dorling, D. (2015). *Injustice: Why social inequality still persists*. Chicago, IL: The Policy Press.

Dovidio, J. F., Brigham, J., Johnson, B., & Gaertner, S. (1996). Stereotyping, prejudice, and discrimination: Another look. In N. Macrae, C. Stangor, & M. Hwestone (Eds.), *Stereotypes and stereotyping* (pp. 1276–1319). New York: Guilford Press.

Dovidio, J. F., Gaertner, S. L., Isen, A. M., & Lowrance, R. (1995). Group representations and intergroup bias: Positive affect, similarity, and group size. *Personality and Social Psychology Bulletin, 21*, 856–865.

Dovidio, J. F., Gaertner, S. L., & Kawakami, K. (2010). Racism. In J. F. Dovidio, M. Hewstone, P. Glick, & V. M. Esses (Eds.), *Sage handbook of prejudice, stereotyping and discrimination* (pp. 312–327). London: Sage.

Downs, A. C., & Lyons, P. M. (1991). Natural observations of the links between attractiveness and initial legal judgments. *Personality and Social Psychology Bulletin, 17*, 541–547.

Doyle, D. M., & Molix, L. (2015). Perceived discrimination and social relationship functioning among sexual minorities: Structural stigma as a moderating factor. *Analyses of Social Issues and Public Policy*. doi: 10.1111/asap.12098

Duck, J. M., Hogg, M. A., & Terry, D. J. (1999). Social identity and perceptions of media persuasion: Are we always less influenced than others? *Journal of Applied Social Psychology, 29*, 1879–1899.

Duclos, S. E., Laird, J. D., Schneider, E., Sexter, M., Stern, L., & Van Lighten, O. (1989). Emotion-specific effects of facial expressions and postures on emotional experience. *Journal of Personality and Social Psychology, 57*, 100–108.

Dugosh, K. L., & Paulus, P. B. (2005). Cognitive and social comparison processes in brainstorming. *Journal of Experimental Social Psychology, 41,* 313–320.

Duncan, J., & Owen, A. W. (2000). Common regions of the human frontal lobe recruited by diverse cognitive demands. *Trends in Cognitive Science, 23,* 475–483.

Dunn, E. W., Aknin, L. B., & Norton, M. I. (2014). Prosocial spending and happiness: Using money to benefit others pays off. *Current Directions in Psychological Science, 23,* 41–47.

Dunn, E., & Ashton-James, C. (2008). On emotional innumeracy: Predicted and actual affective responses to grand-scale tragedies. *Journal of Experimental Social Psychology, 44,* 692–698.

Dunn, E., & Laham, S. A. (2006). A user's guide to emotional time travel: Progress on key issues in affective forecasting. In J. Forgas (Ed.), *Hearts and minds: Affective influences on social cognition and behavior* (pp. 177–193). New York: Psychology Press.

Dunn, E. W., Arknin, L. B., & Norton, M. I. (2008). Spending money on others promotes happiness. *Science, 319,* 1687–1688.

Dunn, J. (1992). Siblings and development. *Current Directions in Psychological Science, 1,* 6–11.

Durrheim, K., Dixon, J., Tredoux, C., Eaton, L., Quayle, M., & Clack, B. (2009). Predicting support for racial transformation policies: Intergroup threat, racial prejudice, sense of group entitlement and strength of identification. *European Journal of Social Psychology, 41,* 23–41.

Dutton, D. G., & Aron, A. P. (1974). Some evidence for heightened sexual attraction under conditions of high anxiety. *Journal of Personality and Social Psychology, 30,* 510–517.

Duus, R., & Cooray, M. (2015). How we discovered the dark side of wearable fitness trackers. *The Conversation.* Retrieved from http://theconversation.com/how-we-discovered-the-dark-side-of-wearable-fitness-trackers-43363

Dweck, C. S., & Legget, E. L. (1988). A social-cognitive approach to motivation and personality. *Psychological Review, 95,* 256–273.

Eagly, A. H. (1987). *Sex differences in social behavior: A social-role interpretation.* Hillsdale, NJ: Erlbaum.

Eagly, A. H. (2009). The his and hers of prosocial behavior: An examination of the social psychology of gender. *American Psychologist, 64,* 644–658.

Eagly, A. H., & Chaiken, S. (1993). *The psychology of attitudes.* Orlando, FL: Harcourt Brace Jovanovich.

Eagly, A. H., & Chaiken, S. (1998). Attitude structure and function. In G. Lindsey, S. T. Fiske, & D. T. Gilbert (Eds.), *Handbook of social psychology* (4th ed., pp. 269–322). New York: Oxford University Press and McGraw-Hill.

Eagly, A. H., Chaiken, S., & Wood, W. (1981). An attributional analysis of persuasion. In J. H. Harvey, W. Ickes, & R. F. Kidd (Eds.), *New directions in attribution research* (pp. 37–62). Hillsdale, NJ: Erlbaum.

Eagly, A. H., Chen, S., Chaiken, S., & Shaw-Barnes, K. (1999). The impact of attitudes on memory: An affair to remember. *Psychological Bulletin, 124,* 64–89.

Eagly, A.H., & Crowley, M. (1986). Gender and helping behavior: A meta-analytic view of the social psychological literature. *Psychological Bulletin, 100,* 283–308.

Eagly, A. H., Eastwick, P. W., & Johannesen-Schmidt, M. (2009). Possible selves in marital roles: The impact of the anticipated vision of labor on the mate preferences of women and men. *Personality and Social Psychology Bulletin, 35,* 403–413.

Eagly, A. H., & Karau, S. J. (2002). Role congruity theory of prejudice toward female leaders. *Psychological Review, 109,* 573–598.

Eagly, A. H., Kulesa, P., Brannon, L. A., Shaw, K., & Hutson-Comeaux, S. (2000). Why counterattitudinal messages are as memorable as proattitudinal messages: The importance of active defense against attack. *Personality and Social Psychology Bulletin, 26,* 1392–1408.

Eagly, A. H., Makhijani, M. G., & Klonsky, B. G. (1992). Gender and the evaluation of leaders: A meta-analysis. *Psychological Bulletin, 111,* 3–22.

Eagly, A. H., & Mladinic, A. (1994). Are people prejudiced against women? Some answers from research on attitudes, gender stereotypes, and judgments of competence. In W. Sroebe & M. Hewstone (Eds.), *European review of social psychology* (Vol. 5, pp. 1–35). New York: Wiley.

Eagly, A. H., & Sczesny, S. (2009). Stereotypes about women, men, and leaders: Have times changed? In M. Barreto, M. K. Ryan, & M. T. Schmitt (Eds.), *The glass ceiling in the 21st century* (pp. 21–47). Washington, DC: American Psychological Association.

Eagly, A. H., & Steffen, V. J. (1986). Gender and aggressive behavior: A meta-analytic review of the social psychological literature. *Psychological Bulletin, 100,* 309–330.

Eastwick, P. W., Luchies, L. B., Finkel, E. J., & Hunt, L. I. (2014). The predictive validity of ideal partner preferences: A review and meta-analysis. *Psychological Bulletin, 140,* 623–665.

Eaton, A. A., Majka, E. A., & Visser, P. S. (2008). Emerging perspectives on the structure and function of attitude strength. *European Review of Social Psychology, 19,* 165–201.

Eaton, A. A., Visser, P. S., Kosnick, J. A., & Anand, S. (2009). Social power and attitude strength over the life course. *Personality and Social Psychology Bulletin, 35,* 1646–1660.

Eberhardt, J. L., Davies, P. G., Purdie-Vaughns, V. J., & Johnson, S. L. (2006). Looking deathworthy: Perceived stereotypicality of black defendants predicts capital-sentencing outcomes. *Psychological Science, 17,* 383–386.

Effron, D. A., & Knowles, E. D. (2015). Entitativity and intergroup bias: How belonging to a cohesive group allows people to express their prejudices. *Journal of Personality and Social Psychology, 108,* 234–253.

Eibach, R. P., & Keegan, T. (2006). Free at last? Social dominance, loss aversion, and White and Black Americans' differing assessments of racial progress. *Journal of Personality and Social Psychology, 90,* 453–467.

Eich, E. (1995). Searching for mood dependent memory. *Psychological Science, 6,* 67–75.

Eid, M., & Diener, E. (2004). Global judgments of subjective well-being: Situational variability and long-term stability. *Social Indicators Research, 65,* 245–277.

Eidelman, S., & Crandall, C. S. (2014). The intuitive traditionalist: How biases for existence and longevity promote the status quo. *Advances in Experimental Social Psychology, 50,* 53–104.

Eidelman, S., Pattershall, J., & Crandall, C. S. (2010). Longer is better. *Journal of Experimental Social Psychology.*

Eisenberg, N., Guthrie, I. K., Murphy, B. C., Shepard, S. A., Cumberland, A., & Carlo, G. (1999). Consistency and development of prosocial dispositions: A longitudinal study. *Child Development, 70,* 1360–1372.

Eisenberger, N. I., & Lieberman, M. D. (2004). Why rejection hurts: A common neural alarm system for physical and social pain. *Trends in Cognitive Sciences, 8,* 294–300.

Eisenman, R. (1985). Marijuana use and attraction: Support for Byrne's similarity-attraction concept. *Perceptual and Motor Skills, 61,* 582.

Eisenstadt, D., & Leippe, M. R. (1994). The self-comparison process and self-discrepant feedback: Consequences of learning you are what you thought you were not. *Journal of Personality and Social Psychology, 67,* 611–626.

Ekman, P. (2001). *Telling lies: Clues to deceit in the marketplace, politics, and marriage* (3rd ed.). New York: Norton.

Ekman, P., & Friesen, W. V. (1975). *Unmasking the face*. Englewood Cliffs, NJ: Prentice-Hall.

Ekman, P., & O'Sullivan, M. (1991). Who can catch a liar? *American Psychologist, 46*, 913–920.

Elfenbein, H. A., & Ambady, N. (2002). On the universality and cultural specificity of emotion recognition: A meta-analysis. *Psychological Bulletin, 128*, 203–235.

Elfenbein, H. A., & Eisenkraft, N. (2010). The relationship between displaying and perceiving nonverbal cues of affect: A meta-analysis to solve an old mystery. *Journal of Personality and Social Psychology, 98*, 301–318.

Ellemers, N. (2014). Women at work: How organizational features impact career development. *Policy Insights from the Behavioral and Brain Sciences, 1*, 46–54.

Ellemers, N., de Gilder, D., & Haslam, S. A. (2004). Motivating individuals and groups at work: A social identity perspective on leadership and group performance. *Academy of Management Review, 29*, 459–478.

Elliot, A. J., & Devine, P. G. (1994). On the motivational nature of cognitive dissonance: Dissonance as psychological discomfort. *Journal of Personality and Social Psychology, 67*, 382–394.

Elliot, A. J., & Niesta, D. (2008). Romantic red: Red enhances men's attraction to women. *Journal of Personality and Social Psychology, 95*, 1150–1164.

Ellison, N., Heino, R., & Gibbs, J. (2006). Managing impressions online: Self-presentation processes in the online dating environment. *Journal of Computer-Mediated Communication, 11*, 415–441.

Ellsworth, P. C., & Carlsmith, J. M. (1973). Eye contact and gaze aversion in aggressive encounter. *Journal of Personality and Social Psychology, 33*, 117–122.

Englehart, J. M. (2006). Teacher perceptions of student behavior as a function of class size. *Social Psychology of Education, 9*, 245–272.

Englich, B., Mussweiler, T., & Strack, F. (2006). Playing dice with criminal sentences: The influence of irrelevant anchors on experts' judicial decision making. *Personality and Social Psychology Bulletin, 32*, 188–200.

Epel, E. S., Blackburn, E. H., Lin, J., Dhabhar, F. S., Adler, N. E., Morrow, J. D., et al. (2004). Accelerated telomere shortening in response to life stress. *Proceedings of the National Academy of Sciences, 101*, 17312–17315.

Epley, N., & Gilovich, T. (2006). The anchoring-and-adjustment heuristic: Why the adjustments are insufficient. *Psychological Science, 17*, 311–318.

Epley, N., & Huff, C. (1998). Suspicion, affective response, and educational benefit as a result of deception in psychology research. *Personality and Social Psychology Bulletin, 24*, 759–768.

Epstude, K., & Mussweiler, T. (2009). What you feel is how you compare: How comparisons influence the social induction of affect. *Emotion, 9*, 1–14.

Escobedo, J. R., & Adolphs, R. (2010). Becoming a better person: Temporal remoteness biases autobiographical memories for moral events. *Emotion, 10*, 511–518.

Esses, V. M., Jackson, L. M., & Bennett-AbuAyyash, C. (2010). Intergroup competition. In J. F. Dovidio, M. Hewstone, P. Glick, & V. M. Esses (Eds.), *Sage handbook of prejudice, stereotyping and discrimination* (pp. 225–240). London: Sage.

Esses, V. M., Jackson, L. M., Nolan, J. M., & Armstrong, T. L. (1999). Economic threat and attitudes toward immigrants. In S. Halli & L. Drieger (Eds.), *Immigrant Canada: Demographic, economic and social challenges* (pp. 212–229). Toronto: University of Toronto Press.

Etcoff, N. L., Ekman, P., Magee, J. J., & Frank, M. G. (2000). Lie detection and language comprehension. *Nature, 40*, 139.

Exline, J. J., & Lobel, M. (1999). The perils of outperformance: Sensitivity about being the target of a threatening upward comparison. *Psychological Bulletin, 125*, 307–337.

Falomir-Pichastor, J. M., Munoz-Rojas, D., Invernizzi, F., & Mugny, G. (2004). Perceived in-group threat as a factor moderating the influence of in-group norms on discrimination against foreigners. *European Journal of Social Psychology, 34*, 135–153.

Fang, R., Chi, L., Chen, M., & Baron, R. A. (2015). Bringing political skill into social networks: Findings from a field study of entrepreneurs. *Journal of Management Studies, 52*, 175–212.

Fazio, R. H. (1990). Multiple processes by which attitudes guide behavior: The MODE model as an integrative framework. In M. P. Zanna (Ed.), *Advances in experimental social psychology* (Vol. 23, pp. 75–109). San Diego, CA: Academic Press.

Fazio, R. H. (2000). Accessible attitudes as tools for object appraisal: The costs and benefits. In G. R. Maio & J. M. Olson (Eds.), *Why we evaluate: Functions of attitudes* (pp. 1–26). Mahwah, NJ: Erlbaum.

Fazio, R. H., & Hilden, L. E. (2001). Emotional reactions to a seemingly prejudiced response: The role of automatically activated racial attitudes and motivation to control prejudiced reactions. *Personality and Social Psychology Bulletin, 27*, 538–549.

Fazio, R. H., Ledbetter, J. E., & Towles-Schwen, T. (2000). On the costs of accessible attitudes: Detecting that the attitude object has changed. *Journal of Personality and Social Psychology, 78*, 197–210.

Fazio, R. H., & Olson, M. A. (2003). Implicit measures in social cognition research: Their meaning and uses. *Annual Review of Psychology, 54*, 297–327.

Fazio, R. H., & Roskos-Ewoldsen, D. R. (1994). Acting as we feel: When and how attitudes guide behavior. In S. Shavitt & T. C. Brock (Eds.), *Persuasion* (pp. 71–93). Boston: Allyn & Bacon.

Feagin, J. R., & Vera, H. (1995). *White racism*. New York: Routledge.

Feinberg, M., Willer, R., & Schultz, M. (2015). Gossip and ostracism promote cooperation in groups. *Psychological Science, 25*, 656–664.

Feingold, A. (1992). Good-looking people are not what we think. *Psychological Bulletin, 111*, 304–341.

Feldman, R. S., Forrest, J. A., & Happ, B. R. (2002). Self-presentation and verbal deception: Do self-presenters lie more? *Basic and Applied Social Psychology, 24*, 163–170.

Ferris, G. R., Treadway, P. I., Perrewe, R. K., Brouber, C. D., & Lux, S. (2007). Political skill in organizations. *Journal of Management, 33*, 290–320.

Feshbach, S. (1984). The catharsis hypothesis, aggressive drive, and the reduction of aggression. *Aggressive Behavior, 10*, 91–101.

Festinger, L. (1954). A theory of social comparison processes. *Human Relations, 7*, 117–140.

Festinger, L., & Carlsmith, J. M. (1959). Cognitive consequences of forced compliance. *Journal of Abnormal and Social Psychology, 58*, 203–210.

Festinger, L., Schachter, S., & Back, K. (1950). *Social pressures in informal groups: A study of a housing community*. New York: Harper.

Fiedler, K., Messner, C., & Bluemke, M. (2006). Unresolved problems with the "I", the "A", and the "T": A logical and psychometric critique of the Implicit Association Test (IAT). *European Review of Social Psychology, 17*, 74–147.

Fielding, K. S., & Hogg, M. A. (1997). Social identity, self-categorization, and leadership: A field study of small interactive groups. *Group Dynamics: Theory, Research, and Practice, 1*, 39–51.

Fink, B., & Penton-Voak, I. (2002). Evolutionary psychology of facial attractiveness. *Current Directions in Psychological Science, 11*, 154–158.

Fischer, P., & Greitemeyer, T. (2006). Music and aggression: The impact of sexual-aggressive song lyrics on aggression-related thoughts, emotions, and behavior toward the same and the opposite sex. *Personality and Social Psychology Bulletin, 32*, 1165–1176.

Fiske, S. T. (2009). Social cognition. In D. Sander & K. R. Scherer (Eds.), *Oxford companion to emotion and the affective sciences* (pp. 371–373). Oxford, UK: Oxford University Press.

Fiske, S. T., Cuddy, A. J. C., Glick, P., & Xu, J. (2002). A model of (often mixed) stereotype content: Competence and warmth respectively follow from perceived status and competition. *Journal of Personality and Social Psychology, 82,* 878–902.

Fiske, S. T., & Stevens, L. E. (1993). What's so special about sex? Gender stereotyping and discrimination. In S. Oskamp & M. Costanzo (Eds.), *Gender issues in contemporary society* (pp. 173–196). Newbury Park, CA: Sage.

Fiske, S. T., & Taylor, S. E. (2008). *Social cognition: From brains to culture.* New York: McGraw-Hill.

Fiske, S. T., & Taylor, S. E. (2013). *Social cognition: From brains to culture* (2nd ed.). Thousand Oaks, CA: Sage.

Fitzsimons, G. M., & Bargh, J. A. (2003). Thinking of you: Nonconscious pursuit of interpersonal goals associated with relationships partners. *Journal of Personality and Social Psychology, 84,* 148–164.

Fitzsimons, G. M., & Kay, A. C. (2004). Language and interpersonal cognition: Causal effects of variations in pronoun usage on perceptions of closeness. *Personality and Social Psychology Bulletin, 30,* 547–557.

Fleming, M. A., & Petty, R. E. (2000). Identity and persuasion: An elaboration likelihood approach. In D. J. Terry & M. A. Hogg (Eds.), *Attitudes, behavior, and social context* (pp. 171–199). Mahwah, NJ: Erlbaum.

Fletcher, G. J. O., Simpson, J. A., & Boyes, A. D. (2006). Accuracy and bias in romantic relationships: An evolutionary and social psychological analysis. In M. Schaller, J. A. Simpson, & D. T. Kenrick (Eds.), *Evolution and social psychology* (pp. 1890–210). New York: Psychology Press.

Flinn, M. V., Ponzi, D., & Muehlenbein, M. P. (2012). Hormonal mechanisms for regulation of aggression in human coalitions. *Human Nature, 23,* 68–88.

Flynn, F. J., Reagans, R. E., Amanatullah, E. T., & Ames, D. R. (2006). Helping one's way to the top: Self-monitors achieve status by helping others and knowing who helps them. *Journal of Personality and Social Psychology, 91,* 1123–1137.

Flynn, R., & Lake, K. B. (2008). If you need help, just ask: Underestimating compliance with direct requests for help. *Journal of Personality and Social Psychology, 95,* 128–141.

Folger, R., & Baron, R. A. (1996). Violence and hostility at work: A model of reactions to perceived injustice. In G. R. VandenBos & E. Q. Bulato (Eds.), *Violence on the job: Identifying risks and developing solutions* (pp. 51–85). Washington, DC: American Psychological Association.

Forbes, G. B., Collinsworth, L. L., Zhao, P., Kohlman, S., & LeClaire, J. (2011). Relationships among individualism-collectivism, gender, and ingroup/outgroup status, and responses to conflict: A study in China and the United States. *Aggressive Behavior, 37,* 302–314.

Forgas, J. P. (2006). *Affect in social thinking and behavior.* New York: Psychology Press.

Forgas, J. P., Baumeister, R. F., & Tice, D. N. (2009). *The psychology of self-regulation.* Sydney, Australia: Psychology Press.

Forrest, J. A., & Feldman, R. S. (2000). Detecting deception and judge's involvement; lower task involvement leads to better lit detection. *Personality and Social Psychology Bulletin, 26,* 118–125.

Fowler, J. H., & Christakis, N. A. (2008). Dynamic spread of happiness in a large social network: Longitudinal analysis over 20 years in the Framingham Heart Study. *British Medical Journal, 337,* 2338–2346.

Frable, D. E., Blackstone, T., & Scherbaum, C. (1990). Marginal and mindful: Deviants in social interactions. *Journal of Personality and Social Psychology, 59,* 140–149.

Frank, T. (2004). *What's the matter with Kansas? How conservatives won the heart of America.* New York: Metropolitan Books.

Franks, A. S., & Scherr, K. C. (2014). A sociofunctional approach to prejudice at the polls: Are atheists more politically disadvantaged than gays and Blacks? *Journal of Applied Social Psychology, 44,* 681–691.

Frederick, S., & Loewenstein, G. (1999). Hedonic adaptation. In D. Kahneman, E. Diener, & N. Schwarz (Eds.), *Well-being: The foundations of hedonic psychology* (pp. 302–329). New York: Russell Sage Foundation.

Fredrickson, B. L. (1995). Socioemotional behavior at the end of college life. *Journal of Social and Personal Relationships, 12,* 261–276.

Fredrickson, B. L. (2001). The role of positive emotions in positive psychology: The broaden-and-build theory of positive emotions. *American Psychologist, 56,* 218–226.

Fredrickson, B. L., & Joiner, T. (2002). Positive emotions trigger upward spirals toward emotional well-being. *Psychological Science, 13,* 172–175.

Freedman, J. L., & Fraser, S. C. (1966). Compliance without pressure: The foot-in-the-door technique. *Journal of Personality and Social Psychology, 4,* 195–202.

Fritzsche, B. A., Finkelstein, M. A., & Penner, L. A. (2000). To help or not to help: Capturing individuals' decision policies. *Social Behavior and Personality, 28,* 561–578.

Frye, G. D. J., & Lord, C. G. (2009). Effects of time frame on the relationship between source monitoring errors and attitude change. *Social Cognition, 27,* 867–882.

Fuegen, K., & Biernat, M. (2002). Reexamining the effects of solo status for women and men. *Personality and Social Psychology Bulletin, 28,* 913–925.

Fuegen, K., & Brehm, J. W. (2004). The intensity of affect and resistance to social influence. In E. S. Knowles & J. A. Linn (Eds.), *Resistance and persuasion* (pp. 39–63). Mahwah, NJ: Erlbaum.

Fujita, K., & Han, H. A. (2009). Moving beyond deliberative control of impulses: The effect of construal levels on evaluative associations in self-control conflicts. *Psychological Science, 20,* 799–804.

Fultz, J., Schaller, M., & Cialdini, R. B. (1988). Empathy, sadness, and distress: Three related but distinct vicarious affective responses to another's suffering. *Personality and Social Psychology Bulletin, 14,* 312–325.

Funk, J. B., Bechtoldt-Baldacci, H., Pasold, T., & Baumgartner, J. (2004). Violence exposure in real-life, video games, television, movies, and the internet: Is there desensitization? *Journal of Adolescence, 27,* 23–39.

Gabaix, X., & Laibson, L. (2006). Shrouded attributes, consumer myopia, and information suppression in competitive markets. *Quarterly Journal of Economics, 121,* 505–540.

Gaertner, S. L., Mann, J. A., Dovidio, J. F., Murrell, A. J., & Pomare, M. (1990). How does cooperation reduce intergroup bias? *Journal of Personality and Social Psychology, 59,* 692–704.

Gaertner, S. L., Mann, J., Murrell, A., & Dovidio, J. F. (1989). Reducing intergroup bias: The benefits of recategorization. *Journal of Personality and Social Psychology, 57,* 239–249.

Gaertner, S. L., Rust, M. C., Dovidio, J. F., Bachman, B. A., & Anastasio, P. A. (1994). The contact hypothesis: The role of common ingroup identity on reducing intergroup bias. *Small Group Research, 25,* 224–249.

Galdi, S., Arcuri, L., & Gawronski, B. (2008). Automatic mental associations predict future choices of undecided decision-makers. *Science, 321,* 1100–1102.

Galinsky, A. D., Magee, J. C., Gruenfeld, D. H., Whitson, J. A., & Liljenquist, K. A. (2008). Power reduces the press of the situation: Implications for creativity, conformity, and dissonance. *Journal of Personality and Social Psychology, 95,* 1450–1466.

Galinsky, A. D., Magee, J. C., Inesi, M. E., & Gruenfeld, D. (2006). Power and perspectives not taken. *Psychologial Science, 17*, 1068–1073.

Galton, F. (1952). *Hereditary genius: An inquiry into its laws and consequences.* New York: Horizon. (Original work published 1870.)

Gantner, A. B., & Taylor, S. P. (1992). Human physical aggression as a function of alcohol and threat of harm. *Aggressive Behavior, 18*, 29–36.

Garcia, D. M., Horstman Reser, A., Amo, R. B., Redersdorff, S., & Branscombe, N. R. (2005). Perceivers' responses to in-group and out-group members who blame a negative outcome on discrimination. *Personality and Social Psychology Bulletin, 31*, 769–780.

Garcia, D. M., Schmitt, M. T., Branscombe, N. R., & Ellemers, N. (2010). Women's reactions to ingroup members who protest discriminatory treatment: The importance of beliefs about inequality and response appropriateness. *European Journal of Social Psychology, 40*, 733–745.

Garcia-Marques, T., Mackie, D. M., Claypool, H. M., & Garcia-Marques, L. (2004). Positivity can cue familiarity. *Personality and Social Psychology Bulletin, 30*, 585–593.

Gardner, R. M., & Tuckerman, Y. R. (1994). A computer-TV methodology for investigating the influence of somatotype on perceived personality traits. *Journal of Social Behavior and Personality, 9*, 555–563.

Gardner, W. I., Pickett, C., & Brewer, M. B. (2000). Social exclusion and selective memory: How the need to belong influences memory for social events. *Personality and Social Psychology Bulletin, 26*, 486–496.

Garling, T., Kirchler, E., Lewis, A., & van Raaij, F. (2009). Psychology, financial decision making, and financial crises. *Psychological Science in the Public Interest, 10*, 1–47.

Gawronski, B., & Bodenhausen, G. V. (2006). Associative and propositional processes in evaluation: An integrative review of implicit and explicit attitude change. *Psychological Bulletin, 132*, 692–731.

Gawronski, B., LeBel, E. P., & Peters, K. R. (2007). What do implicit measures tell us? *Perspectives on Psychological Science, 2*, 181–193.

Gazzola, V., Aziz-Zadeh, L., & Keysers, C. (2006). Empathy and the somatotopic auditory mirror system in humans. *Current Biology, 16*, 1824–1829.

Gelfand, M. J., Raver, J. L., Nishii, L., Leslie, L. M., Lun, J., Lim, B. C., et al. (2011). Differences between tight and loose cultures: A 33–nation study. *Science, 332*, 1100–1104.

Gentile, D. A., Anderson, C. A., Yukawa, S., Ihori, N., Saleem, M., Ming, L. K., et al. (2009). The effects of prosocial video games on prosocial behaviors: International evidence form correlational, longitudinal, and experimental studies. *Personality and Social Psychology Bulletin, 35*, 752–763.

Gentile, D. A., Anderson, C. A., Yukawa, S., Ihori, N., Saleem, M., Kam Ming, L., et al. (2009). The effects of prosocial video games on prosocial behaviors: International evidence from correlational, longitudinal, and experimental studies. *Personality and Social Psychology Bulletin, 35*, 752–763.

Gentile, D. A., & Gentile, J. R. (2008). Violent video games as exemplary teachers: A conceptual analysis. *Journal of Youth and Adolescence, 9*, 127–141.

Gerard, H. B., Wilhelmy, R. A., & Conolley, E. S. (1968). Conformity and group size. *Journal of Personality and Social Psychology, 8*, 79–82.

Giancola, P. R., Levinson, C. A., Corman, M. D., & Godlaski, A. J. (2009). Men and women, alcohol and aggression. *Experimental and Clinical Psychopharmacology, 17*, 154–164.

Gibbons, F. X., Eggleston, T. J., & Benthin, A. C. (1997). Cognitive reactions to smoking relapse: The reciprocal relation between dissonance and self-esteem. *Journal of Personality and Social Psychology, 72*, 184–195.

Giessner, S. R., & van Knippenberg, D. (2008). "License to fail": Goal definition, leader group prototypicality, and perceptions of leadership effectiveness after leader failure. *Organizational Behavior and Human Decision Processes, 105*, 14–35.

Gifford, R., Ng, C. F., & Wilkinson, M. (1985). Nonverbal cues in the employment interview: Links between applicant qualities and interviewer judgments. *Journal of Applied Psychology, 70*, 729–736.

Gigone, D., & Hastie, R. (1997). The impact of information on small group choice. *Journal of Personality and Social Psychology, 72*, 132–140.

Gilbert, D. T. (2002). Inferential correction. In T. Gilovich, D. W. Griffin, & D. Kahneman (Eds.), *Heuristics and biases: The psychology of intuitive judgment* (pp. 167–184). New York: Cambridge University Press.

Gilbert, D. T. (2006). *Stumbling on happiness.* New York: Knopf.

Gilbert, D. T., & Malone, P. S. (1995). The correspondence bias. *Psychological Bulletin, 117*, 21–38.

Gilbert, D. T., & Wilson, T. D. (2000). Miswanting: Some problems in the forecasting of future affective states. In J. Forgas (Ed.), *Feeling and thinking: The role of affect in social cognition.* New York: Cambridge University Press.

Gillath, O., Mikulincer, M., Fitzsimons, G. M., Shaver, P. R., Schachner, D. A. & Bargh, J. A. (2006). Automatic activation of attachment-related goals. *Personality and Social Psychology Bulletin, 32*, 1375–1388.

Gillath, O., Shaver, P. R., Baek, J. M., & Chun, S. D. (2008). Genetic correlates of adult attachment style. *Personality and Social Psychology Bulletin, 34*, 1396–1405.

Gillath, O., Shaver, P. R., Mikulincer, M., Nitzberg, R. E., Erez, A., & van IJzendoorn, M. H. (2005). Attachment, caregiving, and volunteering: Placing volunteerism in an attachment-theoretical framework. *Personal Relationships, 12*, 425–446.

Gladue, B. A., & Delaney, H. J. (1990). Gender differences in perception of attractiveness of men and women in bars. *Personality and Social Psychology Bulletin, 16*, 378–391.

Gladwell, M. (2004, January 12). Big and bad: How the S.U.V. ran over automotive safety. *The New Yorker*, pp. 28–33.

Gladwell, M. (2005). *Blink: The power of thinking without thinking.* New York: Little, Brown.

Gleason, K. A., Jensen-Campbell, L. A., & Ickes, W. (2009). The role of empathic accuracy in adolescents' peer relations and adjustment. *Personality and Social Psychology Bulletin, 35*, 997–1011.

Gleibs, I. H., Haslam, C., Jones, J. M., Haslam, S. A., McNeill, J., & Connolly, H. (2011). No country for old men? The role of a 'Gentlemen's Club' in promoting social engagement and psychological well-being in residential care. *Aging and Mental Health, 15*, 456–466.

Gleibs, I. H., Noack, P., & Mummendey, A. (2010). We are still better than them: A longitudinal field study of ingroup favouritism during a merger. *European Journal of Social Psychology, 40*, 819–836.

Glick, P. (2002). Sacrificial lambs dressed in wolves' clothing: Envious prejudice, ideology, and the scapegoating of Jews. In *Understanding genocide: The social psychology of the Holocaust* (pp. 113–142). New York: Oxford University Press.

Glick, P., & Rudman, L. A. (2010). Sexism. In J. F. Dovidio, M. Hewstone, P. Glick, & V. M. Esses (Eds.), *Sage handbook of prejudice, stereotyping and discrimination* (pp. 328–344). London: Sage.

Goethals, G. R., & Darley, J. (1977). Social comparison theory: An attributional approach. In J. M. Suls & R. L. Miller (Eds.), *Social comparison processes: Theoretical and empirical perspectives* (pp. 259–278). Washington, DC: Hemisphere.

Goetz, J. L., Keltner, D., & Simon-Thomas, E. (2010). Compassion: An evolutionary analysis and empirical review. *Psychological Bulletin, 136*, 351–374.

Goff, P. A., Eberhardt, J. L., Williams, M. J., & Jackson, M. C. (2008). Not yet human: Implicit knowledge, historical dehumanization, and contemporary consequences. *Journal of Personality and Social Psychology, 94,* 292–306.

Goff, P. A., Steele, C. M., & Davies, P. G. (2008). The space between us: Stereotype threat and distance in interracial contexts. *Journal of Personality and Social Psychology, 94,* 91–107.

Goldenberg, L., & Forgas, J. P. (2012). Can happy mood reduce the just world bias? Affective influences on blaming the victim. *Journal of Experimental Social Psychology, 48,* 239–243.

Gollwitzer, P. M. (1999). Implementation intentions: Strong effects of simple plans. *American Psychologist, 54,* 493–503.

Gonzaga, G. C., Keltner, D., Londahl, E. A., & Smith, M. D. (2001). Love and the commitment problem in romantic relations and friendship. *Journal of Personality and Social Psychology, 81,* 247–262.

Goodboy, A. K. (2014). An experimental investigation of the antecedents and consequences of psychological reactance in the college classroom. *Communication Education, 63,* 192–209.

Goodwin, R., Cook, O., & Yung, Y. (2001). Loneliness and life satisfaction among three cultural groups. *Personal Relationships, 8,* 225–230.

Gordon, K. C., Baucom, D. H., & Snyder, D. K. (2004). An integrative intervention for promoting recovery from extramarital affairs. *Journal of Marital and Family Therapy, 30,* 213–231.

Gordon, R. A. (1996). Impact of ingratiation in judgments and evaluations: A meta-analytic investigation. *Journal of Personality and Social Psychology, 71,* 54–70.

Graham, S., & Folkes, V. (Eds.). (1990). *Attribution theory: Applications to achievement, mental health, and interpersonal conflict.* Hillsdale, NJ: Erlbaum.

Grant, A. M., & Gino, F. (2010). A little thanks goes a long way: Explaining why gratitude expressions motivate prosocial behavior. *Journal of Personality and Social Psychology, 98,* 946–955.

Grant, C. M., & Francesca, G. (2010). A little thanks goes a long way: Explaining why gratitude expressions motivate prosocial behavior. *Journal of Personality and Social Psychology, 98,* 946–955.

Gray, H. M. (2008). To what extent and under what conditions are first impressions valid? In N. Ambady & J. Skowronski (Eds.), *First impressions* (pp. 106–128). New York: Guilford Press.

Gray, K., Ward, A. D., & Norton, M. I. (2014). Paying it forward: Generalized reciprocity and the limits of generosity. *Journal of Experimental Psychology: General, 143,* 247–254.

Greenaway, K. H., Haslam, S. A., Cruwys, T., Branscombe, N. R., Ysseldyk, R., & Heldreth, C. (2015). From "we" to "me": Group identification enhances perceived personal control with consequences for health and well-being. *Journal of Personality and Social Psychology, 53,* 53–74.

Greenaway, K. H., Wright, R. G., Willingham, J., Reynolds, K. J., & Haslam, S. A. (2015). Shared identity is key to effective communication. *Personality and Social Psychology Bulletin, 41,* 171–182.

Greenbaum, P., & Rosenfield, H. W. (1978). Patterns of avoidance in responses to interpersonal staring and proximity: Effects of bystanders on drivers at a traffic intersection. *Journal of Personality and Social Psychology, 36,* 575–587.

Greenberg, J. (1993). Justice and organizational citizenship: A commentary on the state of the science. *Employee Responsibilities and Rights Journal, 6,* 249–256.

Greenberg, J., Martens, A., Jonas, E., Eisenstadt, D., Pyszczynski, T., & Solomon, S. (2003). Psychological defense in anticipation of anxiety: Eliminating the potential for anxiety eliminates the effects of mortality salience on worldview defense. *Psychological Science, 14,* 516–519.

Greenberg, J., Pyszczynski, T., & Solomon, S. (1986). The causes and consequences of a need for self-esteem: A terror management theory. In R. F. Baumeister (Ed.), *Public self and private self* (pp. 189–212). New York: Springer-Verlag.

Greene, E., & Bornstein, B. H. (2003). *Determining damages: The psychology of jury awards.* Washington, DC: The American Psychological Association.

Greene, E., & Dodge, M. (1995). The influence of prior record evidence on juror decision making. *Law and Human Behavior, 19,* 67–77.

Greenwald, A. G. (2002). Constructs in student ratings of instructors. In H. I. Braun & D. N. Douglas (Eds.), *The role of constructs in psychological and educational measurement* (pp. 277–297). Mahwah, NJ: Erlbaum.

Greenwald, A. G., & Banaji, M. R. (1995). Implicit social cognition: Attitudes, self-esteem, and stereotypes. *Psychological Review, 102,* 4–27.

Greenwald, A. G., & Farnham, S. (2000). Using the Implicit Association Test to measure self-esteem and self-concept. *Journal of Personality and Social Psychology, 79,* 1022–1038.

Greenwald, A. G., McGhee, D. E., & Schwarz, J. L. K. (1998). Measuring individual differences in implicit cognition: The Implicit Association Test. *Journal of Personality and Social Psychology, 74,* 1464–1480.

Greenwald, A. G., & Nosek, B. A. (2008). Attitudinal dissociation: What does it mean? In R. E. Petty, R. H. Fazio, & P. Brinol (Eds.), *Attitudes: Insights from the new implicit measures* (pp. 65–82). Hillsdale, NJ: Erlbaum.

Greenwald, A. G., Poehlman, T. A., Uhlmann, E. L., & Banaji, M. R. (2009). Understanding and using the Implicit Association Test: III. Meta-analysis of predictive validity. *Journal of Personality and Social Psychology, 97,* 17–41.

Greitmeyer, T., & Osswald, S. (2010). Effects of prosocial video games on prosocial behavior. *Journal of Personality and Social Psychology, 98,* 211–221.

Griffin, J. A., McCune, S., Maholmes, V., & Hurley, K. (2011). Human-animal interaction research: An introduction to issues and topics. In P. McCardle, S. McCune, J. A. Griffin, & V. Maholmes (Eds.), *How animals affect us* (pp. 3–9). Washington, DC: American Psychological Association.

Griskevicius, V., Tybur, J. M., Gangestad, S. W., Perea, E. F., Shapiro, J. R., & Kenrick, D. T. (2009). Aggress to impress: Hostility as an evolved context-dependent strategy. *Journal of Personality and Social Psychology, 96,* 980–994.

Gruber, J., Mauss, I., & Tamir, M. (2011). A dark side of happiness? How, when, and why happiness is not always good. *Perspectives on Psychological Science, 6,* 222–233.

Guéguen, N. (2003). Fund-raising on the Web: The effect of an electronic door-in-the-face technique in compliance to a request. *CyberPsychology & Behavior, 2,* 189–193.

Guéguen, N., Joule, R. V., & Marchand, M. (2013). La technique du leurre: Impact du delai, du sollicituer et di l'implication sur la submission. [The lure technique.] *Canadian Journal of Behavioural Science, 45,* 138–147.

Guimond, S. (2000). Group socialization and prejudice: The social transmission of intergroup attitudes and beliefs. *European Journal of Social Psychology, 30,* 335–354.

Guimond, S., Branscombe, N. R., Brunot, S., Buunk, B. P., Chatard, A., Désert, M., et al. (2007). Culture, gender, and the self: Variations and impact of social comparison processes. *Journal of Personality and Social Psychology, 92,* 1118–1134.

Guimond, S., & de la Sablonniere, R. (2015). Psychological metamorphosis: Understanding the effects of institutions, roles, and dramatic social change on individuals. In R. J. Reynolds & N. R. Branscombe (Eds.), *Psychology of change: Life contexts, experiences, and identities* (pp. 59–76). New York: Psychology Press.

Guinote, A., Judd, C. M., & Brauer, M. (2002). Effects of power on perceived and objective group variability: Evidence that more powerful groups are more variable. *Journal of Personality and Social Psychology, 82,* 708–721.

Gump, B. B., & Kulik, J. A. (1997). Stress, affiliation, and emotional contagion. *Journal of Personality and Social Psychology, 72,* 305–319.

Gunsoy, C., Cross, S. E., Uskul, A. K., Adams, G., & Gercek-Swing, B. (2015). Avoid or fight back? Cultural differences in responses to conflict and the role of collectivism, honor, and enemy perception. *Journal of Cross-Cultural Psychology, 46,* 1081–1102.

Gustafson, R. (1992). Alcohol and aggression: A replication study controlling for potential confounding variables. *Aggressive Behavior, 18,* 21–28.

Hackman, J. R., & Wageman, R. (2007). Asking the right questions about leadership. *American Psychologist, 62,* 43–47.

Hagger, M. S., Wood, C., Stiff, C., & Chatzisarantis, N. L. D. (2010). Ego depletion and the strength model of self-control: A meta analysis. *Psychological Bulletin, 136,* 495–525.

Hahn, A., Judd, C. M., Hirsh, H. K., & Blair, I. V. (2014). Awareness of implicit attitudes. *Journal of Experimental Psychology: General, 143,* 1369–1392.

Halkjelsvik, T., & Jorgensen, M. (2012). From origami to software development: A review of studies on judgment-based predictions of performance time. *Psychological Bulletin, 138,* 238–271.

Hall, J. A., Andrzejewski, S. A., & Yopchick, J. E. (2009). Psychosocial correlates of interpersonal sensitivity: A meta-analysis. *Journal of Nonverbal Behavior, 33,* 149–180.

Hall, J. H., & Fincham, F. D. (2005). Self-forgiveness: The stepchild of forgiveness research. *Journal of Social and Clinical psychology, 24,* 621–637.

Halverscheid, S., & Witte, E. H. (2008). Justification of war and terrorism. *Social Psychology, 39,* 26–36.

Hamerman, E. J., & Morewedge, C. K. (2015). Reliance on luck: Identifying which achievement goals elicit superstitious behavior. *Personality and Social Psychology Bulletin, 41,* 323–335.

Hamilton, D. L., Levine, J. M., & Thurston, J. A. (2008). Perceiving continuity and change in groups. In F. Sani (Ed.), *Self continuity: Individual and collective perspectives* (pp. 117–130). New York: Psychology Press.

Hamilton, G. V. (1978). Obedience and responsibility: A jury simulation. *Journal of Personality and Social Psychology, 36,* 126–146.

Hansen, N., & Sassenberg, K. (2006). Does social identification harm or serve as a buffer? The impact of social identification on anger after experiencing social discrimination. *Personality and Social Psychology Bulletin, 32,* 983–996.

Harmon-Jones, E. (2000). Cognitive dissonance and experienced negative affect: Evidence that dissonance increases experienced negative affect even in the absence of aversive consequences. *Personality and Social Psychology Bulletin, 26,* 1490–1501.

Harmon-Jones, E., Harmon-Jones, C., Fearn, M., Sigelman, J. D., & Johnson, P. (2008). Left frontal cortical activation and spreading of alternatives: Tests of the action-based model of dissonance. *Journal of Personality and Social Psychology, 94,* 1–15.

Harris, C. R. (2003). A review of sex differences in sexual jealousy, including self-report data, psychophysiological responses, interpersonal violence, and morbid jealousy. *Personality and Social Psychology Review, 7,* 102–128.

Harris, L., & Dennis, C. (2011). Engaging customers on Facebook: Challenges for e–retailers. *Journal of Consumer Research, 10,* 338–346.

Harris, L. R., & Weiss, D. J. (1995). Judgments of consent in simulated rape cases. *Journal of Social Behavior and Personality, 10,* 79–90.

Harris, M. B. (1993). How provoking! What makes men and women angry? *Journal of Applied Social Psychology, 23,* 199–211.

Harrison, M. (2003). "What is love?" Personal communication.

Hartwig, M., & Bond, C. F., Jr. (2011). Why do lie-catchers fail? A lens model meta-analysis of human lie judgments. *Psychological Bulletin, 137,* 643–656.

Haslam, C., Cruwys, T., & Haslam, S. A. (2014). "The we's have it": Evidence for the distinctive benefits of group engagement in enhancing cognitive health in aging. *Social Science and Medicine, 120,* 57–66.

Haslam, C., Cruwys, T., Milne, M., Kan, C-H., & Haslam, S. A. (2016). Group ties protect cognitive health by promoting social identification and social support. *Journal of Aging and Health, 28,* 244–266.

Haslam, S. A. (2004). *Psychology in organizations: The social identity approach* (2nd ed.). London: Sage.

Haslam, S. A. (2004). *Psychology in organizations: The social identity approach* (2nd ed.). Thousand Oaks, CA: Sage.

Haslam, S. A., Adarves-Yorno, I., Postmes, T., & Jans, L. (2013). The collective origins of valued originality: A social identity approach to creativity. *Personality and Social Psychology Review, 17,* 384–401.

Haslam, S. A., O'Brien, A., Jetten, J., Vormedal, K., & Penna, S. (2011). Taking the strain: Social identity, social support, and the experience of stress. *British Journal of Social Psychology, 44,* 355–370.

Haslam, S. A., & Platow, M. J. (2001). The link between leadership and followership: How affirming social identity translates vision into action. *Personality and Social Psychology Bulletin, 27,* 1469–1479.

Haslam, S. A., & Reicher, S. D. (2006). Stressing the group: Social identity and the unfolding dynamics of responses to stress. *Journal of Applied Psychology, 91,* 1037–1052.

Haslam, S. A., & Reicher, S. D. (2012). When prisoners take over the prison: A social psychology of resistance. *Personality and Social Psychology Review, 16,* 154–179.

Haslam, S. A., Reicher, S. D., & Birney, M. E. (2014). Nothing by mere authority: Evidence that in an experimental analogue of the Milgram paradigm participants are motivated not by orders but by appeals to science. *Journal of Social Issues, 70,* 473–488.

Haslam, S. A., & Wilson, A. (2000). In what sense are prejudicial beliefs personal? The importance of an in-group's shared stereotypes. *British Journal of Social Psychology, 39,* 45–63.

Haslam, S. A., Reicher, S., & Platow, M. J. (2010). *The new psychology of leadership: Identity, influence and power.* New York: Psychology Press.

Haslam, S. A., Ryan, M. K., Kulich, C., Trojanowski, G., & Atkins, C. (2010). Investing with prejudice: The relationship between women's presence on company boards and objective and subjective measures of company performance. *British Journal of Management, 21,* 484–497.

Haslam, S. A., Ryan, M. K., Postmes, T., Spears, R., Jetten, J., & Webley, P. (2006). Sticking to our guns: Social identity as a basis for the maintenance of commitment to faltering organizational projects. *Journal of Organizational Behavior, 27,* 607–628.

Hassin, R., & Trope, Y. (2000). Facing faces: Studies on the cognitive aspects of physiognomy. *Journal of Personality and Social Psychology, 78,* 837–852.

Hatfield, E. (1988). Passionate and companionate love. In R. J. Sternberg, & M. L. Barnes (Ed), *The psychology of love* (pp. 191–217). New Haven, CT: Yale University Press.

Hatfield, E., Cacioppo, J., & Rapson, R. L. (1994). *Emotional contagion.* New York: Cambridge University Press.

Hatfield, E., & Rapson, R. L. (1993). Historical and crosscultural perspectives on passionate love and sexual desire. *Annual Review of Sex Research, 4,* 67–97.

Hatfield, E., & Sprecher, S. (1986). Measuring passionate lives in intimate relations. *Journal of Adolescence, 9,* 383–410.

Hatfield, E., & Walster, G. W. (1981). *A new look at love.* Reading, MA: Addison-Wesley.

Haugtvedt, C. P., & Wegener, D. T. (1994). Message order effects in persuasion: An attitude strength perspective. *Journal of Consumer Research, 21*, 205–218.

Hawk, S. T., van Kleef., G. A., Fischer, A. H., & van der Schalk, J. (2009). "Worth a thousand words": Absolute and relative decoding of nonlinguistic affect vocalizations. *Emotion, 9*, 293–305.

Hawkley, L. C., Thisted, R. A., Masi, C. M., & Cacioppo, J. T. (2010). Loneliness predicts increased blood pressure: 5-year cross-lagged analyses in middle-aged and older adults. *Psychology and Aging, 25*, 132–141.

Hawkley, L. C., Burleson, M. H., Berntson, G. G., & Cacioppo, J. T. (2003). Loneliness in everyday life: Cardiovascular activity, psychosocial context, and health behaviors. *Journal of Personality and Social Psychology, 85*, 105–120.

Hawkley, L. C., Thisted, R. A., Masi, C. M., & Cacioppo, J. T. (2010). Loneliness predicts increased blood pressure: Five-year cross-lagged analysis in middle-aged and older adults. *Psychology and Aging, 25,* 132–141.

Hawley, P. H., Card, N., & Little, T. D., (2007). The allure of a mean friend: Relationship quality and processes of aggressive adolescents with prosocial skills. *International Journal of Behavioral Development, 32*, 21–32.

Hayden, S. R., Jackson, T. T., & Guydish, J. N. (1984). Helping behavior of females: Effects of stress and commonality of fate. *Journal of Psychology, 117*, 233–237.

Hayward, M. L. A., & Hambrick, D. C. (1997). Explaining the premiums paid for large acquisitions: Evidence of CEO hubris. *Administrative Science Quarterly, 42*, 103–127.

Hayward, M. L. A., Shepherd, D. A., & Griffin, D. (2006). A hubris theory of entrepreneurship. *Management Science, 52*, 160–172.

Hebl, M. R., & Kleck, R. E. (2006). Acknowledging one's stigma in the interview setting: Effective strategy or liability? *Journal of Applied Social Psychology, 32*, 223–249.

Hechanova-Alampay, R., Beehr, T. A., Christiansen, N. D., & Van Horn, R. K. (2002). Adjustment and strain among domestic and international student sojourners: A longitudinal study. *School Psychology International, 23*, 458–474.

Heerdink, M. W., van Klee, A., Homan, A. C., & Fischer, A. H. (2013). On the social influence of emotions in groups: Interpersonal effects of anger and happiness on conformity versus deviance. *Journal of Personality and Social Psychology, 105*, 262–284.

Heider, F. (1958). *The psychology of interpersonal relations.* New York: Wiley.

Heilman, M. E. (2001). Description and prescription: How gender stereotypes prevent women's ascent up the organizational ladder. *Journal of Social Issues, 57*, 657–674.

Heilman, M. E., Block, C. J., & Lucas, J. A. (1992). Presumed incompetent? Stigmatization and affirmative action efforts. *Journal of Applied Psychology, 77*, 536–544.

Helliwell, J. F., Huang, H., & Wang, S. (2014). Social capital and well-being in times of crisis. *Journal of Happiness Studies, 15*, 145–162.

Helliwell, J. F., Layard, R., & Sachs, J. (2015). *World Happiness Report 2015.* New York: United Nations.

Hertzman, C., & Boyce, T. (2010). How experience gets under the skin to create gradients in developmental health. *Annual Review of Public Health, 31*, 329–347.

Hetherington, M. M., Anderson, A. S., Norton, G. N., & Newson, L. (2006). Situational effects on meal intake: A comparison of eating alone and eating with others. *Physiology and Behavior, 88*, 498–505.

Hicks, J. A., Cicero, D. C., Trent, J., Burton, C. M., & King, L. A. (2010). Positive affect, intuition, and feelings of meaning. *Journal of Personality and Social Psychology, 98*, 967–979.

Heilman, M. E., & Okimoto, T. G. (2007). Why are women penalized for success at male tasks? The implied communality deficit. *Journal of Applied Psychology, 92*, 81–92.

Higgins, E. T. (1999). Saying is believing effects: When sharing reality about something biases knowledge and evaluations. In J. M. Levine, L. L. Thompson, & D. M. Messick (Eds.), *Shared cognition in organizations: The management of knowledge* (pp. 33–49). Mahwah, NJ: Erlbaum.

Higgins, E. T., & Kruglanski, A. W. (Eds.). (1996). *Social psychology: Handbook of basic principles.* New York: Guilford Press.

Higham, P. A., & Carment, W. D. (1992). The rise and fall of politicians: The judged heights of Broadbent, Mulroney and Turner before and after the 1988 Canadian federal election. *Canadian Journal of Behavioral Science, 24*, 404–409.

Hilbig, B. E., & Glockner, A. (2014). Personality and prosocial behavior: Linking basic traits and social value orientations. *Journal of Personality and Social Psychology, 107*, 529–539.

Hillen, M. A., de Haes, H. C. J. M., van Tienhoven, G., Bijker, N., van Laarhoven, H. W. M., Vermeulen, D. M., & Smets, E. M. A. (2015). All eyes on the patient: The influence of oncologists' nonverbal communication on breast cancer patients' trust. *Breast Cancer Research and Treatment, 153,* 161–171.

Hilton, N. Z., Harris, G. T., & Rice, M. E. (2000). The functions of aggression by male teenagers. *Journal of Personality and Social Psychology, 79*, 988–994.

Hinsz, V. B. (1995). Goal setting by groups performing an additive task: A comparison with individual goal setting. *Journal of Applied Social Psychology, 25*, 965–990.

Hmieleski, K. M., & Baron, R. A. (2009). Entrepreneurs' optimism and new venture performance: A social cognitive perspective. *Academy of Management Journal, 52*, 473–488.

Ho, S. S., Brossard, D., & Scheufele, D. A. (2008). Effects of value predispositions, mass media use, and knowledge on public attitudes toward embryonic stem cell research. *International Journal of Public Opinion Research, 20,* 171–192.

Hoaken, P. N. S., Giancola, P. R., & Pihl, R. O. (1998). Executive cognitive functions as mediators of alcohol-related aggression. *Alcohol and Alcoholism, 33*, 45–53.

Hochschild, A. R. (1983). *The managed heart: Commercialization of human feelings.* Berkeley: University of California Press.

Hodges, S. D., Kiel, K. J., Kramer, A. D. I., Veach, D., & Villaneuva, B. R. (2010). Giving birth to empathy: The effects of similar experience on empathic accuracy, empathic concern, and perceived empathy. *Personality and Social Psychology Bulletin, 36*, 398–409.

Hoffer, E. (1953). *The passionate state of mind and other aphorisms.* Cutchogue, NY: Buccaneer Books.

Hogg, M. A. (2001). A social identity theory of leadership. *Personality and Social Psychology Reviewer, 5*, 184–200.

Hogg, M. A. (2007). Organizational orthodoxy and corporate autocrats: Some nasty consequences of organizational identification in uncertain times. In C. Bartel, S. Blader, & A. Wrzesniewski (Eds.), *Identity and the modern organization* (pp. 35–59). Mahwah, NJ: Erlbaum.

Holt-Lunstad, J., Smith, T. B., & Layton, J. B. (2010). Social relationships and mortality risk: A meta-analytic review. *PLoS Medicine, 7.* PMID: 20668659.

Hornsey, M. J., de Bruijn, P., Creed, J., Allen, J., Ariyanto, A., & Svensson, A. (2005). Keeping it in-house: How audience affects responses to group criticism. *European Journal of Social Psychology, 35*, 291–312.

Hornsey, M. J., & Imani, A. (2004). Criticizing groups from the inside and the outside: An identity perspective on the intergroup sensitivity effect. *Personality and Social Psychology Bulletin, 30,* 365–383.

Hornsey, M. J., Jetten, J., McAuliffe, B. J., & Hogg, M. A. (2006). The impact of individualist and collectivist group norms on evaluations of dissenting group members. *Journal of Experimental Social Psychology, 42*, 57–68.

Hornsey, M. J., Oppes, T., & Svensson, A. (2002). "It's OK if we say it, but you can't": Responses to intergroup and intragroup criticism. *European Journal of Social Psychology, 32,* 293–307.

Hosoda, M., Stone-Romero, E. F., & Coats, G. (2003). The effects of physical attractiveness on job-related outcomes: A meta-analysis of experimental studies. *Personnel Psychology, 56,* 431–462.

House, J. S., Landis, K. R., & Umberson, D. (1988). Social relationships and health. *Science, 241,* 540–545.

Hovland, C. I., Janis, I. L., & Kelley, H. H. (1953). *Communication and persuasion: Psychological studies of opinion change.* New Haven, CT: Yale University Press.

Hovland, C. I., & Weiss, W. (1951). The influence of source credibility on communication effectiveness. *Public Opinion Quarterly, 15,* 635–650.

Howe, L. C., & Dweck, C. S. (2016). Changes in self-definition impede recovery from rejection. *Personality and Social Psychology Bulletin, 42,* 54–71.

Huang, Y., Kendrick, K. M., & Yu, R. (2014). Conformity to the opinions of other people lasts for no more than 3 days. *Psychological Science, 25,* 1388–1393.

Huesmann, L. R., & Eron, L. D. (1984). Cognitive processes and the persistence of aggressive behavior. *Aggressive Behavior, 10,* 243–251.

Huesmann, L. R., & Eron, L. D. (1986). *Television and the aggressive child: A cross-national comparison.* Hillsdale, NJ: Erlbaum.

Hugenberg, K., & Bodenhausen, G. V. (2003). Facing prejudice: Implicit prejudice and the perception of facial threat. *Psychological Science, 14,* 640–643.

Hummert, M. L., Crockett, W. H., & Kemper, S. (1990). Processing mechanisms underlying use of the balance scheme. *Journal of Personality and Social Psychology, 58,* 5–21.

Hunt, A. M. (1935). A study of the relative value of certain ideals. *Journal of Abnormal and Social Psychology, 30,* 222–228.

Hunt, C. V., Kim, A., Borgida, E., & Chaiken, S. (2010). Revisiting the self-interest versus values debate: The role of temporal perspective. *Journal of Experimental Social Psychology, 46,* 1155–1158.

Huo, Y. J., Binning, K. R., & Molina, L. E. (2010). Testing an integrative model of respect: Implications for social engagement and well-being. *Personality and Social Psychology Bulletin, 36,* 200–212.

Hygen, B. W., Belsky, J., Stenseng, F., Lydersen, S., Guzey, I. C., & Wichstrom, L. (2015). Child exposure to serious life events, COMT, and aggression: Testing differential susceptibility theory. *Developmental Psychology, 51,* 1098–1104.

Hymel, S., & Swearer, S. M. (2015a). Four decades of research on school bullying: An introduction. *American Psychologist, 70,* 293–299.

Hymel, S., & Swearer, S. M. (2015b). Understanding the psychology of bullying: Moving toward a social-ecological diathesis-stress model. *American Psychologist, 70,* 344–353.

Iacoboni, M. (2009). Imitation, empathy, and mirror neurons. *Annual Review of Psychology, 60,* 653–670.

Imhoff, R., & Erb, H-P. (2009). What motivates nonconformity?: Uniqueness seeking blocks majority influence. *Personality and Social Psychology Bulletin, 33,* 309–320.

Insko, C. A. (1985). Balance theory, the Jordan paradigm, and the Wiest Tetrahedron. In L. Berkowitz (Ed.), *Advances in experimental social psychology* (pp. 89–140). New York: Academic Press.

Intergovernmental Panel on Climate Change. (2014). *Synthesis Report: Fifth Assessment Report.* Retrieved from http://ar5-syr.ipcc.ch/

Inzlicht, M., & Ben-Zeev, T. (2000). A threatening intellectual environment: Why females are susceptible to experiencing problem-solving deficits in the presence of males. *Psychological Science, 11,* 365–371.

Isaacowitz, D. M., & Livingstone, K. (2015). Emotion in adulthood: What changes and why? In K. J. Reynolds & N. R. Branscombe (Eds.), *Psychology of change: Life contexts, experiences, and identities* (pp. 116–132). New York: Psychology Press.

Isen, A. M. (1970). Success, failure, attention, and reaction to others: The warm glow of success. *Journal of Personality and Social Psychology, 15,* 294–301.

Isen, A. M. (1984). Toward understanding the role of affect in cognition. In S. R. Wyer & T. K. Srull (Eds.), *Handbook of social cognition* (Vol. 3, pp. 179–236). Hillsdale, NJ: Erlbaum.

Isen, A. M. (2000). Positive affect and decision making. In M. Lewis & J. M. Haviland-Jones (Eds.), *Handbook of emotions* (2nd ed., pp. 417–435). New York: Guilford Press.

Isen, A. M., & Labroo, A. A. (2003). Some ways in which positive affect facilitates decision making and judgment. In S. Schneider & J. Shanteau (Eds.) *Emerging perspectives on judgment and decision research* (pp. 365–393). New York: Cambridge.

Isen, A. M., & Levin, P. A. (1972). Effect of feeling good on helping: Cookies and kindness. *Journal of Personality and Social Psychology, 21,* 384–388.

Istvan, J., Griffitt, W., & Weidner, G. (1983). Sexual arousal and the polarization of perceived sexual attractiveness. *Basic and Applied Social Psychology, 4,* 307–318.

Ito, T. A., Chiao, K. W., Devine, P. G., Lorig, T. S., & Cacioppo, J. T. (2006). The influence of facial feedback on race bias. *Psychological Science, 17,* 256–261.

Iyer, A., Jetten, J., & Tsivrikos, D. (2008). Torn between identities: Predictors of adjustment to identity change. In F. Sani (Ed.), *Self continuity: Individual and collective perspectives* (pp. 187–197). New York: Psychology Press.

Izard, C. (1991). *The psychology of emotions.* New York: Plenum.

Jackman, M. R. (1994). *The velvet glove: Paternalism and conflict in gender, class, and race relations.* Berkeley: University of California Press.

Jackson, T., Soderlind, A., & Weiss, K. E. (2000). Personality traits and quality of relationships as predictors of future loneliness among American college students. *Social Behavior and Personality, 28,* 463–470.

Janis, I. L. (1982). *Victims of groupthink* (2nd ed.). Boston: Houghton Mifflin.

Jetten, J., Branscombe, N. R., Haslam, S. A., Haslam, C., Cruwys, T., Jones, J. M., et al. (2015). Having a lot of a good thing: Multiple important group memberships as a source of self-esteem. *PLoS One, 10,* e0124609.

Jetten, J., Branscombe, N. R., Schmitt, M. T., & Spears, R. (2001). Rebels with a cause: Group identification as a response to perceived discrimination from the mainstream. *Personality and Social Psychology Bulletin, 27,* 1204–1213.

Jetten, J., Haslam, C., Haslam, S. A., & Branscombe, N. R. (2009). The social cure. *Scientific American, September–October,* 26–33.

Jetten, J., Haslam, C., Haslam, S. A., Dingle, G., & Jones, J. M. (2014). How groups affect our health and well-being: The path from theory to policy. *Social Issues and Policy Review, 8,* 103–130.

Jetten, J., Haslam, C., Pugliesse, C., Tonks, J., & Haslam, S. A. (2010). Declining autobiographical memory and the loss of identity: Effects on well-being. *Journal of Clinical Experimental Neuropsychology, 32,* 405–416.

Jetten, J., & Hornsey, M. J. (2014). Deviance and dissent in groups. *Annual Review of Psychology, 65,* 461–485.

Jetten, J., Hornsey, M. J., & Adarves-Yorno, I. (2006). When group members admit to being conformist: The role of relative intragroup status in conformity self-reports. *Personality and Social Psychology Bulletin, 32,* 162–173.

Jetten, J., Schmitt, M. T., Branscombe, N. R., Garza, A. A., & Mewse, A. J. (2011). Group commitment in the face of discrimination: The role of legitimacy appraisals. *European Journal of Social Psychology, 41*, 116–126.

Jetten, J., Spears, R., & Manstead, A. S. R. (1997). Strength of identification and intergroup differentiation: The influence of group norms. *European Journal of Social Psychology, 27*, 603–609.

John-Steiner, V. (2000). *Creative collaboration.* New York: Oxford University Press.

Johnson, B. T. (1994). Effects of outcome-relevant involvement and prior information on persuasion. *Journal of Experimental Social Psychology, 30*, 556–579.

Johnson, J. D., Simmons, C., Trawalter, S., Ferguson, T., & Reed, W. (2003). Observer race and White anti-Black bias: Factors that influence and mediate attributions of "ambiguously racist" behavior. *Personality and Social Psychology Bulletin, 29*, 609–622.

Johnson, M. K., & Sherman, S. J. (1990). Constructing and reconstructing the past and the future in the present. In E. T. Higgins & R. M. Sorrentino (Eds.), *Handbook of motivation and social cognition: Foundations of social behavior* (pp. 482–526). New York: Guilford Press.

Johnston, V. S., & Oliver-Rodriguez, J. C. (1997). Facial beauty and the late positive component of event-related potentials. *Journal of Sex Research, 34*, 188–198.

Johnstone, B., Frame, C. L., & Bouman, D. (1992). Physical attractiveness and athletic and academic ability in controversial-aggressive and rejected-aggressive children. *Journal of Social and Clinical Psychology, 11*, 71–79.

Jones, E. E. (1964). *Ingratiation: A social psychology analysis.* New York: Appleton-Century-Crofts.

Jones, E. E. (1979). The rocky road from acts to dispositions. *American Psychologist, 34*, 107–117.

Jones, E. E., & Davis, K. E. (1965). From acts to disposition: The attribution process in person perception. In L. Berkowitz (Ed.), *Advances in experimental social psychology* (Vol. 2, pp. 219–266). New York: Academic Press.

Jones, E. E., & Harris, V. A. (1967). The attribution of attitudes. *Journal of Experimental Social Psychology, 3*, 1–24.

Jones, E. E., & McGillis, D. (1976). Corresponding inferences and attribution cube: A comparative reappraisal. In J. H. Har, W. J. Ickes, & R. F. Kidd (Eds.), *New directions in attribution research* (Vol. 1). Morristown, NJ: Erlbaum.

Jones, E. E., & Nisbett, R. E. (1971). *The actor and the observer: Divergent perceptions of the causes of behavior.* Morristown, NJ: General Learning Press.

Jones, W. H., Carpenter, B. N., & Quintana, D. (1985). Personality and interpersonal predictors of loneliness in two cultures. *Journal of Personality and Social Psychology, 48*, 1503–1511.

Judge, T. A., & Cable, T. A. (2004). The effect of physical height on workplace success and income: Preliminary test of a theoretical model. *Journal of Applied Psychology, 89*, 428–441.

Jung, M. H., Nelson, L. D., Gneezy, A., & Gneezy, U. (2014). Paying more when paying for others. *Journal of Personality and Social Psychology, 107*, 414–431.

Kahneman, D., & Deaton, A. (2010). High income improves evaluation of life but not emotional well-being. *Proceedings of the National Academy of Science, 107*, 16489–16493.

Kahneman, D., Diener, E., & Schwarz, N. (Eds.). (2003). *Well-being; the foundations of hedonic psychology.* New York: Russell Sage Foundation.

Kahneman, D., & Frederick, S. (2002). Representativeness revisited: Attribute substitution in intuitive judgment. In T. Gilovich, D. Griffin, & D. Kahneman (Eds.), *Heuristics and biases: The psychology of intuitive judgment* (pp. 41–81). New York: Cambridge University Press.

Kahneman, D., Krueger, A. B., Schkade, D., Schwarz, N., & Stone, A. A. (2006). Would you be happier if you were richer? A focusing illusion. *Science, 312*, 1908–1910.

Kahneman, D., & Miller, D. T. (1986). Norm theory: Comparing reality to its alternatives. *Psychological Review, 93*, 136–153.

Kahneman, D., & Tversky, A. (1973). On the psychology of prediction. *Psychological Review, 80*, 237–251.

Kahneman, D., & Tversky, A. (1984). Choices, values, and frames. *American Psychologist, 39*, 341–350.

Kaiser, C. R., Major, B., Jurcevic, I., Dover, T. L., Brady, L. M., & Shapiro, J. R. (2013). Presumed fair: Ironic effects of organizational diversity structures. *Journal of Personality and Social Psychology, 104*, 504–519.

Kaiser, C. R., & Miller, C. T. (2001). Stop complaining! The social costs of making attributions to discrimination. *Personality and Social Psychology Bulletin, 27*, 254–263.

Kaiser, C. R., Drury, B. J., Spalding, K. E., Cheryan, S., & O'Brien, L. T. (2009). The ironic consequences of Obama's election: Decreased support for social justice. *Journal of Experimental Social Psychology, 45*, 556–559.

Kalick, S. M., & Hamilton, T. E. (1986). The matching hypothesis reexamined. *Journal of Personality and Social Psychology, 51*, 673–682.

Kallgren, C. A., Reno, R. R., & Cialdini, R. B. (2000). A focus theory of normative conduct: When norms do and do not affect behavior. *Personality and Social Psychology Bulletin, 26*, 1002–1012.

Kameda, T., & Sugimori, S. (1993). Psychological entrapment in group decision making: An assigned decision rule and a groupthink phenomenon. *Journal of Personality and Social Psychology, 65*, 282–292.

Kandel, D. (1973). Adolescent marihuana use: Role of parents and peers. *Science, 181*, 1067–1070.

Karau, S. J., & Williams, K. D. (1993). Social loafing: A meta-analytic review and theoretical integration. *Journal of Personality and Social Psychology, 65*, 681–706.

Karraker, K. H., & Stern, M. (1990). Infant physical attractiveness and facial expression: Effects on adult perceptions. *Basic and Applied Social Psychology, 11*, 371–385.

Kashy, D. A., & DePaulo, B. M. (1996). Who lies? *Journal of Personality and Social Psychology, 70*, 1037–1051.

Katz, E., & Lazarsfeld, P. F. (1955). *Personal influence: The part played by people in the flow of mass communication.* Glencoe, IL: The Free Press.

Kawakami, K., & Dovidio, J. F. (2001). The reliability of implicit stereotyping. *Personality and Social Psychology Bulletin, 27*, 212–225.

Kawakami, K., Dovidio, J. F., Moll, J., Hermsen, S., & Russin, A. (2000). Just say no (to stereotyping): Effects of training in the negation of stereotypic associations on stereotype activation. *Journal and Personality and Social Psychology, 78*, 871–888.

Keefer, L. A., Landau, M. J., Sullivan, D., & Rothschild, Z. K. (2014). Embodied metaphor and abstract problem solving: Testing a metaphoric fit hypothesis in the health domain. *Journal of Experimental Social Psychology, 55*, 12–20.

Kelley, H. H. (1972). Attribution in social interaction. In E. E. Jones, et al. (Eds.), *Attribution: Perceiving the causes of behavior* (pp. 1–26). Morristown, NJ: General Learning Press.

Kelley, H. H., & Michela, J. L. (1980). Attribution theory and research. *Annual Review of Psychology, 31*, 57–501.

Keltner, D., Gruenfeld, D. H., & Anderson, C. (2003). Power, approach, and inhibition. *Psychological Review, 110*, 265–284.

Kemeny, M. E. (2003). The psychobiology of stress. *Current Directions in Psychological Science, 12,* 124–129.

Kenealy, P., Gleeson, K., Frude, N., & Shaw, W. (1991). The importance of the individual in the 'causal' relationship between attractiveness and self-esteem. *Journal of Community and Applied Social Psychology,1,* 45–56.

Kenworthy, J. B., & Miller, N. (2001). Perceptual asymmetry in consensus estimates of majority and minority members. *Journal of Personality and Social Psychology, 80,* 597–612.

Kessels, L. T. E., Ruiter, R. A. C., Wouters, L., & Jansma, B. M. (2014). Neuroscientific evidence for defensive avoidance of fear appeals. *International Journal of Psychology, 49,* 80–88.

Kiecolt-Glaser, J. K., Gouin, J., Weng, N., Malarkey, W. B., Beversdorf, D. Q., & Glaser, R. (2011). Childhood adversity heightens the impact of later-life caregiving stress on telomere length and inflammation. *Psychosomatic Medicine, 73,* 16–22.

Kilham, W., & Mann, L. (1974). Level of destructive obedience as a function of transmitter and executant roles in the Milgram obedience paradigm. *Journal of Personality and Social Psychology, 29,* 696–702.

Kimmel, A. J. (2004). Ethical issues in social psychology research. In C. Sansone, C. C. Morf, & A. T. Panter (Eds.), *The Sage handbook of methods in social psychology* (pp. 45–61). Thousand Oaks, CA: Sage.

King, B. M. (2013). The modern obesity epidemic, ancestral hunter-gatherers, and the sensory/reward control of food intake. *American Psychologist, 68,* 88–96.

King, D. W., King, L. A., Park, C. L., Lee, L. O., Kaiser, A. P., Spiro, A., et al. (2015). Positive adjustment among American repatriated prisoners of the Vietnam War: Modeling the long-term effects of captivity. *Clinical Psychological Science, 3,* 861–876.

Kitzmann, K. M., Cohen, R., & Lockwood, R. L. (2002). Are only children missing out? Comparison of the peer-related social competence of only children and siblings. *Journal of Social and Personal Relationships, 19,* 299–316.

Klar, Y. (2002). Way beyond compare: The nonselective superiority and inferiority biases in judging randomly assigned group members relative to their peers. *Journal of Experimental Social Psychology, 38,* 331–351.

Kleinke, C. L. (1986). Gaze and eye contact: A research review. *Psychological Bulletin, 100,* 78–100.

Klinenberg, E. (2012). *Going Solo: The extraordinary rise and surprising appeal of living alone.* New York: Penguin Group.

Klinesmith, J., Kasser, T., & McAndrew, T. (2006). Guns, testosterone, and aggression. *Psychological Science, 17,* 568–571.

Klohnen, E. C., & Bera, S. (1998). Behavioral and experiential patterns of avoidantly and securely attached women across adulthood: A 31-year longitudinal perspective. *Journal of Personality and Social Psychology, 74,* 211–223.

Klohnen, E. C., & Luo, S. (2003). Interpersonal attraction and personality: What is attractive — self similarity, ideal similarity, complementarity, or attachment security? *Journal of Personality and Social Psychology, 85,* 709–722.

Ko, S. J., Judd, C. M., & Blair, I. V. (2006). What the voice reveals: Within- and between-category stereotyping on the basis of voice. *Personality and Social Psychology Bulletin, 32,* 806–819.

Kogan, N., & Wallach, M. A. (1964). *Risk-taking: A study in cognition and personality.* New York: Henry Holt.

Komorita, M., & Parks, G. (1994). Interpersonal relations: Mixed-motive interaction. *Annual Review of Psychology, 46,* 183–207.

Konishi, C., Hymel, S., Zumbo, B. D., & Li, Z. (2010). Do school bullying and student-teacher relationships matter for academic achievement? A multilevel analysis. *Canadian Journal of School Psychology, 25,* 19–39.

Koo, M., Algoe, S. B., Wilson, T. D., & Gilbert, D. T. (2008). It's a wonderful life: Mentally subtracting positive events improves people's affective states, contrary to their affective forecasts. *Journal of Personality and Social Psychology, 95,* 1217–1224.

Koole, S. L., Greenberg, J., & Pyszczynski, T. (2006). Introducing science to the psychology of the soul: Experimental existential psychology. *Current Directions in Psychological Science, 15,* 211–216.

Koppensteiner, M. (2013). Motion cues that make an impression: Predicting perceived personality by minimal motion information. *Journal of Experimental Social Psychology, 49,* 1137–1143.

Korsgaard, M. A., Meglino, B. M., Lester, S. W., & Jeong, S. S. (2010). Paying you back or paying me forward: Understanding rewarded and unrewarded organizational citizenship behavior. *Journal of Applied Psychology, 95,* 277–290.

Kosinski, M., Matz, S. C., Gosling, S. D., Popov, V., & Stillwell, D. (2015). Facebook as a research tool for the social sciences. *American Psychologist, 70,* 543–556.

Kotsou, I., Nelis, D., Grégoire, J., & Mikolajczak, M. (2011). Emotional plasticity: Conditions and effects of improving emotional competence in adulthood. *Journal of Applied Psychology, 96,* 827–839.

Kowalski, R. M. (1996). Complaints and complaining: Functions, antecedents, and consequences. *Psychological Bulletin, 119,* 179–196.

Kowalski, R. M. (2001). The aversive side of social interaction revisited. In R. M. Kowalski (Ed.), *Behaving badly: Aversive behaviors in interpersonal relationships* (pp. 297–309). Washington, DC: American Psychological Association.

Kowalski, R. M., Giumetti, G. W., Schroeder, A. N., & Lattanner, M. R. (2014). Bullying in the digital age: A critical review and meta-analysis of cyberbullying research among youth. *Psychological Bulletin, 140,* 73–137.

Kozak, M. N., Marsh, A. A., & Wegner, D. M. (2006). What do I think you're doing? Action identification and mind attribution. *Journal of Personality and Social Psychology, 90,* 543–555.

Krause, N. (2007). Longitudinal study of social support and meaning in life. *Psychology and Aging, 22,* 456–459.

Kray, L. J., Galinsky, A. D., & Wong, E. M. (2006). Thinking within the box: The relational processing style elicited by counterfactual mind-sets. *Journal of Personality and Social Psychology, 91,* 33–48.

Krieglmeyer, R., & Sherman, J. W. (2012). Disentangling stereotype activation and stereotype application in the stereotype misperception task. *Journal of Personality and Social Psychology, 103,* 205–224.

Krizan, Z. I., & Johar, O. (2015). Narcissistic rage revisited. *Journal of Personality and Social Psychology, 108,* 784–801.

Krosnick, J. A., Betz, A. L., Jussim, L. J., & Lynn, A. R. (1992). Subliminal conditioning of attitudes. *Personality and Social Psychology Bulletin, 18,* 152–162.

Kross, E., Verduyn, P., Demiralp, E., Park, J., Lee, D. S., Lin, N., & Ybarra, O. (2013). Facebook use predicts declines in subjective well-being in young adults. *PLoS One, 8,* e69841.

Krueger, P. M., & Chang, V. W. (2008). Being poor and coping with stress: Health behaviors and the risk of death. *American Journal of Public Health, 98,* 889–896.

Kruger, J., & Burrus, J. (2004). Egocentrism and focalism in unrealistic optimism (and pessimism). *Journal of Experimental Social Psychology, 40,* 332–340.

Kulik, J. A., Mahler, H. I. M., & Moore, P. J. (1996). Social comparison and affiliation under threat: Effects on recovery from major surgery. *Journal of Personality and Social Psychology, 71,* 967–979.

Kunda, Z. (1999). *Social cognition: Making sense of people.* Cambridge, MA: MIT Press.

Kunda, Z., & Oleson, K. C. (1995). Maintaining stereotypes in the face of disconfirmation: Constructing grounds for subtyping deviants. *Journal of Personality and Social Psychology, 68*, 565–579.

Kunstman, J. W., & Plant, E. A. (2009). Racing to help: Racial bias in high emergency helping situations. *Journal of Personality and Social Psychology, 95*, 1499–1510.

Kuppens, D., Realo, A., & Diener, E. (2008). The role of positive and negative emotions in life satisfaction judgment across nations. *Journal of Personality and Social Psychology, 95*, 66–75.

Kwan, L. A. (1998). *Attitudes and attraction: A new view of how to diagnose the moderating effects of personality*. Unpublished master's thesis, National University of Singapore.

Laird, J. D. (1984). The real role of facial response in the experience of emotion: A reply to Tourangeau and Ellsworth, and others. *Journal of Personality and Social Psychology, 47*, 909–917.

Lalonde, R. N., & Silverman, R. A. (1994). Behavioral preferences in response to social injustice: The effects of group permeability and social identity salience. *Journal of Personality and Social Psychology, 66*, 78–85.

Lamers, S. M. A., Bolier, L., Westerhof, G. J., Smit, F., & Bohlmeijer, E. T. (2012). The impact of emotional well-being on long-term recovery and survival in physical illness: A meta-analysis. *Journal of Behavioral Medicine, 35*, 538–547.

Lammers, J., Stoker, J. I., Jordan, J., Pollman, M., & Stapel, D. A. (2011). Power increases infidelity among men and women. *Psychological Science, 22*, 1191–1197.

Landau, M. J., Meier, B. P., & Keefer, L. A. (2010). A metaphor-enriched social cogntion. *Psychological Bulletin, 136*, 1045–1067.

Landau, M. J., Solomon, S., Greenberg, J., Cohen, F., Pyszczynski, T., Arndt, J., et al. (2004). Deliver us from evil: The effects of mortality salience and reminders of 9/11 on support for President George W Bush. *Personality and Social Psychology Bulletin, 30*, 1136–1150.

Landau, M. J., Sullivan, D., & Greenberg, J. (2009). Evidence that self-relevant motives and metaphoric framing interact to influence political and social attitudes. *Psychological Science, 20*, 1421–1427.

Langer, E. J., & Rodin, J. (1976). The effects of choice and enhanced personal responsibility for the aged: A field experiment in an institutional setting. *Journal of Personality and Social Psychology, 34*, 191–198.

Langlois, J. H., Kalakanis, L., Rubenstein, A. J., Larson, A., Hallam, M., & Smoot, M. (2000). Maxims or myths of beauty? A meta-analytic and theoretical review. *Psychological Bulletin, 126*, 390–423.

Langlois, J. H., & Roggman, L. A. (1990). Attractive faces are only average. *Psychological Science, 1*, 115–121.

Langlois, J. H., Roggman, L. A., & Musselman, L. (1994). What is average and what is not average about attractive faces? *Psychological Science, 5*, 214–220.

LaPiere, R. T. (1934). Attitude and actions. *Social Forces, 13*, 230–237.

Larsen, J. T., & McKibban, A. R. (2008). Is happiness having what you want, wanting what you have, or both? *Psychological Science, 19*, 371–377.

Latane, B., & Darley, J. M. (1968). Group inhibition of bystander intervention in emergencies. *Journal of Personality and Social Psychology, 10*, 215–221.

Latane, B., & Darley, J. M. (1970). *The unresponsive bystander: Why doesn't he help?* New York: Appleton-Century-Crofts.

Latane, B., & L'Herrou, T. (1996). Spatial clustering in the conformity game: Dynamic social impact in electronic groups. *Journal of Personality and Social Psychology, 70*, 1218–1230.

Latane, B., Williams, K., & Harkins, S. (1979). Many hands make light the work: The causes and consequences of social loafing. *Journal of Personality and Social Psychology, 37*, 822–832.

Laurenceau, J. P., Barrett, L. F., & Pietromonaco, P. R. (1998). Intimacy as an interpersonal process: The importance of self-disclosure, partner disclosure, and perceived partner responsiveness in interpersonal exchanges. *Journal of Personality and Social Psychology, 74*, 1238–1251.

Lazarus, R. A., & Folkman, S. (1984). *Stress appraisal and coping*. New York: Springer.

Lazarus, R. S., Opton, E. M., Nomikos, M. S., & Rankin, N. O. (1985). The principle of short-circuiting of threat: Further evidence. *Journal of Personality, 33*, 622–635.

Leary, M. R., Twenge, J. M., & Quinlivan. E. (2006). Interpersonal rejection as a determinant of anger and aggression. *Personality and Social Psychology Review, 10*, 111–132.

LeBoeuf, R. A., Shafir, E., & Bayuk, J. B. (2010). The conflicting choices of alternating selves. *Organizational Behavior and Human Decision Processes, 111*, 48–61.

Lee, Y. T., & Seligman, M. E. P. (1997). Are Americans more optimistic than the Chinese? *Personality and Social Psychology Bulletin, 23*, 32–40.

Lehmiller, J. J. (2009). Secret romantic relationships: Consequences for personal and relationship well-being. *Personality and Social Psychology Bulletin, 35*, 1452–1466.

Leippe, M. R., & Eisenstadt, D. (1994). Generalization of dissonance reduction: Decreasing prejudice through induced compliance. *Journal of Personality and Social Psychology, 67*, 395–413.

Lemay, E. P., Clark, M. S., & Greenberg, A. (2010). What is beautiful is good because what is beautiful is desired: Physical attractiveness stereotyping as project of interpersonal goals. *Personality and Social Psychology Bulletin, 36*, 339–353.

Lemley, B. (2000, February). Isn't she lovely? *Discover,* 42–49.

Levav, J., & Argo, J. J. (2010). Physical contact and financial risk taking. *Psychological Science, 21*, 804–810.

Levine, J. M., Moreland, R. L., & Hausmann, L. R. M. (2005). Managing group composition: Inclusive and exclusive role transitions. In D. Abrams, M. A. Hogg, & J. M. Marques (Eds.), *The social psychology of inclusion and exclusion* (pp. 139–160). New York: Psychology Press.

Levine, M., Prosser, A., Evans, D., & Reicher, S. (2005). Identity and emergency intervention: How social group membership and inclusiveness of group boundaries shape helping behavior. *Personality and Social Psychology Bulletin, 31*, 443–453.

Levitan, L. C., & Visser, P. S. (2008). The impact of the social context on resistance to persuasion: Effortful versus effortless responses to counter-attitudinal information. *Journal of Experimental Social Psychology, 44*, 640–649.

Levitan, L. C., & Visser, P. S. (2009). Social network composition and attitude strength: Exploring the dynamics within newly formed social networks. *Journal of Experimental Social Psychology, 45*, 1057–1067.

Leyens, J.-P., Desert, M., Croizet, J.-C., & Darcis, C. (2000). Stereotype threat: Are lower status and history of stigmatization preconditions of stereotype threat? *Personality and Social Psychology Bulletin, 26*, 1189–1199.

Li, N. P., Griskevicius, V., Durante, K. M., Jonason, P. K., Pasisz, D. J., & Aumer, K. (2009). An evolutionary perspective on humor: Sexual selection of interest indication? *Social Psychology Bulletin, 35*, 923–936.

Li, N. P., & Kenrick, D. T. (2006). Sex similarities and differences in preferences for short-term mates: What, whether, and why. *Journal of Personality and Social Psychology, 90*, 468–489.

Li, Y. J., Johnson, K. A., Cohen, A. B., Williams, M. J., Knowles, E. D., & Chen, Z. (2012). Fundamental(ist) attribution error: Protestants are dispositionally focused. *Journal of Personality and Social Psychology, 102*, 281–290.

Liberman, A., & Chaiken, S. (1992). Defensive processing of personally relevant health messages. *Personality and Social Psychology Bulletin, 18,* 669–679.

Licata, L., Klein, O., Saade, W., Azzi, A., & Branscombe, N. R. (2012). Perceived outgroup (dis)continuity and attribution of responsibility for the Lebanese civil war mediate effects of national and religious subgroup identification on intergroup attitudes. *Group Processes and Intergroup Relations, 15,* 179–192.

Lickel, B., Hamilton, D. L., & Sherman, S. J. (2001). Elements of a lay theory of groups: Types of groups, relational styles, and the perception of group entitativity. *Personality and Social Psychology Review, 5,* 129–140.

Lickel, B., Hamilton, D. L., Wieczorkowski, G., Lewis, A., Sherman, S. J., & Uhles, A. N. (2000). Varieties of groups and the perception of group entiativity. *Journal of Personality and Social Psychology, 78,* 223–246.

Lickel, B., Rutchick, A. M., Hamilton, D. L., & Sherman, S. J. (2006). Intuitive theories of group types and relational principles. *Journal of Experimental Social Psychology, 42,* 28–39.

Liden, R. C., & Mitchell, T. R. (1988). Ingratiatory behaviors in organizational settings. *Academy of Management Review, 13,* 572–587.

Lieberman, J. D., & Arndt, J. (2000). Understanding the limits of limiting instructions: Social psychological explanations for the failures of instructions to disregard pretrial publicity and other inadmissible evidence. *Psychology, Public Policy, and Law, 6,* 677–711.

Lin, M-C., & Harwood, J. (2003). Accommodation predictors of grandparent–grandchild relational solidarity in Taiwan. *Journal of Social and Personal Relationships, 20,* 537–563.

Linden, E. (1992). Chimpanzees with a difference: Bonobos. *National Geographic,18*(3), 46–53.

Lindsey, E. W., Mize, J., & Pettit, G. S. (1997). Mutuality in parent-child play: Consequences for children's peer competence. *Journal of Social and Personal Relationships, 14,* 523–538.

Lockwood, P., & Kunda, Z. (1999). Increasing the salience of one's best selves can undermine inspiration by outstanding role models. *Journal of Personality and Social Psychology, 76,* 214–228.

Logel, C., Walton, G. M., Spencer, S. J., Iserman, E. C., von Hippel, W., & Bell, A. E. (2009). Interacting with sexist men triggers social identity threat among female engineers. *Journal of Personality and Social Psychology, 96,* 1089–1103.

Lonnqvist, J-E., Leikas, S., Mahonen, T. A., & Jasinskaja-Lahti, I. (2015). The mixed blessings of migration: Life satisfaction and self-esteem over the course of migration. *European Journal of Social Psychology, 45,* 496–514.

Lonnqvist, J. E., Leikas, S., Paunonen, S., Nissinen, V., & Verkasalo, M. (2006). Conformism moderates the relations between values, anticipated regret, and behavior. *Personality and Social Psychology Bulletin, 32,* 1469–1481.

Lopez, F. G., Gover, M. R., Leskela, J., Sauer, E. M., Schirmer, L., & Wyssmann, J. (1997). Attachment styles, shame, guilt, and collaborative problem-solving orientations. *Personal Relationships, 4,* 187–199.

Lord, C. G., & Saenz, D. S. (1985). Memory deficits and memory surfeits: Differential cognitive consequences of tokenism for tokens and observers. *Journal of Personality and Social Psychology, 49,* 918–926.

Lorenz, K. (1966). *On aggression.* New York: Harcourt, Brace, & World.

Lorenz, K. (1974). *Civilized man's eight deadly sins.* New York: Harcourt, Brace, Jovanovich.

Lount, R. B. Jr., & Wilk, S. L. (2014). Working harder or hardly working? Posting performance eliminates social loafing and promotes social laboring in workgroups. *Management Science, 60,* 1098–1106.

Lowery, B. S., Unzueta, M. M., Goff, P. A., & Knowles, E. D. (2006). Concern for the in-group and opposition to affirmative action. *Journal of Personality and Social Psychology, 90,* 961–974.

Lu, L., Yuan, Y. C., & McLeod, P. L. (2012). Twenty-five years of hidden profiles in group decision making. *Personality and Social Psychology Review, 16,* 54–75.

Lun, J., Oishi, S., Coan, J. A., Akimoto, S., & Miao, F. F. (2010). Cultural variations in motivational responses to felt misunderstanding. *Personality and Social Psychology Bulletin, 36,* 986–996.

Luttmer, E. (2005). Neighbors as negatives: Relative earnings and well-being. *Quarterly Journal of Economics, 120,* 963–1002.

Lyness, K. S., & Heilman, M. E. (2006). When fit is fundamental: Performance evaluations and promotions of upper-level female and male managers. *Journal of Applied Psychology, 91,* 777–785.

Lyubomirksy, S. (2001). Why are some people happier than others? *American Psychologist, 56,* 239–249.

Lyubomirsky, S., King, L., & Diener, E. (2005). The benefits of frequent positive affect: Does happiness lead to success? *Psychological Bulletin, 131,* 803–855.

Lyubomirsky, S., Sheldon, K. M., & Schkade, D. (2005). Pursuing happiness: The architecture of sustainable change. *Review of General Psychology, 9,* 111–131.

Maass, A., Cadinu, M., & Galdi, S. (2013). Sexual harassment: Motivations and consequences. In M. K. Ryan & N. R. Branscombe (Eds.), *The Sage handbook of gender and psychology* (pp. 341–358). London: Sage.

Maass, A., & Clark, R. D. III. (1984). Hidden impact of minorities: Fifteen years of minority influence research. *Psychological Bulletin, 95,* 233–243.

MacDonald, T. K., Zanna, M. P., & Fong, G. T. (1995). Decision making in altered states: Effects of alcohol on attitudes toward drinking and driving. *Journal of Personality and Social Psychology, 68,* 973–985.

Mackie, D. M., Devos, T., & Smith, E. R. (2000). Intergroup emotions: Explaining offensive action tendencies in an intergroup context. *Journal of Personality and Social Psychology, 79,* 602–616.

Mackie, D. M., & Smith, E. R. (2002). Beyond prejudice: Moving from positive and negative evaluations to differentiated reactions to social groups. In D. M. Mackie & E. R. Smith (Eds.), *From prejudice to intergroup emotions: Differentiated reactions to social groups* (pp. 1–12). New York: Psychology Press.

Mackie, D. M., & Worth, L. T. (1989). Cognitive deficits and the mediation of positive affect in persuasion. *Journal of Personality and Social Psychology, 57,* 27–40.

Macrae, C. N., Bodenhausen, G. V., Milne, A. B., & Ford, R. (1997). On the regulation of recollection: The intentional forgetting of sterotypical memories. *Journal of Personality and Social Psychology, 72,* 709–719.

Macrae, C. N., Milne, A. B., & Bodenhausen, G. V. (1994). Stereotypes as energy-saving devices: A peek inside the cognitive toolbox. *Journal of Personality and Social Psychology, 66,* 37–47.

Maddux, W. W., Barden, J., Brewer, M. B., & Petty, R. E. (2005). Saying no to negativity: The effects of context and motivation to control prejudice on automatic evaluative responses. *Journal of Experimental Social Psychology, 41,* 19–35.

Madon, S., Jussim, L., & Eccles, J. (1997). In search of the powerful self-fulfilling prophecy. *Journal of Personality and Social Psychology, 72,* 791–809.

Maeda, E., & Ritchie, L. D. (2003). The concept of *Shinyuu* in Japan: A replication of and comparison to Cole and Bradac's study on U.S. friendship. *Journal of Social and Personal Relationships, 20,* 579–598.

Maheswaran, D., & Chaiken, S. (1991). Promoting systematic processing in low-motivation settings: Effect of incongruent information on processing and judgment. *Journal of Personality and Social Psychology, 61,* 13–25.

Maio, G. R., Esses, V. M., & Bell, D. W. (1994). The formation of attitudes toward new immigrant groups. *Journal of Applied Social Psychology, 24,* 1762–1776.

Maio, G. R., Fincham, F. D., & Lycett, E. J. (2000). Attitudinal ambivalence toward parents and attachment style. *Personality and Social Psychology Bulletin, 26,* 1451–1464.

Maisonneuve, J., Palmade, G., & Fourment, C. I. (1952). Selective choices and propinquity *Sociometry, 15,* 135–140.

Major, B. (1994). From social inequality to personal entitlement: The role of social comparisons, legitimacy appraisals, and group membership. In M. P. Zanna (Ed.), *Advances in experimental social psychology* (Vol. 26, pp. 293–348). San Diego, CA: Academic Press.

Major, B., Barr, L., Zubek, J., & Babey, S. H. (1999). Gender and self-esteem: A meta-analysis. In W. B. Swann, J. H. Langlois, & L. A. Gilbert (Eds.), *Sexism and stereotypes in modern society* (pp. 223–253). Washington, DC: American Psychological Association.

Malone, B. E., & DePaulo, B. M. (2001). Measuring sensitivity to deception. In J. A. Hall & F. Bernieri (Eds.), *Interpersonal sensitivity: Theory, measurement, and application* (pp. 103–124). Mahwah, NJ: Erlbaum.

Manago, A. M., Taylor, T., & Greenfield, P. M. (2012). Me and my 400 friends: The anatomy of college students' Facebook networks, their communication patterns, and well-being. *Developmental Psychology, 48,* 369–380.

Mann, T. C., & Ferguson, M. J. (2015). Can we undo our first impressions? The role of reinterpretation in reversing implicit evaluations. *Journal of Personality and Social Psychology, 108,* 823–849.

Marchiori, D., Papies, E. K., & Klein, O. (2014). The portion size effect on food intake: An anchoring and adjustment process? *Appetite, 81,* 108–115.

Marcus, D. K., & Miller, R. S. (2003). Sex differences in judgments of physical attractiveness: A social relations analysis. *Personality and Social Psychology Bulletin, 29,* 325–335.

Markey, P. M., Funder, D. C., & Ozer, D. J. (2003). Complementarity of interpersonal behaviors in dyadic interactions. *Personality and Social Psychology Bulletin, 29,* 1082–1090.

Markus, H. R., & Kitayama, S. (1991). Culture and the self: Implications for cognition, emotion, and motivation. *Psychological Review, 98,* 224–253.

Markus, H. R., & Kitayama, S. (2010). Cultures and selves: A cycle of mutual constitution. *Perspectives on Psychological Science, 5,* 420–430.

Markus, H., & Nurius, P. (1986). Possible selves. *American Psychologist, 41,* 954–969.

Martens, A., Johns, M., Greenberg, J., & Schimel, J. (2006). Combating stereotype threat: The effect of self-affirmation on women's intellectual performance. *Journal of Experimental Social Psychology, 42,* 236–243.

Martin, P. Y., Hamilton, V. E., McKimmie, B. M., Terry, D. J., & Martin, R. (2007). Effects of caffeine on persuasion and attitude change: The role of secondary tasks in manipulating systematic message processing. *European Journal of Social Psychology, 37,* 320–338.

Maruta, T., Colligan, R. C., Malinchoc, M., & Offord, K. P. (2000). Optimists vs. pessimists: Survival rate among medical patients over a 30-year period. *Mayo Clinic Proceedings, 75,* 140–143.

Marx, D. M., Ko, S. J., & Friedman, R. A. (2009). The "Obama effect": How a salient role model reduces race-based performance differences. *Journal of Experimental Social Psychology, 45,* 953–956.

Matsushima, R., & Shiomi, K. (2002). Self-disclosure and friendship in junior high school students. *Social Behavior and Personality, 30,* 515–526.

Mauss, I. B., Evers, C., Wilhelm, F. H., & Gross, J. J. (2006). How to bite your tongue without blowing your top: Implicit evaluation of emotion regulation predicts affective responding to anger provocation. *Personality and Social Psychology Bulletin, 32,* 589–602.

May, J. L., & Hamilton, P. A. (1980). Effects of musically evoked affect on women's interpersonal attraction and perceptual judgments of physical attractiveness of men. *Motivation and Emotion, 4,* 217–228.

Mazzella, R., & Feingold, A. (1994). The effects of physical attractiveness, race, socioeconomic status, and gender of defendants and victims on judgments of mock jurors: A meta-analysis. *Journal of Applied Social Psychology, 24,* 1315–1344.

McCall, M. (1997). Physical attractiveness and access to alcohol: What is beautiful does not get carded. *Journal of Applied Social Psychology, 23,* 453–562.

McCanne, T. R., & Anderson, J. A. (1987). Emotional responding following experimental manipulation of facial electromyographic activity. *Journal of Personality and Social Psychology, 52,* 759–768.

McConahay, J. B. (1986). Modern racism, ambivalence, and the Modern Racism Scale. In J. F. Dovidio & S. L. Gaertner (Eds.), *Prejudice, discrimination, and racism* (pp. 91–125). New York: Academic Press.

McDonald, H. E., & Hirt, E. R. (1997). When expectancy meets desire: Motivational effects in reconstructive memory. *Journal of Personality and Social Psychology, 72,* 5–23.

McInnis, O. A., McQuaid, R. J., Matheson, K., & Anisman, H. (2015). Experience-dependent effects of genes: Responses to stressors. In K. J. Reynolds & N. R. Branscombe (Eds.), *Psychology of change: Life contexts, experiences, and identities* (pp. 25–43). New York: Psychology Press.

McNamee, S., & Wesolik, F. (2014). Heroic behavior of Carnegie medal heroes: Parental influence and expectations. *Peace and Conflict: Journal of Peace Psychology, 20,* 171–173.

Mead, G. H. (1934). *Mind, self, and society.* Chicago: University of Chicago Press.

Mead, N. L., Baumeister, R. F., Gino, F., Schweitzer, M. E., & Ariely, D. (2009). Too tired to tell the truth: Self-control resource depletion and dishonesty. *Journal of Experimental Social Psychology, 45,* 594–597.

Medvec, V. H., Madey, S. F., & Gilovich, T. (1995). When less is more: Counterfactual thinking and satisfaction among Olympic athletes. *Journal of Personality and Social Psychology, 69,* 603–610.

Meier, B. P., Robinson, M. D., & Wilkowski, B. M. (2006). Turning the other cheek: Agreeableness and the regulation of aggression-related primes. *Psychological Science, 17,* 136–142.

Mekawi, Y., & Bresin, K. (2015). Is the evidence from racial bias shooting task studies a smoking gun? Results from a meta-analysis. *Journal of Experimental Social Psychology.*

Mendoza-Denton, R., Ayduk, O., Mischel, W., Shoda, Y., & Testa, A. (2001). Person X situation interactionism in self-encoding (Iam … When …): Implications for affect regulation and social information processing. *Journal of Personality and Social Psychology, 80,* 533–544.

Meyers, S. A., & Berscheid, E. (1997). The language of love: The difference a preposition makes. *Personality and Social Psychology Bulletin, 23,* 347–362.

Miles, L. K., Nind, L. K., & Macrae, C. N. (2010). Moving through time. *Psychological Science, 21,* 222–223.

Miles, S. M., & Carey, G. (1997). Genetic and environmental architecture of human aggression. *Journal of Personality and Social Psychology, 72,* 207–217.

Milfont, T. L., Evans, L., Sibley, C. G., Ries, J., & Cunningham, A. (2014). Proximity to coast is linked to climate change belief. *PLoS One,9*(7), e103180.

Milgram, S. (1963). Behavior study of obedience. *Journal of Abnormal and Social Psychology, 67,* 371–378.

Milgram, S. (1965a). Liberating effects of group pressure. *Journal of Personality and Social Psychology, 1,* 127–134.

Milgram, S. (1965b). Some conditions of obedience and disobedience to authority. *Human Relations, 18,* 57–76.

Milgram, S. (1974). *Obedience to authority.* New York: Harper.

Miller, D. A., Cronin, T., Garcia, A. L., & Branscombe, N. R. (2009). The relative impact of anger and efficacy on collective action is affected by feelings of fear. *Group Processes and Intergroup Relations, 12,* 445–462.

Miller, D. A., Smith, E. R., & Mackie, D. M. (2004). Effects of intergroup contact and political predispositions on prejudice: Role of intergroup emotions. *Group Processes and Intergroup Relations, 7,* 221–237.

Miller, D. T., & McFarland, C. (1987). Pluralistic ignorance: When similarity is interpreted as dissimilarity. *Journal of Personality and Social Psychology, 53,* 298–305.

Miller, D. T., & Morrison, K. R. (2009). Expressing deviant opinions: Believing you are in the majority helps. *Journal of Experimental Social Psychology, 45,* 740–747.

Miller, D. T., & Ross, M. (1975). Self-serving biases in the attribution of causality: Fact or fiction? *Psychological Bulletin, 82,* 213–225.

Miller, D., & Xu, X. (2015). A fleeting glory: Self-serving behavior among celebrated MBA CEOs. *Journal of Management Inquiry* doi: 10.1177/1056492615607975.

Miller, J. G. (1984). Culture and the development of everyday social explanation. *Journal of Personality and Social Psychology, 46,* 961–978.

Miller, P. J. E., & Rempel, J. K. (2004). Trust and partner-enhancing attributions in close relationships. *Personality and Social Psychology Bulletin, 30,* 695–705.

Minson, J. A., & Mueller, J. S. (2012). The cost of collaboration: Why joint decision making exacerbates rejection of outside information. *Psychological Science, 23,* 219–224.

Miron, A. M., Branscombe, N. R., & Schmitt, M. T. (2006). Collective guilt as distress over illegitimate intergroup inequality. *Group Processes and Intergroup Relations, 9,* 163–180.

Miron, A. M., Warner, R. H., & Branscombe, N. R. (2011). Accounting for group differences in appraisals of social inequality: Differential injustice standards. *British Journal of Social Psychology, 50,* 342–353.

Mishra, S. (2014). Decision-making under risk: Integrating perspectives from biology, economics, and psychology. *Personality and Social Psychology Review, 18,* 280–307.

Mitchell, D. B. (2006). Nonconscious priming after 17 years: Invulnerable implicit memory? *Psychological Science, 17,* 925–929.

Miu, A. S., & Yeager, D. S. (2015). Preventing symptoms of depression by teaching adolescents that people can change: Effects of a brief incremental theory of personality intervention at 9-month follow-up. *Clinical Psychological Science, 3,* 726–743.

Mobbs, D., Hassabis, D., Seymour, B., Marechant, J. L., Weiskopf, N., Dolan, R. J., et al. (2009). Choking on the money: Reward-based performance decrements are associated with midbrain activity. *Psychological Science, 20,* 955–962.

Mogilner, C., Kamvar, S. D., & Aaker, J. (2011). The shifting meaning of happiness. *Social Psychological and Personality Science, 2,* 395–402.

Mojzisch, A., & Schulz-Hardt, S. (2010). Knowing others' preferences degrades the quality of group decisions. *Journal of Personality and Social Psychology, 98,* 794–808.

Mondloch, C. J., Lewis, T. L., Budreau, D. R., Maurer, D., Dannemiller, J. L., Stephens, B. R., et al. (1999). Face perception during early infancy. *Psychological Science, 10,* 419–422.

Monteil, J. M., & Nicolas, M. (2000). Effects of context and performance feedback on social comparison strategies among low-achievement students: Experimental studies. *Cahiers de Psychologie Cognitive, 19,* 513–531.

Monteith, M. J., Ashburn-Nardo, L., Voils, C. I., & Czopp, A. M. (2002). Putting the brakes on prejudice: On the development and operation of cues for control. *Journal of Personality and Social Psychology, 83,* 1029–1050.

Monteith, M. J., Devine, P. G., & Zuwerink, J. R. (1993). Self-directed versus other-directed affect as a consequence of prejudice-related discrepancies. *Journal of Personality and Social Psychology, 64,* 198–210.

Montgomery, K. J., Seeherman, K. R., & Haxby, J. V. (2009). The well-tempered social brain. *Psychological Science, 20,* 1211–1213.

Montoya, R. M., Horton, R. S., & Kirchner, J. (2008). Is actual similarity necessary for attraction? A meta-analysis of actual and perceived similarity. *Journal of Social and Personal Relationships, 25,* 889–922.

Moons, W. G., Mackie, D. M., & Garcia-Marques, T. (2009). The impact of repetition-induced familiarity on agreement with weak and strong arguments. *Journal of Personality and Social Psychology, 96,* 32–44.

Moreland, R. L., & Beach, S. R. (1992). Exposure effects in the classroom: The development of affinity among students. *Journal of Experimental Social Psychology, 28,* 255–276.

Moreland, R. L., & Levine, J. M. (2001). Socialization in organizations and work groups. In M. Turner (Ed.), *Groups at work: Theory and research* (pp. 69–112). Mahwah, NJ: Erlbaum.

Morewedge, C. K. (2009). Negativity bias in attribution of external agency. *Journal of Experimental Psychology, 138,* 535–545.

Morf, C. C., & Rhodewalt, F. (2001). Unraveling the paradoxes of narcissism: A dynamic self-regulatory processing model. *Psychological Inquiry, 12,* 177–196.

Morison, L. A., Cozzolino, P. J., & Orbell, S. (2010). Temporal perspective and parental intention to accept the human papilomavirus vaccination for their daughter. *British Journal of Health Psychology, 15,* 151–165.

Morris, M. L., Sinclair, S., & DePaulo, B. M. (2007). No shelter for singles: The perceived legitimacy of marital status discrimination. *Group Processes and Intergroup Relations, 10,* 457–470.

Moscovici, S. (1985). Social influence and conformity. In G. Lindzey & E. Aronson (Eds.), *Handbook of social psychology* (3rd ed.). New York: Random House.

Mugny, G. (1975). Negotiations, image of the other and the process of minority influence. *European Journal of Social Psychology, 5,* 209–229.

Mulder, L. B., van Dijk, E., De Cremer, D., & Wilke, H. A. M. (2006). Undermining trust and cooperation: The paradox of sanctioning systems in social dilemmas. *Journal of Experimental Social Psychology, 42,* 147–162.

Mullen, B., & Cooper, C. (1994). The relation between group cohesiveness and performance: An integration. *Psychological Bulletin, 115,* 210–227.

Mullen, E., & Skitka, L. J. (2006). Exploring the psychological underpinnings of the moral mandate effect: Motivated reasoning, group differentiation, or anger? *Journal of Personality and Social Psychology, 90,* 629–643.

Muller, R., Gertz, K. J., Molton, I. R., Terrill, A. L., Bombardier, C. H., Ehde, D. M., et al. (2016). Effects of a tailored positive psychology intervention on well-being and pain in individuals with chronic pain and a physical disability: A feasibility trial. *Clinical Journal of Pain, 32,* 32–44.

Munkes, J., & Diehl, M. (2003). Matching or competition? Performance comparison processes in an idea generation task. *Group Processes and Intergroup Relations, 6,* 305–320.

Muñoz, L. C., Qualter, P., & Padgett, G. (2011). Empathy and bullying: Exploring the influence of callous-unemotional traits. *Child Psychiatry and Human Development, 42,* 183–196.

Naqvi, N., Shiv, B., & Bechara, A. (2006). The role of emotion in decision making: A cognitive neuroscience perspective. *Current Directions in Psychological Science, 15,* 260–264.

Nadler, A., Harpaz-Gorodeisky, G., & Ben-David, Y. (2009). Defensive helping: Threat to group identity, ingroup identification, status stability, and common group identity as determinants of intergroup help-giving. *Journal of Personality and Social Psychology, 97,* 823.

Nario-Redmond, M. R., & Branscombe, N. A. (1996). It could have better and it might have been worse: Implications for blame assignment in rape cases. *Basic and Applied Social Psychology, 18,* 347–366.

Nario-Redmond, M. R., Noel, J. G., & Fern, E. (2013). Redefining disability, re-imagining the self: Disability identification predicts self-esteem and strategic responses to stigma. *Self and Identity, 12,* 468–488.

Naumann, L. P., Vazire, S., Rentfrow, P. J., & Gosling, S. D. (2009). Personality judgments based on physical appearance. *Personality and Social Psychology Bulletin, 35,* 1661–1671.

Navarro, R. S., Yubero, E., Larrañaga, G., & Martínez, V. (2011). Children's cyberbullying victimization: Associations with social anxiety and social competence in a Spanish sample. *Child Indicators Research, 5,* 281–295.

Nemeth, C. J., Personnaz, B., Personnaz, M., & Goncalo, J. A. (2004). The liberating role of conflict in group creativity: A study in two countries. *European Journal of Social Psychology, 34,* 365–374.

Nenkov, G. Y., & Scott, M. L. (2014). "So cute I could eat it up": Priming effects of cute products on indulgent consumption. *Journal of Consumer Research, 41,* 326–341.

Netchaeva, E., Kouchaki, M., & Sheppard, L. D. (2015). A man's (precarious) place: Men's experienced threat and self-assertive reactions to female superiors. *Personality and Social Psychology Bulletin, 41,* 1247–1259.

The New York Times (June 7, 2014). *Obama on Obama on Climate.* Retrieved from http://www.nytimes.com/2014/06/08/opinion/sunday/friedman-obama-on-obama-on-climate.html?_r=0

Newby-Clark, I. R., & Ross, M. (2003). Conceiving the past and future. *Personality and Social Psychology Bulletin, 29,* 807–818.

Newcomb, T. M. (1956). The prediction of interpersonal attraction. *Psychological Review, 60,* 393–404.

Newcomb, T. M. (1961). *The acquaintance process.* New York: Holt, Rinehart and Winston.

Newell, B. R., & Shanks, D. R. (2014). Unconscious influences on decision making: A critical review. *Behavioral and Brain Sciences, 37,* 1–61.

Newheiser, A-K., & Barreto, M. (2014). Hidden costs of hiding stigma: Ironic interpersonal consequences of concealing a stigmatized identity in social interactions. *Journal of Experimental Social Psychology, 52,* 58–70.

Neyer, F. J., & Lang, F. R. (2003). Blood is thicker than water: Kinship orientation across adulthood. *Journal of Personality and Social Psychology, 84,* 310–321.

Nisbett, R. E., Caputo, C., Legbant, P., & Marecek, J. (1973). Behavior as seen by the actor and as seen by the observer. *Journal of Personality and Social Psychology, 27,* 154–164.

Nisbett, R. E., & Wilson, T. D. (1977). Telling more than we can know: Verbal reports on mental processes. *Psychological Review, 84,* 231–259.

Noel, J. G., Wann, D. L., & Branscombe, N. R. (1995). Peripheral ingroup membership status and public negativity toward outgroups. *Journal of Personality and Social Psychology, 68,* 127–137.

Noor, M., Brown, R., Gonzalez, R., Manzi, J., & Lewis, C. A. (2008). On positive psychological outcomes: What helps groups with a history of conflict to forgive and reconcile with each other? *Personality and Social Psychology Bulletin, 34,* 819–832.

Norenzayan, A., & Hansen, G. (2006). Belief in supernatural agents in the face of death. *Personality and Social Psychology Bulletin, 32,* 174–187.

Norenzayan, A., & Lee, A. (2010). It was meant to happen: Explaining cultural variations in fate attributions. *Journal of Personality and Social Psychology, 98,* 702–720.

Norton, M. I., & Ariely, D. (2011). Building a better America—One wealth quintile at a time. *Perspectives on Psychological Science, 6,* 9–12.

Norton, M. I., Frost, J. H., & Ariely, D. (2006). Less is more: The lure of ambiguity, or why familiarity breeds contempt. *Journal of Personality and Social Psychology, 92,* 97–105.

Norton, M. I., Neal, D. T., Govan, C. L., Ariely, D., & Holland, E. (2014). The not-so-common-wealth of Australia: Evidence for a cross-cultural desire for a more equal distribution of wealth. *Analyses of Social Issues and Public Policy, 14,* 339–351.

Norton, M. I., Sommers, S. R., Apfelbaum, E. P., Pura, N., & Ariely, D. (2006). Color blindness and interracial interaction: Playing the political correctness game. *Psychological Science, 17,* 949–953.

Nussbaum, S., Trope, Y., & Liberman, N. (2003). Creeping dispositionism: The temporal dynamics of behavior prediction. *Journal of Personality and Social Psychology, 84,* 485–497.

O'Brien, L. T., Crandall, C. S., Horstman-Reser, A., Warner, R., Alsbrooks, A., & Blodorn, A. (2010). But I'm no bigot: How prejudiced White Americans maintain unprejudiced self-images. *Journal of Applied Social Psychology, 40,* 917–946.

O'Connor, S. C., & Rosenblood, L. K. (1996). Affiliation motivation in everyday experience: A theoretical comparison. *Journal of Personality and Social Psychology, 70,* 513–522.

O'Leary, S. G. (1995). Parental discipline mistakes. *Current Directions in Psychological Science, 4,* 11–13.

Oakes, P. J., Haslam, S. A., & Turner, J. C. (1994). *Stereotyping and social reality.* Oxford: Blackwell.

Oakes, P. J., & Reynolds, K. J. (1997). Asking the accuracy question: Is measurement the answer? In R. Spears, P. J. Oakes, N. Ellemers, & S. A. Haslam (Eds.), *The social psychology of stereotyping and group life* (pp. 51–71). Oxford: Blackwell.

Oarga, C., Stavrova, O., & Fetchenhauer, D. (2015). When and why is helping others good for well-being? The role of belief in reciprocity and conformity to society's expectations. *European Journal of Social Psychology, 45,* 242–254.

Oettingen, G. (1995). Explanatory style in the context of culture. In G. M. Buchanan & M. E. P. Seligman (Eds.), *Explanatory style* (pp. 209–224). Hillsdale, NJ: Erlbaum.

Oettingen, G., & Seligman, M. E. P. (1990). Pessimism and behavioral signs of depression in East versus West Berlin. *European Journal of Social Psychology, 201,* 207–220.

Oishi, S., Diener, E., & Lucas, R. E. (2007). The optimum level of well-being: Can people be too happy? *Perspectives on Psychological Science, 2,* 346–360.

Oishi, S., Schimmack, U., & Diener, E. (2012). Progressive taxation and the subjective well-being of nations. *Psychological Science, 23,* 86–92.

Olson, M. A., & Fazio, R. H. (2001). Implicit attitude formation through classical conditioning. *Psychological Science, 12,* 413–417.

Olson, M. A., & Kendrick, R. V. (2008). Origins of attitudes. In W. D. Crano & R. Prislin (Eds.), *Attitudes and attitude change* (pp. 111–130). New York: Psychology Press.

Orbach, I., Gilboa-Schechtman, E., Ofek, H., Lubin, G., Mark, M., Bodner, E., Cohen, D., & King, R. (2007). A chronological perspective on suicide—The last days of life. *Death Studies, 31,* 909–932.

Orth, U., Trzesniewski, K. H., & Robins, R. W. (2010). Self-esteem development from young adulthood to old age: A cohort-sequential longitudinal study. *Journal of Personality and Social Psychology, 98,* 645–658.

Osborne, J. W. (2001). Testing stereotype threat: Does anxiety explain race and sex differences in achievement? *Contemporary Educational Psychology, 26,* 291–310.

Oskamp, S., & Schultz, P. W. (2005). *Attitudes and Opinions* (3rd ed.). Mahwah, NJ: Erlbaum.

Pachankis, J. E. (2007). The psychological implications of concealing a stigma: A cognitive-affective-behavioral model. *Psychological Bulletin, 133,* 328–345.

Pachucki, M. A., Jacques, P. F., & Christakis, N. A. (2011). Social network concordance in food choice among spouses, friends and siblings. *American Journal of Public Health, 101,* 217–227.

Packer, D. J. (2014). On not airing our dirty laundry: Intergroup contexts suppress ingroup criticism among strongly identified group members. *British Journal of Social Psychology, 53,* 93–111.

Packer, D. J., & Chasteen, A. L. (2010). Loyal deviance: Testing the normative conflict model of dissent in social groups. *Personality and Social Psychology Bulletin, 36,* 5–18.

Paik, H., & Comstock, G. (1994). The effects of television violence on antisocial behavior: A meta-analysis. *Communication Research, 21,* 516–546.

Palmer, J., & Byrne, D. (1970). Attraction toward dominant and submissive strangers: Similarity versus complementarity. *Journal of Experimental Research in Personality, 4,* 108–115.

Paluck, E. L., Shepherd, H., & Aronow, P. M. (2016). Changing climates of conflict: A social network experiment in 56 schools. *Proceedings of the National Academy of Sciences.* doi:10.1073/pnas.1514483113

Paolini, S., Hewstone, M., Cairns, E., & Voci, A. (2004). Effects of direct and indirect cross-group friendships on judgments of Catholics and Protestants in Northern Ireland: The mediating role of an anxiety-reduction mechanism. *Personality and Social Psychology Bulletin, 30,* 770–786.

Park, B., Wolsko, C., & Judd, C. M. (2001). Measurement of subtyping in stereotype change. *Journal of Experimental Social Psychology, 37,* 325–332.

Park, J., & Banaji, M. R. (2000). Mood and heuristics: The influence of happy and sad states on sensitivity and bias in stereotyping. *Journal of Personality and Social Psychology, 78,* 1005–1023.

Parkinson, B., & Simons, G. (2001). Affecting others: Social appraisal and emotion contagion in everyday decision making. *Personality and Social Psychology Bulletin, 35,* 1071–1084.

Pascoe, E. A., & Smart Richman, L. (2009). Perceived discrimination and health: A meta-analytic review. *Psychological Bulletin, 135,* 531–554.

Patrick, H., Neighbors, C., & Knee, C. R. (2004). Appearance-related social comparisons: The role of contingent self-esteem and self-perceptions of attractiveness. *Personality and Social Psychology Bulletin, 30,* 501–514.

Pavalko, E. K., Mossakowski, K. N., & Hamilton, V. J. (2003). Does perceived discrimination affect health? Longitudinal relationships between work discrimination and women's physical and emotional health. *Journal of Health and Social Behavior, 43,* 18–33.

Peale, N. V. (1952). *The power of positive thinking.* New York: Prentice-Hall.

Pelham, B. W., Carvallo, M., & Jones, J. T. (2005). Implicit egotism. *Current Directions in Psychological Science, 14,* 106–110.

Pentony, J. F. (1995). The effect of negative campaigning on voting, semantic differential, and thought listing. *Journal of Social Behavior and Personality, 10,* 631–644.

Perlini, A. H., & Hansen, S. (2001). Moderating effects of need for cognition on attractiveness stereotyping. *Social Behavior and Personality, 29,* 312–321.

Petrocelli, J. V., Clarkson, J. J., Tormala, Z. L., & Hendrix, K. S. (2010). Perceiving stability as a means to attitude certainty: The role of implicit theories. *Journal of Experimental Social Psychology, 46,* 874–883.

Petrocelli, J. V., & Sherman, S. J. (2010). Event detail and confidence in gambling: The role of counterfactual thought reactions. *Journal of Experimental Social Psychology, 46,* 61–72.

Petrocelli, J. V., Tormala, Z. L., & Rucker, D. D. (2007). Unpacking attitude certainty: Attitude clarity and attitude correctness. *Journal of Personality and Social Psychology, 92,* 30–41.

Pettigrew, T. F. (1981). Extending the stereotype concept. In D. L. Hamilton (Ed.), *Cognitive processes in stereotyping and intergroup behavior* (pp. 303–331). Hillsdale, NJ: Erlbaum.

Pettigrew, T. F. (1997). Generalized intergroup contact effects on prejudice. *Personality and Social Psychology Bulletin, 23,* 173–185.

Pettigrew, T. W. (2007). Still a long way to go: American Black-White relations today. In G. Adams, M. Biernat, N. R. Branscombe, C. S. Crandall, & L. S. Wrightsman (Eds.), *Commemorating Brown: The social psychology of racism and discrimination.* Washington, DC: American Psychological Association.

Pettijohn, T. E. F., II, & Jungeberg, B. J. (2004). Playboy playmate curves: Changes in facial and body feature preferences across social and economic conditions. *Personality and Social Psychology Bulletin, 30,* 1186–1197.

Petty, R. E. (1995). Attitude change. In A. Tesser (Ed.), *Advanced social psychology* (pp. 195–255). New York: McGraw-Hill.

Petty, R. E., & Cacioppo, J. T. (1986). The elaboration likelihood model of persuasion. In L. Berkowitz (Ed.), *Advances in experimental social psychology* (Vol. 19, pp. 123–205). New York: Academic Press.

Petty, R. E., Cacioppo, J. T., Strathman, A. J., & Priester, J. R. (2005). To think or not to think: Exploring two routes to persuasion. In T. C. Brock & M. C. Green (Eds.), *Persuasion: Psychological insights and perspectives* (2nd ed., pp. 81–116). Thousand Oaks, CA: Sage.

Petty, R. E., Wheeler, C., & Tormala, Z. L. (2003). Persuasion and attitude change. In T. Millon & M. J. Lerner (Eds.), *Handbook of psychology: Personality and social psychology* (Vol. 5, pp. 353–382). New York: Wiley.

Petty, R. J., & Krosnick, J. A. (Eds.). (1995). *Attitude strength: Antecedents and consequences* (Vol. 4). Hillsdale, NJ: Erlbaum.

Pew Research Center. (2015). *Climate change and energy issues.* Retrieved from http://www.pewinternet.org/2015/07/01/chapter–2–climate–change–and–energy–issues/

Pfeifer, J. H., Iacoboni, M., Mazziotta, J. C., & Dapretto, M. (2007). Mirroring others' emotions relates to empathy and interpersonal competence in children. *NeuroImage, 39,* 2076–2085.

Phelps, E. A., O'Connor, K. J., Gatenby, J. C., Gore, J. C., Grillon, C., & Davis, M. (2001). Activation of the left amygdala to a cognitive representation of fear. *Nature Neuroscience, 4,* 437–441.

Piff, P. K., Dietze, P., Feinberg, M., Stancato, D. M., & Keltner, D. (2015). Awe, the small self, and prosocial behavior. *Journal of Personality and Social Psychology, 108,* 882–899.

Piff, P. K., Kraus, M. W., Côté, S., Cheng, B. H., & Keltner, D. (2010). Having less, giving more: The influence of social class on prosocial behavior. *Journal of Personality and Social Psychology, 99,* 771–784.

Pinquart, M., & Sorensen, S. (2000). Influences of socioeconomic status, social network, and competence on subjective well-being in later life: A meta-analysis. *Psychology and Aging, 15,* 187–224.

Pittman, T. S. (1993). Control motivation and attitude change. In G. Weary, F. Gleicher, & empirical review. *Psychological Bulletin, 130,* 435–468.

Plant, E. A., & Devine, P. G. (1998). Internal and external motivation to respond without prejudice. *Journal of Personality and Social Psychology, 75,* 811–832.

Plaut, V. C., Adams, G., & Anderson, S. L. (2009). Does attractiveness buy happiness? "It depends on where you're from." *Personal Relationships, 16,* 619–630.

Polivy, J., & Herman, C. P. (2000). The false-hope syndrome: Unfulfilled expectations of self-change. *Current Directions in Psychological Science, 9,* 128–131.

Pollak, K. I., & Niemann, Y. F. (1998). Black and white tokens in academia: A difference in chronic versus acute distinctiveness. *Journal of Applied Social Psychology, 28,* 954–972.

Postmes, T., & Branscombe, N. R. (2002). Influence of long-term racial environmental composition on subjective well-being in African Americans. *Journal of Personality and Social Psychology, 83,* 735–751.

Postmes, T., & Spears, R. (1998). Deindividuation and antinormative behavior: A meta-analysis. *Psychological Bulletin, 123,* 238–259.

Postmes, T., Spears, R., & Cihangir, S. (2001). Quality of decision making and group norms. *Journal of Personality and Social Psychology, 80,* 918–930.

Postmes, T., Spears, R., Lee, A. T., & Novak, R. J. (2005). Individuality and social influence in groups: Inductive and deductive routes to group identity. *Journal of Personality and Social Psychology, 89,* 747–763.

Poteat, V. P., & Spanierman, L. B. (2010). Do the ideological beliefs of peers predict the prejudiced attitudes of other individuals in the group? *Group Processes and Intergroup Relations, 13,* 495–514.

Powell, A. A., Branscombe, N. R., & Schmitt, M. T. (2005). Inequality as ingroup privilege or outgroup disadvantage: The impact of group focus on collective guilt and interracial attitudes. *Personality and Social Psychology Bulletin, 31,* 508–521.

Pozzulo, J. D., & Demopsey, J. (2006). Biased lineup instructions: Examining the effect of pressure on children's and adults' eyewitness identification accuracy. *Journal of Applied Social Psychology, 36,* 1381–1394.

Pozzulo, J. D., & Lindsay, R. C. L. (1999). Elimination lineups: An improved identification for child eyewitnesses. *Journal of Applied Psychology, 84,* 167–176.

Prentice, D. A., & Miller, D. T. (1992). When small effects are impressive. *Psychological Bulletin, 112,* 160–164.

Prentice, D. A., Miller, D. T., & Lightdale, J. R. (1994). Asymmetries in attachments to groups and to their members: Distinguishing between common-identity and common-bond groups. *Personality and Social Psychology Bulletin, 20,* 484–493.

Previti, D., & Amato, P. R. (2003). Why stay married? Rewards, barriers, and marital stability. *Journal of Marriage and Family, 65,* 561–573.

Price, K. H., Harrison, D. A., & Gavin, J. H. (2006). Withholding inputs in team contexts: Member composition, interaction processes, evaluation structure, and social loafing. *Journal of Applied Psychology, 91,* 1375–1384.

Price, M. J. (2015). *At the cross: Race, religion, and citizenship in the politics of the death penalty.* New York: Oxford University Press.

Priller, E., & Schupp, J. (2011). Social and economic characteristics of financial and blood donors in Germany. *DIW Economic Bulletin, 6,* 23–30.

Pronin, E., Berger, J., & Molouki, S. (2007). Alone in a crowd of sheep: Asymmetric perceptions of conformity and their roots in an introspection illusion. *Journal of Personality and Social Psychology, 92,* 585–595.

Pronin, E., Kruger, J., Savitsky, K., & Ross, L. (2001). You don't know me, but I know you: The illusion of asymmetric insight. *Journal of Personality and Social Psychology, 81,* 639–656.

Pronin, E., & Kruger, M. B. (2007). Valuing thoughts, ignoring behavior: The introspection illusion as a source of bias blind spot. *Journal of Experimental Social Psychology, 43,* 565–578.

Pronin, E., Lin, D. Y., & Ross, L. (2002). The bias blind spot: Perceptions of bias in self versus others. *Personality and Social Psychology Bulletin, 28,* 369–381.

Pronin, E., & Ross, L. (2006). Temporal differences in trait self-ascription: When the self is seen as an other. *Journal of Personality and Social Psychology, 90,* 197–209.

Pronin, E., Steele, C. M., & Ross, L. (2004). Identity bifurcation in response to stereotype threat: Women and mathematics. *Journal of Experimental Social Psychology, 40,* 152–168.

Proudfoot, D., Kay, A. C., & Koval, C. Z. (2015). A gender bias in the attribution of creativity: Archival and experimental evidence for the perceived association between masculinity and creative thinking. *Psychological Science, 26,* 1751–1761.

Pruitt, D. G., & Carnevale, P. J. (1993). *Negotiation in social conflict.* Pacific Grove, CA: Brooks/Cole.

Przybylski, A. K., Ryan, R. M., & Rigby, G. S. (2009). The motivating role of violence in video games. *Personality and Social Psychology Bulletin, 35,* 243–259.

Putnam, R. (2000). *Bowling alone.* New York: Simon & Schuster.

Queller, S., & Smith, E. R. (2002). Subtyping versus bookkeeping in stereotype learning and change: Connectionist simulations and empirical findings. *Journal of Personality and Social Psychology, 82,* 300–313.

Quigley, B. M., Johnson, A. B., & Byrne, D. (1995, June). *Mock jury sentencing decisions: A meta-analysis of the attractiveness-leniency effect.* Paper presented at the meeting of the American Psychological Society, New York.

Quinn, D. M., & Chaudoir, S. R. (2009). Living with a concealable stigmatized identity: The impact of anticipated stigma, centrality, salience, and cultural stigma on psychological distress and health. *Journal of Personality and Social Psychology, 97,* 634–651.

Quinn, J. M., & Wood, W. (2004). Forewarnings of influence appeals: Inducing resistance and acceptance. In E. S. Knowles & J. A. Linn (Eds.), *Resistance and persuasion* (pp. 193–213). Mahwah, NJ: Erlbaum.

Quoidbach, J., Dunn, E. W., Petrides, K. V., & Mikolajczak, M. (2010). Money giveth, money taketh away: The dual effect of wealth on happiness. *Psychological Science, 21,* 759–763.

Ranganath, K. A., Smith, C. T., & Nosek, B. A. (2008). Distinguishing automatic and controlled components of attitudes from direct and indirect measurement. *Journal of Experimental Social Psychology, 44,* 386–396.

Read, S. J., & Miller, L. C. (1998). *Connectionist and PDP models of social reasoning and social behavior.* Mahwah, NJ: Erlbaum.

Redersdorff, S., Martinot, D., & Branscombe, N. R. (2004). The impact of thinking about group-based disadvantages or advantages on women's well-being: An experimental test of the rejection-identification model. *Current Psychology of Cognition, 22,* 203–222.

Regan, P. C. (1998). What if you can't get what you want? Willingness to compromise ideal mate selection standards as a function of sex, mate value, and relationship context. *Personality and Social Psychology Bulletin, 24,* 1294–1303.

Reich, J. W., Zautra, A. J., & Potter, P. T. (2001). Cognitive structure and the independence of positive and negative affect. *Journal of Social and Clinical Psychology, 20,* 99–115.

Reicher, S., & Haslam, S. A. (2006). Rethinking the psychology of tyranny: The BBC prison study. *British Journal of Social Psychology, 45,* 1–40.

Reinhard, M. A., & Schwarz, N. (2011). The influence of affective states on the process of lie detection. *Journal of Experimental Psychology: Applied, 18,* 377–389.

Reis, H. T., Maniaci, M. R., Caprariello, P. A., Eastwick, P. W., & Finkel, E. J. (2011). Familiarity does indeed promote attraction in live interaction. *Journal of Personality and Social Psychology, 101,* 557–570.

Reisenzein, R., Bordgen, S., Holtbernd, T., & Matz, D. (2006). Evidence for strong dissociation between emotion and facial displays: The case of surprise. *Journal of Personality and Social Psychology, 91,* 295–315.

Reiss, A. J., & Roth, J. A. (Eds.). (1993). *Understanding and preventing violence.* Washington, DC: National Academy Press.

Reno, R. R., Cialdini, R. B., & Kallgren, C. A. (1993). The transsituational influence of social norms. *Journal of Personality and Social Psychology, 64,* 104–112.

Rensberger, B. (1993, November 9). Certain chemistry between vole pairs. *Albany Times Union,* pp. C-1–C-3.

Reskin, B., & Padavic, I. (1994). *Women and men at work.* Thousand Oaks, CA: Pine Forge Press.

Reynolds, K. J., Turner, J. C., Branscombe, N. R., Mavor, K. I., Bizumic, B., & Subasic, E. (2010). Interactionism in personality and social psychology: An integrated approach to understanding the mind and behavior. *European Journal of Personality, 24,* 458–482.

Rhodes, G., & Tremewan, T. (1996). Averageness, exaggeration, and facial attractiveness. *Psychological Science, 7,* 105–110.

Richard, F. D., Bond, C. F. Jr., & Stokes-Zoota, J. J. (2001). "That's completely obvious … and important": Lay judgments of social psychological findings. *Personality and Social Psychology Bulletin, 27,* 497–505.

Richard, J. F. (2012). Revisiting the whole-school approach to bullying: Really looking at the whole school. *School Psychology International, 33,* 263–284.

Richards, Z., & Hewstone, M. (2001). Subtyping and subgrouping: Processes for the prevention and promotion of stereotype change. *Personality and Social Psychology Review, 5,* 52–73.

Riegelsberger, J., Sasse, M. A., & McCarthy, J. D. (2007). Trust in mediated communications. In A. N. Joinson, K. Y. A. McKenna, T. Postmes, & U.-D. Reips (Eds.), *The Oxford handbook of internet psychology* (pp. 53–60). New York: Oxford University Press.

Riek, B. M., Mania, E. W., Gaertner, S. L., McDonald, S. A., & Lamoreaux, M. J. (2010). Does a common ingroup identity reduce intergroup threat? *Group Processes and Intergroup Relations, 13,* 403–423.

Riemer, H., Shavitt, S., Koo, M., & Markus, H. R. (2014). Preferences don't have to be personal: Expanding attitude theorizing with a cross-cultural perspective. *Psychological Review, 121,* 619–648.

Risen, J. L., & Gilovich, T. (2007). Another look at why people are reluctant to exchange lottery tickets. *Journal of Personality and Social Psychology, 93,* 12–22.

Robbins, T. L., & DeNisi, A. S. (1994). A closer look at interpersonal affect as a distinct influence on cognitive processing in performance evaluations. *Journal of Applied Psychology, 79,* 341–353.

Robins, R. W., Hendin, H. M., & Trzesniewski, K. H. (2001). *Personality and Social Psychology Bulletin, 27,* 151–161.

Robins, R. W., Spranca, M. D., & Mendelsohn, G. A. (1996). The actor-observer effect revisited: Effects of individual differences and repeated social interactions on actor and observer attribution. *Journal of Personality and Social Psychology, 71,* 375–389.

Robinson, E., Thomas, J., Aveyard, P., & Higgs, S. (2014). What everyone else is eating: A systematic review and meta-analysis of the effect of informational eating norms on eating behavior. *Journal of the Academy of Nutrition and Dietetics, 114,* 414–429.

Robinson, E., Tobias, T., Shaw, L., Freeman, E., & Higgs, S. (2011). Social matching of food intake and the need for social acceptance. *Appetite, 56,* 747–752.

Robinson, L. A., Berman, J. S., & Neimeyer, R. A. (1990). Psychotherapy for the treatment of depression: A comprehensive review of controlled outcome research. *Psychological Bulletin, 108,* 30–49.

Roccas, S. (2003). Identification and status revisited: The moderating role of self-enhancement and self-transcendence values. *Personality and Social Psychology Bulletin, 29,* 726–736.

Rochat, F., & Modigliani, A. (1995). The ordinary quality of resistance: From Milgram's laboratory to the village of Le Chambon. *Journal of Social Issues, 5,* 195–210.

Rodrigo, M. F., & Ato, M. (2002). Testing the group polarization hypothesis by using logit models. *European Journal of Social Psychology, 32,* 3–18.

Rogers, R. W. (1980). *Subjects' reactions to experimental deception.* Unpublished manuscript, University of Alabama, Tuscaloosa.

Rogers, R. W., & Ketcher, C. M. (1979). Effects of anonymity and arousal on aggression. *Journal of Psychology, 102,* 13–19.

Rokach, A., & Neto, F. (2000). Coping with loneliness in adolescence: A cross-cultural study. *Social Behavior and Personality, 28,* 329–341.

Romero, D. H., Riggs, S. A., & Ruggero, C. (2015). Coping, family social support, and psychological symptoms among student veterans. *Journal of Counseling Psychology, 62,* 242–252.

Rosenberg, M. (1965). *Society and the adolescent self-image.* Princeton, NJ: Princeton University Press.

Rosenhan, D. L., Salovey, P., & Hargis, K. (1981). The joys of helping: Focus of attention mediates the impact of positive affect on altruism. *Journal of Personality and Social Psychology, 40,* 899.

Rosenthal, R., & Jacobson, L. (1968). *Pygmalion in the classroom: Teacher expectation and pupils' intellectual development.* New York: Holt, Rinehart & Winston.

Ross, L. (1977). The intuitive scientist and his shortcoming. In L. Berkowitz (Ed.), *Advances in experimental social psychology* (Vol. 10, pp. 174–221). New York: Academic Press.

Ross, M., & Wilson, A. E. (2003). Autobiographical memory and conceptions of self: Getting better all the time. *Current Directions in Psychological Science, 12,* 66–69.

Rothman, A. J., & Hardin, C. D. (1997). Differential use of the availability heuristic in social judgment. *Personality and Social Psychology Bulletin, 23,* 123–138.

Rotton, J., & Cohn, E. G. (2000). Violence is a curvilinear function of temperature in Dallas: A replication. *Journal of Personality and Social Psychology, 78,* 1074–1081.

Rowe, P. M. (1996, September). On the neurobiological basis of affiliation. *APS Observer,* 17–18.

Rozin, P., Lowery, L., & Ebert, R. (1994). Varieties of disgust faces and the structure of disgust. *Journal of Personality and Social Psychology, 66,* 870–881.

Rozin, P., & Nemeroff, C. (1990). The laws of sympathetic magic: A psychological analysis of similarity and contagion. In W. Stigler, R. A. Shweder, & G. Herdt (Eds.), *Cultural psychology: Essays in comparative human development* (pp. 205–232). Cambridge, England: Cambridge University Press.

Rubin, J. Z. (1985). Deceiving ourselves about deception: Comment on Smith and Richardson's "Amelioration of deception and harm in psychological research." *Journal of Personality and Social Psychology, 48,* 252–253.

Rubin, K. H., Bukowski, W. M., & Laursen, B. (2011). *Handbook of peer interactions, relationships, and groups.* New York: Wiley.

Rubin, Z. (1970). Measurement of romantic love. *Journal of Personality and Social Psychology, 16,* 265.

Ruder, M., & Bless, H. (2003). Mood and the reliance on the ease of retrieval heuristic. *Journal of Personality and Social Psychology, 85,* 20–32.

Rudman, L. A., & Fairchild, K. (2004). Reactions to counterstereotypic behavior: The role of backlash in cultural stereotype maintenance. *Journal of Personality and Social Psychology, 87,* 157–176.

Ruedy, N. E., Moore, C., Gino, F., & Schweitzer, M. E. (2013). The cheater's high: The unexpected affective benefits of unethical behavior. *Journal of Personality and Social Psychology, 105,* 531–548.

Russell, J. A. (1994). Is there universal recognition of emotion from facial expressions? A review of cross-cultural studies. *Psychological Bulletin, 115,* 102–141.

Rutkowski, G. K., Gruder, C. L., & Romer, D. (1983). Group cohesiveness, social norms, and bystander intervention. *Journal of Personality and Social Psychology, 44,* 542–552.

Ryan, M. K., David, B., & Reynolds, K. J. (2004). Who cares? The effect of gender and context on the self and moral reasoning. *Psychology of Women Quarterly, 28,* 246–255.

Ryan, M. K., & Haslam, S. A. (2005). The glass cliff: Evidence that women are over-represented in precarious leadership positions. *British Journal of Management, 16,* 81–90.

Ryan, M. K., & Haslam, S. A. (2007). The glass cliff: Exploring the dynamics surrounding women's appointment to precarious leadership positions. *Academy of Management Review, 32,* 549–572.

Ryan, M. K., Haslam, S. A., Hersby, M. D., Kulich, C., & Wilson-Kovacs, M. D. (2009). The stress of working on the edge: Implications of glass cliffs for both women and organizations. In M. Barreto, M. K. Ryan, & M. T. Schmitt (Eds.), *The glass it ceiling in the 21st century* (pp. 153–169). Washington, DC: American Psychological Association.

Ryan, R. M., & Deci, E. L. (2000). Self-determination theory and the facilitation of intrinsic motivation, social development, and well-being. *American Psychologist, 55,* 68–78.

Ryan, R. M., & Deci, E. L. (2007). Active human nature: Self-determination theory and the promotion and maintenance of sport, exercise, and health. In M. S. Hagger & N. L. D. Chatzisarantis (Eds.), *Self-determination in sport and exercise* (pp. 1–19). New York: Human Kinetics.

Sadler, P., & Woody, E. (2003). Is who you are who you're talking to? Interpersonal style and complementarity in mixed-sex interactions. *Journal of Personality and Social Psychology, 84,* 80–96.

Sahdra, B., & Ross, M. (2007). Group identification and historical memory. *Personality and Social Psychology Bulletin, 33,* 384–395.

Sanfey, A. G., Rilling, J. K., Aronson, J. A., Nystrom, L. E., & Cohen, J. D. (2003). The neural basis of economic decision making in the ultimatum game. *Science, 300,* 1755–1757.

Sani, F. (2005). When subgroups secede: Extending and refining the social psychological model of schism in groups. *Personality and Social Psychology Bulletin, 31,* 1074–1086.

Sani, F. (2009). When groups fall apart: A social psychological model of the schismatic process. In F. Butera & J. M. Levine (Eds.), *Coping with minority status: Responses to exclusion and inclusion* (pp. 243–266). New York: Cambridge University Press.

Sanitioso, R. B., & Wlodarski, R. (2004). In search of information that confirms a desired self-perception: Motivated processing of social feedback and choice of social interactions. *Personality and Social Psychology Bulletin, 30,* 412–422.

Santaelaa-Tenorio, J., Cerda, M., Villaveces, A., & Galea, S. (2016). What do we know about the association between firearm legislation and firearm-related injuries? *Epidemiologic Reviews, 38,* 140–157.

Sassenberg, K., Jonas, K. J., Shah, J. Y., & Brazy, P. C. (2007). Why some groups just feel better: The regulatory fit of group power. *Journal of Personality and Social Psychology, 92,* 249–267.

Saucier, D. A. (2002). Self-reports of racist attitudes for oneself and others. *Psychological Belgica, 42,* 99–105.

Sawmi, V., Stieger, S., Haubner, T., Voracek, M., & Furnham, A. (2009). Evaluating the physical attractiveness of oneself and one's romantic partner. *Journal of Individual Differences, 30,* 35–43.

Schachter, S. (1951). Deviation, rejection, and communication. *Journal of Abnormal and Social Psychology, 46,* 190–207.

Schachter, S. (1959). *The psychology of affiliation.* Stanford, CA: Stanford University Press.

Schachter, S. (1964). The interaction of cognitive and physiological determinants of emotional state. In L. Berkowitz (Ed.), *Advances in experimental social psychology* (Vol. 1, pp. 48–81). New York: Academic Press.

Schafer, M., Haun, D. B. M., & Tomasello, M. (2015). Fair is not fair everywhere. *Psychological Science, 26,* 1252–1260.

Schein, V. E. (2001). A global look at psychological barriers to women's progress in management. *Journal of Social Issues, 57,* 675–688.

Schmader, T. (2010). Stereotype threat deconstructed. *Current Directions in Psychological Science, 19,* 14–18.

Schmidt, H. G., Mamede, S., Van Den Berge, K., Van Gog, T., Van Saase, J., & Rikers, R. (2014). Exposure to media information about a disease can cause doctors to misdiagnose similar-looking clinical cases. *Academic Medicine, 89,* 285–291.

Schmitt, D. P. (2004). Patterns and universals of mate poaching across 53 nations: The effects of sex, culture, and personality on romantically attracting another person's partner. *Journal of Personality and Social Psychology, 86,* 560–584.

Schmitt, D. P., & Buss, D. M. (2001). Human mate poaching: Tactics and temptations for infiltrating existing mateships. *Journal of Personality and Social Psychology, 80,* 894–917.

Schmitt, M. T., Branscombe, N. R., & Postmes, T. (2003). Women's emotional responses to the pervasiveness of gender discrimination. *European Journal of Social Psychology, 33,* 297–312.

Schmitt, M. T., Branscombe, N. R., Postmes, T., & Garcia, A. (2014). The consequences of perceived discrimination for psychological well-being: A meta-analytic review. *Psychological Bulletin, 140,* 921–948.

Schmitt, M. T., Ellemers, N., & Branscombe, N. R. (2003). Perceiving and responding to gender discrimination at work. In S. A. Haslam, D. van Knippenberg, M. Platow, & N. Ellemers (Eds.), *Social identity at work: Developing theory for organizational practice* (pp. 277–292). Philadelphia: Psychology Press.

Schmitt, M. T., Silvia, P. J., & Branscombe, N. R. (2000). The intersection of self-evaluation maintenance and social identity theories: Intragroup judgment in interpersonal and intergroup contexts. *Personality and Social Psychology Bulletin, 26,* 1598–1606.

Schmitt, M. T., Spears, R., & Branscombe, N. R. (2002). Constructing a minority group identity out of shared rejection: The case of international students. *European Journal of Social Psychology, 32,* 1–12.

Schnall, S., Roper, J., & Fessler, D. M. T. (2010). Elevation leads to altruistic behavior. *Psychological Science, 21,* 315–320.

Schonert-Reichl, K. A. (1999). Relations of peer acceptance, friendship adjustment, and social behavior to moral reasoning during early adolescence. *Journal of Early Adolescence, 19,* 249–279.

Schulz-Hardt, S., Brodbeck, F. C., Mojzisch, A., Kerschreiter, R., & Frey, D. (2006). Group decision making in hidden profile situations: Dissent as a facilitator for decision quality. *Journal of Personality and Social Psychology, 91,* 1080–1093.

Schutte, J. W., & Hosch, H. M. (1997). Gender differences in sexual assault verdicts: A meta-analysis. *Journal of Social Behavior and Personality, 12,* 759–772.

Schwarz, N., Bless, H., Strack, F., Klumpp, G., Rittenauer-Schatka, G., & Simons, A. (1991). Ease of retrieval as information: Another look at the availability heuristic. *Journal of Personality and Social Psychology, 61,* 195–202.

Schwarz, N., & Bohner, G. (2001). The construction of attitudes. In A. Tesser & N. Schwarz (Eds.), *Blackwell handbook of social psychology: Intrapersonal processes* (pp. 436–457). Oxford, UK: Blackwell.

Schwarzer, R. (1994). Optimism, vulnerability, and self-beliefs as health-related cognitions: A systematic overview. *Psychology and Health, 9,* 161–180.

Scutt, D., Manning, J. T., Whitehouse, G. H., Leinster, S. J., & Massey, C. P. (1997). The relationship between breast symmetry, breast size and occurrence of breast cancer. *British Journal of Radiology, 70,* 1017–1021.

Sears, D. O. (2008). The American color line fifty years after Brown v. Board: Many "Peoples of color" or Black exceptionalism? In G. Adams, M. Biernat, N. R. Branscombe, C. S. Crandall, & L. S. Wrightsman (Eds.), *Commemorating Brown: The social psychology of racism and discrimination.* Washington, DC: American Psychological Association.

Sedikides, C., & Gregg, A. P. (2003). Portraits of the self. In M. A. Hogg & J. Cooper (Eds.), *The Sage handbook of social psychology* (pp. 110–138). Thousand Oaks, CA: Sage.

Sedikides, C., Meek, R., Alicke, M. D., & Taylor, S. (2014). Behind bars but above the bar: Prisoners consider themselves more prosocial than non-prisoners. *British Journal of Social Psychology, 53,* 396–403.

Sedikides, C., Wildschut, T., Arndt, J., & Routledge, C. (2008). Nostalgia: Past, present, and future. *Current Directions in Psychological Science, 17,* 304–307.

Segal, M. M. (1974). Alphabet and attraction: An unobtrusive measure of the effect of propinquity in a field setting. *Journal of Personality and Social Psychology, 30,* 654–657.

Selfhout, M., Denissen, J., Branje, S., & Meeus, W. (2009). In the eye of the beholder: Perceived, actual, ad peer-rated similarity in personality, communication, and friendship intensity during the acquaintanceship process. *Journal of Personality and Social Psychology, 96,* 1152–1165.

Seligman, M. E. P., Steen, T. A., Park, N., & Peterson, C. (2005). Positive psychology progress: Empirical validation of interventions. *American Psychologist, 60,* 410–421.

Serota, K. B., Levine, T. R., & Boster, F. J. (2010). The prevalence of lying in America: Three studies of self-reported lies. *Human Communication Research, 36,* 2–25.

Shah, A. K., & Oppenheimer, D. M. (2009). The path of least resistance: Using easy-to-access information. *Current Directions in Psychological Science, 18,* 232–236.

Shah, J. (2003). Automatic for the people: How representations of significant others implicitly affect goal pursuit. *Journal of Personality and Social Psychology, 84,* 661–681.

Shams, M. (2001). Social support, loneliness and friendship preference among British Asian and non-Asian adolescents. *Social Behavior and Personality, 29,* 399–404.

Shanab, M. E., & Yahya, K. A. (1977). A behavioral study of obedience in children. *Journal of Personality and Social Psychology, 35,* 530–536.

Sharp, M. J., & Getz, J. G. (1996). Substance use as impression management. *Personality and Social Psychology Bulletin, 22,* 60–67.

Sharpe, D., Adair, J. G., & Roese, N. J. (1992). Twenty years of deception research: A decline in subjects' trust? *Personality and Social Psychology Bulletin, 18,* 585–590.

Sharvit, K., Brambilla, M., Babush, M., & Colucci, F. P. (2015). To feel or not to feel when my group harms others? The regulation of collective guilt as motivated reasoning. *Personality and Social Psychology Bulletin, 41,* 1223–1235.

Shaver, P. R., & Brennan, K. A. (1992). Attachment styles and the "big five" personality traits: Their connections with each other and with romantic relationship outcomes. *Personality and Social Psychology Bulletin, 18,* 536–545.

Shaver, P. R., Morgan, H. J., & Wu, S. (1996). Is love a "basic" emotion? *Personal Relationships, 3,* 81–96.

Shaver, P. R., Murdaya, U., & Fraley, R. C. (2001). The structure of the Indonesian emotion lexicon. *Asian Journal of Social Psychology, 4,* 201–224.

Shaw, J. I., Borough, H. W., & Fink, M. I. (1994). Perceived sexual orientation and helping behavior by males and females: The wrong number technique. *Journal of Psychology and Human Sexuality, 6,* 73–81.

Shen, H. (2013). Mind the gender gap. *Nature, 495,* 22–24.

Shepperd, J. A., Carroll, P. J., & Sweeny, K. (2008). A functional approach to explaining fluctuations in future outlooks: From self-enhancement to self-criticism. In E. Chang (Ed.), *Self-criticism and self-enhancement: Theory, research and clinical implications* (pp. 161–180). Washington, DC: American Psychological Association.

Shepperd, J. A., & Taylor, K. M. (1999). Social loafing and expectancy-value theory. *Personality and Social Psychology Bulletin, 25,* 1147–1158.

Shepperd, J. A., Waters, E. A., Weinstein, N. D., & Klein, W. M. P. (2015). A primer on unrealistic optimism. *Current Directions in Psychological Science, 24,* 232–237.

Sherif, M. A. (1937). An experimental approach to the study of attitudes. *Sociometry, 1,* 90–98.

Sherif, M., Harvey, D. J., White, B. J., Hood, W. R, & Sherif, C. W. (1961). *The Robbers' cave experiment.* Norman, OK: Institute of Group Relations.

Sherman, J. W., Gawronski, B., Gonsalkorale, K., Hugenberg, K., Allen, T. J., & Groom, C. J. (2008). The self-regulation of automatic associations and behavioral impulses. *Psychological Review, 115,* 314–335.

Sherman, S. S. (1980). On the self-erasing nature of errors of prediction. *Journal of Personality and Social Psychology, 16,* 388–403.

Shnabel, N., & Nadler, A. (2008). A needs-based model for reconciliation: Satisfying the differential emotional needs of the victim and perpetrator as a key to promoting reconciliation. *Journal of Personality and Social Psychology, 94,* 116–132.

Sidanius, J., & Pratto, F. (1999). *Social dominance.* New York: Cambridge University Press.

Sigall, H. (1997). Ethical considerations in social psychological research: Is the bogus pipeline a special case? *Journal of Applied Social Psychology, 27,* 574–581.

Simon, B. (2004). *Identity in modern society: A social psychological perspective.* Oxford: Blackwell.

Simon, B., & Grabow, H. (2014). To be respected and to respect: The challenge of mutual respect in intergroup relations. *British Journal of Social Psychology, 20,* 39–53.

Simon, B., & Klandermans, B. (2001). Politicized collective identity: A social psychological analysis. *American Psychologist, 56,* 319–331.

Simon, L., Greenberg, J., & Brehm, J. (1995). Trivialization: The forgotten mode of dissonance reduction. *Journal of Personality and Social Psychology, 68,* 247–260.

Simonton, D. K. (2009). Historiometry in personality and social psychology. *Social and Personality Psychology Compass, 3,* 49–63.

Sinclair, S., Dunn, E., & Lowery, B. S. (2005). The relationship between parental racial attitudes and children's implicit prejudice. *Journal of Experimental Social Psychology, 41,* 283–289.

Singh, N. A., Clements, K. M., & Singh, M. A. F. (2001). The efficacy of exercise as a long-term antidepressant in elderly subjects: A randomized, controlled trial. *Journal of Gerontology: Psychological Sciences, 56,* M497–M504.

Singh, R., & Teoh, J. B. P. (1999). Attitudes and attraction: A test of two hypotheses for the similarity-dissimilarity asymmetry. *British Journal of Social Psychology, 38,* 427–443.

Sivacek, J., & Crano, W. D. (1982). Vested interest as a moderator of attitude-behavior consistency. *Journal of Personality and Social Psychology, 43,* 210–221.

Siy, J. O., & Cheryan, S. (2013). When compliments fail to flatter: American individualism and responses to positive stereotypes. *Journal of Personality and Social Psychology, 104,* 87–102.

Slonim, G., Gur-Yaish, N., & Katz, R. (2015). By choice or by circumstance?: Stereotypes of and feelings about single people. *Studia Psychologica, 57,* 35–47.

Slotter, E. B., Gardner, W. L., & Finkel, E. J. (2010). Who am I without you?: The influence of romantic breakup on the self-concept. *Personality and Social Psychology Bulletin, 36,* 147–160.

Smalarz, L., & Wells, G. L. (2015). Contamination of eyewitness self-reports and the mistaken-identification problem. *Current Directions in Psychological Science, 24,* 120–124.

Smith, A. E., Jussim, L., & Eccles, J. (1999). Do self-fulfilling prophecies accumulate, dissipate, or remain stable over time? *Journal of Personality and Social Psychology, 77,* 548–565.

Smith, K. D., Keating, J. P., & Stotland, E. (1989). Altruism reconsidered: The effect of denying feedback on a victim's status to empathetic witnesses. *Journal of Personality and Social Psychology, 57,* 641–650.

Smith, S. S., & Richardson, D. (1985). On deceiving ourselves about deception: Reply to Rubin. *Journal of Personality and Social Psychology, 48,* 254–255.

Snyder, C. R., & Fromkin, H. L. (1980). *Uniqueness, the human pursuit of difference.* New York: Plenum Press.

Snyder, M., Tanke, E. D., & Berscheid, E. (1977). Social perception and interpersonal behavior: On the self-fulfilling nature of social stereotypes. *Journal of Personality and Social Psychology, 35,* 656–666.

Solomon, B. C., & Vazire, S. (2014). You are so beautiful…to me: Seeing beyond biases and achieving accuracy in romantic relationships. *Journal of Personality and Social Psychology, 107,* 516–528.

Sommers, S. R. (2006). On racial diversity and group decision making: Identifying multiple effects of racial composition on jury deliberations. *Journal of Personality and Social Psychology, 90,* 597–612.

Sorrentino, R. M., Otsubo, Y., Yasunaga, S., Nezlek, J., Kouhara, S., & Shuper, P. (2005). Uncertainty orientation and social behavior: Individual differences within and across cultures. In R. M. Sorrentino, D. Cohen, J. M. Olson, & M. P. Zanna (Eds.), *Culture and social behavior: The Ontario symposium* (Vol. 10, pp. 181–206). Mahwah, NJ: Erlbaum.

Sotomayor, S. (2014). *My beloved world.* New York: Vintage Books.

Sparrow, B., & Wegner, D. M. (2006). Unpriming: The deactivation of thoughts through expression. *Journal of Personality and Social Psychology, 9,* 1009–1019.

Sparrowe, R. T., Soetjipto, B. W., & Kraimer, M. L. (2006). Do leaders' influence tactics relate to members' helping behavior? It depends on the quality of the relationships. *Academy of Management Journal, 49,* 1194–1208.

Spector, T. (2012). *Identically different: Why you can change your genes.* London: Weidenfeld and Nicholson.

Spencer, S. J., Steele, C. M., & Quinn, D. M. (1999). Stereotype threat and women's math performance. *Journal of Experimental Social Psychology, 35,* 4–28.

Spencer-Rodgers, J., Hamilton, D. L., & Sherman, S. J. (2007). The central role of entitativity in stereotypes of social categories and task groups. *Journal of Personality and Social Psychology, 92,* 369–388.

Spina, R. R., Ji, L.-J., Guo, T., Zhang, Z., Li, Y., & Fabrigar, L. (2010). Cultural differences in the representativeness heuristic: Expecting a correspondence in magnitude between cause and effect. *Personality and Social Psychology Bulletin, 36,* 583–597.

Spunt, R. P., & Lieberman, M. D. (2013). The busy social brain: Evidence for automaticity and control in the neural systems supporting social cognition and action understanding. *Psychological Science, 24,* 80–86.

Stahl, C., Unkelbach, C., & Corneille, O. (2009). On the respective contributions of awareness of unconditioned stimulus valence and unconditioned stimulus identity in attitude formation through evaluative conditioning. *Journal of Personality and Social Psychology, 97,* 404–420.

Stangor, C., & McMillan, D. (1992). Memory for expectancy-congruent and expectancy-incongruent information: A review of the social and social developmental literatures. *Psychological Bulletin, 111,* 42–61.

Stangor, C., Sechrist, G. B., & Jost, T. J. (2001). Changing racial beliefs by providing consensus information. *Personality and Social Psychology Bulletin, 27,* 486–496.

Stasser, G. (1992). Pooling of unshared information during group discussion. In S. Worchel, W. Wood, & J. H. Simpson (Eds.), *Group process and productivity* (pp. 48–67). Newbury Park, CA: Sage.

Stasser, G., Stewart, D. D., & Wittenbaum, G. M. (1995). Expert roles and information exchange during discussion: The importance of knowing who knows what. *Journal of Experimental Social Psychology, 31,* 244–265.

Staub, E. (1989). *The roots of evil.* New York: Cambridge University Press.

Steblay, N. K., Dysart, J. E., & Wells, G. L. (2011). Seventy-two tests of the sequential lineup superiority effect: A meta-analysis and policy discussion. *Psychology, Public Policy, and Law, 17,* 99–139.

Steele, C. M. (1988). The psychology of self-affirmation: Sustaining the integrity of the self. *Advances in Experimental Social Psychology, 21,* 261–302.

Steele, C. M. (1997). A threat in the air: How stereotypes shape the intellectual identities and performance of women and African-Americans. *American Psychologist, 52,* 613–629.

Steele, C. M., & Aronson, J. (1995). Stereotype threat and the intellectual test performance of African Americans. *Journal of Personality and Social Psychology, 69,* 797–811.

Steele, C. M., & Lui, T. J. (1983). Dissonance processes as self-affirmation. *Journal of Personality and Social Psychology, 45,* 5–19.

Steele, C. M., Spencer, S. J., & Aronson, J. (2002). Contending with group image: The psychology of stereotype and social identity threat. *Advances in Experimental Social Psychology, 34,* 379–439.

Steele, C. M., Spencer, S. J., & Aronson, J. (2002). Contending with group image: The psychology of stereotype and social identity threat. In M. P. Zanna (Ed.), *Advances in experimental social psychology* (Vol. 34, pp. 379–440). San Diego, CA: Academic Press.

Steele, C. M., Spencer, S. J., & Lynch, M. (1993). Self-image resilience and dissonance: The role of affirmational resources. *Journal of Personality and Social Psychology, 64,* 885–896.

Stephan, W. G., Boniecki, K. A., Ybarra, O., Bettencourt, A., Ervin, K. S., Jackson, L. A., et al. (2002). The role of threats in the racial attitudes of Blacks and Whites. *Personality and Social Psychology Bulletin, 28,* 1242–1254.

Stephan, W. G., Renfro, C. L., Esses, V. M., Stephan, C. W., & Martin, T. (2005). The effects of feeling threatened on attitudes toward immigrants. *International Journal of Intercultural Relations, 29*, 1–19.

Stephens, N. M., Fryberg, S. A., & Markus, H. R. (2012). It's your choice: How the middle-class model of independence disadvantages working-class Americans. In S. T. Fiske & H. R. Markus (Eds.), *Facing social class: How societal rank influences interaction* (pp. 87–106). New York: Russell Sage Foundation.

Stephens, N. M., Hamedani, M. G., & Destin, M. (2014). Closing the social-class achievement gap: A difference-education intervention improves first-generation students' academic performance and all students' college transition. *Psychological Science, 25*, 943–953.

Sternberg, R. J. (1986). A triangular theory of love. *Psychological Review, 93*, 119–135.

Stewart, T. L., Latu, I. M., Branscombe, N. R., & Denney, H. T. (2010). Yes we can! Prejudice reduction through seeing (inequality) and believing (in social change). *Psychological Science, 21*, 1557–1562.

Stewart, T. L., Latu, I. M., Kawakami, K., & Myers, A. C. (2010). Consider the situation: Reducing automatic stereotyping through situational attribution training. *Journal of Experimental Social Psychology, 46*, 221–225.

Stewart, T. L., Vassar, P. M., Sanchez, D. T., & David, S. E. (2000). Attitudes toward women's societal roles moderates the effect of gender cues on target individuation. *Journal of Personality and Social Psychology, 79*, 143–157.

Stone, J., Lynch, C. I., Sjomeling, M., & Darley, J. M. (1999). Stereotype threat effects on Black and White athletic performance. *Journal of Personality and Social Psychology, 77*, 1213–1227.

Stone, J., Wiegand, A. W., Cooper, J., & Aronson, E. (1997). When exemplification fails: Hypocrisy and the motives for self-integrity. *Journal of Personality and Social Psychology, 72*, 54–65.

Stott, C., Adang, O., Livingstone, A., & Schreiber, M. (2007). Variability in the collective behavior of England fans at Euro2004: 'Hooliganism', public order policing and social change. *European Journal of Social Psychology, 37*, 75–100.

Stott, C. J., Hutchison, P., & Drury, J. (2001). 'Hooligans' abroad? Intergroup dynamics, social identity and participation in collective 'disorder' at the 1998 World Cup Finals. *British Journal of Social Psychology, 40*, 359–384.

Stress in America. (2014). American Psychological Association Survey. Washington, DC: American Psychological Association.

Stroebe, W. (2015). Firearm availability and violent death: The need for a culture change in attitudes toward guns. *Analyses of Social Issues and Public Policy*. doi: 10.1111/asap.12100

Stroebe, W., Diehl, M., & Abakoumkin, G. (1992). The illusion of group effectivity. *Personality and Social Psychology Bulletin, 18*, 643–650.

Stroh, L. K., Langlands, C. L., & Simpson, P. A. (2004). Shattering the glass ceiling in the new millennium. In M. S. Stockdale & F. J. Crosby (Eds.), *The psychology and management of workplace diversity* (pp. 147–167). Malden, MA: Blackwell.

Stürmer, S., & Snyder, M. (2010). Helping "us" versus "them": Towards a group-level theory of helping and altruism within and across group boundaries. In S. Stürmer & M. Snyder (Eds.), *The psychology of prosocial behavior: Group processes, intergroup relations, and helping* (pp. 33–58). Oxford: Wiley & Blackwell.

Suls, J., & Rosnow, J. (1988). Concerns about artifacts in behavioral research. In M. Morawski (Ed.), *The rise of experimentation in American psychology* (pp. 163–187). New Haven, CT: Yale University Press.

Sunstein, C. R. (September 19, 2015). Making government logical. *The New York Times*. Retrieved from http://mobile.nytimes.com/2015/09/20/opinion/sunday/cass-sunstein-making-government-logicalhtml.html

Sutin, A. R., Stephan, Y., & Terracciano, A. (2015). Weight discrimination and risk of mortality. *Psychological Science, 26*, 1803–1811.

Swami, V., Frederick, D. A., Aavik, T., Alcalay, L., Ailik, J., Anderson, D., et al. (2010). The attractive female body weight and female body dissatisfaction in 26 countries across 10 world regions: Results of the international body project I. *Personality and Social Psychology Bulletin, 36*, 309–325.

Swann, W. B. (2005). The self and identity negotiation. *Interaction Studies: Social Behavior and Communication in Biological and Artificial Systems, 6*, 69–83.

Swann, W. B., & Bosson, J. K. (2010). Self and identity. In S. T. Fiske, D. T. Gilbert, & G. Lindzey (Eds.), *Handbook of social psychology* (5th ed., pp. 589–628). New York: McGraw-Hill.

Swann, W. B., Chang-Schneider, C., & McClarty, K. L. (2007). Do people's self-views matter? Self-concept and self-esteem in everyday life. *American Psychologist, 62*, 84–94.

Swann, W. B. Jr., Jetten, J., Gómez, Á., Whitehouse, H., & Bastian, B. (2012). When group membership gets personal: A theory of identity fusion. *Psychological Review, 119*, 441–456.

Swann, W. B., Jr., Rentfrow, P. J., & Gosling, S. D. (2003). The precarious couple effect: Verbally inhibited men + critical, disinhibited women = bad chemistry. *Journal of Personality and Social Psychology, 85*, 1095–1106.

Swap, W. C. (1977). Interpersonal attraction and repeated exposure to rewarders and punishers. *Personality and Social Psychology Bulletin, 3*, 248–251.

Sweeny, K., & Shepperd, J. A. (2010). The costs of optimism and the benefits of pessimism. *Emotion, 10*, 750–753.

Sweldens, S., van Osselaer, S. M. J., & Janiszewski, C. (2010). Evaluative conditioning procedures and the resilience of conditioned brand attitudes. *Journal of Consumer Research, 37*, 473–489.

Swider, B. W., Barrick, M. R., Harris, T. B., & Stoverink, A. C. (2011). Managing and creating an image in the interview: The role of interviewee initial impressions. *Journal of Applied Psychology, 96*, 1275–1288.

Swim, J. K., Aikin, K. J., Hall, W. S., & Hunter, B. A. (1995). Sexism and racism: Old-fashioned and modern prejudices. *Journal of Personality and Social Psychology, 68*, 199–214.

Swim, J. K., & Campbell, B. (2001). Sexism: Attitudes, beliefs, and behaviors. In R. Brown & S. Gaertner (Eds.), *Blackwell handbook of social psychology: Intergroup processes* (pp. 218–237). Oxford, UK: Blackwell.

Tajfel, H. (1978). *The social psychology of the minority*. New York: Minority Rights Group.

Tajfel, H. (1981). Social stereotypes and social groups. In J. C. Turner & H. Giles (Eds.), *Intergroup behavior* (pp. 144–167). Chicago: University of Chicago Press.

Tajfel, H. (1982). *Social identity and intergroup relations*. Cambridge, England: Cambridge University Press.

Tajfel, H., Billig, M., Bundy, R., & Flament, C. (1971). Social categorization and intergroup behaviour. *European Journal of Social Psychology, 1*, 149–178.

Tajfel, H., & Turner, J. C. (1986). The social identity theory of intergroup behavior. In S. Worchel & W. G. Austin (Eds.), *The social psychology of intergroup relations* (2nd ed., pp. 7–24). Monterey, CA: Brooks-Cole.

Talaska, C. A., Fiske, S. T., & Chaiken, S. (2008). Legitimating racial discrimination: A meta-analysis of the racial attitude-behavior literature shows that emotions, not beliefs, best predict discrimination. *Social Justice Research, 21*, 263–296.

Tarrant, M., Branscombe, N. R., Warner, R. H., & Weston, D. (2012). Social identity and perceptions of torture: It's moral when we do it. *Journal of Experimental Social Psychology, 48*, 513–518.

Tausch, N., Hewstone, M., Kenworthy, J. B., & Cairns, E. (2007). Cross-community contact, perceived status differences and intergroup attitudes in Northern Ireland: The mediating role of individual-level vs. group-level threats and the moderating role of social identification. *Political Psychology, 28*, 53–68.

Taylor, K. M., & Shepperd, J. A. (1998). Bracing for the worst: Severity, testing, and feedback timing as moderators of the optimistic bias. *Personality and Social Psychology Bulletin, 24,* 915–926.

Taylor, S. E. (1989). *Positive illusions: Creative self-deception and the healthy mind.* New York: Basic Books.

Taylor, S. E. (2002). *Health psychology* (5th ed.). New York: McGraw-Hill.

Taylor, S. E. (2007). Social support. In H. S. Friedman & R. C. Silver (Eds.), *Foundations of health psychology* (pp. 145–171). New York: Oxford University Press.

Taylor, S. E., & Brown, J. D. (1988). Illusion and well-being: A social psychological perspective on mental health. *Psychological Bulletin, 103,* 193–210.

Taylor, S. E., Helgeson, V. S., Reed, G. M., & Skokan, L. A. (1991). Self-generated feelings of control and adjustment to physical illness. *Journal of Social Issues, 47,* 91–109.

Taylor, S. E., Lerner, J. S., Sherman, D. K., Sage, R. M., & McDowell, N. K. (2003). Are self-enhancing cognitions associated with healthy or unhealthy biological profiles? *Journal of Personality and Social Psychology, 85,* 605–615.

Taylor, S. E., Seeman, T. E., Eisenberger, N. I., Kozanian, T. I., Moore, A. N., & Moons, W. G. (2010). Effects of a supportive or an unsupportive audience on biological and psychological responses to stress. *Journal of Personality and Social Psychology, 98,* 47–56.

Terry, D. J., & Hogg, M. A. (1996). Group norms and the attitude-behavior relationship: A role for group identification. *Personality and Social Psychology Bulletin, 22,* 776–793.

Terry, D. J., Hogg, M. A., & Duck, J. M. (1999). Group membership, social identity, and attitudes. In D. Abrams & M. A. Hogg (Eds.), *Social identity and social cognition* (pp. 280–314). Oxford: Blackwell.

Tesser, A. (1988). Toward a self-evaluation maintenance model of social behavior. *Advances in Experimental Social Psychology, 21,* 181–227.

Tesser, A., & Martin, L. (1996). The psychology of evaluation. In E. T. Higgins & A. W. Kruglanski (Eds.), *Social psychology: Handbook of basic principles* (pp. 400–423). New York: Guilford Press.

Tesser, A., Martin, L. L., & Cornell, D. P. (1996). On the substitutability of the self-protecting mechanisms. In P. Gollwitzer & J. Bargh (Eds.), *The psychology of action* (pp. 48–68). New York: Guilford Press.

Tetlock, P. E., Peterson, R. S., McGuire, C., Change, S., & Feld, P. (1992). Assessing political group dynamics: A test of the groupthink model. *Journal of Personality and Social Psychology, 63,* 403–425.

Thaler, R. H., & Sunstein, C. R. (2009). *Nudge: Improving decisions about health, wealth, and happiness.* New York: Penguin.

Thompson, L. (1998). *The mind and heart of the negotiator.* Upper Saddle River, NJ: Prentice-Hall.

Tice, D. M., Bratslavsky, E., & Baumeister, R. F. (2000). Emotional distress regulation takes precedence over impulse control: If you feel bad, do it! *Journal of Personality and Social Psychology, 80,* 53–67.

Tice, D. M., Butler, J. L., Muraven, M. B., & Stillwell, A. M. (1995). When modesty prevails: Differential favorability of self-presentation to friends and strangers. *Journal of Personality and Social Psychology, 69,* 1120–1138.

Tidwell, M.-C. O., Reis, H. T., & Shaver, P. R. (1996). Attachment, attractiveness, and social interaction: A diary study. *Journal of Personality and Social Psychology, 71,* 729–745.

Tiedens, L. Z., & Fragale, A. R. (2003). Power moves: Complementarity in dominant and submissive nonverbal behavior. *Journal of Personality and Social Psychology, 84,* 558–568.

Toma, C. L., & Carlson, C. L. (2015). How do Facebook users believe they come across in their profiles?: A meta-perception approach to investigating Facebook self-preentation. *Communication Research Reports, 32,* 93–101.

Tomaskovic-Devey, D., Zimmer, C., Strainback, K., Robinson, C., Taylor, T., & McTague, T. (2006). Documenting desegregation: Segregation in American workplaces by race, ethnicity, and sex, 1966–2003. *American Sociological Review, 71,* 565–588.

Tormala, Z. L., & Petty, R. E. (2004). Source credibility and attitude certainty: A metacognitive analysis of resistance to persuasion. *Journal of Consumer Psychology, 14,* 427–442.

Tormala, Z. L., Petty, R. E., & Brinol, P. (2002). Ease of retrieval effects in persuasion: A self-validation analysis. *Personality and Social Psychology Bulletin, 28,* 1700–1712.

Tormala, Z. L., & Rucker, D. D. (2007). Attitude certainty: A review of past findings and emerging perspectives. *Social and Personality Psychology Compass, 1,* 469–492.

Towles-Schwen, T., & Fazio, R. H. (2001). On the origins of racial attitudes: Correlates of childhood experiences. *Personality and Social Psychology Bulletin, 27,* 162–175.

Trafimow, D., Silverman, E., Fan, R., & Law, J. (1997). The effects of language and priming on the relative accessibility of the private self and collective self. *Journal of Cross-Cultural Psychology, 28,* 107–123.

Travis Seidl., J. N., Pastorek, N. J., Lillie, R., Rosenblatt, A., Troyanskaya, M., Miller, B. I., et al. (2015). Factors related to satisfaction with life in veterans with mild traumatic brain injury. *Rehabilitation Psychology, 60,* 335–343.

Tremblay, P. F., & Belchevski, M. (2004). Did the instigator intend to provoke? A key moderator in the relation between trait aggression and aggressive behaviour. *Aggressive Behavior, 30,* 409–424.

Trope, Y., & Liberman, N. (2003). Temporal construal. *Psychological Review, 110,* 401–421.

Tsai, J. (2007). Ideal affect: Cultural causes and behavioral consequences. *Perspectives on Psychological Science, 2,* 242–259.

Turner, J. C. (1991). *Social influence.* Pacific Grove, CA: Brooks/Cole.

Turner, J. C. (2005). Explaining the nature of power: A three-process theory. *European Journal of Social Psychology, 35,* 1–22.

Turner, J. C. (2006). Tyranny, freedom and social structure: Escaping our theoretical prisons. *British Journal of Social Psychology, 45,* 41–46.

Turner, J. C., & Onorato, R. S. (1999). Social identity, personality, and the self-concept: A self-categorization perspective. In T. R. Tyler, R. M. Kramer, & O. P. John (Eds.), *The psychology of the social self* (pp. 11–46). Mahwah, NJ: Erlbaum.

Twenge, J. M., Abebe, E. M., & Campbell, W. K. (2010). Fitting in or standing out: Trends in American parents' choices for children's names, 1880–2007. *Social Psychological and Personality Science, 1,* 19–25.

Twenge, J. M., Baumeister, R. J., Dewall, C. N., Ciarocco, N. J., & Bartels, J. M. (2007). Social exclusion decreases prosocial behavior. *Journal of Personality and Social Psychology, 92,* 56–66.

Twenge, J. M., & Campbell, W. K. (2008). Increases in positive self-views among high school students. *Psychological Science, 19,* 1082–1086.

Twenge, J. M., Konrath, S., Foster, J. D., Campbell, W. K., & Bushman, B. J. (2008). Egos inflating over time: A cross-temporal meta-analysis of the Narcissistic Personality Inventory. *Journal of Personality, 76,* 875–901.

Twenge, J. M., & Manis, M. M. (1998). First-name desirability and adjustment: Self-satisfaction, others' ratings, and family background. *Journal of Applied Social Psychology, 24,* 41–51.

Tybout, A. M., Sternthal, B., Malaviya, P., Bakamitsos, G. A., & Park, S. (2005). Information accessibility as a moderator of judgments: The role of content versus retrieval ease. *Journal of Consumer Research, 32,* 76–85.

Tykocinski, O. E. (2001). I never had a chance: Using hindsight tactics to mitigate disappointments. *Personality and Social Psychology Bulletin, 27,* 376–382.

Tykocinski, O. E. (2008). Insurance, risk, and magical thinking. *Personality and Social Psychology Bulletin, 34,* 1346–1356.

Tyler, Feldman, & Reichert, 2006 — in 12th edition reference list.

Tyler, J. M., & Feldman, R. S. (2004). Cognitive demand and self-presentation efforts: The influence of situational importance and interactions goal. *Self and Identity, 3,* 364–377.

Tyler, T. R., & Blader, S. (2000). *Cooperation in groups: Procedural justice, social identity and behavioral engagement.* Philadelphia: Psychology Press.

Tyler, T. R., & Blader, S. L. (2003). The group engagement model: Procedural justice, social identity, and cooperative behavior. *Personality and Social Psychology Review, 7,* 349–361.

Tyler, T. R., Boeckmann, R. J., Smith, H. J., & Huo, Y. J. (1997). *Social justice in a diverse society.* Boulder, CO: Westview.

U.S. Bureau of Labor Statistics. (2006). *Women in the labor force: A databook.* Report 996. Retrieved from www.bls.gov/news.release/pdf/atus.pdf

U.S. Census Bureau. (2007). *Statistical abstract of the United States: 2007.* Washington, DC: U.S. Government Printing Office.

U.S. Census Bureau, Population Division. (2012). *Projections of the population by sex, race, and Hispanic origin for the United States: 2015 to 2060 (NP2012-T4).* Retrieved from http://www.census.gov/population/projections/data/national/2012/summarytables.html

U.S. Department of Justice. (2003). *Sourcebook of criminal justice statistics.* Washington, DC: U.S. Government Printing Office.

Urbanski, L. (1992, May 21). Study uncovers traits people seek in friends. *The Evangelist,* 4.

Vaillancourt, R. (2010). *Gender differences in police-reported violent crime in Canada, 2008.* Ottawa, Canada: Canadian Centre for Justice Statistics, Statistics Canada. Retrieved from http://www.statcan.gc.ca/pub/85f0033m/85f0033m2010024-eng.pdf

Vakirtzis, A., & Roberts, C. S. (2012). Do women really like taken men? Results from a large questionnaire study. *Journal of Social, Evolutionary, and Cultural Psychology, 6,* 50–65.

Vallone, R. P., Griffin, D. W., Lin, S., & Ross, L. (1990). Overconfident prediction of future actions and outcomes by self and others. *Journal of Personality and Social Psychology, 58,* 582–592.

Van Berkum, J. J. A., Holleman, B., Nieuwland, M., Otten, M., & Murre, J. (2009). Right or wrong?: The brain's fast response to morally objectionable statements. *Psychological Science, 20,* 1092–1099.

Van Boven, L. (2005). Experientialism, materialism, and the pursuit of happiness. *Review of General Psychology, 9,* 132–142.

Van den Bos, K. (2009). Making sense of life: The existential self trying to deal with personal uncertainty. *Psychological Inquiry, 20,* 197–217.

Van den Bos, K., & Lind, E. A. (2002). Uncertainty management by means of fairness judgments. In M. P. Zanna (Ed.), *Advances in experimental social psychology* (Vol. 34, pp. 1–60). San Diego, CA: Academic Press.

Van Dick, R., Wagner, U., Pettigrew, T. F., Christ, O., Wolf, C., Petzel, T., et al. (2004). Role of perceived importance in intergroup contact. *Journal of Personality and Social Psychology, 87,* 211–227.

Van Ginkel, W. P., & Van Knippenberg, D. (2009). Knowledge about the distribution of information and group decision making: When and why does it work? *Organizational Behavior and Human Decision Processes, 108,* 218–229.

Van Lange, P. A. M., & Joireman, J. A. (2010). Social and temporal orientations in social dilemmas. In R. M. Kramer, A. E. Tenbrunsel, & M. H. Bazerman (Eds.), *Social decision making: Social dilemmas, social values, and ethical judgments* (pp. 71–94). New York: Routledge.

Van Overwalle, F. (1998). Causal explanation as constraint satisfaction: A critique and a feed forward connectionist alternative. *Journal of Personality and Social Psychology, 74,* 312–328.

Van Prooijen, J. W., van den Bos, K., Lind, E. A., & Wilke, H. A. M. (2006). How do people react to negative procedures? On the moderating role of authority's biased attitudes. *Journal of Experimental Social Psychology, 42,* 632–645.

Van Straaten, I., Holland, R. W., Finkenauer, C., Hollenstein, T., & Engels, R. C. M. E. (2010). Gazing behavior during mixed-sex interactions: Sex and attractiveness effects. *Archives of Sexual Behavior, 39,* 1055–1062.

Vanderbilt, A. (1957). *Amy Vanderbilt's complete book of etiquette.* Garden City, NY: Doubleday.

Vasquez, M. J. T. (2001). Leveling the playing field — Toward the emancipation of women. *Psychology of Women Quarterly, 25,* 89–97.

Vazire, S., & Mehl, M. R. (2008). Knowing me, knowing you: The accuracy and unique predictive validity of self-ratings and other-ratings of daily behavior. *Journal of Personality and Social Psychology, 95,* 1202–1216.

Vignovic, J. A., & Thompson, L. F. (2010). Computer-mediated cross-cultural collaboration: Attribution communication errors to the person versus the situation. *Journal of Applied Psychology, 95,* 265–276.

Visser, P. S., Bizer, G. Y., & Krosnick, J. A. (2006). Exploring the latent structure of strength-related attitude attributes. *Advances in Experimental Social Psychology, 38,* 1–67.

Visser, P. S., Krosnick, J. A., & Simmons, J. P. (2003). Distinguishing the cognitive and behavioral consequences of attitude and certainty: A new approach to testing the common-factor hypothesis. *Journal of Experimental Social Psychology, 39,* 118–141.

Vogel, T., Kutzner, F., Fiedler, K., & Freytag, P. (2010). Exploiting attractiveness in persuasion: Senders' implicit theories about receivers' processing motivation. *Personality and Social Psychology Bulletin, 36,* 830–842.

Vohs, K. D., Baumeister, R. F., Schmeichel, B. J., Twenge, J. M., Nelson, N. M., & Tice, D. M. (2008). Making choices impairs subsequent self-control: A limited-resource account of decision making, self-regulation, and active initiative. *Journal of Personality and Social Psychology, 94,* 883–898.

Vohs, K. D., Baumeister, R. F., Schmeichel, B. J., Twenge, J. M., Nelson, N. M., & Tice, D. M. (2014). Making choices impairs subsequent self-control: A limited-resource account of decision making, self-regulation, and active initiative. *Motivation Science, 1,* 19–42.

Vohs, K. D., & Heatherton, T. F. (2000). Self-regulatory failure: A resource-depletion approach. *Psychological Science, 11,* 249–254.

Vonk, R. (1998). The slime effect: Suspicion and dislike of likeable behavior toward superiors. *Journal of Personality and Social Psychology, 74,* 849–864.

Vonk, R. (1999). Differential evaluations of likeable and dislikeable behaviours enacted towards superiors and subordinates. *European Journal of Social Psychology, 29,* 139–146.

Vonk, R. (2002). Self-serving interpretations of flattery: Why ingratiation works. *Journal of Personality and Social Psychology, 82,* 515–526.

Vonofakou, C., Hewstone, M., & Voci, A. (2007). Contact with out-group friends as a predictor of meta-attitudinal strength and accessibility of attitudes toward gay men. *Journal of Personality and Social Psychology, 92,* 804–820.

Vorauer, J. D. (2006). An information search model of evaluative concerns in intergroup interaction. *Psychological Review, 113,* 862–886.

Walker, I., & Smith, H. J. (Eds.). (2002). *Relative deprivation: Specification, development and integration.* Cambridge, UK: Cambridge University Press.

Walsh, E. M., & Kiviniemi, M. T. (2014). Changing how I feel about the food: Experimentally manipulated affective associations with fruits change fruit choice behaviors. *Journal of Behavioral Medicine, 37,* 322–331.

Walster, E., & Festinger, L. (1962). The effectiveness of "overheard" persuasive communication. *Journal of Abnormal and Social Psychology, 65,* 395–402.

Walster, E., Walster, G. W., Piliavin, J., & Schmidt, L. (1973). "Playing hard-to-get": Understanding an elusive phenomenon. *Journal of Personality and Social Psychology, 26,* 113–121.

Walster, E. H., Walster, G. W., Berscheid, E., Austin, W., Traupmann, J., & Utne, M. K. (1978). *Equity: Theory and research.* Boston: Allyn & Bacon.

Walton, G. M., & Cohen, G. L. (2007). A question of belonging: Race, social fit, and achievement. *Journal of Personality and Social Psychology, 92,* 82–96.

Walton, G. M., & Cohen, G. L. (2011). A brief social-belonging intervention improves academic and health outcomes of minority students. *Science, 331,* 1447–1451.

Wang, D., Waldman, D. A., & Zhang, Z. (2014). A meta-analysis of shared leadership and team effectiveness. *Journal of Applied Psychology, 99,* 181–198.

Wang, J., Novemsky, N., Dhar, R., & Baumeister, R. F. (2010). Trade-offs and depletion in choice. *Journal of Marketing Research, 47,* 910–919.

Wann, D. L., & Branscombe, N. R. (1993). Sports fans: Measuring degree of identification with their team. *International Journal of Sport Psychology, 24,* 1–17.

Waters, H. F., Block, D., Friday, C., & Gordon, J. (1993, July 12). Networks under the gun. *Newsweek,* 64–66.

Watts, B. L. (1982). Individual differences in circadian activity rhythms and their effects on roommate relationships. *Journal of Personality, 50,* 374–384.

Wayne, S. J., & Liden, R. C. (1995). Effects of impression management on performance ratings: A longitudinal study. *Academy of Management Journal, 38,* 232–260.

Weathington, B. L., Cunningham, C. J. L., & Pittenger, D. J. (2010). *Research methods for the behavioral and social sciences.* Hoboken, NJ: Wiley.

Wegener, D. T., & Carlston, D. E. (2005). Cognitive processes in attitude formation and change. In D. Albarracin, B. T. Johnson, & M. P. Zanna (Eds.), *The handbook of attitudes* (pp. 493–542). Mahwah, NJ: Erlbaum.

Wegener, D. T., Petty, R. E., Smoak, N. D., & Fabrigar, L. R. (2004). Multiple routes to resisting attitude change. In E. S. Knowles & J. A. Linn (Eds.), *Resistance and persuasion* (pp. 13–38). Mahwah, NJ: Erlbaum.

Wegner, D. T., & Petty, R. E. (1994). Mood management across affective states: The hedonic contingency hypothesis. *Journal of Personality and Social Psychology, 66,* 1034–1048.

Weick, M., & Guinote, A. (2010). How long will it take?: Power biases time predictions. *Journal of Experimental Social Psychology, 46,* 595–604.

Weiner, B. (1985). An attributional theory of achievement motivation and emotion. *Psychological Review, 92,* 548–573.

Weiner, B. (1993). On sin versus sickness: A theory of perceived responsibility and social motivation. *American Psychologist, 48,* 957–965.

Weiner, B. (1995). *Judgments of responsibility: A foundation for a theory of social conduct.* New York: Guilford Press.

Weiss, A., Bates, T. C., & Luciano, M. (2008). Happiness is a personal(ity) thing: The genetic of personality and well-being in a representative sample. *Psychological Science, 19,* 205–210.

Weldon, E., & Mustari, L. (1988). Felt dispensability in groups of coactors: The effects of shared responsibility and explicit anonymity on cognitive effort. *Organizational Behavior and Human Decision Processes, 41,* 330–351.

Wells, G. L., Steblay, N. K., & Dysart, J. E. (2015). Double-blind photo lineups using actual eyewitnesses: An experimental test of a sequential versus simultaneous lineup procedure. *Law and Human Behavior, 39,* 1–14.

Weng, H. Y., Fox, A. S., Shackman, A. J., Stodola, D. E., Caldwell, J. Z. K., Olson, M. C., et al. (2013). Compassion training alters altruism and neural responding to suffering. *Psychological Science, 24,* 1171–1180.

Wheeler, S. C., Brinol, P., & Hermann, A. D. (2007). Resistance to persuasion as self-regulation: Ego-depletion and its effects on attitude change processes. *Journal of Experimental Social Psychology, 43,* 150–156.

Whiffen, V. E., Aube, J. A., Thompson, J. M., & Campbell, T. L. (2000). Attachment beliefs and interpersonal contexts associated with dependency and self-criticism. *Journal of Social and Clinical Psychology, 19,* 184–205.

Wilkins, A. C. (2008). "Happier than non-Christians": Collective emotions and symbolic boundaries among Evangelical Christians. *Social Psychology Quarterly, 71,* 281–301.

Wilkinson, R., & Pickett, K. (2010). *The spirit level: Why greater equality makes societies stronger.* New York: Bloomsbury Press.

Williams, J. E., & Best, D. L. (1990). *Sex and psyche: Gender and self viewed cross-culturally.* Newbury Park, CA: Sage.

Williams, K. D. (2001). *Ostracism: The power of silence.* New York: Guilford Press.

Williams, K. D., Harkins, S., & Latane, B. (1981). Identifiability as a deterrent to social loafing: Two cheering experiments. *Journal of Personality and Social Psychology, 40,* 303–311.

Williams, K. D., & Karau, S. J. (1991). Social loafing and social compensation: The effects of expectations of co-worker performance. *Journal of Personality and Social Psychology, 61,* 570–581.

Williams, K. D., & Nida, S. A. (2011). Ostracism: Consequences and coping. *Current Directions in Psychological Science, 20,* 71–75.

Williams, M. J., Paluck, E. L., & Spencer-Rodgers, J. (2010). The masculinity of money: Automatic stereotypes predict gender differences in estimated salaries. *Psychology of Women Quarterly, 34,* 7–20.

Willingham, D. T., & Dunn, E. W. (2003). What neuroimaging and brain localization can do, cannot, and should not do for social psychology. *Journal of Personality and Social Psychology, 85,* 662–671.

Willis, J., & Todorov, A. (2006). First impression: Making up your mind after a 100-ms exposure to a face. *Psychological Science, 17,* 592–598.

Wilson, A. E., & Ross, M. (2001). From chump to champ: People's appraisals of their earlier and present selves. *Journal of Personality and Social Psychology, 80,* 572–584.

Wilson, D. W. (1981). Is helping a laughing matter? *Psychology, 18,* 6–9.

Wilson, J. P., & Petruska, R. (1984). Motivation, model attributes, and prosocial behavior. *Journal of Personality and Social Psychology, 46,* 458–468.

Wilson, R. E., Gosling, S. D., & Graham, L. T. (2012). A review of Facebook research in the social sciences. *Perspectives on Psychological Science, 7,* 203–220.

Wilson, T. D., & Dunn, E. W. (2004). Self-knowledge: Its limits, value, and potential for improvement. *Annual Review of Psychology, 55,* 493–518.

Wilson, T. D., & Kraft, D. (1993). Why do I love thee?: Effects of repeated introspections about a dating relationship on attitudes toward the relationship. *Personality and Social Psychology Bulletin, 19,* 409–418.

Wilson, T., Milosevic, A., Carrol, M., Hart, K., & Hibbard, S. (2008). Physical health status in relation to self-forgiveness and other-forgiveness in healthy college students. *Journal of Health Psychology, 13,* 798–803.

Winograd, E., Goldstein, F. C., Monarch, E. S., Peluso, J. P., & Goldman, W. P. (1999). The mere exposure effect in patients with Alzheimer's disease. *Neuropsychology, 13,* 41–46.

Wisco, B. E., Marx, B. P., Sloan, D. M., Gorman, K. R., Kulish, A. L., & Pineles, S. L. (2015). Self-distancing from trauma memories reduces physiological but not subjective emotional reactivity among veterans with posttraumatic stress disorder. *Clinical Psychological Science, 3,* 956–963.

Wisman, A., & Koole, S. L. (2003). Hiding in the crowd: Can mortality salience promote affiliation with others who oppose one's world view? *Journal of Personality and Social Psychology, 84,* 511–526.

Wohl, M. J. A., & Branscombe, N. R. (2005). Forgiveness and collective guilt assignment to historical perpetrator groups depend on level of social category inclusiveness. *Journal of Personality and Social Psychology, 88,* 288–303.

Wohl, M. J. A., Branscombe, N. R., & Lister, J. J. (2014). When the going gets tough: Economic threat increases financial risk-taking in games of chance. *Social Psychological and Personality Science, 5,* 211–217.

Wohl, M. J. A., Branscombe, N. R., & Reysen, S. (2010). Perceiving your group's future to be in jeopardy: Extinction threat induces collective angst and the desire to strengthen the ingroup. *Personality and Social Psychology Bulletin, 36,* 898–910.

Wohl, M. J. A., Giguère, B., Branscombe, N. R., & McVicar, D. N. (2011). One day we might be no more: Collective angst and protective action from potential distinctiveness loss. *European Journal of Social Psychology, 41,* 289–300.

Wohl, M. J. A., Pychyl, T. A., & Bennett, S. H. (2010). I forgive myself, now I can study: How self-forgiveness for procrastinating can reduce future procrastination. *Personality and Individual Differences, 48,* 803–808.

Wolf, S. (2010). Counterfactual thinking in the jury room. *Small Group Research, 41,* 474–494.

Wood, J. V. (1989). Theory and research concerning social comparisons of personal attributes. *Psychological Bulletin, 106,* 231–248.

Wood, J. V., Perunovic, W. Q. E., & Lee, J. W. (2009). Positive self-statements: Power for some, peril for others. *Psychological Science, 20,* 860–866.

Wood, J. V., & Wilson, A. E. (2003). How important is social comparison? In M. R. Leary & J. P. Tangney (Eds.), *Handbook of self and identity* (pp. 344–366). New York: Guilford Press.

Wood, W., & Quinn, J. M. (2003). Forewarned and forearmed? Two meta-analytic syntheses of forewarning of influence appeals. *Psychological Bulletin, 129,* 119–138.

Wood, W., Quinn, J. M., & Kashy, D. A. (2002). Habits in everyday life: Thought, emotion, and action. *Journal of Personality and Social Psychology, 83,* 1281–1297.

Wright, S. C., Aron, A., McLaughlin-Volpe, T., & Ropp, S. A. (1997). The extended contact effect: Knowledge of cross-group friendships and prejudice. *Journal of Personality and Social Psychology, 73,* 73–90.

Wright, S. C., Taylor, D. M., & Moghaddam, F. M. (1990). Responding to membership in a disadvantaged group: From acceptance to collective protest. *Journal of Personality and Social Psychology, 58,* 994–1003.

Wright, T. A., & Cropanzano, R. (2000). Psychological well-being and job satisfaction as predictors of job performance. *Journal of Occupational Health Psychology, 5,* 84–94.

Wu, L.-Z., Zhang, H., Chiu, R. K., Kwan, H. K., & He, X. (2014). Hostile attribution bias and negative reciprocity beliefs exacerbate incivility's effects on interpersonal deviance. *Journal of Business Ethics, 120,* 189–199.

Wuensch, K. L., Castellow, W. A., & Moore, C. H. (1991). Effects of defendant attractiveness and type of crime on juridic judgment. *Journal of Social Behavior and Personality, 6,* 713–724.

Wyer, R. S., Jr., & Srull, T. K. (Eds.). (1994). *Handbook of social cognition* (2nd ed., Vol. 1). Hillsdale, NJ: Erlbaum.

Xu, J., & Roberts, R. E. (2010). The power of positive emotions: It's a matter of life or death — subjective well-being and longevity over 28 years in a general population. *Health Psychology, 29,* 9–19.

Xu, Y., Farver, J. M., & Pauker, K. (2015). Ethnic identity and self-esteem among Asian and European Americans: When a minority is the majority and the majority is a minority. *European Journal of Social Psychology, 45,* 62–76.

Yeager, D. S., & Dweck, C. S. (2012). Mindsets that promote resilience: When students believe that personal characteristics can be developed. *Educational Psychologist, 47,* 1–13.

Yoder, J. D., & Berendsen, L. L. (2001). "Outsider within" the firehouse: African American and white women firefighters. *Psychology of Women Quarterly, 25,* 27–36.

Yukl, G. A. (1998). *Leadership in organizations* (4th ed.). Englewood Cliffs, NJ: Prentice-Hall.

Yukl, G. A. (2006). *Leadership in organizations* (6th ed.). Upper Saddle River, NJ: Prentice-Hall.

Yukl, G., & Falbe, C. M. (1991). Importance of different power sources in downward and lateral relations. *Journal of Applied Psychology, 76,* 416–423.

Yzerbyt, V. Y., Corneille, O., & Estrada, C. (2001). The interplay of subjective essentialism and entitativity in the formation of stereotypes. *Personality and Social Psychology Review, 5,* 141–155.

Yzerbyt, V. Y., & Demoulin, S. (2010). Intergroup relations. In S. T. Fiske, D. T. Gilbert, & G. Lindzey (Eds.), *Handbook of social psychology* (5th ed., Vol. 2, pp. 1023–1083). Hoboken, NJ: Wiley.

Yzerbyt, V., Rocher, S., & Schradron, G. (1997). Stereotypes as explanations: A subjective essentialist view of group perception. In R. Spears, P. J. Oakes, N. Ellemers, & S. A. Haslam (Eds.), *The social psychology of stereotyping and group life* (pp. 20–50). Oxford: Blackwell.

Zaccaro, S. J. (2007). Trait-based perspective on leadership. *American Psychologist, 62,* 6–16.

Zajonc, R. B. (1965). Social facilitation. *Science, 149,* 269–274.

Zajonc, R. B. (2001). Mere exposure: A gateway to the subliminal. *Current Directions in Psychological Science, 10,* 224–228.

Zajonc, R. B., Heingartner, A., & Herman, E. M. (1969). Social enhancement and impairment of performance in the cockroach. *Journal of Personality and Social Psychology, 13,* 83–92.

Zaki, J. (2014). Empathy: A motivated account. *Psychological Bulletin, 140,* 1608–1647.

Zebrowitz, L. A., Collins, M. A., & Dutta, R. (1998). The relationship between appearance and personality across the life span. *Personality and Social Psychology Bulletin, 24,* 736–749.

Zechmeister, J. S., & Romero, C. (2002). Victim and offender accounts of interpersonal conflict: Autobiographical narratives of forgiveness and unforgiveness. *Journal of Personality and Social Psychology, 82,* 675–686.

Zhang, S., Schmader, T., & Forbes, C. (2009). The effects of gender stereotypes on women's career choice: Opening the glass door. In M. Barreto, M. K. Ryan, & M. T. Schmitt (Eds.), *The glass ceiling in the 21st century* (pp. 125–150). Washington, DC: American Psychological Association.

Zhao, H., & Seibert, S. C. (2006). The big five personality dimensions and entrepreneurial status: A meta-analytical review. *Journal of Applied Psychology, 91,* 259–271.

Zhao, H., Seibert, S. E., & Hills, G. E. (2005). The mediating role of self-efficacy in the development of entrepreneurial intentions. *Journal of Applied Psychology, 90,* 1265–1272.

Zhong, C-B., Bohns, V. K., & Gino, F. (2010). Good lamps are the best police: Darkness increase dishonesty and self-interested behavior. *Psychological Science, 21,* 311–314.

Zhong, C-B., & Leonardelli, G. J. (2008). Cold and lonely: Does social exclusion literally feel cold? *Psychological Science, 19,* 838–842.

Zhou, Z. E., Yan, Y., Che, X.X., & Meier, L. L. (2015). Effect of workplace incivility on end-of-work negative affect: Examining individual and organizational moderators in a daily diary study. *Journal of Occupational Health Psychology, 20,* 117–130.

Zhu, S., Tse, S., Cheung, S-H., & Oyserman, D. (2014). Will I get there? Effects of parental support on children's possible selves. *British Journal of Educational Psychology, 84,* 435–453.

Zillmann, D. (1979). *Hostility and aggression.* Hillsdale, NJ: Erlbaum.

Zillmann, D. (1988). Cognition-excitation interdependencies in aggressive behavior. *Aggressive Behavior, 14,* 51–64.

Zillmann, D. (1994). Cognition-excitation interdependencies in the escalation of anger and angry aggression. In M. Potegal & J. F. Knutson (Eds.), *The dynamics of aggression* (pp. 45–71). Hillsdale, NJ: Erlbaum.

Zillmann, D., Baron, R. A., & Tamborini, R. (1981). The social costs of smoking: Effects of tobacco smoke on hostile behavior. *Journal of Applied Social Psychology, 11,* 548–561.

Zimbardo, P. G. (1970). The human choice: Individuation, reason, and order versus deindividuation, impulse, and chaos. In W. J. Arnold & D. Levine (Eds.), *Nebraska Symposium on Motivation* (Vol. 17, pp. 237–307). Lincoln: University of Nebraska Press.

Zimbardo, P. G. (2007). *The Lucifer effect: How good people turn evil.* New York: Random House.

Zimring, F. E. (2004). Firearms, violence, and the potential impact of firearm control. *Journal of Law, Medicine, and Ethics, 32,* 34–37.

Zuckerman, M., & O'Loughlin, R. E. (2006). Self-enhancement by social comparison: A prospective analysis. *Personality and Social Psychology Bulletin, 32,* 751–760.

Credits

Photo Credits

Cover AntoinetteW/Shutterstock

Chapter 1 Pages 1: oneinchpunch/Fotolia; 3: AF archive/Alamy Stock Photo; 5 (bottom left): uremar/Shutterstock; 5 (bottom right): Konstantin Shevtsov/123RF; 5 (center): Wdstock/iStock/Getty Images Plus/Getty Images; 6 (bottom left): Tomas Abad/Alamy Stock Photo; 6 (bottom right): Rey T. Byhre/Alamy Stock Photo; 9 (bottom left): Auremar/Fotolia; 9 (bottom right): Wavebreakmedia/Shutterstock; 12: Fancy/Alamy Stock Images; 13 (bottom left): Bruce Laurance/DigitalVision/Getty Images; 13 (bottom right): Robert Daly/OJO Images/Getty Images; 16: Uniquely India/Age Fotostock; 17: oneinchpunch/Fotolia; 18: Mark Harmel/Alamy Stock Photo; 24: Warchi/iStock/Getty Images Plus/Getty Images; 28: PeopleImages/E+/Getty Images; 35: Marty Heitner/The Image Works

Chapter 2 Pages 38: Shots Studio/Shutterstock; 40: Syda Productions/Fotolia; 41: Gazmandhu/Shutterstock; 45: Shots Studio/Shutterstock; 47 (bottom left and right): Pechagin/Fotolia; 49 (bottom left): Stocktributor/Fotolia; 49 (bottom right): Gemenacom/Fotolia; 59: Jerry King/Cartoon Stock; 60: Deeaf/Fotolia; 64 (bottom left): Rainbow33/Alamy Stock Photo; 64 (bottom right): Thinkstock Images/Stockbyte/Getty Images; 65: Pictorial Press Ltd/Alamy Stock Photo; 69 (bottom left): micro10x/Shutterstock; 69 (bottom right): Rido/123RF

Chapter 3 Pages 73: Michaeljung/Fotolia; 74: Moviestore collection Ltd/Alamy Stock Photo; 76: Michaeljung/Fotolia; 77 (bottom left): YanLev/Shutterstock; 77 (center): Jochen Schoenfeld/Shutterstock; 77 (bottom right): Johan Larson/Shutterstock; 79 (bottom left): Stokkete/Shutterstock; 79 (bottom right): violetblue/Shutterstock; 81: Uber Images/Fotolia; 83: Wallenrock/Shutterstock; 86 (bottom left): Driving South/Fotolia; 86 (bottom right): Goodluz/Shutterstock; 89: Fotofeel/Fotolia; 96: Paul Chinn/San Francisco Chronicle/Corbis; 98: Matthew T. Carroll/Moment Open/Getty images; 102: Jolopes/Fotolia; 104: Africa Studio/Fotolia

Chapter 4 Pages 107: PeskyMonkey/E+/Getty Images; 108: Gil C/Shutterstock; 110 (bottom): PeskyMonkey/E+/Getty Images; 110 (top): Peter Steiner/The New Yorker Collection/The Cartoon Bank; 112: Ai825/Shutterstock; 113 (bottom): colematt/iStock/Getty Images Plus/Getty Images; 113 (top): Tim Cordell/CartoonStock; 114: B.O'Kane/Alamy Stock Photo; 123 (right): Patronestaff/Fotolia; 123 (left): hurricanehank/Shutterstock; 126: Andresr/Shutterstock; 133 (bottom right): WavebreakmediaMicro/Fotolia; 133 (bottom left): Caiaimage/Getty Images; 134: Bonnie Kamin/PhotoEdit; 135: Tasos Markou/NurPhoto/Sipa USA/Newscom; 140: ZUMA Press, Inc./Alamy Stock Photo

Chapter 5 Pages 145: Andresr/Shutterstock; 147 (top right): Apenigina/Fotolia; 147 (top left): rawpixel/123RF; 148: Justin Bilicki/CartoonStock; 150 (center): Allstar Picture Library/Alamy Stock Photo; 150 (bottom right): Everett Collection Inc./Alamy Stock Photo; 150 (bottom left): Byron Purvis/AdMedia/Newscom; 153: Nicoleta Ionescu/Alamy Stock Photo; 155: Andresr/Shutterstock; 158: Duris Guillaume/Fotolia; 167: Francisco Diez Photography/Moment/Getty Images; 168: Everett Collection Inc / Alamy Stock Photo; 169: Creativa Images/Shutterstock; 172: Pressmaster/Shutterstock; 180: Photographee.eu/Fotolia

Chapter 6 Pages 184: David Zalubowski/AP Images; 185: David Zalubowski/AP Images; 186: Ray Jones/UPI/Newscom; 188: GL Archive / Alamy Stock Photo; 190: Andrew Burton/AP Images; 193: Warren Miller/The New Yorker Collection/The Cartoon Bank; 195 (bottom left): U.S. State Department; 195 (bottom right): federalreserve.gov; 198 (bottom left): Mat Hayward/Shutterstock; 198 (bottom right): Aflo Co., Ltd./Alamy Stock Photo; 200 (left, center and right): Nyla R. Branscombe; 201: Monkey Business/Fotolia; 208 (left and right): Peter Horree / Alamy Stock Photo; 213: GL Archive / Alamy Stock Photo

Chapter 7 Pages 222: AVAVA/Shutterstock; 224 (top left): blueskyimage/123RF; 224 (top right): Jeff Greenberg/PhotoEdit; 225: wavebreakmedia/Shutterstock; 228: Monkey Business Images/Shutterstock; 233: Film Fanatique/Alamy Stock Photo; 234 (bottom left): Allstar Picture Library/Alamy Stock Photo; 234 (bottom right): ZUMA Press, Inc./Alamy Stock Photo; 235: Lemley , 2000., p., 42; 236 (top) Michael Witman/iStock/Getty Images; 236 (bottom left): SuperStock/SuperStock; 236 (bottom right): Image Source/Alamy Stock Photo; 237: Age fotostock/Alamy Stock Photo; 243: AVAVA/Shutterstock; 250: Glasshouse Images/Alamy Stock Photo; 252 (bottom left): Richard Ellis/Alamy Stock Photo; 252 (bottom right): Richard Ellis/Alamy Stock Photo; 253 (bottom right): Consumer Trends / Alamy Stock Photo; 253 (bottom left): NBC Television/Getty Images; 256: Robert Baron

Chapter 8 Pages 259: viappy/Fotolia; 260: mokee81/Fotolia; 263: Begsteiger/Insadco/Age Fotostock; 267 (left and right): Hill Street Studios/Blend Images/Getty Images; 268: Keith Morris/Alamy Stock Photo; 272 (left and right): (c) Philip G. Zimbardo, Inc.; 273: Corepics VOF/Shutterstock; 275: AnnaDe/Shutterstock; 277: viappy/Fotolia; 281: Viacheslav Iakobchuk/Fotolia; 285 (left and right): From The Film Obedience, Copyright 1968 by Stanley Milgram, Copyright renewed 1993 by Alexandra Milgram and distributed by Alexander Street Press.; 293: Gareth Boden/Pearson Education Ltd

Chapter 9 Pages 295: mykeyruna/Shutterstock; 296: Stove-Tec.; 301: mykeyruna/Shutterstock; 302: Sue Ogrocki/AP Images; 306 (top): Tony Dejak/AP Images; 306 (center): HANDOUT/KRT/Newscom; 306 (bottom): Images-USA/Alamy Stock Photo; 307: CandyBox Images/Shutterstock; 310: YankeePhotography/Alamy Stock Photo; 311 (bottom left): John Brueske/ Shutterstock; 311 (bottom right): Sozaijiten; 313: Judie Long / Alamy Stock Photo; 314: Christine Langer-Pueschel/Shutterstock; 315: iStock/Getty Images; 316: vadymvdrobot/Fotolia

Chapter 10 Pages 323: Vladimir Mucibabic/Shutterstock; 325 (right): IPGGutenbergUKLtd/iStock / Getty Images; 325 (left): MindStudio/Pearson Education Ltd; 326: ZUMA Press,Inc./Alamy Stock Photo; 328: Pete Saloutos/Shutterstock; 333: Aaron Amat/Shutterstock; 337 (bottom): SanjMur/Fotolia; 337 (top): Courtesy of Albert Bandura.; 342: Rick Rycroft/AP images; 347: 123RF; 351: Laura Ashley Alamy Stock Photo; 355: Vladimir Mucibabic/Shutterstock

Chapter 11 Pages 358: Hero Images/Getty images; 359 (bottom right): Endostock/Fotolia; 359 (bottom left): Vgstudio/Shutterstock; 361(right): Michaeljung/Fotolia; 361 (left): Minerva Studio/Shutterstock; 362 (left): BlueSkyImage/Shutterstock; 362 (right): Andrey_Popov/Shutterstock; 366 (left): Edyta Pawlowska/Fotolia; 366 (right): DigitalVision/Getty Images; 368: Charles Barsotti The New Yorker Collection/The Cartoon Bank; 370: Ringo Chiu/ZUMA Press/Newscom; 371: Archie Carpenter/UPI/Newscom; 373: J.Scott Applewhite/AP images; 375 (left and right): Nyla R. Branscombe; 377: Hero Images/Getty images; 379 (bottom left): John Lund/Blend Images/Alamy Stock Photo; 379 (bottom right): Luca Bruno/AP images; 381: Production Perig/Fotolia; 395: Morgan DessallesJMP/ABACAUSA.COM/Newscom

Chapter 12 Pages 398: Monkey Business/Fotolia; 399: Stacey Ilyse/ZUMA Press/Newscom; 402: Monkey Business/Fotolia; 404: Antonio Guillem/Shutterstock; 409: Maridav/Fotolia; 411: Monkey Business/Fotolia; 415: Dariush M/Shutterstock.; 416: Skocko/Shutterstock; 418:

Bikeriderlondon/Shutterstock; 423 (bottom left): Wavebreakmedia-Micro/Fotolia; 423 (bottom right): Vojtch Vlk/AGE Fotostock; 426 (top left up): Morgan David de Lossy/Corbis; 426 (top right): Blend Images/Superstock; 426 (top left down): mevans/ E+/Getty Images; 428 (top left): imtmphoto/123RF; 428 (top left): Image 100/Glow Images/Corbis; 430: Chris Madden/Cartoonstock; 433: Monkey Business Images/Shutterstock

Text Credits

Chapter 1 Pages 2: Quote by Dalai Lama; 2: Quote by John Lennon; 2: Quote by Martin Luther King, Jr.; 2: Quote by Bob Marley; 2: Quote by David Byrne; 2: Quote by Robert Alan Silverstein; 2: Quote by Robert Putnam; 7: From "Origami to software development: A review of studies on judgment-based predictions of performance time" by Torleif Halkjelsvik, Magne Jørgensen, Magne in Psychological Bulletin, Vol 138(2), 238-271, © March 2012 American Psychological Association; 11: Nyla Branscombe; 17: From "Choking on the money: Reward-based performance decrements are associated with midbrain activity" by ean Mobbs, Demis Hassabis, Ben Seymour, Jennifer L. Marchant, Nikolaus Weiskopf, Raymond J. Dolan, and Christopher D. Frith in Psychological Science, 20, 955–962, © 2009 Sage Publications; 29: Nyla Branscombe; 32: Nyla Branscombe; 19: Based on data from Montgomery, K. J., Seeherman, K. R., & Haxby, J. V. (2009). The well-tempered social brain. Psychological Science, 20, 1211–1213: Sage Publications, © 2016 by Nyla Branscombe.

Chapter 2 Pages 45: Based on Caruso, E. M. (2008). Use of experienced retrieval ease in self and social judgments. Journal of Experimental Social Psychology, 44, 148–155. © Nyla Branscombe; 46: Based on data from Englich, B., Mussweiler, T., & Strack, F. (2006). Playing dice with criminal sentences: The influence of irrelevant anchors on experts' judicial decision making. Personality and Social Psychology Bulletin, 32, 188–200. © Nyla Branscombe; 52: Based on findings reported by Sparrow, B., & Wegner, D. M. (2006). Unpriming: The deactivation of thoughts through expression. Journal of Personality and Social Psychology, 9, 1009–1019. © Nyla Branscombe; 52: Based on Mark J. Landau, Brian P. Meier, and Lucas A. Keefer. Psychological Bulletin, A Metaphor-Enriched Social Cognition.Vol 136(6), Nov 2010, 1045-1067. American Psychological Association, © Nyla Branscombe; 53: Based on research by Landau, M. J., Meier, B. P., & Keefer, L. A. (2010). A metaphor-enriched social cogntion. Psychological Bulletin, 136, 1045–1067.© Nyla Branscombe; 56: Based on suggestions by Cesario, J., Plaks, J. E., & Higgins, E. (2006). Automatic social behavior as motivated preparation to interact. Journal of Personality and Social Psychology, 90, 893–910. © Nyla Branscombe; 57: Based on data from Dijksterhuis, A., & van Olden, Z. (2006). On the benefits of thinking unconsciously: Unconscious thought can increase post-choice satisfaction. Journal of Experimental Social Psychology, 42, 627–631. © Nyla Branscombe; 61: Based on research by Weick, M., & Guinote, A. (2010). How long will it take?: Power biases time predictions. Journal of Experimental Social Psychology, 46, 595–604. © Nyla Branscombe; 66: Quote by Nathaniel LeTonnerre; 67: Nyla Branscombe.

Chapter 3 Pages 76: Quote by Marcus Tullius Cicero; 83: Nyla Branscombe; 83: Nyla Branscombe; 84: Nyla Branscombe; 90: Nyla Branscombe; 91: From "It Was Meant to Happen: Explaining Cultural Variations in Fate Attributions" by Ara Norenzayan, Albert Lee in Journal of Personality and Social Psychology, Vol. 98, No. 5, 702–720, © 2010 American Psychological Association; 92: Based on data from Norenzayan, A., & Lee, A. (2010). It was meant to happen: Explaining cultural variations in fate attributions. Journal of Personality and Social Psychology, 98, 702–720. American Psychological Association, © Nyla Branscombe; 94: Based on data from Nisbett, R. E., Caputo, C., Legbant, P., & Marecek, J. (1973). Behavior as seen by the actor and as seen by the observer. Journal of Personality and Social Psychology, 27, 154–164, © Nyla Branscombe; 97: From Field theory in social science: Selected theoretical papers by Kurt Lewin in New York: Harper & Row, © 1976 University Of Chicago Press; 100: From ""Forming impressions of personality"" by Solomon E. Asch in The Journal

of Abnormal and Social Psychology, Vol 41(3), 258-290, © July 1946 American Psychological Association; 100: From Gestalt psychologist Kurt Koffka, © by Kurt Koffka; 100: From "Forming impressions of personality" by Solomon E. Asch in The Journal of Abnormal and Social Psychology, Vol 41(3), 258-290, © July 1946 American Psychological Association; 101: From "Forming impressions of personality" by Solomon E. Asch in The Journal of Abnormal and Social Psychology, Vol 41(3), 258-290, © July 1946 American Psychological Association; 103: Nyla Branscombe; 104: Nyla Branscombe.

Chapter 4 Pages 109: "As You Like It Act 2, scene 7 in First Folio, 1623 by William Shakespeare; 111: From "Knowing me, knowing you: the accuracy and unique predictive validity of self-ratings and other-ratings of daily behavior" by Simine Vazire, Matthias R. Mehl in Journal of Personality and Social Psychology, Vol. 95, No. 5, 1202–1216, © 2008 American Psychological Association; 115: From "Why do I love thee?: Effects of repeated introspections about a dating relationship on attitudes toward the relationship." by Timothy D. Wilson, Dolores Kraft in Personality and Social Psychology Bulletin, 19, 409–418, © 1993 Sage Publications; 116: Based on "Temporal differences in trait self-ascription: When the self is seen as an other" by Emily Pronin, Lee Ross in Journal of Personality and Social Psychology, 2006, Vol. 90, No. 2, 197–209, American Psychological Association. © Nyla Branscombe; 119: Based on Oakes, P. J., Haslam, S. A., & Turner, J. C. (1994). Stereotyping and social reality. Wiley-Blackwell. © Nyla Branscombe; 120: Based on data from Guimond, S., Branscombe, N. R., Brunot, S., Buunk, B. P., Chatard, A., Désert, M., et al. (2007). Culture, gender, and the self: Variations and impact of social comparison processes. Journal of Personality and Social Psychology, 92, 1118–1134. American Psychological Association. © Nyla Branscombe; 122: Based on research by LeBoeuf, R. A., Shafir, E., & Bayuk, J. B. (2010). The conflicting choices of alternating selves. Organizational Behavior and Human Decision Processes, 111, 48–61. © Nyla Branscombe; 124: Nyla Branscombe; 130: From "The intersection of self-evaluation maintenance and social identity theories: Intragroup judgment in interpersonal and intergroup contexts" by Michael T. Schmitt, Paul J. Silvia, Nyla R. Branscombe in Personality and Social Psychology Bulletin, 26, 1598–1606, © 2000 Sage Publications; 132: From "Measuring Global Self-Esteem: Construct Validation of a Single-Item Measure and the Rosenberg Self-Esteem Scale" by Robins, R. W., Hendin, H. M., & Trzesniewski, K. H. in Personality and Social Psychology Bulletin, 27, 151-161, © 2001 Sage Publications; 132: "From Society and the adolescent self-image by Morris Rosenberg, © 1965 Princeton University Press; 134: From The power of positive thinking by Norman Vincent Peale, © Prentice hall; 138: Based on data from Schmitt, M.T., Branscombe, N.R., Postmes, T., & Garcia, A. (2014); 139: Nyla Branscombe.

Chapter 5 Pages 147: From Obama on Obama on Climate by Thomas L. Friedman, © June 7, 2014 The New York Times; 149: Nyla Branscombe; 151: Based on Morison, L. A., Cozzolino, P. J., & Orbell, S. (2010). Temporal perspective and parental intention to accept the human papilomavirus vaccination for their daughter. British Journal of Health Psychology, 15, 151–165. John Wiley and Sons. © Nyla Branscombe; 154: Based on Falomir-Pichastor, J. M., Munoz-Rojas, D., Invernizzi, F., & Mugny, G. (2004). Perceived in-group threat as a factor moderating the influence of in-group norms on discrimination against foreigners. European Journal of Social Psychology, 34, 135–153. © Nyla Branscombe; 157: Based on data in Fleming, M. A., & Petty, R. E. (2000). Identity and persua- sion: An elaboration likelihood approach. In D. J. Terry & M. A. Hogg (Eds.), Attitudes, behavior, and social context (pp. 171–199). Mahwah, NJ: Erlbaum. © Nyla Branscombe; 161: Based on research by Clarkson, J. J., Tormala, Z. L., DeSensi, D. L., & Wheeler, S. C. (2009). Does attitude certainty beget self-certainty? Journal of Experimental Social Psychology, 45, 436–439. Petrocelli, J. V., Tormala, Z. L., & Rucker, D. D. (2007). Unpacking attitude certainty: Attitude clarity and attitude correctness. Journal of Personality and Social Psychology, 92, 30–41. © Nyla Branscombe; 165: Nyla Branscombe; 167: From Communication and persuasion: Psychological studies of opinion change by Hovland, C. I., Janis, I. L., & Kelley, H. H., © 1953 Yale University Press; 171: Based on suggestions by Petty, R. E., & Cacioppo, J. T. (1986). The elaboration likelihood model of persuasion. In L. Berkowitz (Ed.), Advances in experimental social psychology (Vol. 19, pp. 123–205) Academic Press. © Nyla Branscombe; 175: From "Individual Differences in Resistance to Persuasion: The Role of Beliefs and Meta-Beliefs" by Pablo Brinõl, Derek D. Rucker, Zakary L. Tormala, and Richard E. Petty in Resistance and Persuasion by Eric S. Knowles, Jay A. Linn, © 2004 Lawrence Erlbaum Associates, Inc.; 176: Based on data from Wheeler, S. C., Brinol, P., & Hermann, A. D. (2007). Resistance to persuasion as self-regulation: Ego-depletion and its effects on attitude change processes. Journal of Experimental Social Psychology, 43, 150–156. © Nyla Branscombe; 178: Nyla Branscombe.

Chapter 6 189: Based on Kaiser, C. R., Drury, B. J., Spalding, K. E., Cheryan, S., & O'Brien, L.T. (2009). The ironic consequences of Obama's election: Decreased support for social justice. Journal of Experimental Social Psychology, 45, 556–559. © Nyla Branscombe; 191: From "Beyond prejudice: Toward a sociocultural psychology of racism and oppression."by Adams, G., Biernat, M., Branscombe, N. R., Crandall, C. S., & Wrightsman, L. S in Commemorating Brown: The social psychology of racism and discrimination, 215–246, © 2008 American Psychological Association; 192: From "Are people prejudiced against women? Some answers from research on attitudes, gender stereotypes, and judgments of competence" by Eagly, A. H., & Mladinic, A. in W. Sroebe & M. Hewstone (Eds.), European review of social psychology (Vol. 5, pp. 1–35), © 1994 John Wiley & Sons; 192: Based on Deaux & Kite, 1993; Eagly & Mladinic, 1994; Fiske, Cuddy, Glick, & Xu, 2002; 195: Based on Ryan, M. K., Haslam, S. A., Hersby, M. D., Kulich, C., & Wilson-Kovacs, M. D. (2009). The stress of working on the edge: Implications of glass cliffs for both women and organizations. In M. Barreto, M. K. Ryan, & M. T. Schmitt (Eds.), The glass it ceiling in the 21st century (pp. 153–169). Washington, DC: American Psychological Association. © Nyla Branscombe; 196: From "Putting the "affirm" into affirmative action: Preferential selection and academic performance" by Brown, R. P., Charnsangavej, T., Keough, K. A., Newman, M. L., & Rentfrow, P. J. in Journal of Personality and Social Psychology, 79, 736–747, © American Psychological Association; 196: Based on Brown, R. P., Charnsangavej, T., Keough, K. A., Newman, M. L., & Rentfrow, P. J. (2000). Putting the "affirm" into affirmative action: Preferential selection and academic performance. Journal of Personality and Social Psychology, 79, 736–747. © Nyla Branscombe; 199: Based on DePaulo, B. M., & Morris, W. L. (2006). The unrecognized stereotyping and discrimination against singles. Current Directions in Psychological Science, 15, 251–254. © Nyla Branscombe; 203: Based on Cottrell, C. A., & Neuberg, S. L. (2005). Different emotional reactions to different groups: A sociofunctional threat-based approach to "prejudice." Journal of Personality and Social Psychology, 88, 770–789. © Nyla Branscombe; 204: Based on DeSteno, D., Dasgupta, N., Bartlett, M. Y., & Cajdric, A. (2004). Prejudice from thin air: The effect of emotion on automatic intergroup attitudes. Psychological Science, 15, 319–324. © Nyla Branscombe; 206: Based on Branscombe & Wann, 1994; Rudman & Fairchild, 2004.© Nyla Branscombe; 209: "Nyla Branscombe; 209: Based on Crandall, C. S., Eshleman, A., & O'Brien, L. T. (2002). Social norms and the expression and suppression of prejudice: The struggle for internalization. Journal of Personality and Social Psychology, 82, 359–378. © Nyla Branscombe; 210: Nyla Branscombe; 218: Based on Powell, Branscombe, & Schmitt, 2005. © Nyla Branscombe.

Chapter 7 226: From The psychology of affiliation by S. Schachter, © 1959 Stanford University Press; 230: Robert Baron; 232: From "What is beautiful is good because what is beautiful is desired: Physical attractiveness stereotyping as project of interpersonal goals" by Lemay, E. P., Clark, M. S., & Greenberg, A. in Personality and Social Psychology Bulletin, 36, 339–353. © 2010 Sage Publications; 235: From as quoted by Judith Langlois in Isn't she lovely? Discover by Lemley, B., © Kalmbach Publishing Co.; 241: Based on Van Straaten, I., Engels, R. G., Finkenauer, C., & Holland, R. W. (2009). Meeting your match: How attractiveness similarity affects approach behavior in mixed-sex dyads. Personality and Social Psychology Bulletin, 35, 685–697. © Robert Baron; 244: Robert Baron; 245: Based on Cottrell et al., 2006. ©

Robert Baron; 249: From Hatfield, E., & Rapson, R. L. (2009). Love. In I. B. Weiner & W. E. Craighead (Eds.). Encyclopedia of Psychology, 4th Edition, © 2009 John Wiley and Sons; 249: From A Triangular Theory of Love by Robert J. Steinberg Psychological Review, 1986, Vol. 93, No. 2, 119-135, © American Psychological Association; 250: From "Measuring passionate lives in intimate relations" by Hatfield, E., & Sprecher, S. in Journal of Adolescence, 9, 383-410, © 1986 Elsevier; 251: From "Secret romantic relationships: Consequences for personal and relationship well-being" by Lehmiller, J. J. Personality and Social Psychology Bulletin, 35, 1452–1466, © Sage Publications; 254: Based on Eagly, A. H., Eastwick, P. W., & Johannesen-Schmidt, M. (2009). Possible selves in marital roles: the impact of the anticipated vision of labor on the mate preferences of women and men. Personality and Social Psychology Bulletin, 35 403–413. © Robert Baron.

Chapter 8 264: From Opinions and social pressure by Asch, S. E. Scientific American, 193(5), 31–35, © 1955 Nature America, Inc.; 264: Robert Baron; 265: Based on Pronin, E., Berger, J., & Molouki, S. (2007). Alone in a crowd of sheep: Asymmetric perceptions of conformity and their roots in an introspection illusion. Journal of Personality and Social Psychology, 92, 585–595. © Robert Baron; 271: From The Lucifer effect: How good people turn evil by Philip Zimbardo, © 2007 Random House; 272: From "Tyranny, freedom and social structure: Escaping our theoretical prisons" by John C. Turner in British Journal of Social Psychology, 45, 41–46. p.45, © 2006 Taylor & Francis; 274: From "Actors Conform, Observers React: The Effects of Behavioral Synchrony on Conformity" by Ping Dong, Xianchi Dai, Robert S Wyer in Journal of Personality and Social Psychology, 108(1):60-75, © 2015 American Psychological Association; 274: Based on Galinsky, A. D., Magee, J. C., Gruenfeld, D. H., Whitson, J. A., & Liljenquist, K. A. (2008). Power reduces the press of the situation: Implications for creativity, conformity, and dissonance. Journal of Personality and Social Psychology, 95, 1450–1466. © Robert Baron; 276: Robert Baron; 276: William Shakespeare, Hamlet, Act 1, Scene 3; 279: From "Measuring impression management in organizations: A scale development based on the Jones and Pittman taxonomy" by Bolino, M. C., & Turnley, W. H. in Organizational Research Methods, 2, 187–206, © 1999 Sage Publication; 279: Based on Cialdini, R. B. (1994). Influence: Science and practice (3rd ed.). New York: Harper Collins. Cialdini, R. B. (2008). Influence: Science and practice (5th ed.) Boston: Allyn & Bacon. © Robert Baron; 282: Based on Gueguen, N. (2003). Fund-raising on the Web: The effect of an electronic door-in-the-face technique in compliance to a request. CyberPsychology & Behavior, 2, 189–193. © Robert Baron; 283: Robert Baron; 286: From "Actors Conform, Observers React: The Effects of Behavioral Synchrony on Conformity" by Ping Dong, Xianchi Dai, Robert S Wyer in Journal of Personality and Social Psychology, 108(1):60-75, © 2015 American Psychological Association; 286: Based on data from Burger, 2009. © Robert Baron; 287: From Obedience to Authority: An Experimental View by Stanley milgram, © 1974 Harper & Row; 288: From "Nothing by mere authority: Evidence that in an experimental analogue of the Milgram paradigm participants are motivated not by orders but by appeals to science" by Haslam, S.A., Reicher, S.D., & Birney, M.E. in Journal of Social Issues, 70, 473–488, © 2014 John Wiley and Sons; 288: Robert Baron.

Chapter 9 298: Based on Gleason, K. A., Jensen-Campbell, L. A., & Ickes, W. (2009). The role of empathic accuracy in adolescents' peer relations and adjustment. Personality and Social Psychology Bulletin, 35, 997–1011. © Robert Baron; 302: Robert Baron; 305: Based on Darley, J. M., & Latané, B. (1968). Bystander intervention in emergencies: Diffusion of responsibility. Journal of Personality and Social Psychology, 8, 377–383. © Robert Baron; 308: Based on Latané, B., & Darley, J. M. (1970). The unresponsive bystander: Why doesn't he help? New York: Appleton-Century-Crofts. © Robert Baron; 312: Robert Baron; 319: From "Elevation leads to altruistic behavior" by Schnall, S., Roper, J., & Fessler, D.M.T. in Psychological Science, 21, 315–320, © 2010 Sage Publications.

Chapter 10 328: Nyla Branscombe; 330: From "Violent video games and hostile expectations: A test of the general aggression model" by Brad J. Bushman Craig A. Anderson in Personality and Social

Psychology Bulletin, 24, 949–960: and Social Psychology Bulletin, 28, 1679–1686, © 2002 Sage Publications; 335: Nyla Branscombe; 336: Based on Anderson, C. A., Berkowitz, L., Donnerstein, E., Huesmann, L. R., Johnson, J. D., Linz, D., Malamuth, N. M., & Wartella, E. (2003). The influence of media violence on youth. Psychology in the Public Interest, 4, 81–110. © Nyla Branscombe; 337: From "Violent video game effects on aggression, empathy, and prosocial behavior in Eastern and Western countries: A meta-analytic review" by Anderson, C. A., Shibuy, A., Uhori, N., Swing, E. I., Bushman, B. J., Sakomoto, A. in Psychological Bulletin, 136, 151–178. p.171, © 2010 American Psychological Association; 339: From "Effects of television violence on memory for commercial messages" by Bushman, B. J. in Journal of Experimental Psychology: Applied, 4, 1–17, © American Psychological Association; 340: Nyla Branscombe; 341: From Canadian Centre for Justice Statistics Profile Series, Gender Differences in Police-reported Violent Crime in Canada, Appendix 1- Table 1, © 2008 Statistics Canada; 344: Based on data from Giancola et al., 2009. © Nyla Branscombe; 348: Nyla Branscombe; 350: Nyla Branscombe; 356: Quote by Jacqueline Schiff; 356: Quote by Terri Guillemets.

Chapter 11 362: Based on Lickel, B., Hamilton, D. L., Wieczorkowski, G., Lewis, A., Sherman, S. J., & Uhles, A. N. (2000). Varieties of groups and the perception of group entiativity. Journal of Personality and Social Psychology, 78, 223–246. © Nyla Branscombe; 364: Based on Jetten, J., Hornsey, M. A., & Adarves-Yorno, I. (2006).When group members admit to being conformist: The role of relative intragroup status in conformity self-reports. Personality and Social Psychology Bulletin, 32, 162–173. © Nyla Branscombe; 367: Based on Hornsey, M. J., Jetten, J., McAuliffe, B. J., & Hogg, M. A. (2006). The impact of individualist and collectivist group norms on evaluations of dissenting group members. Journal of Experimental Social Psychology, 42, 57–68. © Nyla Branscombe; 369: Based on Wohl, M. J. A., Branscombe, N. R., & Reysen, S. (2010). Perceiving your group's future to be in jeopardy: Extinction threat induces collective angst and the desire to strengthen the ingroup. Personality and Social Psychology Bulletin, 36, 898–910. © Nyla Branscombe; 372: Based on Sani, F. (2009). When groups fall apart: A social psychological model of the schismatic process. In F. Butera & J. M. Levine (Eds.), Coping with minority status: Responses to exclusion and inclusion (pp. 243–266). New York: Cambridge University Press. © Nyla Branscombe; 376: Based on Zajonc, R. B. (1965). Social facilitation. Science, 149, 269–274; 383: From "Cultural variations in motivational responses to felt misunderstanding" by Lun, J., Oishi, S., Coan, J. A., Akimoto, S., & Miao, F. F. in Personality and Social Psychology Bulletin, 36, 986–996, © 2010 Sage Publications; 383: Based on Mulder, L. B., van Dijk, E., De Cremer, D., & Wilke, H. A. M. (2006). Undermining trust and cooperation: The paradox of sanctioning systems in social dilemmas. Journal of Experimental Social Psychology, 42, 147–162. © Nyla Branscombe; 384: Based on Lun, J.,

Oishi, S., Coan, J. A., Akimoto, S., & Miao, F. F. (2010). Cultural variations in motivational responses to felt misunderstanding. Personality and Social Psychology Bulletin, 36, 986–996. © Nyla Branscombe; 385: Nyla Branscombe; 386: From Justice in the workplace by Cropanzano, R. pp. 79–103, © 1993 Taylor & Francis; 388: Nyla Branscombe; 390: Nyla Branscombe; 391: From "It's OK if we say it, but you can't": responses to intergroup and intragroup criticism in European" by Matthew J. Hornsey, Tina Oppes and Alicia Svensson in Journal of Social Psychology Volume 32, Issue 3, pages 293–307, © May/June 2002 John Wiley & Sons.

Chapter 12 399: Quote by Friedrich Nietzsche (1889); 400: From My Beloved World by Sonia Sotomayor, © 2013 Knopf Doubleday Publishing Group; 402: Nyla Branscombe; 405: Nyla Branscombe; 406: From "Preventing symptoms of depression by teaching adolescents that people can change: Effects of a brief incremental theory of personality intervention at 9-month follow-up." by Adriana Sum Miu, David Scott Yeager in Clinical Psychological Science, 3, 726-743, © Sage Publications; 407: From "Weight Discrimination and Risk of Mortality" by Angelina R. Sutin, Yannick Stephan, Antonio Terracciano in Psychological Science, 26: 1803-1811, © 2015 Sage Publications; 407: Web page content provided by NAAFA.org; 411: From "Self-Distancing From Trauma Memories Reduces Physiological but Not Subjective Emotional Reactivity Among Veterans With Posttraumatic Stress Disorder" by Blair E. Wisco, Brian P. Marx, Denise M. Sloan, Kaitlyn R. Gorman, Andrea L. Kulish, Suzanne L. Pineles in Clinical Psychological Science, 3(6) 956-963, © 2015 Sage Publications; 413: Nyla Branscombe; 417: Nyla Branscombe; 419: Nyla Branscombe; 421: Based on Bothwell, R. K., Pigott, M. A., Foley, L. A., & McFatter, R. M. (2006). Racial bias in juridic judgment at private and public levels. Journal of Applied Social Psychology, 36, 2134–2149. © Nyla Branscombe; 422: From "Happiness is a personal(ity) thing: The genetic of personality and well-being in a representative sample" by Weiss, A., Bates, T. C., & Luciano, M. in Psychological Science, 19, 205–210, © 2008 Sage Publications; 422: Based on Diener, E. (2000). Subjective Well-Being. The Science of Happiness and a Proposal for a National Index. American Psychologist, 55, 34-43. © Nyla Branscombe; 422: Based on Helliwell, J.F., Layard, R., & Sachs, J. (2015). World Happiness Report 2015. New York: United Nations. © Nyla Branscombe; 424: From "Wealth and happiness across the world: Material prosperity predicts life evaluation, whereas psychosocial prosperity predicts positive feelings" by Diener, E., Ng, W., Harter, J., & Arora, R. in Journal of Personality and Social Psychology, 99, 52–61, © 2010 American Psychological Association; 424: Based on Diener, E., Ng, W., Harter, J., & Arora, R. (2010). Wealth and happiness across the world: Material prosperity predicts life evaluation, whereas psychosocial prosperity predicts positive feelings. Journal of Personality and Social Psychology, 99, 52–61. © Nyla Branscombe.

Name Index

Subject Index

Note: Page numbers followed by "f" indicate figures.